1200 m c
01

BROADCASTING AND GOVERNMENT:

Responsibilities and Regulations

BROADCASTING AND GOVERNMENT:

Responsibilities and Regulations

by

WALTER B. EMERY
J.D., Ph.D.

Professor of Communications, College of Social and Behavioral Sciences, Ohio State University; Member of the Federal Communications Commission Bar, and licensed to practice before the Courts of Ohio and the U. S. District Court, U. S. Court of Appeals for the District of Columbia and the U. S. Supreme Court.

MICHIGAN STATE UNIVERSITY PRESS

To my wife, Olive Helen Emery,
without whose patience and
helpfulness this book would
not have been completed

★
  ★
★
  ★
★

Contents

vii

PART V. THE BROADCASTER
AND ETHEREAL REALITIES

PART VI. A LOOK TO THE FUTURE

Acknowledgments

This book is an outgrowth of many years of experience and study. I began doing research on it as early as 1945 when I was a member of the legal staff of the Federal Communications Commission. My first debt of gratitude, therefore, is to the FCC itself for entrusting me with important responsibilities for a period of almost ten years and making it possible for me to acquire first-hand knowledge concerning the problems of broadcast regulation, without which this book could not have been written.

I am particularly grateful to the late Paul A. Walker, former member and, for a time, Chairman of the FCC. He was appointed as an original Commissioner in 1934 and continued in the job until he retired in 1953. He brought me to the Commission in 1935, and at different periods, while he was there, I served as his legal assistant. I cannot overestimate the value of that association and the influence of his thinking which, to a considerable extent, is reflected in this book.

In my work at the FCC for brief periods in 1935 and 1936 and again from 1943 to 1952, I enjoyed the tremendous advantage of associating regularly with such men as former Commissioner Rosel Hyde (later Chairman) who previously had been General Counsel, and who gave me my first job in what was then the Law Department of the Commission. My continued studies in the field of broadcasting and government and the writing I have done stem, in no small part, from the influence of these thoughtful and dedicated officials.

When I completed the preliminary manuscript of this volume, I submitted some parts of it to different staff members of the FCC and Federal Trade Commission. For their gracious and valuable assistance in reviewing the materials I must give acknowledgment. In so doing, however, I hasten to add that I, and not they, take full responsibility for the content of the book and for what errors of fact or interpretation it may contain. And particularly I want to stress that they cannot be held accountable for any of my criticisms of governmental policies or procedures, or recommendations for remedial action, since I did not solicit their advice or reactions to those parts of the book concerned with such matters.

A special word of thanks is due Gordon A. Sabine, formerly Dean of the College of Communication Arts and now Vice-President for Special Projects at Michigan State University. His genuine and intelligent interest in the subject of this book and the encouragement he gave me throughout the preparation of the first edition was invaluable. I also acknowledge my appreciation to Kay Williams, Alison Cruise, and other members of his secretarial staff who spent many hours typing most of the original manuscript.

I express thanks to Fred S. Siebert, Dean Emeritus of the College of Communication Arts and a distinguished authority in the law of the press, who wrote the Foreword in the original edition and made helpful suggestions, particularly regarding Chapter 22 dealing with legal restrictions on the use of program materials. Also, the original manuscript benefited greatly from the constructive criticisms of my former professorial colleagues in the Department of Television and Radio at Michigan State University. I am indebted to Robert Dye, formerly with Western Michigan University, for valuable assistance in the preparation of the original bibliography.

Since coming to Ohio State University as a professor in 1969, in this and other studies, I have received support and help from Dr. Keith Brooks, an outstanding scholar in communications, formerly Director of the Communications Area and now Chairman of the Department of Speech. It is good to be associated with him and other colleagues at Ohio State University who place a high premium on intellectual inquiry and research.

Finally, I acknowledge the valuable assistance given me by the library staff at Ohio State University in the preparation of this revised and enlarged edition, as well as that given me by the library staff at Michigan State when I was working on the original one.

Foreword

What has been and what should be the function of government in the regulation of broadcasting?

These are the questions which this book attempts to answer. And they are important and difficult questions the answers to which will determine the course of radio and television broadcasting for the next generation.

Most of the legal questions relating to both radio and television broadcasting are relatively new. Very little precedent exists either from the point of view of the regulatory agencies or from that of the broadcasting media, and although some of the problems have been explored, no final answers have been given to some of the most important areas of controversy.

On the one hand, broadcasting is one of the media of mass communication and it is at least in part the inheritor of a long tradition in which the problems of the regulation of the printed media were worked out. For three centuries, the press fought to establish itself as an important element in the political and social structure, and this importance has been recognized by the inclusion of the guaranties of press freedom in the federal and state constitutions. Our society has accepted the principle that although the press may not be completely free of all governmental regulation, it should not be subject to any governmental regulation which impinges on the right of the publisher to express his sentiments, no matter how objectionable, on political and social issues.

To what extent is broadcasting the inheritor of this tradition? Theoretically and practically, broadcasting can perform many of the same essential functions as the press. In practice it has made great strides in this direction. On the other hand, radio and television broadcasting by the nature of their means of transmission must, as compared with the printed media, subject themselves to some degree of government regulation. To what degree has been a question for discussion and some action since the advent of radio, but many of the basic problems have not yet been solved. Because these questions are important, because they have not yet been completely solved, and because their solution is significant for our society, this is an important book.

The author, Walter Emery, is well qualified to discuss the problems of the relation of government to broadcasting. He has been director of a broadcasting station, teacher of broadcasting, attorney and examiner for the Federal

Communications Commission, and student of legal and regulatory problems of broadcasting. In addition, he has been consultant to the Joint Council on Educational Television.

The history of the attempts to reconcile the historical tradition of freedom of expression as applied to broadcasting and the practical necessity for governmental regulation over the use of the air waves is a fascinating study which the author has presented in a concise and readable form. Part VI, A Look to the Future, brings together for the first time various proposals which have been made for changes in the content as well as the structure of governmental regulation of broadcasting.

Fred S. Siebert
Michigan State University

Introduction

It has been a little over a hundred years since Samuel Morse transmitted over a wire from Washington to Baltimore his historic message, "What hath God wrought?" More than eighty years have passed since Bell and Watson, in a little garret on Court Street in Boston, made the discovery that electricity could be made to transmit human speech. More than a half century ago Marconi thrilled the world by sending radio signals across the Atlantic Ocean.

Much of human progress in the past century may be attributed to the discoveries of these men and the tremendous developments in long distance communication which have followed their discoveries. Without the far-flung telegraph, telephone and broadcasting facilities of today, the intricate pattern of modern civilization and world community would be impossible.

A glimpse at the current dimensions of these communications media indicates the vital and indispensable part they have come to play in American life. For the fiscal year 1968, Western Union transmitted more than 62 million messages.[1] Its operating revenues for the calendar year 1968 was 358 million dollars. Its gross plant value was about 917 million dollars. Almost 11,000 offices and 25,857 employees were engaged in carrying on the business.[2]

Telephone companies subject to FCC regulation, in 1968, were operating more than 90 million telephones and had about 49 billion dollars invested in plant facilities.[3] Operating revenues for these companies ran more than 15 billion dollars in 1966.[4] In 1957 it was estimated by the FCC that we Americans used the telephone more than one hundred billion times a year.[5] During the past decade, the use has increased substantially.

In the international field, four cable and six radio companies furnish telegraph and telephone service between the United States and every important point on the globe. In 1968, the overseas telephone calls totaled more than thirteen million—the highest on record. TELEX advanced sharply to 10 million[6] and 24.9 million telegrams were sent abroad. As of December 31, 1966, U.S. carriers had about 620 million dollars invested in overseas plant. About 360 million dollars of which were invested in under-sea cable facilities.[7]

The development of satellite communication is now far advanced. A number of satellites are now in operation providing regular communication

5

service between the United States, Europe, the Pacific area and the Far East. As of June 30, 1969, 68 countries had become members of the International Telecommunications Satellite Consortium (INTELSAT) and were cooperating to the end that mankind may realize the full benefits of satellite technology in global communications.[8]

At the end of the fiscal year 1969, there were, in the United States, 4,254 standard broadcast stations (AM) on the air and 2,018 FM stations authorized and operating. The box score for TV was 857 stations (commercial and noncommercial). For the calendar year 1969, the television broadcasting industry, including the three large networks, their fifteen owned-and-operated stations and 627 other stations, reported revenues of 2.5 billion dollars and profits before tax of 495 million dollars.[9]

The FCC reported in 1969 that more than 3 million homes in the United States were receiving programs via community antenna TV systems (CATV). Increasing interest in CATV systems is being shown throughout the country and continued growth is expected.[10]

Educational broadcasting has now reached large dimensions. In 1969, more than 450 noncommerical stations (AM and FM) were being operated by educational institutions.[11] 195 educational TV stations were on the air distributed throughout the country, serving more than half the population.[12] The passage of Congressional legislation, providing additional funds for the construction of stations and grants-in-aid for the production of programs, has stimulated this growth, and with additional help from Congress further expansion of educational broadcasting is expected.

As important and alluring as public broadcasting has come to be, quantitatively it is only a small part of the total picture. It is not generally realized, that for every station which transmits programs to the general public there are about eighty-five more stations providing other useful services. For example, there were, in 1969, more than 1.7 million stations licensed in the Safety and Special Radio Services.[13] In 1967, Citizens Radio had almost 900,000 licenses outstanding.[14] Amateur licensees operate thousands of transmitters as authorized by the FCC. Many other specialized radio services are being carried on, meeting a multiplicity of communication needs in the country.

These vast radio and broadcasting operations as well as the huge telegraph and telephone industries are so vital to the security and well-being of our people, it is unthinkable that they could be carried on effectively without some governmental regulation. Some have advocated in the past that management should be free to operate these facilities without public regulation. Few persons today, however, seriously entertain such a notion. If for no other reason, in the field of broadcasting the problem of technical interference accentuated by a crowded radio spectrum would be so great that such a system of unrestrained operation would not be feasible.

While there is common agreement that governmental control is necessary, there are honest and intelligent differences of opinion as to how much we should have. On the one extreme, there are some who believe in complete government ownership. In fact, many countries have this system, and private operation as we have it in America is the exception rather than the rule. On the other hand, there are those who urge that regulation should be limited to mere technical matters and that other restraints on free enterprise should be avoided.

There are varying shades of opinion between these two extremes. Speaking with respect to radio, a former chairman of the Federal Communications Commission stated that he believed in "having as few controls of radio as possible" and that government should exert a "minimum of interference with the lives and fortunes of its citizens."[15]

Speaking along the same line but expressing another shade of opinion, one of his predecessors at the FCC stated that what we need is "diversified and balanced control" and to achieve this balance "we must have effective government regulation."[16]

Whatever the individual differences of opinion may be, under the law, we are committed in this country to the basic principle that these communication mechanisms are "clothed with the public interest," and that the people through their government have a right to set the general standards for their operation, and that qualified persons may have the privilege of operating them providing they offer a worthwhile service.

The Federal Communications Commission has the statutory responsibility of regulating the many broadcasting stations which operate in this country as well as all telegraph and telephone facilities which provide interstate and foreign service. Other agencies of government including Congress, the White House, and Federal Trade Commission exercise functions which affect these operations.

The activities of these agencies and the multiplicity of policies and regulations which they have established and administer not only concern the enormous communication industries but they vitally affect the lives of all citizens. There is a real need, therefore, for an up-to-date book which covers the principal functions of these agencies and sets forth briefly the basic policies and rules which govern these industries and the services they provide the American people. This volume attempts to meet this need.

It cannot of course be a substitute for the *Federal Register* and reference services such as *Radio Regulation* by Pike and Fischer which report regularly the complete text of governmental orders, statements of policy and regulations. Nor can it take the place of expert legal and engineering counsel so often needed by the broadcaster and communications carrier to assure full and effective compliance with all governmental requirements. In fact, it is hoped that one of the purposes the book may achieve is to point up the necessity of expert counsel for those engaged in such a complex field of operation.

Avoiding the minutiae of regulation, its design is to bring together in one handy volume basic information essential to an understanding of how our unique regulatory system developed and how it operates and generally what qualification tests and rules of conduct must be complied with by those entrusted with the privilege of operating these communication media.

This book is mainly concerned with the FCC and its control of broadcasting. To understand fully, however, the factors that brought the FCC into being, some knowledge of the early developments of the telegraph and telephone industries is essential. Hence the chapter, "A Talking World," in Part I is included.

Since the FCC has the responsibility of regulating all telegraph and telephone service of an interstate and foreign character, what it does or does not do in these fields may be related to or may influence its actions with respect to broadcasting. It is appropriate, therefore, that some reference be made to its functions in these fields.

The work is divided into six major divisions. Part I discusses the primary technological, economic and social factors which led to the creation of the American system of broadcasting, combining private enterprise and limited governmental regulation. In addition to the developments in wire and wireless communication (including the fierce struggle for survival between the telegraph and telephone industries), there is a review of the mushroom growth of radio broadcasting following the First World War. Included in this review are some of the early microphone celebrities and types of programming which emerged, and the problems which plagued the young industry—technical interference and "chaos in the ether", wave piracy, hucksterism, censorship and monopoly—and the resulting public concern which precipitated legislative action and the establishment of the Federal Radio Commission in 1927 and its successor, the FCC, in 1934.

Part II defines the statutory powers and functions of the FCC and describes its organization and administrative machinery. Included is a discussion of conflicting points of view as to the extent of its powers and a historical review of legislative and administrative actions which have led to its present organizational structure and pattern of operation. There is a special chapter on the Federal Trade Commission and its controls over broadcast advertising. A glimpse is also taken at other agencies of government—federal, state and local—which have influence or exercise controls over special areas and phases of broadcasting.

Part III is concerned with the broadcasting spectrum and the rules governing frequency allocation for the various classes of radio and television services—Standard Broadcast (AM), Frequency Modulation (FM), Television, International Broadcasting, and Auxiliary and Experimental Radio. Problems of classification, utilization and conservation of radio frequencies, with which the FCC is currently faced, are also discussed.

Parts IV and V deal with the hard facts of regulation—governmental requirements which must be met to get a license, responsibilities which must be assumed and conduct which must be avoided if one is to keep a license. As an outgrowth of the quiz scandals and payola practices, Congress, in

1960, enacted legislation imposing new restraints and responsibilities on radio and TV stations. All these, as well as other important license requirements, are fully covered.

Part VI analyzes some of the current problems of regulation and suggests clarifying legislation and other remedial measures, which, the author believes, would make regulation more effective.

Finally, it is believed that the reader will find the Appendix to be most useful. It contains those parts of the Communications Act, as amended which are related to broadcasting; a detailed and documented chronology of the FCC and its leadership from 1934 to 1970; recent FCC policy statements on program responsibilities of radio and television stations and other helpful reference materials.

In the preparation of this work, a high premium has been placed upon completeness and accuracy of documentation. Where Commission cases are referred to, citations in both the *FCC Reports* and Pike and Fischer's *Radio Regulation* (RR)* are given if the publications were available at the times the cases were decided. The FCC suspended publication of its annual reports of decisions from 1950 to 1957 and Pike and Fischer did not begin their publication until 1945.

Where references are made to the *Federal Register* (Fed. Reg.), the Pike and Fischer citations are also given, if the matter referred to did not occur prior to 1945. Where specific FCC rules and regulations are recited, their section numbers are given and their locations in Pike and Fischer are also indicated. The complete text of cited regulations may also be found under the appropriate section numbers in Title 47, Telecommunications, *Code of Federal Regulations* (CFR).

Footnotes appear at the end of each chapter. Many of them contain not only the citations of documentary sources but clarifying, explanatory and supplementary materials that may be of interest and use to the reader.

This second edition includes many new and important broadcast policies and regulations adopted by the FCC since this book was first published in 1961. For example, the chapter on International Broadcasting has been greatly revised and expanded. New FCC pronouncements and court decisions regarding the "fairness doctrine", new FM, CATV and toll TV regulations, new developments in educational broadcasting, recent FCC and court decisions relating to "indecent" programming, unauthorized transfers of control, forfeitures, an updated chronology of FCC leadership—these and many other materials of interest to all students of broadcast regulation, much of which did not appear in the original publication, have been included in this new and revised edition.

---

*Pike and Fischer's *Radio Regulation* (RR) is one of the most valuable sources of information in the field of broadcasting law and regulations. It is published at 2000 L St., N.W. in Washington, D.C. Educational institutions offering instruction or doing research in this field would do well to subscribe to it.

NOTES

1. Federal Communications Commission, *35th Annual Report* for the *Year 1969*, p. 66.
2. *Ibid.*
3. *Ibid.*, pp. 59, 64.
4. *Ibid.*, p. 591
5. *Ibid.* p. 64.
6. *Ibid.*, pp. 70, 71.
7. *Ibid.*
8. *Ibid.*, p. 75.
9. *Ibid.*, p. 2.
10. *Ibid.*, p. 4; see also Ralph Smith, "The Wired Nation," *The Nation*, May 18, 1970.
11. *Ibid.*, pp. 2, 128.
12. *Ibid.*, 126.
13. *Ibid.*, p. 6.
14. *FCC, 34th Annual Report*, 1967, p. 73.
15. McConnaughey, George C., an address at the Meeting of One Hundred of Miami Beach, Florida, January 8, 1957, FCC Release No. 40143.
16. Walker, Paul A., an address before the Third Annual Radio Conference sponsored by Stephens College, November 18, 1944.

PART I

Prologue to Regulation

CHAPTER 1

A Talking World

Do you not know that all the world is all now one single whispering gallery?—WOODROW WILSON

The vastness and efficiency of modern communication media contrast sharply with the limited and crude facilities in use during the early period of our nation's history. There were no telephones, no radios, and no ocean cables. There was some tinkering with telegraphy but its utility for communication had not yet been demonstrated. The postal service had been established, but stage coach travel was slow and it took days and days to get a message across the oceans, and communications to and from foreign countries required weeks and even months to reach their destinations.

The semaphore system had come into use and its enthusiasts envisioned its development on a nation-wide basis. Consideration was given to a plan by which intelligence could be relayed visually from city to city, using signalling stations placed a few miles apart.[1] But this system had obvious limitations. It could not be used at night or during cloudy weather. Considering its limited utility, it would be expensive to establish and maintain.

The pressing need for improved methods of communication in a rapidly expanding nation stimulated experimental studies. As early as 1837, Samuel Morse and Alfred Vail had demonstrated that intelligence could be transmitted over wires and recorded by means of electromagnetism.[2] The equipment which they first used had little to suggest the efficiency of modern telegraphic apparatus. After some improvements, however, Morse pleaded with Congress for an appropriation to build an experimental line between Washington and Baltimore. He aroused interest, but some Congressmen were skeptical. He was called a "crank" and ridiculed for visionary ideas. Some Congressmen thought it would be questionable politics to approve a subsidy to carry on a project which they associated with "mesmerism" and "animal magnetism."[3]

Despite the mockery, Morse was able to muster enough votes to get an appropriation. On March 3, 1843, Congress passed a bill giving him $30,000 to construct his telegraph line.[4] A year later the line was completed, and on May 24, 1844 it was formally opened with special ceremonies in the old Supreme Court room in the Capitol. Congressional leaders and other high government officials heaped praises and congratulations upon the proud and happy Morse.[5]

A New Era of Social and Economic Growth.   The use of electromagnetic energy for long distance communication had definitely proved its worth. Henceforth it was destined to play an increasingly important part in the social and economic progress of the nation and the world.

By 1856, many telegraph companies had been organized and lines between many major cities had been established. This expansion continued at a rapid pace during the War between the States. In October, 1861, a line was completed to San Francisco providing service across the country.[6] President Lincoln, despite reverses at Bull Run, was not too busy to acknowledge receipt of several messages which came over the line during the first few days of its operation.[7]

The successful use of wire communication during the War gave impetus to its peace time development. The social and economic utility of this new facility was now generally recognized. Important negotiations and transactions, which formerly required weeks and even months to accomplish could now be completed in a few hours or days, and the parties were thus enabled to devote time and capital saved to new enterprises.

There followed a period of intense rivalry between telegraph companies. Cut-throat competition was the order of the day. Rates were drastically cut in some sections of the country. While a few small companies were able to survive this period of ordeal, many were unable to stand up against unrestrained competition and the economic power of giant monopoly.

While the war of wires was being waged, scientists were making new discoveries and developing new techniques. Technical improvements increased the carrier capacity of the wires. The development of apparatus for automatic transmission made it possible to send and record several thousand words per minute.

These developments and improvements were enormously helpful to news reporting. Following the construction of the Morse wire in the early days, telegraphic news reports carried by such papers as the *National Intelligencer* and the *Washington Madisonian* became popular features with the reading public. During the years that followed, with the improvement and extension of wire facilities, news agencies such as the Associated Press developed a thriving business. By the turn of the century, the newspapers of the country were sending news messages over Western Union facilities totaling hundreds of millions of words per year.

As Robert Thompson has pointed out in his excellent book, *Wiring a Continent,* the growth of the telegraph had a profound effect upon the life of the nation. He was referring to the early period of telegraph history, but what he had to say applies equally well to developments which came later. "Men from all walks of life and for a variety of reasons, employed the new means of communication."[8] Persons away from home could keep in close touch with their families. Urban life was made more secure by the use of telegraph for police and fire alarms. The farmer, merchant, banker, broker, the capitalist and the journalist constantly were broadening their base of operations as it became possible to transmit and receive intelligence quickly over hundreds and thousands of miles. In fact, the telegraph was a vital factor in the development of the American system of free enterprise.

Wires, Cables and World Community. Not all the developments by any means took place in this country. Scientists in Germany, Russia, France and other European countries did important experimental work in electrical communication and it achieved considerable growth in these countries during the forties and fifties. It had made a beginning during those early years in India, Australia, China, Japan, Turkey and some countries in Central and South America.[9]

It was only natural for men to begin thinking of connecting links among nations. Early in his career, Morse had predicted the spanning of the Atlantic and the ultimate development of a world-wide telegraphic network. After long and heroic efforts with many disheartening setbacks, the Atlantic Telegraph Company, under the courageous leadership of Cyrus Field, completed the construction of the first Atlantic cable.[10]

On August 5, 1858, a few days after the cable was laid, the New York *Evening Post* commented that "the hearts of the civilized world will beat in a single pulse, and from that time forth forevermore, the continental divisions of the earth will in a measure lose their conditions of time and distance . . ."

A few days later, the Queen of England sent a message over the cable to the President of the United States in which she prophesied that it would prove an additional link between Great Britain and the United States, "whose friendship is founded upon their common interest and reciprocal esteem."[11] President Buchanan replied, expressing the hope that the cable might "prove to be a bond of perpetual peace and friendship between the kindred nations, and an instrument destined by Divine Providence to diffuse religion, civilization, liberty and laws throughout the world.[12]

The first Atlantic cable functioned spasmodically for a time and then went completely dead. The approach of the War between the States prevented any immediate attempts to put down another one. Within one year after the War, however, two new cables were in successful operation providing a continuous flow of intelligence between the United States and Europe.[13] By 1870, a large part of the world was embraced by a network of telegraph wires. This expanding web of wires was having a vital effect upon international relations and the development of world community.

The Ring of the Magneto-Bell. While this vast telegraphic expansion was taking place, scientists were experimenting with the idea that human speech might be transmitted over wires. In 1876, Alexander Graham Bell, working in his laboratory in Boston, demonstrated that it could be done.[14] He had worked out an apparatus which included an electro-magnet, a U-shaped iron bar with a coil of wire wrapped around one limb and a thin plate of iron attached to the other. A membrane diaphragm was stretched across the tube to serve as a mouthpiece. After some experimentation, he was able to produce undulations of electric current in the circuit, corresponding to the vibrations in the voice, thereby transmitting continuous and intelligible speech.

Bell took advantage of every opportunity to demonstrate how the new contrivance worked. He exhibited it at the great Centennial Exposition in Philadelphia in 1876 where thousands of people from all parts of the world had a chance to view its operations.[15] The novelty of it interested people but few at that time realized its possibilities. Most persons considered it something to play with and afford amusement. They thought little of its economic and social utility.

The telephone instruments which were first used in the seventies were crude and inefficient. A crank had to be turned vigorously. One talked into an odd appearing mouthpiece, and yelling often was necessary to overcome the howls and hisses of static so that one might be heard and understood at the other end of the line. The telephone was built in separate parts and the connections between the magneto bell, transmitter and battery were run around and tacked on the wall. It was troublesome, expensive and unsightly. The pictures of the original telephone as carried in the advertisements of that day present an amazing contrast to the dial telephone of today so compactly built that it can be put in an overcoat pocket.[16]

Improvements came quickly. The original telephone with separate, sprawling parts was soon replaced with one more compactly built. The new model had the magneto bell mounted on a base board, behind which were concealed in a box all connecting wires for the transmitter. The battery box was attached to the baseboard and served as a miniature desk on which one could write while conversing on the phone.[17]

Public interest in the use of the telephone increased so fast that by March, 1881, there was only one city in the country with more than 15,000 people that did not have a telephone exchange.[18] There were frequent comments in magazines regarding the increasing value of these telephones to community life. In cases of sickness, fire, theft or other emergencies, they saved life and property. Business men were finding them essential to the development of trade. They facilitated social contacts and group enterprise.

The Struggle for Supremacy. The growth of telephonic communication presented a real threat to the telegraph industry. The telephone offered a convenience and personal contact not provided by the telegraph. It was one thing to read a short, printed message from a friend 200 miles away but it was something else to hear that friend's voice over the telephone. To meet the competition of the expanding telephone service, Western Union began building telephone exchanges of its own throughout the country.[19]

The Bell company retaliated by bringing suit for infringement of its patent. The legal contest was settled out of court in 1879, Western Union admitting the validity of the Bell patents. The Bell company agreed to purchase the Western Union telephone system and to stay out of the telegraph business.[20]

This arrangement gave the Bell interests a clear field for the development of telephone service. They organized a new company in 1890 and under the leadership of Theodore N. Vail, moved forward rapidly. Vail had already formulated plans for a nation-wide system of inter-connected telephones, using long distance lines. Five years later, the American Telephone and Telegraph Company was established in New York for the purpose of providing long distance service.[21] On October 18, 1892, Bell sent the first message over a wire from New York to Chicago, and by the end of the century telephone toll service had become a flourishing business.

Technological developments had improved the quality of long distance communication. A report of the American Institute of Electrical Engineers published in 1904 gave a good summary of major improvements. The efficiency of long distance circuits had been vastly improved. A large part of the country was supplied with long distance lines built of sturdy copper wire. Improved equipment replaced the clumsy hand-operated magneto machines which required the subscriber to furnish his own current and keep his battery in working condition. The old system had been superseded by the single central station battery, a few cells of which were able to do the work of many and could be maintained more economically and efficiently. In most large cities, underground cables had replaced the appalling and unsightly maze of wires above the streets.[22]

In 1905, the Bell system as a whole had more than 4 million subscribers and handled on an average more than 7,000 calls per minute, 460,000 an hour and close to 11 million a day. The distance of the calls varied from a few feet to more than 1600 miles. The Bell company was handling nearly forty times as many messages as the telegraph companies. More than 30,000 towns and cities were connected by the wires of the system.[23]

This was not all. Beginning in the early nineties, numerous smaller companies not connected with the Bell system were established. By 1901, independent exchanges were being operated in 45 states and in the territories, with an investment of 100 million dollars and over a million telephones.[24]

Not all the development had occurred in the United States. In 1878, only two years after Bell had invented the telephone, public telephone exchanges were opened in London, Manchester and Liverpool. By 1891, Glasgow, Paris and Berlin were operating similar exchanges. The expansion continued, and in 1910 all the principal cities in the world had telephone service. It was estimated there were about ten million telephones in use, nearly two-thirds of which were in this country. The total number had almost reached the 15 million mark by 1915.[25]

Wireless Wizardry. But the telephonic achievements which evoked exclamatory utterances from journalists of that day could not compare with the wireless wonders which were already on the way. As previously men-

17

tioned, in 1901 Marconi thrilled the world with the transmission of electro-magnetic signals across the Atlantic Ocean.[26] In March, 1903, the first transoceanic radiogram appeared in the London *Times*. A few years later, De Forest transmitted speech across his laboratory, using an audion amplifier which he had invented.[27] This made voice amplification possible and was the basis for the development of radio telephony.

By 1915, the American Telephone and Telegraph Company had inaugurated regular telephone service between New York and San Francisco. It was this same year, with the use of the Audion tube, that Bell engineers were able to span the Pacific and Atlantic oceans by means of radio telephony.[28]

World War I brought many improvements in radio communication. By 1925, transoceanic telephony using radio waves had been developed to the point that it was almost as reliable as that by wire and cable. During the next few years, tele-communications developed rapidly and literally revolutionized the pattern of living in many parts of the world.

On December 31, 1932, telegraph and cable companies then reporting to the Interstate Commerce Commission had capital assets amounting to more than 250 million dollars. Western Union and International Telephone and Telegraph Corporation transmitted over 125 million messages that year. The telephone industry had an investment of over 5 billion dollars with an annual income running more than a billion. In 1932, there were over 17 million telephones in use in the country. There were nearly ninety million miles of wire, more than enough to reach from the earth to the moon and back again more than 150 times.[29]

In 1934, the year the Federal Communications Commission was created, a vast network of wires extended to every major part of the globe with more than 32 million telephones in use. What a century before had been a multiplicity of provincial habitations, widely separated by time and space and scattered over the face of the earth, was now a talking world with the various parts literally linked together by wires and electromagnetic waves.

1. Harlow, Alvin F., *Old Wires and New Waves* (New York, 1936), pp. 32, 33.
2. Bureau of the Census, *Telephones and Telegraphs* (Washington, D. C., 1902), pp. 112, 113.
3. Harlow, *op. cit.*, pp. 84, 85.
4. *Ibid.*, p. 86.
5. Morse, Edward Lind, *Samuel F. B. Morse, Letters and Journals*, Vol. 2 (Boston, 1914), pp. 221-229.
6. Harlow, *op. cit.*, p. 313.
7. *Ibid.*
8. Thompson, Robert, *Wiring a Continent* (Princeton, 1947), pp. 444, 445.
9. Shaffner, Tal. P., *The Telegraph Manual; a Complete History and Description of the Semaphoric, Electric and Magnetic Telegraphs of Europe, Asia, Africa and America, Ancient and Modern* (Pudney and Russell, 1859).
10. Walter, Kellogg Towers, *From Beacon Fire to Radio* (New York, 1924), pp. 117-124.
11. *Ibid.*, p. 125.
12. *Ibid.*
13. *Ibid.*, p. 136.
14. Bureau of the Census, *op. cit.*, p. 66.
15. *Ibid.*
16. Rhodes, Fredrich Leland, *Beginnings of Telephony* (New York, 1929); and Kingsbury, John E., *The Telephone and Telephone Exchanges* (Longmans Green, 1915).
17. *Ibid.*
18. Bureau of the Census, *op. cit.*, p. 66.
19. *Ibid.*
20. *Ibid.*
21. Casson, Herbert N., *The History of the Telephone* (New York, 1910), pp. 173, 174.
22. *Ibid.*
23. *Ibid.*
24. MacNeal, Harry B., *The Story of Independent Telephony* (The Independent Pioneer Telephone Association, Washington, D. C.).
25. Casson, *op. cit.*, pp. 245-273; also Bureau of Census, *op. cit.*, 1906, pp. 68-78.
26. *The Radio Industry, The Story of Its Development*, as told by leaders of the industry (Chicago, 1928), p. 29.
27. *Ibid.*, pp. 55, 56.
28. *Ibid.*, p. 130.
29. Federal Communications Commission, *Report, Special Telephone Investigation*, 1937.

CHAPTER 2

Eliminating the Static

*The ether is a public medium and its use must be for public benefit. . . .
The dominant element for consideration in the radio field is, and always will
be, the great body of the listening public, millions in number, countrywide
in distribution.* —HERBERT HOOVER

The technological development of radio and its effective use in telegraphic and telephonic communication paved the way for broadcasting.
From about 1910 to the end of the first World War, sporadic, experimental
attempts were made to broadcast programs for general reception. For example, in 1910, standing on the stage of the Metropolitan Opera House in New
York City, Enrico Caruso sang an aria into a paper cone attached to
a musician's tripod. Inside the cone was a vibrating diaphragm attached
to a telephone wire which ran to the laboratory of the young scientist,
Lee W. De Forest, located some distance away. The voice of the world
famous tenor was carried over this wire and then transmitted through space
by De Forest to wireless operators on various ships at sea.[1]

As early as 1909, a radio telephone transmitting station in San Jose,
California (later assigned call letters KQW) began broadcasting. In 1917,
station 9XM at the University of Wisconsin (subsequently identified as
WHA) began experimental broadcasts of musical programs.[2]

During this early period, amateur operators, or "hams" as they were
popularly called, scattered in various parts of the country, with transmitting
and receiving equipment located in pantries, basements and attics, were
entertaining one another with small talk and recorded music and were
exchanging ideas on the wonders of wireless telephony. In 1916, one of
these amateur operators by the name of David Sarnoff (later to become one
of the great leaders in the broadcast industry) proposed that regular musical
and talking programs be presented by radio. He suggested the manufacture
of a "radio music box," complete with amplifying tubes and a loudspeaker
telephone. He expressed confidence that within a few years millions of these
sets could be sold to the general public.[3]

Early Microphone Celebrities.   His confidence was fully justified. Following the first World War, there was a rapid development in the radio art.
With technological improvements which came out of the War, imaginative

business men such as Sarnoff applied their minds to the development of broadcasting as a means of public entertainment and enlightenment, at the same time foreseeing its vast commercial possibilities.

Great talent was brought before the microphones. For example, Fritz Kreisler caused a sensation when he performed over KDKA in Pittsburgh's Carnegie Hall on January 26, 1922.[4] Likewise, people were thrilled over the broadcast of grand opera by a station in Chicago.[5] John McCormack, noted Irish tenor, and Lucrezia Bori, Metropolitan opera star, gave their initial radio performances on the New York station WEAF in January, 1925. Many persons in the New York area heard them and the theatres complained of the competition.[6]

Lighter music was featured by some stations and attracted large audiences. There were the Kansas City Night Hawks who brought jazz music and night club atmosphere to millions of fans in the Midwest. WOS in St. Louis featured Harry M. Snodgrass, known popularly as "King of the Ivories," at that time serving a three year term for forgery in the Missouri State Prison. Vincent Lopez became a national celebrity as he and his traveling orchestra broadcast popular rhythm over WEAF and other stations. The harmony team of Jones and Hare, "The Happiness Boys," made their debut on WEAF in December, 1923 and "The National Barn Dance" was in full swing several months later on WLS in Chicago.[7]

During the early twenties, station WEAF was broadcasting the popular news analysis of H. V. Kaltenborn, then Associate Editor of the *Brooklyn Daily Eagle* and whose fame spread rapidly, soon making him a national figure. About the same time, Harold "Red" Grange, famous All-American half-back, was bringing dramatic accounts of sports events over the facilities of WOC in Davenport, Iowa. Station WJZ in New York broadcast a World Series game for the first time in October, 1921 and about two years later Graham McNamee presented a play-by-play report of the Series in his first network sports assignment.[8]

For the first time in history a speech in the halls of Congress was broadcast when President Harding read his message on December 6, 1923. Woodrow Wilson broke his silence of four years when on Armistic Day of the same year he addressed the American public through microphones installed in his home.[9]

Advertising Values Recognized. The value of radio as an advertising medium was being increasingly recognized. For example, during the early twenties, numerous commercial companies used the facilities of station WEAF in New York to advertise their products. There was The Eveready Hour sponsored by the National Carbon Company, which urged listeners to buy the dry-cell Eveready battery for their receiving sets. To attract listeners, the company featured celebrities such as John Drew, Julia Marlowe, George Gershwin, Weber and Fields, and Irvin S. Cobb.[10] More and more advertisers sponsored programs, featured high priced talent and enlarged the markets for their products or services.

Educational and Religious Uses. The educational values of radio were not overlooked during those early years. For example, Judith Waller, one of the great pioneer women in commercial radio, became widely known for her contributions to public service broadcasting, including her early leadership in the University of Chicago Round Table. In May, 1923, WJZ in New York began the first University of the Air, featuring talks on economic problems of the day.[11]

Many colleges and universities had their own stations and were bringing to eager listeners professional lectures, inter-collegiate debates, musical and dramatic shows and market reports. By 1925, some institutions were offering formal instruction by radio and there was much talk among educators about extending its use for the teaching of a wide variety of subjects to the general public.

Religious programs were featured by many stations in those early days. On January 2, 1921, KDKA broadcast the first "Church of the Air." As early as 1922, the "Great Commoner," William Jennings Bryan, was transmitting via radio his message of salvation to vast number of churched and unchurched people. In 1925, Reverend Howard O. Hough established the "First Radio Parish Church in America," a non-sectarian organization, using the facilities of Station WCSH in Portland, Maine. Father James R. Cox of Pittsburgh became widely known for his presentation of the Catholic message from the Old St. Patrick's Church through the facilities of WJAS.[12]

The "Peddlers of the Air". But all was not sweetness and light. There were the "peddlers of the air" who victimized listeners with their "get rich quick" schemes. Astrologers, fortune tellers, experts on dandruff and falling hair and other quacks found ready access to the microphones in many communities.

The mercenary medicine men presented a special problem. Hucksters such as Dr. John R. Brinkley made extravagant claims for their medicine and cures, swelling their bank accounts with cash which flowed in daily from unsuspecting and trusting listeners. Dr. Brinkley broadcast a program of hillbilly music and medical talks over his station KFKB in Milford, Kansas. In connection with this program he advertised his famous "goatgland" operation as a sure and effective means of revitalizing elderly gentlemen. He openly defied the American Medical Association and through his broadcast braggadocia and buffoonery attracted literally thousands of older men from all parts of the United States to his clinic in Milford. There he performed "revitalizing" operations for a fee which averaged about $750.

For years he exploited a publicly owned radio channel to hawk his medical quackery. Finally, the Federal Radio Commission cancelled his license and put a stop to his predatory practice in Kansas.[13] Unable to operate on an assigned frequency in this country, he subsequently secured a high-powered transmitter in Mexico and beamed his medical gullery back into this country, using the call letters XER. He established new hospitals in Del Rio, Texas and Little Rock, Arkansas where he continued his "revitalizing" therapy. For ten years thereafter he carried on his "border raids" and come-on games until in 1941 a wholesale reallocation of frequencies and reductions in transmitting power of stations along the border, resulting from a treaty with Mexico and other North American countries, dealt a death blow to his 100,000-watt XER.[14]

Robert J. Landry in his book, *The Fascinating Radio Business,* has given an interesting account of the hawking activities of Brinkley and other radio hucksters during those early days:

Brinkley was definitely the most colorful of the motley assortment of self-promoters who came to radio in the early years. There were hysterical clergymen, enemies of Wall Street, enemies of chain stores, enemies of Catholics, Jews and Negroes, promoters of patented heavens. Tea-leaf Kitty from Jersey City went on the radio and offered to answer any three questions in a sealed envelope for one dollar. The meaning of the stars, the stock market, the future life could all be learned by enclosing cash. Falling hair or teeth could be arrested—just write. Fortunes in real estate could be made overnight—just write. Home cures for this, that or the other thing were available—just write.[15]

Frenzied Competition for Radio Audience. In the whole history of scientific discovery there perhaps has never been so rapid a development of knowledge for popular use as in the field of radio. In 1920 there were only about three radio stations providing regular program service to the public. By 1924, there were more than 500 on the air with programs available to most of the homes in the country. The sales of radio receivers and other apparatus at that time were averaging about a million dollars a day. It was estimated that over 200,000 persons were employed in the broadcasting industry.[16] In homes, offices, workshops and hotels, in cities, towns and rural areas, Americans were huddled around receivers with earphones clamped to their skulls listening in awe and wonderment to programs coming through the "ether" from stations far and near.

Broadcasters vied with one another for the listener's attention and interest. Advertisers were looking for the programs and talent that would attract the most listeners and provide the best market for services and goods. Some stations stepped up their power, jumped frequencies and changed hours of operation at will in a frenzied effort to enlarge their coverage areas, reach larger audiences, and achieve competitive advantage.

While some broadcasters entered into agreements with respect to power, use of frequencies and hours of operation, there were many others who refused to do so. In deliberate, cut-throat fashion, some broadcasters attempted to interfere with and drown out the signals of lower-powered stations. Francis Chase, Jr., in his informal history of broadcasting, *Sound and Fury,* has described the general situation at that time as one where "chaos rode the air waves, pandemonium filled every loud-speaker and the twentieth century Tower of Babel was made in the image of the antenna towers of some thousand broadcasters who, like the Kilkenny cats, were about to eat each other up."[17]

The Growth of Networks. Network operation had reached a fairly advanced stage by 1925. Its development had come rapidly. On January 4, 1923, with a special circuit set up between WEAF in New York City and WNAC in Boston, a program originating at WEAF was transmitted simultaneously by the two stations. According to official reports, this was the first network broadcast.[18]

WEAF was then owned by the American Telephone and Telegraph Company. At that time the Bell company claimed exclusive rights under certain patents and patent-licensing agreements to sell radio time and operate "toll broadcasting stations." By the end of 1925, it had expanded its network to include 26 stations as far west as Kansas City. The company was selling time to advertisers over a basic network of 13 stations at $2600 per hour with a gross income of about $750,000 per year.[19]

The Radio Corporation of America also got an early start in network broadcasting. In the spring of 1923, RCA acquired control of WJZ in New York City and later that year constructed and started operating WRC in Washington. Its first network broadcast occurred in December, 1925, and included WJZ and the General Electric Company station WGY in Schenectady.[20]

Because of the restrictive policy of the AT&T in refusing to furnish wire service to broadcasting stations not licensed under that company's patents, RCA was hampered in the early development of its network. For a time, the radio company was compelled to use telegraph wires. Their transmission quality was much inferior to that of the telephone lines operated by the Bell system.[21] Also, since the telephone company claimed the exclusive right to sell time for broadcasting, RCA made no charge for the use of its facilities and was handicapped in developing the commercial aspects of its network.[22]

In 1926, the Telephone Company withdrew from the broadcasting field and transferred its radio properties to RCA, Westinghouse, and General Electric, and agreed to make its lines available to RCA for network purposes.[23]

That same year, RCA formed a corporation, the National Broadcasting Company, to take over its network business with the outstanding stock owned by RCA, General Electric, and Westinghouse. Subsequently, RCA purchased all the stock interests of GE and Westinghouse in NBC and the latter company became a wholly owned subsidiary of RCA.[24]

The Columbia Broadcasting System was organized in 1927. Its original network consisted of 16 stations. By this time, NBC had increased its outlets to 48. This made a total of 64 stations affiliated with the two chain systems, providing regular network service to every part of the country.[25]

The Listeners Become Critical. With the continued growth of cities and metropolitan areas, expanding industries, and developments in transportation, life in America was taking on an increasingly complex pattern. It was far removed from the simple life of the early American Indians who found smoke rings and fire-arrows adequate to meet their needs for long distance communication. Telegraph, telephone and radio had facilitated this remarkable social and economic growth and had become an indispensable part of a highly developed civilization. Communication lines and channels had become the nerve fibers through which the organization of a great democratic nation of 120 million people was made to function.

More and more the average citizen realized this. He became increasingly conscious that his individual comfort and happiness as well as that of the community and nation were dependent upon the efficiency of these media. The security of his home, family, and job, the welfare of his local institutions —the church, the school and other community enterprises—all were tied up with communications service. In the language of the courts, these public utilities were "clothed with the public interest," and the citizen was voicing more concern with the way they were managed and operated.

He became more critical. The free and unrestrained transmissions of radio operators on ships at sea too often interfered with the music, speeches, baseball scores, weather reports and market information that he and thousands of others were trying to get from broadcast stations.

Many listeners complained of excessive and offensive advertising on radio programs. They deplored frequent interruptions by sponsors advertising hair nets, soaps, facial creams, etc.

Censorship, Monopoly and Demagoguery Deplored.　　There was complaint against censorship. Political speakers didn't like the idea of having to submit manuscripts to station managers, who often deleted portions of the speeches. Men like the elder Robert La Follette and Norman Thomas insisted there should be no censorship of their radio speeches because of the prejudice or fears of station managers.

There were bitter attacks against the growth of monopoly in the radio industry. Frequent editorials in newspapers and magazines deplored the growing concentration of control in a few large companies. The Federal Trade Commission condemned what it termed an illegal monopoly in the manufacture and sale of radio apparatus.[26] In 1924, Station WHO in Des Moines, Iowa refused to carry the speech of Senator La Follette in behalf of his candidacy for President on the Progressive ticket. He asserted that "a monopoly had been formed to prevent him from going on the air."[27]

In a letter to the *New York Times* dated August 28, 1924, Congressman Emanuel Celler protested against what he termed an "absolute monopoly" in radio. He charged that the monopoly was "manifesting itself against candidates for public office who desire to use the radio for campaign purposes."[28]

There were general grumblings at the time about propagandists, religious zealots and unprincipled persons with axes to grind and a motley of demagogues and hucksters seeking to reach radio audiences with their peculiar brands of publicity. There were protests against radio programs not in good taste, and the excessive use of phonograph recordings was vehemently condemned.

With respect to radio, the decade from 1920 to 1930 can most certainly and appropriately be referred to as "the roaring twenties." A fast and furious growth in the industry, wave piracy, offensive advertising, monopoly and other disturbing conditions brought demands from the public that the government do something to correct the situation generally thought to be a "conglomerate mess."

Interference Becomes Intolerable. Herbert Hoover, then Secretary of Commerce, found much of his time taken up answering letters, telegrams and telephone calls from listeners complaining about technical interference. Typical of the complaints were those which came as a result of two church broadcasts in Washington. For three successive Sundays in 1922, two stations in the Capitol City broadcast services from these churches at the same time on the same wave length. The result was anything but heavenly. What poured from the receivers was a pain-provoking jumble of noise that was more conducive to neuroses than quiet religious worship. Large numbers of distressed listeners appealed to Secretary Hoover to straighten out the tangle. "Dante's Inferno can be no worse than the noises that come to us in Florida," wrote one distraught listener to the Secretary.

From every section of the country came similar appeals for relief from static and interference. For example, on May 15, 1922, the Radio Broadcasting Society of America asked Secretary Hoover to revoke the license of Station WJZ in New York, alleging that it wantonly interfered with the operation of fifteen other stations.[29]

Hoover was tremendously interested in the problems of broadcasting and was eager to improve a situation which some authorities thought was threatening to kill the art and industry. However, his authority to regulate radio was limited. By a 1910 Congressional Act, it was made unlawful for a ship carrying fifty or more persons to leave any port of the United States unless equipped with efficient radio communication facilities.[30] The Secretary of Commerce and Labor (as he was then called) was given the power to make regulations for the proper execution of this law.

The Titanic disaster of 1912 prompted Congress to strengthen the safety provisions of the 1910 law. A new act was passed implementing treaty obligations of the United States in connection with the use of radio by ships at sea, and specifying procedure to be followed in transmitting and answering distress calls. Other provisions of the 1912 Act required every radio station to secure a license from the Secretary of Commerce and Labor, made compulsory the employment of a licensed operator, and specified bands of frequencies for different classes of stations.[31]

But still the law gave the Secretary no discretionary power. There were no general standards by which he could choose among applicants for stations. He had no authority to specify particular frequencies, power, hours of operation or the period of a license. There were certain regulations in the law designed to prevent or reduce interference between stations, but in large measure, broadcasters chose their own wave lengths and operated much as they pleased.

Hoover and his staff gave a great deal of thought to what might be done to correct the situation. Because of his interest in their problems, troubled broadcasters and listeners sought his help and advice. As an unofficial arbiter, he was able to settle many serious conflicts and disturbances in the radio field. He became convinced, however, that the serious impediments to effective broadcasting in this country could not be removed until the government was given actual and not nominal authority to regulate the radio industry. Accordingly, he called a conference of radio experts to discuss the possibilities of new and remedial legislation.

New Legislation Recommended. The meeting assembled in Washington, D.C. on February 27, 1922. After two months of study and investigation, the conference unanimously recommended the immediate extension of the regulatory powers of the government, and drafted technical provisions for submission to Congress.[32]

Wallace H. White, Jr., the Congressman from Maine, took the lead in drafting a bill along the lines suggested, and stated that the proposed legislation would provide for a "traffic cop of the air." In submitting the report of the Committee on the Merchant Marine and Fisheries which had held hearings on the bill, Congressman White said in part:

On December 27, 1922, there were in operation in the country 21,065 transmitting radio stations. Of these, 16,898 were amateur stations, 2,762 were ship stations, 569 were broadcasting stations, 39 were coast stations, 12 were transoceanic stations, and there were a few others not necessary to be enumerated . . . There are, however, in addition to them, receiving stations to the estimated number of 2,000,000.

He further pointed out that 279 government stations were using 122 of the total wave lengths then available, leaving only 29 for more than 17,000 private stations of all classes. He said:

There must be an ordered system of communication on the air into which all users of the ether must be fitted or there can be no intelligible transmission by this means. It is as difficult for two stations in the same locality to simultaneously transmit on the same wave length as it is for two trains to pass each other upon the same track. A schedule for transmission of messages in the air is as essential as a schedule for the movement of trains upon land. The primary purpose of the pending bill is to give the Secretary of Commerce such powers of regulation and control as are needed to relieve the present congestion and to bring about a more orderly and efficient use of the ether.[33]

Despite the chaotic situation, the House and Senate could not agree on legislation, so Hoover called a second conference in 1923. Important commercial, scientific, and public organizations were represented. Since Congress had failed to act, the main purpose of the meeting was to work out administrative methods to reduce the ever-increasing interference to radio reception. The result was a recommendation for reallocation of frequencies which would place all broadcasting stations in a band from 550 to 1,350 kilocycles and assign other frequencies for amateur, government and marine use. The Department of Commerce adopted the recommendations and the interference problem was considerably alleviated.[34]

But Hoover was still concerned over the inadequacy of the law. There were thousands of radio stations of various types operating in the United States and along the coasts. He was expected to see that they were inspected but he had only a few men to do the work. He kept urging Congress to give the government more power to regulate broadcasting and additional money to employ adequate personnel

Hoover Calls More Conferences.   Congress continued to study the problem and Hoover continued to call conferences. At the Third National Radio Conference which assembled on October 6, 1924, he declared that "we must have traffic rules, or the whole ether will be blocked with chaos, and we must have safeguards that will keep the ether free for full development."[35]

In a statement to the press on December 31, 1924, he referred to both the appreciative and critical attitudes of the public regarding radio and its impact upon American life:

Listeners are becoming more and more appreciative of the real service of radio and increasingly critical, both as to the character of the matter furnished them and as to the efficiency with which it reaches them.

The whole broadcasting structure is built upon service to the listeners. They are beginning to realize their importance, to assert their interest and to voice their wishes. Broadcasting must be conducted to meet their demand, and this necessarily means higher character in what is transmitted and better quality in its reproduction to the ears of the listener.

The broadcasters as a whole are alive to the situation. There is a growing realization on their part of the public responsibilities they assume in conducting an agency so greatly affecting the cultural progress of our people.[36]

At the Fourth National Radio Conference in November, 1925, he reiterated the need for effective regulation. "We must face the actualities frankly," said this engineer who later was to become President. "We can no longer deal on the basis that there is room for everybody on the radio highways. There are more vehicles on the roads than can get by, and if they continue to jam in, all will be stopped."[37]

"We hear a great deal about freedom of the air, but there are two parties to freedom of the air, and to freedom of speech, for that matter. Certainly in radio I believe in freedom for the listener . . . Freedom cannot mean a license to every person or corporation who wishes to broadcast his name or his wares, and thus monopolize the listener's set."[38]

He further observed that "we do not get much freedom of speech if 150 people speak at the same time at the same place". With 578 independent stations in operation, he expected that there would be a wide latitude for the expression of opinions on social, political and religious questions. He did not feel, however, that any broadcaster could rightly complain that he had been deprived of free speech if he was compelled to prove that there was "something more than naked commercial selfishness in his purpose."[39]

He then stated a philosophy that was to become the basis for government regulation of broadcasting in this country from that day to this; that "the ether is a public medium, and its use must be for public benefit;" and that the main "consideration in the radio field is, and always will be, the great body of the listening public, millions in number, countrywide in distribution. There is no proper line of conflict between the broadcaster and the listener . . . Their interests are mutual, for without the one the other could not exist."[40]

The Radio Act of 1927. That 1925 conference recommended legislation giving the Federal government authority to issue licenses, assign wave lengths, and determine the power of broadcast stations. But the Conference cautioned against extending governmental authority "to mere matters of station management, not affecting service or creating interference."[41] Governmental censorship was strongly opposed.

Two important developments the following year made new legislation imperative. A Federal court held that a station owner could not be punished for disregarding a frequency assignment made by the Secretary of Commerce.[42] Shortly thereafter, the Attorney General sounded the death knell for Federal regulation under the then existing law when he ruled that the Act of 1912 gave the Secretary no authority to limit frequency, power or time used by any station.[43]

Congress had been holding hearings intermittently for several years but never had been able to agree on legislation. The chaotic condition of radio in 1926, however, intensified the determination of Congressional leaders to compromise differences and get a law passed. The public was fed up on the nightly chorus of heterodyne squeals caused by a multiplicity of broadcasters operating on the same channels. Congress was impelled to act.

Out of the 1926 Congressional hearings, in which leaders in government, education, religion, industry and labor urged Congress to remedy the intolerable situation, came a bill which the House and Senate finally agreed upon. It became law on February 23, 1927.[44]

This Radio Act of 1927, while imperfect in some respects, was an important step in the direction of effective radio regulation. It provided for a commission of five members with authority to grant, renew or revoke station licenses. It was provided that after one year, all authority was to be vested in the Secretary of Commerce except that he would have no authority to revoke a license and would be required to refer to the Commission all applications for licenses, renewals or modifications thereof, about which there might be any controversy.

It was definitely established by the Act that the radio spectrum belonged to the public and that a broadcaster acquired no ownership rights in a frequency when granted a license. Before he could be granted a license or a renewal of one, he was required to show that the public interest would be served. Thus the government was given authority to make a systematic assignment of frequencies and, within limitations, to set standards and make rules for the operation of radio stations.[45]

Actually, the authority provided in the law never became vested in the Secretary of Commerce. Congress from time to time extended the one year limitation and the Federal Radio Commission continued to function as originally provided until the passage of the Communications Act of 1934 when all authority to regulate radio was vested in the Federal Communications Commission.

The Federal Radio Commission established the regular broadcasting band from 550 to 1,500 kilocycles, and provided for a 10 kilocycle separation between stations. A general reallocation of frequencies brought about a more equitable distribution of radio facilities throughout the country and eliminated much of the station interference.

"Radio Became the Fifth Estate". With the help of this new "traffic cop of the air," general radio reception rapidly improved. Interference was reduced. Static continued to be some bother, but became less troublesome as the years passed. Head phones were soon replaced by attractive table sets and cabinet models. By 1930, national networks were doing a flourishing business. Plans were underway for the erection of an immense structure in the heart of New York City to cost $250,000,000. It was to cover three square blocks and rise 60 stories in the air. It was to be called Radio City, house the studios of the National Broadcasting Company and become the radio center of the world.

Will Rogers was thrilling millions of listeners with his down-to-earth philosophy and humor. Jack Pearl, popularly known as Baron Munchausen, had become top billing with his comedy on the Lucky Strike Hour. He was the forerunner of a galaxy of radio stars who captivated the American people with their talent—Ed Wynn, Eddie Cantor, George Jessel, Joe Penner, and a host of others. There were the entertainment teams—the Duncan Sisters, Amos 'n Andy, Bergen and McCarthy, Fibber McGee and Molly, to mention only a few. Paul Whiteman's orchestra and the New York Philharmonic Symphony had become network features and were being heard regularly from coast to coast.

The superbly modulated and melodious voice of Milton J. Cross was reaching the eager and appreciative ears of music lovers throughout the country as he announced the broadcasts of the Metropolitan Opera. Walter Damrosch had achieved his ambition to broadcast musical education to the nation. The Columbia Broadcasting System was bringing to the classrooms of America "The School of the Air," offering a variety of subjects designed to supplement formal instruction. The inimitable Ted Husing was reporting important sports events to millions of excited fans. The CBS "Church of the Air" had become an established radio pulpit for every major religious faith. Father Charles E. Coughlin was causing a national furor, espousing the cause of his National Union for Social Justice over an independent network.

In 1932, Harold La Fount, then a member of the Federal Radio Commission, reported that there were 17 million radio receivers in homes throughout the country.[46] Popular stars such as Kate Smith were estimated to have audiences approaching the 5 million mark.[47] According to a survey covering 16 groups of stations and embracing 93 cities, almost 25 million dollars were spent for radio advertising during 1932, with about half the amount expended to promote the sale of food, beverages, drugs, toilet articles, automobiles, and tobacco.[48]

Ted Husing, in his delightful book, *Ten Years Before the Mike*, attempted in 1935 to recapture the psychology of broadcasting during that early period:

. . . Big names of the stage, screen and concert platforms began to appear in the broadcast schedules. With symphony orchestras broadcasting Beethoven and eminent clergymen starting "churches of the air," the most finical artists could no longer look on radio as a cheap toy. As a result, delight undreamed of by the masses, music, drama, comedy, romance, travel, enlightenment of every sort—in a word (consulting my Webster), culture, pressed down and running over—began to flow freely from early morning till late night alike into the hovels of Pittsburgh steel workers and the mansions of Southampton millionaires. Radio became the Fifth Estate.[49]

Inadequate Regulation of Telephone and Telegraph Service. Rules established by the Federal Radio Commission had helped to alleviate the chaos which had characterized radio in its formative years and had given impetus to the rapid and healthy development of the broadcasting industry. This Commission, however, had no authority to regulate telephone and telegraph companies now doing an enormous interstate business. In 1910, Congress had provided for the Federal regulation of these companies but the law was never adequate.[50] Regulatory authority had been assigned to the Interstate Commerce Commission, but that agency was largely concerned with railroad transportation, and communications received comparatively little attention.

Numerous state commissions had been established but their ability to regulate industries which had become national in scope was seriously limited. They were powerless to regulate communication services extending across state lines and into foreign countries.

Felix Frankfurter, then a professor of law at Harvard University, expressed the opinion in 1930 that throughout the United States the machinery of utility regulation had shown strain. He made note of the growing public feeling that not only had the purposes for which these state commissions had been designed—to serve the interests of the consumers—not been realized, but that actually the regulatory systems had been operating to defeat these purposes.[51]

In 1932, Dr. W.W. Splawn, Special Counsel for the House Committee on Interstate and Foreign Commerce, which had undertaken a special study of communications companies in the United States, wrote that the "American people are entitled to know if they are being over-charged for service" and stressed the need for more effective regulation. He expressed the feeling held by many at the time that a new Federal commission should be created to make an intensive study of telephone and telegraph companies with particular respect to their accounts, their methods, of figuring depreciation, their operating expenses, their contracts for service, and their political activities.[52]

The telegraph and telephone industries more and more were making use of radio for point to point communication in both their domestic and foreign business. At the same time, the expansion of the broadcasting industry depended greatly upon the use of wire and cable facilities, particularly in the development of network operations.

As previously pointed out, prior to 1926, the Bell System had owned and operated broadcast stations. It had established its own network, manufactured and sold broadcast transmitting equipment, and furnished wire facilities to other broadcasters. It restricted the use of wire facilities to promote its own broadcasting activities and to protect its patent position.

After July, 1926, when the company sold its stations, it limited its radio activities to the furnishing of wire facilities to broadcasters. By reason of its patent position, its extensive wire networks, and its restrictive policies, it had attained a dominant position in the broadcasting field. Despite this monopoly, and the almost total dependence of broadcasters upon the Bell System for network operation, the telephone company, prior to 1934, had not committed itself to the principle that the furnishing of wire service to broadcasters was a part of its public service responsibility.[53]

There was increasing public awareness of the inter-dependency of the radio and telephone business as well as that of the telegraph companies. It became apparent that the efficiency, economy and growth of these media depended greatly upon how well their operations were coordinated. It followed, therefore, that effective regulation of any one of them required an understanding of the others and the working relationships of them all.

Accordingly, experts in the communications field such as Dr. Splawn felt there was imperative need for the establishment of a comprehensive national policy covering all these media, with a single Federal agency designed and equipped to administer the policy and make rules implementing it.

Roosevelt and the FCC. It was the perception of this need that prompted President Roosevelt to initiate a study of the over-all problem during the summer of 1933. Pursuant to his directive, the Secretary of Commerce appointed a governmental committee to consider the formulation of a national policy.[54] This committee found that regulation at the Federal level was divided among various governmental agencies. Radio was under the jurisdiction of the Federal Radio Commission; to a limited extent, as already mentioned, the Interstate Commerce Commission was authorized to regulate interstate telephone and telegraph carriers but did very little to exercise its powers; minor jurisdictions over wire services, at one time or another, had been vested in the Postmaster General and the President. The Committee was of the opinion that this division of authority was not conducive to effective regulation and recommended that a new Federal commission be created to which all existing authority would be transferred.[55]

David Sarnoff, President of the Radio Corporation of America, appeared before the House Committee on Interstate and Foreign Commerce on May 16, 1934 and testified in support of the principle of unified regulation of the communications industry. He said:

> We have always believed in the necessity for effective regulation of communications by a single governmental agency, and we pledge our complete support to the President's views as expressed to Congress in his message of February 26, in which he urged the creation of a single agency to be vested with the authority now lying in the Federal Radio Commission, together with that authorized over communications now vested in the Interstate Commerce Commission.
>
> To make this authority complete, I would suggest that the present authority of the Postmaster General over communications covered in the Post Roads Act, which includes the power to fix rates for governmental telegrams, be also transferred to the new Commission. Similarly, the power of the Executive Department, covering the granting and regulation of cable landing licenses, should likewise be transferred to the new Commission. Only in this manner can the United States develop a unified and progressive communications policy, both national and international.
>
> Foreign nations give much thought to the control and effective planning of their international communication services. The creation of a single Federal regulatory body in this country will mark a most constructive step in the communications history of the United States. We therefore hope that the Communications Act of 1934 will become law and that under that law the Federal Communications Commission will be promptly established.[56]

Many other important leaders in industry, government and education supported Mr. Sarnoff's point of view. And after extensive hearings and debate, the Congress enacted the Communications Act of 1934, abolishing the Federal Radio Commission and creating the Federal Communications

Commisssion with authority to regulate all interstate and foreign communication by means of wire or radio. The President signed the bill and it became law on June 19, 1934.[57]

Thus it was that the basic Federal law governing communications was established. It was an outgrowth of a long evolutionary process which had been going on for many decades. The law has now been in effect for more than thirty-seven years. It has been amended from time to time, but its basic features remain very much the same today as they were in 1934 when the law was adopted.

The story of how the Communications Act of 1934 and the FCC came into being is the story of America's struggle to achieve maximum benefits from communications under a system of democratic, free enterprise. Both literally and figuratively, our people sought to eliminate static in the field of communications. They chose private ownership and management but insisted that there be government regulation for the protection of the public interest.

In the next part of this book, the more important features and provisions of this law as adopted in 1934, will be reviewed and the powers, functions and organizational structure of the FCC which it created will be described. The study, of course, will have more meaning and value if made in terms of the technical, social, economic and cultural developments discussed in this and the preceding chapter.

1. Shurick, E.P.J., *The First Quarter Century of American Broadcasting* (Kansas City, 1946), pp. 28-29; also, Husing, Ted, *Ten Years Before the Mike* (New York, 1935), pp. 17-18.

2. Shurick, *Ibid.*, pp. 46-47.

3. Dunlap, Jr., Orin Elmer, *Dunlap's Radio and Television Almanac* (New York, 1951), p. 58.

4. Shurick, *op.cit.*, p. 66.

5. Landry, Robert, Jr., *This Fascinating Radio Business* (New York 1946), p. 161.

6. *New York Times*, January 2, 1925, pp. 1,3.

7. Shurick, *op. cit.*, pp. 59-61, 71, and personal recollections of the author.

8. *Ibid.*, pp. 121, 129-30.

9. *Ibid.*, pp. 265-266.

10. Chester, Giraud and Garrison, R. Garnet, *Radio and Television* (New York, 1950), p. 25; also, see Goldsmith, Alfred N. and Lescarboura, Austin C., *This Thing Called Broadcasting* (New York, 1930).

11. Shurick, *op.cit.*, pp. 141-142, 303.

12. *Ibid.*, 312-314, 320.

13. KFKB *Broadcasting Association*, FRC, June 13, 1930, affirmed 60 App. D.C. 79, 47 F. (2d) 670 (1931).

14. Pike and Fischer, *Radio Regulation*, Vol. I, pp. 41:201-202; contains background report on original North American Regional Broadcast Agreement which became effective March 29, 1941 and Mexico's ratification of this agreement.

15. Landry, *op.cit.*, p. 48.

16. Third National Radio Conference, *Recommendations for Regulation of Radio* (Washington, D. C., 1924), p. 2.

17. Chase, Francis Jr., *Sound and Fury* (New York, 1942), p. 21.

18. Federal Communications Commission, *Report on Chain Broadcasting*, Commission Order No. 37, Docket No. 5060 (Washington, D. C., May, 1941), p. 6.

19. *Ibid.*

20. *Ibid.*

21. *Ibid*, p. 7.

22. *Ibid*, pp. 7-8.

23. *Ibid.*

24. *Ibid.*

25. *Ibid.*, pp. 21-23.

26. *New York Times*, January 28, 1924, p. 1; also *Federal Trade Commission Report* No. 1686, December 1, 1923.

27. *New York Times*, October 17, 1925, p. 3.

28. *Ibid.*, September 5, 1924, Section I, p. 17.

29. *Ibid.*, July 23, 1922, Section I, p. 17.

30. 36 Stat. 629 (1910).

31. 37 Stat. 199 (1912).

32. First National Radio Conference, *Proceedings* (Washington, D.C., February 27, 1922).

33. *House Reports,* (Vol. 1, 67th Congress, 3rd and 4th Sessions, 1922, 1923, Report No. 1416), p. 2.

34. *Radio Service Bulletin*, Bureau of Navigation, Department of Commerce, (April 2, 1923), pp. 9-10.

35. Third National Radio Conference, *Recommendations for Regulation of Radio* (Washington D.C., October 6-10, 1924), pp. 1-2.

36. *New York Times,* January 1, 1925, p. 22.

37. Fourth National Radio Conference, *Proceedings and Recommendations for Regulation of Radio* (Washington, D.C., November 9-11, 1925), p. 6.

38. *Ibid,* p. 7.

39. *Ibid.*

40. *Ibid.*

41. *Ibid.* p. 34.

42. *United States v. Zenith Radio Corporation,* 12 F. (2nd) 616 (1926).

43. 35 Op. Att. Gen. 126 (1926).

44. 44 Stat. 1162-1174.

45. For good analysis of its provisions see Cushman, Robert E., *The Independent Regulatory Commissions* (New York, 1941), pp. 302-310.

46. *New York Times,* May 25, 1932, p. 22.

47. Landry, *op. cit.,* p. 306.

48. *Advertising and Selling,* November 26, 1930, p. 40.

49. Husing, *op. cit.,* pp. 107-108.

50. 36 Stat. 539, June 18, 1910.

51. Frankfurter, Felix, *The Public and Its Government* (New Haven, 1930), p. 93.

52. *Preliminary Report on Communications Companies* (H.R. 1273, 73rd Congress, 2nd Session, April 18, 1934), p. XXXI.

53. Federal Communications Commission, *Proposed Report, Telephone Investigation, Pursuant to Public Resolution No. 8, 74th Congress,* p. 470. Chapter 13 of this report, pp. 454-470, contains a detailed and accurate account of the Bell system's involvement in broadcasting activities up until 1934.

54. Senate Committee Print, S. Doc. 144, *Study of Communications by an Interdepartmental Committee,* (73rd Congress, 2d Sess. 1934).

55. *Ibid.*

56. *Hearings before the Committee on Interstate and Foreign Commerce, House of Representatives* (H.R. 8301, 73rd Cong., April 10, 1934), pp. 292-293.

57. 48 Stat. 1064, June 19, 1934.

PART II

The Basis and Scope
of Governmental Controls

CHAPTER 3

The Statutory Powers and Functions
of the FCC

*When one segment of society, whether it be government or industry or some
other, is vested with unlimited authority over radio, then freedom is threatened and democracy suffers. It is diversification and balance of control that
we want in American radio.* —PAUL A. WALKER*

One of the distinctive features of the Communications Act of 1934 is that
it envisages private ownership and operation of telegraph, telephone and
broadcasting facilities. Prior to the passage of the Act, however, there had
been some pressures on Congress from time to time to establish a system
of government ownership patterned after systems adopted in other countries. In the early days, for example, Samuel Morse tried to persuade Congress to take over telegraph communication. He thought it would be better
if the government would assume complete control of its use and development.[1] He was supported in this view in 1845 by the Postmaster General
who stated that "the use of an instrument so powerful for good or evil
cannot with safety to the people be left in the hands of private individuals . . . "[2]

Many years later, in 1913, Postmaster General Burleson, influenced by
Congressional agitations, publicly declared:

A study of the constitutional purposes of the postal establishment leads to the
conviction that the Post Office Department should have control over all means of
the communication of intelligence. The first telegraph line in this country was
maintained and operated as a part of the postal service, and it is to be regretted that
Congress saw fit to relinquish this facility to private enterprise . . . [3]

He observed that in other countries the government owned and operated
communications services and he advocated that the government in this
country do the same.[4]

There was a resurgence of this type of advocacy at the time of America's
entrance into the First World War. It again reached a high pitch during the

*Former chairman of the FCC.

39

depression years as revolutionaries and agitators, encouraged by the social anxiety of the period, attempted a demolition job on the free enterprise system.

But Congress, always influenced by the traditional conservatism of the American community, consistently resisted this panacean advocacy. Unwilling to run the risk of what Justice Holmes called "interstitial detriments"[5] that may result from radical and abrupt social change, Congress rejected the idea of government ownership of communications media in this country.

At the same time, as heretofore pointed out, telecommunications had become so vital to American life that the public demanded that they be more strictly regulated by the government. And it was this growing psychology in the early thirties that precipitated Congressional action, resulting in the Communications Act of 1934. A basic feature of the law, therefore, is its establishment of a national policy regarding these media which makes the public interest paramount and sets up administrative machinery to execute this policy. At the same time, it provides for private operation with legislative restrictions against governmental intrusion and control. Important sections of the law as they pertain to broadcasting are reproduced in Appendix I, including the Communications Act Amendments, 1960, adopted by the 86th Congress and approved by the President on September 13, 1960. Amendments since 1960 also have been added.

Scope and Limits of Federal Authority. As stated in Section I, the broad purpose of the Communications Act (hereinafter sometimes referred to as the Act) is "to make available, so far as possible, to *all* the people of the United States, a *rapid, efficient, nation-wide,* and *world-wide* wire and radio communication *service* with adequate facilities at *reasonable* charges . . . " (emphasis supplied), and the Federal Communications Commission was created, with centralized authority to carry out this policy and enforce the provisions of the Act.[6]

As pointed out in the previous chapter, the Radio Act of 1927 was repealed and the powers and functions of the Federal Radio Commission were assigned to the new agency. The limited authority with respect to wire communications vested in the Interstate Commerce Commission and the Postmaster General were likewise transferred.[7]

In the establishment of the 1934 Act, Congress was careful not to encroach upon the authority of state governments. Section 2 makes it emphatic that no part of the Act applies to communications which are purely intrastate in character.[8] Its application is limited to interstate and foreign communication.[9] The FCC, therefore, cannot prescribe rules for communication services which are strictly local in character and do not cross state boundaries. For example, the rates charged and the service provided in connection with telephone calls and telegrams transmitted and received over wires that do not cross state boundaries are not regulated by the FCC. These are regulated by state public utility commissions. Congress recognized, however, that information available to these state agencies might be useful in dealing with interstate and foreign communication and provided in the Act that the FCC might "avail itself of such cooperation services, records, and facilities" as might be provided by any State commission.[10]

Under the "commerce clause" of the Constitution, Congress had the power to establish a federal agency to regulate interstate and foreign communications.[11] In the early administration of the Communications Act, however, the question was raised whether radio transmissions not crossing state lines constituted "interstate commerce" and were subject to federal jurisdiction. The courts answered this question in the affirmative. In 1933, the Supreme Court said that "no state lines divide the radio waves, and national regulation is not only appropriate but essential to the efficient use of radio facilities."[12]

Since any radio emission, regardless of its range, may affect or cause interference to other radio signals crossing state lines, it is subject to the regulatory authority of the FCC.[13] As Judge Freed in *U.S. v. Betteridge,* (N.D. Ohio, E. Div., 43 F. Supp. 53, 55) pointed out, because of the natural characteristics of electromagnetic waves "all transmissions of energy communications or signals by radio, either use an interstate or foreign channel of transmission or so affect interstate or foreign channels as to require the regulation of their use" if the purposes of the Communications Act are to be carried out effectively. [14]

What this means is that the FCC has exclusive regulatory jurisdiction with respect to any type of radio transmission, and can require every station regardless of its power and range to have a license and to operate under rules established by the Commission. Attempts by state governmental agencies to exercise authority in this field are invalid and have been so held by the Federal courts.[15]

Monopoly Condoned and Condemned. When the Act was adopted, the telegraph and telephone industries had come to be recognized as "natural monopolies" in this country. History had shown the folly of free competition with wasteful duplication of facilities. Yet experience had also demonstrated that monopolies often resulted in abuse of power with infliction of unreasonably high and discriminatory rates upon the public. As protection against these predatory practices, Congress subjected both services and charges of interstate and foreign "carriers for hire" to FCC regulations.

Section 201 of the Act makes it the duty of these telegraph and telephone companies to furnish service on request and to connect with one another to establish through routes.[16] The section further declares that these public utilities must be fair and reasonable in their "charges, practices and classifications." Section 202 prohibits preferences in charges or services and 203 requires the publication of all rate schedules.[17]

The FCC was given authority to determine and prescribe reasonable charges and standards of service and to require carriers subject to the Act to file an inventory of all or any parts of their properties, classified by units and showing original costs and estimated costs of reproduction less depreciation. The Commission was also given "free access" to all properties of the carriers and their "accounts, records, and memoranda."[18]

While recognizing and sanctioning regulated monopoly in domestic wire communication services, Congress wanted to encourage competition between cable and radio in the foreign communication business. Wires and cables were first used for regular telegraph and telephone service between the United States and other countries. Subsequently, wireless transmission was developed, and, as heretofore pointed out, by 1934 radio telegraphy and telephony had become well established in the overseas service. Congress was concerned that no arrangements or agreements of any kind should be made which might unduly restrain competition between cable and radio as two separate and distinct means of international communication.[19] Accordingly, Section 314 of the Act provides that any such contrivances or deals involving unfair methods of competition are unlawful.[20]

Broadcasting: a Field of Free Competition. Unlike the telegraph and telephone industries, Congress recognized the field of broadcasting as one of free competition. Radio and television stations broadcasting programs intended to be received by the general public are not considered to be "common carriers for hire."[21] The Commission, therefore, was not given any authority to require stations to make their facilities available to every member of the public who might request them and has no power to determine or regulate the rates charged for the sale of broadcasting time.

To guard against the tendencies toward monopolistic control in broadcasting which had already developed in 1934, Congress declared in Section 313 of the Act that "all the laws of the United States" relating to unlawful restraints of trade are applicable to the manufacture and sale of radio apparatus and to broadcasting in general.[22] The section further provides that if any broadcaster is found guilty of the violation of any such laws the court hearing the case may revoke the license of the station. In the event the court assesses this extreme penalty, Section 311 prohibits the Commission from granting any further radio authorizations to the guilty party.[23]

Public Ownership of Broadcast Channels. The tangible facilities including wire and cables and other physical apparatus used by telephone and telegraph "carriers" and broadcasting stations are privately owned. While the use of these properties is regulated by the FCC, the actual title to the properties is vested in the carrier companies and the broadcast licensees. This is not true with respect to broadcast channels which they employ. Section 301 asserts with crystal clarity that one of the purposes of the Act is "to maintain the control of the United States over all the channels of interstate and foreign radio transmission."[24] It is provided that these channels can be used for limited periods of time only under licenses granted by federal authority and that no such license is to be construed as creating "any right beyond the terms, conditions, and periods of the license."[25]

The law states that "no station license shall be granted by the Commission until the applicant therefore shall have signed a waiver of any claim to the use of any particular frequency or of the ether as against the regulatory power of the United States because of the previous use of the same, whether by license or otherwise."[26]

General Powers of the FCC. Section 303 of the Act sets forth the general powers of the FCC with respect to broadcasting. The Commission is authorized to classify stations, prescribe the nature of their service, determine what power and type of technical facilities they shall use, the time they shall operate, where they shall be located and the areas they shall serve. It also may inspect equipment and installations and may designate and cause to be published the call letters of stations.[27]

One of the most important powers is that of allocating channels to the various classes of broadcasting service and the assignment of frequencies for station operation. In these functions, the Commission is under a statutory mandate to make "a fair, efficient, and equitable distribution of radio service" among the various states and communities.[28]

To prevent a recurrence of the bedlam in the ether which had bedeviled radio in earlier years, the framers of the 1934 Act gave the Commission specific authority to make regulations "necessary to prevent interference between stations."[29] But it was not enough simply to perform "traffic cop" functions. To carry out its powers and keep pace with a dynamic and fast growing industry, the Commission was required to "study new uses for radio, provide for experimental uses of frequencies and generally encourage the larger and more effective use of radio in the public interest.[30] It was also given authority to make such rules and regulations and prescribe such restrictions and conditions as might be necessary to carry out the provisions of the Act.[31]

Authority To Regulate Network Stations. At the time the Radio Act of 1927 was passed there was Congressional concern that networks might acquire monopolistic controls and unduly restrict competition in the industry. In the debates on the 1927 Act, Senator Dill expressed the feeling of anxiety prevalent in Congress and among independent broadcasters:

... the various radio organizations, including the Radio Corporation of America and the American Telephone and Telegraph Co., are going ahead and building up the chain stations as they desire without any restrictions because the Secretary of Commerce has no power to interfere with them. Unless this proposed legislation shall be enacted they will continue to do so and they will be able by chain-broadcasting methods practically to obliterate the independent small stations . . . [32]

While the commission would have the power under the general terms of the bill, the bill specifically sets out as one of the special powers of the Commission the right to make specific regulations for governing chain broadcasting . . . [33]

This section of the bill, providing that the Radio Commission had the power to "make special regulations applicable to radio stations engaged in chain broadcasting", was passed and became Section 4 (h) of the Radio Act of 1927.[34] It was carried over verbatim and appears as Section 303 (i) of the 1934 law, giving the FCC the same power to make such regulations.[35] It was the exercise of this authority by the FCC which subsequently resulted in the adoption of the network regulations which now control the relations between the networks and their station affiliates and to which detailed reference is made in Chapter 18.

It should be noted here that only licensees of stations and not networks as such are covered by Section 303 (i). If these stations are affiliates, and their relationships with networks affect their ability to operate in the public interest, then the Commission is empowered by law to make special rules governing their operations. It goes without saying that the effect of exercising this power is an indirect control over the network organizations.

There has been growing sentiment in Congress during the past ten years in favor of amending the law, giving the FCC direct regulatory authority over the networks. For example, a bill introduced in Congress in February, 1960 (HR 11340) by Congressman Oren Harris would bring TV and radio networks under FCC control, requiring "operating certificates" for networks with proscriptions against illegality in programs, failure to exercise control over matter broadcast, giving unfair advantages in matter broadcast to products and services in which networks have interests, and making contracts with affiliates not deemed to be in the public interest.

Again, on June 1, 1967, Congressmen John D. Dingell and John E. Moss introduced House Bill 10481 (90th Congress, 1st Session). Proposed as an amendment to Section 2a of the Communications Act, the bill would bring television networks and their programs under the direct control of the FCC. Among other things, the bill would make the "fairness doctrine" and Section 315 of the Act (equal treatment for political candidates) applicable to these networks; require them to provide a "balanced program structure;" impose restrictions on the amount of programs they may own and control; limit the amount of programming they may make available to their affiliates; prohibit agreements which would allow TV networks to interrupt or suspend football games and other specified athletic events to broadcast commercial advertisments; and forbid network ownership of any business which promotes professional games.

Furthermore, the bill would require networks to make available programs to the maximum number of television broadcasting stations; and would forbid them from exercising any influence or controlling the rates charged by their affiliates for non-network programs, or from engaging directly or indirectly as sales representatives for independent stations, "except for the sale of program time or other services connected with network broadcasting."

All network contracts with stations would be required to be filed with the FCC and would be open to public inspection. And any such contracts would be prohibited which would "unreasonably" restrict use by an affiliated station of its own productions, or those furnished by other networks and program distributors.

Finally, the FCC would be authorized to establish "any other rules and regulations with respect to television networks for the purpose of insuring that their operation will be in the public interest."

As reported by *Broadcasting* (June 5, 1967, p. 30), some members of Congress expressed the view that the bill perhaps was intended for propaganda purposes, or to express Congressional displeasure with some current practices of networks, but with no serious thought that the bill would be enacted into law. But Congressman Moss insisted that the proposal was to be taken literally, that it "was an attempt to set up a system of fair broadcasting, to let free enterprise work."

No action was taken on the bill. However, in February, 1968, Congressmen Dingell and Moss introduced a similar one (H. R. 15267). As of April 29, 1968, the bill was still resting in the House Interstate and Foreign Commerce Committee and no hearings had yet been held. Some segments of the broadcast industry have expressed strong opposition to the proposed legislation, and whether Congress will provide for FCC regulation of the networks is problematical.

Licensing Powers.   Of all the powers possessed by the FCC none is more important than that which pertains to its licensing functions. Section 308 (a) of the Act gives the Commission authority to grant construction permits and station licenses or modifications or renewals thereof. Paragraph (b) of the same section specifies that all such applications "shall set forth such facts as the Commission by regulation may prescribe as to citizenship, character, and financial, technical, and other qualifications of the applicant to operate the station," and other information pertaining to ownership of facilities, proposed frequency, power, hours of operation, and the purposes for which the station is to be used.[36]

At any time after the filing of an application, or during the period of a license, the Commission may require from the applicant or the licensee additional information to determine whether the application should be granted or denied or the license should be revoked.[37] Such information must be submitted in written form under oath or affirmation.[38]

No construction permit or station license, or any rights pertaining thereto may be transferred, assigned or disposed of in any manner without the prior approval of the Commission. Section 310 (b) requires the filing of a written application for such transfer or assignment and the written consent of the Commission.[39]

If upon examination of any application, it appears that the applicant is not qualified or that a grant would not serve the public interest, the Commission has the power to deny the application. The applicant, however, must be given an opportunity for a public hearing before the decision is made final, as provided in Section 309 (b).[40]

If the licensee fails to operate substantially as required by his license or fails to observe or violates any provision of the Act or regulation of the Commission, the agency may issue a cease and desist order with respect to the offense. In the case of willful or repeated violations of the law or regulations as described in Section 312, the more serious penalty of license revocation may be assessed. Before either a cease and desist order or license revocation can become final, however, the licensee must be given the opportunity for a hearing as prescribed in paragraphs (c), (d), and (e) of Section 312.[41]

As is discussed more fully in Chapter 21, Congress recently amended Section 503, granting the FCC authority to impose forfeitures for willful and repeated violations of the Act, certain sections of the Criminal Code, United States treaties, or FCC regulations.

Station Operators. The Commission has the responsibility of classifying and prescribing the qualifications of station operators and issues licenses in accordance therewith. Subject to the right of an operator to a formal hearing as provided in Section 303 (2), the Commission is vested with power to suspend and revoke his license if convincing evidence shows him guilty of any of the following offenses:

1. Violation of any provision of the Act, treaty or other agreement binding on the United States or rules implementing the same.

2. Failure to carry out a lawful order of the master of a ship.

3. Willful damage to any radio installations.

4. Transmission of superfluous radio communications containing profane or obscene words; or willful transmissions of false or deceptive signals or communications.

5. Willful and malicious interference with any other radio communications.

6. Obtaining or attempting to obtain for himself or another an operator's license by fraudulent means.[42]

Program Controls. Section 326 of the Act specifically prohibits the Commission from censoring radio and television programs. It reads:

Nothing in this Act shall be understood or construed to give the Commission the power of censorship over the radio communications or signals transmitted by any radio station and no regulation or condition shall be promulgated or fixed by the Commission which shall interfere with the right of free speech by means of radio communication.[43]

There have been differences of opinion as to what this provision means. Some have contended that it precludes any concern on the part of the Commission with the program service of licensees, except in cases where there are violations of specific laws. This view was strongly espoused by former Commissioner T.A.M. Craven. On November 19, 1958, the FCC adopted a public notice proposing to make certain revisions in Section IV of its renewal application form 303.[44] The changes proposed pertained to that part of the application form which elicited information regarding past program service of a station and that intended for the future. Commissioner Craven dissented to the proposed changes, contending that the Commission exceeds its authority when it requires applicants for broadcast facilities to file any program information except that which may be requested to determine whether a specific law would be or is being violated. He believes that the First Amendment to the Constitution and Section 326 of the Act forbid the Commission from exercising any authority over broadcast programming except where infractions against lottery laws and the like may be involved.[45]

Others have interpreted Section 326 differently. Relating it to other provisions of the Act, they believe that, while the Commission cannot tell a station what particular program or programs it can or cannot present, it does have the authority and the responsibility to review the over-all operation of a station when it comes up for renewal of its license to determine whether its operation has been in the public interest. This interpretation seems to be correct as confirmed by the legislative history of the Radio Act of 1927, the Communications Act of 1934, and the consistent administrative practice of the two commissions and court decisions.

Early Administrative Practice. The law directs the Commission to grant licenses and renewals of these licenses *only* if public interest, convenience and necessity will be served thereby. The original Federal Radio Commission which was established in 1927 assumed from the beginning that program service was an important factor in making this determination. The renewal application forms used by it contained questions as to the amount of time devoted by the station to various types of programs.[46]

From 1927 to 1934, this original commission made reports to Congress regarding its practice of evaluating program service in connection with its consideration of renewal applications. By the time Congress was considering the replacement of the 1927 law with the Communications Act of 1934, there appeared to be little doubt that the government did have the authority and the responsibility to take program performance into account.

In Congressional hearings on one of the bills which culminated in the 1934 law, the National Association of Broadcasters presented a statement upholding this regulatory authority. It read in part as follows:

It is the manifest duty of the licensing authority in passing upon applications for licenses or the renewal thereof, to determine whether or not the applicant is rendering or can render an adequate public service. Such service necessarily includes broadcasting of a considerable proportion of programs devoted to education, religion, labor, agricultural and similar activities concerned with human betterment. In actual practice over a period of seven years, as the records of the Federal Radio Commission amply prove, this has been the principal test which the Commission has applied in dealing with broadcasting applications.[47]

In hearings upon the same bill, the Chairman of the Federal Radio Commission testified that "it is the duty of the Commission in passing on whether or not that station should be relicensed for another period, to say whether or not its past performance during the last license period has been in the public interest"[48] Fully informed of the procedure which had been followed by the Federal Radio Commission, Congress re-enacted the relevant provisions in the Communications Act of 1934.

When the 1934 Act was being considered by Congress there was a great deal of public agitation and pressure for a provision in the law which would require stations to set aside substantial portions of their broadcast time to be used by educational institutions and other non-profit organizations. In fact, the public feeling was so strong that 23 Senators voted for the Wagner-Hatfield Amendment which proposed to allocate 25 per cent of all radio broadcasting facilities to educational, religious, agricultural, labor, cooperative, and similar non-profit-making interests. While Congress did not adopt the amendment,[49] it did pass Section 307 (c) of the Act directing the FCC to make a study of the proposal and report to Congress its findings.[50]

The Commission did make a study, and in its report to Congress in 1935 it advised against the adoption of the legislative proposal. Its main reason for opposing it was that it already had adequate authority to achieve the ends that Congress had in mind. The Report in part said:

> The Commission feels that present legislation has the flexibility essential to attain the desired ends without necessitating at this time any changes in the law.
> In order for non-profit organizations to obtain the maximum service possible, cooperation in good faith by the broadcasters is required. Such cooperation should therefore, be under the direction of the Commission.[51]

FCC Program Powers Recognized by the Courts. From the very beginning, therefore, the FCC took the attitude that it did have the power to take into account program service as an important factor in its public interest determinations. Its view had been supported not only by legislative history and prior administrative practice, but by court decisions as well.

In the KFKB case referred to in the previous chapter, in which Dr. Brinkley's application for a renewal of license was denied, the Federal Radio Commission said:

> The Commission is expressly precluded by the Radio Act of 1927 from exercising any power of censorship. At the same time, the Commission must, under the statutory standard, reach a decision that the nature of the program broadcast is in the public interest, convenience and necessity before it may grant an application. Upon the evidence adduced, the Commission feels constrained to hold that the practice of a physician's prescribing treatment for a patient whom he has never seen, and bases his diagnosis upon what symptoms may be recited by the patient in a letter addressed to him, is inimical to the public health, and safety, and for that reason is not in the public interest.
> The testimony in this case shows conclusively that the operation of Station KFKB is conducted only in the personal interest of Dr. John R. Brinkley. While it is to be expected that a licensee of a radio broadcasting station will receive some remunera-

tion for serving the public with radio programs, at the same time the interest of the listening public is paramount, and may not be subordinated to the interests of the station licensee. A license to operate a radio broadcasting station is a franchise from the public, and the licensee is a trustee for the public. Station KFKB has not been operated in the interest of the listening public and we, therefore, find that public interest, convenience and necessity will not be served by granting the application for renewal of its license.[52]

The United States Court of Appeals for the District of Columbia sustained the Commission's decision, holding that under Section 11 of the Radio Act of 1927 the Federal Radio Commission was "necessarily called upon to consider the character and quality of the service to be rendered and that in considering an application for renewal of a license an important consideration is the past conduct of the applicant."[53]

In its argument to the Court of Appeals, the Commission had contended that there had been no attempt on its part "to scrutinize broadcast matter prior to its release," and that administrative review of the station's past conduct was not censorship.[54] The Court agreed with this point of view.

In a 1932 case, the Court of Appeals again reaffirmed this position. A Reverend Dr. Shuler owned KGEF in Los Angeles. The Commission denied his application for renewal of license on grounds that he attacked religious organizations, public officials, the courts, institutions and individuals; that these attacks often were not based upon facts; and that, in general, the programs of the station tended to be "sensational" in character rather than instructive or entertaining.[55] On appeal, the Court sustained the Commission's decision. In its opinion the Court said:

If it be considered that one in possession of a permit to broadcast in interstate commerce may, without let or hindrance from any source, use these facilities, reaching out, as they do, from one corner of the country to the other, to obstruct the administration of justice, offend the religious susceptibilities of thousands, inspire political distrust and civic discord, or offend youth and innocence by the use of words suggestive of sexual immorality, and be answerable for slander only at the instance of the one offended, then this great science, instead of a boon, will become a scourge, and the nation a theatre for the display of individual passions and the collision of personal interests. This is neither censorship nor previous restraint, nor is it a whittling away of the rights guaranteed by the First Amendment, or an impairment of their free exercise . . . [56]

Dr. Shuler appealed the case to the U.S. Supreme Court, but his petition for a writ of *certiorari* was denied.[57] This left no doubt, from a judicial point of view, that the Federal Radio Commission had the authority to evaluate past program performance in connection with its consideration of renewal applications.

Judicial Sanction of Network Regulations. The language prohibiting censorship, which appeared in Section 29 of the Radio Act of 1927, was reproduced verbatim in Section 326 of the Communications Act of 1934. It came up for consideration again by the Federal courts in connection with their review of the FCC's network regulations.

It is interesting to note that former Commissioner Craven, in 1941, when he was serving his first term as a member of the FCC, dissented to the Commission's adopting of the network regulations on much the same grounds that he objected to requiring applicants and licensees to furnish information regarding program service. In a nineteen-page dissent, in which former Commissioner Norman Case joined, he said:

... The type of regulation specified by Congress for broadcasting clearly envisioned that the Communications Commission should not regulate the programs, the business practices or business policies of broadcast licensees.[58]

The network regulations were vigorously contested in the courts. Contentions similar to those made in the earlier cases were made that the Commission's powers were limited to technical matters, and that the right of free speech within the purview of the First Amendment and Section 326 of the Communications Act was abridged. The Supreme Court rejected these arguments and upheld the legal validity of the regulations. In answer to the contentions of the appellants, the Court said:

The Commission's licensing function cannot be discharged, therefore, merely by finding that there are no technological objections to the granting of a license. If the criterion of 'public interest' were limited to such matters, how could the Commission choose between two applicants for the same facilities, each of whom is financially and technically qualified to operate a station? Since the very inception of Federal. regulation of radio, comparative considerations as to the service to be rendered have governed the application of the standard of 'public interest, convenience, or necessity.'[59]

The Court further said:

... we are asked to regard the Commission as a kind of traffic officer, policing the wave lengths to prevent stations from interfering with each other. But the Act does not restrict the Commission merely to supervision of the traffic. It puts upon the Commission the burden of determining the composition of that traffic.[60]

FCC Authority Limited by Public Interest Considerations. While possessing a wide range of discretion in the exercise of its powers, the Commission must always be guided by the "public interest, convenience, or necessity." If at any time, it fails to comply with this standard, the courts are available for redress.

For example, in choosing among applicants for limited radio facilities, the Commission may exercise administrative discretion, but the law requires that its judgments be based upon public interest considerations. Parties who are aggrieved by actions unsupported by substantial evidence or by "arbitrary" or "capricious" actions, not in accord with this statutory requirements, may secure relief through appeal to the courts.

In this connection, the following discourse of the United States Supreme Court in a 1952 case is pertinent:

With the chaotic scramble for domestic air space that developed soon after the First World War, Congress recognized the need for a more orderly development of the air waves than had been achieved under prior legislation. Although the Radio Act of 1912 had forbidden the operation of radio apparatus without a license from the Secretary of Commerce and Labor, judicial decision left him powerless to prevent licensees from using unassigned frequencies, to restrict their transmitting hours and power, or to deny a license on the ground that a proposed station would necessarily interfere with existing stations. See *National Broadcasting Co. v. United States,* 319 U.S. 190, 212. Congress thereupon, in the Radio Act of 1927, created the Federal Radio Commission with wide licensing and regulatory powers over interstate and foreign commerce.

Congress did not purport to transfer its legislative power to the unbounded discretion of the regulatory body. In choosing among applicants, the Commission was to be guided by the 'public interest, convenience, or necessity', a criterion we held not to be too indefinite for fair enforcement. *New York Central Securities Corp. v. United States,* 287 U.S. 12. The statutory standard no doubt leaves wide discretion and calls for imaginative interpretation. Not a standard that lends itself to application with exactitude, it expresses a policy, born of years of unhappy trial and error, that is 'as concrete as the complicated factors for judgment in such a field of delegated authority'. *Federal Communications Comm'n v. Pottsville Broadcasting Co.,* 309 U.S. 134, 138.

Congress might have made administrative decision to license not reviewable. Although it is not suggested—or implied by the grant of power to review—that Congress could not have reserved to itself or to the Commission final designation of those who would be permitted to utilize the air waves, precious as they have become with technological advance, it has not done so. On the other hand, the scope of this Court's duty to review administrative determinations under the Federal Communications Act of 1934, 48 *Stat.* 1064, as amended, 47 U.S.C., Section 151 *et seq.,* has been carefully defined. Ours is not the duty of reviewing determinations of 'fact' in the narrow, colloquial scope of that concept. Congress has charged the courts with the responsibility of saying whether the Commission has fairly exercised its discretion within the vaguish, penumbral bounds expressed by the standard of 'public interest'. It is our responsibility to say whether the Commission has been guided by proper considerations in bringing the deposit of its experience, the disciplined feel of the expert, to bear on applications for licenses in the public interest.[61]

In the foregoing discussion, the principal features of the Communications Act and the general scope of the FCC's statutory authority have been analyzed. The next chapter describes the administrative and organizational structure developed by the FCC to exercise its powers and perform its functions.

1. Morse, Edward Lind, *Samuel F. B. Morse, His letters and Journals* (New York, 1914), Vol. 2. pp. 228, 232, 240.

2. *Annual Report of the Postmaster General,* Document No. 2, December 1, 1845, p. 861.

3. *Report of the Postmaster General for the Fiscal Year Ended June 30, 1913,* Miscellaneous Reports, p. 15.

4. *Ibid.*

5. Holmes, Oliver Wendell, "Ideals and Doubts," 10 *Ill.,* L. R. 2 (1915).

6. 48 Stat. 1064.

7. 48 Stat. 1101-1102.

8. 48 Stat. 1065.

9. *Ibid.*

10. 48 Stat. 1098.

11. *General Electric Company v. Federal Radio Commission,* 31 F. (2d) 630 (App. D.C. 1929).

12. *Federal Radio Commission v. Nelson Brothers,* 53 Sup. Ct. 627, 633-634.

13. *United States v. Gregg,* 5F. Supp. 848 (S.D. Texas 1934); also see *C. J. Community Services, Inc., v. FCC,* 100 U. S. App. D.C. (379, 246 F. (2d) 660, 15 RR 2029 (1957).

14. *U.S. v. Betteridge,* 43 F. Supp. 53, 55 (N.D. Ohio, E. Div.).

15. See *City of New York v. Federal Radio Commission,* 59 App. D.C. 129, 36 F. (2d) 115 (1929); *Radio Station WOW v. Johnson,* 326 U.S. 120 (1944); *DuMont Laboratories v. Carroll,* 86 F. Supp. 813, 5 RR 2053 (E.D. Pa. 1949).

16. 48 Stat. 1070.

17. *Ibid.*

18. *Ibid.,* 1071.

19. 68 *Cong. Rec.* 2579; also see *MacKay Radio and Telephone Company v. Federal Communications Commission,* 97 F. (2d) 641, 645 (1938).

20. 48 St. 1087-1088.

21. 48 Stat. 1066; also see *Federal Communications Commission v. Sanders Bros.,* 309 U.S. 470 (1940).

22. 48 Stat. 1087.

23. 48 Sta.. 1086.

24. 48 Stat. 1081.

25. *Ibid.*

26. *Ibid.*

27. 48 Stat. 1081.

28. 48 Stat. 1082-1083.

29. 49 Stat. 1475.

30. 48 Stat. 1082.

31. *Ibid.*

32. 50 Stat. 191.

33. 68 *Cong. Rec.* 2881. See also statements by Representative White, 68 *Cong. Rec.* 2579-2580, and by Senator Dill, 69 *Cong. Rec.* 12,352.

34. 68 *Cong. Rec.* 2881.

35. 44 Stat. 1164.

36. 48 Stat. 1082.

37. 48 Stat., 1084-1085.

38. *Ibid.*

39. *Ibid.*

40. 48 Stat. 1086.

41. 48 Stat. 1085.

42. 66 Stat. 716-717.

43. 48 Stat. 1082-1083.

44. 48 Stat. 1091.

45. *In the Matter of Amendment of Section IV (Statement of Program Service) of Broadcast Application Forms 301, 303, 314 and 315,* FCC Docket No. 12673, 1 RR 98:21. Also see "The Active Eyebrow—a Changing Style for Censorship," by W. Theodore Pierson, a distinguished attorney in Washington, D. C., who takes a similar view. His analysis of this issue from a legal and cultural point of view appears in *Television Quarterly,* Vol. 1, February, 1962, pp. 14-21.

46. *Hearing on Jurisdiction of Radio Commission,* House Committee on Merchant Marine and Fisheries (1928), p. 26.

47. Report by Federal Communications Commission, *Public Service Responsibility of Broadcast Licensees* (March 7, 1946), p. 10; also, *Hearings on Jurisdiction of Radio Commission,* House Committee on Merchant Marine and Fisheries (1928) p. 26.

48. *Hearings on H.R. 8301,* 73rd Cong., p. 117.

49. *Ibid.,* pp. 350-352.

50. 48 Stat. 1084.

51. Federal Communications Commission, *Report to Congress Pursuant to Section 307 (c) of the Communications Act of 1934,* January 22, 1935.

52. Transcript of Record, No. 5240, in *KFKB Broadcasting Association, Inc. v. Federal Radio Commission,* 60 App. D.C. 79, 47 F. (2d) 670 (1931); Statement of Facts and Grounds for Decision, p. 13.

53. *Ibid.,* p. 672.

54. *Ibid.*

55. Transcript of Record, No. 5561, in *Trinity Methodist Church South v. Federal Radio Commission,* 61 App. D.C. 311, 62 F. (2d) 850 (1932), p. 970.

56. *Ibid.*

57. *Ibid.,* 288 U.S. 599 (January 16, 1933).

58. Federal Communications Commission, *Report on Chain Broadcasting,* Commission Order No. 37, Docket No. 5060 (May 1941) p. 117.

59. *National Broadcasting Company v. United States,* 319 U.S. 190, 216-17 (May 10, 1943).

60. *Ibid.,* p. 215. There have been more recent court cases which sustain the Commission's authority to regulate programming. For example, see the so-called Red Lion Case, 395 U.S. 367 (decided June 9, 1969). The complete text of the opinion appears in Appendix V. Also see *Reuben B. Robertson* (20 RR 2d 381-388), which contains a memorandum from the FCC General Consul to the Commission in which he states that the *Red Lion* decision of the Supreme Court gives the Commission "broad authority to establish general program standards founded on clear public interest considerations without running afoul of Section 326 or the First Amendment."

61. *FCC v. RCA Communications, Inc.,* 346 U.S. 89-91 (June 8, 1953).

CHAPTER 4

How the FCC Is Organized and Conducts Its Business

In the last analysis, much depends on whether administration is heavy-handed and burdensomely bureaucratic or whether it is flexible and imaginative. —MARSHALL E. DIMOCK*

As prescribed in Section 4 of the Communications Act, the FCC is composed of seven commissioners chosen by the President with the advice and consent of the Senate, one of whom the President designates as Chairman.[1] As specified in the same section, the terms of the first commissioners ran for one, two, three, four, five, six and seven years, respectively, with all successive appointments made for seven years and until their successors are appointed and have qualified, except that they may not continue to serve beyond the expiration of the next session of Congress subsequent to the end of their fixed term. A person chosen to fill a vacancy is appointed only for the unexpired term of the Commissioner whom he succeeds.[2]

The Communications Act has very little to say about the qualifications of commissioners. It does require that they be citizens of the United States and no more than four of them may be members of the same political party. For the service they perform for the American people they draw annual salaries of $38,000 except for the Chairman who gets $40,000.[3] (See Appendix II for biographical studies).

Legislative Restrictions on Commissioners. As specified in the Act, while serving on the Commission, members are prohibited from having a financial interest in any of the following activities, enterprises or companies:
1. The manufacture or sale of radio apparatus or equipment for wire or radio communication.
2. Any kind of radio transmission of energy.
3. Any wire or radio communication.
4. Companies furnishing services or such apparatus to those engaged in wire or radio communication or to those manufacturing or selling such equipment.

*Professor and Head, Graduate Government Department, New York University.

5. Any company owning stock, bonds, or other securities of any such companies.[4]

The commissioners are further prohibited from participating in any hearing or proceeding in which they have a pecuniary interest and may not be employed by or hold any official relationship to any person subject to any of the provisions of the Communications Act. They may not own stocks, bonds, or other securities of any corporation over which the FCC has any jurisdiction. Nor may they be otherwise employed, or engaged in any other business, vocation or profession while they are on the Commission.[5] Formerly, they could accept reasonable honorariums or compensation for the presentation or delivery of publications or papers. 1960 legislation, however, now prohibits this. (See 1960 Amendments to Act in Appendix I).

If a member terminates his service prior to the expiration of his appointed term, he must wait for a year before he may represent any person before the Commission in a professional capacity. This restriction does not apply, however, if he continues to serve out his appointed term.[6]

Transaction of Business. The seven commissioners function as a unit, and exercise general supervision over the work of the agency.[7] The Chairman, however, as provided in Section 5 (a) of the Act, serves as the chief executive officer of the Commission. It is his duty to preside at all meetings of the Commission, and to represent the agency in all legislative matters, (except that any other commissioner may present his own or minority views). He also represents the Commission in all matters requiring conferences or communications with other governmental officers, departments or agencies, and generally coordinates and organizes the work of the Commission.[8]

Four members of the Commission constitute a quorum for the transaction of business.[9] General sessions of the Commission are required to be held at least once a month at its principal offices in Washington, D.C. Special meetings, however, may be held elsewhere in the United States if economy and convenience will be served.[10] Biographical material pertaining to present FCC commissioners and past chairmen appears in Appendix 2. Also, a brief chronology of significant FCC events is set forth there.

The Commission has the legislative authority to take actions, make rules and regulations and issue orders, not contrary to law, as may be necessary to carry out its functions and may conduct proceedings in a manner "as will best conduce to the proper dispatch of business and to the ends of justice."[11]

Every vote and official action of the Commission must be recorded, and its proceedings (excluding its business meetings) shall be open to the public upon request of any interested party. One statutory exception to this is that the Commission may withhold publication of records or proceedings containing secret information affecting the national defense.[12]

Reports to Congress. A special matter of business required by law is the preparation and transmission of an annual report to Congress. This report must contain (1) information collected and considered by the Commission to have value in the settlement of questions relating to regulation of inter-state and foreign transmissions by wire and radio; (2) information as to its work and accomplishments, and the adequacy of its staff and equipment. As further implementation of this statutory requirement, the Commission makes monthly reports to the Senate Commerce Committee on the nature and number of broadcast applications that have been pending for more than three months together with the reasons for the processing delays. In addition, the report includes all hearings which have been closed for more than six months and the case has not been finally disposed of. A former requirement for biographies of all persons employed during the year, their FCC positions and salaries, together with names of those who left the employ of the agency, was repealed in 1952.[13]

Personnel and Expenditures. Legislative authority for the selection of staff personnel appears in paragraphs (1) and (2) of Section 4(f) of the Act.[14] Subject to civil-service laws and the Classification Act of 1949, the Commission is authorized to appoint "officers, engineers, accountants, attorneys, inspectors, examiners, and other employees" as are necessary to carry out its functions.[15] It is provided that each commissioner may appoint a legal assistant, engineering assistant, administrative assistant, and a secretary to serve in his office, and may prescribe the duties of each.[16] In filling these particular jobs, he may disregard the civil-service laws but must comply with the requirements of the Classification Act of 1949.[17]

Paragraph (g) of Section 4 authorizes expenditures out of available appropriations as are necessary for the performance of Commission functions. All such expenditures, including necessary transportation expenses of commissioners or their employees, incurred while conducting any official business outside the city of Washington, are allowed and paid on the presentation of itemized vouchers approved by the Chairman or by such other members or officers as may be designated by the Commission.[18]

Original Organization of the FCC. The Communications Act, as adopted in 1934, provided that the Commission might divide itself into not more than three divisions, each to consist of at least three members. It was further provided that the Commission might direct that "any of its work, business or functions" might be assigned or referred to any division for action. In case of referral, the division was authorized to act on the assigned matter with all the jurisdiction and powers conferred by law upon the full Commission, and its action had the same force and effect as if taken by the Commission.[19]

As originally passed, the Act also authorized the agency to assign or refer any portion of its work to an individual commissioner or to a board composed of one or more employees. This authority, however, did not extend to investigations instituted on the Commission's own motion, or to those specifically required by the Act. Nor was it applicable to contested proceedings requiring the taking of testimony at public hearings, unless agreed to by the parties involved.[20]

Any action taken by an individual commissioner or a board with respect to an assigned matter had the same force and effect as if taken by the Commission. It was provided, however, that any party affected by any order, decision, or report of such commissioner or board might file a petition for rehearing by the Commission or a division. Any action by a division upon such a petition was subject to review by the Commission.[21]

Pursuant to these provisions, immediately after its creation, the FCC established three divisions—Broadcast, Telephone, and Telegraph—each composed of two members with the Chairman of the Commission acting *ex officio* as a third member of each division.[22] The agency exercised, authority over all matters not assigned to any division, and specifically retained jurisdiction over the allocation of frequency bands to the various classes of radio service and all matters involving two or more divisions. Pursuant to Section 405 of the Act, the full Commission was required to dispose of petitions requesting rehearing of cases decided by a division.[23]

This system of compartmentalized regulation did not prove satisfactory. There were jurisdictional disputes within the Commission. Differences in work load among the divisions required some commissioners to assume more responsibility than others. Because of the interrelationships of the telegraph, telephone and broadcast industries, a commissioner's competency in one area of regulation was limited by his lack of experience and knowledge in the others. As Harry Warner has pointed out, "the division system was not conducive to cooperation and mutual understanding, vested an unnecessary share of responsibility and power in each division and prevented a rounded development of each commissioner's knowledge and experience."[24]

FCC Divisions Abolished.   Having become dissatisfied with the system, the Commission abolished the Telegraph, Telephone and Broadcast divisions on October 13, 1937 and assumed full responsibility for all their functions.[25] Henceforth, the Commission acted as a unit in regulatory matters relating to the three industries, with each commissioner having an equal voice in all policy determinations and other regulatory matters.

The organization at the staff level, as it was established at the time the Commission began operations in 1934, was not changed. There was the Secretary and his assistants responsible for keeping records, maintaining dockets, and performing other functions essential to daily operations. There were four departments with the heads thereof directly responsible to the full Commission. The Legal Department headed by a General Counsel, was concerned with such matters as applications and complaints, carried on investigations, and handled litigation involving the Commission. Cooperating closely, was the Department of Examiners.

The technical work was done by the Engineering Department with a Chief Engineer in charge. This included research on radio propagation, the installation, operation and maintenance of radio equipment, and such matters as the preparation and presentation of expert testimony at hearings conducted by the Commission. A special section of this department participated in international conferences concerned with the technical aspects of wire and radio communication and channel allocations. Still another section operated in the field, conducting examinations for radio operators, monitoring and inspecting station operations and assisting in field investigations.

The fourth department was the Accounting, Statistical and Tariff Department headed by a Chief Accountant. Its work was concerned with classification of services, depreciation and cost analysis, determination of rate schedules, and statistical studies relating to the communications industries.

Staff Organization Proves Inefficient. This departmental organization, with work arranged and divided on the basis of specialized knowledge and skills, was maintained for more than fifteen years. In the middle forties, however, faced with the prospect of a greatly increased work load after the War, the Commission began to think seriously in terms of a reorganization of its staff to achieve more economical and efficient operation. In August, 1945, Charles S. Hyneman, who had been serving as Director of the Foreign Broadcast Intelligence Service, a wartime service of the FCC, was assigned the task of helping work out a new organization.[26]

He was busy at the job for more than a year and a half. In his book, *Bureaucracy in a Democracy,* published in 1952, he described the organizational situation and problems at the FCC as he had found them while he was there. He pointed out that no man below the seven commissioners was in a position to coordinate and direct the work of the agency effectively. With respect to the manner in which the staff then disposed of cases, he wrote:

. . . Accountant, engineer, and lawyer negotiate in order to decide what questions shall be taken up next and how much work shall be done on the particular case. If agreement is reached (and it usually is) as to how men in the three divisions shall relate their work on a particular case, the individuals who actually do the work get their instructions from different superior officers and the original agreement is readily upset because someone forgets his part of the agreement or neglects to tell somebody else that a more pressing matter has arisen and he has reassigned his man to another task. The practical consequence of this situation is that the work which men in three different divisions do on a specific case is not well timed. Sometimes the case which should have gotten up before the commission last month, and which is scheduled to get there this month, does not actually get there until month after next. And it is not because men who analyze the cases lack competence or loaf on the job; it is because there is no one (short of the commissioners themselves) who has authority extending over all three divisions and is able to coordinate the work.[27]

After a detailed discussion of the operational demerits of this system, Mr. Hyneman stated that the commissioners had to choose between two sets of values:

They can organize the staff according to specialized knowledge or skill, suffer delays, and incur excessive costs in getting matters brought before them for attention, but have the assurance that the commissioners will get a full disclosure of the important considerations which they ought to take into account in making their decisions. Or the commissioners can organize the staff according to the industry (or area of affairs) to be regulated, have the assurance that there are men below them with ample authority to coordinate and direct all of the work on each and every problem that comes before the commissioners, and take a chance that these men will not, consciously or unconsciously, prejudice the decisions of the commissioners by failure to make available to them the information and points of view which they ought to consider. . . .[28]

The Hoover Commission, after a careful study of regulatory commissions, in 1949 made recommendations with respect to their internal organization. Its task force had recommended that agencies like the FCC, whose staff were organized on a professional basis (e.g., with legal, engineering and accounting departments) reorganize on a functional basis in terms of the second alternative suggested by Mr. Hyneman.[29]

The Hoover Commission, in its report to Congress, favored vesting all administrative responsibility of the regulatory agency in its chairman, but had nothing to say about how the staff should be organized.[30]

Congress Becomes Concerned. Congress became increasingly concerned with the mounting backlog of work at the FCC and was especially unhappy about the slowness with which many cases were decided. After more than a decade of study including lengthy public hearings, the Senate Committee on Interstate and Foreign Commerce recommended that the Communications Act of 1934 be amended to provide, among other things, for a reorganization of the Commission along functional lines and to center administrative responsibility in the Chairman.

In its report to Congress on these amendments, submitted January 25, 1951, the Senate Committee said:

Section 5 of the bill is a revision of Section 5 of the law which deals with the organization of the Commission. The existing section of the law is an anachronism in that it provides for a permissive divisional organization of the Commission, which was adopted briefly shortly following enactment of the law in 1934 and then dropped. . . .

The most important subsection, and in the committee's opinion one of the most important of the entire bill here recommended, is subsection (b) which would reorganize the Commission into a functional organization. To make clear what the effect of this subsection would be, it should be explained that the Commission has been organized into three principal bureaus—Engineering, Accounting, and Legal. It also has, of course, other subsidiary sections and units but the bulk of its licensing work flows upward through these three bureaus. Regardless of the type of case involved, each of these three bureaus must independently, or occasionally in consultation, pass upon applications and other types of cases. Whether or not this system is responsible, the fact remains that the Commission's backlog of cases has continued to mount to alarming proportions. Hearing cases rarely get out in less than 2 years; some have been before the Commission as long as 4 to 7 years.

Citizens and taxpayers are entitled to greater consideration and better service from their Government than this.

Moreover, under this system, the three bureaus have become self-contained and independent little kingdoms, each jealously guarding its own field of operations and able to exercise almost dictatorial control over the expedition of a case. They can, and have, set at naught the best efforts of individual Commissioners to spur action.[31]

Communications Act Amended Requiring Establishment of Functional Organization. After consideration of reports from both Houses as well as the Conference Report,[32] Congress amended Section 5 of the Communications Act to provide for the changes recommended.[33] As amended, the section required the Commission, within six months, to "organize its staff into (1) integrated bureaus, to function on the basis of the Commission's principal workload operations, and (2) make such other divisional organizations as the Commission may deem necessary."[34] It was further required that each such integrated bureau should include "such legal, engineering, accounting, administrative, clerical, and other personnel" as the Commission might determine to be necessary.[35]

This amendment further directed the Commission to set up a new unit in the agency consisting of a "review staff" to assist in the preparation of summaries of evidence taken at adjudicatory hearings and by the compilation of facts material to exceptions and replies filed by interested parties after initial decisions and before oral argument, and "by preparing for the Commission or any member or members thereof, without recommendations and in accordance with specific directions from the Commission or such member or members, memoranda, opinions, decisions, and orders."[36]

Congress was concerned that this "review staff" be an independent group able to perform accurate and objective reporting functions, and with this end in mind provided (1) that it should be directly responsible to the Commission and not a part of any bureau or divisional organization thereof; (2) that none of its work should be supervised or directed by anyone other than a member of the review staff whom the Commission would designate as head of such staff; and (3) that no employee of the Commission not a member of the review staff should be allowed to perform any of the review functions.[37]

The original language of Section 5 of the Communications Act was further amended to provide for greater flexibility in the delegation of authority, and references to the Commission's authority to organize itself into "divisions" were deleted from the law.

Except for certain adjudicatory cases designated for hearing by the Commission and which must be conducted by it or an examiner as required by the Administrative Procedure Act,[38] the Commission was authorized to delegate functions as follows. It can, when necessary to the proper functioning of the Commission and prompt and orderly conduct of its business, "assign or refer any portion of its work, business, or functions to an individual commissioner or commissioners or to a board composed of one or more employees of the Commission."[39] Any such assignment may be amended, modified or recinded at any time, and any person aggrieved by any action taken under such an assignment may file an application for review by the Commission.[40] The Commission, upon approval of such an application, may "affirm, modify, or set aside such order, decision, report or action," or order a rehearing thereon as provided in Section 405 of the Act.[41]

Actually, the functional organization required by the 1952 amendments, for the most part had already been established by the FCC before they were passed. The first step in the staff reorganization was taken in early 1950 and had been fully completed by March, 1952.[42]

Present FCC Organization.   As it operates today, the FCC is divided into five bureaus and a number of staff offices. The functions of these various units, as described in Part 0 of the Commission's Rules and Regulations, are briefly set forth below.

Broadcast Bureau.   Among the more important functions of the Broadcast Bureau are (1) the processing of applications for broadcasting stations; (2) participation in hearings involving applications and rule making proceedings; (3) studying frequency allocations and drafting plans for their use in the broadcast services; (4) studying and establishing technical requirements for broadcasting equipment; (5) participation in government, industrial and international conferences concerning broadcast services and (6) the making of recommendations to the Commission concerning the promulgation of broadcasting rules and standards as well as recommendations relating to other functions mentioned.

The work load of the Broadcast Bureau is distributed among the Office of the Chief and seven divisions: namely, Broadcast Facilities, Renewal and Transfer, Complaints and Compliance, Rules and Standards, License, Hearing, and Research and Education.[43]

A special *Office of Network Study* has been established in the Bureau to compile data relating to radio and television network operations to help the Commission develop and maintain an adequate regulatory program.[44]

Common Carrier Bureau.   The work of the Common Carrier Bureau is handled by the Office of the Chief and six divisions: International and Satellite Communication, Domestic Rates, Domestic Radio, Domestic Services and Facilities, Field Operations, and Economic Studies. The Bureau develops, recommends, and administers policies and programs with respect to the regulation of rates, services, accounting and facilities of communication carriers involving the use of wire, cable, radio and space satellites. It performs the following functions (1) advises and represents the Commission on matters relating to common carrier regulation; (2) participates in international conferences involving such matters; (3) collaborates with representatives of state regulatory commissions and with the National Association of

Railroad and Utilities Commissioners in the conduct of cooperative studies of regulatory matters of common concern; (4) participates in adjudicatory hearings in which important common carrier issues are involved; (5) advises and assists its members of the public and the industries regulated regarding communication matters; (6) makes recommendations to the FCC regarding the use of space satellites for purposes other than common carrier communication; and (7) exercises such other authority as may be delegated by the Commission pursuant to Section 5(d) of the Communications Act of 1934, as amended.[45]

Safety and Special Radio Services Bureau. As previously mentioned, for every station broadcasting to the general public there are many others providing special radio services. It is the main function of the Safety and Special Radio Services Bureau to issue authorizations for these special operations. It also initiates any rulemaking proceedings with respect to them, studies frequency assignments and technical requirements for equipment, participates in international conferences and collaborates with other governmental agencies and industry groups interested in the problem of safety and special radio services, and plans and executes an enforcement program for such services, including educational campaigns conducted in collaboration with the Field Engineering and Monitoring Division.

In addition to the Office of the Chief, there are five divisions in the Bureau: Legal, Advisory and Enforcement; Industrial and Public Safety Rules; Industrial and Public Safety Facilities; Aviation and Marine; and Amateur and Citizens.[46]

Field Engineering Bureau. Another important phase of the Commission's work is handled by the Field Engineering Bureau. This consists of the Office of the Bureau Chief, the Engineering and Facilities Division, the Field Offices Division and its associated field organization consisting of district offices, sub-offices, marine offices and mobile enforcement units; and the Monitoring Systems Division with its widely distributed monitoring stations.

The location of these various field offices and monitoring stations, including specific mailing addresses, are listed in Section 0.121 of the Commission's Rules and Regulations (1 RR 53: 133-139).

This bureau is responsible for all engineering activities in the field relating to broadcast stations including station inspections, monitoring, direction finding, signal measurement, and investigation.[47] It also administers and enforces rules for commercial radio operators, and conducts examinations and issues licenses to these operators. It processes data to determine whether proposed new or modified antenna structures will create hazards to air travel; participates in international conferences relating to communications and cooperates with the Office of Emergency Communications in plans for national defense.[48] It also exercises a wide range of responsibilities in the nonbroadcast field such as inspection of radio facilities on ships at sea, and performs a variety of other tasks as set forth in Sections 0.111-0.115 of the Commission Rules.

Cable Television Bureau. The Cable Television Bureau is responsible for the planning, development and execution of regulatory programs for CATV systems and related private and common carrier microwave radio facilities. It conducts programs involved in the licensing and regulation of Community Antenna Relay Stations after coordination with the Broadcast Bureau. The Bureau coordinates with the Common Carrier Bureau in the licensing and regulation of CATV related common carrier microwave facilities and with the Safety and Special Radio Services Bureau in the licensing and regulation of Business Radio Service facilities. It also reviews and evaluates CATV system operations to assure compliance with the Commissioner's rules and regulations.

Office of Hearing Examiners. All of these various bureaus are served by the Office of Hearing Examiners. In 1946, Congress passed the Administrative Procedure Act which, among other things, provides for the appointment of hearing examiners in the FCC and other federal administrative agencies. Under the provisions of this act, these examiners preside at and conduct adjudicatory proceedings assigned them by the agency and issue initial decisions. They are appointed subject to Civil Service laws, and cannot be removed from their offices except for good cause established by the Civil Service Commission after opportunity for hearing.[49]

Their functions are separated from those of other units in the Commission and, with limited exceptions, they are not permitted to consult with any person or party on any factual issue in a hearing unless upon notice and with opportunity for all parties to participate. They may not be supervised or directed by any FCC officer, employee, or agent engaged in the performance of investigative or prosecuting functions. In other words, they serve in a judicial role and are completely independent in the preparation of their opinions.

The Chief Hearing Examiner has administrative duties which include the assignment of examiners to preside at hearings and the time and place of hearings and the maintenance of hearing calendars. Upon advice of other examiners he recommends to the Commission changes in rules and regulations to simplify and expedite conduct of hearings; secures and prepares reports for the Civil Service Commission or other governmental agencies concerned with operations of the Office of Hearing Examiners; and serves as liaison for the Commission and the Examiners in securing advice or information from outside sources concerning the improvement of administrative procedures applicable to hearing cases.[50]

Review Board. The Review Board is composed of three or more Commission employees (there are five members at the present time). Its functions consist of reviewing initial decisions and other hearing matters referred to it by the Commission. It acts on certain interlocutory matters which arise during the course of hearings, and perform such additional duties not inconsistent with these functions as may be assigned to it by the Commission.[51]

Office of Opinions and Review.   This office consists of legal, accounting, engineering and other personnel whose job is to assist and make recommendations to the Commission and to individual commissioners designated to review initial decisions in adjudicatory cases.[52] Previously, as pointed out above, this office was prohibited by Section 5(c) of the Communications Act from making recommendations of the Commission as to actions to be taken on such cases. It could perform no duties other than to assist the Commission in adjudicatory matters by preparing summaries of evidence presenting in initial hearings, and by compiling facts material to exceptions and replies thereto filed by the parties. However, on August 31, 1961, Section 5(c) of the Act was repealed (P. L. 87-192, 75 Stat. 420, 107 *Cong. Rec.* 14576-14581, August 3, 1961) and the Commission was given freedom to seek the advice of these experts upon the basis of their study and analyses of evidence and pleadings in cases.

Office of Executive Director.   Administrative affairs of the FCC are planned and directed by the Executive Director who is responsible to the Chairman of the Commission and cooperates generally with the staff in the development and improvement of administrative procedures. He is concerned with employment of personnel, budget, and the general housekeeping functions of the FCC. Also, under the direction of the Defense Commissioner, and with the advice and assistance of the heads of the several bureaus and offices, he coordinates the defense activities of the Commission. The units in his office consist of the following divisions: Budget and Fiscal, Data Processing, Management Information, Administrative Service, Property Management, Personnel and Emergency Communications.[53]

General Counsel.   This official and his staff represent the Commission in all litigation matters and, among other functions, advises the Commission with respect to proposed legislation concerning communications and assists in the preparation of Commission reports to Congress relating thereto; interprets general procedural rules of the agency as well as statutes, international agreements and regulations affecting its operation. He cooperates with other officers in rendering advice with respect to rulemaking matters and proceedings affecting more than one Bureau in the Commission. He carries on legal research as directed by the Commission and cooperates with the Common Carrier Bureau and the Office of Chief Engineer on all matters pertaining to space satellite communications. The units in the General Counsel's office consist of the following divisions: Litigation, Legislation, Administrative Law and Treaties, and Enforcement and Defense.[54]

The Office of Chief Engineer has the following primary duties and responsibilities: (a) plans and directs broad programs looking toward the more effective use of communications in the public interest; (b) advises the Commission and the various Bureaus on matters of applied technical research; (c) advises and represents the Commission on the allocation of radio frequencies, including international agreements pertaining thereto; cooperates with the General Counsel in advising the Commission with respect to general frequency allocation proceedings not within the jurisdiction of any single Bureau; maintains liaison with other agencies of government and with technical experts representing foreign governments, and deals with members of the public and the industries concerned.

This office also collaborates with the several Bureaus in the formulation of standards of engineering practice and the rules and regulations related thereto, and advises the Commission on such matters.

In addition to the Chief Engineer's immediate office, there are the following divisions: Research, Technical, Laboratory, and Frequency Allocation and Treaty.[55]

The Secretary signs Commission correspondence and documents. He is the custodian of the Commission's seal and records. He maintains minutes and records of Commission actions and the dockets of hearing proceedings, and is responsible for their accuracy, authenticity and completeness. With a few exceptions, all papers destined for Commission consideration should be addressed to him at his offices in Washington, D.C.[56]

An important source of information for members of the public is the *Office of Information* which is responsible for releasing public announcements of the Commission. It is the contact point for the press, the industry and the public to secure the latest facts regarding the Commission and its activities.[57]

Commission Delegations of Authority.   There are three basic categories of delegated authority made by the Commission pursuant to Section 5 (d) of the Communications Act of 1934, as amended: (1) delegations to act in matters and proceedings of a non-hearing nature, usually made to bureau chiefs and other members of the Commission's staff, and sometimes to individual commissioners and boards or committees of commissioners; (2) delegations to rule on interlocutory matters in hearing proceedings and made to the Review Board and the Chief Hearing Examiner; and (3) delegations to individual commissioners, to panels of commissioners, or to the Review Board, to review initial decisions of an adjudicatory nature.[58]

The Commission, by vote of a majority, may delegate functions of a continuing and recurring nature by adoption of rules which must be published in the *Federal Register.* It may, at any time amend, modify, or rescind any such rule. Also, the Commission similarly may delegate authority for the disposition of some particular matter or proceeding by simple order, and which must be noted in the *Federal Register* and associated with the record of that matter or proceeding.[59]

The responsibility for the general administration of internal affairs of the commission is delegated to the Chairman of the Commission. This authority includes actions of routine or non-routine character not involving basic policy determinations. On important matters requiring action he may only present recommendations to the Commission.[60]

As provided in Section 0.212 of the Rules, in the absence of a quorum of the Commission, the Chairman or Acting Chairman may convene a board, of Commissioners or those present and able to act. This Board may then act upon all matters normally acted upon by the Commission en banc, except the following:

(1) The final determination on the merits of an adjudicatory or investigatory matter in hearing status or of any rule making proceeding, unless the Board finds that the public interest would be disserved by awaiting action by a Commission quorum.

(2) Petitions for reconsideration of Commission actions.

(3) Applications for review of actions taken pursuant to delegated authority.[61]

The *Telegraph Committee,* composed of three commissioners, is authorized to act on all applications or requests of carriers engaged principally in record communication to construct, acquire, operate or extend telegraph lines, for temporary or emergency telegraph service, for supplementing existing telegraph facilities, or for discontinuance, reduction or impairment of telegraph service. The *Telephone Committee,* composed of three commissioners, has similar authority with respect to carriers engaged in telephone communication. A *Subscription Television Committee* of three members is authorized by the Commission to act upon requests and other matters pertaining to trial subscription television operations conducted in accordance with the provision of the Third Report (Docket No. 11279), with the exception of applications for authority to carry on trial subscription television operations on stations not previously engaged in such operations.[62]

The Commission designates one of its members to serve as *Defense Commissioner* and two others to serve as alternates. The Defense Commissioner directs the defense activities of the Commission and has the following duties: keeps the Commission informed as to significant developments in the field of emergency preparedness and defense mobilization; (2) represents the Commission in national defense matters requiring conferences or communications with other governmental officers, department, or agencies; (3) acts as defense coordinator in representations with other agencies regarding plans for the continuity of essential functions of the FCC under national emergency conditions, and serves as the principal representative of the FCC to the Inter-agency Emergency Planning Committee of the Office of Emergency Planning; and (4) serves as the principal representative to the Inter-agency Civil Defense Committee of the Office of Civil Defense, Department of the Army, and is contact man to the National Communications System.[63]

It is his job to take such measures as will assure continuity of the Commission's functions under emergency conditions with a minimum of interruption. And, in the event of enemy attack, or the imminent threat thereof, or other disaster, resulting in the inability of the FCC to function at its offices in Washington, D.C., he assumes all the duties and responsibilities of the Commission and Chairman, until relieved or augmented by other commissioners or members of the staff.[64]

Working with and under the Defense Commissioner is the *Emergency Communications Division* which, in cooperation with FCC staff officials, prepares plans for the continuity of Government functions of the Commission in the event of national emergency. The *Division* is composed of the Chief, the Secretariat of a National Industry Advisory Committee, and FCC Mobilization Planning Officer, the Emergency Communication Systems Division, and an Emergency Communications Resources Plans Division.[65]

The Emergency Communication Systems Branch develops and recommends plans and procedures for (1) the construction, activation, deactivation of broadcast facilities and services, continuance or suspension thereof, and the uses of personnel in times of national emergency. It does the same for the Safety and Special Radio Services. It also provides advice to achieve industry protection as is necessary to "maintain the integrity of the facilities and station licensees and promote a national program to stimulate disaster preparedness and damage control." The guidance includes the organization and training of employees, advice regarding personnel shelter, evacuation and relocation plans, protection of records, continuity of management, security, repair and recovery of facilities, decentralization and dispersal of facilities, and establishment of mutual aid associations.[66]

Emergency Relocation Board. This board, to be convened at the Commission's relocation headquarters, performs the functions of the Commission in the event of the inability of the Commission to function at its offices in Washington, D.C., resulting from disaster or the threat of enemy attack, under any one of the following conditions:

(1) If specified by directive of the President.

(2) In the absence thereof, upon receipt of a warning signal indicating that an attack on the capital is likely.

(3) In the absence of either a directive or warning signal immediately following an actual attack.

The Board is to be comprised of such Commissioners as may be present and able to act or, if no Commissioner is available or able to act, the occupants of the following positions, in the order listed, shall assume Board functions: The Chief of the Field Engineering Bureau, General Counsel, Chief Engineer, Chief of the Safety and Special Radio Services Bureau, Chief of the Broadcast Bureau, Chief of the Common Carrier Bureau, the Executive Director, and lower ranking administrative officials as enumerated and in the order specified in Section 0. 186 of the Rules. As described in section 0.11-0.186 of the Commission Rules, its organization is as follows:

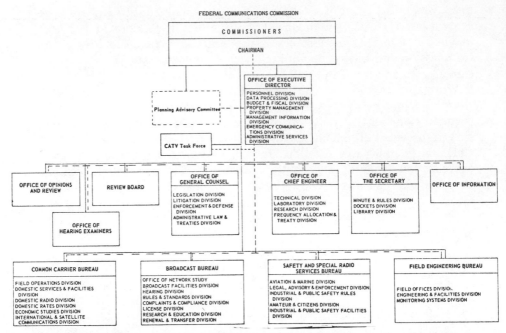

FEDERAL COMMUNICATIONS COMMISSION

*The CATV Task Force has been replaced by the Cable Television Bureau since this chart was described by the FCC rules.

FCC Facilities and Work-load. To maintain the various offices described above and perform its functions, the Commission had only 1,501 employees at the close of fiscal year 1969. Total annual appropriations for 1969 were more than twenty million dollars.[67] Average employment for 1969 was 1,458 and was divided as follows:[68]

	Washington	Field	Total
Commissioners' Offices	41	—	41
Review Board	23	—	23
Office of Opinions and Review	21	—	21
Office of Hearing Examiners	23	—	23
CATV Task Force	24	—	24
Office of Information	9	—	9
Office of Executive Director	174	21	195
Office of Secretary	35	—	35
Office of General Counsel	44	—	44

	Washington	Field	Total
Office of Chief Engineer	69	18	87
Common Carrier Bureau	135	17	152
Safety and Special Radio Service	135	21.9	156.9
Broadcast Bureau	243	—	243
Field Engineering Bureau	76	327	403
Total	1,052	412.2	1,458.

In 1959, the Commission had about 2.5 million radio authorizations outstanding. During that year the Commission received or dispatched over 1,500,000 pieces of mail.[69] As pointed out in the Introduction, in 1969 the number of broadcast authorizations had substantially increased, and in the Safety and Special Radio Services alone there were more than 1.8 million stations and 7 million licensed transmitters, not to mention the enormously enlarged dimensions of the telephone industry, and the growth of satellite communications, all of which has added greatly to the regulatory burdens of the Commission. The Commission must process and dispose of an increasingly large number of petitions and motions, oppositions and replies, protracted cases involving the taking of volumes and volumes of testimony, protests, court appeals and many other matters relating to the Commission's adjudicatory functions. With a comparatively small staff and limited resources, it goes without saying that effective regulation of the communications industries is difficult, if not impossible. This problem is discussed more fully in Chapter 23.

1. 74 Stat. 407.
2. *Ibid.*, p. 408.
3. 5 USC, Sections 5314 (19), 5315 (57).
4. 48 Stat. 1066-67.
5. 66 Stat. 711.
6. *Ibid.*
7. *Ibid.*
8. 66 Stat. 712-713.
9. 48 Stat. 1068.
10. *Ibid.*, 1067 and 66 Stat. 714.
11. 48 Stat. 1068; also see 50 Stat. 191.
12. *Ibid.*
13. 50 Stat. 712; deletion referred to, 74 Stat. 245, 249.
14. 66 Stat. 711.
15. *Ibid.*
16. *Ibid.*
17. *Ibid.* The Classification Act of 1949 (separate from the Communications Act) requires that all jobs in the Federal Civil Service be classified and job descriptions approved by the Civil Service Commission.
18. 48 Stat. 1067; also, 66 Stat. 711-712.
19. 48 Stat. 1068-1070.
20. *Ibid.*
21. *Ibid.*
22. FCC Order No. 1, 1 FCC 3-4 (1934).
23. 48 Stat. 1095.
24. Warner, Harry P., *Radio and Television Law* (New York, 1953), p. 150.
25. Commission Order No. 20, 4 FCC 41.
26. Hyneman, Charles S., *Bureaucracy in a Democracy* (New York, 1950), p. xii.
27. *Ibid.*, p. 506.
28. *Ibid.*, p. 509.
29. Committee on Independent Regulatory Commissions; *A Report with Recommendations Prepared for the Commission on Organization of the Executive Branch of the Government,* (Appendix N); Government Printing Office, 1949.
30. *Ibid.*
31. Senate Report No. 44, 82nd Congress, 1st Session, submitted January 25, 1951; 97 *Cong. Rec.* 658.
32. House Report No. 2426, 82nd. Congress, 2nd. Session, submitted July 1, 1952; 98 *Cong. Rec.* 8807.
33. 66 Stat. 712-713.
34. *Ibid.*
35. *Ibid.*
36. *Ibid.*
37. *Ibid.*
38. 60 Stat. 244 (June 11, 1946).
39. 66 Stat. 713.
40. *Ibid.*, 713-714.
41. *Ibid.*
42. FCC, *Sixteenth Annual Report* (1950), pp. 15-18; also see *Nineteenth Annual Report* (1953), pp. 13-14.
43. FCC Rules and Regulations Concerning Radio, Section 0.72; Fed. Reg. 4606 (1960).

44. *Ibid.*, Section 0.80.
45. *Ibid.*, Sections 0.91-0.92.
46. *Ibid.*, Sections 0.131-0.132.
47. *Ibid.*, Sections 0.111-0.115.
48. *Ibid.*
49. Administrative Procedure Act, Section 11, 60 Stat. 237.
50. FCC Rules, Sections 0.151-0.152.
51. *Ibid.*, Sections 0.161, 0.361, 0.365.
52. *Ibid.*, Section 0.171.
53. *Ibid.*, Sections 0.5(b) (1), 0.11-0.17.
54. *Ibid.*, Sections 0.41-0.47.
55. *Ibid.*, Sections 0.31-0.37.
56. *Ibid.*, Sections 0.51-0.56.
57. *Ibid.*, Section 0.61.
58. *Ibid.*, Section 0.201.
59. *Ibid.*, Sections 0.201-0.203.
60. *Ibid.*, Section 0.211.
61. *Ibid.*, Section 0.212.
62. *Ibid.*, Sections 0.214-0.218.
63. *Ibid.*, Section 0.181.
64. *Ibid.*
65. *Ibid.*, Section 0.183.
66. *Ibid.*
67. *FCC, 35th Annual Report for the Fiscal Year 1969,* pp. 1, 20.
68. *Ibid.*, p. 20.
69. *FCC Annual Report to Congress,* 1959, pp. 23-24.

CHAPTER 5

Other Governmental Agencies Concerned with Broadcasting

Any betrayal of public confidence by any station blackens the eye of all broadcasters. . . . Repairs are needed and you can make them. And if you need help from the government, it will be forthcoming. But don't lose faith in your own capacity, for if you do, you lose faith in freedom. —EARL W. KINTNER*

The Federal Trade Commission.   While the FCC is the principal governmental agency with which the broadcaster must be concerned, there are many others at federal, state and local levels which exercise powers and perform functions which affect his operations. One of these is the Federal Trade Commission, whose basic function is to prevent "unfair methods of competition" and "unfair or deceptive acts or practices in commerce."[1] Since one of the primary concerns of this agency is with false and misleading advertising, its regulations and activities impinge directly upon the commercial broadcaster who depends largely upon advertising for revenue to sustain his operations.

The Federal Trade Commission was created by the Federal Trade Commission Act passed by Congress in 1914.[2] This act provided that the Commission should have five members appointed by the President and subject to approval of the Senate. It provided that the original Commissioners were to be appointed for three, four, five, six and seven year terms, with successive appointments running for seven years. As is the case with the FCC, any person chosen to fill a vacancy is appointed only for the unexpired term of the Commissioner he succeeds. Not more than three Commissioners may be members of the same political party and no Commissioner may engage in any other business, vocation or employment.

The Chairman is designated by the President and is vested with the administrative management of the agency. Headquarters for the agency are located in Washington, D. C. FTC investigational work is carried on by a division of deceptive practices, supported by eleven field offices in Houston,

*Former Chairman, Federal Trade Commission.

Falls Church, Va., New York; Washington, Atlanta, Cleveland, Chicago, Kansas City, Seattle, San Francisco, and New Orleans.[3]

As reported in the *United States Government Organization Manual* for 1968, the chart on the following page describes the FTC organization.

The statutory authority of the Commission is prescribed by the Federal Trade Commission Act of 1914, mentioned above, and as amended by the Wheeler-Lea Act of 1938 and the Oleomargarine Act of a later date. Originally, the Law prohibited only "unfair methods of competition." This made it necessary in every case of false or misleading advertising for the Commission to prove some injury to competition. The 1938 amendment, however, provided that any unfair or deceptive act or practice in commerce, regardless of its effect on competition, is unlawful.[4] This not only protects industry from unfair competition but protects all consumers from deceptive advertising.

Section 5 of the Federal Trade Commission Act makes unlawful any false radio or television advertising designed to induce listeners to purchase any commodities which move in interstate or foreign commerce.

What Is "False Advertising?" And what is "false advertisment" within the meaning of the Act? Sec. 15 states that it is an advertisement "which is misleading in a material respect." In determining whether any advertisement is misleading, "there shall be taken into account (among other things) not only representations made or suggested by statement, word, design, device, sound, or any combination thereof," but also the extent to which it fails to reveal material facts regarding consequences which may result from the use of the commodity under the conditions prescribed in the advertisement or under conditions considered to be customary or usual. The law further states that "no advertisement of a drug shall be deemed to be false if it is disseminated only to members of the medical profession, contains no false representations of a material fact, and includes, or is accompanied in each instance by truthful disclosure of, the formula showing quantitatively each ingredient of such drug."

The same section provides that, in the case of oleomargarine or margarine, an advertisement shall be deemed misleading in a material respect if . . . "representations are made or suggested by statement, word, grade designation, design, device, symbol, sound, or any combination thereof, that such oleomargarine or margarine is a dairy product . . ."

In the case of foods, drugs, devices or cosmetics, Section 12 of the Act declares false advertising to be unlawful whether or not these particular goods move in interstate or foreign commerce. The Act defines the term "food" to mean "(1) articles used for food or drink for man or other animals, (2) chewing gum, and (3) articles used for components of any such article."

The term "drug" includes "(1) articles recognized in the official United States Pharmacopoeia, official Homeopathic Pharmacopoeia of the United States, or official National Formulary, or any supplement to any of them; and (2) articles intended for use in the diagnosis, cure, mitigation, treat-

FEDERAL TRADE COMMISSION

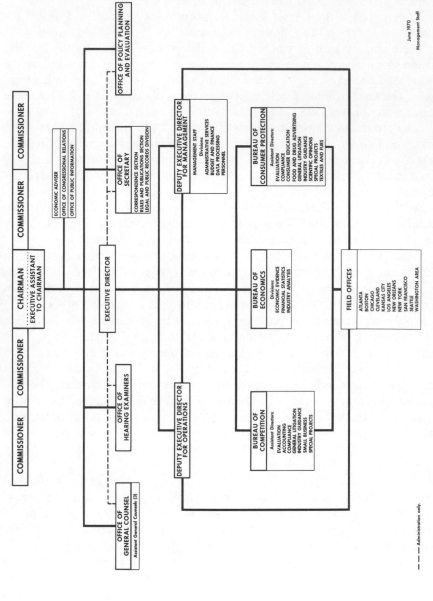

June 1970
Management Staff

COMMISSIONER | COMMISSIONER | CHAIRMAN | COMMISSIONER | COMMISSIONER

EXECUTIVE ASSISTANT TO CHAIRMAN

ECONOMIC ADVISER
OFFICE OF CONGRESSIONAL RELATIONS
OFFICE OF PUBLIC INFORMATION

OFFICE OF POLICY PLANNING AND EVALUATION

EXECUTIVE DIRECTOR

OFFICE OF SECRETARY
CORRESPONDENCE SECTION
RULES AND PUBLICATIONS SECTION
LEGAL AND PUBLIC RECORDS DIVISION

OFFICE OF HEARING EXAMINERS

OFFICE OF GENERAL COUNSEL
Assistant General Counsels (3)

DEPUTY EXECUTIVE DIRECTOR FOR OPERATIONS

DEPUTY EXECUTIVE DIRECTOR FOR MANAGEMENT
MANAGEMENT STAFF
Divisions:
ADMINISTRATIVE SERVICES
BUDGET AND FINANCE
DATA PROCESSING
PERSONNEL

BUREAU OF COMPETITION
Assistant Directors:
EVALUATION
ACCOUNTING
COMPLIANCE
GENERAL LITIGATION
INDUSTRY GUIDANCE
SMALL BUSINESS
SPECIAL PROJECTS

BUREAU OF ECONOMICS
Divisions:
ECONOMIC EVIDENCE
FINANCIAL STATISTICS
INDUSTRY ANALYSIS

BUREAU OF CONSUMER PROTECTION
Assistant Directors:
EVALUATION
COMPLIANCE
CONSUMER EDUCATION
FOOD AND DRUG ADVERTISING
GENERAL LITIGATION
INDUSTRY GUIDANCE
SCIENTIFIC OPINIONS
SPECIAL PROJECTS
TEXTILES AND FURS

FIELD OFFICES
ATLANTA
BOSTON
CHICAGO
CLEVELAND
KANSAS CITY
LOS ANGELES
NEW ORLEANS
NEW YORK
SAN FRANCISCO
SEATTLE
WASHINGTON AREA

– – – – Administration only.

ment, or prevention of disease in man or other animals; and (3) articles (other than food) intended to affect the structure or any function of the body of man or other animals; and (4) articles intended for use as a component of any article specified in clause (1), (2), or (3); but does not include devices or their components, parts, or accessories.

The Act defines "device" to include "instruments, apparatus, and contrivances, including their parts and accessories, intended (1) for use in the diagnosis, cure, mitigation, treatment, or prevention of disease in man or in other animals; or (2) to affect the structure or any function of the body of man or other animals."

The term "cosmetic" embraces "(1) articles to be rubbed, poured, sprinkled, or sprayed on, introduced into, or otherwise applied to the human body or any part thereof intended for cleansing, beautifying, promoting attractiveness, or altering the appearance, and (2) articles intended for use as a component of any such articles; except that such term shall not include soap."

Particular attention is called to the fact that Section 15 requires the FTC to consider not only direct falsehoods, but also failure to reveal material facts respecting consequences resulting from the use of the product. Under the authority of this section, the Commission requires the inclusion of warning statements in advertisements of potentially harmful products.[5]

Failure to Disclose Material Facts. Mention should also be made of cases involving advertisements which misrepresent the value of products for treatment purposes by failing to disclose material facts. For example, in one case, the FTC held that certain advertisements promoting the sale of medicinal preparations for use in treatment of conditions of the hair and scalp were misleading and unlawful. The manufacturer had falsely represented their therapeutic effect for the prevention of baldness and had falsely claimed that they would stimulate the growth of hair and prevent excessive hair fall. The Commission ordered the company to discontinue such advertisements on the grounds that they failed to reveal the fact that the vast majority of cases of excessive hair fall and baldness are known to dermatologists as male pattern baldness and that in cases of that type, the preparation in question would not stop excessive hair fall, prevent or overcome baldness or have any favorable influence on its underlying cause.[6]

Another type of advertising which has been subject to critical examination by the FTC is that which includes television demonstrations which are represented as proving the value of a product when in fact they do not. In a case decided June 11, 1959, the Commission, while it did not find the evidence sufficient to support the particular complaint involved, did enunciate clearly the principle that the use of such a demonstration, if untrue, constitutes an unfair trade practice within the meaning of Section 5 of the FTC Act, since it has "the tendency and capacity to mislead purchasers into believing they are buying a product which has been demonstrated or proven to have a certain quality or characteristic. The law is well settled that the public is entitled to buy what it thinks it is buying . . ."[7]

A 1965 case (*Federal Trade Commission v. Colgate-Palmolive Co. et al.*, 380 US 374) involved three minute television commercials advertising shaving cream. The announcer claimed that the cream, because of its moisturizing power, when applied to "tough, dry sandpaper" could be shaved in a "stroke." The Federal Trade Commission issued a cease and desist order, holding that the test exhibited in the TV commercial was not genuine because of the undisclosed fact that plexiglass was applied to the sandpaper and that this was a misrepresentation of the product and a deceptive practice in violation of Section 5 of the Federal Trade Commission Act. On appeal, the U.S. Supreme Court upheld the decision of the Commission.

In a 1967 case, the question was whether a TV commercial advertising a tonic known as Geritol was deceptive in claiming the use of the product affords relief of iron deficiency anemia. The FTC contended that the advertisement must affirmatively disclose the negative fact that a great majority of the persons who experience the symptoms of tiredness, loss of strength, run-down feeling, or irritability do not have vitamin or iron deficiency. The U.S. Circuit Court of Appeals of the Sixth Circuit upheld the Commission's position stating that there was "substantial evidence to support the finding of the Commission that most tired people are not so because of iron deficiency anemia, and the failure to disclose this fact is false and misleading because the advertisement creates the impression that the tired feeling is caused by something which Geritol can cure," (*J.B. Williams Company, Inc. and Parkson Advertising Agency, Inc. v. Federal Trade Commission,* 381 F. 884).

Administrative Procedure.   Certain types of cases involving deceptive advertising are disposed of by administrative settlement or stipulation procedure established by the Commission. Where these processes are not successful in securing compliance with the law, formal complaints are issued against offenders and matters are set down for public hearing before examiners with counsel for the Commission assuming the general burden of proof. After all evidence is submitted and the record closed, the Examiner issues an initial opinion which may be reviewed by the Commission on its own initiative or at the request of the respondent in the proceeding.

If the allegations in the complaint are sustained by the evidence, the hearing examiner (or the Commission on appeal or review) then issues an order requiring the respondent to cease and desist from the false or misleading advertising. Subject to final review by the Federal Courts, the order becomes final. Failure to comply with the order subjects the offender to suit by the government in a U. S. District Court for recovery of a civil penalty of not more than $5,000 for each violation.[8]

In addition to the regular proceedings, the Commission may, in some cases, bring suit in a United States District Court and request the Court to enjoin the dissemination of advertisements of food, drugs, cosmetics, and devices intended for use in the diagnosis, prevention or treatment of disease, whenever the Court has reason to believe that such a proceeding would be in the public interest. If the Court grants the request, the injunction remains in effect until the Commission has dismissed the complaint or it has been set aside by the Court on review, or until an order of the Commission to cease and desist has become final.[9]

Where it is proved that the use of a commodity is injurious to health or where there is intent to defraud or mislead, Section 14 of the Federal Trade Commission Act states that the offender is guilty of a misdemeanor and conviction subjects him to a fine of not more than $5,000 or imprisonment of not more than 6 months, or both. Succeeding convictions may result in a penalty of not more than $10,000 and not more than 1 year's incarceration, or both.[10]

Applicability of this criminal provision, however, is limited to the "manufacturer, packer, distributor or seller of the commodity to which the false advertisement relates," and specifically precludes publishers, broadcasting stations, or advertising agencies or media, providing they furnish the Commission on request the name and post office address of the party for whom the advertising was disseminated.[11]

The statute provides that the Commission shall certify this type of case to the Attorney General for institution of appropriate court proceedings.[12]

Complaints May Be Filed by Members of Public. Members of the public may file complaints with the Commission regarding deceptive and misleading advertising. No formality is required. A letter alleging deception with facts to support the charges is all that is required. Upon receipt of any such complaint, the Commission, through appropriate offices, considers the matter and determines whether to institute formal proceedings. It is the policy of the Commission not to disclose the identity of the complainant.[13]

If the Commission determines there is a valid basis for formal action, as provided by the law, it may proceed against the offender on one or all of three grounds: attacking the objectionable advertising as (1) an "unfair method of competition;" (2) as a "deceptive practice;" or (3) if food, drugs, cosmetics or devices are involved, as "misleading in a material respect."[14]

General Types of False Advertising. Several general types of deceptive advertising have been matters of serious concern to the Federal Trade Commission. One of these involves misrepresentations of one's business status or the advantages or connections which he may have, or claim to have, in the conduct of his business. Examples of this type are:

that certain distinguished authorities or personages are connected with his business;
that he has certain valuable contacts and arrangements with others;
that his business is for charity;
that he has Government endorsement;
that his business is an educational, religious or research institute or is non-profit in character;

77

that he maintains scientific laboratories;
that the medical profession or the dental profession has endorsed his product;
that certain scientific tests have been made of his product;
and a host of other similar misrepresentations.[15]

A second type of advertising with which the FTC has been concerned is that which is deceptive concerning the comparative merits of products. For example, the audio portion of a TV commercial may well be within legal limits on the comparative merits of two products and at the same time the video portion may give the false and misleading impression of undesirability or unworthiness of the competitive product through slight-of-hand performances or other trick devices which may be skillfully employed.[16] There have been numerous cases involving this kind of deception in which the Commission has issued cease and desist orders.[17]

As mentioned above, false claims as to the efficacy of drugs and medicines constitute a third general type of advertising which has been declared unlawful. A fourth involves fictitious pricing or misrepresentation of comparative prices. Another is the bait-switch kind which advertises for sale at a low price a product described as desirable, and then when the customer offers to buy it on the terms suggested, he is switched to other merchandise either because the advertiser does not want to sell the article advertised or actually may not have it in stock, or for some other reason not in accord with fair business practice.[18]

Guides have been adopted by the Federal Trade Commission for the use of its staff in evaluation of pricing representations in advertising. While the guides do not purport to be all inclusive, the Commission has said "they are directed toward the elimination of existing major abuses and are being released to the public in the interest of obtaining voluntary, simultaneous and prompt cooperation by those whose practices are subject to the jurisdiction of the Federal Trade Commission. The text of these guides against deceptive advertising is reproduced in Appendix III.

Cigarette Advertising. On January 11, 1964, after about two years of study, the Advisory Committee to the Surgeon General of the U.S. Public Health Service, consisting of ten physicians and scientists concluded that "cigarette smoking is a health hazard of sufficient importance in the United States to warrant appropriate remedial action."[19] Because of the great public interest and concern engendered by this report, the Federal Trade Commission issued a notice of proposed rulemaking, looking toward the establishment of a regulation which would require all labeling and advertising of cigarettes to contain warnings of health hazards which might result from smoking cigarettes.[20] After long hearings on the matter, the FTC, on June 22, 1964, issued a trade regulation which, in effect, would require, after January 1, 1965, all packs and containers in which cigarettes are sold to the public to contain an affirmative warning that cigarette smoking is dangerous to health and may cause death from cancer and other diseases,* and that after July 1, 1965, all cigarette advertising, including that on radio and television, contain a similar warning.[21]

After extended hearings, Congress enacted the Federal Cigarette Labeling and Advertising Act which became law on July 27, 1965.[22] This act required that beginning January 1, 1966, every package of cigarettes must display conspicuously and legibly the following words: "Caution: Cigarette Smoking May Be Hazardous to Your Health." The law further said that (1) no different statement relating to smoking and health need be on the package and (2) until July 1, 1969 no advertisement was required to contain any such words of caution if the packages were labeled in accordance with the law.

Following passage of this legislation, the Federal Trade Commission issued a statement vacating the requirements of its regulation and setting forth what it considered to be its regulatory authority and responsibilities regarding cigarette advertising. A part of its statement follows:

The Labeling Act explicitly states that, except as otherwise specifically provided, the authority of the Commission with respect to unfair or deceptive acts or practices in the advertising of cigarettes is not affected. The act does not change the substantive legal standards under the Federal Trade Commission Act applicable to cigarette advertising; any cigarette advertisement that violates the standards of that act is unlawful, notwithstanding enactment of the Labeling Act. Congress has made clear that the Commission should continue to apply the established standards of present law to cigarette advertising, and prohibit any advertising, found to violate the law . . . During the period in which the Commission is prevented by the terms of the Labeling Act from requiring a health statement in cigarette advertising, it will continue to monitor current practices and methods of cigarette advertising and promotion, and take all appropriate action consistent with that act to prohibit cigarette advertising that violates the Federal Trade Commission Act.[23]

. . . .

Voluntary Cigarette Advertising Code. During the Senate hearings on the labeling bill, Robert B. Meyner, Administrator of the cigarette advertising code, testified that cigarette manufacturers are required to submit all their advertisements in advance to him and that he, acting in a judicial capacity, determines whether they may be used.[24] The code became effective January 1, 1965, and prohibits cigarette advertising in school and college publications, testimonials from athletes or other celebrities who may have special appeal to youth, and any advertising which makes unfounded representations with respect to health.

Following passage of the Labeling Act, the late Senator Robert Kennedy

*The effective date was subsequently extended to July 1, 1965, pending conclusion of Congressional hearings on the matter.

introduced legislation that would require stronger health warnings on packs and in advertisements as well; that would impose limits on expenditures for cigarette advertising; give the FCC control of the type of programs that may carry such ads, and limit the time of day they may be presented on the air. He stated, however, that he would prefer a cooperative solution by the industry that would eliminate the necessity for legislative action. His main concern, he said, was that cigarette appeals encourage youth to begin smoking.[25]

In response to his appeal and that of Senator Warren G. Magnuson, in February, 1968, the P. Lorillard Company, one of the biggest tobacco advertisers, announced that it would not sponsor the CBS-TV's coverage of the National Football League games during that year and would not advertise on any nonnews TV show starting before 9 p.m., and would keep the size of the audience's youth group in mind in considering programs starting before 10 p.m.[26]

The influence of Congress and the threat of further Congressional action had effect. Also, through its voluntary compliance procedure, the Federal Trade Commission was in a position to give guidance to the industry and through informal processes to prevent deceptive advertising and false claims regarding cigarette smoking. If and when commercials on radio and TV tended to negate the idea that cigarette smoking might cause injury to health, the Commission, under the law, was clearly authorized to institute formal action to prohibit such commercials.

Subsequently, the FTC, in a report to Congress, recommended an outright ban of all cigarette advertising on radio and television. If unwilling to take such action, the FTC alternately suggested to Congress that limitations be put on the hours and types of programs on which cigarette advertising might appear, and on the over-all volume of advertising. One FTC Commissioner urged that the industry make voluntary changes so that drastic action by the FTC would not be necessary (*Code News*, NAB, July, 1968, p. 4).

The Labeling Act expired July 1, 1969 and Congress did not extend it. The Federal Trade Commission in 1969 proposed to bar or to impose severe limitations on cigarette advertising. The National Association of Broadcasters, in July, 1969, opposed an outright ban and suggested a gradual phase out. (See *Broadcasting*, July 21, 1969, pp. 22-23).

In early November, 1969, the Senate Commerce Committee voted to recommend the prohibition of cigarette advertising over the airwaves, effective January 2, 1971. Congress passed the legislation, banning all cigarette advertising via radio and TV.

Increased workload. As reported in the 1967 FTC Report, pp. 18-19, the volume of work in the Bureau of Deceptive Practices in the FTC has been steadily increasing from year to year. In 1966, complaints from the public and commercial interests increased 45 percent over 1965. In 1967 there was an additional increase of 10 percent. During 1967, the Commission conducted more than one thousand formal investigations of complaints of deceptive advertising.

Stations have Legal Right to Refuse False Ads.   Broadcasting stations and print media can avoid FTC investigations, by refusing advertising which appears to be false, misleading or otherwise harmful to the public interest. Most contracts for the sale of time or publication space provide for this. A clause often incorporated in such contracts, and recommended by Standard Rate and Data Service, reads: "The right is reserved to reject or exclude copy which is unethical, misleading, extravagant, challenging, questionable in character, in bad taste, detrimental to public health or interest, or otherwise inappropriate or incompatible with the character of the publication or that does not meet with the approval of the Federal Trade Commission."

FTC Monitoring Services.   During recent years the FTC has given increasing attention generally to false advertising on radio and television. It has a staff which regularly scans samples of commercial continuity of stations. A 1960 form letter used by the FTC to elicit this information from stations also appears in Appendix V.

In October, 1956, a Radio and Television Advertising Unit was established by the Commission whose purpose is to monitor both aural and video presentations over broadcast media to discover any false advertising claims. A sizeable number of employees is assigned to the unit and is actively engaged in the work in Washington and the various branch offices. Also, all professional members of the FTC staff have been requested by the Commission to report misleading radio and television advertising coming to their attention during off-duty hours, when that advertising appears to violate the FTC Act. This supplements the regular monitoring activities of the Commission.

This monitoring unit employs equipment which records both aural and visual commercial continuity broadcast by stations. If an initial study suggests malpractice, an investigation of the matter is undertaken by a project attorney of the Commission. If he recommends prohibitive action against the advertiser and is supported by officials in charge of litigation and by the Commission, the advertiser is then formally charged with having engaged in unfair methods of competition or unfair or deceptive acts, and is brought to trial before an examiner as previously described.

FTC Warns Against Illegal Huckstering.   In the late fifties, the Federal Trade Commission stepped up its monitoring activities. Public reaction then against rigged television shows and offensive advertising practices prompted the Commission to issue an official warning that it would scrutinize more carefully "advertising excesses that dance on the edges of the law." On November 1, 1959, the Commission announced that it had received many complaints from the public about TV advertising practices and was ready to "strike fast and hard" at "illegal huckstering by the irresponsible few."

The announcement further stated that the FTC would double its monitoring staff, make continuous rather than spot checks on all network commercials and speed investigations on non-network advertising throughout the country. Monitoring practices and investigations have greatly increased in recent years.

The Importance of Government Regulation Stressed. The importance of governmental regulation in the advertising field is indicated by the following remarks taken from a speech by Charles A. Sweeney, former Director of the Bureau of Deceptive Practices, delivered in New York at the annual meeting of the Division of Food, Drug and Cosmetic Law, American Bar Association, July 12, 1957:

The increasingly important role of advertising as an essential of our continuously expanding economy not only justifies but demands such attention by the Federal government. The Commission is seriously mindful that the importance of advertising, especially in the field of foods and drugs because of the health aspect, has grown with our expanding economy and also in direct proportion to the lessening of direct, personal contact between producer and consumer. Few would deny today that advertising is indispensible to the maintenance and continued expansion of our American standard of living and our economic well-being.

It follows logically that the more important advertising becomes to the nation and its well-being, the greater the public interest in maintaining its integrity. That interest flows from the dependence of the buyer on this facility for knowledge essential to his intelligent selection of those goods which best suit his needs.

The seller has an equal interest in the integrity of advertising because of his desire to invest his advertising money with assurance that potential purchasers will have sufficient confidence in his claims to persuade them to select his products. This is an immediate and pressing interest. However, beyond that immediate interest, the seller must expect to rely increasingly upon the medium of advertising to acquaint the public with new products to be developed. For that reason any lessening of confidence in advertising not only will diminish the value of his advertising dollar but jeopardize or for practical purposes destroy this medium of contact upon which his business future so largely depends.

It is vital, for these reasons, that all of us recognize our common interest in utilizing the agencies and procedures provided by Congress to maintain the integrity and believability of advertising, of such importance to our economy and individual business well-being.

Food and Drug Administration. Not to be disregarded by the broadcaster are the functions and activities of the Food and Drug Administration. This agency, among other things, is charged with the responsibility of enforcing the Federal Food, Drug and Cosmetic Act.[27] It is empowered to prevent the misbranding and mislabeling of commodities. It is an operating division of the U.S. Department of Health, Education and Welfare, whose administrative officers have wide discretion in promulgating standards of quality for the marketing and sale of consumer goods.

There are the offices of the Commissioner, two Associate and two Assistant Commissioners, and their staff in Washington, D.C., with 18 district offices and many inspection stations distributed throughout the United States, equipped with testing laboratories and staffed with chemists and other technical personnel.[28] When violations of rules and regulations with respect to quality and labeling of commodities are discovered, the FDA can resort to a number of corrective procedures as provided by law. It may attempt to secure compliance with rules and regulations by informal, administrative agreement in much the same manner as the Federal Trade Commission.[29] Or it may condemn adulterated or misbranded products offered for sale.[30] It also may recommend to the Department of Justice the seizure of such products, or the institution of injunction actions and criminal prosecutions.[31]

There is a working agreement between the Federal Trade Commission and the Food and Drug Administration by which it is acknowledged that the primary concern of the former agency is with advertising and that of the latter is with mislabeling.[32] The agreement provides for a close relationship between the agencies involving exchanges of information, and is designed to avoid jurisdictional conflicts and duplication of efforts and to strengthen enforcement procedures.

The Department of Health, Education and Welfare. As authorized by the ETV Facilities Act of 1962, this Department, out of Congressional appropriations, makes available matching funds for the construction of educational radio and TV facilities. Since 1962, a large number of such grants have been made to educational institutions and organizations throughout the country for his purpose. This Federal, financial assistance has been a great boon to the development of noncommercial, educational broadcasting stations in the United States. The ETV Facilities Act was adopted as an amendment to Title III of the Communications Act of 1934, as amended, and the full text appears in Appendix I.

The Corporation for Public Broadcasting. As a part of the ETV Facilities Act, Congress has authorized the creation of the Corporation for Public Broadcasting. While the Act states that the Corporation is not an agency or establishment of the United States government, at the present time it is largely funded by Congress (it is authorized to receive private moneys), and the members of its board of directors are appointed by the President with the advice and consent of the Senate.

It is a nonprofit, nonpolitical organization, and its purposes, broadly stated, are to provide financial aid for the planning and production of high quality noncommercial, educational radio and TV programs, and to assist in the development of systems of interconnection for the distribution of these programs throughout the United States. It does not produce programs itself, but receives and makes grants-in-aid to others (creative individuals, groups and organizations, educationally disposed) to produce programs and to distribute them for wide reception. The full text of that part of the ETV Facilities Act relating to the Corporation appears as an amendment to the Communications Act in Appendix I.

The President.   As provided in Section 305 of the Communications Act, the President of the United States assigns all radio frequencies used by the Federal government. More than half of all available spectrum space is used by the various agencies of the Government including the expanding military establishment.

If he finds it necessary, the President is authorized by Section 606 of the Communications Act to exercise certain emergency powers in time of war. He may direct carriers to give communications preference or priority if they are essential to national defense and security. This section makes it unlawful for any person, during a war in which the United States may be engaged, to obstruct or retard interstate or foreign communication by radio or wire and the President is authorized to use the armed services to prevent any such obstruction or retardation of communications.[33]

Upon proclamation by the President that there exists war or a threat of war, or a state of public peril, disaster or other national emergency, or in order to preserve neutrality of the United States, he may suspend as he sees fit the rules and regulations applicable to any or all radio stations as prescribed by the FCC and may cause the closing of any such station. He may order the removal of its apparatus and equipment or he may authorize the use or control of any station or device, its apparatus and equipment by any department of the government under such rules as he may prescribe with just compensation to the owners.[34]

By an Executive Order issued December 10, 1951, the President delegated to the FCC, subject to certain limitations, the authority vested in him with respect to radio stations, except those owned and operated by any department or agency of the U.S. Government. With respect to government stations, subject to certain limitations, the authority vested in the President has been delegated to the head of each department or agency with which the stations are involved.[35]

The President has the advice and help of the Office of Emergency Planning whose purpose is to provide effective leadership in our national mobilization effort, including both current defense activities and readiness for any future national emergency.[36]

The Director of OEP, on behalf of the President, directs, controls, and coordinates all mobilization activities of the executive branch of the government. Pursuant to Executive Order 11051 of September 27, 1962, he assists and advises with the President respecting telecommunication functions in the executive branch including: (1) the coordination of the development of telecommunication policies, standards, plans and programs among the various government agencies to assure maximum security to the United States in time of national emergency with a minimum interference to non-government activities and (2) assigning radio frequencies to government agencies.[37] The Director coordinates his activities in this regard with the Federal Communications Commission. He is assisted by the Interdepartmental Radio Advisory Committee representing the various agencies of the government and by the Office of Telecommunications Management, of which an Assistant Director for Telecommunications is head.[38] The functions of this Assistant Director are not restricted to mobilization but are of continuing nature during normal as well as abnormal conditions.[39]

Mention has already been made of the President's power to appoint the members of the FCC and FTC and to designate their chairmen. While the law specifies that a limited number of commissioners may be members of the same political party, it goes without saying that the President has wide latitude in appointing those whom he thinks will reflect his own political and administrative ideas. Since the chairmen of these agencies hold their positions subject to the will of the President, their official conduct, needless to say, may be affected by attitudes and opinions which prevail at and radiate from the White House. A sense of loyalty and, in some cases, a realization that the same President may still be in office when time for reappointment of these members of FCC and FTC, can have a subtle, but none the less real influence upon their thinking and behavior.

The Congress.　Since their appointments and reappointments depend upon approval of the Senate, it is only natural that Commissioners should be concerned with what the Senators think of their actions. This is particularly true with respect to the Senate Commerce Committee. Every presidential appointment and reappointment to one of these commissions must be approved by this Committee. Accordingly, opinions on communications matters expressed by any Senator, particularly those of the Committee, are likely to receive careful consideration by commissioners.

Also, under the direction of its Chairman and with the assistance of staff experts, this Senate Committee makes continuing studies of problems in interstate and foreign commerce and has important responsibilities with respect to the initiation of legislation in the broadcasting field. There is a close liaison between the Committee staff and that of the commissions and the exchange of information is most helpful in the development of legislation designed to improve regulatory processes.

The importance of other Congressional committees should be mentioned. The Committee on Interstate and Foreign Commerce in the House, like its counterpart in the Senate, is concerned with the operations of the FCC, FTC, and numerous other governmental bureaus. The appropriations committees of Congress also are able to influence the policies and activities of these commissions because of their power to approve or disapprove budget proposals submitted by these agencies.

Special Congressional committees have been appointed from time to time to investigate the operations of the FCC and other commissions and to study particular aspects of their operations and regulatory problems. The investigations and reports of these Congressional committees on occasions have affected, and often seriously disrupted, the normal operations of these commissions. This is discussed more fully in Chapter 23.

The influence of individual Congressmen should not be overlooked. Because of inquiries, complaints and pressures from their constituents, they may be in frequent contact by telephone or correspondence with FCC and other government officials. In fact, a substantial portion of the correspondence of these agency officials is related to communications from individual Congressmen speaking in behalf of the people or of interests "back home." While it would be difficult to calculate their precise effects, it is safe to say that there have been times when these congressional communications have affected materially the consideration and ultimate outcome of matters pending before these bureaus.

The Courts.   In the event that any parties over which the FCC, FTC and FDA have jurisdiction violate laws which these agencies administer, or fail to comply with lawful orders issued by them, the Federal District Courts are available to enforce compliance. For example, Section 401 of the Communications Act provides that these courts, upon application of the Attorney General of the United States at the request of the FCC may issue writs of mandamus commanding compliance with provisions of the law.[40] Similarly, these courts have authority to compel compliance with laws administered by the Federal Trade Commission and the Food and Drug Administration.[41]

Mention has already been made in Chapter 3 of Section 313 of the Communications Act which relates to the enforcement of the anti-trust laws. As pointed out, this section declares that all laws of the U.S. forbidding monopolies and restraints of trade are applicable to the manufacture and sale of radio apparatus and to interstate and foreign radio communications. The section further provides that whenever any civil or criminal proceeding is instituted in a Federal Court to enforce or review the orders of the Federal Trade Commission or other government agency with respect to these anti-trust laws, if the Court finds any radio licensee to be guilty, it may, in addition to the penalties imposed by the laws, revoke the license. Thereupon all rights under such license would cease subject of course to the licensee's right to appeal to a higher court.

Section 402 of the Communications Act provides that appeals may be taken from decisions and orders of the FCC to the United States Court of Appeals for the District of Columbia in any of the following cases:

(1) By any applicant for a construction permit or station license whose application is denied by the Commission.

(2) By any applicant for the renewal or modification of any such instrument of authorization whose application is denied by the Commission.

(3) By any party to an application for authority to transfer, assign, or dispose of any such instrument of authorization, or any rights thereunder, whose application is denied by the Commission.

(4) By an applicant for authorization to locate and operate a broadcast studio or other place from which programs are transmitted or delivered to a radio station in a foreign country for the purpose of having them reach consistently the United States, whose application has been denied by the

Commission or whose permit has been revoked by the Commission.

(5) By the holder of any construction permit or station license which has been modified or revoked by the Commission.

(6) By any other person who is aggrieved or whose interests are adversely affected by any order of the Commission granting or denying any application described above.

(7) By any person upon whom an order to cease and desist has been served under Section 312 of the Communications Act.[42]

It is provided in Section 402 that the decision of the District Court of Appeals on any of the above matters shall be final, subject, however, to review by the Supreme Court of the United States upon writ of *certiorari.*[43]

Section 402 sets forth detailed procedural requirements for appeals.[44] The appellate court may confirm or overturn the decision of the Commission. In the latter case, it remands the decision of the Commission to carry out the judgment of the Court.[45]

The laws governing the functions of the Federal Trade Commission and the Food and Drug Administration also provide for appeals to the U.S. Circuit Courts from decisions and orders of these agencies.[46]

The Department of Justice. The Department of Justice is the agency generally responsible for the enforcement of Federal laws. Its affairs and activities are under the direction of the Attorney General, who supervises and directs the activities of U.S. district attorneys and marshals in the various judicial districts.

As provided in Section 401 (c) of the Communications Act, it is the duty of any district attorney of the United States, upon application by the FCC to institute in the proper court and prosecute under the direction of the Attorney General all necessary proceedings for the enforcement of any provisions of the Act and for punishment of any violations thereof.[47] Similar assistance of the Attorney General and these district attorneys is available to the FTC and FDA, as provided in the laws governing these agencies.[48]

Special mention should be made of the anti-trust and criminal divisions of the Department of Justice. These divisions are particularly concerned with the enforcement of Federal anti-trust laws by criminal actions and by civil suits in equity aimed to protect and restore competitive conditions to the American system of free enterprise. The Criminal Division has responsibility for and supervision over the enforcement of Federal criminal laws generally. Both are directed by Assistant Attorney Generals who are responsible to the Attorney General.

Prosecution of violations of Sections 313 and 314 of the Communications Act pertaining to anti-trust laws and preservation of competition in the broadcasting industry is the responsibility of the Anti-Trust Division. Violations of Section 1304 and 1464 of the U.S. Criminal Code, making it unlawful to broadcast lotteries and indecent and profane language, and violations of Section 14 of the Federal Trade Commission Act forbidding false advertising and Section 301 of the Food, Drug and Cosmetics Act prohibiting the mislabeling of foods, drugs and other commodities are prosecuted by the Criminal Division.

State and Local Agencies of Control.   While the Federal Communications Commission has the primary responsibility for the regulation of broadcasting, the activity is affected to a considerable extent by governmental agencies and requirements at state and local levels. While by no means covering the many requirements and areas of activity of these agencies, the following are some of the more important ones which impinge upon broadcasting.

A large majority of radio and television stations are operated by corporations. In all states there exist general laws which prescribe procedure which must be followed in establishing corporations including those engaged in the broadcasting business. A certificate of incorporation must be approved by the Secretary of State or equivalent officer in the state government and the charter under which the station operates must authorize broadcasting activities.

While state statutes rarely expressly require corporations to adopt by-laws, they usually provide that they may do so and the implication is strong that they should. A failure to do so may in some cases actually lead to violation of state statutes in the transaction of corporate business.[49]

In drafting the charter and by-laws, the prospective broadcaster should consult with legal counsel familiar with corporation law in the state where the business is to be carried on.

State and Local Taxation.   The Commerce Clause of the Federal Constitution prohibits states and localities from assessing any tax which directly or indirectly places an undue burden on or discriminates against interstate commerce. This rule, however, has not always operated to free interstate business such as broadcasting from all such levies. Some state courts have held that stations may be subject to a state tax if it is directed only at the local aspects of broadcasting.

While there is no uniform pattern for taxing radio and television stations at state and local levels, several types of levies have been made. One is the gross receipts tax. For example, the state of New Mexico imposed a 2 percent privilege tax on gross receipts derived from local business firms, but excluded gross receipts from network advertising originating in other states and those from national spot advertising on the grounds that they were interstate in character and therefore not subject to state assessment.[50]

Hawaii passed a law imposing a similar tax on the gross receipts of radio stations. Honolulu Station KPOA contested the validity of the tax in the courts, contending that all broadcasting is interstate in character, that Congress had preempted the subject matter of radio broadcasting to the exclusion of state and territorial legislation of every kind, including taxation, and that the assessments made against the station were invalid and unconstitutional.

The tax was upheld by the courts. It was held that Hawaii might levy a tax on gross receipts of a radio station located within the territory, where the station's broadcasts have commercial value only within the territory and income from broadcasts to the mainland by short-wave relay are excluded. Such a tax was held not to be a burden on interstate commerce. The fact that Congress had preempted the radio field and required broadcasters to secure licenses did not render them immune from taxation. It was reasoned by the courts that the character of radio communication does not prohibit a tax upon the state business any more than the interstate character of railroads, power companies, telephone, telegraph and express companies prevent taxes which do not aim to control interstate commerce.[51]

In an early case, *Fisher's Blend,* 297 U.S. 650, 56 S.Ct. 608, 80 L. ed. 956 (1936), a state occupation tax measured by gross receipts from two radio stations in the state of Washington was involved. In that case, the Court held that since the stations' income was derived from interstate commerce, the tax measured by gross receipts was a burden on interstate commerce. The Court indicated, however, that a gross receipts tax directed solely at a local aspect of broadcasting would not be invalid.

The cases seem to show, therefore, that the courts must be satisfied that a tax measured by gross receipts is in some way related to activity within the state, either because the event taxed is a "local one," like the sale of advertising, or because the taxed income is intrastate commerce or is allocable to intrastate commerce.

The City of New York has worked out an apportionment formula by which interstate companies are taxed for the privilege of doing business there. The regulations there require that a radio station apportion to the City as "wholly taxable receipts" that "proportion of the gross receipts from the sale of sponsored time" which the number of radio families within the city bears to the total number of radio families covered by the station.[52]

Some municipalities have resorted to flat license taxes as a means of obtaining revenue from broadcasting stations. The courts have sustained this type of tax where it is shown that some proportion of the programs broadcast either originate in the local studios, are sponsored by local advertisers, or are primarily intended to reach a local audience. There have been exceptions though. An ordinance requiring all firms or persons operating a radio station to pay a license tax was struck down in *Whitehurst v. Grimes,* 21 F. (2d) 787 (E.D. Ky. 1927) as a direct tax on the business of radio broadcasting which the court said was interstate commerce and exclusively committed to the national government. *Tampa Times v. Burnett,* 45 F.Supp. 166 (S.D. Fla. 1942) was a similar case.

In 1961, taxes were being imposed on broadcast advertising by taxing authorities in five states: Arizona, Delaware, Indiana, New Mexico and West Virginia. An unsuccessful attempt was made in 1951 to impose a privilege tax on Oklahoma stations and a 5 percent tax on gross receipts of these stations. The privilege tax or license would have consisted of ten cents per watt, or $5,000 for a 50 kw station.[53]

In a 1959 ruling of the U.S. Supreme Court, it was held that the state might impose a tax on the net income of national business concerns, even though they may not have tangible assets in the taxing state, provided the levy is limited to that portion of the income derived from sales solely within the taxing state. (See 358 U.S. 450 Feb. 1959).

This decision appeared to make broadcast stations, station representatives, advertising agencies, program syndicators and networks liable for taxes in all states where they do business and derive income. According to *Broadcasting Magazine* for March 2, 1959, page 32, some 35 states then imposed corporation taxes on companies located within their borders. Prior to the recent Supreme Court decision, companies had never paid income tax to a state in which they had no tangible property or assets.

The current practice with respect to taxation on broadcasting stations varies with the taxing authorities and courts in the different states and communities. With states and municipalities under increasing pressure to find new sources of revenue to meet the rising costs of government, it may be that stations will be called upon more and more to share in these costs.

Municipal Regulations. Some mention should be made of municipal regulations which impinge upon the broadcaster. These may include local ordinances to prevent interference to radio reception from various sources such as diathermy machines, industrial heating devices, and all types of electronic equipment capable of radiating electro-magnetic energy. Also, municipalities, by means of zoning and safety ordinances regulate the height and location of transmitting towers. These regulations are considered to be a valid exercise of state police power and designed to prohibit "nuisances" and other evils which affect the security and safety of the community.[54]

In a 1951 Pennsylvania case it was held that state and local authorities may not censor movies presented on television. In *Allen B. Dumont Laboratories v. Carroll,* 184 F. (2d) 153 (1951), the United States Court of Appeals for the Third District held that Congress had fully occupied the field of television regulation to the exclusion of any regulation by the states; that it had the constitutional right to do so, and that therefore a state could not censor motion picture films used in television broadcasts. The U.S. Supreme Court denied a writ of *certiorari* in the case, sustaining the decision of the lower court.[55]

Despite the decision in this case, some legal authorities feel that perhaps the Courts have not spoken the last word on this matter and there is speculation to the effect that in some cases, such as those involving unquestionable obscenity in films shown on television, judicial interpretation might take a different turn.[56]

When State Controls of Broadcasting May Be Exercised: A Landmark Case. In a 1963 New Mexico case, the U.S. Supreme Court upheld a state statute that prohibited the advertisement by any means of prices or terms relating to eye glasses.[57] A newspaper and radio station which carried advertisements by an optometrist were enjoined by a trial court and the Supreme Court of Mexico upheld the injunction. On appeal to the U.S. Supreme Court, the newspaper and station contended that the statute and injunction were an undue burden on interstate commerce, and that the state's jurisdiction was preempted by federal legislation.

The U.S. Supreme Court conceded that both the newspaper and radio station, being located close to the Texas border and serving readers and listeners in both states, were engaged in interstate commerce, but said that under the particular facts of the case, it did not follow that there was an unconstitutional burden on this commerce. Said the Court:

> Without doubt, the appellants' radio station and newspaper are engaged in interstate commerce, and the injunction in this case has unquestionably imposed some restraint upon that commerce. But these facts alone do not add up to an unconstitutional burden on interstate commerce. As we said in Huron Portland Cement Co. v. City of Detroit, 362 U.S. 440, upholding the applications of a Detroit smoke abatement ordinance to ships engaged in interstate and international commerce: "In determining whether the state has imposed an undue burden on interstate commerce, it must be borne in mind that the Constitution when conferring upon Congress the regulation of commerce, . . . never intended to cut the State off from legislating on all subjects relating to the health, life, and safety of their citizens, though the legislation might indirectly affect the commerce of the country. Legislation, in a great variety of ways, may affect commerce and persons engaged in it without constituting a regulation of it, within the meaning of the Constitution. Sherlock v. Alling, 93 U.S. 99, 103; Austin v. Tennessee, 179, U.S. 343; Louisville & Nashville R. Co. v. Kentucky, 183 U.S. 503; The Minnesota Rate Cases, 230 U.S. 352; Boston & Maine R. Co. v. Armburg, 285 U.S. 234; Collins v. American Buslines, Inc., 350 U.S. 528; 362 U.S. at 443-444".[58]

The Court went on to say:

> Like the smoke abatement ordinance in the Huron case, the statute here involved is a measure directly addressed to protection of the public health, and the statute thus falls within the most traditional concept of what is compendiously known as the police power. The legitimacy of state legislation in this precise area has been expressly established. Williamson v. Lee Optical Co., 348 U.S. 483. A state law may not be struck down on the mere showing that its administration affects interstate commerce in some way. "State regulation, based on the police power, which does not discriminate against interstate commerce or operate to disrupt its required uniformity, may constitutionally stand. Huron Portland Cement Co. v. City of Detroit, supra, at 448".[59]

. . . .

In dealing with the contention that New Mexico's jurisdiction to regulate radio advertising has been pre-empted by the Federal Communications Act, we may begin by noting that the validity of this claim cannot be judged by reference to broad statements about the "comprehensive" nature of the federal regulation under the Federal Communications Act. ". . . Statements concerning the 'exclusive jurisdiction' of Congress beg the only controversial question: whether Congress intended to make its jurisdiction exclusive." California v. Zook, 336 U.S. 725, 731. Kelly v. Washington, 302 U.S. 1, 10-13. In areas of law not inherently requiring national uniformity, our decisions are clear in requiring that state statutes, otherwise valid, must be upheld unless there is found "such actual conflict between the two schemes of regulation that both cannot stand in the same area, [or] evidence of a congressional design to preempt the field." Florida Avocado Growers v. Paul, 373 U.S. 132.

. . . .

Finally, there has been no showing of any conflict between this state law and the federal regulatory system, or that the state law stands as an obstacle to the full effectiveness of the federal statute. No specific federal regulations even remotely in conflict with the New Mexico law have been called to our attention. The Commission itself has apparently viewed state regulation of advertising as complementing its regulatory function, rather than in any way conflicting with it. . . . As in Colorado Anti-Discrimination Communication v. Continental Air Lines, Inc., 372 U.S. 714 at 724, we are satisfied that the state statute "at least so long as any power the [Commission] may have remains 'dormant and unexercised', will not frustrate any part of the purpose of the federal legislation".[60]

In a long concurring opinion, Mr. Justice Brennan set forth what he considered to be the important tests in determining whether federal legislation displaces state regulation on any given subject: Is the subject matter clearly one "by its very nature admitting only of national supervision? Is there evidence of congressional intent exclusively to occupy the field? As a practical matter, can both regulations be enforced without impairing the federal superintendence of the field? . . ."

Justice Brennan, under the particular facts of this case, had no difficulty in answering the first two questions in the negative and in finding that, constitutionally, both federal and state regulations were valid and could operate without conflict.[61] He warned, however, that the decision in this case did not intimate any "view of the constitutionality of several other superficially similar forms of state regulation of broadcasting. In supporting this point he said:

. . . First, nothing here said suggests that a system of state regulation, although not in direct conflict with federal law, would pass muster if it was so pervasive and so burdensome upon broadcasters as to interfere substantially with the overall purposes of federal regulation. Cf. Allen B. Dumont Labs. v. Carroll, supra. Second, nothing said answers the problem of the situation, factually closer to that at bar but legally quite distinct, which would be presented if a State in which nationwide network material originates, sought to restrict network advertising under a statute enacted for the protection only of that State's consumers. Such regulation might well exceed the scope of the State's legitimate interests, and involve a constitutionally illegitimate attempt to control communications beyond its borders. Cf. Bibb v. Navajo Freight Lines, Inc., 359 U.S. 520; Southern Pacific Co. v. Arizona, 325 U.S. 761,775. Third, nothing said here may be read to sustain the constitutionality of applications of local advertising regulations which threaten to make it impossible for a local station to transmit network broadcasts because of their sponsorship.... While the States's interest might be no different from that protected by this New Mexico statute, the more drastic effect of the regulation upon the exercise of the broadcaster's federal license and his access to network material might well require a different result. All that the Court decides today is that this New Mexico statute may constitutionally be enforced against radio broadcasters equally with other news media doing business in New Mexico.[62]

In summary, what the Judge and the Court seemed to be saying is that a state's authority to regulate advertising or any other aspect of broadcast operations will depend upon whether the regulation is a legitimate exercise of police powers concerned with the health, safety and well-being of the state; whether the evidence clearly indicates a congressional design to preempt the field; and whether the state action defeats, frustrates or conflicts with any purpose of federal legislation or regulations which implement it. And the answers to these questions must be determined on the basis of the facts in each individual case. What may be valid State regulation of some particular phase of broadcasting under one set of circumstances may not be valid under another. (In point, see *People v. Eller Telecasting Co. of Arizona*, Court of Appeal, Fourth Appelate District, California, December 4, 1970, 20 RR 2d 2131, which involved TV advertising across state boundaries, and in which the California Court said the facts were different in the New Mexico case discussed above in 374 U.S. 424, and in terms of that Supreme Court decision the California Court held that an injunction against an Arizona TV station transmitting advertising of glasses into California, contrary to law, was an undue burden on interstate commerce and unconstitutional.)

1. 52 Stat. 111 (1938).
2. 38 Stat. 717 (1914).
3. Federal Trade Commission, *Annual Report* (1967), p. III.
4. Wheeler-Lea Act, approved March 21, 1938, 52 Stat. 111, amending the Federal Trade Commission Act.
5. For excellent discussion of this matter, see "Remarks of Charles A. Sweeney," Legal Advisor for Radio and Television Bureau of Investigation, Federal Trade Commission, before The Nutrition Foundation, Inc. and Institute of Food Technology, Northern California Section, Berkeley, California, January 15, 1959. See also *Aronberg v. FTC*, 132 F(2d) 165 and *Gelb v. FTC*, 144 F(2d) 580.
6. See Sweeney, *Ibid.* Also, *In the Matter of Ward Laboratories, Inc. et al.*, FTC Docket No. 6346, decided March 4, 1959.
7. See *In the Matter of Hutchinson Chemical Corporation and Herman S. Hutchinson*, FTC Docket No. 7140.
8. 52 Stat. 114.
9. *Ibid.*, 115.
10. *Ibid.*
11. *Ibid.*, 116.
12. *Ibid.*, 116-117.
13. Federal Trade Commission, *Annual Report* (1957), p. 19.
14. *Ibid.*, pp. 6, 7.
15. Scott, Harold T., former Legal Adviser, Radio and Television Advertising, Federal Trade Commission; address to New Jersey Pharmaceutical Association, January 28, 1958.
16. *Ibid.*, p. 5.
17. See Federal Trade Commission, Annual Reports (1955, 56, 57 and 58).
18. *Ibid.*
19. *Smoking and Health, Report of Advisory Committee to Surgeon General of the Public Health Service*, U.S. Department of Health, Education, and Welfare, January 11, 1964, p. 33.
20. *Trade Regulation for the Prevention of Unfair or Deceptive Advertising and Labeling of Cigarettes in Relation to the Health, Hazards of Smoking and Accompanying Statement of Basis and Purpose of Rule*, Federal Trade Commission, June 22, 1964, Appendix C.
21. *Ibid.*, pp. 151-153.
22. Public Law 89-92, 79 Stat. 282.
23. 111 Cong. Rec. 20680-20681, August 17, 1965.
24. See Governor Meynor's complete testimony; Hearings before the Committee on Commerce, U.S. Senate, on S. 559 and S. 547, Bills to Regulate Labeling of Cigarettes and for Other Purposes, March 30, 1965, pp. 562-585.
25. Senate Bill 1803, May 17, 1967; Senate Bills 2394 and 2395, September 12, 1967; also, see *Broadcasting* magazine, November 6, 1967, p. 30.
26. *Broadcasting*, February 12, 1968, p. 26.
27. 52. Stat. 1041 (1938).
28. *U.S. Government Organization Manual* (1967-68), pp. 378-380.
29. 52 Stat. 1043-45.
30. *Ibid.*
31. *Ibid.*
32. "The Regulation of Advertising", 56 Columbia L.R. 1036-1037 (November, 1956).
33. 48 Stat. 1104-5.

34. *Ibid.*

35. Executive Order on Emergency Control of Stations and Facilities, Executive Order No. 10312, signed December 10, 1951, 16 Fed Reg. 12452.

36. *U.S. Government Organization Manual* (1967-68), pp. 67-70.

37. Executive Order 11051, September 27, 1962.

38. *U.S. Government Organization Manual* (1967-68), p. 68.

39. *Ibid.*

40. 48 Stat. 1092.

41. 52 Stat. 114, and 1043-45.

42. 66 Stat. 718-19.

43. *Ibid.,* 720.

44. *Ibid.,* 719.

45. *Ibid.,* 720.

46. 52 Stat. 112-13 and 1055-56.

47. 48 Stat. 1093.

48. 52 Stat. 116-117 and 1046.

49. See Olek, Howard L., *Non-Profit Corporations and Associations* (Englewood Cliffs, N.J., 1956), p. 173.

50. N.M. Stats., Section 76-1404 (1941).

51. *McGaw v. Tax Commissioners of Hawaii,* 40 Haw. 121, 9 RR 2055 (1953); affirmed *sub. nom. McGaw v. Fase,* 11 RR 2004 (9 Cir., October 30, 1954).

52. Article 214 of the New York City Regulations, *Radio Broadcasting Stations; Allocation of Receipts from Radio Broadcasting,* issued under the General Business and Financial Tax Law.

53. See *Broadcasting* (November 11, 1957), p. 27.

54. For an excellent and comprehensive discussion of local ordinances affecting broadcasting see Rhyne, Charles S., *Municipal Regulations, Taxation and Use of Radio and Television,* Report No. 143 (1955), National Institute of Municipal Law Officers, Washington, D.C.

55. 340 U.S: 929.

56. See Rhyne, *op. cit.,* pp. 43-44.

57. 374 U.S. 424; 10 L ed 2d 983; 83 S Ct 1759; decided June 17, 1963.

58. 374 U.S. p. 428.

59. *Ibid.,* pp. 428-29.

60. *Ibid.,* 429-30.

61. *Ibid.,* p. 432.

62. *Ibid.,* pp. 433-447.

PART III

Character, Classification and Utilization of Radio Frequencies

CHAPTER 6

The Nature, Measurement and Uses
of Radio Waves

*I must confess to a feeling of profound humility in the presence of a
universe which transcends us at almost every point. I feel like a child who
while playing by the seashore has found a few bright colored shells and a few
pebbles while the whole vast ocean of truth stretches out almost untouched
and unruffled before my eager fingers.*— ISAAC NEWTON

As pointed out in Chapter 3, Section 303 of the Communications Act
requires the FCC to classify broadcasting stations, assign bands of frequencies to the various classes of stations and prescribe the nature of their uses
and services. Pursuant to this statutory mandate, the Commission has established detailed regulations providing for a systematic allocation of frequencies and classification of stations for different types of broadcasting service.
Some knowledge of the nature of electromagnetic energy and the broadcast
spectrum is necessary before these regulations can be fully understood and
evaluated.

Broadcasting makes use of electromagnetic energy which exists in the
form of waves. These waves travel at the speed of light (186,000 miles per
second). To understand their properties and behavior, it is helpful to compare them with water and sound waves.[1] A pebble dropped in a pool causes
an up and down movement of the water which is propagated on the surface
in all directions with a certain velocity. Similarly, sound waves result from
the movement or vibration of some physical material or body causing alternate condensations and rarefactions of air which we are able to "hear"
because we possess auditory equipment which can detect varying conditions of the air.[2]

Electromagnetic waves are characterized by varying frequencies and
lengths. The frequency is the number of cycles of vibration per second. The
wave length is the distance the wave travels in one cycle. Or it may be
described as the distance between the crests of the troughs of the wave.

The frequency is usually expressed in kilocycles (1000 cycles per second)
and abbreviated *kc* or in megacycles (1 million cycles per second) abbreviated *mc.* For example, a station operating on a frequency of 600,000

99

cycles per second is referred to as a 600 kc operation.

Radio communication is accomplished by transforming air vibrations into electromagnetic waves. This is done by a process called transduction. The sound waves set up by the voice or a musical instrument in a broadcasting studio strike a thin metal diaphragm in a microphone. An electrical current having the same vibrations is produced, and is carried by wire to amplifying tubes. These tubes increase the intensity of the current but do not change the frequency. This "audio-frequency" current, as it is called, is imposed on the carrier wave transmitted by the station. Electrical impulses oscillating back and forth between the antenna and the ground system of the station result in the emission of the carrier wave. This wave travels through space to a receiving set where the carrier current is modified so that sound currents corresponding with those at the broadcasting station are obtained, amplified and made intelligible to the human ear.[3]

The strength or field intensity of a wave at any receiving point depends upon numerous factors including the power and efficiency of the transmitting facilities, the distance from the transmitter to the receiver, the frequency, time of day, season, meteorological conditions, characteristics of the transmission path, etc.[4]

The field strength of a wave at any given point is measured in terms of volts or fractions thereof per meter. Unless in close proximity to the station, the electric field is always less than one volt per meter. Within a few miles the measure is in terms of millivolts per meter. As the wave travels farther and diminishes in intensity, it is measured in terms of microvolts per meter.[5]

The existence of other electric fields in an area of reception may produce interference problems. These "interference fields," as they are called, may result from a number of causes: atmospheric electricity or static, electrical devices such as diathermy machines and radio stations operating on the same or adjacent channels. In order for radio reception to be satisfactory, the field intensity of the desired wave must be strong enough and the receiving equipment good enough to overcome interference from the other electric fields existing in the area.[6]

Electromagnetic energy manifests itself in ways other than radio waves. It may take the form of electricity or be in the form of light, X-rays or cosmic rays, depending upon wave lengths and frequencies. When laid out in numerical order, these make up what is called the electromagnetic spectrum. Roughly, this is analogous to a piano key board with low frequency notes at one end and ascending in numerical order to the higher notes at the other. Similarly, it may be compared to a color sequence with the red end of the spectrum representing the lower frequencies and the blue end representing the higher ones.

At the lower part of the electromagnetic spectrum are the electrical waves which are comparatively long and have low frequencies. Above these, are the radio frequencies, starting at about 10,000 cycles per second with the wave being over 18 miles in length. At the upper end of this part, the waves have a frequency as high as 300,000 megacycles per second and measure only about one twenty-fifth of an inch in length. Above the radio spectrum in the area of visible light the waves become almost infinitesimal and have frequencies of millions of megacycles per second.[7]

The vast range of frequencies in the radio spectrum itself has been divided and classified by international agreement as follows:[8]

Very Low Frequency (VLF)	Below 30 kc/s
Low Frequency (LF)	30 to 300 kc/s
Medium Frequency (MF)	300 to 3,000 kc/s
High Frequency (HF)	3 to 30 mc/s
Very High Frequency (VHF)	30 to 300 mc/s
Ultra High Frequency (UHF)	300 to 3,000 mc/s
Super High Frequency (SHF)	3 to 30 gc/s
Extremely High Frequency (EHF)	30 to 300 gc/s

Propagation Characteristics of Radio Frequencies. Just as the various parts of the electromagnetic spectrum as a whole differ in their form and behavior, so do the various frequency ranges within the radio spectrum itself exhibit different characteristics. For example, some radio waves travel in straight lines from the point of transmission to the point of reception. They are called direct waves. Others tend to follow the curvature of the earth and are called ground waves. Still others travel away from the earth and are reflected back. They are referred to as sky waves.

From about 35 to 250 miles above the earth, there are several layers of ionized atmosphere. These various strata make up what is called the ionosphere. They are formed as the ultra-violet rays from the sun reach the upper regions of air and electrify or ionize them. Their thickness and height vary from hour to hour with changes in the intensity flow of these rays from the sun. Radio waves traveling upward, striking the ionosphere, and reflecting back to earth, are called sky waves and constitute an important resource for radio transmission.

The four principal layers of the ionosphere are D, E, F_1 and F_2. During the daytime, the D layer lies about 37 miles above the earth. This is primarily a region of radio wave absorption, although some very long waves are reflected by it and provide some radio service. The E layer is about 70 miles above the earth. Still higher at about 140 miles is the F_1 region. Above this, at heights ranging from 185 to 250 miles is the heavily ionized F_2 strata.

These ionized layers reflect radio waves in much the same way that a mirror reflects light. A broadcast station transmits a wave which strikes the ionosphere, is reflected back to earth, and in a series of skips may travel a great distance before its energy is finally exhausted.

With respect to the utility of the different types of waves, in the lower frequencies (10 to 200 kc), ground waves predominate. These are capable of traveling long distances and their reception is comparatively stable and free from fading. To overcome atmospheric noises to which these frequencies are subject, however, greater power must be used, requiring high powered transmitting equipment and involving greater costs. Effective and profitable use of these frequencies is made to provide long distance point-to-point communication.

In the lower part of the next frequency range (200 to 2,000 kc), the ground waves continue to be important. Their attenuation, however, is more affected by the conductivity of the soil and irregularities of terrain over which they must travel and structures such as buildings, wire lines, etc., which lie in their pathway. These frequencies are useful for such services as aural broadcasting since they provide reasonably stable and moderately long distance transmission during both day and night. Like the frequencies in the 10 to 200 kc range, however, they must have substantial transmitting power to override atmospheric noises and be most effective.

Toward the top of the 200 to 2,000 kc range, relatively short distance ground-wave service is possible, especially over paths with poor conductivity. At these upper levels, skywaves become more important. While they are subject to the changes in the ionosphere, they are useful for long distance communication at night.

From 2 to 30 megacycles, skywaves become predominate. At night time when ionospheric conditions are favorable, long distance communication within this range can be achieved with relatively low transmitting power.

Frequencies above 30 mc are seldom reflected back to earth by the ionosphere. Useful propagation in this upper frequency range is achieved, however, with waves which travel directly from transmitting to receiving attennas and those which are reflected from the surface of the ground. Generally, the strength of the direct waves within line of sight is inversely proportional to the distance from the transmitter. Their effective use is for the most part limited to line-of-sight distance, and the height of the transmitting and receiving antennas are the principal factors which determine range of reception.[9]

Radio Service Classifications. In 1927, when the Federal Radio Commission was established, there was comparatively little knowledge regarding the propagation characteristics of the different bands of frequencies. The result was that many of the early assignments did not prove to be the most economical and efficient. As the years passed, however, the FRC and its successor the FCC, and the radio industry, through research and experimentation, acquired a better understanding of frequency behavior and, accordingly, the FCC has been able to parcel out the radio spectrum for more effective utilization.

The Commission has established three broad classifications of radio services; (1) Common Carrier, (2) Safety and Special Services, and (3) Broadcast. Common carrier services include wire and wireless facilities available to the general public for private messages, both domestic and international. The long lines telephone system in the country now measures many billions of miles. Of this number, more than a third involve radio transmission including radio links, TV microwave relays, ship-to-shore telephone, etc.

Microwave radio continues to carry a heavy load in the common carrier wideband transmission field. Use of microwave radio for telephone, telegraph, video, and data transmission is expanding both in scope and volume. During the fiscal year 1967, more than 10,000 applications were filed with the FCC requesting new or modified domestic common carrier radio facilities. This represented an increase of about 20 percent over the preceding year. As the Commission has pointed out, this increasing use of and demand for radio facilities by telephone and telegraph companies "has created critical and increasingly complex problems in providing frequency spaces and maintaining interference-free common carrier operations."[10]

Safety and Special Radio Services make up the largest part of radio operations licensed by the FCC, including about fifty different types. Major classifications, as determined by the Commission, include Marine, Aviation, Public Safety, Industrial, Land Transportation, Citizens, Amateur, and Disaster Radio Services. In 1969 there were 1,769,387 Safety and Special Radio stations licensed by the Commission. This was an increase of more than 100,000 over the preceding year. These stations were using more than 7,000,000 transmitters, and the demand for additional facilities is rapidly increasing.[11]

In the Public Safety, Industrial, and Land Transportation categories there are twenty-one different types of radio service being provided. Authorized facilities are being used for police and fire protection, highway maintenance, forestry conservation, national defense, and as an aid in disaster and emergency situations. Wide use of radio is being made by industry throughout the country—by public utilities, by oil and gas industries, manufacturing concerns, etc. The Business Radio Service makes radio facilities available for a multiplicity of business and professional activities. Also, the FCC has been generous in providing frequencies for railroads, truckers, taxicabs, motor clubs, garages, and construction companies.[12]

Citizens Radio now has more licensed stations than all other two-way radio services combined (more than 848,000 were authorized in 1968). The Commission recently has described these facilities and the regulatory problems connected with their use:

The service permits use of comparatively inexpensive transmitting equipment designed for low-power, short-distance communications. Although hobby-type or recreational communications are banned, those relating to necessary personal and business activities of the licensees are permitted. Specialized uses include the remote control, by radio, of objects or devices, such as garage door openers, model aircraft, and radio paging systems in hospitals and factories.[13]

It goes without saying that ship and aeronautical transportation are greatly dependent upon the uses of radio communication. In the Aviation

Radio Services, as prescribed by the FCC, there are seventeen classifications of aircraft and ground stations, and the regulation of these services requires close and continuous coordination with other government agencies and many technical and advisory groups.[14]

Mention should be made of the Amateur Radio Service. For 58 years ham operators, so-called, have been providing emergency radio communications for the public. In 1968, there were 261,503 authorized stations. There has been a steady increase in these amateur operations during recent years.[15]

The Broadcast Services, as classified by the Commission, include standard broadcasting (AM), frequency modulation (FM), non-commercial educational FM, television, and international. Added to these are the experimental, auxiliary and special broadcast services. There has been an enormous growth in these services as pointed out in the Introduction.

On July 23, 1958, the Commission authorized the first new international broadcast station since World War II. It is located at Belmont, California and its programs are beamed to Latin America. One other international broadcast station has been licensed by the FCC at Scituate, Massachusetts. All other international broadcast stations in this country are governmentally owned and operated by the United States Information Agency.[16]

Types of Radio Stations and Their Frequency Assignments. Part 2 of the FCC Rules and Regulations defines the exact nature and limits of each type of radio service and station.[17] Included in this part of the rules is a table of frequency allocations which has been adopted by the Commission, specifying the particular frequency bands to be used by each of these types of services and stations.[18]

Frequencies between 10 and 535 kilocycles are assigned largely to radiotelegraph stations and radio beacons used by ships and aircraft. The frequencies between 535 kc and 1605 kc are set aside for standard (Am) broadcast stations. Above this familiar AM band and extending to 25 megacycles are portions of the radio spectrum assigned to long distance radio telegraph and telephone communication, to ships at sea, planes in the air and international broadcasting.

In the region between 25 and 890 megacycles are the channel allocations for a variety of services including public safety, citizens radio, land transportation, industrial, etc. Also, FM and TV broadcasting occupy portions of this spectrum range. FM stations operate on channels between 88 and 108 megacycles. VHF television stations, receivable on standard sets, use specified frequencies within the 54 to 216 megacycle range. UHF TV stations are confined to the portion of the spectrum between 470 and 890 megacycles.

Beyond 890 megacycles, extending as high as 30,000 megacycles, space has been assigned to radio navigation, common carrier and mobile services and many other specialized radio services. Beyond the 30,000 mc point, frequencies are assigned mainly for experimental purposes and for developmental work in connection with new and improved services and equipment.

It is not possible to spell out an exact spectrum chart, because assignments of some of the radio services are widely scattered in different parts of the spectrum. For example, as of August 5, 1968, the amateur service carried on by more than 266,000 "hams" (as they are popularly called), uses the following widely distributed frequencies: 1800-2000 kc, 3500-4000 kc, 7000-7300 kc, 14,000-14,350 kc, 21,000-21,450 kc, 28 to 29.7 mc, 50-54 mc, 144-148 mc, 220-225 mc, 420-450 mc, 1215-1300 mc, 2300-2450 mc, 3500-3700 mc, 5650-5925 mc, 10,000 to 15,000 mc, 21,000 to 22,000 mc, and numerous bands above 30,000 mc. Similar scattering of assignments is to be found in various parts of the radio spectrum between 5950 kc and 26,100 kc for international broadcasting stations.

The Commission has provided in its rules that the assignment and use of frequencies for different types of radio service must be in accordance with the table of frequency allocations mentioned above. In individual cases the Commission may authorize, on a temporary basis only, the use of a frequency or frequencies not in accordance with the table, if no harmful interference will be caused to an existing service, and provided exceptional circumstances justify such irregular utilization.[19]

Planning for More Effective Utilization of the Radio Spectrum. Increasing demands for spectrum space have presented serious allocation problems in recent years. The government, including the rapidly expanding military establishment, industry, education and a multiplicity of other social and business segments of our society have been clamoring for additional space in the radio spectrum to meet new communication needs. Existing broadcast services, to which reference has just been made, suffer because of overcrowding conditions in the limited areas of the spectrum to which they are assigned.

The problem of reappraising frequency allocations for government, military and civilian uses and working out plans for a more effective utilization of frequencies in these different areas, has become a critical and perplexing one. It has engaged the serious attention of the White House, Congress, the FCC, the broadcasting industry and numerous other governmental and business groups making use of radio.

On June 8 and 9, 1959, the Communications Subcommittee of the House Interstate and Foreign Commerce Committee, listened to a panel of experts discuss frequency allocation problems. Representatives of the Office of Civilian and Defense Mobilization, the Federal Aviation Agency, Department of Defense, the FCC, and the broadcasting and telecommunications industries, participated in the conference. The Chairman of the President's Special Advisory Committee on Communications, and several other distinguished experts also were involved.[20]

A number of suggestions were made at this conference to help meet the allocations problem. One group recommended that a Federal Spectrum Authority be established. Such an authority would have jurisdiction over the entire radio spectrum and would be empowered to make a division of frequencies and settle conflicts between government and non-government users. As described by a leading trade journal, it would be the "spectrum czar and bring to an end the amorphous dual jurisdiction exercised by the President and the FCC, established in 1934 in the Communications Act."[21]

Another group at the meeting urged the creation of a governing body or single administrator to exercise jurisdiction over the government portion of the spectrum. Still others suggested the establishment of a Presidential commission to study the matter of allocations. Certain members of the broadcasting industry called for a complete Congressional investigation of the spectrum before any move is made toward establishing new agencies of management and control.

On July 28, 1959, pursuant to studies growing out of the June conference, Congressman Oren Harris, Chairman of the House Interstate and Foreign Commerce Committee, introduced a bill in the House to establish in the executive branch of the government an independent agency to be known as the Frequency Allocation Board, composed of three members appointed by the President and approved by the Senate. The functions of the Board as stated in the bill would be as follows:

(1) to conduct on a continuing basis a thorough and comprehensive study and investigation of, and to develop long-range plans for, the utilization of the radio spectrum, including (but without being limited to) the allocation of radio frequencies in the radio spectrum between, and the utilization of such radio frequencies by, federal government users and non-federal government users, in order to ascertain the effectiveness of the utilization of the radio spectrum by, and the division of the radio spectrum among, federal government users and non-federal government users in the light of the needs of the national security and international relations of, and economic, social, educational and political activites in the United States, and the general welfare of its people;

(2) from time to time on its own initiative, or on application of the Federal Communications Commission or the Government Frequency Administrator, subject to section 206 and to international agreements to which the United States is a party, to allocate radio frequencies for federal government use and non-federal government use, as the Board deems appropriate, and to modify or cancel any such allocation;

(3) to advise the President in connection with matters concerning the foreign relations of the United States insofar as such matters relate to the utilization and division of the radio spectrum.

(4) The Board shall maintain tables of radio frequency allocations for federal government use and non-federal government use and shall make such tables available for public inspection.[22]

The bill would establish a Government Frequency Administrator to act for the President in the allocation of government frequencies among military and other federal government users.

The President's power over the radio spectrum in times of war and national emergency and the FCC's authority over frequency assignments for civilian uses would not be disturbed.

In its August 3, 1959 issue, *Broadcasting* magazine made the following editorial comment regarding the bill:

First tangible recognition of the need for complete overhauling of management of the critically important radio spectrum allocations as between government and non-government users is given in a bill (HR 8426) quietly introduced in the House last week. It would create a three-man Frequency Allocation Board—a sort of super-FCC but with power far broader than that vested in the FCC or perhaps in any other independent agency. Because of the bill's significance and scope, it must be assumed that its author, Chairman Oren Harris (D-Ark.) of the House Commerce Committee, does not expect passage at this session, now within weeks of adjournment. Rather, it looks to us like a trial balloon for study by interested groups during the Congressional recess.

There can be no doubt about the sincerity of Mr. Harris' intentions. He wants efficient management of the spectrum, to prevent hoarding of valuable frequencies by government but, at the same time, to protect the national security. Because broadcasters have a life-and-death stake in the sensitive allocation areas, particularly the vhf range in which tv and fm are assigned, extreme care and diligence must be exercised in appraising the new bill.

Is too much power given to three men? Should provision be made for appeal from board rulings? Should usual administrative procedures be followed in the functioning of the board or of the Government Frequency Administrator who would function under the President? Is the FCC unduly stripped of allocation functions?

These are just a few of the questions that crop up in a casual reading of the Harris Bill. It is for these reasons that all entities in broadcasting, who are responsible for direct service to the public, must give priority to analysis and interpretation of the Harris Bill.[23]

As is the case with so many bills introduced in Congress, this one never was adopted. However, concern over the growing shortage of spectrum space continued. A science panel assembled under the aegis of the Department of Commerce issued a report in October, 1966 calling attention to the tremendous growth in all kinds of electromagnetic services and the increasing need for radio frequencies. The panel recommended creation of an organization of "high level competence" in the Department of Commerce to do comprehensive research on the overall problem of spectrum utilization.[24] Congress was asked to appropriate from ten to fifty million dollars per year to finance the studies.[25]

In the February 5, 1968 issue of *Broadcasting* it was reported that "a battle that major broadcaster groups regard as one of the most significant that they have been called on to fight is now shaping up in Washington." The issue, the report went on to say, has to do with the entire spectrum space allocated to television. "The first engagement in the fight is now under way—with land mobile users, who are applying pressure in their effort to obtain for their use a portion of the spectrum allocated to television.[26]

On July 17, 1968, the Commission adopted notices of proposed rule making to provide more spectrum space for land mobile services. Among the proposals to be considered was one to use UHF TV channels, fourteen through twenty-five, in the twenty-five largest urbanized areas of the United States. Comments and reply comments were due to be filed with the FCC not later than December 2, 1968 and January 31, 1969, respectively, (FCC 68743, Docket 18261; 33 FR 10943). Much to the dismay of many broadcasters, suggestions were being made in official circles in February, 1968 that it might be necessary to shift television to wires and cables and use the vacated space for other radio services. However, in a meeting that same month with President Johnson's special telecommunications task force, officials of the National Association of Broadcasters showed no inclination to support such proposals or any other wholesale changes in spectrum allocation or management.[27]

The Task Force, which had a study under way for some time, was under a Presidential directive to report its findings by the middle of August, 1968.[28] With civilian and military communication needs growing at a rapid rate, it was expected that some drastic allocation changes would be made. Many experts and authorities in the radio field are agreed that the present situation is chaotic and wasteful and there is critical need for corrective action. The growing importance of radio services to the well-being of our national life makes imperative conservation and more effective utilization of the spectrum.

The Presidential Task Force in its *Final Report* issued December 7, 1968 recommended some drastic changes in the Federal regulatory apparatus and its organizational structure to help accomplish this and other purposes. Some of its more important conclusions and recommendations are mentioned in Chapter 23.

1. Filgate, John Thomas, *Theory of Radio Communication*, (Brooklyn, N.Y., 1929), p. 2.

2. Morecroft, John H., *Elements of Radio Communication* (New York, 2nd edition, 1934).

3. *Ibid.*, pp. 203-229.

4. *Ibid.*, pp. 97-102.

5. *Ibid.*, p. 98.

6. *Ibid.*, 111-112; Also see Warner, Harry, *Radio and Television Law* (New York, 1953), 225-227.

7. See Head, Sydney, *Broadcasting in America* (Boston, 1956), pp. 8-12 for an informative discussion on this subject.

8. Section 2.101, 1 RR 52:561, 47 CFR 199, 30 Fed. Reg. 7156.

9. Much of the foregoing discussion of the propagation characteristics of different frequencies is based upon the excellent study of the Joint Technical Advisory Committee of the Institute of Radio Engineers, Radio-Television Manufacturers Association, *Radio Spectrum Conservation* (New York, 1952).

10. *Ibid.*, p. 77.

11. FCC, *35th Annual Report/Fiscal Year 1968*, pp. 146-147.

12. FCC, *33rd Annual Report* 1967, pp. 101-105.

13. *Ibid.*, p. 103.

14. *Ibid.*, p. 96-97.

15. *Ibid.*, p. 104.

16. FCC, *24th Annual Report* (1958), p. 118.

17. 23 Fed. Reg. 10437 (1958); Section 2.1, 47 CFR, 191-1981, 1 RR 52:531-544.

18. 23 Fed. Reg. 10440-63 (1958); Section 2.106, 47 CFR, 202-253, 1 RR 52: 575-606.

19. FCC Rules and Regulations, Section 2, 102, 25 Fed. Reg. 13976.

20. *Broadcasting*, June 15, 1959, pp. 60-62.

21. *Ibid.*, p. 60.

22. 89th Congress (1st Session) H.R. 8426, July 28, 1959, referred to the Committee on Interstate and Foreign Commerce.

23. *Broadcasting*, August 3, 1959, p. 104.

24. *Ibid.*, October 24, 1966, pp. 27-30.

25. *Ibid.*, p. 27.

26. *Ibid.*, February 5, 1968, p. 19.

27. *Ibid.*, February 26, 1968, p. 56.

28. *Ibid.*

CHAPTER 7

Standard Broadcast Stations (AM)

I believe we have a reasonably competitive system in AM. Some would say too much competition, but I think such persons would be reluctant to accept any alternatives there may be for the competitive system. — ROSEL H. HYDE*

As mentioned in the preceding chapter, standard broadcast or amplitude modulation (AM) stations, as they are called, operate on channels in the band of frequencies, 535-1605 kilocycles.[1] This space is only a small fraction of the entire radio spectrum now in use. The many broadcast stations that operate in this small space are licensed to transmit programs primarily intended to reach the general public as distinguished from point-to-point communication.[2]

Within this "standard broadcast band" there are 107 channels, each channel having a 10 kc spread.[3] The frequency at the center of the channel is known as the carrier frequency and is the one on which the station operates. For example, if a station operates on an assigned frequency of 600 kc, its channel or band of frequencies is from 595 to 605 kc, and the channel is designated by the assigned carrier frequency. Beginning at 540 kc and continuing in successive steps of 10 to 1600 kc, there are 107 carrier frequencies assigned and used by standard broadcast stations.[4]

Types of AM Service Areas and Channels. These standard broadcast stations use both ground and sky waves. The area surrounding such a station, receiving a ground wave signal strong enough to overcome ordinary interference and not subject to objectionable fading, is called the *Primary Service* area. As indicated in the previous chapter, primary coverage of a station depends upon numerous factors including the power of the station, the particular frequency, the character of the soil and topography over which the ground wave must travel, the extent of man-made noise in the area, certain atmospheric conditions, etc. For example, a station operating with 1 kw power in Texas on 550 kc frequency would provide primary service to a substantially larger area than a station operating on the same frequency in New Hampshire. The reason is that the low flat terrain and type of soil of the Lone Star state is more conducive to electromag-

*Former Chairman of the FCC.

netic wave transmission than is the hilly and rocky terrain of New England.

Roughly and empirically estimated, stations with different powers provide good, reliable ground wave service the following average distances:[5]

Power	Average Radius Miles
100 watts	30
250 watts	41
1kw	63
5kw	93
10kw	115
50kw	160

These values are averages only and cannot be used to calculate the precise coverage of any particular station. These coverage figures are no doubt too high for some stations, especially the low-powered stations.[6]

Beyond the primary service area lies the *intermittent* service area, served by the groundwave but subject to some interference and fading.

The *secondary service* area is that receiving skywaves which are not subject to objectionable interference but which do not always provide the best reception because of variations in intensity.[7] The range of these secondary service areas may vary from less than one hundred miles to a thousand miles or more. The service, however, in these extended areas, for the reason suggested, is not consistently dependable.

Ionospheric absorption of skywaves during daylight hours prevent their effective use for daylight broadcasting, and from sun-up to sun-set AM stations are dependent entirely upon groundwave propagation. After dark, however, as heretofore pointed out, the skywaves are reflected back to earth by the ionosphere and with reasonably good transmitting power and with no interference from other stations, they make possible at night a wider coverage area often reaching far beyond the groundwave contours. It should be pointed out that these skywaves at night, while providing extended service, may introduce complications which reduce the groundwave coverage.

In 1939, after extensive public hearings, the FCC adopted revised rules governing these AM stations.[8] Previously, the Commission had established three categories of channels for these stations: clear, regional and local. The revised rules retained these categories but in addition prescribed four general classes of stations.[9]

As defined in the FCC Rules, a *clear channel* is one on which stations operate with wide coverage. Their primary service areas and a substantial part of their secondary ones are protected from objectionable interference from other stations.[10]

A *regional channel* is one on which several stations may operate with no more than 5 kilowatts power and whose primary service area may be limited to a certain field intensity contour by interference from other stations operating on the same channel.[11]

The *local channel* is one assigned for the use of stations serving small areas whose power cannot exceed 250 watts during night time and 1000 watts during days, and whose primary service areas may be restricted by the operation of other stations on the same channel.[12]

Classes of Am Stations and Frequency Assignments. As described in the FCC Rules, a *Class I station* is a dominant one operating on a clear channel with not less than 10 and not more than 50 kilowatts power, and designed to achieve relatively wide coverage. Its primary service area is free from all objectionable interference. Its secondary area is protected except that it may be subject to some interference from distant stations on the same channel or from those operating on adjacent channels.[13]

There are 47 clear channels assigned for station operation. These stations, so assigned, are classified as I-A and I-B groups. Section 73.182 states that I-A stations shall operate during night time on the same channels, except for certain ones specified in Section 73.22.[14]

The I-A stations are afforded protection during daytime to the 0.1 mv/m groundwave contour from stations on the same channel and to the 0.5 mv/m groundwave contour from those on adjacent channels. During night time, the I-A's are protected to the 0.5 mv/m, 50% skywave contour from stations on the same channel, and to 0.5 mv/m groundwave contour from those on adjacent channels.[15]

The 1-B group operate with power not less than 10 or more than 50 kw and the channels they occupy[16] may also be assigned to other Class I or Class II stations operating unlimited time.[17] During night time hours, a I-B station is protected to its 500 uv/m, 50 percent skywave contour and during the day to its 100 uv/m groundwave contour from stations operating on the same channel. It is protected both day and night from stations on adjacent channels to its 500 uv/m groundwave contour.[18]

The Class II station is a secondary one on a clear channel with its primary service area limited by and subject to interference as may be received by Class I stations.[19] This type of operation is restricted to power not less than 250 watts nor more than 50 kilowatts.[20] When necessary, a Class II station must use a directional antenna or other means to avoid causing interference within the normally protected service areas of Class I or other Class II stations.[21]

These Class II stations normally provide primary service only, the extent of the coverage depending upon location, power and frequency of the station. It is recommended by the Commission that they be so located that the interference received from other stations will not limit their service areas to greater than the 2500 uv/m groundwave contour at night and 500 uv/m groundwave contour daytime.[22]

The following frequencies are assigned to Class II stations which do not deliver over 5 microvolts per meter groundwave or over 25 microvolts per meter 10 per cent time skywave at any point on the Canadian border, and for night-time operation are located not less than 650 miles from the nearest point on the border: 690, 740, 860, 990, 1010 and 1580 kilocycles.[23]

In the continental United States, Class II stations operating daytime only with power not exceeding 1 kw and which do not deliver over 5 microvolts per meter groundwave at any point on the Mexican border, and those in Alaska, Hawaii, Puerto Rico, and the Virgin Islands which do not deliver over 5 microvolts per meter groundwave or over 25 microvolts per meter 10 per cent time skywave at any point on that border, use the frequencies 730, 800, 900, 1050, 1220 and 1570 kilocycles.[24]

The Class III stations operate on regional channels and are designed to provide service primarily to metropolitan districts and contiguous rural areas.[25] These stations are divided into A and B groups. The III-A stations operate with power not less than one or more than five kilowatts and are normally protected to their 2500 uv/m groundwave contours at night and their 500 uv/m groundwave contours daytime. Class III-B stations operate with power not less than 0.5 kw, or more than 1 kw nighttime and 5 kw daytime. Their service areas are normally protected to the 4000 uv/m contour at night and to the 500 uv/m contour during daytime.[26]

The Class III-A and III-B stations are assigned to the following frequencies designated as regional channels: 550, 560, 570, 580, 590, 600, 610, 620, 630, 790, 910, 920, 930, 950, 960, 970, 980, 1150, 1250, 1260, 1270, 1280, 1290, 1300, 1310, 1320, 1330, 1350, 1360, 1370, 1380, 1390, 1410, 1420, 1430, 1440, 1460, 1470, 1480, 1590 and 1600 kc.[27]

A Class IV station is one which operates on a local channel and is designated to render service primarily to a city or town and the suburban and rural areas contiguous to it.[28] The power of such a station may not be less than 100 watts nor more than 250 watts at night and 1 kw daytime.[29] The FCC Rules provide that it shall be protected to its 0.5 mv/m contour.[30] The following frequencies have been designated by the Commission as local channels and are assigned for use by Class IV stations: 1230, 1240, 1340, 1400, 1450 and 1490 kc.[31]

Previously, the Commission permitted the assignment of Class IV stations to regional channels under certain conditions. A revision of Section 73.29 of the Commission's Rules covering Radio Broadcast Services prohibited this, except that stations which had already been authorized at the time the rule was revised were not required to change their frequencies or power. Such stations, however, are afforded no protection against interference from Class III stations.[32]

Increase of Power for Local Stations Authorized.   On May 28, 1958, the Commission adopted an order amending its rules to permit Class IV stations to increase their daytime power to 500 watts and, under certain conditions, to increase their power to 1 kw. It was set forth in the order, however, that

113

increase in nighttime power for these stations would not be allowed, nor could directional antennas be used to reduce presently required separations between these Class IV stations.[33]

The Commission announced that Class IV applications for increase in power would be processed on a case-by-case basis except for two geographical locations. Stations requesting boosts in power were not permitted to locate within an area 62 miles or less from the U.S.-Mexican border or in an area covering approximately the southern half of Florida, south of 28 degrees north latitude and 80-82 degrees west longitude. These limitations were made in deference to agreements with other North American countries. Prior to the adoption of the May 28, 1958 order, the Community Broadcasters Association, Inc. had filed a petition with the Commission requesting a mandatory power increase for all Class IV stations or, in the alternative, blanket permission to increase power. The Commission denied this request, however, stating that it would decide each application on its merits.[34]

Of the 107 standard broadcast channels, 60 have been designated as clear channels and are assigned for use by Class I and Class II stations. Forty-six of these are used by the United States and the remainder are distributed among other nations of North America in accordance with the North American Regional Broadcast Agreement. Forty-one additional channels are designated as regional and are assigned for use by Class III-A and III-B stations. Six others are local channels on which Class IV stations operate.

The Clear Channel Controversy. Efforts of smaller stations to secure additional power and the almost wild scramble for spectrum space by many eager and enterprising have-nots in our society—all this is tied in with the long struggle to break up the clear channels and provide more frequencies for new stations in areas not now receiving adequate radio service.

In February, 1945, the Commission instituted a public hearing to explore the problems and consider proposals for improving the situation. For forty days the Commission listened to testimony on a number of issues. Evidence was received on such questions as (1) whether the number of clear channels should be increased or decreased; (2) what minimum and maximum power should be authorized for clear channel stations; (3) whether and to what extent power above 50 kw for such stations would affect the economic ability of other stations to operate in the public interest; (4) whether the present geographical distribution of clear channel stations and the areas they serve represent an optimum distribution of radio service throughout the country; (5) whether it is economically feasible to relocate clear channel stations so as to serve those areas which do not presently receive service; (6) what new rules, if any, should be promulgated to govern the power or hours of operation of Class II stations operating on clear channels; (7) what changes should be made with respect to geographical location, frequency, authorized power or hours of operation of any presently licensed clear channel station; (8) whether the clear channel stations render a program service particularly suited to rural needs; and (9) the extent to which service areas of clear channel stations overlap.[35]

Parties in that proceeding advocated numerous and diverse approaches to the problem of achieving more efficient use of the clear channels and of improving the deficiencies in the present service available to the public on these channels. Proposals for revising the clear channel allocations ranged all the way from exclusive nighttime use of selected clear channels by a single station operating at substantially higher powers than the present maximum of 50 kw, to the reclassification of selected clear channels as "local channels" on which it would be possible to assign over a hundred and fifty stations operating at maximum powers of 250 watts. Between these extremes a wide variety of proposals were submitted.[36]

As the Commission has pointed out, the record in the case "reflected two basically divergent views concerning the measures best calculated to improve the efficient use of the clear channel frequencies. Some parties urged that the chief goal should be to improve the capacity of the major clear channel stations (particularly the Class I-A stations) to provide a satisfactory signal to wide areas, and that this should be achieved by substantially increasing their power and by limiting (and, during the nighttime hours, excluding) co-channel stations. Other parties contended that the most desirable objective would be to increase the number of unlimited time stations on the clear channels and to reduce the degree of protection now afforded the latter throughout wide service areas."[37]

In June, 1946, the Commission announced the adoption of the policy of dismissing applications for station assignments or modifications of station assignments which were not permissible under the existing rules pending a resolution of the clear channel case.[38]

In May, 1947, a separate proceeding was initiated (FCC Docket 8333) to determine whether and the extent to which limitations should be imposed on daytime skywave radiation toward Class I-A and I-B stations operating on clear channels.[39]

In December, 1947, the two proceedings were consolidated and on January 19, 20, and 21, 1948, the Commission heard oral arguments on both matters.[40]

The proceedings, however, were again separated by the Commission in 1953, and in November, 1956, the Clear Channel Broadcasting Service filed a petition to reopen the record in the Clear Channel case, and again consolidate it with the daytime skywave case and afford opportunity to bring the records up to date. In response to this, the Daytime Broadcasters' Association promptly filed a petition requesting that the clear channel proceeding be dismissed, that the freeze on clear channel assignments be lifted, and that the Commission institute rule making on the Association's earlier request that daytime stations be authorized to operate additional hours.[41]

On September 17, 1957, as is more fully discussed later in this chapter, the FCC granted the request of the daytime broadcasters to consider the proposal to increase the hours for operation of their stations, but denied their request to dismiss the clear channel proceeding and remove the freeze on the processing of applications for Class II stations on the clear channel frequencies.[42]

On April 15, 1958, the Commission reopened the record in the clear channel case, stating that "it would be inappropriate, and inconsistent with sound and fair procedure, to attempt to arrive at final conclusions solely on the basis of the out-dated record before us."[43] At the same time, the Commission proposed to eliminate the exclusive nighttime use of Class I-A clear channels in New York, Chicago, Philadelphia, Pittsburgh, Rochester, Cleveland, Detroit, and St. Louis. The Commission also proposed to assign additional Class I stations to 12 western cities located in less well-served areas and to consider the possible assignment of Class II stations on those channels to other parts of the country that do not now have any primary groundwave service.[44]

In July, 1959, the Commission announced that it had instructed its staff to draw up a new proposal for rulemaking which, if adopted, would permit the assignment of some unlimited time Class II stations on Class I-A channels. These Class II stations, the Commission stated, would be not less than 10 kw in power, and their locations would be determined on the basis of need in areas without primary radio service.[45] Subsequently, the Commission did issue a proposal for rulemaking which would authorize new Class II stations on clear channels in the western part of the country where local broadcast facilities are limited.[46]

Clear channel stations vigorously protested the proposal. The Commission, however, after prolonged consideration of many petitions and much argument, on September 13, 1961, decided that thirteen of the twenty-five I-A clear channels would be available for duplication, and that one additional full-time station might be assigned to each of these channels. The decision was made effective October 30, 1961.[47]

Implementation of the decision, however, was delayed by petitions for reconsideration, by a Congressional resolution asking a year's delay, and by court appeals. Pending final effectuation of the regulation, the House of Representatives by a vote of 198 to 87 approved a resolution recommending that the FCC authorize clear channel stations to operate with higher power than 50 kw to assure better service to rural areas and asked the Commission to delay for a year plans to duplicate any of these channels.[48]

The Commission yielded to this Congressional pressure and in the meantime several of the clear channel stations filed appeals to the Commission's regulation in the Court of Appeals in the District of Columbia. While the matter was still pending in court and less than a week before the expiration of the one year delay, the chairman of the House Interstate and Foreign Commerce Committee wrote to the FCC chairman asking that the moratorium on duplication of the 13 channels be further extended, and suggested that the Commission request permission of the Court of Appeals to recall the duplication order pending the securing of more information by the Committee.[49]

The Commission declined to ask the Court to do so, and in its response to the Committee Chairman stated that the FCC had not ruled out the possibility of granting higher power, at least for the twelve clear channels not included in its order, and expressed the opinion that proposed duplication on the other thirteen would not result in substantial loss to their service areas. The FCC noted also that in all cases of duplication clear channel stations would be protected to their 0.5 mv/m 50% skywave contours.[50]

On October 31, 1963, the Court of Appeals, by unanimous decision, upheld the Commission's order. The Court affirmed the Commission's right to break down the thirteen Class 1-A channels and to hold up for further consideration the question of authorizing higher power (more than 50 kw) for stations operating on these channels.[51]

At the time of the Court's decision there were fifteen applications for stations on eight of the clear channels which were made available for duplication.[52] The *1968 Broadcasting Yearbook* reveals that a number of these applications have been granted with service now being duplicated by stations in Idaho, New Mexico, Wyoming, Oregon, and Montana. Availabilities for service duplication are set forth in Section 73.22 of the Commission's Rules.[53]

As yet the Commission has taken no action with respect to the remaining 12 I-A channels. In its 1964 annual report, the Commission said:

. . . One possibility is authorizing "higher power" for the class I-A stations on these channels, or some of them, in the order of 500 or 750 kw compared to the present maximum of 50 kw. A number of "experimental" applications have been filed by these stations for such facilities. Most of these present problems as to interference to stations on adjacent channels, and studies are underway to see if these problems can be resolved. Consideration can then be given to the general "higher power" question, which has long been a subject of controversy.[54]

Field Intensity Requirements for AM Service Areas. As specified by the Commission, the field intensities of radio signals necessary to render primary service to different types of reception areas are as follows:

Area	Field Intensity Groundwave
City business or factory areas	10 to 50 mv/m
City residential areas	2 to 10 mv/m
Rural—all areas during winter or Northern areas during the summer	0.1 to 0.5 mv/m
Rural—southern areas during summer	0.25 to 1.0 mv/m

117

As Section 73.182(f) of the FCC Rules provides, all these values are based on an absence of objectionable fading, the usual noise level in the areas, and an absence of limiting interference from other broadcast stations. The values apply both day and night, but generally, fading or interference from other stations limits the primary service at night in all rural areas to higher values of field intensity than those recited.[55]

In determining the population of the primary service area, the following signal intensities are considered adequate to overcome man-made noise in towns of the population specified:

Population	Field Intensity Groundwave
Up to 2,500	0.5 mv/m
2,500 to 10,000	2.0 mv/m
10,000 and up	Values same as those listed in paragraph above for different types of cities.

The Commission has pointed out that these values are subject to wide variations in individual areas and especial attention must be given to interference from other stations. These specific values are not considered satisfactory in any case for service to the city in which the main studio of the station is located.[56]

Secondary service is delivered in the areas where the skywave for 50 per cent or more of the time has a field intensity of 500 uv/m or greater. To provide satisfactory secondary service in cities, it is considered necessary that the skywave signal approach the value of the groundwave required for primary service. But the secondary service is necessarily subject to some interference and extensive fading whereas the primary service area is not. Class I stations only are assigned on the basis of providing secondary service.[57]

The intermittent service is rendered by the groundwave and begins at the outer boundary of the primary service area and extends to the point where the signal has no further service value. This point may be where the signal has an intensity or low as only a few microvolts in some areas and as high as several millivolts in others, depending on noise level, interference from other stations, or objectionable fading at night. Only Class I stations are assigned so that their intermittent service areas are protected from interference from other stations.[58]

Time Classifications for Stations. Each broadcasting station is authorized to operate in accordance with specified time classifications. These classifications are:

Unlimited time
Limited time
Daytime
Share-time
Specified hours

Unlimited Time stations operate without any restrictive time limits. Those authorized on a *limited time* basis are the Class II stations (secondary) which operate on clear channels only. They are permitted to operate during the day and until local sunset if located west of the dominant station on the clear channel. If located east thereof, they must close down when the sun sets at the dominant station. They may also operate during the night hours when the dominant station is off the air.[59]

Daytime stations operate during the hours between average monthly local sunrise and average local sunset. The opening and closing hours of operation for such stations are specified in their licenses. For example, a Class II daytime station operating on 1570 kc in the east central part of Illinois has the following sign-on and sign-off schedule:

January	7:15 A. M.	to 5:00 P. M.
February	6:45 A. M.	to 5:30 P. M.
March	6:00 A. M.	to 6:00 P. M.
April	5:15 A. M.	to 6:30 P. M.
May	4:45 A. M.	to 7:00 P. M.
June	4:30 A. M.	to 7:15 P. M.
July	4:30 A. M.	to 7:15 P. M.
August	5:00 A. M.	to 6:45 P. M.
September	5:30 A. M.	to 6:00 P. M.
October	6:00 A. M.	to 5:15 P. M.
November	6:30 A. M.	to 4:45 P. M.
December	7:00 A. M.	to 4:30 P. M.

In 1960, the Commission amended its rules to permit daytime stations to sign off at 6:00 P.M. during months when local sunset is later than 6:00 P.M. (see Report No. 13-28, Pike and Fischer RR, July 27, 1960.)

As already indicated, the limitation and irregularity of these hours have been matters of grave concern to many daytime broadcasters. Reference has already been made to the petition filed by the Daytime Broadcasters Association, Inc. requesting that all daytime stations be authorized to operate from 5:00 A.M. or local sunrise (whichever would be earlier) to 7:00 P.M. or local sunset (whichever would be later) in lieu of the sunrise to sunset hours prescribed in the present rules.

In its petition, DBA asserted that there was a large unsatisfied need for local service during pre-sunrise and post-sunset hours. It was pointed out that in the United States over 900 communities, with a total population of more than 7,500,000, did not have available to them any locally licensed radio outlets other than daytime-only stations. It was argued by DBA that extended hours were necessary for daytime stations, notwithstanding the resulting interference to existing radio broadcast services, in order that the needs of these communities and surrounding areas for broadcast service might be more fully met.[60]

On September 19, 1958, the Commission denied this petition.[61] On October 20, 1958, DBA asked the Commission to reconsider its decision or, in the alternative, permit all daytime stations to operate from 6:00 A.M. or local sunrise (whichever is earlier) to 6:00 P.M. or local sunset (whichever is later). On January 7, 1959, the Commission refused to reconsider its decision regarding the "5 to 7" request and dismissed the DBA alternative request for "6 to 6" operation. At the same time, the Commission stated that it was not apprised of sufficient facts concerning the changes envisaged in the standard broadcast structure to render a decision upon the merits of the alternative request. Accordingly, the Commission instituted a formal inquiry to elicit further information.[62]

After receiving comments from interested parties and studying the record in the proceeding, on July 8, 1959, the Commission denied the "6 to 6" request. The reasons for the denial were succinctly set forth in paragraph 19 of the decision:

Upon careful review of the comments which have been filed, and a review of our decision in Docket No. 12274, we conclude that the losses of standard broadcast radio service, both groundwave and skywave in the various areas affected, which would result from an extension of the hours of operation of stations licensed for daytime operation must be determinative herein. We are unable to find an expression of any local need which is impossible of substantial fulfillment under existing rules for station licensing and which is so great or so pressing as to warrant widespread disruption of the existing radio service now enjoyed thereunder and relied upon daily by millions of citizens. Particularly, would it be undesirable and unwarranted to permit such disruption in those instances where the result as shown by the data would simply be the taking of regular service from rural farm areas and from small urban communities, which need radio vitally, and giving more stations— serving less area—to city and principal urban areas which are already relatively well supplied not only with standard broadcast radio programs but with other facilities for relaxation, intellectual stimulus, information and recreation. Moreover, this conclusion is strongly reinforced by a comparison of the 1,761,622 persons in 357 communities, now receiving only skywave service, who would gain in lieu thereof a local groundwave service, with the 25,631,000 persons in 1,727,000 square miles, now receiving skywave service, who would lose entirely the standard broadcast radio service now available to them.[63]

Despite this decision of the Commission, daytime stations continued to press for authority to operate before sunrise. In fact, the pressure became so strong that by July, 1962 the House of Representatives had approved a bill which would have permitted daytime stations in single station markets to go on the air before sunrise and would have authorized the FCC on a discretionary basis to permit other daytimers to do the same.[64] The Senate failed to act on the bill and it did not become law. However, the FCC had some second thoughts on the matter and after further study proposed to make some concessions to the daytimers. A further notice of proposed rule making was issued (FCC 62-1241) on November 30, 1962 and comments on the proposal were solicited from interested parties. Though modified somewhat from what had been proposed, rules were finally adopted June 28, 1967 and made effective August 15 thereafter.[65]

Why did the Commission reverse itself and authorize this pre-sunrise service? While recognizing that some interference would be caused with loss of service to some specific areas, with reduction in power for pre-sunrise operation and limiting operation to only a part of the clear channels, the Commission concluded that, on an overall basis, the general public would stand to gain.[66] In further justification of its decision the Commission in part said:

. . . the resolution of this proceeding necessarily represents a balance between considerations and objectives which are to some degree in conflict—the provisions for needed pre-sunrise service on the one hand, particularly in situations where it has been in existence before and has come to be relied upon by listeners, and on the other hand, protection of the existing service of unlimited-time stations against an inordinate amount of loss through interference, and thus inefficient use of the channels involved. It is also apparent, as it has been for some time, that pre-sunrise use of daytime facilities by United States stations must be brought into line with this country's obligations, under pertinent international agreements, to protect the stations of other nations in the North American Region from objectionable interference. With respect to the regional channels, we are persuaded, after careful consideration of the record herein and the above considerations, that the most appropriate balance can be achieved by permitting virtually all Class III stations, with 500 watts power, using their daytime modes of operation (directional or nondirectional), except where lesser power is required to meet international obligations as mentioned above.

In reaching this conclusion, we have taken into account the many considerations which have been so vigorously urged by those taking the various opposing positions, and the numerous counterproposals, urged upon us. We recognize that, as many fulltime stations urge, permitting pre-sunrise operations by daytimers (and by fulltimers) may cause substantial interference to the licensed service of fulltime stations; it may well be true . . . that the losses will often, perhaps usually, exceed the gains if strict engineering stands are applied. But in our judgment the record herein establishes that the pre-sunrise service rendered by daytime-only stations is, by and large, a valuable one, and one should be permitted. In our view, as a general proposition the gains outweigh the losses, when all factors, such as the location of the areas of service and interference with respect to the stations gaining and losing, and the extent of other service, are taken into account. We note the contention . . . that rural areas will lose the badly needed service of wide-coverage fulltime regional stations. But we also note that, with few exceptions, the fulltimers did not establish the extent to which listeners in such areas (usually at some distance from the station) actually rely on and need their service. Their showing in this respect fell short of daytimers' showing.[67]

A number of petitions for reconsideration were filed with the Commission, all of which were denied.[68]

On May 10, 1968, the Circuit Court of Appeals (Second Circuit), by unanimous decision, upheld the regulations, and settled a complex and troublesome question which had plagued the broadcasting industry and the Commission for more than a decade.[69]

While the case was pending in the Circuit Court of Appeals, the Commission proceeded to grant many requests for Pre-sunrise Service Authority (PSA). By the use of its Univac III machine, it was planning to determine the stations eligible for PSA'S and in what cases authorizations of less than 500 watts would be required to comply with the rules prohibiting interference to other stations.[70] As of the end of May, 1968, the Commission had granted a large number of pre-sunrise authorizations and many others were in the offing.

Share time stations are restricted in their operation in accordance with a specified division of time with one or more stations using the same channel.

Some stations are authorized to operate *specific* hours as stated in their licenses. (The minimum schedule for this type of station as well as all other stations are prescribed in Sections 73.71-83.)

New Commission Freeze Imposed on All AM Applications. As reported by Pike and Fischer in *Radio Regulation* (Report 21-28, July 17, 1968), on July 18, 1968, the FCC announced a freeze on all new applications for AM stations, regardless of type, in order to make a study to decide (1) whether there exists a significant national need for more such stations or whether major changes in existing stations should be made to provide more and better programming for areas of the country now inadequately served; (2) whether presently available spectrum space in the AM band should be conserved for future uses; (3) whether any future allocation system should view AM and FM broadcasting as a single aural service; and (4) whether making further assignments on a demand basis would be an unwise use of valuable spectrum space.

On September 4, 1969, the Commission instituted a rule to revise AM assignments. The rules governing the acceptance and consideration of standard broadcast applications would be substantially more restrictive than the present rules. The Commission summarized the changes as follows:

(a) Applications for daytime-only facilities (new and major changes) would be accepted only if they will provide a substantial "first primary service" benefit.

122

(b) Applications for major changes in authorized nighttime facilities would be subjected to the same "first primary service" standard as present applications for new nighttime facilities.

(c) In determining whether a substantial area of population would receive a first primary service, existing FM as well as AM service would be taken into account.

(d) Applications for new stations would not be accepted if there is an available FM channel which the applicant could use and provide the same substantial service benefit.[71]

1. FCC Rules and Regulations, Part 3, Section 73.1, 1 RR 53:601.
2. *Ibid.*
3. *Ibid.*, Section 73.3, 1 RR 53:601.
4. *Ibid.*
5. *Fifth Annual Report of Federal Radio Commission (1931),* 30-31.
6. See Warner, Harry P., *Radio and Television Law* (New York, 1953), p. 233-34.
7. Section 73.11, 1 RR 53:603.
8. 4 Fed. Reg. 2714 (1939).
9. Section 73.21, 1 RR 53:609-610.
10. Section 73.21, 1 RR 53:609.
11. Section 73.21(b), 1RR 53:610.
12. Section 73.21(c), 1 RR 53:614.
13. Section 73.182, 1 RR 53:772.
14. Section 73.182(a) (1) (i), 1 RR 53:772. Clear channels are: 640, 650, 660, 670, 700, 720, 750, 760, 780, 820, 830, 840, 870, 880, 890, 1020, 1040, 1100, 1120, 1160, 1180, 1200 and 1210 kc. See Section 73:25(a) of FCC Rules.
15. *Ibid.*
16. 73.182(a) (1) (ii). See Sections 73.25(b).
17. Section 73.182(a) (1) ii, 1 RR 53:772.
18. *Ibid.* A note under Section 73.25(b) of the FCC Rules states that Class I and II stations are prohibited from delivering over 5 microvolts per meter groundwave or 25 microvolts per meter 10 per cent time skywave at any point of land in the Bahama Islands, and such stations operating at night shall be located not less than 650 miles from the nearest point of land in these islands.
19. Section 73.21(a) (2), 1 RR 53:609.
20. Section 73.182(2), 1 RR 53:773.
21. Section 73.21(2), 1 RR 53:609.
22. Section 73.182(a) (2), 1 RR 53:773.
23. Section 73.25(c), 1 RR 53:620.
24. Section 73.25(d), 1 RR 53:620.
25. Section 73.21(b), 1 RR 53:610.
26. *Ibid.* Also, Section 73.182(a) (3) (i), 1 RR 53:773.
27. Section 73.26, 1 RR 53:622.
28. Section 73.21(c) (1), 1 RR 53:610. The FCC no longer grants authority for 100 watt operation on these channels. However, stations previously authorized to so operate are permitted to continue to do so.
29. *Ibid.*
30. Section 73.182(a) (4), 1 RR 53:773.
31. Section 73.27, 1 RR 53:622
32. Section 73.29, 1 RR 53:625.
33. FCC Docket No. 12064, 11 RR 1541.
34. See *Broadcasting,* April 13, 1959, p. 54; also see Decision of the Commission denying petition for reconsideration and making its order final. 17 RR 1548a.
35. See *In the Matter of Clear Channel Broadcasting in the Standard Broadcast Band;* FCC Docket 6741, 1 RR 53; lix, p. 53:liii. The chronology of the Clear Channel case is recited succinctly here.
36. *Ibid.*, 23 Fed. Reg. 2612 (1958); 1 RR 53:xlix.
37. *Ibid.*
38. *Ibid.*
39. *Ibid.*
40. *Ibid.*

41. 1 RR 53:lv.
42. *Ibid.*
43. 1 RR 53:1.
44. *Ibid.*, 1 RR 53:lx5iii, lxix, and lxx.
45. *Broadcasting*, July 27, 1959, p. 60.
46. FCC Docket No. 6741, 24 Fed. Reg. 7739 (1959).
47. FCC Docket No. 6741, 26 Fed. Reg. 886, 21 RR 1801.
48. *Broadcasting*, July 9, 1962, p. 38.
49. *Ibid.*, July 1, 1963, p. 56.
50. *Ibid.*, July 8, 1963, pp. 64-66.
51. 325 F. (2d) 637-644.
52. *Broadcasting*, November 4, 1963, pp. 82-84.
53. 1 RR 53:108.
54. FCC, *30th Anniversary Report*, 1964, p. 77.
55. Section 73.182(f), 1 RR 53:775.
56. Section 73.182(g), 1 RR 53:776.
57. Section 73.182(i), 1 RR 53:776.
58. Section 73.182(j), 1 RR 53:777.
59. Section 73.23, 1 RR 53:612-13.
60. *In the Matter of Inquiry into the Advisability of Authorizing Standard Broadcast Stations to Operate with Facilities Licenses for Daytime Operation from 6:00a.m. or Local Sunrise (whichever is earlier) to 6:00p.m. or Local Sunset (whichever if later)* FCC Docket No. 12729, 1 RR 53:xix at 53:xxiii and 53:xxiv.
61. *Ibid.*
62. *Ibid.*
63. 18 RR 1689.
64. *Broadcasting*, July 9, 1962, p. 38.
65. 32 Fed. Reg. 10437; 10 RR (2d) 1580.
66. 10 RR(2d) 1580; 32 Fed. Reg. 10437.
67. *Ibid.*, pp. 1600-1601.
68. *Broadcasting*, August 21, 1967, pp. 60-61.
69. 396 F (2)601; 13 RR 2d 2001.
70. *Broadcasting*, September 4, 1967, p. 62.
71. 17 RR 2d 1524:34 Fed. Reg. 14384. The FCC's *Memorandum and Order* is less restrictive on Class IV broadcast stations. The rationale for the new AM rules is fully stated in the Commission's lengthy statement, 17 RR 2d 1524-1544.

CHAPTER 8

Frequency Modulation Broadcasting (FM)

First to make use of the 3-electrode tube for generating continuous electric waves which made radio broadcasting feasible, inventor of the long and widely used superheterodyne receiving circuit, and inventor of the new broadcasting by frequency modulation that so well avoids static as almost to defy the lightning. He is one of the leaders in accomplishing the miracle of radio communication, a reality so inconceivably novel that the imagination of no poet, no author of tales or fables, had ever anticipated. —Citation of the National Association of Manufacturers in selecting Edwin Armstrong as one of the National Modern Pioneers in 1940.

Prior to Pearl Harbor, great technological advances in the techniques of broadcasting had been made, but the remarkable developments which came out of the ensuing war surpassed any which had taken place before. Dazzling before a weary and war-ridden world were the brilliant prospects of a new electronics era destined to revolutionize life on this planet and to provide a valuable tool for exploration of outer space.

Advantages of FM. Frequency Modulation or FM, a new radio technique developed during the 1930's by Major Edwin F. Armstrong, had demonstrated its superior utility in military operations and was on the verge of a vast expansion in broadcasting.[1] Engineers had discovered and demonstrated that FM had several major advantages over Amplitude Modulation (AM) used in standard broadcasting.

First, it was discovered that FM was not affected nearly so much by static. Because atmospheric and electrical noises consist primarily of amplitude variations, they often got into the standard radio sets and ruined reception. FM, on the other hand, had an inherent advantage in avoiding these noises. Even though a storm might be raging, attended by frequent bursts of thunder and flashes of lightning, or though an electric train might be roaring past the door, radio reception would remain clear.

Another advantage was its ability to reproduce the entire tonal range from the deepest base to the highest overtones. Many music lovers found it more pleasurable to listen to symphony orchestras via FM because the varied tones produced by the different instruments in the studio came through with balance and clarity.

Also, FM made possible the operation of stations much closer together on the same channel without objectionable interference. This meant that many more towns and cities might have their own radio stations.[2]

Prior to the Second War, the FCC had held public hearings to explore the possibilities of FM broadcasting.[3] And on May 22, 1940, the Commission allocated 35 channels to the FM service in the 43-50 megacycle band. Five months later, there were fifteen stations in the country authorized to engage in FM broadcasting.[4] By the time of the World War II freeze on civilian construction which was imposed in 1941, the number had increased to about thirty.[5]

Post War Growth. It was not until after the War, however, that the enormous potential for FM broadcasting became generally recognized. Its superior advantages having been demonstrated in war maneuvers, there developed a wave of enthusiasm for its peace time use. Responding to this enthusiasm, the Commission conducted a series of allocation hearings, and on June 27, 1945, allocated the 88 to 108 mc band as the "permanent home" of FM. Of the 100 channels made available, the first twenty were assigned to non-commercial operation for educational groups and institutions.[6]

By July 1, only three days after the allocations were made, there were more than 400 applications for new FM stations on file with the FCC and the Commission had received hundreds of requests for information and application forms.[7]

But FM did not attain quickly the large measure of success envisioned by its enthusiasts. The expansion of standard broadcasting after the war and the flooding of the market with low-priced AM receiving sets and with comparatively few FM receivers available—all combined to make it difficult for FM stations. Many were compelled to leave the air for lack of audience and advertising revenue.

In 1949, just four years after the FM allocations were made, there were more than 700 commercial FM stations in operation. By 1956, this number had dropped to 530 and a large number of these were duplicating AM services.[8] By 1958, there had been an increase, and a new wave of enthusiasm for FM was sweeping the country.

The following figures show the pattern of decline and growth of commercial FM from 1949 to 1969:[9]

Year	Grants	Deletions	Pending Applications	Licensed
1949	57	212	65	377
1950	35	169	17	493
1951	15	91	10	534
1952	24	36	9	582
1953	29	79	8	551
1954	27	54	5	529
1955	27	44	6	525
1956	31	37	10	519
1957	40	26	24	519
1958	98	24	57	526
1959	153	19	71	578
1960	165	22	114	700
1961	200	20	97	829

Year	Grants	Deletions	Pending Applications	Licensed
1962	138	39	147	955
1963	42	26	191	1,090
1964	183	18	258	1,141
1965	207	13	233	1,317
1966	197	18	211	1,494
1967	214	7	181	1,638
1968	158	15	210	1,812
1969	101	13	225	1,985

Year	CP's on Air	Total on Air	CP's Not on Air	Total Authorized
1949	360	737	128	865
1950	198	691	41	732
1951	115	649	10	659
1952	47	629	19	648
1953	29	580	21	601
1954	24	553	16	569
1955	15	540	12	552
1956	11	530	16	546
1957	11	530	31	560
1958	22	548	86	634
1959	44	622	147	769
1960	41	741	171	912
1961	60	880	203	1,092
1962	57	1,012	179	1,191
1963	30	1,120	87	1,207
1964	40	1,181	190	1,371
1965	26	1,343	222	1,565
1966	21	1,515	229	1,744
1967	70	1,708	243	1,951
1968	38	1,850	244	2,094
1969	33	2,018	163	2,181

Previous Plan for Assigning FM channels. When the FM service was shifted to its present space in the spectrum (88 to 108 mc), the band of 20 megacycles was divided into 100 channels, each 200 kc in width. These channels were designated by number, from 201 to 300. The lowest 20 were reserved for noncommercial educational use and the remaining 80 were set aside for commercial operations. 20 of these 80 commercial channels, interspersed through the FM spectrum from Channel 221 to Channel 296, were allocated for use by low-power "Class A" stations. The other 60 were allocated for use by high-powered "Class B" stations.

In 1945, at the time of spectrum shift, the Commission put into effect a tentative table of assignments, under which particular "Class B" FM channels were assigned to particular cities. In August, 1958, however, the Commission abandoned this plan of assignment and deleted the FM table.[10] It then followed the practice of making FM assignments on the same basis as it made AM assignments—grants were made at any location if applicants could show that they were legally, technically and financially qualified, and that their proposed operations were in accordance with the Rules and would not cause objectionable interference to existing co-channel or adjacent-channel stations.

Revision of FM Broadcast Rules. The sudden and rapid growth of FM which followed caused the Commission to reassess the merits of this assignment pattern. Accordingly, on July 5, 1961, the FCC issued a public notice discussing the possibility of making basic revisions in the FM Broadcast Rules.[11] The Commission said that two general questions would be explored:

(1) whether the system at that time of making station assignments was the one best suited for the optimum development of the FM broadcast service, or, if not, what changes should be instituted; (2) how the development and expansion of the FM service could be achieved without the serious administrative burdens and great delays inherent in the system then being employed.[12]

In a subsequent Report released on August 1, 1962, the Commission concluded that future FM grants should be made according to a table which would assign specific FM channels to specific cities, as in television, and pursuant thereto adopted a schedule of minimum mileage separations to underlie the construction of such a table.[13] On July 30, 1963 the Commission adopted a final Table of Assignments for future FM stations and which continues to serve as a basis for the assignment of frequencies and the establishment of new FM stations.[14]

In the proceedings leading up to the final Report, the Commission was pressed to adopt other assignment systems. The largest group of petitioners urged the Commission to return to a plan under which new or changed FM assignments were required to provide protection to the 1 mv/m contour of other existing stations or proposed stations. Under this plan, each station "would be treated as operating with its actual or proposed facilities—rather than maximum permissible facilities—and most parties would permit the use of all available assignment tools, including measurement data, to determine the location of relevant service contours.[15]

Some of the petitioners wanted to make the protection of 1 mv/m contours absolute. Still others wished a complete return to the traditional AM system in which "service gains are weighed against service losses in each case in order to determine whether a new application should be granted." In support of the protected contour system, many parties in the proceeding favored the use of directional antennas to reduce the required spacing between stations on the same or adjacent channels.[16]

A second group of petitioners, while accepting the principle of a table and mileage separations based upon assumed operation with maximum facilities, plead for shorter spacings than those adopted by the Commission. And some in this group would couple these shorter distances between stations with a "demand" system rather than a fixed table of assignments—i.e., a system allowing an applicant to apply for a new FM facility at any place where the required mileage separations could be met. A few parties objected to the Zone system as proposed by the Commission and asked for its elimination or modification.[17]

The Commission rejected all these alternative proposals. It contended that the "protected contour" system was "inherently inefficient from a strictly engineering point of view," and that the total area receiving satisfactory service from all stations would be considerably less than under a system which allows spacings between stations on the basis of assumed operation with relatively maximum facilities.[18] The Commission further expressed concern that the "protected contour" plan fails to provide for long term objectives. "As increasing numbers of stations are 'squeezed-in' at near minimum facilities", said the Commission, "these stations, and nearby submaximum stations, are forever precluded from increasing their height and power. This is precisely the state of affairs we wish to prevent in an age of rapidly expanding metropolitan areas."[19]

In its July 30, 1963 Report and Order, the Commission stated further its basic rationale for adopting the new FM system:

The Table of Assignments and the mileage separations used to construct it reflect basic engineering and policy judgments as to the future role of FM. In our recent notice of rule making concerning revision of the AM rules, 13 / we expressed the view that AM and FM should be regarded as complementary parts of a single aural service.

It is our belief that FM stations can best fulfill their role within the total aural service in two ways. First, FM can be used to provide local aural service to communities of moderate size which, for one reason or another, have been unable to obtain any AM station or which do not receive adequate nighttime local AM service. For the most part, we have tried to do this job with Class A stations which have a relatively limited service radius (15 miles at maximum facilities) and are, therefore, more appropriate for smaller communities than for larger metropolitan complexes. FM's second role is more significant. Departing from past practice in the AM service, where 90% of existing stations operate with one kilowatt power or less, we have set aside 75% of all commercial FM channels for stations which will be able to provide interference-free service over relatively wide areas and we have adopted mileage separations which will allow a large proportion of these stations to achieve maximum facilities. These decisions reflect our judgment that the wide coverage FM station is the vehicle by which FM may best be developed as a complementary aural service to AM. In previous paragraphs we noted four specific areas of need in which wide coverage FM stations may play vital roles not wholly fulfilled by AM services: (a) the need to provide service from central city stations to burgeoning suburban

13 / FCC 63-468 [25 RR 1615], May 17, 1963 (Docket No. 15084).

communities; (b) the need to provide primary aural service to nighttime "white areas" lying some distance from large communities; (c) the need to provide the best possible stereophonic transmission over stations which must be spaced on the basis of assumed monaural services; and (d) the need to provide signals of adequate strength to serve what is expected to be a substantially increased FM automotive audience in the future. To these factors may be added a further consideration pertaining to the nature of the FM service itself. Many of the most successful FM operations thus far have been stations which have directed their programming appeal toward minority and specialized audiences. We believe that in order to compete successfully in larger metropolitan areas with television and long established AM operations, many FM stations will find it desirable to continue to provide alternative program choices in this manner. Except in the most concentrated centers of population, this type of operation cannot achieve maximum success without a relatively extensive service area. A station providing interference-free coverage for a radius of only ten or fifteen miles is seldom able to provide service to enough people interested in limited appeal programming to survive. We believe that a wider base of economic support is necessary for such operations which, for the most part, fulfill needs not served by AM facilities.[20]

Zones. Under the plan adopted for purposes of allocation and assignments of FM channels, the FCC divided the United States into three zones. Zone 1 consists of most of the United States. Zone 1-A includes Puerto Rico, the Virgin Islands and that portion of the State of California which is located south of the 40th parallel. Zone II covers Alaska, Hawaii, and the rest of the United States not located in either Zone I or Zone I-A.

Classes and Service Requirements of FM Stations. The Rules classify commercial FM stations into A, B and C groups. The A group consists of those designed to render service to a relatively small community, city, or town, and the surrounding rural area. Such stations may not operate with less than 100 watts nor more than 3 kilowatts effective radiated power and their antennas must not exceed 300 feet above average terrain.[21]

The following frequencies are designated as Class A channels and are assigned for use by Class A stations:[22]

Frequency	Channel No.	Frequency	Channel No.
92.1	221	110.1	261
92.7	224	100.9	265
93.5	228	101.7	269
94.3	232	102.3	272
95.3	237	103.1	276
95.9	240	103.9	280
96.7	244	104.9	285
97.7	249	105.5	288
98.3	252	106.3	292
99.3	257	107.1	296

Class B-C channels and Class B and C stations. Except for the channels listed above, all FM channels from 222 through 300 (92.3 through 107.9 Mc/s) are classified as Class B-C channels, and, except for restrictions applicable to Alaska and Hawaii (to be discussed later), are assigned for use in Zones I and I-A by class B stations only, and for use in Zone II by Class C stations only. There are no Class C stations in Zones I or I-A and no Class B stations in Zone II.[23]

A Class B Station is one which operates on a Class B-C channel in Zone I or Zone I-A, and is designed to render service to a sizeable community, city, or town, or to the principal city or cities of an urbanized area, and its environs.[24] The Commission Rules provide that such stations licensed after September 10, 1962, must not operate with less than 5 kw nor more than 50 kw effective radio power and with an antenna height of not more than 500 feet above average terrain. Antenna heights may exceed this figure provided the effective radiated power is reduced to an amount less than the normal minimum specified and is calculated in accordance with curves set forth in Figure 3 of Section 73.333 of the Rules.[25] In Puerto Rico, antenna heights up to 2,000 feet above average terrain may be used with effective radiated powers permitted up to 25 kw. The Rules say, however, that higher antennas may be authorized provided the transmitting power is reduced so that the station's 1 mv/m contour will be no further from the station's transmitter than it would be if power of 25 kw and antenna height of 2,000 feet were being employed. For powers above 25 kw (up to 50 kw) no antenna heights are authorized which result in greater coverage than that which can be obtained with the normal specifications for power and antenna.[26]

A Class C station is a station which operates on a Class B-C channel in Zone II, and is designed to render service to a community, city, or town, and large surrounding area. Such stations, if authorized after September 10, 1962, may not operate with less than 25 kw nor more than 100 kw effective radiated power and their coverage may not exceed that which can be obtained from 100 kw and an antenna height of 2,000 feet above average terrain. As with Class B stations, the length of the antenna may exceed the standard maximum, provided it is compensated for by appropriate reduction of power.[27]

FM Applications Must Comply with the Table of Assignments. Section 73.202b of the Rules contains a list of the cities throughout the United States with the particular commercial FM channels assigned to each city.[28] Applications for such stations will be accepted for filing by the FCC in the 48 coterminous states only on the channels set forth in the Table of Assignments and only in communities recited therein. There is one exception. An application to construct a station in a town or city not listed in the Table may be filed if the channel requested is Class A and the place is located within ten miles of a listed community. Or if a channel B/C is sought the place must be within fifteen miles of the listed community. These rules apply provided no other channel in the listed community has been similarly assigned to another community and provided that the unlisted community has not already removed a channel from any other listed community.[29] Applications which do not comply with these requirements will not be considered by the Commission.[30]

Any change in the Table requires the filing of a formal petition with a showing that the proposal will comply with mileage separation requirements and that the public interest will be served. Since the Table was established in 1963 it has been amended many times, and as of June, 1969 a sizeable number of petitions requesting additional changes were on file awaiting action of the Commission.[31]

International Agreements and Other Restrictions on Use of Channels.

All authorizations for FM stations are subject to the provisions of any agreements the United States may have with Canada concerning FM assignments. Section 73.204 states that the "Commission may decide after consultation with Canada that an application should not be granted; or if, pursuant to an agreement providing for timely objection after grant, Canada files such objection, the Commission may on its own motion set aside the grant pending consideration."[32] In such case, the Commission gives notice of such action.

The frequency 89.1 Mc/s (channel 206) was formerly reserved in the New York area for the use of the United Nations "with the equivalent of an antenna height of 500 feet above average terrain and effective radiated power of 20 kw.[33] However, recently New York University and Fairleigh Dickinson University have been granted a share time assignment on this frequency (17 RR 2d 104).

Furthermore, in Alaska, the frequency band 88-100 Mc/s has been allocated exclusively to Government radio services and the so-called non-Government fixed services and none of these channels are available in that state for FM assignments. Likewise, the frequency band 98-108 Mc/s is allocated for non-broadcast use in Hawaii and none of the frequencies in that range may be assigned there for FM broadcast stations.[34]

Minimum Mileage Separations. Petitions to amend the Table of Assignments will be dismissed and no application for a new Commercial FM station, for a change of an existing station, or increase in antenna height or effective radiated power, or change in location of an existing station will be accepted by the FCC for filing if the proposal does not comply with the prescribed mileage separations as set forth in the table below. Proposed stations of the respective classes shown in the left-hand column of the Table must be located no less than the specified distances from existing co-channel stations and first adjacent-channel stations (200 kc/s removed) and second and third adjacent-channel stations (400 and 600 kc/s removed), which distances are shown in the right-hand columns of the table. The Rules state that these prescribed separations apply regardless of which class station is the new one being proposed (e.g., the spacing required between a new Class

A station and an existing one of the C class is the same as it would be between a new Class C station and an existing A one). The Rules further state that the separation requirements between Class B and Class C stations apply only across zone lines.[35]

Class of Station and Frequency Separation (kc/s)

*Class of station	Class A				Class B				Class C			
	Co-ch	200 kc/s	400 kc/s	600 kc/s	Co-ch	200 kc/s	400 kc/s	kc/s 600	Co-ch		200	200	600
A.............	65	40	15	15	—	65	40	40	—	105	65	65
B....................................					150	65	40	40	170	135	65	65
C...									180	150	65	65

Note: Stations or assignments separated in frequency by 10.6 or 10.8 Mc/s (53 or 54 channels) will not be authorized unless they conform to the following separation table:

Class of Stations	Required spacing in miles
A to A...........................	5
B to A...........................	10
B to B...........................	15
C to A...........................	20
C to B...........................	25
C to C...........................	30

*Educational FM stations are discussed later in this chapter.

Stations which are separated from other stations on the same channel or on adjacent channels less than the specified distances specified above may apply for changes in their facilities provided the requested changes conform to the requirements set forth in Section 73.213(a) of the Rules:

Section 73.213(b) states that stations already authorized to use facilities in excess of those specified above are allowed to continue to operate with such facilities. Greater facilities (up to the maximum specified for a particular class station) may be used if, by use of a directional antenna, radiation in any direction in which a short separation exists is reduced to no more than that permitted by the preceding table.[36]

Duplication of FM and AM Programming. Licensees of FM stations in cities of over 100,000 population may devote no more than 50 per cent of the average FM broadcast week to programs duplicated from an AM station owned by the same licensee in the same local area. Duplication is defined by the Commission to mean "simultaneous broadcasting of a particular program over both the AM and FM station or the broadcast of a particular FM program within 24 hours before or after the identical program is broadcast over the AM station."[37]

This rule was adopted by the Commission in August, 1964.[38] By various orders, however, the time was extended and the rule did not become effective until March 31, 1966.[39] Sometimes before the rule was established, the Commission had expressed the opinion that the time had come "to move significantly toward the day when AM and FM stations can be regarded as component parts of a total aural service. We believe that the ultimate role of FM broadcasting is to supplement the aural service provided by AM stations and that, eventually, there must be an elimination of FM stations which are no more than adjuncts to AM facilities in the same community..."[40]

It goes without saying that when the Commission announced that it proposed to require separate programming it caused a great stir among AM licensees who were duplicating their programs via FM facilities. In fact, as the Commission pointed out, in the early sixties almost half of the FM stations reported no revenues and were "presumably" duplicating the programs of AM stations 100 per cent of the time.[41] The wave of reaction which resulted no doubt had much to do with the Commission's providing for waivers of the rule where the "public interest" seemed to justify. And so, paragraph (c) of Section 73.242 was adopted and currently is in effect. It reads:

Upon a substantial showing that continued program duplication over a particular station would better serve the public interest than immediate non-duplication, a licensee may be granted a temporary exemption from the requirements of paragraph (a) of this section. Requests for such exemption must be submitted to the Commission, accompanied by supporting data, at least 6 months prior to the time the non-duplication requirement of paragraph (a) of this section is to become effective as to a particular station. Such exemption, if granted, will ordinarily run to the end of the station's current license period, or if granted near the end of the license period, for some other reasonable period not to exceed 3 years.[42]

Following the adoption of the rule, a sizeable number of AM licensees requested waivers. Some were granted, but in most cases the petitions were denied. It is clear that a heavy burden of proof is required by the FCC to justify the granting of such waivers.

Subsidiary Communications Authorizations. On March 22, 1955, the Commission adopted rules providing for the issuance of Subsidiary Communications Authorizations (SCA's) to FM broadcasters. These authorizations made it possible for the FM stations to present specialized programs consisting of news, music, time, weather, and other similar program categories, and were designed to serve business establishments and bolster station revenue.[43]

Originally, FM stations were allowed to conduct these subsidiary operations on a "multiplex" basis at any time, or temporarily on a "simplex" basis providing they were transmitted outside regular broadcasting hours. When programs are "multiplexed", they cannot be heard on ordinary FM receivers since they are sent on subchannels simultaneously with regular programs on the main channel.

When the programs are "simplexed", they can be heard on standard FM receivers because they are transmitted on the same carrier frequency used for broadcasting. Special receivers sold or leased to commercial subscribers eliminate or amplify certain portions of the programs (usually the spoken words) by means of an inaudible supersonic (beep) signal.[44]

When simplex operation was authorized in 1955, the Commission emphasized that it was for a year only because of the unavailability of multiplex equipment and that, to protect the FM broadcast service, it would be necessary ultimately for all these subsidiary operations to be conducted on a multiplex basis only.[45]

Authority to carry on simplex transmissions was extended for a year, but by July 1, 1957, multiplex equipment was available in sufficient quantities and since that time no further simplex operations have been authorized. The Commission, however, granted stations additional time to convert from simplex to multiplex equipment. As of July 30, 1958, 82 FM stations held SCA authorizations for multiplex operation.[46]

The Contest Over Simplex Operations. Station WFMF in Chicago contested the validity of the Commission's rules governing the SCA service insofar as they excluded such operation on a simplex basis. On appeal, the Commission contended that functional programming consisting of the presentation of a highly specialized program format with the deletion of advertising from the subscribers' receivers, and the exaction of a charge for these services, was "point-to-point" communication and not broadcasting within the meaning of Section 3(o) of the Communications Act.[47] The Court of Appeals, however, held otherwise. The court in part said:

. . . Broadcasting remains broadcasting even though a segment of those capable of receiving the broadcast signal are equipped to delete a portion of that signal . . . Petitioner, for example, has acquired a high degree of popularity with the Chicago free listening audience. Moreover, it receives substantial and growing revenues from advertisers specifically desiring to reach that audience. In this light, a finding that the programming of petitioner and broadcasters comparably situated is not directed to, and intended to be received by the public is clearly erroneous. Transmitted with the intent contemplated by Section 3(o), such programming therefore has the requisite attributes of broadcasting.[48]

Judge Danaher wrote a dissenting opinion. He stated that WFMF and the entire radio industry were on notice that the Commission would authorize only "multiplex" transmission by which there might be simultaneous sending of two or more signals within a single channel. "The Commission," he said, "made it abundantly clear that an FM broadcast band, already allocated to a particular area in the public interest, was not to be converted in large degree to commercial or industrial operations where the subscribers, and not the public, would control the receiving sets, decide when they should operate, at what volume, and what portions of what programs were to be deleted.[49]

He further declared that the Commission had decided as a matter of policy, "that FM bands were to be used for the purpose for which they had been allocated, and that functional music operations might be authorized on those FM bands only in a manner subsidiary to the main broadcasting service from which the licensee was to draw its financial sustenance. Its policy was evolved in the public interest, and was designed to achieve a far more effective use of the allocated FM frequencies, with greater opportunity to more licensees to achieve economically feasible FM broadcasting ... The Commission simply decided that the specialized simplex service was not to be permitted to pre-empt the valuable spectrum space allocated to FM frequencies intended to be devoted to broadcasting. This was a public interest determination required to be made by law. Thus the Commission's rule-making was entirely within the Commission's competence."[50]

The Commission filed a petition for rehearing which was denied by the full court on January 16, 1959.[51] An appeal was taken by the Commission to the U.S. Supreme Court. But on October 12, 1959 the Supreme Court refused to review the case, thereby, in effect, sustaining the lower court's ruling that the FCC's regulation requiring all SCA operations of FM stations to use multiplexing was illegal.[52]

On July 2, 1958, the Commission issued a *Notice of Inquiry* soliciting comments from the public on a number of questions relating to the feasibility of and the extent to which subsidiary FM communications should be authorized.[53] On March 11, 1959, the Commission enlarged the scope of the inquiry to afford interested parties an opportunity to submit further data and opinions directed specifically to the matter of stereophonic programming on a multiplex basis. Comments were requested with respect to the following questions:[54]

(a) Should stereophonic broadcasting by FM broadcast stations on a multiplex basis be permitted on a regular basis, and, if so, should such broadcasting take the form of a broadcast service to the general public, or should it be available only on a subscription basis under Subsidiary Communications Authorizations, or both?

(b) What quality and performance standards, if any, should be applied to a multiplex sub-channel used for stereophonic broadcasting?

(c) Should a specific sub-carrier frequency or frequencies be allocated for stereophonic broadcasting?

(d) Should the quality and performance standards applicable to the main channel be further relaxed, beyond the point already permitted for SCA operations, to accommodate stereophonic broadcasting and, if so, to what extent?

(e) What transmission standards regarding cross-talk between the main channel and stereophonic sub-channel should be adopted?

(f) Should FM broadcast stations engaging in stereophonic broadcasting be required to use a compatible system which allows listeners tuned only to the main channel to hear an aurally balanced program?

The March 11, 1959 *Notice* specified that statements should be filed on or before June 10, 1959. On June 3, 1959, however, the Commission extended the date to December 11, 1959. Subsequently, the date for filing comments was further extended to March 15, 1960.[55]

The outcome of all this was that on May 9, 1960, the Commission issued a report and order amending its rules to enlarge the scope of multiplex subcarrier operations by FM stations, but refused to permit transmissions unrelated to broadcasting.[56]

About a year later, it amended its rules to permit FM stations to transmit stereophonic programs on a multiplex basis. A number of systems proposed were rejected by the Commission—some because "of inferior frequency response and stereo separation together with excessive cross-talk and high stereo subchannel noise characteristics," another because of "its inability to handle orchestral dynamics in a manner that will produce an acceptable subjective stereophonic effect," and still another because of its "detrimental effect on the monophonic listener." The system adopted (identified as System 4-4A) said the Commission, "would have negligible effect on the monophonic listener", would involve less cost, would be comparatively free from distortion, and "its use would not ipso facto displace SCA operation.[57]

Termination of "Simplex" Transmissions. The rationale, as stated by the Commission in its original order, calling for a cessation of "simplex" operation was that such transmissions were non-broadcast in character. As previously mentioned, the courts held such an order and regulation to be invalid on this ground. On March 29, 1963, the Commission proposed, once again, to eliminate "simplexing", but on different grounds than those found to be objectionable by the Court of Appeals. The Commission said that the simplex operator, because of contractual arrangements with subscribers, was inhibited from providing programming which would meet the varied and changing needs of the public, that subscriber orientation in programming tended toward abdication of licensee control, that the FM broadcasting industry no longer needed "simplexing" as an economic crutch and that multiplex operators suffered an unfair competitive disadvantage because of less service area and higher costs of receiving equipment.[58]

With few exceptions, all parties filing comments in the proceeding endorsed or accepted in principle the proposed elimination of "simplex" operations. WFMF in Chicago, however, again vigorously objected. But again, though for different reasons, the Commission issued an order requiring

WFMF and a few other stations engaged in "simplex transmissions" to terminate the practice.[59]

SCA Regulations. Section 73.293 of the present Rules states that permissible uses of Subsidiary Communications Authorizations must fall within one or both of the following categories:

(1) Transmission of programs which are of a broadcast nature but which are of interest primarily to limited segments of the public wishing to subscribe thereto. Illustrative services include: background music; storecasting; detailed weather forecasting; special time signals; and other material of a broadcast nature expressly designed and intended for business, professional, educational, religious, trade, labor, agricultural or other groups engaged in any lawful activity.

(2) Transmission of signals which are directly related to operation of FM broadcast stations; for example: relaying of broadcast material to other FM and standard broadcast stations; remote cueing and order circuits; remote control telemetering functions associated with authorized STL operation, and similar uses.[60]

It is further provided in this section that applications for SCA's must be submitted on FCC Form 318, and that each application shall specify the particular purposes for which the facility is to be used. There are no restrictions as to time when SCA operations shall be conducted, so long as the programming on the main channel is broadcast simultaneously.[61]

Section 73.295 has a number of provisions which should be noted:

(a) Operations conducted under an SCA must conform to the uses as proposed in applications which are granted by the Commission and licensees may not engage in other activities without prior FCC permission.

(b) Superaudible and subaudible tones and pulses may, when authorized by the FCC, be used by SCA holders to activate and deactivate subscribers' multiplex receivers, but the use of these or any other control techniques to delete main channel material is prohibited.

(c) In all arrangements with outside parties, SCA holders must retain control over all material transmitted over the station's facilities, with the right to reject any material which it deems inappropriate or undesirable. Any sub-channel leasing agreements must be reduced to writing and filed with the Commission within thirty days from the time of execution.

(d) Logging, announcement and other detailed requirements pertaining to broadcasting on main FM channels (as in Sections 73.282, 283, 284, 287, 288 and 289) are not applicable to material transmitted on sub-carrier frequencies.

(e) However, to the extent that SCA circuits transmit programs, each licensee or permittee must maintain a daily program log in which a general description of the programs shall be entered once during each broadcast day. In the event of a change in the general programming, an entry must be made describing the change and indicating the time it occurred.

(f) A daily operating log must be maintained in which the following entries are required (subcarrier interruptions of five minutes or less excluded): times when subcarrier generator is turned on and off; and times when modulation is applied to and removed from the subcarrier; and a notation describing the results obtained in determining the frequency of each SCA subcarrier.[62]

Daily checks must be made to make sure that the operation on a subchannel does not deviate more than 500 cycles per second from the frequency authorized by the Commission and operations must comply with the technical standards which are specifically set forth in Section 73.319 of the Rules.[63]

Stereophonic broadcasting. Section 73.332 prescribes in detail the transmission standards for stereophonic broadcasting. As provided in Section 73.297, any FM station may, without further authority, transmit such programming in accordance with these standards, provided, however, that the Commission and the Engineer and Charge of the radio district in which the station is located is notified within ten days of the installation of equipment to be used (type-accepted) and the commencement of stereophonic programming. The Rules further state that daily checks must be made to insure that the pilot subcarrier frequency is kept at all times within the prescribed two cycle per second tolerance.[64]

Non-Commercial Educational FM. The Commission has established a special class of FM stations—Non-Commercial Educational FM broadcast stations. As previously indicated, the frequencies set aside for these stations include those between 88 and 92 megacycles. These twenty channels are assigned for educational use and commercial interests may not apply for them.

As pointed out in Chapter 3, when Congress was considering legislation to establish the FCC, there was a great deal of public support for a requirement that all broadcasting stations set aside substantial portions of broadcasting time for educational and cultural programs. This proposal was not adopted, but Congress did pass Section 307(c) of the Communications Act directing the Commission to make a study of it.[65]

Pursuant to this legislative mandate, the Commission conducted a hearing on the matter and invited educators and other interested parties to testify. Among the educational witnesses who testified in that 1935 proceeding was Dr. H. L. Ewbank of the University of Wisconsin. He urged the FCC to earmark a number of broadcasting channels to provide for non-commercial stations and that these be reserved for qualified educational agencies.[66]

This proposal was revived ten years later when the Commission conducted hearings on the allocation of frequencies above 25 megacycles to which reference was made earlier in this chapter. Educators representing such national organizations as the National Educational Association and the American Council on Education urged the Commission to reserve channels for educational FM broadcasting.[67] Accordingly, as pointed out above, on June 27, 1945, the Commission reserved 20 of the 100 FM channels (88 to 92 megacycles) for this purpose and in 1946 promulgated special rules governing the operation of stations on these channels.[68]

Progress Since 1944. In September, 1944, one institution of higher learning, the University of Illinois, was operating an FM station. At that time, construction permits had been granted to the Universities of Iowa, Kentucky and Southern California but the stations were not yet on the air. As of the same date, public school systems in Chicago, New York, San Francisco, and Cleveland were operating FM stations.[69]

With the assignment of special channels for education in 1945, the interest of educators was stimulated. The U.S. Office of Education was especially helpful in disseminating information regarding the availability of FM channels for education and urged schools to take advantage of the new opportunity.[70]

By December, 1945, more than 40 educational institutions had filed applications for new educational FM stations. Four years later, 58 such stations had been authorized.

Since that time, though the growth of educational FM has not been rapid, it has been steady as shown by the following figures:[71]

Year	Grants	Deletions	Pending Applications	Licensed
1949	18	7	9	31
1950	25	4	3	61
1951	19	6	2	82
1952	12	2	2	91
1953	13	1	3	106
1954	9	2	1	117
1955	7	3	1	121
1956	13	4	5	126
1957	17	5	2	135
1958	11	3	6	144
1959	16	8	2	150
1960	20	4	11	161
1961	21	3	4	176
1962	11	1	12	192
1963	30	1	4	213
1964	20	1	11	231
1965	17	2	12	259
1966	32	2	19	281
1967	44	-	17	303
1968	40	6	18	335

Year	CP's on Air	Total on Air	Not on Air	Total Authorized
1949	3	34	24	58
1950	1	62	20	82
1951	1	83	12	95
1952	1	92	12	104
1953	0	106	10	116
1954	0	117	6	123
1955	3	124	3	127
1956	0	126	10	136
1957	0	135	13	148
1958	3	147	10	157
1959	4	154	11	165
1960	4	165	16	181

Year	CP's on Air	Total on Air	Not on Air	Total Authorized
1961	10	186	13	199
1962	9	201	8	209
1963	8	221	17	238
1964	12	243	14	257
1965	3	262	10	272
1966	10	291	11	302
1967	15	318	26	344
1968	13	348	30	378

Eligibility and Program Requirements. As provided in Section 73.501 of the Commission rules, the following channels are available for non-commercial educational FM broadcasting:[72]

Frequency (mc)	Channel No.	Frequency (mc)	Channel No.
88.1	201	90.1	211
88.3	202	90.3	212
88.5	203	90.5	213
88.7	204	90.7	214
88.9	205	90.9	215
89.1	206	91.1	216
89.3	207	91.3	217
89.5	208	91.5	218
89.7	209	91.7	190
89.9	210	91.9	220

Only non-profit educational organizations are eligible to apply for licenses to operate these educational FM stations. In determining eligibility of publicly supported educational organizations, the Commission takes into account whether they are accredited by their respective state departments of education. With respect to privately controlled educational organizations or institutions, their rating by regional and national accrediting associations is considered as a factor in determining eligibility. While the rules do not bar the holding of licenses by educational organizations without accreditation, they do place a heavier burden of proof on them to show that they are truly educational in character and have the resources and qualifications to operate an educational station in the public interest.[73]

The applicants for these educational FM stations must show that they will be used for the advancement of educational programs. The rules provide that the facilities may be used to "transmit programs directed to specific schools in a system or systems for use in connection with regular courses as well as routine and administrative material pertaining thereto and may be used to transmit educational, cultural, and entertainment programs to the public."[74]

At the time FM channels were reserved for education, there was considerable interest in the development of state-wide educational FM networks.

Wisconsin did establish one which is still in operation today. Others were planned but did not materialize. In anticipation of network developments, the Commission provided in Section 3.502 of its Rules that in considering the assignment of a channel for noncommercial educational FM broadcasting, it would take into account the extent to which an application meets the requirements of any state-wide plan for such broadcasting, provided the plan affords fair treatment to public and private educational institutions at the various levels of learning and is otherwise fair and equitable.[75] This rule is still in effect but has had little applicability because plans for statewide educational FM networks have not developed on as wide a basis as was expected when the rule was adopted.

Section 73.503 of the rules provides that each educational FM station is required to furnish a "non-profit and non-commercial broadcast service." No sponsored or commercial program may be transmitted and commercial announcements of any character are prohibited. These educational stations may transmit the programs of commercial stations. If they do, however, the rules say that all commercial announcements and references must be deleted.[76]

A public notice issued by the FCC on March 16, 1960, stating that all stations must identify on the air the suppliers of free records used in broadcasts, seemed to conflict with these rules governing noncommercial FM operations. This March 16 public notice was an interpretation by the FCC of Section 317 of the Communications Act which requires sponsorship identification of broadcast programs.[77] Under this interpretation, a failure of the educational FM station to identify the donors of records (those supplied the station without cost and not those sold), would have been a violation of Section 317 of the Act. At the same time, such identification would have contravened the Rules of the FCC against the use of commercial plugs on this type of station.

This conflict put educational FM broadcasters in the awkward position of not being able to use free records, and they were compelled to limit their broadcasts to recordings which they bought.

Subsequent legislation by Congress, however, corrected this situation. As provided in Section 508 of the Communications Act, stations (both commercial and noncommercial) may use "free" records without being required to identify the donors.[78]

Formerly, programming regulations pertaining to educational FM stations were amended on May 6, 1970, largely for clarification purposes. Section 73.503, paragraph (c) and (d) has been added to read as follows:

(c) A noncommercial educational FM broadcast station may broadcast programs produced by, or at the expense of, or furnished by persons other than the licensee, if no other consideration than the furnishing of the program and the costs incidental to its production and broadcast are received by the licensee. The payment of line charges by another station, network, or someone other than the licensee of a noncommercial educational FM broadcast station, or general contributions to the operating costs of a station, shall not be considered as being prohibited by this paragraph.

(d) Each station shall furnish a non-profit and noncommercial broadcast service. Noncommercial educational FM broadcast stations are subject to the provisions of § 73.289 to the extent that they are applicable to the broadcast of programs produced by, or at the expense of, or furnished by others; however, no announcements promoting the sale of a product or service shall be broadcast in connection with any program.

NOTE 1. Announcements of the producing or furnishing of programs or the provision of funds for their production may be made no more than twice, at the opening and at the close of any program. The person or organization furnishing or producing the program shall be identified by name only, and no mention shall be made of any product or service with which it may have a connection.

NOTE 2. Announcements of general contributions of a substantial nature which make possible the broadcast of programs for part, or all, of the day's schedule may be made no more than three times during the broadcast day. (See 19RR 2d 1501; paragraphs (d) and (e) and notes relating thereto of Section 73.503).

As previously pointed out, the number of educational FM stations has been growing steadily. A factor favorable to this development was the adoption of a rule by the FCC authorizing these stations to operate with power of 10 watts or less.[79] The equipment and cost requirements for these stations are comparatively low. Some manufacturers have package deals which make it possible to secure the basic equipment for such a station at relatively low costs.

Rules Classifying Stations and Governing Frequency Assignments. In its first Report and Order issued on August 1, 1962 having to do with revision of FM broadcast rules, the Commission made a few minor changes relating to allocation of channels for non-commercial, educational FM broadcasting. For purposes of assigning frequencies the United States was divided into the three zones; Zone I, Zone I-A, and Zone II, having the same boundaries as those specified for commercial FM.[80] New Rules were established dividing these stations into the following four classes:[81]

(1) Class D—educational stations operating with no more than 10 watts transmitter power output, and eligible for assignment on any of the above listed channels reserved for education.

(2) Classes A, B, or C—educational stations operating with more than 10 watts transmitter output, with particular classifications depending on the effective radiated power and antenna height above average terrain, the zone in which the station's transmitter is located and determined on the same basis as prescribed in the rules covering stations.

The Commission has not as yet prescribed any minimum effective radiated power or antenna height for stations operating on channels reserved for educational FM broadcasting. However, as will be pointed out later, proposals looking toward action have been made and are likely to be effectuated in the near future.

One basic change in rules governing noncommercial, educational FM was made in the August 1, 1962 Report and Order mentioned above. Stations operating on frequencies on the top three reserved channels (218, 219 and 220) are subject to certain mileage-separation restrictions in order to control the impact of transmissions to and from the bottom three commercial channels (221A, 222 and 223).[82] Aside from these restrictions, educational FM stations are still assigned on the basis of protecting interference within the 1 mv/m contour of other stations on the reserved channels.[83]

Proposed Changes. On November 14, 1966, the Commission issued a Public Notice of Inquiry in which it stated:

Based on our experience with television allocations and the commercial FM Table of Assignments, and the need for negotiations with the Canadian Government for a border agreement for the educational channels, we have tentatively reached the conclusion that a nationwide Table of Assignments for educational FM stations would best serve the educational radio needs of the country and would be the most effective and efficient manner in which the valuable portion of the spectrum may be utilized. We are, therefore, inviting comments on the proposed manner of making FM channels available to the various communities and the educational interests of the country. We are also inviting comments on various tentative criteria to be used in drafting up an educational FM Table of Assignments . . .[84]

The Commission further stated that as regards classes of stations, powers and antenna heights, and minimum station and assignments separations, it proposed to adopt the same standards as are applicable to commercial FM stations. Comments, however, were invited as to whether the limits on facilities and separations should be different.[85]

Some skepticism was expressed as to the value of some ten watt FM operations and questions were raised as to whether they should be restricted or even continued. After pointing out that, as of September, 1966, there were 158—slightly more than half—of the educational FM stations operating with transmitting power of 10 watts or less, the Commission said:

. . . These stations present certain problems. Operation with such limited power does not usually represent an efficient use of scarce spectrum space, since coverage is often limited to a few miles. *3/* In addition, while these stations are often high-quality operations, presenting programming consistent with the educational purpose for which the non-commercial educational FM band is designed, in numerous instances it appears that they are really routine light entertainment media, similar to many commercial radio stations only without commercials. In this respect they appear to reflect what was in many cases their origin—an attempt to expand and replace carrier-current "campus radio" operations. In our view, therefore, the time

3/ With an antenna height of 100 ft. a.a.t., and 10 watts ERP, a 10-watt station provides a 1 mv/m signal out to about two miles.

may well be at hand when proper use of the increasingly crowded educational FM band requires restrictions on the further authorization and continuance of 10-watt operations, and comments are invited on the following proposals:

(1) No further authorization of 10-watt stations or other facilities not meeting the minimum for Class A stations. However, upon a showing of need and public interest, waivers of this rule may be requested in specific situations.

(2) Existing 10-watt stations may continue to operate on this basis, and will be included in the Table and protected on the basis of the regular separations applicable to the class of channel on which they are assigned (Class A or Class B/C). _4/_ However, the 10-watt licensee will be permitted to operate on this basis only until the end of his present license period, and will then be required either to propose facilities meeting the minimum for his channel or surrender his authorization. As in the case of new stations, waiver of the provisions will be considered in individual cases.

(3) Consideration will be given to rule-making proposals to change the educational Table of Assignments by deleting one or more 10-watt assignments in favor of regular assignments elsewhere, and unless a 10 watt licensee indicates that before the end of his license period he will apply for at least the regular minimum facilities, his assignment may be deleted effective at the end of the license period; and if he so indicates and then does not so apply the assignment may be deleted without further procedings.[86]

Dates for filing comments in the proceeding were extended a number of times, the latest one being until May 11, 1967.[87] As of June 15, 1970, the Commission had not taken final action on its proposals. However, in view of the critical shortage of spectrum space and the increasing pressures on the Commission to achieve more efficient utilization of FM channels, some revisions in the rules along the lines proposed appear to be in the offing.

Inquiry Regarding Use of Low Power FM Translator Stations.
Large areas, particularly in the West, are still without satisfactory FM service. With regard to this need, on February 1, 1967, the Commission began consideration of the feasibility of using 1 watt FM translators (FCC Docket 17159) similar to those used in television.[88] Pursuant to this inquiry, developmental broadcast authorizations were granted to the China Lake Community Council, China Lake, California and to Station KPEN in San Francisco. The China Lake transmitter is located on Laurel Mountain near Ridgecrest, using a power of 1 watt, began retransmitting a signal from a distant FM station on April 14, 1967. KPEN received authority to develop co-channel equipment designed to improve the reception of its signal in certain shadow areas such as Concord and Walnut Creek, California. It began operation on April 28, 1967.[89]

_4/_ This may not be possible in those cases where the actual spacings of existing 10-watt stations are well below the proposed minimums. In such cases the 10-watt operation will, of course, be permitted to continue.

1. See Armstrong, Edwin H., "A Method of Reducing Distrubances in Radio Signaling by a System of Frequency Modulation", 24 Proceedings of the Institute of Radio Engineers, No. 5, May, 1936, p. 689.

2. Walker, Paul A. and Emery, Walter B., "Post War Communications and Speech Education", *Quarterly Journal of Speech,* Vol. 30, No. 4, December, 1944, pp. 399-401. In this article, two former FCC officials discuss the advantages of FM transmission.

3. FCC Log. *A Chronology of Events in the History of the Federal Communications Commission from Its Creation on June 19, 1934, to July 2, 1956,* compiled by the FCC Office of Reports and Information, July, 1956, p. 21.

4. FCC News Release, Mimeograph No. 44578, October 31, 1940.

5. FCC News Release, Mimeograph No. 46405, January 15, 1941.

6. FCC Docket No. 6651. Also see *Broadcasting,* May 28, 1945, pp. 17, 24, 26, 28.

7. *FCC Annual Report,* 1945, pp. 19-20.

8. *Ibid.,* 1958, p. 131.

9. FCC, *35th Annual Report/Fiscal Year 1969,* p. 128.

10. 21 RR 1657. See 10 Fed. Reg. 12006, 14526, 12 Fed. Reg. 1369, and 26 Fed. Reg. 6130.

11. 21 RR 1958, 23 Fed. Reg. 6110.

12. *Ibid.* 21 RR 1657, 26 Fed. Reg. 6130.

13. *Ibid.*

14. 23 RR 1801, 27 Fed. Reg. 7765.

15. 23 RR 1859, 28 Fed. Reg. 8077.

16. 23 RR 1861, 28 Fed. Reg. 8077.

17. *Ibid.*

18. *Ibid.*

19. 23 RR 1863, 28 Fed. Reg. 8078.

20. 23 RR 1867-1868.

21. Section 73.206, 1 RR 53:983, 47 CFR 129.

22. *Ibid.*

23. Section 73.206(b) (1), 1 RR 53:983, 47 CFR 129-130.

24. Section 73.206(b) (2), 1 RR 53:983, 47 CFR 129-130.

25. Section 73.206(b) (3), and 73.211 (b) (2), 1 RR 53-983, 989, 47 CFR 129-30, 133.

26. Section 73.211(b) (3), 1 RR 53:989, 47 CFR 133.

27. Section 73.206(b) (4) and (5), 1 RR 53:984, 47 CFR 129-130.

28. Section 73.202(b), 1 RR 53:912-919, 47 CFR 112-128.

29. Section 73.203(a) and (b), 1 RR 53:981, 47 CFR 128.

30. Section 73.203(a), 1 RR 53:981, 47 CFR 128-129; also see 30 Fed. Reg. 12711.

31. 1 RR 53:931-955.

32. Section 73.204(a), 1 RR 53:981, 47 CFR 129.

33. Section 73.204(b), 1 RR 53:982, 47 CFR 129.

34. Section 73.204(c) and (d), 1 RR 53:982, 47 CFR 129.

35. Section 73.207(a), 1 RR 53:984, 47 CFR 130.

36. Section 73.213(b) and (c), 1 RR 53:992, 47 CFR 135.

37. Section 73.242(a), 1 RR 53:1017, 47 CFR 140.

38. 2 RR (2d) 1658, 29 Fed. Reg. 9492.

39. 4 RR (2d) 1567, 7 RR (2d) 99.

40. 25 RR 1622.

41. *Ibid.*
42. 1 RR 53:1017-1018, 47 CFR 140.
43. 11 RR 1589, 20 Fed. Reg. 1825.
44. FCC, *Annual Report,* 1958, p. 116.
45. *Ibid.*
46. *Ibid.*
47. *Functional Music, Inc. v. Federal Communications Commission, Functional Music, Inc. v. United States et. al.,* U.S. Court of Appeals, District of Columbia Circuit, November 7, 1958, 274 F. (2d) 543; reported in 17 RR 2152.
48. 17 RR 2158; 274F. (2d).
49. *Ibid.,* p. 2160; 274 F. (2d).
50. *Ibid.*
51. *Broadcasting,* January 19, 1959, p. 9.
52. 361 U.S. 813, 80 S.C. Rep. 50, October 12, 1959.
53. FCC Docket No. 12517, 23 Fed. Reg. 5284.
54. 24 Fed. Reg. 1997.
55. 24 Fed. Reg. 10416.
56. 19 RR 1619.
57. 21 RR 1615.
58. FCC 63-303, March 29, 1963.
59. 2 RR 2d 1683.
60. 1 RR 53:1096, 47 CFR 158.
61. *Ibid.*
62. 1 RR 53:1097-1098, 47 CFR 158.
63. *Ibid.,* 1098; 47 CFR 158.
64. 1 RR 53:1099, CFR 159.
65. 48 Stat. 1084.
66. See transcript of record upon which was based the FCC's *Report to Congress Pursuant to Section 307(c) of the Communications Act of 1934,* January 22, 1935.
67. Testimony in FCC Docket No. 6651, 1944-45.
68. These rules were promulgated March 8, 1946, 11 Fed. Reg. 2839 (1946).
69. Emery and Walker, *op. cit.,* pp. 401-402.
70. *Ibid.*
71. FCC, *34th Annual Report/Fiscal Year 1968,* p. 116.
72. 1 RR 53:1151, 47 CFR 181.
73. Section 73.503, 1 RR 53:1152, 47 CFR 181.
74. *Ibid.*
75. Section 73.502, 1 RR 53:1151, 47 CFR 181.
76. *Ibid.,* Section 73.503, CFR 181.
77. *In the Matter of Public Notice* (FCC 60-239), March 16, 1960, entitled "Sponsorship Identification of Broadcast Material," 25 Fed. Reg. 2406 (1960); 19 RR 1569.
78. For a full understanding of what is meant by "free" records, the full text of Section 508 of the Communications Act should be consulted. See Appendix I.
79. 13 Fed. Reg. 4922, September 27, 1948.
80. Section 73.504, 1 RR 53:1153, 47 CFR 181.
81. *Ibid.,* 47 CFR 181-182.
82. *Ibid.*
83. 23 RR 1829.
84. Docket No. 14185, 1 RR 53:69, 31 Fed. Reg. 14755.
85. 1 RR 53:70, 31 Fed. Reg. 14756.
86. 1 RR 53:71, 31 Fed. Reg. 14756.
87. 1 RR 53:73, 32 Fed. Reg. 4182.7031.
88. FCC, *33rd Annual Report/Fiscal Year 1967,* p. 52.
89. *Ibid.,* pp. 52-53.

CHAPTER 9

Television

So swiftly that America has barely awakened to its significance, television has reached from city to city across the nation. It has brought into millions of homes the magic of its immediacy and reality—transmissions of sight and sound combined, with an impact on practically all phases of life.
—DAVID SARNOFF

As early as June, 1936, the FCC had promulgated rules governing visual broadcasting but because of the newness of the medium, did not establish any fixed standards for operations.[1] Considerable research and experimentation were carried on and by late March, 1939, there were 23 licensed TV stations authorized to engage in experimental broadcasting.[2] In the spring of 1939 and again in 1940, the rules governing television were revised.[3] The 1940 revised rules prescribed two classes of television stations:[4]

(1) "Experimental Research Stations" for the development of the television art in its technical aspects;
(2) "Experimental Program Stations" for the development and improvement of program service.

Subsequently, in March, 1941, a formal hearing was initiated by the Commission to consider the establishment of engineering standards, and to determine when television broadcasting should be placed upon a commercial basis.[5]

The outcome of this hearing was the adoption, on April 30, 1941, of rules and regulations and Standards of Good Engineering Practice governing commercial and experimental television stations.[6]

The Commission allocated 18 channels to television, the first nine being located in the 50 to 186 mc. band, and the second nine in the 186 to 294 mc. band.[7]

By January, 1942, there were a number of commercial and experimental television stations licensed to operate.[8] But the freeze on television construction brought on by the War halted, for the time being, the development of television for civilian use.[9]

After the cessation of hostilities, when it became evident that television

149

would expand rapidly, the Commission began a long study looking toward amendment of its rules to provide for a systematic and efficient plan of allocating frequencies to meet the needs of the growing service. After public hearings, the Commission adopted a nation-wide allocation table and made 13 channels available for television broadcasting.[10] Subsequently, channel 1 was deleted from the television assignments and made available to fixed and mobile radio services. The Commission then proposed a distribution of the twelve VHF channels to a total of more than 340 cities in the United States.[11] However, in June and July, 1948, the Commission became concerned that the mileage separations it had proposed for TV stations were insufficient. Accordingly, it institutued further rule making proceedings and in September, 1948 declared a temporary freeze on all new television applications.[12]

These hearings continued intermittently until the latter part of 1951. In April, 1952, the Commission issued its final order in the proceedings, establishing a new fixed table of television assignments.[13]

During the hearings, there were some who urged the Commission not to adopt a nation-wide table of assignments and permit, as is the case in AM broadcasting, the assignment of frequencies in terms of community needs and in accordance with established engineering standards. The Commission rejected this proposal, stating reasons as follows:

13. The Communications Act of 1934, among other things, establishes as a responsibility of the Commission the 'making available to all people of the United States, an efficient nationwide, radio service,' (Section 1) and the effectuation of the distribution of radio facilities in such a manner that the result is fair, efficient and equitable and otherwise in the public interest from the standpoint of the listening and viewing public of the United States (Section 303 and 307b). Our conclusion that these standards can best be achieved by the adoption of a Table of Assignments is based upon three compelling considerations: A Table of Assignments makes for the most efficient technical use of the relatively limited number of channels available for the television service. It protects the interests of the public residing in the smaller cities and rural areas more adequately than any other system for distribution of service and affords the most effective mechanism for providing for noncommercial educational television. It permits the elimination of certain procedural disadvantages in connection with the processing of applications which would otherwise unduly delay the overall availability of television to the people . . .[14]

The Commission assigned 70 UHF (Ultra High Frequency) channels between 470 and 890 megacycles in addition to the 12 VHF (Very High Frequency) channels between 54 and 216 megacycles which were already in use. At the same time, the new table of television assignments made available more than 2000 TV channels in almost 1300 communities throughout the United States, its territories and possessions.

Also, as a result of an impressive showing by educational organizations and interests in the TV allocation hearings, the Commission made channel assignments in 242 communities for noncommercial educational use, 80 of which were VHF and 162 UHF. As of the end of the fiscal year 1958, the FCC had increased the number to 86 VHF and 171 UHF.[15] Since that time, as will be explained later, the Commission has revised its table of TV assignments and many more channels, both educational and commercial, have been added and are available to a vastly larger number of communities in the country.

The Early Growth of Commercial Television. Once the Commission had established the fixed table of assignments, television showed an amazing growth. By the end of 1958, it was estimated that over 90 percent of the population was within service range of at least 1 TV station and that over 75 percent were within range of two or more stations. Nearly 50 million TV sets were in use with more than 80 percent of the homes having one or more such sets.[16]

As of April 25, 1960, *Broadcasting Magazine* reported 526 commercial television stations in operation.[17] Of this number, 449 were VHF and 77 UHF. Also, as of the same date, there were 119 applications for new stations on file and awaiting action of the Commission.[18]

While VHF television had advanced rapidly, UHF was having serious problems. As the Commission said:[19]

. . . It is generally recognized, however, that the greatest difficulties are encountered in achieving successful operation of stations in the UHF band. Since there are only 12 channels in the VHF bands, it was contemplated in 1952 that extensive use of the 70 channels in the UHF band would be required to attain a nation-wide TV service. However, UHF stations have had great difficulty in getting established and in competing with VHF stations. The head start by the VHF system, the present disparity in performance between UHF and VHF transmitting and receiving equipment, and the small number of sets in use and being manufactured that are capable of receiving both UHF and VHF signals are the principal reasons for the difficulties experienced by UHF stations. Other factors, such as the preference of advertisers and other program sources for VHF and UHF outlets, have flowed from the principal reasons and aggravate the UHF difficulties.

The Television Allocations Study Organization (TASO), established in 1957 to study the technical aspects of both VHF and UHF, made its final report in March, 1959. Much of the report was unfavorable to UHF in its state of development at that time.

The Report concluded that (1) a UHF signal deteriorates more rapidly than a VHF signal as the distance from the transmitter increases; (2) a UHF receiving antenna is less efficient than a comparable VHF antenna; and (3) a UHF station costs more to operate than a comparable VHF outlet.

Factors favorable to UHF were found to be (1) the signal is almost impervious to man-made electrical noise and atmospheric interference; (2) within limits of its signal range, UHF is on a par with VHF when it is operating over a level, smooth, treeless terrain.[20]

151

While the TASO study was a comprehensive one, as the report indicated, there was need for further research. Some experts believed that as more was learned regarding the propagation characteristics of UHF frequencies and as sending and receiving equipment was improved, the outlook for UHF television would become brighter.

In its 1961 budget proposal to Congress, the FCC earmarked two million dollars for a UHF research program as a follow-up of the TASO study. Subject to Congressional appropriation, the Commission announced that it would construct a superpower UHF transmitter in the Manhattan area of New York, that receivers would be placed throughout the city, and that a broad scale study over a two-year period would be made to determine the full capabilities of UHF in terms of both technical operation and programming.[21]

Congress did appropriate money, as requested, and the FCC initiated the project. An experimental station was operated for a year on top of the Empire State Building where all seven VHF stations in New York City have their transmitting antennas. With 5,000 UHF receivers distributed throughout an area within a twenty-five mile radius, the FCC made measurements of signal quality. And in July, 1962, the Commission reported, on the basis of 800 measurements, that a "passable or better picture" was received from the UHF station at 77 percent of the locations with an indoor antenna and at 95 percent of the locations with an outdoor antenna. This, according to the Report, was almost as good as VHF reception, with 88 and 98 percent respectively for VHF Station WCBS on Channel Two, and 90 and 97 percent for VHF Station WABC on Channel Seven.[22]

One important finding of the Commission was that elaborate outside antennas were not necessary to get satisfactory UHF reception. Where VHF programs could be received with indoor antennas so could UHF programs. Where outdoor antennas were needed for VHF reception, they were also required for UHF.[23]

New York City officials were so impressed with the success of the experimental project that they filed an application with the FCC to purchase the station. The Commission granted the application, and for a purchase price of $384,000 the City became the owner and regular licensee of the station.[24]

On November 1, 1962, Newton H. Minow, then FCC Chairman, speaking at ceremonies in connection with the assignment of the license to New York City, said:

"[Channel 31's] success in the most difficult reception area of the country shows that UHF will work anywhere and paves the way for the growth of commercial and non-commercial TV."[25]

Many other officials, educators and broadcasters attending the ceremonies made similar comments. A consensus of government and non-government engineers who worked on the project indicated agreement with this view.[26] The experiment seemed to corroborate closely the conclusions of TASO—that UHF worked as well as VHF up to about forty miles from the transmitter. Beyond this, there was deterioration in signal quality, and at seventy miles UHF reception was virtually nil.[27]

The New York experiment generated a new wave of enthusiasm for UHF television. UHF got its biggest boost, however, from Congress. The Commission, for sometime, had been pressing Congress to pass legislation requiring all TV to be equipped to receive UHF as well as VHF programs. On July 10, 1962 Congress responded and passed the all-channel TV receiver law.[28] As authorized by this legislation, the Commission prohibited the shipment in interstate commerce of any TV receiver not equipped for UHF reception manufactured after April 30, 1964.[29] This removed one of the greatest barriers to UHF growth—the scarcity of receivers and comparatively few people able to view the programs.

Advisory Committee on UHF.   On March 12, 1963, the Commission established the Committee for the Full Development of All-Channel Broadcasting.[30] The Committee was composed of three groups, one concerned with equipment and technical rules, another with station operations and program availability, and the third with consumer information. Among the members were representatives of the major networks, the Electronic Industries Association, Maximum Service Telecasters, Committee for Competitive Television, National Association of Broadcasters, National Association of Educational Broadcasters, and numerous other organizations.

Shortly thereafter, as a part of its overall plan to foster UHF expansion, the Commission, on October 24, 1963, proposed a revised allocation plan for UHF channels which it was expected could add over 400 new channel assignments to the television table.[31]

In February, 1965, the Advisory committee on UHF completed a major portion of its work and issued a report dealing with all-channel receivers, UHF antennas and receiving systems, transmitting and studio equipment, and other aspects of UHF operations. On June 3, thereafter, the Commission issued a revised table of UHF channel allocations which became effective July 15, 1965 and March 28, 1966.[32] This made available over 1,000 UHF assignments in the continental United States, of which about 500 were reserved for educational, noncommercial stations. The total was actually less than the FCC had previously proposed. In its 1965 Annual Report, the Commission explained the reason for this:

. . . it was decided not to assign commercial channels to cities less than 25,000 population except where a demand has been shown. It was believed that the needs of these smaller cities may be better served by a new type of "community" TV station, operating with relatively small facilities. With stations of lesser power, it is possible to make many more assignments on each channel because they can be separated from each other at less distances without undue interference. Since few stations are now authorized on channels 70 to 83, it was tentatively decided to reserve these channels for this type of station.

Moreover, with respect to channels 14 through 69, the plan is by no means a saturated one. In many parts of the country it will be possible to make further assignments on these channels where needed. By means of the electronic computer, the Commission will be constantly informed as to remaining availabilities so as to maintain a fair and equitable distribution of assignments among the various States and communities.[33]

Various proposals regarding use of these channels (70-83) had been made. It was suggested that some might be used for high-powered educational and commercial stations in places where critical needs could not be met by assignment of channels below 70. Also the land mobile services have been pressing for additional spectrum space for a number of years and had suggested the use of these channels for their activities. And, as pointed out in Chapter Six, page 108, the Commission had proposed to allocate in large cities some channels in the UHF band to these mobile services. Much lower channels, however, had been proposed.

In May, 1970, the Commission, after long consideration, did issue an order permitting landmobile stations to share one or two of the seven UHF channels in the ten largest urban areas, subject to Commission review at the end of five years (*Broadcasting*, May 18, 1970, pp. 66-68, and June 15, 1970, pp. 35-36).

In a following order dated May 20, 1970, in Docket No. 18262 (FCC 70-519), the Commission reallocated a portion of the TV spectrum comprising UHF channels 70-83 from the broadcasting service to the land mobile service. Accordingly, the FCC abandoned these channels for use by educational institutions and emphasized the importance that educators more fully develop the 2500-2690 MHz frequency band for Instructional Television Fixed Service (FCC Docket No. 14744, FCC 70-640, I RR 54:269, 35 Fed. Reg. 10462). The nature of this instructional TV service is discussed hereinafter on pages 197-98 in Chapter 11.

The TV Table of Assignments and How It May Be Amended. Section 73.606 of the Rules contains a list of the cities throughout the United States with the particular TV channels assigned to each city. Those marked with an asterisk are reserved for education.[34]

Only channels which are listed in the Table of Assignments may be applied for. To make any changes in this table requires the filing of a formal petition with the Commission and a showing that the proposed changes will comply with the requirement for mileage separation of stations operating on the same or adjacent channels and that the public interest will be served.

As provided and graphically described in Section 73.609 of the Rules, the country is divided into three zones. For stations operating on the same channels, or co-channel stations as they are called, the minimum mileage separations in the various zones are as follows.[35]

Zone	Channels 2-13	Channels 14-83
I	170 miles	155 miles
II	190 miles	177 miles
III	220 miles	205 miles

For stations operating on adjacent channels, the minimum mileage separations for all zones are:[36]

Channels 2-13	Channels 14-83
60 miles	55 miles

Since the TV Table of Assignments was established many petitions to make channel changes have been filed with the FCC. Some have been granted while others have been denied, the action of the Commission depending upon the facts of each case and whether the public interest seemed to justify the proposed change. For information on all changes in the Television Table of Assignments approved by the FCC since the table was adopted in 1952, 1 RR 53:1341-1362 should be consulted.

Non-Commercial Educational Television. In the post-war television hearings, to which reference has been made above, educators made an impressive showing regarding the possibilities of using television for educational purposes. More than 70 witnesses appeared before the Commission and urged that TV channels be reserved for the exclusive use of education. More than 800 colleges, universities, state boards of education, school systems, and public service agencies submitted written statements urging the Commission to make the reservations. Distinguished professors pointed out how television could be used to extend the services of educational institutions in the sciences, arts, humanities, vocational education and other important areas of learning. As the Joint Council on Educational Television has pointed out, mayors, parent teacher groups, chambers of commerce, libraries, art associations, newspapers, civic groups, municipal boards, clergymen, prominent members of Congress, men representing both of the major political parties, and others either testified or submitted written statements in behalf of these educational TV assignments.[37]

The Joint Council and a host of educational organizations including the American Council on Education, the National Education Association, the

National Association of Land-Grant Colleges and Universities, the National Association of Broadcasters, the Council of Chief State School Officers joined in the crusade. The result of these joint efforts, as already pointed out, was the reservation of 242 channels (the number now is more than 600 VHF and UHF) for the exclusive use of education with each state receiving a large number of assignments.

The reservation of these channels parallels in a striking way the passage of the Morrill Act in 1859. This Act made available large areas of land in the public domain to help establish public colleges. From this has developed a nation-wide system of land-grant institutions that has become favorably recognized throughout the world. Similarly, the FCC's historic act of 1952 setting aside another part of the public domain, the broadcasting spectrum for educational use has opened up a new and valuable frontier in American education.[38]

Following the FCC's action in 1952, numerous states held state-wide meetings to arouse interest in the activation of these reserved channels. Many committees were organized throughout the country to study the financial, programming and engineering problems of building educational stations.

Numerous governors and legislatures took definite steps to investigate the potentialities of educational television. Numerous foundations including the Fund for Adult Education, Ford Foundation, Twentieth Century Fund, Payne Fund, and others were early contributors to the educational TV movement.

On December 3, 1952, the Fund for Adult Education announced the formation of the National Citizens Committee on Educational Television with Milton S. Eisenhower and Marion B. Folsom as co-chairmen. Two days later, the Fund announced the formation of a National Educational Television and Radio Center. The purpose of this center, financed with an original grant of over a million dollars, was to aid in the exchange, circulation, and development of quality films and kinescopes to be used by educational television stations.[39]

In May, 1953, only one of the reserved TV channels had been activated. By the end of 1954, however, eight educational stations were on the air. Eight additional stations were in operation by the end of 1955 followed by five more in 1956, six in 1957, eight in 1958, and seven as of April, 1960.[40] On September 1, 1970, as reported in *Broadcasting,* there were more than 200 on the air.

With this many educational television stations on the air, and numerous others under construction or in the advanced planning stage—plus state-wide networks and others being contemplated—there can be no doubt that educational TV has reached an advanced stage in its development and may now be considered firmly rooted in American life.

What the Joint Council on Educational Television said in 1954 is even more true today:[41]

The stresses and strains of this atomic age have imposed new problems on the citizen and the society in which he lives. His physical and psychological security is threatened in a tense and competitive world. Health, home, livelihood, retirement, social unrest, war—these and many other areas of individual concern make him eager to secure new and continuing knowledge. As our report shows, educational stations are now offering a wide variety of informational and instructional programs designed to help supply this knowledge speedily and effectively.

The American citizen also wants to make the most effective use of his leisure time and to benefit more fully from the cultural resources and influences so abundant in this country and other parts of the world. Accordingly, educational television stations are bringing into his home the reality and beauty of famous museums, art galleries, educational centers, parks and gardens, and historical sites. Also, they are making it possible for him to see and hear—on a regular basis—distinguished scholars in the fields of science, philosophy, literature, and so forth, and artists in the fields of painting, sculpture, music, dance, and drama.

It is clear that educational television has made and is making real progress. There are problems but these are gradually but surely being overcome. The facts clearly show that educational television is having a tremendous effect upon the educational and cultural life of the nation.

Eligibility and Operating Requirements for Educational TV Stations.
Eligibility requirements for educational television stations are essentially the same as those for educational FM stations. Section 73.621 of the FCC Rules states that they may be licensed only to non-profit, educational organizations upon a showing that they will be used primarily to serve the educational needs of the community; for the advancement of educational programs; and to furnish a non-profit and non-commercial television broadcast service. In determining eligibility of public and private educational institutions to hold licenses, as is the case with educational FM stations, the factor of accreditation is also taken into account.[42]

While the rules that classify the services and prescribe the purposes for which educational FM and TV were substantially the same, there were a few differences. Section 73.621 of the Rules pertaining to licensing requirements and character of service contained some language and provisions which did not appear in Section 73.503 covering the same subject regarding educational FM stations. For example, paragraph (a) of Section 73.621 was a bit more expansive than paragraph (a) of Section 73.503. It read:

(a) Except as provided in paragraph (b) of this section, noncommercial educational broadcast stations will be licensed only to non-profit educational organizations upon a showing that the proposed station will be used primarily to serve the educational needs of the community; for the advancement of educational programs; and to furnish a non-profit and non-commercial television service.[43]

The language of paragraph (d) and (e) of Section 73.621 relating to educational TV stations did not appear at all in Section 73.503 of the non-commercial educational FM rules. These paragraphs stated:

157

(d) An educational station may not broadcast programs for which a consideration is received, except programs produced by or at the expense of or furnished by others than the licensee for which no other consideration than the furnishing of the program is received by the licensee. The payment of the charges by another station or network shall not be considered as being prohibited by this paragraph.

(e) To the extent applicable to programs broadcast by a noncommercial educational station produced by or at the expense of or furnished by others than the licensee of said station, the provisions of Section 73.654 relating to announcements regarding sponsored programs shall be applicable, except that no announcements (visual or aural) promoting the sale of a product or service shall be transmitted in connection with any program; provided, however, that where a sponsor's name or product appears on the visual image during the course of a simultaneous or rebroadcast program, either on the backdrop or in similar form, the portions of the program showing such information need not be deleted.[44]

These former rules required some interpretation. They prohibited educational TV stations from broadcasting any program for which pay is received. Exceptions to this permitted the broadcast of recorded programs furnished by others or the use of programs, the costs of producing which are defrayed by others, provided the programs constituted the only consideration derived by the station. Also, the rules did not preclude a commercial network or station from paying line charges in connection with the furnishing of programs to educational TV stations.

In adopting the rules, it was the Commission's intention that educational TV stations should not sponsor the sale of goods, and commercial announcements were prohibited. In order that these stations might carry outstanding educational programs made available by commercial networks, the Commission did not require the deletion of visual images or pictorial material containing the name of the sponsor or his product. Aural commercials, however, in connection with such network programs, were required to be deleted by the educational TV station.

Business institutions did and have supplied many fine programs on educational TV stations. Simple identification on the air of the institutions furnishing the programs did not contravene the rules against advertising on these stations, so long as the design was not to promote the business of the institution or the sale of its goods. However, the interpretation by the Commission of Section 317 of Communications Act (to which reference was made in the preceding chapter), which required stations, both commercial and non-commercial, when using free recordings to identify the commercial distributors, presented somewhat the same dilemma for educational TV stations that it did for educational FM stations. As previously pointed out, however, recent legislation by Congress has eliminated the confusion.

Because of some differences in language of the rules pertaining to educational TV and FM stations, the Commission, on May 6, 1970, adopted an order clarifying language of the rules and making other changes to comform to the regulations of both the educational TV and FM services. Section 73.503, paragraphs (d) and (e) have been added to read:

(d) A noncommercial educational television station may broadcast programs produced by or at the expense of, or furnished by persons other than the licensee, if no other consideration than the furnishing of the program and the costs incidental to its production and broadcast are received by the licensee. The payment of line charges by another station, network, or someone other than the licensee of a non-commerical educational television station, or general contributions to the operating costs of a station, shall not be considered as being prohibited by this paragraph.

(e) Each station shall furnish a non-profit and noncommercial broadcast service. However, noncommercial educational television stations shall be subject to the provisions of § 73.654 to the extent that they are applicable to the broadcast of programs produced by, or at the expense of, or furnished by others, except that no announcements (visual or aural) promoting the sale of a product or service shall be broadcast in connection with any program: *Provided, however,* that where a sponsor's name or product appears on the visual image during the course of a simultaneous or rebroadcast program either on the backdrop or in similar form, the portions of the program showing such information need not be deleted.

Announcements of the furnishing or producing of programs may be made no more than twice, at the opening and at the close of any program. The person or organization furnishing or producing the program shall be identified by name only, and no mention shall be made of any product or service with which it may have a connection.

Announcements of general contributions of a substantial nature which make possible the broadcast of programs for part, or all, of the day's schedule may be made no more than three times during the broadcast day. (See 19 RR 2d 1501; paragraphs (d) and (e) and notes related thereto of section 73.621).

1. Fed. Reg. 536 (1936). For full story of Commission's concern with television and development of rules governing the service prior to the War see Warner, Harry P., *Radio and Television Law* (New York, 1953), pp. 620-667.

2. FCC Mimeograph No. 32563, February 27, 1939.

3. FCC Docket No. 5806, February 29, 1940, 5 Fed. Reg. 933 (1940).

4. FCC Mimeograph No. 39404, February 29, 1940, *Ibid.*

5. FCC Mimeograph No. 47053, January 28, 1941.

6. FFC Mimeograph No. 49832, May 2, 1941, 6 Fed. Reg. 2284.

7. *Ibid.*

8. FCC Mimeograph No. 57820, January 1, 1942.

9. FCC Memorandum Opinion, Mimeograph No. 59725, April 27, 1942.

10. FCC Docket No. 6780, November 21, 1945.

11. FCC Report and Order, Docket No. 8487, May 5, 1948.

12. FCC Log, *op. cit.*, p. 62; also Section 13 Fed. Reg. 5182 (1948).

13. FCC Sixth Report and Order, 17 Fed. Reg. 3905-4100, May 2, 1952.

14. *Ibid.*, P. 3906.

15. FCC *Annual Report,* 1958, p. 108.

16. *Ibid.*, p. 101.

17. *Broadcasting,* April 25, 1960, p. 104.

18. *Ibid.*

19. FCC *Annual Report,* 1958, p. 102.

20. *Broadcasting,* March 16, 1959, pp. 165-183.

21. See *Broadcasting,* April 25, 1960, p. 82, for report on and discussion of this research project. The project was authorized, and on October 5, 1960, the FCC announced that "the New York project for which Congress appropriated two million dollars is under the direction of the Commission's Chief Engineer and a special unit, aided by technical advice of the cooperating committees." (FCC Public Notice-B 94811, Oct. 5, 1960)

22. *Broadcasting,* November 5, 1962, p. 70.

23. *Ibid.*

24. *Ibid.*

25. *Ibid.*

26. *Ibid.*

27. *Ibid.*

28. 76 Stat. 150-151.

29. FCC *Annual Report,* 1963, p. 66.

30. *Ibid.*, p. 68.

31. FCC *Annual Report,* 1964, p. 68.

32. 30 Fed. Reg. 7711, 8680, 8681; 31 Fed. Reg. 2932. For *Report* see 5 RR 2d 1587, 6 RR 2d 1643.

33. FCC *Annual Report,* 1965, p. 111.

34. FCC Rules, Section 73.606, 47 CFR 201-208, 1 RR 53:1322-1328.

35. Section 73.610, 47 CFR 209, 1 RR 53:1383.

36. Section 73.610, 47 CFR 209-210, 1 RR 53:1383-1384.

37. Joint Council on Educational Television, *Four Years of Progress in Educational Television,* (Washington, D.C. 1956), p.20.

38. *Ibid.*, p. 1.

39. Based on information in files of JCET. Additional information about the functions of these organizations and the services they have provided may be obtained from the Joint Council on Educational Telecommunications, Washington, D.C.

40. *Ibid.* See JCET *Educational Television Factsheet,* April 1960.
41. JCET, *Four Years of Progress in Educational Television, op. cit.,* pp. 18-19.
42. Section 73.621, 1 RR 53:715, 716, 47 CFR 213.
43. *Ibid.*
44. *Ibid.*

CHAPTER 10

American Broadcasting Overseas*

We here have an obligation to do everything within our power to strengthen the Voice of America. The voice that reaches out from our shores must be firm and clear. It must speak the truth in all the basic tongues of mankind. It must be heard throughout the world. The Voice of America must play its part in the fulfillment of the prophecy that "nation shall speak peace unto nation."—CHARLES R. DENNY**.

International Broadcast Stations

Several international broadcast stations are authorized to operate in the United States. These stations, as defined by the Rules of the Federal Communications Commission, are those whose transmissions are intended to be received directly by the general public in foreign countries. Seven discrete bands of frequencies between 5,950 and 26,100 kilocycles have been allocated by the FCC for this service.[1]

Section 73.788 of the FCC Rules provides that these stations "shall render only an international broadcast service which will reflect the culture of this country and promote international good will, understanding and cooperation. Any program solely intended for, and directed to an audience in the continental United States does not meet the requirements of this service."[2]

FCC Form 309 is used to apply for a construction permit to build one of these international broadcast stations.[3] This is followed by the submission of FCC Form 310 which requires proof that the construction has been satisfactorily completed and requests a license for operation.[4]

The Commission has stated that a license will be issued only after the applicant has satisfactorily shown that:

* Reprint of Chapter 32 in author's book, *National and International Systems of Broadcasting: Their History, Operation and Control* (1969), with permission of publisher, Michigan State University Press, East Lansing.
**Former FCC Chairman.

(1) there is a need for the service;

(2) necessary program resources are available;

(3) directive antennas and other technical facilities will be used to deliver maximum signals to the "target" area or areas for which the service is designed;[5]

(4) competent personnel will be used;

(5) the applicant is technically and financially qualified and possesses adequate facilities to carry forward the service proposed; and finally,

(6) the public interest will be served by the proposed international broadcast operation.[6]

Such stations are licensed for unlimited time operation. However, certain stations receive frequency authorizations four times a year with hours for operation and target areas specified.[7] International stations must operate with not less than fifty kilowatts of power and their signals must have a strength of at least one hundred and fifty microvolts per meter fifty percent of the time in the distant target area.[8]

Assignment of Frequencies.   Section 73.702 of the Rules says that frequencies in the bands allocated to the international broadcast service will be assigned to authorized stations for use at certain hours and for transmission to stated target areas.[9] Licensees may request the use of specific frequencies for particular hours of operation by filing informal requests in triplicate with the Commission six months prior to the start of a new season.[10] These requests are honored to the extent that interference and propagation conditions permit.[11]

Not more than one frequency is authorized for use at any one time for any one program transmission except in instances where a program is intended for reception in more than one target area and the intended target areas cannot be served by a single frequency.[12]

In 1955, the World Wide Broadcasting Company, the former licensee of international broadcasting station WRUL,[13] petitioned the Commission to reconsider its prohibition against using more than one frequency for transmitting programs to the same area. The station contended that other nations, particularly Russia, employ multiple frequencies to transmit programs to the same area causing interference to certain frequencies used by U.S. international stations, making it necessary for the latter to use more than one to insure reception in a particular area.

The Commission denied the petition on the grounds that such multiple frequency transmission to the same area is inconsistent with Article XLIII of the Convention of the International Telecommunications Union which requires the Commission to limit the number of frequencies and spectrum space to the minimum necessary to render satisfactory service. The Commission said, however, it would "take appropriate action" to protect the station from harmful interference caused by foreign stations operating in violation of international agreements.[14]

The Commission has stated that "all specific frequency authorizations will be made only on the express understanding that they are subject to immediate cancellation or change without hearing whenever the Commission determines that interference or propagation conditions so require and that each assignment of 'frequency hours'[15] for a given season is unique unto itself and not subject to renewal, with the result that completely new assignments must be secured for the forthcoming season."[16]

Section 73.792 of the Rules describes the geographic areas to be served by an international broadcast station.[17] Licensees sending programs to several of these areas must specify one as *primary*, and state the reasons for the choice, with special reference to the nature and special suitability of the proposed programming.[18]

Commercial Programs Permitted. International broadcast stations are permitted to carry commercial or sponsored programs provided no more than the name of the sponsor and the name and general character of the commodity or service is advertised.

Section 73.788 of the Rules gives several other restrictions on advertising: (1) a commodity advertised must be one regularly sold or being promoted for sale on the open market in the foreign area to which the program is directed; (2) commercial continuity advertising an American utility or service to prospective visitors must be particularly directed to such persons in the foreign countries where they reside and to which the program is directed; and (3) where an international attraction such as a world fair or resort is being advertised, the oral continuity must be consistent with the purpose and intent of the provisions in this Section.[19]

Operational Requirements. The FCC Rules contain specific requirements regarding the equipment and operation of international broadcast stations. These technical requirements, relating to power, frequency control, antenna design, auxiliary and alternate main transmitters, changes in equipment and keeping and preserving logs, are in many ways substantially the same as those governing other broadcast stations. However, some differences are necessary because of the service's special character. For example, antennas must be so designed and operated that the field intensity of the signal toward the specific country served will be 3.16 times the average effective signal from the station.[20] Moreover, station identification, program announcements, and oral continuity must have international significance and be communicated in a language suitable to the foreign areas for which the service is primarily intended.[21]

Licenses for international broadcast stations are issued for one year only.[22] Unless otherwise directed by the Commission, each renewal application must be filed at least ninety days prior to the expiration date of the license.[23] FCC Form 311 is used in applying for the renewal.[24] A supplementary statement must also be submitted showing the number of hours the station has operated on each assigned frequency, listing contract and private operations separately,[25] and reporting reception, interference and conclusions regarding propagation characteristics of assigned frequencies.[26]

THERE are only three private international broadcasting stations operating in the United States under the regulations discussed above: WINB, Red Lion, Pennsylvania; WNYW, Scituate, Massachusetts; and KGEI, Belmont, California. The Voice of America, however, an instrument of the United States Information Agency (USIA), is the official U.S. Government radio, and, as such, operates a large number of high-power stations beaming programs to many parts of the world.

Section 305(a) of the Communications Act of 1934 states that radio stations belonging to and operated by any agency of the United States Government are not subject to the regulatory powers of the FCC as set forth in Sections 301 and 303 of the Act.[27] The only exception is that government stations (not including those on government ships beyond the continental limits of the United States) when transmitting a radio communication or signal relating to government business must conform to Commission regulations designed to prevent interference with other radio stations and the rights of others.[28]

Accordingly, the President, through delegated authority, assigns the frequencies to the USIA for the Voice of America transmissions. The VOA's program policies and pattern of operation are determined by the USIA. The Director of the Agency reports to the President through the National Security Council. Since one of the Voice's chief functions is to report and interpret to foreign peoples policies and actions of the U.S. Government and promote national security, its activities are closely coordinated with the White House, the State Department, the Office of Civil and Defense Mobilization, the military establishment and other government organizations concerned with the country's position and participation in world affairs.[29]

The Voice, with headquarters and central studios in Washington, began on February 4, 1942. On the first day of its operation, with the Nazis on the rampage in Europe, a VOA announcer broadcast in German via shortwave these words: "Daily, at this time, we shall speak to you about America and the war. The news may be good or bad—we shall tell you the truth." This, say the VOA officials, has continued to be the guiding principle of all programming.[30]

After the war, the program services were expanded. Statesmen, educators, artists, writers, businessmen and laborers were brought before the microphones to express their ideas about the American way of life and world affairs in general. News reporting was greatly increased. Other program features were added. Since the operation was financed by the Federal Government and programs had to be approved by officials in Washington, convenience and economy dictated that headquarters be moved there. In 1954, the offices and studios were moved into the Health, Education and Welfare Building. Subsequently, new transmitters were built and the old ones improved. Overseas program centers were built, and a world-wide network of correspondents was established.

The Voice has grown rapidly since 1954 and now has thirty-eight transmitters in the United States and fifty-four abroad, with a combined output of more than fifteen million watts. Programs are sent via microwave and telephone lines from Washington to the domestic broadcasting sites where they are relayed by short-wave to overseas relay stations which in turn boost them to the intended reception areas. The VOA operates transmitters in Greenville, North Carolina; Marathon, Florida; Dixon and Delano, California; and Bethany, Ohio. The Greenville operation is said to be the world's largest broadcasting facility, having an output of almost five million watts, equal to the transmitting power of nearly one hundred of the largest commercial stations in the United States.

The overseas establishment of the Voice includes transmitting installations at Woofferton, England; Munich, Germany; Tangier, Morocco; Thessaloniki and Rhodes, Greece; Okinawa; the island of Luzon in the Philippines; Colombo, Ceylon; Monrovia, Liberia; and Hue, Vietnam. New transmitters are being built in northern Thailand, northern Greece and the Philippines.

In addition to the overseas booster stations, there are more than five thousand foreign-owned and operated stations in many parts of the world that carry programs produced and supplied by the Voice. In fact, about thirteen thousand hours of its programs are carried each week by these stations.[31]

The VOA now broadcasts more than eight hundred and fifty hours weekly in thirty-seven languages to an overseas audience estimated in the tens of millions.[32] The programs are varied, with about fifty percent devoted to up-to-the-minute news and commentaries on current developments throughout the world.

In addition to the straight news, the Voice prepares and broadcasts many commentaries, analyzing and interpreting important national and international events. In preparing these commentaries, it has access to a wide variety of informational services, including the White House, the State Department, other government agencies, the commercial news services and its own reporters.

The VOA's charter states the following guiding principles for news analysis and reporting:

1. VOA will establish itself as a consistently reliable and authoritative source of news. VOA news will be accurate, objective and comprehensive.

2. VOA will represent America, not any single segment of American society. It will therefore present a balanced and comprehensive projection of significant American thought and institutions.

3. As an official radio, VOA will present policies of the United States clearly and effectively. VOA will also present responsible discussion on these policies.[33]

Another important component of Voice programs is music. A brochure published by the VOA contains the following discussion of its musical broadcasts:

Music, considered as the greatest common denominator in attracting and holding a radio audience, occupies an important place in VOA programming. Music is one of the few genuine American products which can be offered to foreign listeners first hand. Music is not thought of solely in terms of entertainment but also as an important means of conveying a message, telling a story. The Voice has created programs that cut across historical, educational, cultural and religious lines. For example, by projecting a series of programs called *Music in Our Schools,* VOA also reflected the activities and interest of American youth in cultural fields. Another series, *Musical Folkways,* used music to relate the entire history of the founding and development of the United States and its democratic principles.

There are some 600 symphony orchestras in the United States. The world is generally familiar with the Big Three—the New York Philharmonic, and the Boston and Philadelphia symphony orchestras—but the Voice of America records concerts by many other orchestras representative of various sections of the country. It covers numerous music festivals: the Aspen Music Festival in Colorado, the Berkshire Festival in Massachusetts, the Newport Jazz Festival in Rhode Island, and the Folk Festival in North Carolina.

Popular music and jazz fill the widely-listened-to program, *Music USA.* Music selections are often accompanied by interviews with leading personalities in the jazz and popular fields on various aspects of style, development and history of American music.

. . .

In most musical programs of the Voice of America, music, with its universal message is an end in itself. But music is also used in many narrative programs to add diversity and interest. In both cases, whether used incidentally or as the principal ingredient of a program, music displays an aspect of living culture in the United States and the creative people who contribute to it.[34]

Various other types of programs are presented. Well-known statesmen, scientists, philosophers, authors, clergymen and others discuss a wide range of important topics and public issues in forums which reflect, in general, contemporary thinking in the United States. Also, some of the finest dramatic, artistic and literary talent is brought before the microphones to give the world a balanced view of American culture.[35]

The Soviet Union stopped jamming VOA programs in 1963. Although it is costly and not very effective, Communist China, Bulgaria and Cuba continue to jam the VOA's programs. Nevertheless, the response to Voice programs is reported to be good. For example, in replies to announcements during a single week, in 1964, the Voice received thirty-five thousand letters from listeners in Latin America, including fifteen hundred from Cuba. Over twenty-five thousand Brazilians responded, and broadcasts in English brought in over eighty-five thousand replies from almost every country in the world including Communist China.[36] Total audience mail now runs over two hundred thousand letters a year.

In 1965, the Voice spent $28,819,536 to finance its operations, and the expenditures for 1966-67 were over thirty-two million.[37] In addition, more than twenty-six million dollars was requested from Congress in 1966 to construct new and improve existing facilities.[38]

While the Voice is concerned with radio, the USIA provides many television programs for stations overseas. Regular series have been produced by the Agency for countries such as Japan, Nigeria, Thailand and Latin America. Some USIA programs have been carried by more than eighty stations throughout Latin America. Broadcasts such as "Let Us Continue" (how democratic life continues even if a President is assassinated), "Some of Our Voices" (new cultural developments) and "Adventures in English" are a few of the USIA television programs which have been widely seen in other countries.

Radio in the American Sector (RIAS)

RIAS, a radio station in West Berlin owned and operated by the United States Information Agency, began as a wired radio system in early 1946, sending out news and recorded music to several hundred telephone subscribers. Its audience grew rapidly and it soon took to the air with a larger variety of entertainment and educational broadcasts.

It now provides two separate programs. Its principal program (RIAS I) is broadcast twenty-four hours daily by one three hundred kilowatt and one one hundred kilowatt medium-wave transmitter, plus one twenty kilowatt short-wave facility at night. All these facilities are located in West Berlin. Two FM stations there also carry this program. RIAS also uses one VOA one hundred kilowatt transmitter in Munich. In Hof, in Bavaria, RIAS also maintains a forty kilowatt installation and one FM station.[39]

The second program (RIAS II), on the air during the evening and other select times, repeats some RIAS I broadcasts, including those that may have special political or cultural significance and musical programs that appeal to a more sophisticated audience.

With its two programs, RIAS broadcasts thirty-three hours each weekday, thirty-five hours on Saturday and forty hours on Sundays and holidays.[40]

The station, with a staff of almost five hundred, presents a wide variety of programming—straight news, educational broadcasts, music (chamber, choral and orchestral, ranging from classical to modern), drama, religious programs, light entertainment such as quiz shows and situation comedies and other special features. Ninety percent of all these programs are produced by the RIAS staff and facilities.

Officials of the station have stated:

RIAS is today, more than ever, the bridge between the Free World and the people of the Soviet Zone of Germany. When Walter Ulbricht began the erection of the Wall the morning of August 13, 1961, the manifold contacts between East and West came abruptly to a halt. . . . Radio, and to a lesser extent, television, remain the only media of exchange between the Free World and the unwilling inmates of the "German Democratic Republic." RIAS now carries an even heavier responsibility than before in informing the East Berliners and the East Germans of the true nature of events in their own country and in the world, and in providing continuing cultural contacts with the West.[41]

In this connection, RIAS provides regular political commentaries. The station has explained its pattern of broadcasting in this regard:

While the basic philosophy of RIAS is that the facts speak for themselves, it is imperative that RIAS expresses its own opinion on the significance of particular events in the public eye at the moment. When RIAS takes a stand on such an issue, it is clearly labeled as commentary. Thus, its main political commentary is introduced with the words, "And now, our evening commentary," followed by the author's name. When comments on developments outside Germany are necessary, the commentary may be written in Berlin, or by the RIAS correspondent in the country indicated. This correspondent is generally a German journalist with an international reputation, also representing a major German newspaper. In this case, the commentary is by the individual concerned, and carries his name. All commentaries are succinct; rarely do they exceed 6 minutes.[42]

In addition to the two or three daily commentaries, RIAS supplements its hourly newscasts with analysis and interpretation designed to help put current events in perspective for East Germans. On RIAS I, the news commentaries and analyses are interspersed with popular music nine hours each day. On RIAS II, the news and commentaries are often presented in much greater depth for more discerning listeners.

RIAS has further stated that "roundtable discussions are frequently used to present divergent but basically free opinion on matters of political and cultural interest. The traditional European political cabaret is not used to make fun of the problems of the people in the Soviet Zone, but rather to point out in a light vein the understanding and sympathy of the free peoples for those problems. . . ."[43]

Radio Free Europe

THE early operations of RIAS and its broadcasts to East Germany were influential in the development of plans for Radio Free Europe (RFE), a private American network with five stations broadcasting to the communist East European countries. While he was the U.S. Commander in Germany in 1948-49, General Lucius D. Clay was greatly impressed with the RIAS broadcasts. Upon his return to the United States, he proposed a similar operation "to break the Communist monopoly of communications in the satellite states of centrál Eastern Europe."[44] This led to the organization of the National Committee for a Free Europe in 1949 by a group of distinguished American citizens. The Committee, now called Free Europe, Inc., is a private, nonprofit organization incorporated under the laws of New York and managed entirely by U.S. citizens and organizations. Almost one hundred organizations in the United States make financial contributions to the operation. Solicitations for funds are made over the national networks and contributions come in from many individuals over the country.

The RFE's main offices in New York City are maintained by a staff of about ninety-seven. Its operations include the publication of *East Europe*, a monthly journal of information and opinion regarding affairs in the communist world which is circulated in eight countries. Another of the Committee's functions is to provide liaison with national and international organizations established by exiles from nine communist countries in Eastern Europe.

The most important function is Radio Free Europe, initiated July 4, 1950. Its studios in Munich and thirty-one transmitters (combined power of over 2,260,000 watts) in Portugal and West Germany make up one of the largest broadcast operations in the world. In 1966, the RFE averaged about nineteen hours of broadcasting a day to Poland, Czechoslovakia and Hungary, twelve hours to Rumania and about seven and one-half hours to Bulgaria.[45] Only the languages of these countries were used in its programs.

That same year, news reports occupied about seventeen percent of its broadcast schedules with politically significant programs running to forty-four percent. Music took about twenty-five percent of the total time. The remaining fourteen percent consisted of religious programs representing all faiths, educational and cultural features, dramatic shows (some satirical) and special programs for farmers and other labor groups.[46]

RFE programs have included reports on outstanding cultural events in the West, including interviews with well-known personalities. Direct coverage of a European music festival, transmission from backstage at an American jazz concert, and live broadcasts of important dramatic and operatic performances typify the many special programs which RFE has carried.

As a basis for preparing the news commentaries, radio stations in communist countries are extensively monitored and hundreds of communist publications are studied. Information derived from the reports of western observers and interviews with travelers and refugees from the Eastern European countries are also useful in the analysis and interpretation of news reports from foreign stations and news agencies.[47]

Exiles from the communist countries within the station's coverage area make up the personnel of the broadcast departments. They write and broadcast the programs under the direction of an American director who is assisted by a staff of specialists in East European affairs.

It has been estimated that eighty-four million people live in the five countries covered by the RFE and that more than half the families in these countries have sets capable of receiving its programs. RFE surveys have indicated that about thirty-eight percent of the persons in Bulgaria, forty-one percent in Czechoslovakia, forty-five percent in Rumania, fifty-two percent in Hungary and fifty-six percent in Poland listen to its programs at least twice a week. There are no laws *per se* against listening to the RFE, although the radio stations and the press in the reception countries frequently attack its operations. RFE has also reported that there is a large amount of jamming of the Czechoslovak and Bulgarian programs but states that, through imaginative engineering techniques and transmission of the same program on multi-channels, ninety percent of the RFE signals reach the target areas unimpaired.[48]

A West European Advisory Committee (WEAC) of the prominent citizens counsels the RFE on matters of policy. In May 1967, this Committee held its eleventh session. Eminent political and intellectual leaders from eleven West European countries held discussions with Free Europe officials on "Building Bridges to East Europe," and the RFE's role in East-West communication.[49]

RFE's Philosophy of International Broadcasting

THE Free Europe Committee's philosophy of broadcasting, the mission of RFE and its criteria for programming have been presented in various materials published by the Committee. One of the RFE's important principles, that all peoples have a right to secure pertinent facts and opinions concerning world developments, is confirmed by Article XIX of the Universal Declaration of Human Rights. RFE believes that a free flow of information across national boundaries is essential to individual and national freedom everywhere. Since Eastern European countries do not accept this principle, RFE feels it is a moral responsibility to broadcast to these countries.

A second tenet of its philosophy is that people ultimately can reach intelligent decisions if they have access to the important facts. And it conceives as a major task the making of public opinion in East Europe more enlightened and a more effective force for democracy.

Moreover, the station views the communist governments as unpopular with the people and believes they will continue to be so as long as these regimes suppress individual liberties. And, while totalitarianism may compel obedience for a time, the yearning of the people for freedom will ultimately prevail and they will insist on a return of their rights.

RFE officials look upon the communist regimes of East Europe as quite different from other types of authoritarian governments to which the station does not broadcast. The Communists, it is said, are hostile to the "free

171

world" and determined to remake it in the Marxist image. As a part of an international "camp," they are committed to aggressive action and force, if necessary, to attain their goals.

In carrying out its mission, RFE seeks to break the news monopoly exercised by the East European governments and to provide citizens in these countries with full information about important developments within as well as outside their national boundaries. It hopes to convince these peoples that the communist system must fail since it is antipathetic to human aspirations, and that their destiny is more logically and properly linked with the democracies of the West.

RFE Criteria for Selection of Broadcasting Materials

In a July 15, 1964 statement regarding the sources for RFE newscasts, the RFE staff said:

RFE newscasts must be accurate, objective, truthful and complete as possible. In general, unconfirmed, opinionated, or interpretive material will not be used in newscasts. Newscasts must carefully avoid slanting or taking material out of context. Primary responsibility for newscasts lies with the individual broadcasting departments, whose selection and presentation of newscast material is guided by the needs and interests of their audiences and the general objectives of RFE.[50]

Another important aspect of the RFE operation is the separation of the news reports and editorials. While the station does broadcast editorials, they are always labeled as such and may not be included as integral parts of newscasts.

RFE officials wish to create an image of credibility. Accordingly, they insist that news be carefully checked for accuracy, that the commentaries be as objective as possible, and that the program schedules be well balanced, even to the extent of presenting views which are contrary to those held by the station. For example, one program, "Press Review," which covers a wide spectrum of national and international opinion on important current topics, is especially designed for this purpose.

Radio Liberty

The American Committee for Liberation, like the Free Europe Committee, is a private organization of prominent U.S. citizens. It was incorporated January 18, 1951, under the laws of New York. Its expressed purpose is to promote democracy in the Soviet Union. Those who shape the Committee's policies state that their main purpose is to help bring about the "liberation" of peoples in the Soviet Union and the "establishment of a genuine representative government responsible to the will of the people."[51]

It is financed by private interests in the United States and receives no revenue from foreign countries. The President and his high-level staff direct the varied activities of the organization from the New York offices.

One of its principal functions is research which is conducted through its Institute for the Study of the USSR. The Institute maintains a library of more than fifty-five thousand volumes, including a large number of books and periodicals dating to Imperial Russia. And through microfilm processes it has developed a complete file of the Russian publications, *Pravda* and *Izvestia*, dating to 1917.

The Committee has a large research staff of Soviet scholars, many of whom left the USSR for political reasons. With the aid of these scholars and other specialists, it publishes authoritative materials on the Soviet Union in English, Russian, French, German, Spanish, Turkish, Arabic, Ukrainian and other languages.

Other activities have included sponsoring international symposia with world-renowned experts discussing important current developments in Russia, and schools for the study of the Russian language attracting students from the United States, Canada, Europe, Africa, Asia and Australia. The Institute has also provided facilities for research by scholars who have fellowships with universities and other educational organizations.

The Committee's most important activity is the operation of Radio Liberty with studios in Munich. This station broadcasts twenty-four hours a day, over seventeen transmitters in West Germany, Spain and Formosa with a combined output of 1,840,000 watts. Whereas RFE directs its programs to five countries in Eastern Europe, Radio Liberty beams its programs largely to the Soviet Union and the Soviet armies in East Germany, Poland and Hungary. These programs are broadcast in seventeen languages spoken in the USSR.

Radio Liberty's programming centers is a reconstructed former airport building at Oberwiesenfeld on the outskirts of Munich. The staff consists mostly of former Soviet citizens—more than two hundred officials, writers, scientists, teachers and politicial leaders—representing more than a dozen nationalities in their homeland.

Two programs are presented over the station. The First Program begins at seven o'clock in the evening, Moscow time, and runs for two hours. This two hour segment is repeated around the clock. The Second Program begins at nine o'clock in the evening, runs for one hour, and is repeated throughout the evening and most of the next day.

A review of one week's broadcasts in 1965 (said to be typical of the station's operation) on the First Program showed the following schedules for Sunday and Monday of that week.[52]

Sunday: 7:00 P.M.—News; 7:15—Newsmagazine; 7:30—Suggested by a Listener: Russia Yesterday, Today and Tomorrow—Present-day Soviet Society in a Historical Perspective; 7:50—Paths to Peace—An Analysis of Practical Approaches to Peace and Ways to Insure It; 8:00—News; 8:15—Panorama; 8:30-9:00—Discussion: The Youth Show—Life, Travel, Recreation, Student Affairs, Education, and Opportunities in the Free World.

Monday: 7:00—News; 7:15—News Features; 7:30—Doctor's Talk; 7:40 —Listeners Present Their Views: Answers to Letters; 8:50—A Service for the Consumer: Technology in Everyday Life; 9:00—News; 9:15—News Features; 9:30—Book-of-the-Week Program—The Bookshelf—Books Banned in the USSR or Unknown Fiction and Nonfiction; 9:40—A Cultural Critic Looks at Soviet Literature and Art; 9:50-10:00—Africa-Asia-Latin America: The Developing World—Reports from Radio Liberty Correspondents.

Other First Program features which appeared later in the week included an analysis of "Problems of Stalinism"; reports on "The United Nations at Work"; a variety show with interviews, music, verse and commentary, and a panel discussion involving a clergyman, historian, journalist and economist, discussing religion and ethics, problems of ideology, life in the USSR and Soviet and world economy.

News and commentary constitute a large part of Radio Liberty's programming. The network denotes much attention to reports of events and affairs within the Soviet Union and the communist bloc. Radio Liberty's officials have stated that RL "discloses what the Soviet rulers would conceal. It reports accurately what the Soviet media distort. No less important, it lifts to a level of significance many events, within or outside the USSR, which the Kremlin buries in a few lines."[53]

The schedules on the Second Program for the same week were designed for special audiences. The programs for Sunday were: 7:00 P.M.—This is Jazz—interviews with top musicians—new trends in serious jazz—original Soviet music banned in the USSR, arranged and played by leading U.S. artists; 7:30—News; 7:45—Topical Feature—discussion of where Communism is being built; 7:55-8:00—Topical Commentary.

On Monday the Second Program included: 7:00—Analysis of Soviet Communist Party Affairs; 7:30—News; 7:45-8:00—Topical Features. Some of the offerings later in the week were discussions of cultural trends, science, art, literature, and economic theory and practice. A thirty minute period was devoted to drama, in which plays and literature which had been banned in the Soviet orbit were presented and analyzed.

In connection with its program preparation, Radio Liberty monitors more than sixty Soviet radio stations and screens more than two hundred Soviet publications. It also has its own research unit as does RFE, the wire service of UPI and Reuters, and numerous publications in the West.[54]

In his Annual Report to the Board of Trustees of the Radio Liberty Committee, dated November 30, 1964, the President said:

Radio Liberty's chief purpose is to give the Soviet citizen that information and that view of the world that he would get if the press, radio, and TV of his country were not controlled by a dictatorship. Although the Soviet citizen is primarily interested in what is going on inside his own country, he is still very much concerned about what is happening to the rest of the world, especially when those happenings have particular relevance to himself. The VOA and the BBC, of course, attempt to satisfy his curiosity in this respect, but they are limited to the extent that they are the official voices of governments. In addition to its heavy emphasis on the internal Soviet scene, Radio Liberty devotes a great deal of energy to filling out the Soviet citizen's knowledge of the free world.[55]

The Communications Satellite Corporation (COMSAT)

THE growth of satellite communication in recent years has been spectacular. Experimentation in the United States, Russia and other countries has greatly improved the technology in a relatively short time. Outer space was first penetrated by man-made vehicles less than twelve years ago, and as John Johnson, the Vice-President of the Communications Satellite Corporation, has said: "The simultaneous development of rocket propulsion and advances in electronic technology opened up a totally new resource for economic exploitation. For the first time man was able to place mechanisms of considerable size far above the earth's atmosphere, to control their position and movement with amazing precision, and to utilize them to serve his scientific and economic interests."[56]

Early in 1961 the FCC and Congress became seriously concerned with these new developments. It was apparent that some systematic regulatory plan would have to be devised to provide for the orderly growth of satellite communications at both the domestic and international level. The FCC appointed an ad hoc committee to study the problems. Both the House and the Senate conducted protracted hearings, exploring frequency allocation needs and considering various regulatory proposals. Some witnesses urged that the Government should own and operate the satellites. Others contended that a monopoly should be granted to communication carriers such as the American Telephone and Telegraph Company, subject to limited control by the Government. Still others urged the adoption of a compromise plan—the establishment of a private corporation with a limited amount of stock owned by communication carriers and the rest by the general public.[57]

The last plan won the support of Congress, and on August 31, 1962, the President signed the Communication Satellite Act authorizing the establishment of a corporation with the authority to develop a communications satellite system in the United States.[58]

In establishing this law, Congress stressed the international aspects of satellite communication, stating that "it is the policy of the United States to establish, in conjunction and in cooperation with other countries, as expeditiously as practicable a commercial communications satellite system, as part of an improved global communications network, which will be responsive to public needs and national objectives, which will serve the communication needs of the United States and other countries, and which will contribute to world peace and understanding."[59]

175

"The new and expanded telecommunication services," said the Congress, "are to be made available as promptly as possible and are to be extended to provide global coverage at the earliest practicable date. In effectuating this program, care and attention will be directed toward providing such services to economically less developed countries and areas as well as those more highly developed, toward efficient and economical use of the electromagnetic frequency spectrum, and toward the reflection of the benefits of this new technology in both quality of services and charges for such services."[60]

In order to achieve the objectives and carry out the purposes of the Act, Congress provided that the President should:

(1) aid in planning and development and foster the execution of a national program for the establishment and operation, as expeditiously as possible, of a commercial communications satellite system;

(2) provide for continuous review of all phases of the development and operation of such a system, including the activities of a communications satellite corporation authorized under title III of this Act;

(3) coordinate the activities of governmental agencies with responsibilities in the field of telecommunication, so as to insure that there is full and effective compliance at all times with the policies set forth in this Act;

(4) exercise such supervision over relationships of the corporation with foreign governments or entities or with international bodies as may be appropriate to assure that such relationships shall be consistent with the national interest and foreign policy of the United States;

(5) insure that timely arrangements are made under which there can be foreign participation in the establishment and use of a communications satellite system;

(6) take all necessary steps to insure the availability and appropriate utilization of the communications satellite system for general governmental purposes except where a separate communications satellite system is required to meet unique governmental needs, or is otherwise required in the national interest; and

(7) so exercise his authority as to help attain coordinated and efficient use of the electromagnetic spectrum and the technical compatibility of the system with existing communications facilities both in the United States and abroad.[61]

The Act also provides that the National Aeronautics and Space Administration (NASA) should cooperate in research and development; consult with the Corporation with respect to the technical aspects of the communications satellite system; and, upon request, provide satellite launching and associated services.[62]

This legislation gives the FCC overall regulatory authority over the Corporation to insure effective competition in the procurement of equipment and services; to see that all authorized communications carriers have nondiscriminatory use of and access to the facilities of the satellite system and under reasonable regulations and charges; to institute, through appropriate proceedings,[63] new service to a particular point upon advice from the Secretary of State and NASA that will be technically feasible and will serve the national interest; to prescribe accounting regulations, approve technical characteristics of the operational system and terminal stations; and to "grant appropriate authorization for the construction and operation of each satellite terminal station, either to the Corporation or to one or more authorized carriers or jointly to the Corporation and carriers, basing the grants upon the public interest without reference to either the Corporation or carriers."[64]

Furthermore, the law empowers the FCC to authorize the Corporation to issue new shares of stock and negotiate loans, if the FCC determines such to be in the public interest. Finally, the Act specifies that no substantial additions to the facilities of the system or satellite terminal stations may be made without the FCC's approval in terms of the public interest. Moreover, subject to procedural requirements in Section 214 of the Communications Act of 1934, as amended, the FCC may, on its own initiative, require that such additions be made if it finds the public interest will be served.[65]

The law provides that the President should appoint the incorporators, by and with the consent of the Senate, to serve as the initial Board of Directors until the first annual meeting of the stockholders and that these incorporators should arrange for an initial stock offering and take the necessary action to establish the Corporation, as approved by the President.[66]

Section 303 (a), as amended, states that there shall be a Board of Directors made up of fifteen U.S. citizens, three appointed by the President, subject to Senate approval, four elected annually by the common carriers and eight by other stockholders. The terms of the three presidential appointees run for three years except, to provide for a staggered arrangement, the terms of two of the original appointees were limited to one and two years.[67] If a vacancy occurs, the replacement gets only the unexpired part of the term of the Director he succeeds.

Congress defined the purposes and powers of the Corporation:

(1) to plan, initiate, construct, own, manage and operate itself or in conjunction with foreign governments or business entities a commercial communications satellite system;

(2) furnish, for hire, channels of communication to United States communications common carriers and to other authorized entities, foreign and domestic; and

(3) own and operate satellite terminal stations when licensed by the Commission under Section 201 (c) (7).

(4) conduct or contract for research and development related to its mission;

(5) acquire the physical facilities, equipment and devices necessary to its operations, including communications satellites and associated equipment and facilities, whether by construction, purchase or gift;

(6) purchase satellite launching and related services from the United States Government;

(7) contract with authorized users, including the United States Government, for

the services of the communications satellite system; and

(8) develop plans for the technical specifications of all elements of the communications satellite system.[68]

To carry out these purposes, the Corporation is given the usual powers conferred upon stock corporations doing business in the District of Columbia by the D.C. Business Corporation Act.[69]

Section 404 of the COMSAT law requires that the President make an annual report to Congress describing the activities and accomplishments of the communications satellite system. It also calls for annual reports to Congress from the Corporation and the Federal Communications Commission. Pursuant to this mandate, on March 17, President Lyndon Johnson submitted his report for 1967. He referred to the creation of the International Telecommunications Satellite Consortium (INTELSAT), and the recent progress in satellite communications that has been made at the domestic and international level through the cooperative efforts of various agencies of the Federal Government and more than fifty-five countries that are now members of INTELSAT. (Now there are more than 70.)

The American Forces Network—Europe *

From Wasserkuppe, a tiny remote village, to Munich, a sophisticated metropolitan city, and from a lonely patrol along the Czech border to a full-scale field operation in southern Bavaria—regardless of where the G.I. serves, he can twist his radio dial and listen to the American Forces Network (AFN). As a significant part of the Overseas Military Information Program, AFN provides entertainment, news, and special events to literally hundreds of thousands of American military personnel and their families; it has done so for the more than 20 years that the American military has been present in Europe.

The network went on the air for the first time on July 4, 1943, broadcasting from London to five 50-watt transmitters located throughout the British Isles, using space and equipment loaned by the British Broadcasting Corporation. When the Allied invasion force crossed the channel on June 6, 1944, AFN followed immediately as "mobile broadcasting units attached to U.S. First, Seventh, and Ninth Armies."[70] After Germany surrendered, AFN's headquarters was located in the *schloss*, a 14th Century Von Bruening Castle in Hoechst, a village just outside Frankfurt. The headquarters remained there until June 1966, when it moved into an ultramodern $2

---

*The American Forces Network in Europe is one of the best known radio services in the world. Although programmed by and for Americans, its activities and scope are nearly unknown to most people living in the United States. Major Ovid L. Bayless, who worked as a consultant with AFN during the summer of 1966, and at present is Associate Professor of Speech and English at the United States Air Force Academy, is the author of this article, which appeared in the Spring 1968 issue of the *Journal of Broadcasting*. It is reprinted with the permission of the author and the *Journal.*

million facility located adjacent to *Hessicher Rundfunk,* the German radio station in downtown Frankfurt. This present AFN,[71] its personnel, organization, facilities, and programming bring the American serviceman in Europe closer to home, and, incidentally, provides Europeans with an additional American "voice."

Personnel and Organization.   The AFN Headquarters assigns personnel, on a permanent basis, to seven different studio-transmitter locations in West Germany. Frankfurt is the network's key station and headquarters; other stations are located in Berlin, Munich, Stuttgart, Kaiserslautern, Nuremberg, and Bremerhaven. Most local productions originate from Frankfurt, where nearly half the network's approximately 232 engineers, announcers, newsmen, and so forth, are located. Both Army and Air Force personnel man the network, with the Army providing roughly 85% of the people. Since AFN is not an orthodox military unit, and since it has a unique function, it has a large portion of civilian employees. Over half of AFN's authorized manpower spaces are civilian, either American or local nationals, who mainly work in either programming or engineering.

The organizational structure of the network compares with most military units in that it has an officer-in-charge and staff heads for personnel, administration, logistics, engineering, and programming. The officer-in-charge, an Army lieutenant colonel, is responsible to the Public Affairs Division, Headquarters U.S. Army Europe, though he maintains close liaison with Headquarters U.S. Air Forces Europe.[72] Military officers are in charge of personnel, administration, and logistics, while civilians head engineering and programming. The station manager is the ranking man at each outlying station, and he is responsible to the network officer-in-charge.

Facilities.   The network has thirty AM transmitters compared with only six FM. Twenty-nine AM and five FM transmitters blanket central and southern Germany. Berlin, situated in the heart of East Germany, operates both an AM and an FM transmitter. Berlin required an FM transmitter because a portion of the city's American Sector was unable to get adequate AM reception, according to Lt. Col. Victor Bloecker, former officer-in-charge.

The most powerful transmitter in the network is located at Frankfurt; it has 150,000 watts of power, which is three times the maximum authorized in the U.S., and operates on a frequency of 872 kc; Munich (1106 kc) has a 100,000-watt transmitter. Four other studio-transmitter locations, Berlin (935 kc), Kaiserslautern (611 kc), Nuremberg (611 kc), and Stuttgart (1142 kc) have 10,000-watt transmitters, and Bremerhaven (1142 kc) has 5,000 watts. Besides the Berlin station, AFN has FM transmitters at Augsburg, Frankfurt, Stuttgart, Pirmasens, and Illesheim. The network installed these FM facilities primarily because of the increasd number of FM receivers owned by Americans in these areas of troop concentration.

Twenty-three well-situated AM repeater-transmitters insure primary coverage for the U.S. serviceman in the less populated areas of Germany.

In addition to these, the network also operates three FM repeater-transmitters in the Netherlands. Engineering personnel of the studio-transmitter station nearest the repeater facility are responsible for routine maintenance on the repeater-transmitters. Engineers dispatched from the headquarters in Frankfurt handle more serious trouble on a call basis.

The network is presently negotiating for transmitter locations for Belgium in order to provide broadcast support to the NATO and SHAPE headquarters which were moved from Paris in the Spring of 1967. AFN ceased broadcasting in France in the fall of 1967 when its Bel Manior transmitter, near Paris, went off the air at the end of September. AFN's outlets in France were the last U.S. elements to be withdrawn from that country.

Programming and Audience. The AFN programming format is much like traditional network radio in the U.S. "before television." The normal broadcast day runs nineteen hours, from 6:00 a.m. until 1:05 a.m. Record and variety shows, both local and transcribed from Armed Forces Radio and Television Services (AFRTS) in Los Angeles, are presented throughout the day aimed primarily at the serviceman's wife and off-duty personnel. Most of the shows originate in the Frankfurt studios, since most of the program material is located there and since the network reserves only three hours each day for programming by the local outlet.

The Frankfurt music library contains 1,500,000 music selections and 250,000 complete shows, enough material to program regularly for six years without repeating; AFN boast that this is the largest radio library in the world. A typical morning schedule includes a "request" show to start the day, followed by the Ira Cook show, Don McNeill's "Breakfast Club," and Arthur Godfrey. The afternoon format includes more request music, "Musical Heritage," and the "Jim Ameche Show." The programming shifts to country music at 4:05 p.m., with a 55-minute request show from Frankfurt. The evening schedule includes a 55-minute block of uninterrupted instrumental music of the David Rose variety, followed by a 55-minute block of drama, such as *The Whistler,* and *Suspense.* The typical total broadcast week, classified by program type, is presented in Table I.

TABLE 1

Program Classification

Program Type	AFN Program Schedule	AFRTS Recommended Program Schedule
News	14.5%	11.3%
Information	5.1	10.0
Education	2.3	3.6
Variety	11.2	7.3

Program Type	AFN Program Schedule	AFRTS Recommended Program Schedule
Sports*	3.1	2.6
Drama	5.4	1.4
Religion	3.0	2.6
Music	55.4	61.2

*During football and baseball season this increases to nearly 8%

The most important aspect of AFN programming is its news, which is presented every hour (five minutes) except when three major newscasts (thirty minutes) are aired at 7:00 a.m., 6 p.m., and 10:00 p.m. Through the facilities of AFRTS in New York and Los Angeles, AFN has more news input sources than any other single mass communication medium. In addition to wire service from Associated Press and United Press International, the network obtains news feeds via shortwave from all four major radio networks in the United States. Furthermore, AFN has two correspondents[73] of its own, located in the German cities of Bonn and Frankfurt. Greater dimension is provided AFN's current events coverage by its own special events production crew which interviews noted personalities when they visit Europe; *On the Scene and Eucom* (European Command) *Report* are two of the shows that give AFN a personality of its own in terms of local coverage.

The central programming axiom is that AFN will air no show that has propaganda overtones. The news programs are "straight" news presentations that are free of editorializing. Any news in depth show normally is taken from one of the major radio networks and involves a respectable journalist. For example, programs like *David Brinkley Reports* are quite often aided during one of AFN's major newscasts.

Since most G.I.'s are sport fans, AFN has a heavy sport format which runs throughout the year. To avoid preempting regular shows, the network broadcasts professional baseball only on the weekend, Saturday and Sunday evenings. The games are taped earlier and aired regularly during the season at 9:05 p.m. Network policy is to broadcast one National League game and one American League game every weekend if possible, and also to broadcast games involving teams that are in contention for the pennant. AFRTS relays these regular season games to AFN via shortwave, but for the World Series AFRTS uses a transatlantic cable to insure that AFN gets satisfactory reception. Atmospheric conditions often limit or prohibit broadcasting special events from the United States and costs and higher Signal Corps priorities prevent using the cable on a regular basis.

The network broadcasts college and professional football and basketball each Saturday and Sunday during the season. AFRTS does an excellent job of feeding AFN with highly attractive contests. For example, during the fall of 1965 AFN aired such college games as Notre Dame and Army, Texas vs. Arkansas, Air Force vs. Army, Michigan State vs. Notre Dame, and Army vs. Navy. The 1965 Professional Football contests included Green Bay vs. Baltimore, Cleveland vs. Dallas, and Chicago vs. Baltimore. The season was climaxed with the championship games of both the National and the American Football Leagues, plus the Cotton Bowl and the Rose Bowl. For the 1966 basketball season, AFN carried games such as Boston College vs. Providence, Army vs. Navy, Kentucky vs. Tennessee, Detroit Pistons vs. Cincinnati Royals, and Boston Celtics vs. Philadelphia 76ers. To supplement the AFRTS sport schedule, the AFN sports staff covers important sports events on the Continent, such as service football championships and the races at *Le Mans.*

The heavy emphasis on American news and sports no doubt means that AFN's most loyal listeners are the quarter of a million or so American servicemen and their families; the entire AFN programming schedule aims specifically for these people. Nevertheless, AFN has a large non-American audience; with signals beaming "from Scandinavia to Italy and from Ireland to Austria"[74] an indigenous audience of millions could hardly be denied. Just how many millions is not known though estimates range from 20 million[75] to 50 million.[76]

For Europeans desiring to learn English, listening to AFN is an excellent instructional device. The younger Europeans have grown up with AFN and it has provided adjunct instruction for those engaged in studying English in the classroom. Other Europeans, those not particularly interested in learning English, listen to AFN mostly for entertainment. Jack Gould of *The New York Times* suggests that many Europeans dial AFN because it has an established credibility, nurtured over the past 20 plus years.[77]

The AFN listening audience is increased considerably by Americans residing in Europe who are not associated with the Department of Defense. These include State Department personnel, employees of large U.S. companies, and tourists. During the summer months especially, the large influx of Americans who flock to the Continent greatly swells the audience. Hundreds of cards and letters from tourists indicate that AFN not only keeps them posted on the latest news and special events from home, but that it entertains them as well.

Conclusion. As long as United States foreign policy requires that a substantial number of American troops be stationed in Europe, no doubt the American Forces Network will continue to provide entertainment, news, and special events. During the serviceman's normal three year tour in Europe, he will keep track of the happenings at home through several different avenues; AFN radio is one of the most important. Throughout his stay he knows he can hear many familiar programs, the stateside news immediately, and the nation's most exciting sports events; AFN links the serviceman and "back home." And Europeans will continue to listen to

AFN for entertainment, to learn English and to get objective news. For these reasons AFN will not only remain an integral part of the Overseas Military Information Program, but it will also be what Gould calls "an admirable ambassador on the airwaves."

1. Section 73.701(a), FCC Rules and Regulations; 1 RR 53:851. Section 73.2(c); 1 RR 53:853.

2. Section 73.788(a); 1 RR 53:869.

3. Section 73.711(a); 1 RR 53:857.

4. An FCC requirement, but apparently not covered by a regulation.

5. A target area, as defined by Section 73.701(m); 1 RR 53:851, is a geographic area in which the reception of particular programs is specifically intended and in which adequate broadcast coverage is contemplated.

6. Section 73.731; 1 RR 53:859. Also, see *Report of Commission*, 13 RR 1501.

7. Section 73.761; 1 RR 53:865.

8. Sections 73.702(d) and 73.751; 1 RR 53:853, 861.

9. 1 RR 53:852.

10. *Ibid.* Four seasons are defined by the FCC Rules: March and April; May, June, July and August; September and October; and November, December, January and February.

11. *Ibid.*

12. Section 73.702(f); 1 RR 53:854.

13. Station WRUL is now owned by the Church of Jesus Christ of Latter Day Saints and is known as Radio New York World Wide, Inc., WNYW.

14. FCC Docket No. 10962; 13 RR 1510a.

15. The term "frequency hour," as defined by Section 73.701(b); 1 RR 53:851, means one frequency used for one hour.

16. Section 73.702(a); 1 RR 53:852.

17. 1 RR 53:873.

18. Section 73.702(b); 1 RR 53:852.

19. Section 73.788; 1 RR 53:869.

20. Section 73.753; 1 RR 53:861.

21. Section 73.787(b); 1 RR 53:868.

22. Section 73.718; 1 RR 53:859.

23. Section 1.539; 1 RR 51:267.

24. Section 1,539(d) (2); 1 RR 51:268.

25. "Contract operations," as defined by Section 73.701(n), means any non-government operation of an international broadcast station pursuant to a contract with an agency of the U.S. Government and subject to government control as to program content, target areas to be covered, and time of broadcast. These operations no longer exist. "Private operation," as defined by paragraph (0) of the same Section, is any operation not of a contract character. See 1 RR 53:852.

26. Section 73.791; 1 RR 53:872.

27. 48 Stat. 1083.

28. *Ibid.*

29. See *United States Government Organization Manual*, 1959-60, pp. 506-510; also, see *Annual Reports* of the USIA, 1954-59.

30. *VOA*, published by the Broadcasting Service of the United States Information Agency, 1964, p. 7.

31. *Facts About the USIA* (Washington: U.S. Government Printing Office, 1964), p. 6.

32. Radio Moscow leads in foreign broadcasting with 1,620 hours per week. Radio Peking presents twelve hundred hours and the United Arab Republic nine hundred and twenty hours weekly. The British Broadcasting Corporation, with eight hundred hours a week, follows the VOA.

33. *VOA*, p. 15.

34. *Ibid.,* p. 17.

35. *Ibid.,* p. 7.

36. *Facts about the USIA,* p. 7.

37. Committee on Appropriations, Congress, House, Committee on Appropriations Hearings, Departments of State, Justice, Commerce, the Judiciary and related agencies; Appropriation for 1967, 88th Congress, 2nd Session, 1966, p. 625; also, 90th Congress, 1st Session, 1967, p. 651.

38. *Ibid.,* 1967, p. 764.

39. *RIAS, the Free Voice of the Free World,* published by RIAS, West Berlin.

40. Information received from RIAS in West Berlin as of October 23, 1967.

41. *RIAS, the Free Voice of the Free World,* p. 3.

42. *Ibid.,* pp. 10-11; also, more recent reports from RIAS.

43. *Ibid.*

44. *Radio Free Europe, What It Is—What It Does,* Radio Free Europe (One English Garden, Munich, Germany).

45. *Thumbnail Sketches of Radio Free European Programs,* Radio Free Europe (Two Park Avenue, New York), p. 1; this has been updated by October 1967 correspondence.

46. *The Job Ahead,* Free Europe, Inc., 1965, published in 1966, p. 4; updated by October 1967 correspondence.

47. *Ibid.,* p. 9.

48. *Radio Free Europe.*

49. *The Job Ahead,* p. 10.

50. Statement supplied the author by RFE when he visited the Munich operation in 1965.

51. American Committee for Liberation, *The Most Important Job in the World,* updated, p. 1.

52. The author received this weekly program schedule from officials at Radio Liberty in Munich when he was visiting there and studying RL's operation in May 1965.

53. American Committee for Liberation, p. 5.

54. *Radio Liberty Russian-Language Program Schedule,* with informational notes, published by Radio Liberty (30 East 42nd Street, New York, N.Y., 10017).

55. Radio Liberty Committee, *The President's Annual Report to the Board of Trustees,* November 30, 1964, p. 14.

56. John A. Johnson, "Satellite Communications: The Challenge and the Opportunity for International Coorperation," *Federal Communications Bar Journal,* FCC Bar Association, XIX, No. 3 (1964-65), 89. This is an excerpt from a speech Mr. Johnson gave before the Washington World Conference on World Peace Through Law; Working Session II—Section II, September 14, 1965.

57. See Hearings before the Committee on Commerce, United States Senate, 87th Congress, 2nd Session, on S. 2814, *A Bill to Provide for the Establishment, Ownership, Operation, and Regulation of a Commercial Satellite System, and for Other Purposes;* April 10, 11, 12, 13, 16, 24 and 26, 1962 (Washington: U.S. Government Printing Office, 1962). Also, see Hearings before the Committee on Interstate and Foreign Commerce, House of Representatives, 87th Congress, 1st Session, July 25, 26, 27, and 28, 1961 (Washington: U.S. Government Printing Office, 1962).

58. *U.S. Statutes at Large,* 87th Congress, 2nd Session, Vol. 76, 1962, pp. 419-427.

59. *Ibid.,* p. 419.

60. *Ibid.*

61. *Ibid.,* p. 421.

62. *Ibid.*

63. *Ibid.*, p. 422.

64. *Ibid.*

65. *Ibid.*, p. 423.

66. *Ibid.*

67. *Ibid.;* See amendment to Section 303(a), Public Law 91-3, 91st Congress, S 17, March 12, 1969, which makes the number of (public and carrier) directors proportionate to the percentage of stock held by each group of shareholders.

68. *Ibid.*, p. 425.

69. *Ibid.*

70. "The Servicemen's Voice in Europe," *Army in Europe*, USAREUR Pamphlet 360-43, July, 1966, p. 6.

71. In the course of this investigation the author received the assistance of a great many people; he is especially grateful to Lt. Col. Victor Bloecker, Lt. Col. William Ellington, former officers-in-charge, and Lt. Col. Henry L. Cody, present officer-in-charge. He specifically acknowledges the help of Mr. Robert J. Harlan, present Program Director. Several members of the AFN staff were also most helpful: Capt. Eugene Bickley, Chief Warrant Officer Robert Moore, Mr. George Kaso, Mr. Harry Bean, Mr. Frank Mortensen, Mr. Jimmy Lunsford, Mr. Shelby Whitfield, and Sergeant Major Samuel Summer.

72. The U.S. Air Forces in Europe operate the only Armed Forces Television on the continent, three stations in Germany: Ramstein, Spangdahlem, and Berlin. The Ramstein program is relayed to Wiesbaden and Rhein Main Air Base which in turn rebroadcasts it over low-powered translators.

73. Until recently the network also had correspondents in London, Paris, and Berlin.

74. Jack Gould, "A Voice that Europe Trusts," *The New York Times*, April 17, 1966.

75. *Ibid.*

76. *This is AFN Europe.* (Undated), p. 1. This publication is available at the Headquarters, American Forces Network, Bertram Strasse, Frankfurt, Germany.

77. Gould, op. cit.

CHAPTER 11

Auxiliary and Other Special Types
of Broadcasting

. . . these radio waves are made to perform all sorts of work. . . .
*Since they are public property, the deciding factor in determining how
many channels a certain type of service shall have, and who shall be entrusted with a channel within a type of service, must be the public interest.*
                                                                    —WAYNE COY*

FCC rules provide for the use of numerous auxiliary facilties which contribute greatly to the economy, efficiency and quality of the regular broadcast services already discussed. Without these adjunct operations, the football game far removed from the station studio could not be brought into our
homes; an inaugural parade in Washington could not be transmitted to the
television viewers throughout the nation; inhabitants in many small, isolated communities in the West would have no local television service; and
much of the variety, immediacy and color that now characterize broadcasting in general would be missing.

Each of these important auxiliary services is subject to special regulations
established by the FCC, and each has been assigned the use of particular
bands of frequencies in the radio spectrum. Space will not permit a detailed
discussion of these regulations and channel allocations. It is hoped, however, that the reader will find the following informational highlights helpful.

Remote Pickup Stations. All broadcast stations (standard, FM, Noncommercial FM, and TV) are eligible to apply for and use remote pickup
transmitters for a variety of purposes to support their regular operations.[1]
These pickup units are used to send programs from remote points to the
main transmitter for simultaneous or delayed broadcasting and for the
transmission of information and orders pertaining to such programs. They
may be authorized to operate on a mobile or fixed basis.[2]

Special temporary authority may be granted to operate, as remote pickup
stations, equipment already authorized for use by another class of station

*Former chairman of the FCC.

or equipment which, under the Communications Act of 1934, does not require a construction permit.[3]

These applications for temporary authority may be filed informally but should reach the Commission at least ten days previous to the date of operation. If received in less time, the Commission will accept the application if sufficient reasons for the delay are stated.[4]

These informal requests must set forth full particulars as to the purpose of the temporary remote pickup operation; give the name of the licensee whose equipment is to be used, the call letters, the type of equipment and the frequency or frequencies to be employed, time and date, location, transmitter power, and type of emission proposed.[5]

The frequencies used must be those especially assigned to the remote pickup broadcast service. Other frequencies under the jurisdiction of the FCC may be requested if effective transmission on the assigned ones is not possible and the programs to be broadcast relate to events of national interest and importance. In any case, it must be shown that the operation will not cause interference to any existing station. Under no circumstances, will frequencies in the so called Special Radio Emergency Service be authorized for these remote pickup operations.[6]

Special Rules for Miniature Low Power Auxiliary Stations. On July 30, 1958, the Commission adopted special rules for the operation of tiny transmitting devices, inconspicuously worn on the person, and used mainly for cueing and directing participants in rehearsals of programs as well as actual broadcasts. This small, portable equipment is a happy substitute for the clumsy telephonic apparatus and extension cords formerly used in the production of elaborate programs and has contributed further to the versatility of the broadcast media.

Only licensees of broadcast stations are eligible to use this auxiliary apparatus, and then only in connection with activities of a specified station or combination of stations. Their transmissions must be intended for reception at a point within the same studio, building, stadium or similarly limited indoor or outdoor area.

Only one application prepared in duplicate is required to be filed for one or more of these transmitting units, provided they are designed for operation in a common frequency band and are to be used with the same broadcast station or combination of such stations in a single city.

Adding further to the utility of this apparatus, the rules permit one licensee to use it in conjunction with broadcast stations of other licensees in the same area. If, however, it is to be used this way in other locations for a consecutive period of more than one day, the FCC Engineer in Charge of the radio district where the station is located and the FCC Engineer in the district where the operation is conducted must be notified in writing at least two days in advance of the operation.[7]

The power of these small pickups is limited to 1 watt and their operation is subject to the condition that no harmful interference will be caused to other stations of a fixed or mobile character.[8] Persons without operators' licenses may use them, but a licensed operator must be available to make immediate correction of any improper operation. If any adjustments or repairs are needed, they should be made by him or under his direction.[9]

Call letters are not assigned to these stations. An announcement, however, must be made over the transmitting unit at the beginning and end of each period of operation, identifying the type of operation, its location, and the call sign of the broadcast station with which it is being used.[10] Section 74, 437(e) authorizes these pickups only in bands 26.10-26.48 mc/s., 450-451 mc/s and 942-952 mc/s.

Aural Broadcast STL (Studio-Link) and Intercity Relay Stations. STL stations are fixed installations which serve the purpose of connecting studios of broadcast stations (excluding international broadcasting stations) with their transmitters which, for some reason or another, it has been necessary or desirable to locate some distance away, often on a mountain top or other remote point to achieve efficient operation and satisfactory coverage.[11]

Relay Stations are fixed stations for the transmission of aural program material between broadcasting stations other than international broadcast stations, for simultaneous or delayed broadcast.[12]

Both types of stations may employ multiplexing to provide additional communication channels for the transmission of aural program material, operational communiciations, or material authorized to be sent over an FM broadcast station under a valid Subsidiary Communications (SCA). However, they may not be used solely for the transmission of operational and subsidiary communications. The FCC has defined operational communications as "cues, orders, and other communications directly related to the operation of the broadcast station as well as special signals used for telemetry or for control of apparatus used in conjunction with the broadcasting operation."[13]

The Rules provide that all program material, including subsidiary communications, carried over these STL and Intercity relays must be intended for use by broadcast stations owned or under common control of a licensee or licensees of these auxiliary stations.[14] Furthermore, Section 74.531(e) of the Rules states, with respect to STL stations, that if "multiplexing is employed for the simultaneous transmission on more than one aural channel, the STL transmitter must be capable of transmitting the multiple channels within the channel on which STL station is authorized to operate and with adequate technical quality so that each broadcast station utilizing the circuit can meet the technical performance standards stipulated in the rules governing that class of broadcasting station."[15] Furthermore, the Rule provides that if multiplex is employed during regular operation of the STL station, the additional circuits must be in operation at the time that the required periodic performance measurements are made of the overall broadcasting system from the studio microphone input circuit to the broadcast transmitter output circuit."[16]

A single broadcast licensee may be authorized by the FCC to operate more than one aural STL or Intercity relay upon a satisfactory showing that there is need for different program circuits for more than one broadcast over a path which, due to terrain or distance, a single relay is unable to provide.[17] If plural facilities are to be used, this information must be clearly set forth in the application for construction permit or license.[18]

One of the conditions of the license for these auxiliary operations is that their transmitting and receiving locations must be specified along with the direction of the main radiation lobe of the transmitting antenna.[19] These stations may be operated by remote control provided certain conditions are met, such as having adequate safeguards to prevent improper operation of the equipment, having needed repairs made by technically qualified persons. Other conditions are set forth in Section 74.533 of the Rules.[20]

Directional antennas are required. Normally only frequency modulation may be employed. Limitations on transmitting power, emission and bandwidth, and equipment and operational requirements, plus regulations concerning antenna structure, marking and lighting, the keeping of records and station identification are set forth in detail in Sections 74.534 through 74.582.

Television Auxiliary Broadcast Stations. There are four types of these stations: (1) a television pickup station, which is mobile in character, and is used to transmit programs and related communications from remote points to television stations, which in turn broadcast the programs for public reception; (2) TV-STL stations of a fixed character, used to carry TV programs and related communications from the studios to the main TV transmitter; (3) TV Intercity Relays operating at fixed intermediate points which receive programs from one city and send them on to another; and (4) fixed TV translator relays which receive and project TV signals to television broadcast translator stations.[21]

As is the case with auxiliary operations solely of an aural character, TV-STL or TV intercity relay stations may employ multiplexing to provide additional communication channels for the transmission of their aural program material and operational communications. These include voice transmissions, telemetry and alerting, fault reporting, and control signals, all of which must be directly related to the technical operation of the associated television broadcast station or the STL or intercity relay system of which the multiplexed transmitter is a part. The aural programming may include the sound accompanying the visual presentation carried by the STL or intercity relay system, or it may include any aural material intended for broadcast by AM, FM or other TV broadcast stations, owned by or under the common control of the licensee of the STL or intercity transmission facility.[22]

The Commission has stated that auxiliary stations will be authorized only in those cases where they are employed primarily to transmit programs for use by their associated TV broadcast stations. However, they may be opera-

190

ted at any time for the transmission of aural program material and operational communications whether or not there is visual presentation, provided no harmful interference is caused to TV pickup, STL, or intercity relay stations carrying television broadcast programs.[23]

Only licensees of television broadcast stations can apply for any of these auxiliaries. A separate application is required for each transmitter, and the frequency desired must be specified. Applications for new pickup TV facilities or for renewal of licenses of existing ones, must designate the television broadcast stations with which they are to be associated and must specify the areas expected to be covered by the proposed operations.[24] In the event a licensee has two or more television broadcast stations located in different communities and applies for a new TV pickup facility, or for renewal of license of an existing one, it must designate the television broadcast station with which it is to be principally operated, and may not then use it in connection with another television broadcast station in a different city for more than ten days out of a thirty day period.[25]

TV translator relays are authorized to receive only the signals of television broadcast stations or other translator relays and send them on to television translator stations for simultaneous retransmission. These signals must be received directly through space, converted to channels made available under Section 74.602(h) of the Commission Rules, and suitably amplified as required. Applications for such TV translator relays must designate the television broadcast stations whose programs are to be relayed and the broadcast translator stations with which the relay facilities are to be operated.[26]

Temporary authority may be granted for the operation, as an auxiliary broadcast facility, the equipment of another licensed television broadcast station, or other class of station. An application for this temporary authority can be made informally but must be filed with the Commission at least ten days prior to the time the proposed operation is to begin. Among other things, the application must provide full particulars as to the purpose of the request, supply information as to the type of equipment to be used, the power output, emission, frequency or frequencies to be employed, and the time, date and location of the proposed operation.[27]

Remote control operation is permitted provided the Commission is notified at least ten days prior to such operation and the notification is accompanied by a detailed description of the proposed remote control installation with a showing that it complies with conditions set forth in Section 74.634 of the Rules designed to insure responsible and efficient transmissions. As is the case with aural auxiliary broadcast stations, the Rules prescribe certain power limitations, emission and bandwidth; set forth equipment and operational requirements, and state the manner records are to be kept and how stations are to be identified.[28]

Television Broadcast Translator Stations. These are defined by the FCC as those which retransmit the signals of a television broadcast station, another television broadcast translator station, or a television translator relay station, and do it by means of direct frequency conversion and amplification without significantly altering any of their characteristics other than frequency and amplitude.[29] There are both VHF and UHF translators. Boosters, so-called, may be used to retransmit and reradiate UHF translator signals so long as the only character change is in the amplitude.[30]

Originally, the Commission granted only UHF broadcast translator stations.[31] However, in 1960, the Rules were amended to permit low power VHF translators also.[32] When the Commission proposed this amendment, many segments of the broadcast industry objected. For example, one station averred that the "unrestricted use of VHF translators in areas now served by UHF television stations poses an economic threat to UHF stations. Where such translators would bring in the programs of distant VHF stations, the local station would be deprived of audience and advertising revenue."[33]

The concern about economic impact was not limited to existing UHF stations. Numerous VHF stations voiced the opinion that the "diversion of audience and the duplication of programs carried by local TV stations or the bringing in of programs from distant TV stations which might otherwise be carried by the local station would seriously impair their ability to obtain advertising revenue.[34]

Despite these and other objections presented by organizations representing the broadcast industry, the Commission concluded that the public interest justified the authorization of VHF translators. The Commission said:

The matter of economic impact said to be exerted upon regular TV stations by translators was studied in great detail in Docket No. 12443. There are two areas of public interest involved and in some cases they may not be compatible. The economic welfare of TV broadcasting stations is certainly a matter of public interest. The availability of more than one TV service is also a matter of public interest. As between TV broadcast stations, competition is generally to be encouraged because it usually results in better programming. On the other hand, competition for audience between a TV broadcast station representing a substantial investment and operating under strict technical requirements and a TV translator representing a modest investment and required to observe only minimal standards, may present problems. We have, however, found no way to write a rule of general applicability which would not be arbitrary. The only feasible way of meeting the problem is to consider each case on its merits . . . TV station licensees who believe that the grant of a specific application would cause economic injury are privileged to state their opposition prior to the grant of an application . . . we reject proposals which would by rule automatically restrict the use of TV translators because of the existence of a local TV station or stations.[35]

An applicant for this type of station as provided by the Rules, must be specific as to frequency desired and must endeavor to select channels that will not cause interference to the reception of other stations. Any one of the twelve standard VHF television channels (two to thirteen inclusive) may be assigned to a VHF translator provided no interference is caused to other operations on the same or adjacent channel. Exceptions to this are channels five and six which are allocated for nonbroadcast use in Alaska and Hawaii and may not be used for VHF translators.[36]

The Commission has stated that UHF channels (seventy to eighty-three) may be assigned to UHF translators provided the site of their operations are not located:

(1) Within twenty miles of a television broadcast station or city which is assigned the second, third, fourth, fifth, or eighth channel above or below that requested.
(2) Within fifty-five miles of a television broadcast station or city which is assigned an adjacent channel.
(3) Within sixty miles of a television broadcast station or city which is assigned the seventh channel above or the seventh or fourteenth channel below that requested.
(4) Within seventy-five miles of a television broadcast station or city which is assigned the fifteenth channel below that requested.
(5) Within 155 miles of a television broadcast station or city which is assigned the same channel as that desired unless it appears in the Table of Assignments set forth in Section 73.606(b) of the Rules, and has been assigned to the city in which the proposed translator is to be operated and the channel is not already occupied by a television broadcast station in that city.[37]*

As to eligibility for licenses, any qualified individual, organization, broadcast station licensee, or local civil governmental body, upon making an appropriate showing of financial ability, may qualify. Only one channel may be assigned to each translator station. The Commission frowns upon the establishment of VHF translators in areas receiving satisfactory UHF service unless it can be clearly shown that intermixture will serve the public interest.[38]

Any authorization for a VHF translator may be terminated by the Commission upon giving sixty days notice, if community conditions have changed so greatly that such operation can no longer be justified in terms of the public interest.[39]

In some small "shadowed" areas, reception can be improved by the use of UHF translators. One or more of these may be licensed to UHF translator stations to fill in the gaps where the translator transmission alone may not

*The Commission, in its *First Report and Second Notice of Inquiry* in Docket No. 18262, issued May 21, 1970, reallocated channels 70-83 (806-890 MHz) from the television translator service to the Land Mobile Radio service. Simultaneously, the Commission released a *Notice of Proposed Rule Making* in Docket No. 18861, proposing to authorize UHF television translators on channels 14-69 (470-806 MHz) in lieu of the higher band. In the same document, the Commission proposed to authorize 1,000 watt UHF translators on channels allocated in the Television Table of Assignments which were "idle", i.e., either not used by a television station or authorized but not built after a prolonged period of time, and construction not likely to be completed in the near future.

be adequate to provide satisfactory service. Section 74.733 sets forth the requirements for transmitting apparatus, provides that the booster installation must comply with the standards of good engineering practice, must not cause objectionable interference to the reception of any station, broadcast or nonbroadcast, other than the parent translator. However, it is expected that even this will be kept to a minimum.[40]

The boosters may be unattended, and the translator stations themselves may transmit without licensed operators. But to do so, they must meet certain requirements, as set forth in Section 74.734 of the Rules.[41]

Power limitations of television broadcast translator stations, emission and bandwidth requirements, antenna location, equipment specifications and operational requirements are set forth in detail in Sections 74.735 through 74.781. For example, changes in equipment require the prior approval of the Commission, frequency tolerances are specified, operation is prohibited except when the primary station is transmitting its signals, and cessation of operation for a period of thirty days or more, except for causes beyond the control of the licensee, will result in cancellation of the license.[42]

As is the case with other types of broadcast stations, licensees of TV translators must maintain records of their current instrument of authorization, official correspondence with the Commission, contracts, permission for rebroadcasts, etc. If the station operates with more than 100 watts peak visual power, it must transmit its call sign in International Morse Code every 30 minutes while on the air. Automatic devices may be used for this purpose. Under the Rules, one watt translators need not be identified at all. Translators of more than one watt peak visual output power up to and including 100 watt translators must be identified, but need not use call letters. They may arrange to be identified by their primary stations (the stations whose programs they retransmit). If they choose self-identification, they may be done by frequency shift keying ("FSK") or by amplitude modulation of the FM aural carrier. Translators of more than 100 watts must identify themselves in one of these two ways.[43]

Television Broadcast Booster Stations. The Commission has provided for a special class of booster stations to serve primary television stations operating in the UHF band. Regulations for this type of operation are found in Sections 74.801 through 74.883. The purpose of these adjunct facilities, as stated by the Commission, is to provide means "whereby the licensees of television broadcast stations operating in the UHF television broadcast band may provide service to areas of low signal intensity in any region which would be encompassed by the theoretical Grade A contour, assuming operation with an effective radiated power of 5,000 kilowatts from an antenna 2,000 feet above average terrain over a transmission path of normal terrain."[44] Under these assumptions, the Commission further states that the distance from a UHF television broadcast station to this theoretical contour is 68 miles.[45]

Certain restrictions are imposed on these boosters which should be mentioned. They may retransmit only the signals of their primary stations. They may not operate at any location more than 68 miles from their primary stations, and must not produce a field strength beyond this range greater than 5 millivolts per meter at a height of 30 feet above ground. Their transmissions must be designed for direct reception by the general public and they may not be used for point-to-point communication. They may be licensed only to television stations broadcasting in the UHF band and must be used solely for retransmitting the signals of these primary stations. While no numerical limit is placed upon the number of such boosters which a single licensee may operate, the Rules require that a separate application must be filed for each booster and a separate authorization for its operation be granted.[46]

Transmitting power is limited to that which is necessary to provide an adequate signal over the area intended to be served by the booster. In no event, however, will the Commission authorize operation with more than 5 kilowatts (ERP) of peak visual power. Nor will any such booster be permitted to operate at a location, and with an effective radiated power and with antenna height above average terrain, that would produce a predicted field strength of more than 5 millivolts per meter at any place more than 68 miles from the primary station.[47]

Remote control operation, of course, is permitted provided the transmitter is equipped with automatic devices which, when the primary station is not on the air, will render the booster inoperative and which may be activated by a coded signal or tone transmitted from the primary station.

Frequencies (aural and visual) of the booster must be identical with those of the primary station. Operation is limited to periods when the primary station is on the air. While no regular schedule of operations is required, it is expected that unwarranted interruptions in service will be avoided. Discontinuance of operation for more than thirty days, except for causes beyond the control of the licensee, results in automatic forfeiture of the license.

Other regulations pertaining to operator requirements, marking and lighting of antenna structures, keeping of records and station identification appear in Sections 74.863 through 74.883. Among other things, the station must keep posted at the transmitter location the license and any other instrument of authorization, display the call letters of the station and the assigned channel of the primary station at the booster site on the structure supporting the antenna so as to be visible to a person standing on the ground; have a first or second-class operator on duty at the transmitter, except, if the booster is remotely controlled. An unlicensed person at the primary station may turn on and off the power if under instructions from an operator on duty. Appropriate marking and lighting is required, and operating logs must be maintained and kept on file for a period of two years.

Boosters of this type are not assigned call letters, but must identify themselves by retransmission of the call letters of the primary stations.[48]

Commission Authorized to Grant Licenses to Existing Repeaters . During the fifties, more than 300 "repeater" stations, so-called, were installed and were operating in the United States without having been authorized by the FCC.[49] These were low power devices for the reception, amplication and retransmission of television signals, irrespective of whether the output channel was the same as the input channel, or was a different channel in the case of VHF translators.

A proposal to license these devices on a regular basis had been under consideration for a number of years but the FCC's jurisdiction over these operations was questioned in *C. J. Community Services, Inc. v. Federal Communications Commission*, 100 U. S. App. D. C. 379; 246 F. (2d) 660; 15 RR 2033 (1957). In that case, however, the Court held that the Commission did have jurisdiction over these "repeater" stations and that operation of them, causing interference to authorized stations was a violation of the Act. The Court said further that the Commission had a statutory duty to provide for the issuance of appropriate licenses and suggested that it might "well" get on with rulemaking proceedings."[50]

The Commission was reluctant to take action against these stations since they were providing broadcast service in many areas of the country and had widespread support. It sought help from Congress. On April 14, 1959, it announced that it was recommending to Congress that the Communications Act be amended to legalize and permit the licensing of these repeater stations under certain conditions and, if this was done, to allow up to one year for those in operation to comply with technical requirements to avoid interference to other stations.[51]

The Commission further pointed out that Section 319 of the Act prohibits the Commission from licensing broadcast facilities constructed without a prior permit. Accordingly, said the Commission, Congress would need to amend this section before the Commission could grant licenses to these repeater stations already installed.[52]

Shortly after this announcement, in April, 1959, legislation was introduced in Congress designed to give the Commission the authority requested.[53]

Pending Congressional action, the Commission announced that unlicensed repeaters would have until September 30, 1959, to comply with regulations. Subsequently, the Commission extended the time to June 29, 1960.[54]

The Commission's request for statutory power to validate their operations was approved by Congress on July 7, 1960. Section 319 of the Communications Act was amended by the addition of the following language:

If the Commission finds that the public interest, convenience and necessity would be served thereby, it may waive the requirement of a permit for construction of a station that is engaged solely in rebroadcasting television signals if such station was constructed on or before the date of enactment of this Act.[55]

Accordingly, the Commission adopted Section 74.790 of the Rules, setting forth the conditions under which these VHF repeater stations might secure valid licenses.[56] They were required to request temporary licenses no later than October 31, 1960. Upon proper written request, they were granted authority to operate until October 31, 1961. On or before this latter date, each station was required to take all necessary steps to comply with basic statutory requirements before the Commission would grant regular licenses. It should be noted that the legislation authorizing the Commission to issue licenses without having first granted construction permits, applied *only* to repeater stations in operation on or before the enactment date (July 7, 1960), and had no applicability to any broadcast station, repeater or otherwise, that might be built later.[57]

Instructional Television Fixed Stations. In July, 1963, the FCC established this new class of service to meet the needs of educators for the transmission of visual and aural instructional material to students enrolled in courses of formal instruction.[58] Multiple frequencies in the 2,500-2,690 megacycle band were allocated for this educational activity. The Commission has pointed out that it is not a substitute for conventional ETV broadcast service, but is viewed as "an important adjunct, making instructional television programming available to school systems in communities without ETV stations and easing the problem of TV broadcast channel shortages in many communities."[59] At the end of 1969, there were ninety-four ITFS systems in operation. Forty-nine additional stations were under construction and sixteen new applications were pending action of the Commission.[60]

In October, 1965, a National Committee for the Full Development of Instructional Television Fixed Service was established. It is made up of FCC representatives and members of the educational community, and its purpose is to assist in planning for efficient use of ITFS frequencies throughout the country. The Committee provides information and acts as liaison between the Commission and educators interested in the development of the ITFS service. Under a procedure adopted in December, 1966, the Commission supplies local subcommittees with copies of parts of ITFS applications which have been filed to enable them to participate in cooperative planning for the more effective utilization of frequencies.[61]

While space does not permit discussion of all the regulations pertaining to this new service, mention may be made of some. For example, the licensee is limited to the assignment of no more than four channels for use in a single area of operation. It is expected that applicants will proceed expeditiously to activate channels requested, and evidence must be submitted showing serious intention to construct facilities and not simply to reserve channels for future use.[62]

The Rules further provide that these stations, in addition to their use for classroom instruction, may be employed to transmit "visual and aural material to selected receiving locations for in-service training and instruction in special skills and safety programs, extension of professional training, informing persons and groups engaged in professional and technical activities of current developments in their particular fields, and other similar endeavors."[63] Also, "during periods when the circuits provided by these stations are not being used for the transmission of instructional and cultural material, they may be used for the transmission of material directly to the administrative activities of the licensee, such as the holding of conferences with personnel, distribution of reports and assignments, exchange of data and statistics, and other similar uses."[64] However, the Commission has warned that these stations will not be licensed solely for "the transmission of administrative traffic."[65]

As to eligibility for licenses, the Commission has stated that only institutional or governmental organizations "engaged in the formal education of enrolled students or to a nonprofit organization formed for the purpose of providing instructional television material..." may qualify.[66] Any nonprofit organization which qualifies to operate a noncommercial educational television broadcast station is eligible to apply for an instructional TV license (see pp. 157-58).

No numerical limit is placed on the number of stations which may be authorized for operation by a single licensee, though, as pointed out above, there is a limitation on the number of channels that may be used. As is the case with some other auxiliary services, operational requirements are less rigid than those which apply to public TV broadcasting. Remote control and unattended operation are permitted when signals of another station are being relayed, provided among other things the transmitter is equipped with automatic circuits which will permit radiation only when a signal coming from the principal or other station is present at the input terminals of the instructional TV apparatus. But means must be provided for turning on and off the transmitter at a place which can be reached promptly at all hours and in all seasons.[67] And the apparatus must be so installed to prevent tampering or operation by unauthorized persons. The station is not required to adhere to any regular schedule and, unless specified in the license, the hours of operation are unlimited.[68] Identification of call signs is required at the beginning and end of each period of operation and once each hour the station is on the air. However, the hourly ID may be deferred if it would interrupt a single consecutive demonstration, lecture, or other similar discourse, or otherwise impair the continuity of a program in progress. In such cases, the announcement should be made at the first normal break in the program.[69] For more detailed information regarding power limits, frequency tolerance, equipment, and other operational requirements, Section 74.935 through 74.981 should be consulted.

Community Antenna TV Systems. In 1968, the FCC estimated that in nearly 3,000 localities over the country, community antenna TV systems (CATV) were in operation. They served about three million homes or about ten million viewers. This was nearly six per cent of the total TV audience in the United States, estimated at about 182 million.[70]* These CATV systems employ receiving antennas which pick up signals from regular TV stations and relay them by wire or cable to customers who pay a fee for the service. In some cases, the signals of distant TV stations are transmitted by micro-wave facilities supplied by common carriers and fed into the local cable distribution system. CATV systems also are privately owned facilities authorized to relay cable programs, as licensed through the Antenna Relay Service (section 74.1030 IRR 54:879).

Originally, these cable systems were not required to secure authorizations from the FCC. Since they do not transmit over the air to the general public, the Commission took the position, at first, that it had no regulatory jurisdiction over their operations.[71] But by 1959 the number had grown to about seven hundred, serving as many as a half million people, and important segments of the broadcasting industry as well as Congress pressed the Commission to reconsider its position.[72]

Some objected to the cable systems on the grounds that they unfairly and unlawfully pirated the programs of regularly licensed TV stations. Some owners of small, local stations without network affiliations protested having to compete with cable carriers that picked up network shows from distant points and micro-waved them to the CATV units where they were distributed to local customers.

In hearings before a Senate subcommittee on communications in July, 1959, a number of broadcasters from western states urged that CATV operators be required to secure licenses from the FCC; that they be required to secure permission of originating stations to distribute their programs; and that the FCC be required to take into account the impact of cable antenna and booster operations on local stations.[73]

With the continued growth of CATV systems, the Commission, under great pressure from broadcasters feeling the pinch of cable competition, took steps to minimize the economic impact on local TV stations.** On February 14, 1962, in *Carter Mountain Transmission Corporation*, the Commission asserted jurisdiction over common-carrier microwave facilities serving CATV systems and beyond this concluded that in the "public interest" the FCC had jurisdiction over the regulatory uses of cable programming.[74] This decision was subsequently sustained by the federal courts.[75]

Shortly thereafter, the Commission began intensive studies and ac-

*It is estimated that as of January 1, 1970 there were 2,350 CATV systems serving 4.5 million subscribers (1970-71 *Television Factbook*, Services Volume No. 40).

**Originally, the most vehement requests for the assertion of FCC jurisdiction came from small market stations with network affiliations (see Notice of Inquiry and Notice of Proposed Rule Making in Docket 15971, 1 FCC 2d 453(1965), and *First Report and Order* in Docket 14895, 38 FCC 683 (1965).

cumulated additional data on the over-all CATV situation. As an outgrowth of these studies, on April 23, 1965, the Commission adopted rules governing the grant of microwave authorizations to be used to relay TV signals to CATV systems. In general, these rules provided that any microwave-served CATV system, upon request, was required to carry the programs of local stations and refrain from duplicating their programs fifteen days before and after local broadcast.[76]

At the same time, the Commission instituted a further rule making proceeding. Contrary to its earlier position, in Part I of its order, the Commission asserted that it did have and should exercise jurisdiction over the CATV systems not served by microwaves and proposed to impose the same requirements on them as were applicable to those served by microwave facilities.[77] In Part II of the proceeding, the Commission initiated an inquiry looking toward possible rule making on broader questions and problems—the effects of CATV developments on independent UHF stations in major markets, possible limits on long distance extension of stations' programs by CATV systems, CATV program origination, and the over-all economic impact of CATV systems, on the American system of broadcasting. Part II also included a *Notice of Proposed Rule Making*, suggesting measures, interim or final, which might be adopted to deal effectively with some of the more pressing problems.[78]

Still doubtful as to its exact authority over CATV, the Commission had been urging Congress to enact legislation to clarify the matter. On March 3, 1966, H.R. 13286 was introduced and Congress began protracted hearings on the matter.[79] The following day, the Commission, under mounting pressure from the broadcast industry, adopted its *Second Report and Order*, establishing regulations covering CATV systems whether or not fed by microwave facilities.[80] CATV systems having fewer than 50 subscribers and those serving apartment houses under common ownership were excluded.[81] The Rules require CATV systems to carry, at the request of TV stations and up to channel capacity, programs of all stations providing a grade A or grade B signal to the CATV area of operations, and all 100 watt translator stations in the CATV community.[82]

Furthermore, the regulations specified that no CATV system operating within the predicted grade A contour of any TV broadcast station in the top 100 markets in the country could bring in the programs of any station which would extend that station's coverage beyond its grade B contour unless, after a public hearing, the Commission determined it to be in the public interest.[83] This, however, was not made applicable to CATV systems in operation as of February 15, 1966.[84]

In May, 1967, the Commission proposed to amend the regulations to make them less restrictive. "At present", said the Commission, "a CATV system must carry—with exceptions—the signal of any television station placing a predicted grade B or better contour over the CATV system's community. A CATV system in a top-100 market cannot import the distant signal of any television station without either a hearing, or, in the alternative, a waiver of Section 74.1107(a) of the Commission's Rules.* This rule has led to anomalous results, as where only two of three competing VHF signals in a market reach a community, or where the signals of a UHF station in the market do not reach as large an area as those of competing VHF stations, or where the CATV system must give priority in carriage to a VHF station over a closer UHF station."[85]

The effect of this proposed rule, if adopted, would be to allow a CATV system in a community within the predicted Grade B contour of any television station in one of the top 100 markets to carry the programs of any other station operating in any community within the market area. As the Commission said, what is proposed is a refinement of standards, "placing on a competitive footing all stations in a given market."[86]

In July, 1967, the Commission proposed further to amend the Rules to allow CATV systems to bring in the programs of distant educational TV stations without the necessity of an evidentiary hearing as now required by Section 74.1107 of the Rules. "We believe," said the Commission, "that sufficient experience has accumulated to indicate that in most top 100 cases no significant objection is voiced to the carriage of distant educational television signals. . . . This change, if adopted, would still permit the Commission to consider any case where objections are raised by local educational authorities pursuant to Section 74.1109 or the Rules . . ."[87] In both notices there were dissenting opinions. Interested parties were given opportunity to file comments.**

Following publication of these two notices the Commission continued to be plagued with increasingly difficult regulatory problems in the CATV field. As a result, the Commission, on December 12, 1968, issued another notice of rule-making much broader in scope, and instituted a far-reaching inquiry into CATV's present and future rule in the national communications structure.[88] After discussing the general nature and scope of the inquiry, the Commission indicated some specific areas of study with which it would be concerned.

The Commission stated that it had in mind authorizing CATV systems to originate their own programs, said it would explore the question as to whether advertising should be permitted, would look into the matter of requiring these systems to observe national regulatory policies which apply to broadcasting, such as equal treatment of political candidates, sponsorship identification, and the fairness doctrine as it applied to the discussion of controversial subjects of public importance.

Other proposals and topics for review concerned diversification of owner-

*The provisions of the Rule and of the Commission's proposal do not apply to CATV systems located outside the top 100 markets. They do not need permission to import distant signals, except when a "timely" objection is filed as provided in Section 74.1105 of the Rules.
**By order of the Commission (FCC 69-1039) the staff was granted delegated authority to act on any unopposed proposal to import distant educational TV signals in the 100 largest TV markets.

ship, the use of CATVs for common carrier purposes in addition to the carriage of broadcast programs, reporting requirements, technical standards, and importation of distant television programs. Many other areas of study were listed as falling within the scope of the inquiry.

On October 24, 1969, the Commission issued an order establishing rules covering some of the proposals made in the December 12, 1968 *Notice* and withholding action on others pending further study. The Commission, in part, stated:

... we wish to emphasize that in this complex rule-making proceeding, it would be wholly impracticable to attempt to issue a comprehensive set of rules governing all aspects. Rather, we shall split off parts for action, deferring action on other parts pending further analysis or further proceedings. Thus while we act here on CATV origination, whether it should be required, whether commercials should be allowed, and certain basic requirements such as equal opportunities for political candidates, fairness, and sponsorship identification, we have not acted on the related diversification issues. Clearly, with origination, there should be multiple ownership rules, particularly with respect to cross-ownership of broadcasting and CATV facilities in the same area. But since the diversification issues require lengthier analysis and study, we act now, as we can, in the above noted areas. For, it is we think, of the utmost importance that we supply needed guidance to the industries involved, to State and municipal entities, and to other interested persons, as to the Federal regulatory policies in this vital area. Moreover, we note that Congress is considering legislation in this area. While the legislation is believed to be aimed essentially at resolving the unfair competition issues treated in Part IV of the *Notice,* our policies in the origination area (Part III) may also be relevant to the Congress in its consideration of the above noted legislation. We think it desirable, therefore, that Congress be fully informed of these policies, so that it may take them into account, either as appropriate background to the legislation or as matters to be included in the legislation. We state, as we have before, that in this important new area we welcome Congressional review and whatever guidance Congress may wish to afford.[89]

The complete text of the proposal and notice of inquiry runs more than fifty pages. It is not feasible to cover the full text here, but broadcasters and CATV operators and students of the media would do well to study it carefully since it reflects the Commission's current thinking on many important regulatory areas concerning CATV and, as indicated by the Commission, will serve as a basis for important future FCC actions affecting the industry.

The new rules, as adopted by the above order, provide that any CATV system may originate programs without restriction and, beginning April 1, 1971, any system with 3,500 subscribers or more will be required to originate programs to a "significant extent." (*Memorandum Opinion and Order* in Docket 18397, 23 FCC 2d 825.) This means the programs will have to include more than mere announcements of time, weather conditions, and services such as music and entertainment. Also, it means that these larger systems will have to have some kind of video cablecasting equipment for the production of local live and delayed programming. The Commission has explained that this requirement of "origination to a significant extent" may be met by the use of tapes and films produced by others and by CATV network programming.

The Commission has also provided that CATVs may present advertising at the beginning and end of each cablecast and at natural intermissions or breaks in the program. Except for these natural breaks, no interruptions of the program continuity by commercials will be allowed.

The new rules further say that CATVs must observe the requirements of the Communications Act and regulations concerning equal opportunities for political candidates, the fairness doctrine, and Section 317 of the Act pertaining to sponsor identification.[90]

In response to inquiries, requesting clarification of the Rules, the Commission issued a *Public Notice*, dated November 25, 1969, declaring that, as of December 1, 1969, any local franchise provision which prohibits a cable system, with fewer than 3,500 subscribers, from originating programs or carrying advertising, is invalid. In the *Notice* the Commission pointed out that, while the new rules make origination mandatory on and after April 1, 1971 only for systems with 3,500 or more subscribers, its policy, as stated in the order establishing the rules, is to encourage voluntary origination by smaller systems. The Commission further indicated that it intended to explore further the question whether systems with fewer than 3,500 subscribers should be required to originate programs and, if so, what the cut-off point should be.

The *Notice* of November 25, also stated that under the new rules (Section 74.1117) any cable system, regardless of size, was free to advertise at the beginning and end of each cable program, and at "natural intermissions or breaks within a cablecast."[91]

On June 24, 1970, the FCC adopted several actions relating to CATV: (1) a proposal to permit CATVsystems in the top 100 markets to import tour distant signals, subject to a specified payment for public broadcasting, deletion of commercials from the outside and substitution of commercials on local broadcast stations, with first priority on independent UHF stations; (2) a proposal to prohibit local cross-ownership of CATV systems by television stations and asked the commission as to limitation of multiple ownership of cable systems on a nationwide and regional basis; (3) possibilities were considered as to twenty and forty channel systems, with possibilities of two-way communication and the use of distinct community channels exclusively devoted to public service programs, and comments were invited on proposed technical standards of operation; (4) the commission affirmed the program origination rules as proposed in 1968; (5) new rules were adopted prohibiting CATV systems from "siphoning off" programs without charge on toll TV stations, and a proposal would prohibit regular telecasts of sports events of transmissions for charge on toll TV (STV) and CATV in a commu-

203

nity within any one year preceding a five year period; and further comments were invited the FCC as to the effect of local and state regulation of cable television and their relationship to federal regulation, and as to what limitation of franchise fees on these cable services. (See FCC Docket 18397 regarding all these FCC actions: *Second Further Notice of Proposed Rule Making*, 1 RR 54 235-248, FCC News Report No. 6103, 35 Fed. Reg 11045; *Notice of Proposed Rule Making and of Inquiry*, 1 RR 54: 249-256, FCC 70-674(49443), FCC News Report No. 6104; *Notice of Proposed Rule Making*, 1 RR 54: 257-262, 35 Fed. Reg. 11044, FCC 70-675 (49425), FCC News Report 6102: *Notice of Proposed Rule Making*, 1 RR 54-263-267, 35 Fed. Reg. 11040, FCC 70-678 (49190), FCC News Report No. 6105; *Notice of Proposed Rule Making*, 1 RR; 273-286, 35 Fed. Reg. 11036, FCC 70-679 (49433), FCC News Report 6107.)

Judicial Sanction of FCC Authority.   Recently, the Courts have held that the FCC does have authority to regulate community antenna systems, though it has been contested vigorously by interested parties. In *United States et al. v. Southwestern Cable Co. et al* (decided by the U. S. Supreme Court, June 10, 1968, 392 U. S. 157, 13 RR 2d 2045), the Court held that the FCC had such authority under Section 2 of the Communications Act and the fact that CATV systems are not common carriers or broadcasters does not mean that they are not subject to regulation by the Commission under this section.[92] The protesting cable systems in this case were engaged in interstate communication, said the Court, even though the programs which they intercepted "emanate from stations located within the same state in which the CATV system operates."[93]

The Court further stated, "that television broadcasting consists in very large part of programming devised for, and distributed to, national audiences; respondents thus are ordinarily employed in the simultaneous retransmission of communications that have very often originated in other states. The stream of communication is essentially uninterrupted and properly indivisible. To categorize respondents' activities as intrastate would disregard the character of 'the television industry', and serve merely to prevent the national regulation that 'is not only appropriate' but essential to the efficient use of radio facilities. *Federal Radio Commission v. Nelson Bros. Co.,* 289 U.S. 266, 279."[94]

In another recent case, *Black Hills Video Corp. v. FCC* (decided by the U.S. Eighth Circuit Court of Appeals, August 7, 1968), in line with the Supreme Court opinion, the Circuit Court upheld the authority of the Commission to regulate CATV systems, whether they be "off-the-air" operations or "microwave-fed," and rejected the contention, among others, that the Commission's rules violate constitutional rights.[95]

A long-awaited decision of the Supreme Court in the case, *Fortnightly Corp. v. United Artists Television, Inc.* (decided June 17, 1968, 13 RR 2d 2061) laid to rest the long standing question as to whether CATV systems infringe the law by carrying, without licenses, the programs of TV stations containing copyrighted materials. The Supreme Court said no. The case turned on the question whether CATV operators, in terms of the Copyright Act of 1909, "perform" the programs that they receive and carry. Answering this question in the negative, the Court said:

The television broadcaster in one sense does less than the exhibitor of a motion picture or stage play; he supplies his audience not with visible images but only with electric signals. The viewer conversely does more than a member or a theater audience; he provides the equipment to convert electronic signals into audible sound and visible images. Despite these deviations from the conventional situation contemplated by the framers of the Copyright Act, broadcasters have been judicially treated as exhibitors, and viewers as members of a theater audience. Broadcasters perform. Viewers do not perform. Thus, while both broadcaster and viewer play crucial roles in the total television process, a line is drawn between them. One is treated as active performer; the other, as passive beneficiary.

When CATV is considered in this framework, we conclude that it falls on the viewer's side of the line. Essentially, a CATV system no more than enhances the viewer's capacity to receive the broadcaster's signals; it provides a well-located antenna with an efficient connection to the viewer's television set. It is true that a CATV system plays an "active" role in making reception possible in a given area, but so do ordinary television sets and antennas. CATV equipment is powerful and sophisticated, but the basic function the equipment performs is little different from that performed by the equipment generally furnished by a television viewer. If an individual erected an antenna on a hill, strung a cable to his house, and installed the necessary amplifying equipment, he would not be "performing" the programs he received on his television set. The result would be no different if several people combined to erect a cooperative antenna for the same purpose. The only difference in the case of CATV is that the antenna system is erected and owned not by its users, but by an entrepreneur.

The function of CATV systems has little in common with the function of broadcasters. CATV systems do not in fact broadcast or rebroadcast. Broadcasters select the programs to be viewed; CATV systems simply carry, without editing, whatever programs they receive. Broadcasters procure programs and propagate them to the public; CATV systems receive programs that have been released to the public and carry them by private channels to additional viewers. We hold that CATV operators, like viewers and unlike broadcasters, do not perform the programs that they receive and carry.[96]

For a number of years, Congress has been considering changes in the Copyright Act of 1909 upon which the Supreme Court decision was based. At this writing, new legislation seems imminent, and conceivably proposed revisions of the law now pending in Congress could require the cable companies to pay copyright fees, at least under some conditions. Vested interests have been and still are battling in the halls of Congress over the matter. What the legislative outcome will be is still uncertain.[97]

Subscription Television. Another special broadcast service recently authorized by the Commission is subscription television. On February 10,

1955, the FCC adopted a Notice of Proposed Rule Making to authorize this service and invited interested parties to file comments regarding the proposal.[98] The Notice listed numerous questions as to its legal validity and its possible effects on the public interest.

In the comments filed in response to the Notice, three systems for subscription TV were submitted for consideration and approval: (1) *Phonevision,* supported by Zenith Radio Corporation and Teco, Inc.; (2) *Subscriber-Vision* endorsed by Skiatron Electronics and Television Company and Skiatron Television, Inc., and (3) *Telemeter,* proposed by International Television Corporation.

During the week of September 15, 1957, the FCC was informed of two other methods: *Bi-Tran,* developed by Blonder-Tongue Laboratories, Inc., and *Teleglobe* by Teleglobe Pay-Television System, Inc.[99]

Briefly, the operating principles of these systems are as follows. Phonevision, Subscriber-Vision and Telemeter contemplate the encoding and scrambling of both images and sound transmitted via TV. Each requires the use of a decoding device attached to the receiver. Phonevision, and Subscriber-Vision would involve periodic billings, while Telemeter would require deposit of coins in a box associated with the decoder. All three systems provide, in different ways, for the dissemination to subscribers of information on how to activate the decoders and the procedure for recording charges and making payments.

Teleglobe involves the sending of the TV picture by conventional methods but the sound part of the transmission would be sent by wire and made available only to subscribing members of the public.

The Bi-tran system envisages simultaneous transmission of two programs on a single channel, one of which would be available without charge as at present, and the other subject to a fee and used for subscription TV operations.

The proponents of these various systems filed detailed comments urging the Commission to authorize the new service. The Joint Council on Educational Television filed a brief comment taking no definite position on the merits, but saying that educators should have the privilege of using subscription TV if the new service should be authorized.

The three major commercial networks vigorously objected. They were joined by the National Association of Radio and Television Broadcasters. The Joint Committee on Toll Television (said to represent a large percentage of the motion picture exhibitors in the country) and some television stations registered their disapproval.

Following the issuance of a Notice of Further Proceedings in May, 1957, the FCC announced that it had concluded that it had the statutory authority to authorize toll TV.[100] While the Communications Act of 1934 did not specifically authorize the Commission to approve toll TV, the Commission, in justifying its action, relied upon certain general provisions of the Act. In the First Report, reference was made to Section 301 which states that a basic purpose of the Act is "to provide for the use" of radio channels "under licenses granted by Federal authority."

The Commission also made reference to paragraphs (b), (e) and (g) of Section 303 of the Act which empower the Commission to prescribe the nature of the service to be rendered by each class of radio station; to regulate the kind of apparatus it uses, and to study new uses for radio, provide for experimental uses of frequencies, and generally encourage the larger and more effective use of radio in the public interest.

While acknowledging limitations on its power (such as the statutory bar against censorship) the Commission declared that there was nothing in the language of the Communications Act suggesting Congressional intent to prohibit the authorization of toll TV.

The Commission took note of arguments made against the legal validity of the system—that Section 1 of the law states the basic purpose of the Act to be that of providing communications facilities to *all* the people; that Section 3 (o) defines broadcasting as "the dissemination of radio communications intended to be received by the public" and that Congress, in passing the law, did not contemplate program service being made available only to such persons as were able and willing to pay a charge for it.

The Commission's response to these arguments was that Section 1 states the purpose of the Communications Act in broad terms but does not preclude the authorization of special services. For example, the Commission said, reference in the Act to "all the people of the United States" does not prevent the Commission from licensing stations for safety and other special purposes. Also, the Commission pointed out that it already licenses FM stations to provide musical programs to restaurants, department stores, etc., —establishments that pay a fee for the service, and that the basic operating principles of subscription TV are essentially no different.

After considerable analysis of the legislative history of the Communications Act as it relates to toll TV, the Commission concluded that it did have the statutory power to authorize the service and that the only real question is whether the public interest will be served. In this connection, the Commission stated two fundamental issues:

(1) Will toll TV supplement the program choices, and provide an increase in financial resources that will increase the numbers of services to the public than under the present system?

(2) Or will it seriously impair the capacity of the present system to provide advertiser-financed programming now free of direct charge to the public?

Arguments by Proponents. Proponents of toll TV argued that under our present system of broadcasting, advertisers for the most part determine the type of programs that go out over the air; that their main concern is to reach the largest possible audience and that there is not the diversity and variety of programming that there might be; that with toll TV the listeners will determine the programs and that broadcasts of opera, Shakespearean drama, etc., while not attracting huge audiences, will attract enough viewers to make them economically worthwhile. They have argued that programs will be presented without commercials and that this will appeal to the general public.

Arguments by Opponents. Opponents of pay-as-you-see TV argued that the public is asked to pay for what it now gets without charge and that the present broadcasting system will be destroyed. They argued that if toll TV can attract large audiences, enormous revenue will be derived which will tend to attract the best talent away from conventional TV; that with the loss of economic support from advertisers, the networks and stations will not be able to supply outstanding sustaining programs. They contend that toll TV can't offer anything the public doesn't already get. Why charge? Toll TV will be seeking the same big profits anyway, they say.

Trial Period. The Commission considered these various arguments and decided to authorize toll TV on a trial basis, but to reserve judgment on whether it should be approved on a permanent basis. The Commission said:

... While a trial may not be expected to give, in itself, a complete demonstration of the effects of a subsequently expanded subscription television service—should it be found desirable later to authorize it—it could, nevertheless, provide useful information concerning what subscription television can offer, how the public responds to what is offered, how the service would operate in practice, what, if any, abuses require curbing, whether it imposes a genuine threat to the free service (as distinguished from a challenge to that service to meet fresh competition of a new kind) what legislative and administrative safeguards would be desirable and effective, and a host of other important questions, such as the desirability of standardizing the equipment used, on which a largely argumentative record affords inadequate basis for final conclusions and decisions at this time.[101]

Conditions of Trial Operations. In authorizing trial operations the FCC set forth a number of conditions:

(1) During the trial period any single toll TV system was limited to three markets.

(2) Authorizations were limited to cities having at least four commercial television stations. This was to make sure of continuing availability of free program service and at the same time allow maximum opportunities for competition between toll TV and the present system.

(3) Both VHF and UHF stations were eligible.

(4) Applications would be accepted from any holder of a construction permit or license for a television station or any person who filed an application on FCC Form 301 requesting a construction permit and asking for a waiver of the rules as then precluded subscription TV.

(5) Systems could not cause interference to other stations and the reception had to be good.

(6) Any franchise holder had to provide the service to all stations in the community who wanted it.

(7) The station had to be free to use more than one system if it wanted to.

(8) The contracts between the franchise holder for TV operation and the station had to be so worded as to permit any station contracting to present programs under one system to transmit them under any other system that meets the technical requirements of the Commission. Thus, more than one station would be free to participate in the trial operation of any individual system, more than one system would have an opportunity to be tried in the community, and any single station would have an opportunity if it desired and was authorized, to transmit subscription programs under more than one system.

(9) Licensees would be responsible for the choice of programs and had to participate in determining the charges made to all subscribers.

(10) Programs had to begin no later than six months after authorization unless more time was granted for good cause.

(11) Minimum hours of free programs were required to be broadcast.

(12) Periodical reports were to be made to the Commission on the status of the trial operations.

(13) Technical regulations governing regular stations, such as the keeping of logs, were made applicable to toll TV operations.

Congressional Reaction. Following adoption of the report authorizing subscription TV under these conditions, the House Interstate and Foreign Commerce Committee, conducted six days of public hearings on the matter. Thereafter, on February 6, 1958, the Committee adopted the following resolution:

Resolved, that it is the sense of this Committee that the public interest would not be served by the granting of authorizations for subscription television operations as contemplated by the Federal Communications Commission in its First Report, adopted October 17, 1957, in Docket Number 11279, because

(1) It has not been established to the complete satisfaction of this Committee that authority to license such operations comes within the power of the Commission under the provisions of the Communications Act of 1934; and

(2) Such operations might lead at least to a partial blacking-out of the present system in particular communities, if not throughout the United States.[102]

Subsequently, numerous bills were introduced in both houses to prohibit or place restriction on toll TV service and the Commission was informed that further Congressional hearings would be held on the subject.

In response, the Commission issued its Second Report on the matter, February 26, 1958, announcing that no applications for authorizations to conduct trial toll TV operations would be processed until thirty days following the *sine die* adjournment of the 85th Congress.[103]

More than a year having elapsed since this announcement, the Commission, on March 23, 1959, issued a Third Report in the proceeding stating that applications for trial subscription television operations would be accepted under conditions previously announced except that the trial of any particular television system would be limited to a *single* city and not to *three* as previously provided. Another new limiting factor added was that authorizations would be granted only on condition that the public would not be called upon to purchase any special receiving equipment.[104]

This action was followed two days later by the adoption of a resolution by the Senate Interstate and Foreign Commerce Committee (by a vote of 11 to 10) stating that it had no reservations to the approval of toll TV as contemplated in the Commission's Third Report.[105]

The Zenith Radio Corporation announced in late March, 1960 that it had entered into an agreement with the RKO General Company to conduct a three year experiment in toll TV in Hartford, Connecticut under the conditions recently prescribed by the FCC. It announced that the two companies would request the Commission's approval for the ten million dollar experiment.[106]

Subsequently, Hartford Phonevision Company (subsidiary of RKO General, Inc.) filed an application with the FCC for authority to conduct trial subscription TV operations over its station WHCT (channel 18) in Hartford. On September 28, 1960, the FCC designated this application for a public hearing. In announcing this action, the Commission stressed that questions relating to a general toll TV service would have to await further hearings and the consideration of appropriate legislation.[107] The only matter, therefore, which the Commission proposed to decide in that hearing was whether to authorize the limited trial operation proposed for a three-year period in Hartford.

The Commission did conclude that a trial operation should be authorized and the Hartford station began operation on June 29, 1962. Its authorization was extended for three years on May 21, 1965, and further extended in 1968.[108] In the meantime, the Commission appointed a Committee (Commissioners Lee, Cox and Wadsworth) to study the data subsequently submitted by the Hartford operation. Shortly after the close of fiscal year 1967, this Committee issued a report containing proposals regarding toll television.[109] It was recommended that "over-the-air subscription television" (STV) be established as a permanent broadcast service and comments were subsequently invited as to what technical rules and equipment standards should be adopted. Oral argument on the proposals was held before the Commission on October 2, 1967.[110]

On November 16, 1967, the House Interstate and Foreign Commerce Committee adopted a resolution asking the Commission to withhold action for one year or until the Communications Act is amended specifically authorizing toll television service.[111]

As proposed by the FCC Committee STV authorizations were to be granted only in communities within the primary coverage areas (grade A contours) having at least five or more commercial TV stations, the STV facility being counted as one of the five. While there would be no requirement for minimum or maximum hours of STV programming, the toll TV station would have to provide a minimum number of hours of non-STV broadcasts as specified by the Commission.[112]

The service was to be available to both UHF and VHF stations, but only one authorization would be allowed in any one community. Charges and service conditions would have to be applied uniformly; STV decoders, attached to receiving sets, would have to be leased and could not be sold to subscribers; the showing of feature films more than two years old and not more than ten would be prohibited; older ones would be permitted, but the number would be strictly limited by the FCC; the amount of time devoted to films and sports programming would be limited to 90 per cent and some "educational and cultural" programming would be expected during the remaining hours; and no commercials would be permitted.[113]

CATV carriage and nonduplication rules, discussed above, would be applicable to the conventional (non-STV) programming of a toll TV station. However, CATV systems would not be required to carry STV programming, though, with FCC approval, an STV station could make arrangements with CATV systems within its coverage areas (grade A and B) to have them carry its programs over their cables.[114]

On December 12, 1968, the Commission finally issued a Fourth Report and Order establishing, on a permanent basis, a subscription television service (STV).* The Commission related the thirteen year history of the case, including the results of the Hartford experiment mentioned above. It reviewed the fifteen regulatory issues which had been raised by parties during the long proceeding, and concluded that the FCC had the statutory power to authorize STV and that, in so doing, the public interest would be served.[115]

To protect so-called "free" broadcasting, some limitations were imposed upon the new service. The new rules, prescribing the nature and limitations of STV, stated that (1) authorizations are to be issued only to the licensees, or the holders of construction permits, or to applicants for commercial TV facilities; (2) an authorization for an STV operation may be granted only to stations whose principal area of service is located entirely within the grade A contour of five or more commercial TV stations (including the station of the applicant); (3) no more than one STV station may be operated in one single community; (4) no advertising (except announcements promoting STV programs) is allowed during STV programming; (5) some limitations apply to the showing of feature films which have been generally released in theatres anywhere in the United States more than two years prior to their use on STV; (6) sports events may not be carried live on STV broadcasts if those events have been regularly televised in the community via "free" television during the previous two years; (7) STV stations, in addition to the

*With some modifications the Commission adopted the proposals of the Subscription Television Committee.

211

subscription programs, must also broadcast the minimum number of hours of "free" television, as required of all TV stations under Section 73.651 of the Commission's Rules.[116]

On September 4, 1969, the Commission adopted technical standards for Subscription Television and specified detailed requirements for the filing of applications.[117] Less than three weeks later the Court of Appeals in the District of Columbia, having previously received an appeal from the National Association of Theatre Owners, upheld the Commission's authority to establish and regulate the toll TV service.[118] The Supreme Court of the United States, on February 24, 1970, denied *certiorari.* [119]

1. FCC Rules and Regulations, Section 74.432; 1 RR 54:197.
2. Section 74.401; 1 RR 54:191.
3. Section 74.433; 1 RR 54:199.
4. *Ibid.*
5. *Ibid.*
6. *Ibid.*
7. Section 74.437(f); 1 RR 54:202.
8. Section 74.437(g); 1 RR 54:202.
9. Section 74.437(h); 1 RR 54:203.
10. Section 74.437(i); 1 RR 54:203.
11. Section 74.501(a)(b) and Section 74.601; 1 RR 54:221, 241; also see *FCC Annual Report,* 1958, p. 118.
12. *Ibid.*
13. Section 74.531(c); 1 RR 54:223.
14. Section 74.531(d); 1 RR 54:223.
15. Section 74.531(e); 1 RR 54:223.
16. *Ibid.*
17. Section 74.532(b); 1 RR 54:224.
18. Section 74.532(c); 1 RR 54:224.
19. Section 74.532(d); 1 RR 54:224.
20. Section 74.533(a); 1 RR 54:224.
21. Section 74.601; 1 RR 54:241.
22. Section 74.631(d); 1 RR 54:247.
23. *Ibid.,* 1 RR 54: 247-248.
24. Section 74.632(a); 1 RR 54:249.
25. Section 74.632(d); 1 RR 54:249.
26. Section 74.632(e); 1 RR 54:249.
27. Section 74.633; 1 RR 54:250.
28. Section 74.634; 1 RR 54:250-251.
29. Section 74.701(a); 1 RR 54: 271.
30. Section 74.701(b)(c)(d)(e); 1 RR 271.
31. 21 Fed Reg. 3684(1956); 13 RR 1561.
32. 25 Fed. Reg. 7317 (Aug. 4, 1960); 20 RR 1536.
33. *Ibid.,* 1538.
34. *Ibid.*
35. *Ibid.,* 1539-1540.
36. Section 74.702 (a) (b); 1 RR 54:271.
37. Section 74.702(c); 1 RR 54:272.
38. Section 74.732(a) (b) (c) (d); 1 RR 54:275.
39. Section 74.732 (2) (f); 1 RR 54:276.
40. Section 74.733; 1 RR 54:277-278.
41. Section 74.734; 1 RR 54:279.
42. Section 74.735, 74.781; 1 RR 54:279-287.
43. Section 74.781 and 74.783; 1 RR 54:287.
44. Section 74.831; 1 RR 54:303.
45. *Ibid.*
46. Section 74.831-832; 1 RR 54: 303-304.
47. Section 74.835; 1 RR 54: 304.
48. Section 74.834, 74.861, 74.863; 1 RR 54: 304-311.
49. FCC Public Notice 72034, April 14, 1959; 18 RR 1514a.
50. 100 U. S. App. D. C. 379; 246 F(2d) 660; 15 RR 2033(1957).

51. FCC Public Notice 72034, April 14, 1959; 18 RR 1514b.

52. *Ibid.*

53. S. C. R. 4 and H. C. R. 62, 86th Congress, First Session; also see *Broadcasting,* April 20, 1959, p. 76-77.

54. FCC Public Notice 72034, April 14, 1959; 18 RR 1514.

55. Public Law 86-609. approved July 7, 1960; 74 Stat. 363.

56. Section 74.790; 1 RR 54:810.

57. *Ibid.*

58. 25 RR 1785; also see 2 RR(2d) 1615; also see 28 Fed. Reg. 8103.

59. FCC *34th Annual Report/Fiscal Year 1968,* p. 29.

60. *FCC, 35th Annual Report/Fiscal Year 1969, p. 38.*

61. *Ibid.*

62. Section 74.901(c); 1 RR 54:851.

63. Section 74.931(b); 1 RR 54:851.

64. Section 74.931(c); 1 RR 54:851.

65. *Ibid.*

66. Section 74.932; 1 RR 54:851-852.

67. Section 74.934; 1 RR 54:853.

68. Sections 74.933(1) and 74.963(a); 1 RR 54:852, 861.

69. Section 74.982(a)(b)(c); 1 RR 54:865.

70. *FCC Annual Report/Fiscal Year 1968,* p. 46.

71. See *FCC Report and Order,* Docket No. 12443, April 14, 1959, 18 RR 1573, for comprehensive opinion of Commission that it had no authority to regulate CATV systems. The Commission contended at that time that CATV systems were not common carriers nor were they engaged in broadcasting as defined by the Communications Act and, therefore, concluded that there was no FCC jurisdiction. The opinion said that these systems were engaged in interstate commerce but that Congress would have to enact legislation before the Commission could regulate them.

72. *Broadcasting,* June 29, 1959.

73. *Ibid.,* July, 1959, pp. 64-69.

74. 32 FCC 459, 1181; 22 RR 193, 194h.

75. U. S. Court of Appeals, District of Columbia Circuit, May 23, 1963; 25 RR 2055; 321 F 2d 359; *cert. den.,* 375 U. S. 951.

76. 4 RR 2d 1725; 30 Fed. Reg. 6038.

77. *Ibid.,* pp. 1691-1694.

78. *Ibid.,* pp. 1695-1705.

79. H. R. 13286, March 3, 1966.

80. 6 RR 2d 1717; 31 Fed. Reg. 4540.

81. Section 74.1101; 1 RR 54:901.

82. Section 74.1103; 1 RR 54:902.

83. Section 74.1107; 1 RR 54:906.

84. *Ibid.*

85. 32 Fed. Reg. 7537.

86. *Ibid.*

87. 32 Fed. Reg. 10664.

88. 15 FCC (2d) 417; 33 Fed. Reg. 19028.

89. 17 RR 2d 1571-1572; 34 Fed. Reg. 1.

90. *Ibid.,* and see Rules in 1 RR 54:1101 and 54:1111-54:1119.

91. 17 RR 2d 1676-1677; FCC Public Notice, November 25, 1969; FCC 69-1276, 40096. In regard to these matters of program origination and advertising by cable systems, the Commission expressed the opinion that under the doctrine of "pre-emption" any local franchise provisions contrary to these Federal regulations would be invalid, but that local authorities who grant the cable franchises are free "to

impose additional affirmative obligations which are not inconsistent with Federal regulatory policies. 'See Head v. New Mexico, 374 U. S. 424; 25 RR 2087 (1963)).

92. 13 RR 2d 2045; 392 U. S. 157.

93. 13 RR 2d 2052; 392 U. S. 168-169.

94. 13 RR 2d 2052-2053; 392 U. S. 169.

95. 13 RR 2d 2128; 399 F. 2d 65.

96. 13 RR 2d 2066-2068; 392 U. S. 398-401.

97. For background on the Congressional proceedings relating to revision of Copyright laws which would affect community antenna systems, the issues involved, and bills pending in the House and Senate, see reports on House Hearings held by Subcommittee, No. 3, of the Committee on the Judiciary on House Bill 4347 and Report thereon (H. Rept. No. 2237, 89th Congress, Second Session, October 12, 1966); Report No. 83, 90th Congress, 1st Session, March 8, 1967, which accompanied H. R. 2512 and which grew out of and reflected some changes in H. R. 4347; Hearings before the Subcommittee on Patents, Trademarks, and Copyrights of the Senate Committee on the Judiciary, 90th Congress, 1st Session, pursuant to S. Res. 37 on S. 597, April 6, 11 and 12, 1967; S. 543, a revised bill introduced by Senator McClellan in the Senate, 91st Congress, 1st Session, January 10, 1969.

98. Docket 11279(FCC 55-165); 20 Fed. Reg. 988(1955).

99. *Ibid.* (FCC 57-1153); 16 RR 1509(1957).

100. *Ibid.*, p. 1513; also see Commission's letter to Honorable Oren Harris, Chairman, Interstate and Foreign Commerce Committee, July 3, 1957, 15 RR 1689; also see *Notice of Further Proceedings* of May 23, 1957, 22 Fed. Reg. 3758(1957), and Memorandum of Law Concerning Authority of the Federal Communications Commission to Authorize Subscription Television Operations of the same date, 15 RR 1692(1957).

101. *Ibid.*, 1522.

102. See Hearings before House Committee on Interstate and Foreign Commerce, 85th Congress, 2d Session, on Subscription Television, January 14, 15, 16, 17, 21, 22 and 23, 1958. The text of the Committee resolution was reported by the FCC in its *Second Report* in Docket 11279 in 16 RR 1539-1540.

103. FCC Docket 11279; 23 Fed. Reg. 1574(1958); 16 RR 1539.

104. *Ibid.*, 1540a; 24 Fed. Reg. 2534(1959); see other changes and conditions in FCC *Third Report.*

105. 16 RR 1540 j.

106. See *Broadcasting,* April 4, 1960, pp. 35-37, for full report on plans for this experiment.

107. FCC Public Notice-B, No. 94442, September 28, 1960, 25 Fed. Reg. 9572 (1960).

108. 30 FCC 301; 20 RR 754(1961); 14 RR (2d) 1603; 30 Fed. Reg. 7187.

109. 32 Fed. Reg. 10606; 10 RR (2d) 1617(1967).

110. 14 RR 2d 1602.

111. 14 RR 2d 1606-1607.

112. See 32 Fed. Reg. 10606; 10 RR 2d 1617(1967).

113. *Ibid.*

114. *Ibid.*

115. For a full discussion of the history and issues involved in the case, see 14 RR 2d 1601(1969); 15 FCC 2d 466; 33 Fed. Reg. 19149.

116. See Sections 73.641, 73.642, 73.643, 73.644; 1 RR 53:1451-1456, 47 CFR 218.

117. 17 RR 2d 1509; 34 Fed. Reg. 14370.

118. U. S. Court of Appeals, District of Columbia, September 30, 1969; 17 RR 2d 2010.

119. 397 U. S. 922(1970).

CHAPTER 12

Experimental Radio and Broadcast Services

Except as otherwise provided in this Act, the Commission from time to time, as public convenience, interest, or necessity requires shall study new uses for radio, provide for experimental uses of frequencies, and generally encourage the larger and more effective use of radio in the public interest.
—Section 303 (g) of the Communications Act of 1934.

Section 303(g) of the Communications Act requires that the FCC "study new uses for radio, provide for experimental uses of frequencies, and generally encourage the larger and more effective use of radio in the public interest."[1] The Commission has implemented this provision by the establishment of various classes of experimental stations and the adoption of rules governing their operations.

Experimental Radio. Part 5 of the Commission's Rules and Regulations sets forth elaborately the licensing and operating requirements for experimental radio stations. The Commission has classified these stations into two groups: (1) those authorized to do research in the radio art not related to the development of an established or proposed new service, or to provide essential communications for research projects which could not be carried on without the use of such communications; and (2) those authorized to experiment with the development of data, or techniques for an existing or proposed radio service.[2]

These experimental radio operations are non-broadcast in character; that is, they may involve the experimental study of the propagation characteristics of certain frequencies, or the use of radio energy in connection with research projects in industry, or the development of improved transmitting or receiving equipment, etc.—projects in which broadcasting to the general public is not involved or is not an essential part.

Application and Licensing Procedure. Part 5 of the FCC Rules and Regulations, Sections 5.1 through 5.411, provide for the establishment of these stations, define their purposes, and prescribe the requirements for their operation.[3]

Applications to construct land (fixed and mobile) stations in this service, or to modify permits, must be filed on FCC Form 440. A separate application must be filed for each station. Where mobile units are to be used in connection with one operation, these several units may be requested in the one application.[4]

FCC Form 403 is used to request licenses for operation after construction has been completed or to modify licenses already granted.[5]

The rules specify that FCC Form 405 must be used to apply for renewal of licenses. In this connection Section 5.55 (g) states that "a blanket application may be submitted for renewal of a group of station licenses in the same class in those cases where the renewal requested is in exact accordance with the terms of the previous authorizations. The individual stations covered by such applications shall be clearly identified thereon. Unless otherwise directed by the Commission, each application for renewal of license shall be filed at least 60 days prior to the expiration date of the license to be renewed."[6]

The rules provide for the filing of informal requests (usually in letter form) for special permission to operate these stations on a temporary basis in a manner different to that specified in the authorization, providing the requests in no way conflict with Commission rules. These requests must give the name and address of applicant; explain the purpose of the request and the need for special action; and inform the Commission regarding the class, type, location and date of the proposed operation. They must also specify equipment to be used, frequency desired, power output, type of radio emission and antenna height.[7]

In connection with all formal applications for construction permits for these experimental stations, a supplemental statement must be submitted with facts showing that the applicant is qualified to do the project proposed; that qualified personnel and adequate technical and financial resources are available; that an organized plan of experimentation has been worked out which promises to make a constructive contribution to the radio art, and that laboratory developments have reached the stage where actual transmission by radio is essential to further progress; and that harmful interference will not be caused to other stations.[8]

In addition, a statement must be submitted by the applicant confirming his understanding that all frequencies are assigned for experimental purposes only, and that the granting of authority to experiment as proposed shall not be construed as a finding by the Commission that the frequencies assigned are the best suited for the project, or that the applicant is qualified to operate any station other than experimental or that he may be so authorized. And finally, he must confirm his understanding that there will be no obligation on the part of the Commission to make provision for his type of operation on a regular basis.[9]

Operational Requirements.   Sections 5.101 through 5.166 of FCC Rules contain the technical standards and operation requirements for these experimental radio stations. Requirements regarding frequency stability, types of emission that may be used, modulation, transmitter control and measurements, power and antenna heights, etc. are specifically set forth.[10]

The Commission expects adherence to these regulations, but in keeping with the exploratory and experimental character of these services, the Commission wisely allows some exceptions, "provided the applicant makes a satisfactory showing that the nature of the proposed program of experimentation precludes compliance therewith."[11]

These stations may make only such transmissions as are necessary to the conduct of the applicant's specified research project, and, unless permitted in the instrument of authorization, must not retransmit signals of any other station, or transmit programs intended for public reception.[12]

Unless specifically exempted, each station must announce its call letters at the end of each complete transmission. This is not required where the project calls for "continuous, frequent or extended use of the transmitting apparatus." In such case, the call letters should be announced at least every thirty minutes.[13]

Licensed operators are required. Their licenses together with that of the station must be conspicuously posted at the principal point of operational control. Records of operation must be maintained, and tower lights must be regularly checked as specified in the rules.[14]

Reports to the FCC on Experimental Program. The normal license period for experimental radio stations is for two years only[15], as against a period of three years for regular broadcast stations. Except in the case of stations providing essential communications for research projects, a report on the results of the experimental program authorized by the Commission must be submitted with and made a part of each application for renewal of license. The Commission may request other reports as it deems necessary during the period of a license, to evaluate the progress of the experimental program.[16]

Stations falling in the research group, as defined by the Commission and mentioned above, must include in their reports filed with renewal applications description of the experimentation conducted; detailed analysis of the results obtained; copies of publications covering the experimental work; a list of patents issued as a result of the research; and the number of hours the stations operated on each frequency assigned.[17]

Where a renewal of license is being requested for a radio facility essential to a research project not concerned with the radio art, the Commission requires a showing of need for continuing the authorization as part of the renewal application.[18]

With respect to stations classified as developmental, in addition to submitting the above data, they must provide comprehensive information as to the practicability of service operations, interference encountered, signals employed, and prospects for public support for the new service if established.[19]

Student Authorization for Radio Experimentation. On July 23, 1953, the Commission adopted special rules to encourage radio experimentation by students and instructors in educational institutions. These rules are reported at 23 Fed. Reg. 5775, and 1 RR 55:56-57. These authorizations may, in the discretion of the Commission, be granted to students of seventh grade or higher level.

As provided in Section 5.402 of the rules, an application may be filed in letter form, in duplicate, signed under oath and shall contain the following information:

(1) Name and adress of applicant.

(2) A statement that the applicant is a citizen of the United States.

(3) Applicant's school and grade.

(4) A detailed description in narrative form of the project including the type and purpose of operation.

(5) Place of operation—street address, name of building, or other specific location.

(6) Date(s) of operation including the exact hours, when known, as well as the duration of each period of operation.

(7) Equipment to be used. If manufactured, list name of manufacturer and type number. For other equipment, describe in detail and furnish a circuit diagram.

(8) Frequency(ies) desired and range of frequencies which could be employed.

(9) The method by which the frequency of operation will be determined.

(10) Frequency tolerance.

(11) The means by which this tolerance will be maintained.

(12) DC place power input to final radio frequency stage. If not known, indicate any known power rating of equipment and state whether this is power output of transmitter or radiated power, and whether average or peak.

(13) Type of emission, including a description of the modulation that will be applied, if modulated.

(14) Description of the antenna to be used, including height above ground.

Dimensions of Experimental Radio.   In its 1958 annual report, the Commission pointed out several types of experiments being carried on in the experimental radio services.[20] For example, studies were being made to determine the height of the various reflecting layers in the ionosphere, which information is useful in making high frequency propagation forecasts.

Other licensees were investigating "scatter" phenomena, so called, which is developing as a new mode of long range communication, using VHF.

Experimental studies were being conducted, investigating propagation characteristics at the frequency of 8 kilocycles, which is just below the commonly accepted lower boundary of the radio spectrum. The antenna being used for the study was a section of high voltage power line several miles in length.

Other important experimentation in the development of new radio equipment is being carried on by colleges, universities, manufacturing concerns, and private laboratories, using radio frequencies assigned by the Commission in the experimental services.

"Another function of the experimental radio services," the Commission stated in 1958, "is to provide short-term authorizations for field-strength surveys and equipment demonstrations to prospective purchasers of new radio equipment. The demand for this type of operation has increased approximately 400 per cent in a little over 4 years and is still climbing. Experimental applications processed during the year totaled 2,854 as compared with 1,055 in 1952 and authorizations increased from 369 to 834."[21]

Because of the tremendous growth in experimental radio operations, there is the increasing problem of finding frequencies to meet the demand. More and more, researchers are compelled to share frequencies, and care must be exercised to see that regularly established services are not disrupted and that maximum utility from experimental frequencies is achieved.

Experimental Broadcast Services. In addition to stations in the experimental radio service, the Commission has provided in its rules for the establishment of experimental broadcast stations whose operations include the presentation of programs for public reception.

There are three types of these stations. One is the *Experimental Television Broadcast Station.* It is defined as one licensed for experimental transmission of "transient visual images of moving or fixed objects for simultaneous reception and reproduction by the general public." It of course also involves the transmission of synchronized sound and any license for such a station authorizes aural as well as visual transmissions.[22]

Its purpose is to carry on research and experimentation for the advancement of television broadcasting which may include tests of equipment, training of personnel, and experimental programs as are necessary.[23]

A second type of experimental broadcast station provided for in the Commission rules is that involving *Facsimile* transmission.[24] FM stations may transmit still pictures, graphs, and printed or written matter to the general public on a simplex or multiplex basis. In the past a few authorizations have been granted for transmission of facsimile, but no stations are now engaged in this type of broadcasting.

The *Developmental Broadcast Station* is a third type. Its purpose is to carry on research and development primarily in radiotelephony for the advancement of broadcasting in general.[25] This kind of station may broadcast programs only when they are necessary to the experiments being conducted, but no regular program service may be carried on unless specifically authorized by the FCC.[26] Section 4.382 of the Rules states that if the license authorizes the carrying of programs, the developmental broadcast station may transmit the programs of a standard, or FM broadcast station or networks, provided, that during the broadcast a statement is made identifying the source of the programs and announcing that the program is being presented in connection with the experimental operation.[27]

Application and Licensing Procedure. FCC Form 309 is used in applying for permits to establish these three types of experimental broadcast facilities.[28] As is true with experimental radio stations already discussed, it must be shown in the application for each type of experimental broadcast station that the proposed operation complies with the general provisions of the Communications Act; that a definite program of technical research and experimentation has been worked out which indicates reasonable promise of substantial contribution to the development of the particular art; that the applicant has qualified personnel and is capable of proceeding immediately with such a program; and that the transmission of radio signals is essential to the proposed experimental research.[29]

Similar to the requirements in the experimental radio services, a supplemental statement must be filed with the application confirming the applicant's understanding that all operation upon the frequency requested is for experimental purposes only; that the frequency requested may not be the best suited for the particular project; and that it need not be allocated for any service that may be developed as a result of the experimentation; and that the frequency assignment is subject to change or cancellation without advance notice or hearing.[30]

After an application is granted, during the period of construction, the permittee (after notifying the Commission and the Engineer in Charge of the district in which the station is located) is free to conduct equipment tests.[31] Once these tests show compliance with conditions of the permit and technical requirements of the FCC, a license application may be filed on FCC Form 310 showing the station to be in satisfactory operating condition.[32] The station may then conduct service or program tests, provided, the Engineer in Charge of the district and the Commission are notified at least two days (not including Sundays, Saturdays and legal holidays) in advance of the beginning of such broadcasting.[33]

Each license specifies the maximum power that may be used by the station, and in no event may the actual operating power for an experimental broadcast station exceed more than 3 per cent of that authorized by the license. A 5 per cent tolerance is allowed for all types of these stations.[34] The license is issued subject to the condition that no objectionable interference will be caused other stations.[35]

More than one frequency may be assigned for these experimental broadcast operations provided the applicant has made an adequate showing of need, but the Commission does not authorize the exclusive use of any frequency by a single licensee.[36] Where interference will result from the simultaneous operation of experimental broadcast stations, licensees must try to arrange a satisfactory time division so that the interference will be avoided. If an agreement cannot be reached, then the Commission specifies the time division.[37]

Sections 74.103, 74.202, and 74.302 provide that the frequencies which are allocated for aural and TV broadcasting are listed in the Commissions Table of Frequency Allocations and are frequencies which may be assigned for experimental, facsimile, or developmental broadcasting.[38]

No person may own more than one experimental broadcast or facsimile station unless a showing is made that the character of the programs of research requires a licensing of two or more separate stations.[39] This limitation on ownership, however, does not appear in the rules relating to developmental and other types of experimental stations discussed in this chapter.

Licenses for these stations are granted for one year, and renewal applications (FCC Form 311) must be filed 60 days prior to the expiration of the licenses.[40] With respect to the experimental TV stations, a report must accompany the renewal application showing the following:

(1) Number of hours the station has operated.
(2) Full data on research and experimentation conducted including the type of transmitting and studio equipment used and their mode of operation.
(3) Data on expense of research and operation during the period covered.
(4) Power employed, field intensity measurements and visual and aural observations and the types of instruments and receivers utilized to determine the station service area and the efficiency of the respective types of transmissions.
(5) Estimated degree of public participation in reception and the results of observations as to the effectiveness of types of transmission.
(6) Conclusions, tentative and final.
(7) Program for further developments in television broadcasting.
(8) All developments and major changes in equipment.
(9) Any other pertinent developments.[41]

Less detailed reports are required to be submitted with applications for renewal of licenses of facsimile and developmental broadcast stations. A statement, however, must be filed showing the number of hours of operation, the research and experimentation conducted, developments and major changes in equipment, conclusions drawn from the study and a suggested program for further developments of the facsimile or developmental broadcast service.[42]

Equipment and Technical Operation. Licensees of these three types of broadcast stations may make changes in the equipment if (1) the operating frequency is not permitted to deviate more than the allowed tolerance; (2) the emissions are not outside the authorized band; (3) the power output complies with the license and the regulations governing the same; and (4) the transmitter as a whole or output power rating of the transmitter is not changed.[43] Section 74.351 (d) of the rules states that this last limitation does not apply to developmental broadcast stations licensed to operate in connection with the development and testing of commercial broadcast equipment.[44]

The Rules provide that experimental broadcast television and developmental stations must maintain their operating frequencies within the tolerance specified in their instruments of authorization. The same applies to facsimile stations.[45]

The necessary means must be provided and sufficient observations must be made to insure that these stations operate within the allowed frequency tolerance.[46] Each frequency measurement and the exact time it is made and the method employed must be entered in the station log.[47]

No regular schedule of operation must be maintained, but each type of station must actively conduct a program of research and experimentation substantially in accord with that proposed in the original application unless otherwise authorized by the Commission.[48]

Other operation requirements set forth in the rules include the maintenance of adequate records showing the operating hours of the station, programs transmitted, frequency checks, pertinent remarks concerning transmission, points of program origination and receiver location when relay or pickup stations are involved, and research and experimentation conducted.[49] Where antenna structures are required to be illuminated, inspections of the lighting must be made and recorded as specified in Part 17 of the Rules to which reference is made in Chapter 16.[50] All station records must be retained for a period of two years.[51]

No charge of any kind may be made by these experimental broadcast stations for the production or transmission of programs.[52] Call letters and station location must be announced at the beginning and end of each operation and at least once every hour during the broadcast period.[53]

Rebroadcasting of programs is not permitted without the prior written consent of the originating stations and, upon application, without securing the written authority of the Commission.[54]

One or more first or second class operators must be on duty at the place where the transmitting apparatus is located and in actual charge of its operation. He may be employed for other duties or for the operation of other broadcasting facilities so long as the operation of the transmitter at the experimental station is not unfavorably affected.[55]

Dimensions of Experimental Broadcasting. The Commission reported that there were 20 experimental TV stations in operation in 1968.[56] They were carrying on research in a number of fields.

This research during the past decade has ranged from the development of a hand-carried TV camera and transmitter to experimentation with directional antennas. One study related to repeater stations. Studies have indicated that a repeater, operating on the same channel as its parent station, can improve UHF coverage in mountainous terrain. Among other researches, comparative studies have been made with respect to UHF and VHF transmissions.

Applicants for the developmental type of operation usually are AM or FM licensees, and permission for short-term special operation may be granted to these licensees without their having to submit formal applications. Only three such authorizations were outstanding in 1968.[57]

1. 48 Stat. 1082.
2. FCC Rules and Regulations, Section 5.3(c), (d) and (e); 1 RR 55:12.
3. Sections 5.1-5.411; 1RR 55:11-58.
4. Section 5.55; 1 RR 55:15-17.
5. *Ibid.*
6. *Ibid.*
7. Section 5.56; 1 RR 55:18-19.
8. Section 5.57; 1 RR 55:19.
9. *Ibid.*, 55:19-20.
10. Sections 5.101-5.166; 1 RR 55:31-40.
11. Section 5.107; 1 RR 55:34.
12. Section 5.151(b); 1 RR 55:35.
13. Section 5.152; 1 RR 55:35.
14. Sections 5.155, 5.156, 5.157, 5.163; 1 RR 55:35-39.
15. Section 5.63; 1 RR 55:22.
16. Sections 5.204; 1 RR 55:51-52.
17. *Ibid.*
18. Section 5.204(d); 1 RR 55:52.
19. Section 5.255(d); 1 RR 55:55.
20. *FCC Annual Report,* 1958, pp. 171-172.
21. *Ibid.,* p. 172.
22. Section 74.101; 1 RR 54:625.
23. Section 74.102; 1 RR 54:625.
24. Section 74.201; 1 RR 54:651.
25. Section 74.301; 1 RR 54:681.
26. Section 74.382; 1 RR 54:685.
27. *Ibid.*
28. Section 1.533(2); 1 RR 51:265.
29. Sections 74.131, 74.231, 74.331; 1 RR 54:676, 652, 682.
30. Sections 74.112, 74.312; 1 RR 54:626, 682.
31. Section 74.13; 1 RR 54:103.
32. *Ibid.,* and Section 1.536(2); 1 RR 51:266.
33. *Ibid.*
34. Section 74.132, 74.232, 74.332; 1 RR 54:627, 653, 682.
35. Sections 74.131(c); 1 RR 54:133.
36. Sections 74.103, 74.131(b), 74.202, 74.231(b), 74.302, 74.331(b); 1 RR 54: 625, 627, 651, 652, 681, 682.
37. Sections 74.131(b), 74.231(b),74.331(b); 1 RR 54:133, 152, 172.
38. Section 2.106; 1 RR 52:165-190.
39. Sections 74.134, 74.234; 1 RR 54:134, 153.
40. Section 1.539(d) (2); 1 RR 51:268.
41. Section 74.113; 1 RR 54:132.
42. Sections 74.213, 74.313; 1 RR 54:152, 172.
43. Sections 74.151, 74.251, 74.351; 1 RR 54:134, 153, 173.
44. Sections 74.351(d); 1 RR 54:173.
45. Sections 74.161, 74.261, 74.361; 1 RR 54:134, 153.
46. Sections 74.162, 74.262, 74.362; 1 RR 54:654, 683.
47. *Ibid.*
48. Sections 74.163, 74.263, 74.363; 1 RR 629, 654, 683.
49. Sections 74.181, 74.281, 74.381; 1 RR 54:630, 655, 685.
50. Sections 74.167, 74.267, 74.367; 1 RR 54:630, 655, 684.

51. Sections 74.781, 74.281, 74.381; 1 RR 54:630, 655, 685.
52. Sections 74.182, 74.282, 74.382; 1 RR 54:630, 631, 655, 686.
53. Sections 74.183, 74.283, 74.383; 1 RR 54:631, 656, 686.
54. Sections 74.184, 74.284, 74.384; 1 RR 54:631, 656, 686.
55. Sections 74.166, 74.266, 74.366; 1 RR 54:629, 654, 684.
56. *FCC Annual Report,* 1968, p. 113.
57. *Ibid.*

PART IV

Problems of Getting
on the Air

CHAPTER 13

Qualifying for a License

The application for a construction permit shall set forth such facts as the Commission by regulation may prescribe as to the citizenship, character, and the financial, technical, and other ability of the applicant to construct and operate the station. . . .—Section 319 (a) of the Communications Act of 1934

Just anybody cannot get a license to operate a radio or television station. The Communications Act gives the FCC considerable discretion in determining the minimum qualifications for authority to operate stations, but in certain cases it specifically prohibits the Commission from granting licenses.

Statutory Ineligibility. The framers of the Communications Act were fearful that subversive elements might acquire control of the communications facilities to the detriment of national security. As early as 1932, the Secretary of the Navy had written to the Chairman of the Senate Interstate Commerce Committee stating that stations owned or controlled by foreign interests might be used "in espionage work and in the dissemination of subversive propaganda." He further declared:

It is not sufficient that the military forces have authority to assume control of radio stations in war. A certain amount of liaison between radio company executives and departmental officials responsible for government communications is required in peace time. Familiarity on the part of commercial executives of American radio companies with communication operating methods, plans, and developments of the military departments of the government is certainly to the best interests of the nation. Some of these matters are of a very secret nature. For the Navy Department to initiate and carry out this important contact with commercial companies, the divulging of confidential plans to directors is necessary. This is obviously impossible with even one foreigner on the board.

International companies must have agreements between their subsidiaries and the parent companies for a free exchange of information. Foreign personnel are transferred from one subsidiary to another so as to obtain intimate knowledge of the methods and equipment employed by other branches. It is impossible for a military service to work in close cooperation with or disclose its new developments to an organization which has foreign affiliations of this nature and employs foreign personnel.[1]

To make sure that the communications systems of the country would be absolutely free of foreign control, Congress adopted Section 310 (a) of the Communications Act prohibiting the granting of a license to any alien, foreign government, or any corporation organized under the laws of any foreign government. No corporation can hold a license if any officer or director is an alien or if more than *20%* of the stock is owned or voted by aliens or foreign governments or corporations.

Paragraph 5 of this section gives the FCC discretionary power to refuse a license to any corporation directly or indirectly controlled by another corporation of which any officer or more than *25%* of the stock is owned or voted by aliens, foreign governments or corporations or representatives thereof.

The FCC has consistently and strictly enforced the provisions of this section. Individuals applying for broadcasting facilities are required to prove their citizenship. Corporate applicants likewise must show that they are not subject to alien or foreign control.

In a 1938 case, the Commission denied an application for a construction permit when one of the individuals in a partnership was foreign born and claimed derivative United States citizenship through his stepfather but failed to present his certificate of derivative citizenship and did not prove that he had taken the oath to defend the constitution or had renounced his allegiance to his native country.[2]

In a 1939 case, the Commission held that the president and principal stockholder of an applicant corporation who was born abroad did not meet the legal requirements of Section 310 though he had come to this country when he was two years of age and claimed derivative citizenship through the naturalization of his father.[3]

The Commission was satisfied, however, with a "marginal" showing in another 1939 case, consisting of oral testimony by a stockholder in an applicant company as to the citizenship of an officer. The FCC gave credence to the testimony because the witness had been associated with the officer in a business way for many years and was well acquainted with his family.[4]

In 1955, the Commission held that a sufficient showing was made of compliance with paragraph 5 of Section 310(a) of the Act by a corporation with a large number of stockholders, where a sampling indicated that less than 25% of the stock was held by aliens or foreign governments or corporations, and no evidence was submitted to question the reliability of the sampling method used. The Commission recognized, however, that this method of proof might not be acceptable in all cases and under other circumstances.[5]

Monopolistic Practices. Section 313 of the Communications Act provides that if a court finds a party guilty of violating any of the anti-trust laws, it may, in addition to other penalties imposed, revoke any broadcasting license held by that party. In case of such court revocation, the

Commission is directed to refuse any further permits or licenses to the offender.

In view of the mandatory features of Section 311, companies holding radio or television licenses and who are engaged in the manufacture, sale or trading of broadcasting equipment that enters or affects interstate or foreign commerce, must be particularly cautious to avoid any kind of arrangements or activities which might subject them to prosecution for monopolistic practices and unlawful restraints of trade.

Other Legal Disabilities. As will be discussed more fully later, persons desiring to operate broadcasting stations must first file written applications with the FCC asking for authority to construct the facilities and for licenses to operate them once construction is completed. In fact, except in cases of emergency involving danger to life or property or national security, Section 308(a) of the Communications Act specifically forbids the FCC from granting a construction permit, license or renewal of license without a written application having first been filed.

As set forth in Section 309(a) of the law, the Commission must be able to find that the public interest will be served before granting authority to build or operate a station. To aid the Commission in this function, the applicant is required to set forth in writing such facts as the Commission by regulation may prescribe as to his "citizenship, character, and financial, technical and other qualifications." In each case, the Commission must study these facts and be satisfied that the applicant is legally, financially, technically and otherwise qualified to operate a station in the public interest.

A corporation, partnership, association or other type of joint enterprise must establish itself as a legal entity and show its authority to engage in broadcasting activities before it can qualify for a construction permit or license. For example, two individuals, claiming to be a partnership, applied for a station, but the application was denied for the reasons that there was no written partnership agreement between the parties and they were not legally bound by any written instrument to contribute anything to the joint venture.[6]

In another case, involving a limited partnership,[7] the Commission held that the applicant was not legally qualified to receive a grant where it failed to show the statutory authority upon which it relied for its right to exist as a legal entity and presented for the record no partnership agreement or binding contract on the parties to contribute to the partnership funds.

Every profit and non-profit corporation is required to give evidence of its incorporation under state law and establish its legal identity and show that broadcasting falls within the scope of its purposes and powers as set forth in its charter. The Federal Radio Commission, predecessor of the FCC, stated in 1932 that a "corporation has only such powers as are expressly granted in its charter or which are necessary for the carrying out of its express powers and the purposes of its incorporation."[8] This does not mean in every case that the instrument of authorization must specifically provide for broadcasting. The important test is whether it can reasonably be construed that the operation of a broadcasting station is appropriate or essential to the accomplishment of the general purpose set forth in the charter. Many educational institutions, for example, have qualified for licenses, even though the charter or the statutes which authorize their activities make no specific mention of broadcasting.

Financial Qualifications. As may be implied from Sections 308(a) and 319(a) of the Communications Act and prescribed in paragraph (3) of Section 73.24(c) of the Commission's Rules governing broadcast stations, there is a positive burden of proof on every applicant to show that he has the financial resources to build and operate the type of station proposed. In an early 1935 case, despite a showing by an applicant that he could secure money from friends to buy station equipment, his application was denied by the Commission on the grounds that he did not have enough finances to erect the station and maintain its operation and there was no proof that the station would be self-supporting.[9]

That same year, the Commission refused to grant a construction permit to an applicant because he proposed to build a station with money he had borrowed without security, the loan to be repaid in five years. On appeal, however, the Court of Appeals of the District of Columbia overruled the Commission and held that in the absence of a Commission rule or statutory prohibition against the use of borrowed funds, the applicant's plan for financing, with assured resources for five years, was adequate and that the Commission erred in disapproving it.[10]

In a later decision, an application of a California corporation for a television station was denied on the grounds that the applicant had only $32,500 available for construction and initial operation of the station. The estimated costs of construction ran almost $26,000, which did not include the cost of a monitor. With reference to the matter of financial inability the Commission said:

Where we consider the initial cost of operation for any reasonable period of time in the light of funds available to the applicant, together with our uncertainty with regard to the cost of composite equipment and the fact that no allowance has been made for the RCA monitor . . . that contingencies may arise which the applicant has not considered in its cost estimate . . . a substantial question as to the adequacy of the operating expense allocated for the purchase of film . . . we are unable to conclude that the applicant is financially qualified to construct, own and operate the proposed station.[11]

The Commission has established no hard and fast rules with respect to financial qualifications. Decisions have been based largely upon the facts of each case. Generally, the Commission has been fairly liberal in making grants where there is a reasonable proof that funds are on hand or will be available or can be secured to assure the construction and initial operation of the station. In making decisions on financial ability, the agency has taken into account such factors as costs of construction, estimated expense of operation for the first year, the size and type of market and possibilities of income, the previous income of the applicant, his present financial assets and liabilities, and ability of prospective donors or creditors, if any, to fulfil their pledges and commitments.

Technical Qualifications. The construction and operation of a broadcasting station requires special technical knowledge and skills. To qualify therefore for a permit or license, technical ability must be demonstrated. In an early 1936 case, the Commission stated a point of view which it more or less has followed through the years:

An indispensable element in passing upon any application for station licenses is the technical qualifications of the applicant. This does not mean that the applicant in every case must be personally qualified technically, but it does mean that if he is not personally qualified technically and does not propose to operate the station himself but through employees, then he should show that he has a competent staff to operate the proposed station for him, and their technical qualifications.[12]

In another 1936 case, a permit to build a station was denied on the grounds that technical ability of the applicant himself was insufficient and he declined to state the names of persons to whom he would entrust technical control.[13]

Where a Michigan company was seeking a special type of broadcasting station, the application was denied for the reason that no showing was made that there would be an adequate staff of engineers and technical facilities to effectuate the program of research and experimentation proposed. The company proposed to use the technical facilities of a university but this was held to be insufficient since the governing board of the institution had made no commitment in this regard and, in fact, had refused to assume any expense for such an operation.[14]

In a 1955 television case, the Commission stated that it did not expect an applicant to "achieve perfection in its first day of operation," and that the question with respect to technical qualifications is whether "staffing, studio and equipment plans are *adequate* to effectuate to a *reasonable* degree the programs it has promised." (Italics supplied).[15]

Character Qualifications. In addition to legal, financial and technical competencies, the Commission is given wide latitude in considering the general character qualifications of those seeking station licenses. This stems from the public interest features of the Communications Act and the fact that the Commission can require applicants to supply information regarding their character and behavior as it may relate to their ability to operate a station in the public interest. (See Sections 308(a) and 319(a) of the Communications Act). Since the use of a publicly owned channel is in the nature of a public trust, the Commission has attached great importance to elements of character such as honesty and reliability, moral, financial and social responsibility and respect for law and order.

In a 1937 case, the District Circuit Court of Appeals sustained the FCC in its denial of an application for a construction permit where, in addition to financial inability, the applicant failed to "make frank, candid, and honest disclosures of its organizational set-up, stock ownership, and connection with another licensee."[16] This same court took a similar position in a 1946 case where the Commission had questioned the honesty and candor of an applicant.[17]

In 1951, the application of a corporation for an FM station was denied, various misrepresentations of facts having been made and one of the three stockholders having demonstrated a lack of character qualifications because he had been "intemperate in his writings, sermons and broadcasts and was an expert in vituperation and vilification."[18] There again, on appeal, the Court confirmed the Commission's decision.

In some cases, where parties have failed to disclose material facts in applications regarding past conduct which is questionable, the Commission has resolved doubts in their favor, especially when the misconduct did not appear to have been willful and the parties have high professional standing and reputations for good character in the communities where they live. For example, the Commission decided that the failure of the principal stockholder in an applicant corporation to disclose his connection with a bankrupt corporation and to reveal that a number of his assets were in fact owned by his wife did not warrant a finding that there was intentional deception. There was an implication in the language of the Commission that the principal stockholder had not shown the highest degree of candor, but because of his generally good reputation and professional competency, the Commission gave him the benefit of the doubt.[19]

Public Responsibility and Respect for Law. In administrative practice, an applicant's sense of public responsibility and respect for law have always been considered by the FCC to be important character elements. Where serious deficiencies in these respects have appeared, the agency has not hesitated to disqualify applicants.

In 1950, the U.S. Appellate Court for the District of Columbia agreed with the Commission in refusing a construction permit to a newspaper that had attempted to suppress competition by coercing advertisers to enter into exclusive contracts, and had refused to make space available to business concerns which also advertised over the local radio station, and also refused to print any reference to the station except unfavorable ones. Whether this conduct actually violated the anti-trust laws the Court said was immaterial. It was enough that the behavior standards of the applicant in its business affairs and dealings with the public raised serious questions as to its ability to meet the requirements and responsibilities of a broadcast licensee.[20]

It has been held in another case that failure of a corporation to comply with state corporation laws reflects upon its character qualifications to become a licensee. The Commission declared that failure to comply with the state laws was a disqualifying factor plus the fact that two of the three incorporators had not looked at the application before it was filed and its preparation and submission to the Commission were carried on in "a confused and slipshod manner" and indicated a lack of ability and sense of responsibility essential for the operation of a radio station in the public interest.[21]

Certain individuals were disqualified from securing a license on the grounds that in the conduct of their private business, over a long period of time, they had violated and disregarded the regulatory laws of the states and the federal government. Even though their record did not involve any civil or criminal judgments against them, still the Commission and the Courts decided that they had not demonstrated sufficient sense of responsibility to qualify.[22]

In a later case, however, the fact that an applicant had been indicted on three occasions for alleged offenses but had been acquitted each time, was not considered by the Commission to reflect adversely on his character to operate a station.[23] Nor was arrest and conviction for giving a worthless check considered a reflection on the applicant's moral character when it was shown that through an oversight in the rush of business his bank account had been inadvertently overdrawn and when he had deposited funds immediately to take care of the check upon discovery of the error.[24]

In 1951, after a long study on the part of the FCC and its staff, the agency made a statement of uniform policy which it proposed to follow in cases where applicants have been involved in law violations. The Commission said:

In determining that an applicant is qualified to be a broadcast licensee the Commission must examine all pertinent conduct of the applicant. If an applicant is or has been involved in unlawful practices, an analysis of the substance of these practices must be made to determine their relevance and weight as regards the ability of the applicant to use the requested radio authorization in the public interest. Such a determination must be made on the facts of each case and no blanket policy may be enunciated. However, violation of a federal law, whether deliberate or inadvertent, raises sufficient question regarding character to merit further examination. Violation of federal laws does not necessarily make the applicant ineligible for a radio grant, since there may be extenuating or countervailing considerations. Innocent violations are not as serious as deliberate ones.

Another matter of importance is whether the infraction of law is an isolated instance or whether there have been recurring offenses which establish a definite pattern of misbehavior. Also there must be more concern with recent violations than with those which occurred in the remote past and have been followed by a long period of adherence to law and exemplary conduct. It is irrelevant to a determination of qualifications whether the finding of violation is in a civil or criminal case and the particular tribunal which makes the finding is not significant. And the Commission may consider and evaluate the conduct of an applicant insofar as it relates to matters entrusted to the Commission even though no suit alleging illegal conduct has been filed or has not been heard or finally adjudicated.[25]

In the Commission's Report, of which the above is a summary, certain basic considerations were set forth as guides to be followed in making a case to case determination of character qualifications where law violations are involved. These may be stated as follows:

(1) Was the violation willful or inadvertent?
(2) Was the infraction an isolated instance or have there been recurring offenses?
(3) Has the applicant been engaged in violations over a long period of time so as to show an antipathetic attitude toward the laws of the United States?
(4) Has the applicant recently engaged in illegal practices?
(5) Is the applicant presently engaged in such practices?

Involvement in Anti-Trust Litigation.

While the Report had general applicability with respect to violation of all laws, the Commission's main concern was with violation of the anti-trust laws. The Report stressed the point that in setting up the Communications Act, Congress conceived as one of the Commission's major functions the preservation of competition in the radio field and the protection of the public interest. Accordingly, it was made clear that the Commission would view with much concern the proclivity of applicants to monopolize and drive out competition and would make it a major consideration in its determination of character qualifications to operate broadcast stations in the public interest.[26]

In *National Broadcasting Company v. United States,* 319 U.S. 190, 222, the Court gave judicial sanction to the Commission's point of view in this matter. In that case the Court had said that the Commission could exercise its judgment as to whether violations of the anti-trust laws disqualify an applicant from operating a station in the public interest and "might infer from the fact that the applicant had in the past tried to monopolize radio, or had engaged in unfair methods of competition, that the disposition so manifested would continue and that if it did it would make him an unfit licensee."[27]

During the period of time that the Commission had under study the adoption of its policy with respect to law violations, it withheld action on a number of applications for new broadcast facilities and for renewal of existing licenses filed by large companies with records of involvement in anti-trust litigation. One of these was Westinghouse Radio Stations, Incorporated. Westinghouse Electric, the parent company, had been named as a defendant in a number of anti-trust suits, but only once had it been found to have violated the laws against monopolies. The parent company also had been involved in several anti-trust proceedings resulting in consent decrees but in which there was no admission of guilt or court conviction.[28]

After a careful study of Westinghouse's record, the Commission concluded that there was insufficient evidence of character taint to warrant denial of license renewals. Accordingly, in April, 1952, the renewal applications were granted.[29] On April 1, 1953, the Commission granted the application of the company to increase the operating power of Station WOWO, action on which had been delayed until the disposition of the anti-monopoly questions. Subsequently, on June 29, 1955, the Commission issued its decision in a Portland, Oregon case involving four conflicting television applications for Channel 8 in that city, Westinghouse being one of the four applicants. While the company did not prevail in that comparative proceeding, the Commission again found no basis on which to impugn the character of the company because of alleged monopolistic practices, and the decision in the case favorable to another applicant turned on other grounds.

The Commission held that no adverse findings should be made against an applicant because of litigation in which it has been involved where the evidence consists chiefly of a recitation of the litigation without a showing of facts as they relate to the conduct of the applicant, and where no pattern of illegal conduct is proved. Facts of conduct and not mere allegations are important.

The Commission further said that *nolo contendere* decrees do not constitute proof of facts.[30] Nor do consent decrees reflect upon the conduct of the applicant where they are remote in time and no pattern of misbehavior can be established because of them.[31]

Paramount's Involvement in Anti-Trust Litigation. A more difficult case for the Commission to decide involved applications of Paramount Television Productions, Inc., and its subsidiary companies, seeking renewals of licenses and construction permits for numberous television stations. Along with those of Westinghouse, the applications of Paramount were kept in a pending status while the Commission was formulating its policy with respect to law violations mentioned above.

The Paramount companies had been involved in anti-trust litigation for more than 20 years. These cases included complaints alleging monopolistic practices and restraints of trade, both at federal and state levels.[32] On May 3, 1948, the United States Supreme Court handed down decisions in three cases involving anti-trust complaints against several companies owning or operating motion picture theatres and engaged in the production and distribution of films.[33] Paramount was one of the defendants in these cases. Proceedings in these cases were started in 1938 with a suit filed by the Government against Paramount Pictures, Inc., and several other motion picture companies, alleging violations of Section 4 of the Sherman Act.

The complaint charged that Paramount and other defendants, as distributors and exhibitors of motion picture films, had conspired to restrain and monopolize interstate trade in the exhibition of films in most of the larger

237

cities of the country, and that they were guilty of a vertical combination of producing, distributing and exhibiting films contrary to the provisions of the Sherman Act.

Before the trial on these charges was held, negotiations for a settlement were undertaken, resulting in a consent decree entered on November 20, 1940. The consent decree contained no admission or adjudication of any issues of law or fact, other than the admission that the complaint stated a cause of action. The decree reserved to the government the right at the end of a three-year period to seek further relief. At the end of this period, the government, feeling that the decree had not proved effective, moved for trial against all the defendants.

After lengthy proceedings, the Federal District Court found the defendants substantially guilty of all the allegations of the complaint. On appeal to the Supreme Court, the judgment was affirmed with respect to charges of unreasonable restraints of trade. On certain questions relating to divorcement and arbitration, the District Court's findings were reversed and the matters sent back for redetermination.

In affirming the District Court's findings that the defendants had engaged in price-fixing conspiracies, the Supreme Court said:

The District Court found that two price-fixing conspiracies existed—a horizontal one between all the defendants, a vertical one between each distributor—defendant and its licensees. The latter was based on express agreements and was plainly established. The former was inferred from the pattern of price-fixing disclosed in the record. We think there was adequate foundation for it too. It is not necessary to find an express agreement in order to find a conspiracy. It is enough that a concert of action is contemplated and that the defendants conformed to the arrangement.[34]

In regard to the defendants' policies in granting clearances,[35] the Supreme Court upheld a finding that these arrangements were unreasonable and that many of them "had no relation to the competitive factors which alone could justify them."[36]

Furthermore, the lower court's findings were affirmed, that the defendants had been guilty of unfair competition in that they operated theatres, normally competitive, as units with profit-sharing agreements and had discriminated against independent exhibitors through various kinds of contract provisions. Other trade practices that were found to be unreasonable restraints of trade included formula deals, and block-booking. In regard to the latter practice the Supreme Court said:

. . . Block-booking prevents competitors from bidding for single features on their individual merits. The District Court (66 F. Supp. 349) held it illegal for that reason and for the reason that it 'adds to the monopoly of a single copyrighted picture that of another copyrighted picture which must be taken and exhibited in order to secure the first.' . . . The Court enjoined defendants from performing or entering into any license in which the right to exhibit one feature is conditioned upon the licensee's taking one or more other features. We approve that restriction.[37]

The District Court found that the defendants had a particular monopoly in the ownership of theatres, having interest in over 17% of the theatres in the United States from which they received 45% of the total domestic film rental. It found that in the 92 cities having populations over 100,000 at least 70% of all the first run theatres were affiliated with one or more of the defendants. The District Court enjoined the defendants from expanding their theatre holdings.[38]

The Supreme Court remanded the question of theatre ownership to the lower court. On remand of the case, Paramount entered into a consent decree under the terms of which it was split into two companies, not under common control, one to be concerned with pictures and the other with theatres. Under a plan of reorganization the old company was dissolved and its assets transferred to two new companies, namely Paramount Pictures Corporation and United Paramount Theatres, Inc.

The FCC was concerned that Paramount's monopolistic practices might carry over into the television field. It had received reports to the effect that Paramount and other motion picture industries had refused to make any of their films available for use by television stations. There also were restrictions imposed by some of these companies as to the appearances of actors under contract to the studio on television programs and to the use on television of stories or plays whose rights had been acquired by the studio.[39]

With respect to the weight to be attached to involvement in anti-trust litigation as regards character qualifications, attorneys for Paramount made a number of points which should be mentioned here. One point stressed was that anti-trust laws are highly complex and often-times difficult to understand; that a great deal of uncertainty as to the meaning of these laws prevails among businessmen, lawyers and the courts; that some practices now prohibited by the courts were formerly sanctioned by them. It was argued, therefore, because of the complexity and uncertainty of meaning of the anti-trust laws, that big business should not be charged with moral dereliction for violating them.[40]

It was further contended by legal counsel for Paramount that its involvement in the litigation described above had no real connection with the radio industry. "It does not reflect the character or qualifications of the defendant to serve the public interest." Nor was there any "claim in the Paramount case that the public was not adequately served by motion pictures, no was there any claim of an exclusion of any picture from the public. On the contrary, it was conceded that the public in this case was not only given adequate, but the very best of theatre and amusement facilities." The counsel concluded, therefore, "public interest in radio, in the sense it is used in the Communications Act, is not even remotely involved in the Paramount case;" and further, "it cannot be fairly said that this type of activity in another field—activity of a kind which the government and the courts themselves were not certain about until recently—it cannot be said that such activity gives the slightest indication that businessmen would have a tendency toward monopoly in a different field."[41]

Despite these arguments, the Commission was unable to conclude that a grant of Paramount's pending applications for new broadcasting facilities and for renewal of its existing licenses would serve the public interest. Accordingly, they were designated for public hearing.

After a prolonged hearing in which Paramount's record and qualifications were thoroughly explored, the Commission granted the applications. The decision declared that with respect to Paramount and its subsidiaries who were existing licensees with records as broadcasters, it was impracticable to attempt to delve into and evaluate the entire history, remote as well as recent, of their activities in fields other than radio communications which might have involved anti-trust violations. The Commission further said that in general it would not consider any such activities which occurred more than three years before the filing of the applications.[42]

Subsequently, the Commission approved a merger of Paramount with the American Broadcasting Company. In the decision approving the merger, it was held that the policies of the motion picture concern with respect to its past use of film, talent or stories on television did not constitute a bar to a grant of license and transfer applications.[43]

In a case decided by the Commission in June, 1953, in which a question was raised as to whether recent conduct involving violation of the anti-trust laws was an absolute bar to getting a license, it was held that "a single violation or even a number of them, *ipso facto*, did not disqualify an applicant." Even though the applicant may have engaged in unlawful practices, in each case an analysis of the substance of these practices must still be made to determine their relevance and weight in terms of his ability to use the requested facilities in the public interest.[45] In support of this position the Commission quoted from its report setting forth policies to be followed in assessing qualifications of law violators, adopted in 1951 and referred to earlier in this chapter. This quotation is as follows:

Violations of Federal laws, whether deliberate or inadvertent, raise sufficient question regarding character to merit further examination. While this question as to character may be overcome by countervailing circumstances, nevertheless, in every case, the Commission must view with concern the unlawful conduct of any applicant who is seeking authority to operate radio facilities as a trustee for the public. This is not to say that a single violation of a federal law or even a number of them necessarily makes the offender ineligible for a radio grant. There may be facts which are in extenuation of the violation of law. Or, there may be other favorable facts and considerations that outweigh the record of unlawful conduct and qualify the applicant to operate a station in the public interest.[46]

No Hard and Fast Rules for Character Qualifications. No hard and fast rules can be drawn with respect to what constitutes adequate character qualifications to operate broadcasting stations in the public interest. The foregoing discussion with random reference to a few of the more important cases decided by the Commission simply suggests some types of behavior on the part of applicants, both individual and corporate, about which the FCC has raised questions. The Commission, by statute, is given wide latitude in determining character qualifications. Guiding principles have been established to which the public has a right to expect reasonable adherence by the FCC, but in the last analysis, each case must stand on its own merits, and be decided in terms of the particular facts involved. In any case, where the facts raise questions as to character and suggest inability to operate a station in the public interest, the burden of proof is always on the applicant to resolve any doubts and show that he does have the ability and can meet the requirements of law.

NOTES

1. Part of letter from the Secretary of Navy to the Chairman of the Senate Interstate Commerce Committee, March 22, 1932, Hearings on S. 2910, 73rd Congress, 2nd Session, p. 69.

2. *Sam Klaver,* 6 FCC 536 (1938).

3. *Mountain Top Trans Radio Corporation,* 7 FCC 180 (1939).

4. *Kentucky Broadcasting Corporation,* 6 FCC 776 (1939).

5. *Westinghouse Radio Stations, Inc.,* 10 RR 878 (1955).

6. *Carter and Wolfe,* 2 FCC 544 (1935).

7. *Chicago Broadcasting Association,* 3 FCC 277 (1936).

8. *Sun-Gazette Company* (FRC Docket No. 1300, March 18, 1932).

9. *Carl C. Struble,* 2 FCC 115.

10. *Heitmeyer v. FCC,* 68 App. D.C. 180; 95 F.(2d) 91 (1937).

11. *Orange Belt Telecasters,* 9 RR 1002a (1954).

12. *W.H. Kindig,* 3 FCC 313, 315, (1936).

13. *E.L. Clifford,* 2 FCC 573, (1935).

14. *Ann Arbor Broadcasting Co., Inc.,* 5 FCC 284, (1938).

15. *WKRG-TV, Inc.,* 10 RR 225 (1955), 268b.

16. *Greater Western Broadcasting Association v. FCC,* 68 U.S. App. D.C. 119, 94 F.(2d) 244.

17. *Calumet Broadcasting Corporation v.FCC,* 82 U.S. App. D.C. 59; 160 F. (2d) 285.

18. *Independent Broadcasting Co. v. FCC,* 89 U.S. App. D.C. 396; 193 F.(2d) 900; 7 RR 2066 (1951).

19. *Cherokee Broadcasting Company,* 13 RR 725 (1956).

20. *Mansfield Journal Co. v. FCC,* 86 U.S. App. D.C. 102; 180 F.(2d) 28, 5 RR 2074 e.

21. *Royal Broadcasting Corporation,* 6 RR 717 (1951).

22. *Bulova and Henshel (Mester),* 11 FCC 137, 3 RR 125 (1946), affirmed 70 F. Supp. 118, 332 U.S. 749 (1947).

23. *James A. Noe,* 4 RR 1441 (1949).

24. *Harold H. Thoms,* 7 FCC 108 (1939).

25. *In the Matter of Establishment of a Uniform Policy to be Followed in Licensing of Radio Broadcast Station Cases in Connection with Violations by an Applicant of Laws of the United States other than the Communications Act,* Docket No. 9572, 16 Fed. Reg. 3187 (1951); 1 RR 91:32 (1951).

26. *Ibid.*

27. 319 U.S. 190, at 222.

28. *Westinghouse Radio Stations, Inc.,* 10 RR 911 (1955).

29. *Ibid.*

30. A *nolo contendere* plea in a criminal prosecution is one which, without admitting guilt, subjects the defendant to conviction, but does not preclude him from denying the truth of the charges in a collateral proceeding.

31. *Westinghouse, op. cit.*

32. FCC Docket 7279, Vol. 3., Paramount Exhibit 4, San Francisco Hearing (TV).

33. *United States v. Paramount Pictures, Inc., et al.,* 334 U.S. 131; *United States vs. Griffith et al.,* 334 U.S. 100; *Schine Chain Theatres, Inc., et al. v. United States,* 334 U.S. 100.

34. *Ibid.,* p. 142.

35. A Clearance is the period of time elapsing between runs of the same feature in the same area.

36. *United States v. Paramount Pictures, Inc., et. al., op. cit.,* p. 146.

37. *Ibid.,* p. 157-58.

38. *Ibid.,* p. 167.

39. FCC Docket 9572, 16 Fed. Reg. 3187 (1951).

40. *Ibid.,* p. 92.

41. *Ibid.,* p. 9.

42. *Paramount Television Productions, Inc., et. al.* (Dockets 10031-10032); 16 Fed. Reg. 8159 (1951).

43. *Paramount Pictures, Inc.,* 8 RR 135 (1952).

44. *ABC-Paramount Merger Case,* 8 RR 541 (1952).

45. *The Loraine Journal Co.,* 9 RR 406 (June 4, 1953).

46. *Ibid.,* p. 406.

CHAPTER 14

Competing with Other Applicants for Broadcast Facilities

The selection of an awardee from among several qualified applicants is basically a matter of judgment, often difficult and delicate, entrusted by the Congress to the administrative agency. The decisive factors in comparable selections may well vary; sometimes one applicant is superior to another in one respect, whereas in another case one applicant may be superior to its rivals in another feature. And . . . the Commission's view of what is best in the public interest may change from time to time. Commissions themselves change, underlying philosophies differ, and experience often dictates changes . . . All such matters are for the Congress and the executive and their agencies. . . . They are not for the judiciary. —JUDGE E. BARRETT PRETTYMAN, *230 F. (2d)204*

A single applicant for a broadcast station must show that he meets all the statutory requirements as set forth in the previous chapter. Furthermore, as set forth therein, he must show that he is financially, technically, legally and otherwise competent and possessed of good character before the Commission can grant him a license. His burden of proof, however, may become much heavier if he is competing with others for the same facilities. In such a case, he must show not only that he meets the minimum requirements of the statute, but that he is *better* qualified than the other applicants and that his plans and proposals for the establishment of a station will *better* serve the public interest.

As the U.S. Appellate Court for the District of Columbia has said, "a choice between two applicants involves more than the basic qualifications of each applicant. It involves a comparison of characteristics. Both A and B may be qualified, but if a choice must be made, the question is which is the better qualified. Both might be ready, able and willing to serve the public interest. But in choosing between them, the inquiry must reveal which would better serve that interest. . . .Comparative qualities and not mere positive characteristics must then be considered."[1]

In comparing qualities, the Commission has attempted to employ various criteria in determining which one, among multiple applicants, is best qualified to serve the public interest. At best, these criteria can be considered no more than guide posts, and the weight to be given any decisional factor in a comparative case is dependent upon the circumstances of that particular case.[2]

Local Ownership. In choosing among contenders for broadcasting facilities, the Commission has tended to prefer applicants owned and controlled by persons who reside and have their roots in the community where the station is to operate. This is based on the theory that they are likely to be more familiar with and responsive to local needs than non-residents and thus better qualified to operate a station in the "public interest." As will be pointed out later, however, in some cases applicants have overcome the disadvantage of non-residence by showing superior qualifications in other respects, including past broadcast experience and record of performance.

In an early 1935 case, involving two applications for the same radio channel, the Commission preferred an applicant company, of which a 51% stockholder had published a daily newspaper in the locality for many years and had been closely indentified with local affairs, over an applicant that had no affiliation other than property investments in the community.[3]

Since that time, as revealed in a long line of cases, in comparing the qualifications of applicants, the factor of local ownership and residence has continued to hold a central position in the thinking of the Commission.[4]

Where local applicants have been able to show diversified ownership, representing various professions and business interests in the community, with participation and leadership in civic affairs, they have strengthened their positions in competitive proceedings. Furthermore, where they have proposed to integrate the ownership and management of stations and to recruit a competent staff from among citizens living in the local area, they have scored additional points of preference.

A typical expression of the Commission's attitude and judgment on these matters is found in the case, *Scripps-Howard Radio, Inc.*, 4 RR 525, decided in 1948. This involved two conflicting applications for a station in the same locality. As between the two, the Commission preferred the applicant corporation whose stockholders had diversified backgrounds, most of whom had resided in the local area for many years and had been active in the civic and philanthropic life of the community. The losing applicant was a newspaper organization controlled by a board of five directors, only one of whom lived in the city; two other officers of the corporation lived there but had no real voice in the establishment of policies and the management of the corporation.[5]

Broadcast Experience. The FCC has consistently viewed experience in broadcasting or related fields as an important aspect of qualifications in deciding cases involving competing applicants. For example, in *Utah Radio Educational Society,* 3 FCC 246 (1936), the Commission preferred an applicant whose principals were experienced in radio engineering as against an individual applicant without any radio experience. In a recent case, *Toledo Blade Co.*, 25 FCC 251, 15 RR 739 (1958), the Commission held that an applicant whose principals had had extensive experience in the operation of a local radio station over a long period of time was entitled to preference over applicants showing lesser experience. Other cases in point are *Scripps-Howard Radio, Inc.*, 11 RR 985 (1956); *Richmond Newspapers, Inc.*, 11 RR 1234 (1955); and *WHDH, Inc.*, 22 FCC 761, 13 RR 507 (1957).

Record of Past Performance. Since the early part of 1950, the Commission's decisions have reflected increasing emphasis upon the quality of past performance in the broadcast field as a determinative factor in comparative cases. For example, in *Petersburg Television Corporation*, 10 RR 567 (1954), it is stated that such factors as local residence, civic participation and integration of ownership and management are at most the basis for presumption of greater probability that programming commitments will be carried out or that the applicant will be sensitive to the area's needs, and are of minor importance where the applicants have a record of good past performance in the operation of broadcasting stations in the area.

In a 1954 case, the Commission concluded that an applicant which had compiled an outstanding operational record at its several broadcast stations over a period of years was entitled to a slight preference over an applicant with no record of past broadcast performance, but which had a higher degree of local ownership and integration.*

The Commission has taken the position that past broadcast records and broadcast experience are separate factors entitled to independent appraisal and weight and not to be considered as a single decisional factor in comparative cases. (See *Toledo Blade Co.*, cited above.)

It is not necessary to discuss them here since they are dealt with in various chapters in Part V of the book, but there are many negative factors that can weigh against applicants in competitive proceedings. Violations of FCC rules and regulations, failure to report accurately or willful misrepresentation of facts to the Commission, unauthorized transfers of control of a station, abdication of licensee responsibility, failure to provide program service that meets the tests of public interest as prescribed by the FCC— these and many other types of derelictions (discussed at length in later chapters), if part of a broadcaster's record, can work to his disadvantage if he is seeking additional radio or TV facilities in a competitive hearing.

Programming as an Element in Comparative Cases. In comparative proceedings, the program proposals of applicants are scrutinized carefully. In varying degrees, the Commission has given points of preference to applicants whose program proposals appear better designed to serve the particular needs and interests of the area in which the station will operate. Often

---

*See Walter B. Emery, "Nervous Tremors in the Broadcast Industry," *Educational Broadcasting Review* , June 1969, pp. 43-47; but also see later statement of FCC (18RR 2d 1901), January 14, 1970, which seemed to take a different turn.

these points of preference become determinative in the outcome of a case.

The FCC decisions reveal both quantitative and qualitative comparisons of proposed plans for program service submitted by competing applicants. Depending upon the circumstances of the case, the Commission has awarded decisional preferences for superiority in over-all program design. In some instances, particular types of program service proposed such as local live programs planned especially to meet the needs of the area, including the discussion of vital issues of public interest in the community or religious and educational programs involving the local churches and schools, coverage of the local news—these and other specific features have tipped the scales in favor of some applicants.

It is only by a study of the particular facts in a case and the full text of the decision that one can understand fully the basis on which the Commission prefers one application over another. For example, since program rating in competitive cases is always a relative matter, the preferential weight to be given a proposal for full news coverage might depend upon the particular journalistic skills of the applicant as well as the community need for this type of service. Or a proposal to broadcast agricultural programs in an area largely urban in character would not have as much decisional significance as it would in one with a large rural population.

While the decisions of the Commission do not reveal any precise rating scales or standards of evaluation in connection with programming, excerpts from the conclusions in a few cases will suggest some guiding principles which have motivated the agency's thinking and judgment.

In *Tribune Co.*, 9 RR 719 (1954), the Commission expressed the view that local live programming is a factor of great importance in comparative consideration of broadcast applicants, but that a greater percentage is not itself determinative. Of more significance is the content and the promise for implementation of the proposal and the assurance of its effectuation.

Again, in *KTBS, Inc.*, 10 RR 811 (1955), the point was made that slight differences in emphasis and allocation of time are not important in appraisal of program proposals. Quantitative and statistical measurement is not enough. Furthermore, ordinarily proposals to carry network programs do not warrant points of preference but arrangements for broadcasting local live programs are considered more important in showing how the needs of the area will be served.

The primary question in program evaluation is whether the applicants have planned and propose a diversified, well-rounded service for the community, and mere differences percentages of time to be devoted to various program types are not considered important. [7]

Numerical superiority, however, may achieve decisional significance if the statistical difference involves a kind of programming that clearly and effectively will serve community interests. [8]

The Commission has recognized that program proposals may be skillfully prepared but the important consideration is the basic competency of the applicant to provide a service which will meet the needs of the community from day to day.[9]

In a variety of comparative cases, the Commission has given preferential consideration to proposals to provide instructional broadcasts for inschool viewing,[10] to present programs dealing with "cultural arts,"[11] to provide time to local organizations for talks and discussions,[12] and to carry a "considerable number of regular agricultural programs."[13]. Also, the Commission has made favorable mention of proposals to make time available for diversified, religious programs,[14] and to cover both national and local news and engage a special staff to prepare and present the newscasts.[15]

As reflected in various cases, applicants have scored points of preference for superior program plans based upon personally conducted surveys and discussions with leaders of civic, educational, religious and other community groups;[16] and for more comprehensive, detailed and well balanced program plans with specific limitations upon the amount of commercial programming to be carried by the station.[17] Also, commitments for larger and more competent staffs have elicited favorable comment from the Commission.[18]

Illustrative of the Commission's concern that applicants make careful studies of local needs and problems and plan programs accordingly, is a 1949 Michigan case.[19] This proceeding involved three applications for a station to operate on the frequency 1320 kc, with 1 kw power, unlimited time. Two of the applicants requested the facility in Lansing, Michigan. The third wanted it in Charlotte, Michigan, only twenty miles away. Since the applications were conflicting and mutually exclusive, the Commission designated them for a comparative hearing.

The successful applicant was station WILS in Lansing. In denying the Charlotte application, the Commission said:

The Charlotte Broadcasting Company has not demonstrated that the need of the Charlotte community for an outlet for local self-expression is more than merely theoretical. The applicant has not made a single contact with people in the Charlotte community who might cooperate with the proposed station in putting on musical, dramatic, educational or agricultural programs. . . .While the applicant's policy calls for sustaining time for civic and fraternal organizations there is no specific provision for programs by those organizations in the program schedule. Although the program schedule calls for 43.9 per cent of the operating time to be devoted to live programs, no arrangements have been made to secure talent for these programs with the single exception of a discussion with the President of the Ministerial Association with respect to religious programs. . . .

The preferential weight given to each of these program items has varied with the circumstances and comparative situation in each case. Not every aspect however of an applicant's program performance or his projected plans for the future gets favorable consideration. For example, in certain

decisions, the Commission has declared its unwillingness to give any decisional weight to the fact that one network affiliation rather than another is
anticipated,[20] or because one applicant intends to use network programs
more during prime listening hours as against another who plans to present
more wire and recorded broadcasts.[21] Nor will the Commission attach any
importance to a failure to subscribe to a news film service where adequate
arrangements otherwise have been made for local news film and leased wire
service.[22]

In a number of cases, the agency has asserted unequivocally that it is not
concerned one way or another whether religious programs are carried on
a sustaining or commercial basis.[23] In *Southland Television Co.*, 10 RR 699
(1955), it attached no significance to the fact that one applicant emphasized
film programs while other applicants stressed network programming.[24]

Limitations on Ownership of Stations. The Commission has established
rules limiting the number of radio and television stations which may be
owned or controlled by one party. Section 73.35 of the Rules covering
standard (AM) broadcast stations provides that no license may be granted
to any party who already owns, operates or controls another such station
serving substantially the same primary service area, except on a showing
that the public interest will be served. This is known as the duopoly rule and,
in most cases, has served as a bar to the ownership or control of more than
one station of the same class in a single community.

There have been exceptions to this rule, however. The Commission has
said it would not grant duplicate facilities to the same party or interests
unless it could be "overwhelmingly" shown that it would meet a community
need which would otherwise not be met.[25] In a 1941 Hawaiian case,[26] the
FCC did permit the Hawaiian Broadcasting System, which already was
operating three of the only four stations in the Islands to acquire an additional one in the area. While expressing concern over the concentration of
control which would result, the agency concluded that foreign language
programs designed to promote Americanism and democratic principles
which were proposed by the Hawaiian Company would serve an "overwhelming" need there and that a grant was justified.

In *Lubbock County Broadcasting Co.*, 4 RR 493 (1948), the Commission
said that each case involving multiple ownership must be decided on its
merits and that Section 73.35 of the Rules is not an absolute bar to a grant
in every instance where there is overlap of service areas of two stations
under common control.[27]

The prohibition against owning more than one station also applies even
though the stations may be located in different communities, if, on the basis
of the particular facts in the case, the Commission believes this multiple
ownership would result in an undue concentration of control of broadcasting facilities contrary to the public interest.[28] Regardless of the facts, the
rules preclude the single ownership of more than seven standard broadcast
(AM) stations in the country.[29]

These same limitations with respect to multiple ownership apply to FM and television stations. Section 73.240 of the FCC Rules prohibits the ownership and control of more than seven FM stations.[30] Section 73.636 makes the same restriction applicable to television, except with the qualification that no more than five of the stations may be VHF, with the ownership and control of two additional UHF stations permitted.[31]

The Commission has not made these restrictive rules applicable to FM and television stations authorized for educational, non-commercial operation only. As previously pointed out, the special rules governing these stations provide that local and state school systems may use them for administrative and instructional purposes and no limit is placed on the number that a local or state educational organization may operate.

Despite the limitations on multiple ownership of commercial stations, the Commission has permitted the ownership by a single party of one AM, one FM and one TV station in the same community. However, on March 27, 1968, the Commission issued a notice of proposed rule making looking toward a change in the regulation. "One of the purposes," said the Commission, "of the Multiple Ownership Rules is to promote maximum diversification of programming sources and viewpoints. It is well established that "the widest possible dissemination of information from diverse and antagonistic sources is essential to the welfare of the public . . . " *Associated Press v. United States,* 326 U.S. 1, 20; *Scripps-Howard Radio, Inc. v. FCC,* 89 U.S. App. D.C. 13, 19, 189 F 2d 677, cert. den. 342 U.S. 830.

Accordingly, the Commission proposed to amend sections 73.35, 73.240 and 73.636 to provide:

(a) No license for a standard broadcast station shall be granted to any party if such party already owns or controls an FM or television station in the market applied for;

(b) No license for an FM broadcast station shall be granted to any party if such party already owns or controls an unlimited time standard broadcast or a television station in the market applied for.

(c) No license for a television broadcast station shall be granted to any party if such party already owns or controls an unlimited time standard broadcast or an FM broadcast station in the market applied for. (See I RR 53:181-183).

The Commission, however, did not propose to require divestiture, by any licensee, of existing facilities. The proposed regulation would be applicable only when new broadcast facilities are being requested. The Commission requested comments from the public and extended the time for filing until August 15, 1968. On March 25, 1970, the Commission adopted an order providing for new multiple ownership rules, prohibiting common ownership of a TV and AM station if the Grade A contour of the former encompasses the entire community of the latter, or if the 2 mv/m contour of the latter encompasses the community of the license of the former. The same principle applies to FM stations in relation to TV or AM stations, with the 1 mv/m contour of the FM station being the criterion.

There are exceptions. Class IV stations licensed to communities of less than 10,000, and not having a TV facility, may own an FM station in the same market. An FM licensee, however, may not obtain a daytime only AM license in the same market.

If for good reason, an AM-FM operation in the same market may assign or transfer the combined facility to a party who does not have any station in that community (18 RR 2d 1735, April 6, 1970). At time of this writing, petitions for reconsideration were pending, but it is expected that the rules will be finally adopted.

In competitive proceedings involving conflicting commercial applications, the matter of multiple ownership and possible concentration of control may become an important decisional factor. For example, in a 1947 case involving two applications for a new radio station in Grenada, Mississippi, the decision turned on this point. The Commission said:

The chief distinction between the applicants, and the one which we believe is decisive, is the fact that (one) is the licensee of three other standard broadcast stations in Mississippi, while (the other) has no other broadcast interests. . . .It is our view that, unless there are countervailing considerations the public interest would be better served in choosing between two applicants by granting the application of the one which as compared with its competitor has fewer broadcast interests since such would tend towards a greater diversity of the ownership of broadcast stations.[32]

Some other competitive cases in which multiple ownership and diversification of control of mass media have been considered by the FCC as decisional factors are: *Triad Television Corporation,* 25 FCC 848, 16 RR 501 (1958); *Sucesion-Luis Pirallo-Castellaros,* 26 FCC 109, 16 RR 113 (1959).*

A superior record of performance[33] or a closer identity with the community and a better program proposal in terms of local need[34]—these and other factors in comparative cases have been strong enough at times to overcome the multiple ownership and concentration of control factors. In the final analysis, the real test is: Which applicant is most likely to serve the interests and needs of the community taking into account all the pertinent facts?

It should be mentioned that the seven station ownership limitation of the FCC has been challenged in the courts. On May 21, 1956, the U. S. Supreme Court, however, affirmed the Commission's authority to impose such a restriction. The court held that the Commission was not barred from adopting rules that declare a present intent to limit the number of stations to

*See reference to article by author, "Nervous Tremors in the Broadcast Industry," p. 246, for a discussion of more recent cases in which the Commission shows increasing concern regarding multiple ownership of mass media, especially where print media are involved, and make this an important decisional factor in comparative cases.

prevent a concentration of control inimicable to the public interest and that the limitations were reconcilable with the Communications Act of 1934 as a whole. The Court did declare, however, that if any applicant could show adequate reasons in the public interest why the rules should be amended or waived in his case, he was entitled to a full hearing before the Commission, should he desire it.[35]

As Judge Miller indicated, in *McClatchy Broadcasting Co. v. FCC,* there is no fixed and inflexible standard by which all comparative cases can be decided. As he said, the Commission "has the duty, in choosing between competing applicants, to decide which would better serve the public interest. Where that interest lies is always a matter of judgment and must be determined on an *ad hoc* basis.[36]

As FCC Examiner Gifford Irion has pointed out, "dogmatic rules are not well adapted to administrative law, especially in comparative cases . . . There is no simple or easy method for deciding between applicants."

He has added, however, that

. . . there is good reason for saying that primary principles do not—or should not —change. If public interest requires selecting the party who will provide the best service and who gives the greatest assurance of so doing, then this must hold true in every case. The evidence by which he proves these things will, of course, vary from case to case, and that is why no single criterion should be invariably predominant. The task of counsel in a comparative proceeding is to form a theory of his client's case and to present the evidence so that one area of comparison leads logically into another. Ordinarily he will be unable to gain a preference on every point, but he certainly should have some rational theory explaining why the points on which he does prevail are those which should govern. If this standard of advocacy were maintained, not only during the hearing proper, but also on appeal to the full Commission, it may be fairly assumed that the decisions, both initial and final would likewise take on a desired quality of logic and consistency.[37]

In 1965, the FCC adopted a policy statement setting forth the important decisional factors in determining the winning applicants in competitive hearings.[38] An FCC pronouncement on competitive hearings, involving regular renewal applicants, later was adopted on January 14, 1970 (FCC 70-62, 40869; 22 FCC 2d 424; 18 RR 2d 1901). The crux of this policy was that a renewal applicant, in a competitive case, acquired a preference if he could show that his station had rendered a "substantial service." On February 17, 1971, the Commission issued a *Notice of Inquiry,* proposing to define what is meant by "substantial service," and asked the public for alternative suggestions. (See FCC Docket 19154, FCC 71-159.)

1. *Johnson Broadcasting Co. v. FCC,* 85 U.S. App. D.C. 40, 175 F.(2d) 351, 4 RR 2138 (1949).

2. *Hearst Radio Inc.,* 6 RR 994 (1951). For a detailed consideration of the various criteria used by the FCC in deciding competitive cases, see digest of cases in 2 RR M-2001 to M-2884.

3. *United States Broadcasting Corporation,* 2 FCC 208 (1935).

4. See *H. K. Glass,* 2 FCC 365 (1936); *Voice of Greenville,* 4 FCC 321 (1937); *Capital Broadcasting Co., Inc.,* 6 FCC 72 (1938); *Herbert L. Wilson,* 9 FCC 56 (1941); *Julio M. Conesa,* 11 FCC 200, 3 RR 158 (1946); *Town Talk Broadcasting Co.,* 11 FCC 919, 3 RR 769 (1947); *Norman Broadcasting Co.,* 13 FCC 1133; 5 RR 120 (1949); *Aladdin Radio and Television, Inc.,* 9 RR 1 (1953); *Mid-Continent Television, Inc.,* 9 RR 1271 (1953); *Southland Television Company,* 10 RR 699 (1955); *WKAT, Inc.,* 22 FCC 1254, 12 RR 1 (1957); *Hi-Lane Broadcasting Co.,* 13 RR 1017 (1957).

5. Other cases: *Southern Tier Radio Service,* 11 FCC 171, 3 RR 211 (1946); *Midwest Broadcasting Co.,* 11 FCC 817, 3 RR 764 (1947); *Wichita Broadcasting Co.,* 11 FCC 1010, 3 RR 865 (1947); *Kendrick Broadcasting Co.,* 9 RR 425 (1953); *City of Jacksonville,* 12 RR 113 (1956); *WHPH, Inc.,* 22 FCC 761, 13 RR 507 (1957); *Queen City Broadcasting Co.,* 23 FCC 113; 15 RR 645 (1957).

6. *McClatchy Broadcasting Company,* 9 RR 1190 (1954). Other cases along the same line: *Petersburg Television Corporation,* 10 RR 567 (1954); *Scripps-Howard Radio, Inc.,* 11 RR 985 (1956); *St. Louis Telecast, Inc.,* 22 FCC 625, 12 RR 1289 (1957).

7. *WOOD Broadcasting Corporation,* 10 RR 1119 (1956).

8. *WMBD, Inc.,* 11 RR 533 (1956).

9. *Television East Bay, Inc.,* 14 RR 1 (1956).

10. *WKRG-TV, Inc.,* 10 RR 225 (1955).

11. *Brush Moore Newspapers, Inc.,* 11 RR 641 (1956).

12. *Hi-Lane Broadcasting Company,* 13 RR 1017 (1956).

13. *Radio Station KFH Co.,* 11 RR 1 (1955).

14. *Richmond Newspapers, Inc.,* 11 RR 1234 (1955).

15. *Oregon Television, Inc.,* 9 RR 1401 (1954).

16. *Tuscaloosa Broadcasting Company,* 11 FCC 487 (1946).

17. *Bay State Beacon, Inc.,* 12 FCC 567 (1947), 3 RR 1455.

18. *Orlando Daily Newspapers, Inc.,* 11 FCC 760, 3 RR 624 (1946).

19. *Loving Broadcasting Company,* 5 RR 48 (1949).

20. *WSAV, Inc.,* 10 RR 402 (1955).

21. *WREC Broadcasting Service,* 10 RR 323 (1955).

22. *Superior Television, Inc.,* 11 RR 1173 (1956).

23. *WJR, The Goodwill Station, Inc.,* 9 RR 227 (1954); *Tampa Times Co.,* 10 RR 77 (1954); *KTBS Inc.,* 10 RR 811 (1955).

24. *Southland Television Co.,* 10 RR 699 (1955).

25. *Genesee Radio Corporation,* 5 FCC 183 (1938).

26. *The Hawaiian Broadcasting System,* 8 FCC 379 (1941).

27. *Lubbock County Broadcasting Co.,* 4 RR 493 (1948).

28. Section 3.35 (b), FCC Rules and Regulations, 1 RR 53:160.

29. *Ibid.*

30. Section 3.240, 1 RR 53:417.

31. Section 3.636, 1 RR 53:641.

32. *Grenada Broadcasting Co.,* 12 FCC 1319 (1947); 3 RR 1159.

33. *Penn Thomas Watson,* 12 FCC 180.

34. *Norfolk Broadcasting Corporation,* 12 FCC 395, 3 RR 1699 (1947).

35. *United States et. al. v. Storer Broadcasting Company,* 351 U.S. 192, 13 RR 2161.

36. 239 F. 2d 15 (1956).

37. Irion, H. Gifford, "FCC Criteria for Evaluating Competing Applicants," *Minnesota Law Review,* Vol. 43, No. 3, p. 479, January, 1959. This is an excellent analysis of the criteria applied by the Commission and is based upon a detailed analysis of cases decided by the FCC. The problems of applying these criteria are clearly presented. Mr. Irion has served as an examiner with the FCC for a number of years and his opinions on this subject are an outgrowth of long study and experience.

38. 1 FCC (2d) 393; 5 RR (2d) 1901 (1965).

PART V

The Broadcaster and Ethereal Realities

CHAPTER 15

Getting Authority to Build a Station: Procedural Steps

The determination of any particular proceeding requires a determination of the public interest, reached through procedure designed to give full protection to individual rights. —GEORGE E. STERLING*

The detailed procedure for getting a license to operate a radio or television station is set forth in Part I of the FCC's Rules, entitled "Practice and Procedure." Part 73 of the Rules, "Radio Broadcast Services," explains the kind of showing an applicant must make before an authorization for a new standard broadcast station or an increase in existing facilities will be granted.

The purpose of this chapter is to provide a general understanding of the problems involved and the basic steps to be followed if a broadcast authorization is to be secured. The procedure is substantially the same whether the operation contemplated is standard (AM), frequency modulation (FM), television, or international broadcast.

As already stated, except under certain emergency conditions set forth in Section 308(a) of the Communications Act of 1934, the Commission is prohibited from granting construction permits, station licenses, or modifications thereof, or renewal of licenses, without *written* applications first having been filed.[1] As pointed out in Chapter 3, these applications must provide the Commission with certain types of information as specified in Section 308(b) of the Act.

Pursuant to this statutory mandate, FCC Application Form 301 has been designed. It has a flexible format and is required to be used to apply for authority to build a new AM, FM or television station or to make changes in existing broadcasting facilities.

With respect to standard broadcast stations, the requirements of Section 73.24 of the Commission's rules should be noted.[2] This section provides that an authorization for such a station will be issued *only* after a satisfactory showing has been made in regard to certain matters.

*Former member of the FCC.

Showing Fair Distribution of Frequencies. First, the applicant must show that the frequency assignment requested "will tend to effect a fair, efficient, and equitable distribution of radio service among the several states and communities." This provision implements Section 307(b) of the Communications Act.

Following passage of the Radio Act of 1927, Congress became concerned that the Federal Radio Commission was concentrating grants of licenses in the Northern and Eastern parts of the country. Congressmen from the South and West protested this trend.[3] The result was the adoption of the Davis Amendment to help correct this situation.[4] Under this Amendment, the Federal Radio Commission was required to make an equal allocation of broadcasting facilities among five zones which had been established and to see that a fair distribution was made among the states in each zone according to population. The Radio Commission worked out a quota system based upon the population of each zone.[5]

With the demise of the 1927 Act, the Davis Amendment was embodied in Section 307(b) of the Communications Act of 1934. It was soon found, however, that allocation of facilities based largely on population did not lead to a "fair, efficient and equitable" distribution. The sparsely settled areas tended to suffer. Congress, therefore repealed the Davis Amendment in 1936. As amended, Section 307(b) now reads:

In considering applications for licenses, and modifications and renewals thereof, when and insofar as there is demand for the same, the Commission shall make such distribution of licenses, frequencies, hours of operation, and of power among the several States and communities as to provide a fair, efficient, and equitable distribution of radio service to each of the same.[6]

This is a very general and flexible provision which has been used by the Commission to justify preference of one applicant in a community which has no radio station over another in a second community which already has broadcasting facilities.[7] In other cases, the Commission has preferred one application over another because more people would be served by a proposed operation than by another.[8]

Showing That Overlap and Interference Will Not Result. A second showing required to be made in an application, is that the proposed assignment and operation will not cause overlap or objectionable interference to other stations. In seeking a new daytime only AM station or for major changes in such facilities, section 73.24 requires a showing that certain ground-wave contours (as set forth in section 73.37) will not prohibit overlap. For nighttime proposals a showing is required that objectionable nighttime interference will not be involved (objectionable nighttime interference caused by the operation of stations on the same or adjacent channels due to ionospheric reflections is considered to exist when certain ratios of desired to undesired signals occur). Precise methods for determining whether prohibited overlap may occur during daytime hours or whether nighttime proposals may involve objectionable interference in the standard broadcast band are set forth by the Commission in sections 73.182, 73.183, 73.184, 73.185, 73.186 and 73.187 of the Technical Standards.[9] In selecting a suitable frequency and preparing the necessary technical showing, the services of a competent engineer are required.

Showing Financial, Legal, Technical and Character Qualifications. Paragraphs (c) and (d) of Section 73.24 call for a showing in the application that the applicant is financially and legally qualified and possesses good character and other qualifications. Paragraph (e) requires proof that the "technical equipment proposed, the location of the transmitter, and other technical phases of operation comply with the regulations governing same, and the requirements of good engineering practice." These paragraphs simply implement statutory provisions which have already been discussed in Chapter 13.

Showing That International Agreements Are Not Violated. Since radio waves do not stop at national boundaries, arrangement and agreements must be made with other countries to avoid objectionable interference and to achieve desirable international objectives. Accordingly, Paragraph (f) of Section 73.24 requires a showing in the application that the location and operation of a proposed station will not violate international agreements. Accordingly, Paragraph (f) of Section 73.24 requires a showing in the application that the location and operation of a proposed station will not violate international agreements with foreign countries designed to prevent interference among domestic and foreign stations. For example, we are signatories to what is known as the North American Regional Broadcasting Agreement. Canada and countries to the south of us are parties to the agreement. The Commission has scrupulously adhered to these agreements and has not permitted assignments or operations in this country which would interfere with those in other countries.[10]

Other Requirements. Paragraph (g) of Section 73.24 requires that an application for a standard broadcast station (AM) show that not more than one per cent of the population within the 25 millivolt per meter contour of the station shall reside in the one volt per meter area in the immediate vicinity of the transmitter. The rule does not apply where no more than 300 persons live within the one volt per meter contour. The rationale for this rule is that the signal of the station within a mile or so of the transmitter is so strong that it tends to override the signals of other stations and limits the inhabitants in this nearby area to the one local station. It is desirable, therefore, that the transmitter be located so that this limitation will affect as few people as possible.

Finally, the Commission says in Paragraph (j) of Section 73.24 that an application for an AM station must show that "the public interest, convenience, and necessity will be served through the operation under the proposed assignments."

Programming Information Required. Information regarding program service which an AM or FM applicant proposes to provide is required in Section IV of Application Form 301. Numerous and detailed exhibits must be prepared and submitted with the application. In Part I of this section, the applicant is required to state in an exhibit the methods used to ascertain the needs and interests of the public to be served by the station. This information must include (1) identification of representative groups, interests and organizations which were consulted and (2) the major communities or areas which applicant will principally undertake to serve. Also, the significant needs and interests of the public which the applicant expects to serve (including national and international matters) must be set forth, and, excluding entertainment and news, typical and illustrative programs designed to meet these needs and interests must be listed. While not required to be submitted with the application, sufficient records upon which these representations are based must be kept on file by the station for three years and be available on request for inspection by the Commission during this period.

Furthermore, in Part III of Section IV, the number of hours that the station proposes to broadcast during a normal week of operation must be stated. The minimum time to be devoted to news, public affairs, and other types of programs, exclusive of entertainment and sports, must be indicated. There are specific interrogatories as to the amount of time to be devoted to local and regional news and the staff and other facilities and services to be used in providing this news.

Other questions call for information regarding the applicant's policy with respect to making time available for the discussion of public issues, the amount of time to be devoted to particular areas of programming in the entertainment field, how and to what extent this will contribute to the "over-all diversity of program services available in the area or communities to be served," and the number of public service announcements to be broadcast during a typical week, and network affiliations, if any, must be reported. If the application is for an FM station, the number of hours, if any, must be reported, and the number of hours, if any, that the programming will duplicate that of an AM station must be indicated. Section 73.242(a) of the Commission Rules defines duplication as simultaneous broadcasting of a particular program over both AM and FM stations or the broadcast of a particular FM program within 24 hours before or after the identical program is broadcast over the AM station.

In Part V, the applicant is required to state the maximum percentage of commercial material which he proposes for normal broadcasting during different segments of the day, and under what circumstances and how often he would expect to exceed this amount. Moreover, the Commission wants to know who will be in charge of operations, who will make the day-to-day decisions regarding programming, and whether he will be a full time employee, what general policies or code with respect to programming and advertising standards has been established by the station, and how many people are to be employed. If, as an integral part of station identification announcements, the applicant expects to make reference to any business or activity other than broadcasting in which it or its affiliate or any stockholder is engaged, examples of these announcements must be submitted and their approximate frequency must be indicated. And finally, the applicant must state how it expects to keep itself informed as to the requirements of the Communications Act and the Commission's Rules and Regulations, and how it plans to ensure compliance from its employees.

In Section IV of the application form, the Commission gives applicants notice that the replies to questions therein constitute "a representation of programming policy upon which the Commission will rely in considering the application." Accordingly, applicants are cautioned to devote time and care and use their best judgment in preparing these replies. It is not expected by the Commission, however, that licensees "will or can adhere inflexibly in day-to-day operation" to the program representations made.

Controversial Character of Section IV. The announcement of the Commission in early 1961 that it proposed to adopt a new program reporting form for television and radio broadcast stations evoked much controversy. Proceedings were instituted on February 21, 1961, but the final application form was not approved until July 27, 1965 (Docket No. 13961). During this period, many comments were filed with the Commission, some favoring the adoption of more stringent program requirements for stations, others strongly opposing any such action. The bulk of the opposition came from the broadcast industry. Networks, broadcasting stations, state associations of broadcasters, and other segments of the industry registered their concern. For example, the following is a part of a lengthy objection filed by the Michigan Association of Broadcasters:

The instant proposal . . . is an enormous leap beyond the pale of limited control as practiced by the Commission in the past. As opposed to the present three page form which has been in use for many years, we are now confronted with a proposed one which is three times as long, which would require the preparation of numerous tables and eighteen lengthy exhibits, necessitating hundreds of additional man-hours of work from station management, staff, and legal counsel to secure, record, and report a voluminous amount of program information in a form which is far more detailed and prescriptive in character, and which would impose a heavy drain on the energies of station personnel needed for the creative and qualitative aspects of programming. We submit that the proposal is such an extreme departure from long and consistent administrative practice, is so unreasonable and capricious in its demands, and would give the government such an overpowering hand in the area of broadcast programming, that by no stretch of the imagination could it be expected to merit judicial sanction . . .

Aside from the unlawful character of the proposal, we cannot believe that the Commission would wish to inflict so many detailed, unrealistic burdens on AM and FM broadcasters . . .

We do not believe that this onerous compiling and reporting of minutiae is necessary for the Commission to determine whether a station has operated in the public interest. Furthermore, even assuming that it might have some value for regulatory purposes, the Michigan Association of Broadcasters does not see how, as a practical matter, the Commission staff could effectively review this data, let alone the Commission itself which must be concerned with the ever widening field of broadcast regulation and the mounting stack of agenda items upon which it must pass judgment each week. In view of the Commission's huge backlog in the processing of applications for new stations and renewal of licenses for existing ones, it is inconceivable to us how the Commission and its staff could give more than a superficial and perfunctory examination to the loads of information data which would pour into the offices of the Commission from every area and community in the country. Yet the efforts which broadcasters would have to make to supply the data would compel the hiring of additional personnel and the spending of thousands of extra dollars.

On the other hand, some groups such as the National Council of Churches of Christ, and other church groups strongly favored the adoption of stricter program requirements for stations, arguing that the Communications Act requires stations to operate in the public interest, that many fall below this standard and that the Commission has a statutory duty to require that stations measure up in terms of their obligation to serve community interests and needs. To accomplish this, these groups contended that the Commission should elicit more rather than less program information in applications, and that stations should be held to strict account when coming up for renewal of their licenses.

As a result of the many comments filed and prolonged study, the Commission made some modifications in its proposals. To ease the administrative burden on broadcasters, some interrogatories in Section IV were eliminated. For purposes of clarification some were re-worded. In its final report and order adopting the present application form, the Commission, in part, said:

A number of comments have included extensive constitutional, legal, and philosophical arguments concerning the role of this Commission and its duty, or lack of authority, in the field of programming. That these matters are serious and basic is evident. The Commission's views in the matter, however, have been set forth in some detail in its "Report and Statement of Policy Re: Commission *En Banc* Program Inquiry" (FCC 60-970, 25 F.R. 7291, 20 RR 1902, released July 29, 1960).* Many of the arguments now presented have been disposed of in that report and other Commission pronouncements in this area. Suffice it to say here that the Commission finds the proposals adopted herein to be in accordance with its statutory duties and authority and warranted in the public interest.

The Commission, throughout this proceeding, has made every effort to accede to reasonable suggestions. It has been our intention to seek only information we deem necessary in fulfilling our statutory functions and to do it with the least expense, inconvenience and burden to licensees and applicants (5 RR 2d 1775, 30 Fed. Reg. 19195).

*This report appears in full in Appendix IV.

One part of the Report and Order concerning deviations of licensees from program representations made in their applications should be especially noted. It reads:

> ... Because the proposals as to programming and commercial matter are representations relied upon by the Commission in determining whether grant of an application is in the public interest, licensees are given the responsibility to advise the Commission whenever substantial changes occur. It is not possible to define what would constitute a substantial change so that it may be applied in every case. This is a judgment to be made by the licensee in the exercise of sound judgment. It does not require that every departure from programming and commercial proposals is to be reported to the Commission. Obvious examples of the type of program format alteration which would be reported are a station deciding as a matter of policy to increase the maximum percentage of commercial matter which it proposes to allow, or if the station determines that it is exceeding these proposed maximums approximately 10 percent of the time. If the type of change raises serious public interest questions, the licensee will be so advised and an inquiry may be made in order to ascertain complete details. However, silence on the part of the Commission is not to be construed as indicating that the Commission has passed on the matter. The station's performance in the public interest will be evaluated in any event at the time of next renewal (5 RR 2d 1776, 30 Fed. Reg. 19196).

Technical Aspects of the Application. Section V of the form covers the technical aspects of the application. It must be prepared and signed by one having engineering knowledge. It calls for such information as frequency, hours of operation and power requested; location of station, transmitter and main studio; description of equipment including frequency and modulation monitors, antenna system, various coverage contours as proposed for day and night operation, and the methods employed to determine these contours; and maps clearly showing antenna location, general character of the city or metropolitan area to be served, buildings and other structures, and location of other transmitters and stations within a ten mile radius.

Unlike FM or TV assignments, where the allocations are based on established channel and mileage separations, AM station assignments are greatly complicated by numerous complex variables such as ground conductivity, skywave propagation conditions, highly suppressed multi-element directional antenna systems and groundwave field intensity measurement data. As a result, considerably more technical data are required of applicants for AM facilities than for those seeking FM or TV authorizations.

Section V-G calls for specific information regarding the proposed antenna and site which is submitted by the FCC for review by federal aviation authorities. Types of information requested include a list of landing areas within ten miles of the antenna site, exact distance to nearest airway within five miles, and the height of the proposed tower.

Commission Procedure for Processing Broadcast Applications. Three copies of the application and all exhibits must be prepared. Two additional copies (a total of five) of Section V-G and associated exhibits are required.

The application must be personally subscribed and verified by the party in whose name it is filed or by one of the parties if there be more than one; or if a corporate applicant, by one of the officers of the company. Only the original need be signed and verified; the copies may be conformed.

If the applicant is physically disabled or absent from the continental United States, his attorney may execute and file the application. In his verification, however, he must set forth the grounds of his belief as to all matters not stated upon his knowledge and the reason why the applicant has not supplied the information or is unable to do so.

Except for Section V-G, information called for in Form 301 need not be refiled if it has already been submitted to the Commission in some other FCC form. This incorporation by reference is acceptable providing the form number, date of filing, and specific paragraph of the document containing the information are indicated, and the applicant states there has been "no change since the date of filing." In this connection, the Commission warns that any such incorporation makes the information referred to as well as the entire document containing it, whether confidential or otherwise, open for public inspection.*

All applications for radio and television stations are required to be filed with the Secretary of the Commission.[11] They may be mailed or delivered personally to the Secretary's office at 1919 M Street, N.W., Washington, D.C. At the time of filing, the applicant must give public notice in the principal area proposed to be served by the station. Instructions as to type of notice are set forth in detail in Section 1.580 of the Commission's Rules. Upon receipt in the Secretary's office, applications are dated and forwarded to the Broadcast Bureau for review.[12] If a preliminary review shows the application to be substantially incomplete or defective, it is returned to the applicant with a brief statement concerning its defects. Or if there are only minor omissions, it may be accepted for filing and a letter addressed to the applicant requesting additional information.[13]

When the application appears to be in complete form, copies are distributed to appropriate staff members in the Broadcast Bureau. The Chief of the Bureau may act on all requests for broadcast authorizations if they comply fully with the requirements of the Communications Act and the regulations relating to delegations of authority to the staff, and if they are not contrary to Commission policy and standards, are not mutually exclusive with any other application, and if no formal protest or other substantial objection has been filed.[14]

The Commission previously reserved to itself the power to act on all applications for new stations or for major changes in broadcast facilities.

*With the exception of certain technical data, information required of applicants for TV facilities is much the same as that required of AM and FM. Since the 301 Application Form (AM, FM and TV) runs more than forty pages, it is not reproduced in this volume. However, copies can be secured from the U.S. Printing Office in Washington, D.C. at nominal cost. Since it is a public document copies may be duplicated freely by those wishing to use it for instructional purposes.

The present rule, however, widens the scope of the Broadcast Chief's authority, but it goes without saying that it requires him to exercise more careful and critical judgment to ensure that the law, and FCC regulations and policies are complied with. In case of doubt, he is obligated to send the application to the Commission for action. This is particularly true if it raises questions about which there may be substantial disagreement among Commissioners as to what action should be taken.

Applications for new broadcasting stations or for major changes in facilities already authorized may not be granted by the Commission earlier than 30 days from the date that the Commission gives public notice that such applications have been accepted for filing.[15] Each is given a file number and is processed as nearly as possible in the order in which it is filed, except that the Broadcast Bureau is authorized to group together those which involve interference conflicts and where it appears that they must be designated for a consolidated public hearing.[16]

Formerly, Commission Rules provided that applications for non-commercial educational stations might be acted upon at any time after "Public Notice" was given of their acceptance by the FCC. Congressional legislation, however, has precluded such grants earlier than 30 days from the date of notice of filing.[17]

After the FCC staff has made an engineering, legal and accounting study of an application, if Commission action is required, a memorandum is prepared and the Chief of the Broadcast Bureau places it on the agenda for Commission action. If there are questions concerning the qualifications of the applicant, or if the proposed operation of the new station would cause objectionable interference to an existing one, or the staff feels that there are other reasons why a grant of the application would be against the public interest, these matters are set forth in the memorandum for the consideration of the Commission.

Upon the basis of the information submitted by the staff, the Commission determines the action to be taken. If it appears that the public interest will be served, the application is granted and a construction permit is issued.[18] On the other hand, if the Commission is unable to make such a finding, the applicant and all interested parties are informed of any objections or questions. The applicant then may make a formal reply. If, upon consideration of this reply, the Commission is still in doubt, the application is then designated for a public hearing on the unresolved questions. The burden of meeting the specified issues and proving that a grant of the application will serve the public interest then falls upon the applicant.[19]

Pre-Grant Procedure. Section 309(c) of the Act formerly specified that grants of applications were subject to protest for a period of thirty days. During that time, any party in interest might formally register opposition and request a public hearing.[20] Congress, however, in 1960 Amendments to the Communications Act, abolished the protest procedure and in lieu thereof provided that any party in interest may file with the Commission a petition to deny any application (whether as originally filed or as amended) at any time prior to the day the Commission grants it. The petitioner must serve a copy of such a petition on the applicant. The applicant is afforded an opportunity to make a formal reply. If the application and the pleadings raise serious questions as to whether a grant of the application will serve the public hearing, the Commission must designate the application for public hearing on specified issues, giving due notice to the applicant and other parties in interest. On the other hand, if the application and the petition raise no material questions, the Commission must make the grant, deny the petition, and issue a concise statement of reasons for denying the petition.[21] (For more detailed information regarding petitions, interventions, and other pre-grant procedure, see 1960 Amendments to Communications Act in Appendix I.)

Hearing Procedure. As provided in Section 1.593 of the Rules, when an application is set for hearing, the Commission mails an order to the applicant setting forth the reasons for the Commission's action and the issues to be heard.[22] If there are competing applications for the same channel, they will be designated for a consolidated hearing and all applications will be notified by the Secretary of the issues on which their qualifications will be compared and the basis on which the winner will be selected.

The notice of hearing is published in the *Federal Register,* and, when possible, at least 60 days advance notice is provided.[23]

Any applicant has the right to withdraw or ask dismissal of an application without prejudice prior to its designation for hearing, but after that time such requests are considered only upon written petition served upon all parties involved in the proceeding and are granted by the Commission only for good cause shown.[24]

If an applicant desires to avail himself of the opportunity for a public hearing, he or his attorney must file with the Commission in triplicate a written appearance within twenty days from the mailing of the FCC hearing notice by the FCC Secretary, stating that the applicant will appear and present evidence on the issues specified. Unless a request is made to dismiss the application prior to the expiration of the 20 days or a petition is filed to accept an appearance at a later date, a failure to enter an appearance within the prescribed period will result in a dismissal of the application with prejudice for failure to prosecute.[25]

While hearings may be conducted by one or more Commissioners, in most cases, an examiner is designated to preside in accordance with Section 11 of the Administrative Procedure Act.[26] Under the law, the examiner is an independent officer, empowered to administer oaths, issue subpoenas, examine witnesses, rule on questions of evidence, take depositions, regulate the course of hearings, maintain decorum, hold conferences for the settlement or simplification of issues with the consent of parties, and perform other functions essential to the conduct of adjudicatory proceedings by Federal administrative agencies.[27]

After the taking of testimony, the examiner officially closes the record and, after certification, files it in the office of the Commission Secretary. Ten days are allowed for necessary corrections of the transcript.[28]

The applicant and other parties may file with the examiner proposed findings of fact and conclusions of law which become a part of the record in the case. These are required to be filed within 20 days after the record is closed, unless additional time is allowed.[29]

Upon the basis of the complete record, the examiner prepares an initial decision which must contain findings of fact and conclusions, as well as the reasons therefor, upon all material points in the case, and must contain a recommendation as to what disposition of the case should be made by the Commission. The initial decision is transmitted to the Secretary who makes it public immediately and files it in the docket of the case.[30]

Appeal and Review of Initial Decisions. As provided in Section 1.276(a) of the Rules, within 30 days of the public release of an initial decision, or such other time as the Commission may specify, any of the parties may appeal to the Commission by filing exceptions.[31] The Commission, on its own motion, may, within 20 days after the time for filing exceptions expires, order that an initial decision shall not become final pending review by the Commission.[32]

Either on its own intiative or upon appropriate requests from a party, the agency may take one or more of several actions with respect to initial decisions which are subject to review. It may (1) hcar oral argument on the exceptions; (2) require the filing of briefs; (3) before or after oral argument or the filing of exceptions or briefs reopen the record and/or remand the proceedings to the presiding officer to take further testimony or evidence or make further findings or conclusions. The Commission may itself issue a supplemental initial decision or cause one to be issued by the presiding officer.[33]

Section 1.153 also provides that unless exceptions are filed within the required time, or unless the Commission takes one or more of the actions enumerated in the preceding paragraph, the initial decision becomes final and effective after 50 days from time of public release of the full text thereof.

Any exception to an initial decision must point out with particularity alleged errors and must contain specific references to the page or pages of the transcript, exhibit or order on which the exception is based.[34]

Within the time allowed for the filing of exceptions any party may file a statement in support of an initial decision, in whole or in part. Such a supporting statement, as well as any exception, may be accompanied by a separate brief or memorandum of law which is limited to 50 double-spaced typewritten pages. Ten days, or such other time as the Commission may specify, are allowed for the filing of reply briefs to which the same page limitation applies.[35]

If exceptions have been filed, any party may request oral argument not later than five days after the time for filing replies to the exceptions has expired.[36] If no request for oral argument is filed within the time allowed, parties are deemed to have waived their rights thereto. Those wishing to participate in an oral argument must file written notice of intention to appear and participate within five days from the date of the Commission's order. A failure to do so constitutes a waiver of the opportunity to participate.[37]

Following oral argument, the Commission issues a final decision in the case.[38] This decision contains findings of fact and conclusions upon all material issues, as well as the reasons therefor; rulings on all relevant and material exceptions filed, and an appropriate order granting or denying the application.[39]

Within 30 days from the day the full text of a final decision is released, or, if such a document not issued, from the date of "Public Notice" announcing the action, petitions for reconsideration and rehearing may be filed with the Commission. Only persons aggrieved or whose interests are adversely affected by the decision may file such petitions. Persons not parties to the proceeding must show clearly what their interests are and show good reason why they were unable to participate.[41]

Petitions for reconsideration or for rehearing, as provided in Section 1.191 of the Rules, may request numerous types of relief including (1) reconsideration; (2) reargument; (3) reopening of the proceeding; and (4) amendment of any finding of the Commission.[42] The rule provides, however, that only newly discovered evidence or that which should have been taken in the original proceeding will be admissible in a rehearing.[43] It also states that the filing of a petition under this section, without a special order of the Commission, does not excuse any person from complying with or obeying any decision, order, or requirement of the Commission, or operate in any manner to stay or postpone the enforcement thereof. But if good cause can be shown, the Commission may stay the effectiveness of its order pending a decision on the petition.[44]

Court Review of FCC Decisions. Any applicant for a construction permit, competitive or otherwise, whose application has been denied by the Commission, may appeal the decision to the United States Court of Appeals for the District of Columbia. As provided in Section 402 of the Communications Act, notice of appeal must be filed with the Court within 30 days following public notice of the decision, and must contain a concise statement of the nature of the proceedings, the reasons for the appeal and proof of service of a true copy of the notice and statement upon the Commission.[45]

Within five days of an appeal, the Commission must notify all interested parties and within thirty days must file with the Court a copy of the order complained of, a full statement in writing of the facts and grounds relied upon in support thereof, and the originals or certified copies of all papers and evidence presented to and considered by it in reaching its decision.[46]

The Court is required to hear and determine the appeal at the earliest convenient time. As provided in Section 10(e) of the Administrative Procedure Act, the Court may set aside the decision of the Commission if the findings and conclusions are "arbitrary, capricious or involve an abuse of discretion, or otherwise are contrary to law, or if not supported by substantial evidence."[47]

Section 402(h) of the Communications Act describes the procedure and disposition of a case in the event of court reversal. It reads:

In the event that the court shall render a decision and enter an order reversing the order of the Commission, it shall remand the case to the Commission to carry out the judgment of the court and it shall be the duty of the Commission, in the absence of the proceedings to review such judgment, to forthwith give effect thereto, and unless otherwise ordered by the court, to do so upon the basis of the proceedings already had and the record upon which said appeal was heard and determined.[48]

Paragraph (j) of the same Section provides that "the court's judgment shall be final, subject, however, to review by the Supreme Court of the United States. Under Section 1254 of Title 28 of the United States Code, the appellant, the Commission or any interested party intervening in the appeal, or the circuit court itself, may petition the higher court to review the case.[49]

1. 48 Stat. 1084.
2. FCC Rules and Regulations, Section 73.24, 1 RR 53:613.
3. 69 *Cong. Rec.* 4489 (1928).
4. Act of March 28, 1928, 45 Stat. 373.
5. FRC General Order No. 40, *Second Annual Report of FRC* (1928), 11.
6. Act of June 5, 1936, 49 Stat. 1475.
7. See Warner, Harry P., *Radio and Television Law* (New York, 1953), p. 293, for discussion of this point.
8. *Ibid.*, pp. 294-297.
9. Section 73.182 *et al.*, 1 RR 53:772-849.
10. See various treaties with countries in this hemisphere, 1 RR 41:1-254.
11. Section 1.564; 1 RR 51:281.
12. *Ibid.*
13. *Ibid.*
14. Section 0.281, 1 RR 50:215.
15. Section 309(b); Communications Act Amendments, 1960, approved September 13, 1960.
16. Section 1.571(c), 1 RR 51:289.
17. Section 309(b); Communications Act Amendments, 1960.
18. Section 1.591; 1 RR 51:315.
19. Section 1.593; 1 RR 51:316.
20. 70 Stat. 3.
21. Sections 309(d) and (e); Communications Act Amendments, 1960.
22. Section 1.593; 1 RR 51:316-317.
23. Section 1.221(b); 1 RR 51:163.
24. Section 1.221(c); 1 RR 51:163.
25. Section 1.221(c); 1 RR 51:163.
26. Section 1.241(a); 1 RR 51:171.
27. Section 1.243; 1 RR 51:171-172.
28. Section 1.258; 1 RR 51:176a.
29. Section 1.263; 1 RR 51:176b.
30. Section 1.264; 1 RR 51:177
31. Section 1.276(a); 1 RR 51:180-181.
32. *Ibid.*
33. Section 1.276(c); 1 RR 51:179.
34. Section 1.277(a); 1 RR 51:180.
35. Section 1.277(c); 1 RR 51:181.
36. *Ibid.*
37. *Ibid.*
38. Section 1.282; 1 RR 51:182.
39. *Ibid.*
40. Section 1.104(b); 1 RR 51:136.
41. Section 1.106(b); 1 RR 51:137.
42. Section 1.106(d); 1RR 51:137.
43. Section 1.106(1); 1 RR 51:139.
44. Section 1.106(n); 1 RR 51:139.
45. 66 Stat. 719.
46. *Ibid;* also Rule 37(a) and (b), Title VII, Federal Communications Commission, General Rules, U. S. Court of Appeals, D. C. Circuit; 1 RR 40:28.
47. Section 10(e); Administrative Procedure Act, 60 *Stat.* 237.
48. 1 RR 10:123.
49. *Ibid.*

CHAPTER 16

Building the Station and Getting a License

Upon the completion of any station for . . . which a permit has been granted, and upon it being made to appear to the Commission that all the terms, conditions, and obligations set forth in the application and permit have been fully met, and that no cause or circumstance arising. . . since the granting of the permit would . . . make the operation . . . against the public interest, the Commission shall issue a license . . . for the operation of said station. —Section 319(c) of the Communications Act of 1934

When an application is granted by the Commission, whether it be with or without a hearing, the applicant receives a construction permit to build the station. The construction of the station must proceed in exact accordance with the specifications and conditions set forth in the authorization. If any changes are to be made, the prior approval of the Commission may be secured by filing an application for modification of permit. The same form (301) is used for this purpose as is used for the original application.

At this point, a few words of caution are appropriate. Section 319 (a) of the Communications Act prohibits the Commission from granting a license for the operation of any station the construction of which is begun or is continued unless a permit for this construction has been granted.[1] The reason Congress adopted this provision in the law was to free the Commission from any pressure for a license which might be exerted because of expenditures made before a construction permit was granted.[2]

The Commission has interpreted this statutory prohibition to mean that an applicant is denied the right to operate a station constructed in whole or in part without a permit having been previously issued. This does not mean that premature construction precludes the Commission from issuing a permit, or that it is to be held against a competing applicant in a comparative proceeding, if the construction was not undertaken by that applicant for the purpose of influencing or "pressuring" the Commission into a favorable decision.[3]

Mention should be made of an amendment to Section 319(d) of the Act which provides that the FCC may waive the requirement for a permit for the construction of a station that is "engaged solely in rebroadcasting television signals if such station was constructed on or before the date of the enactment" of the amendment (74 Stat. 363). This was designed to make possible the validation of a large number of community antenna TV systems constructed without permits first having been received from the FCC.

In line with the statutory mandate in Section 319(b), the Commission requires that construction of a television station must be completed within 18 months, and construction of a radio station must be completed within 12 months from the date the permit is authorized unless, upon proper request, additional time is granted due to causes beyond the control of the permittee which have prevented completion within that period.[4]

During the eight months, studios must be built or arranged for; a tower and antenna must be erected; a transmitter, monitors, indicating instruments, and various other kinds of equipment, depending on the type of station, must be secured and installed. Required technical studies must be completed, such as field intensity measurements for stations employing directional antennas.

Technical Standards and Requirements. In the building of the station, how much and what types of equipment must be installed? What are the specifications as to performance? The answers to these questions are set forth in detail in Part 73 of the Commission's Rules.

The importance of these technical rules and standards cannot be overestimated. It is essential that the transmissions of a broadcasting station be efficient and reliable, free of objectionable interference and otherwise acceptable if a maximum utility from the channel on which the station operates is to be achieved and the public interest is to be fully served. This would not be possible without some regulations and uniform technical standards specifing types of equipment to be used and quality of performance required.

While the technical standards provide for some flexibility, the Commission has cautioned that "it is not expected that material deviation therefrom as to fundamental principles will be recognized unless full information is submitted as to the reasonableness of such departure and the need therefor."[5]

The Commission has further said that these standards will be changed from time to time as the radio art progresses and as new engineering knowledge is acquired.[6]

It is not possible within the limits of this chapter to cover all the detailed technical rules and standards. The purpose here is simply to present some of the high lights which must be taken into account by those who hold construction permits and have been authorized by the FCC to build stations. For detailed technical requirements regarding the various types of equipment and standards of performance of AM, FM, Television and International Broadcast stations, Part 73 of the Rules should be studied.

Transmitters. Transmitting equipment must be capable of satisfactory operation in terms of the authorized power of the particular type of station. The limits of modulation, as precisely prescribed in the Rules, and the degree of carrier shift and the amount of hum and extraneous noise are specifically limited. The design of transmitters must be such that they may readily be adjusted. Adequate provision must be made for changing power output to compensate for excessive variations in line voltage or other factors which affect the output. Automatic frequency control equipment must be installed, capable of maintaining operation on the assigned frequency or within specified limits thereof.[7]

The transmitter and associated equipment must be so constructed and adjusted that emissions are not radiated outside the authorized band which would cause interference to the communications of other stations.[8]

The utility and efficiency of the transmitter depend to a great extent upon its location. The Commission, therefore, has specified four primary objectives to be kept in mind in selecting a site for a transmitter. These are: (1) to serve adequately the center of population in which the studio is located and to give maximum coverage to adjacent areas; (2) to cause and experience minimum interference to and from other stations; (3) to present a minimum hazard to air navigation; (4) to insure maximum field intensities and adequate service to both business and residential sections.[9]

Transmitters must have suitable indicating instruments for determination of operating power and other equipment as is necessary for proper adjustment, operation and maintenance of the indicating instruments, the scale permitted, and the degree of accuracy which is required.[10]

Auxiliary and Alternate Main Transmitters. Upon a showing of need for an auxiliary transmitter, the Commission may issue a license for one under the following conditions which are set forth in the Rules. It may be installed either at the location of the main transmitter or at another location; it must be ready for operation if the regular transmitter fails or is being modified or repaired; it must have control equipment capable of maintaining operation on the assigned frequency as required by the Commission; and its maximum rated power may be less but in no case more than that authorized for station operation.[11]

The Commission may authorize the use of alternate main transmitters providing a technical need is shown. Such authorization may be justified where the station is on a twenty-four hour schedule and alternate use of transmitters is needed to maintain continuous and satisfactory operation, or when developmental work requires alternate operation. It is required that the two transmitters be located at the same place and have the same power rating, except where the operating power during the day is different from that at night when appropriate variations in power ratings of transmitters is permitted. Also, the external effects from both transmitters must be substantially the same as to frequency range and audio-harmonic generation.

Radiating Systems. Each broadcasting station is required to have an efficient radiating system which complies with the Standards of Good Engineering Practice. The antenna system must meet the minimum requirements for height or field intensity.

As the Commission has pointed out, to obtain maximum efficiency from antennas, good ground systems must be employed, involving the use of a sizeable number of evenly spaced buried radial wires. Also, if the location of the transmitter site in the center of a city necessitates placing the antenna on top of a building for best service, this building should not be surrounded by taller structures, especially if they are located in the direction which the antenna is particularly designed to serve. When higher than the antenna itself, they tend to cast radio shadows which may materially reduce the coverage of the station.

The Commission has cautioned against locating broadcasting stations in areas with high signal intensities caused by overhead electrical power and telephone lines, or where the wiring and plumbing are old and improperly installed. These conditions give rise to what is called "cross-modulation interference". Antennas are only permitted in down-town sections when the power of the station does not exceed 500 watts.

Important considerations to be taken into account in locating technical facilities outside the urban areas include the topography in the vicinity of the station, the ground conditions and the type of soil between the transmitting site and the principal area to be served, distance to airport and airways, and space dimensions for the antenna and ground system.

Modulation and Frequency Monitors. Each broadcast station must have in operation, either at the transmitter or at the place where the transmitter is controlled, both frequency and modulation monitors of the types approved by the Commission. Only monitoring equipment which meets the specifications set forth in the Rules may be used in the construction and operation of the station.[12]

This requirement does not apply to low power non-commercial educational FM stations. With respect to them, Section 73.552(d) of the Rules reads:

(d) The licensee of such noncommercial educational FM broadcast station licensed for transmitter power output of 10 watts or less shall provide for the measurement of the station frequency by a means independent of the frequency control of the transmitter. The station frequency shall be measured (1) when the transmitter is initially installed, (2) at any time the frequency determining elements are changed, and (3) at any time the licensee may have reason to believe the frequency has shifted beyond the tolerance specified by the Commission's rules.

Safety Regulations. The construction and operation of technical facilities of all broadcast stations must comply with numerous safety regulations. For example, high voltage equipment including transformers, filters, rectifiers and motor generators must be protected to prevent injury to operating personnel. The antenna and associated parts must be constructed so as not to constitute a hazard to life or limb; metering equipment with a potential of more than 1,000 volts, must be protected by suitable devices and be so installed that it may be read easily and accurately without the operator having to risk contact with high powered circuits.[13]

Transmitter panels or units must be wired in accordance with standard switchboard practice. The monitors and the radio frequency lines to the transmitter must be totally shielded. This also applies to the crystal chamber, together with the conductor or conductors to the oscillator circuit.[14]

Installations must be constructed in suitable quarters providing for the comfort of operators. Studio equipment should be designed to comly with normal safety. There are no specific requirements with respect to design and acoustical treatment of studios except that noise level should be kept as low as reasonably possible.[15]

Construction, Marking and Lighting of Antenna Towers and Supporting Structures. Part 17 of the Commission Rules contains specific requirements with respect to the location, construction, marking and lighting of antenna towers and structures. These Rules were issued pursuant to provisions in the Communications Act which vest in the Commission the authority to issue licenses in terms of the public interest and to require the painting and/or illumination of broadcasting towers and supporting structures to avoid menace to air travel.[16]

Proposed antenna sites and structures involving no hazard to air navigation are considered and approved by the FCC itself. Under other conditions, however, applications for broadcasting towers are referred to the Federal Aviation Administration for special study.

Type Accepted Equipment. Transmitters, frequency and modulation monitors and other kinds of broadcast equipment, may be type-accepted by the Commission upon request of manufacturers, provided data is submitted showing that they meet technical requirements set forth in the Rules. Application for type approval may be in the form of a letter addressed to the Secretary of the Commission, specifying the particular Rules under which approval is requested and describing the equipment and stating the size and weight of each component. In most instances, the Commission advises the applicant to ship the equipment prepaid to the Chief, Laboratory Division, P. O. Box 31, Laurel, Maryland together with operating instructions and circuit diagrams.[17]

A separate request for type acceptance must be submitted for each different type of equipment. It must be filed in triplicate and signed by the applicant or his duly authorized agent who must certify that the facts asserted are true and correct. Additional certification by a qualified engineer who performed or supervised the equipment test is also required.

Lists of type-approved and type-accepted equipment are available for inspection at the Commission's offices in Washington, D.C. and at each of its field offices. These are published in three parts:

Part A, television Broadcast Equipment
Part B, aural Broadcast Equipment
Part C, Other than Broadcast Equipment

Files containing information about equipment submitted by the manufacturers and other persons pursuant to the Commission's Rules are not open to public inspection.

If equipment for sale has been type-accepted by the Commission, persons authorized to build stations may purchase it and use it for construction without further approval of the Commission.

Getting the License. The equipment used and the construction of the station must comply with all the technical standards and requirements set forth above. Once this is accomplished, tests must be made and proofs of performance submitted to the Commission. An applicaton for a license to cover the construction permit must then be filed. FCC Form 302 is used for this purpose. It is a comparatively short form calling for information as to the beginning and completion dates of construction; the actual building costs incurred and current financial position of the station. The most important part of the application must be prepared by an engineer describing equipment installed and reporting tests and measurements of performance.

Having filed the license application and given proof of good station performance, a request may then be made for Commission authority to begin program tests. The Rules require that this request be filed with the Commission at least 10 days in advance of the time desired for commencement of the tests. At the same time, the Engineer in Charge of the District in which the station is located must be notified.

The Commission reserves the right to change the date for the beginning of program tests or to suspend them if the public interest requires. They remain valid, however, unless suspended or revoked by the Commission, during the time the license application is under consideration. As soon as the Commission acts on the application, the program test authority is automatically terminated.

If all the terms of the construction permit have been met and the operation of the station is shown to be in accordance with the Rules and Standards, the Commission grants a license for regular operation as required by Section 319(c) of the Act. That section reads:

Upon the completion of any station for the construction of which a permit has been granted, and upon it being made to appear to the Commission that all the terms, conditions, and obligations set forth in the application and permit have been fully met, and that no cause or circumstance arising or first coming to the knowledge of the Commission since the granting of the permit would, in the judgment of the Commission, make the operation of such station against the public interest, the Commission shall issue a license to the lawful holder of said permit for the operation of the station. Said license shall conform generally to the terms of said permit . . .[18]

Section 307(d) of the Act provides that no license for a broadcasting station may be issued for more than three years and Commission Rules limit the normal license to this period.[19] In order to relieve the workload of the Commission staff, however, original licenses are issued to expire in accordance with staggered schedules and usually run less than three years. Expiration dates for original licenses are specified in the Rules depending upon the state in which stations are located.[20] Renewals are granted at three year intervals thereafter, except in the case of International Broadcast Stations where licenses run for one year only.[21]

By the 1960 Communications Act Amendments, referred to in Chapter 15, Section 307(d) was amended, giving the Commission authority to grant licenses for shorter periods than three years, if, in its judgment, public interest would be served.[22] Accordingly, the Commission has amended its rules, providing for license terms less than three years if the public interest justifies (see Section 73.34 of FCC Rules).

Each license granted by the Commission must contain a statement that (1) the licensee acquires no right in the use of the frequencies assigned beyond the term specified nor in other manner than that authorized; (2) that the rights granted under the license may not be assigned or otherwise transferred in violation of the Act; and (3) that the license is subject to Section 606 of the Act, giving the President emergency war-time powers.[23]

1. 48 Stat. 1089.
2. See *WSAV, Inc.*, 10 RR 402, 430 J (1954), for discussion of the legislative history of Section 319(a) of the Act. Also see H.R. Rep. No. 417 to accompany H.R. 4557, P.L. 321, 83rd Congress, 1st Sess. (1953), 68 Stat. 35 (1954).
3. *Ibid.*, Also see *WJIV-TV, Inc. v. Federal Communications Commission*, U.S. Court of Appeals, D.C. (January 12, 1956), reported in 13 RR 2049.
4. For example, see Section 1.598; 1 RR 51:322.
5. FCC Technical Standards, Section 73.181(d); 1 RR 53:771.
6. Standard Broadcast Technical Standards, Section 73.181(e); 1 RR 53:771.
7. See Section 73.40 of FCC Rules, 1 RR 53:655 for Standard Broadcasting and other appropriate sections covering transmitters in the FM and television service.
8. *Ibid.*
9. See Sections 73.188, 73.315; 1 RR 53:827-831, 1123-1124 for detailed information regarding transmitter locations of AM and FM stations. These sections of the Rules should be consulted carefully. Regarding television, transmitter location must accord with the mileage separations and maximum field intensity requirements prescribed by Sections 73.610, 73.611, 73.685; 1 RR 53:1383-1386, 1565-1567.
10. Sections 73.39, 73.258, 73.688; 1 RR 53:651-655, 1038-1039, 1576-1577.
11. Sections 73.63, 73.64, 73.321, 73.555, 73.556, 73.637, 73.757, 73.758; 1 RR 53:689-692, 1136-1137, 1165-1167, 1410-1411, 1671-1672.
12. Sections 73.56, 73.60, 73.252, 73.253, 73.552, 73.553, 73.691, 73.692, 73.-693, 73.794, 73.754, 73.757, 73.758; 1 RR 53:685-688, 1032-1034, 1162-1165, 1601-1606, 1671-1673.
13. Sections 73.40(b), 73.46(b); 1 RR 53:657, 662.
14. *Ibid.*
15. *Ibid.*
16. Section 303(q), Communications Acts of 1934, 48 Stat. 1083.
17. Sections 2.551-2.593; 1 RR 52:831-850.
18. 66 Stat. 718.
19. 66 Stat. 714.
20. Sections 73.34, 73.218, 73.518, 73.630; 1 RR 53:635-636, 1003-1004, 1157-1158, 1404-1405.
21. Section 73.718; 1 RR 53:1669.
22. 74 Stat. 889.
23. *Ibid.*

CHAPTER 17

Technical Requirements for Operation of Broadcast Stations

One of the most essential duties incumbent upon the licensee of a broadcast station is that of insuring the continuous efficient operation of the transmitting equipment and failure of this equipment, due to causes reasonably within human control, whereby the public is deprived of service, denotes a state of carelessness and mismanagement which the Commission will not condone. —4 FCC 521 (1937)

The FCC has established detailed technical requirements for the operation of all broadcast stations (AM, FM, non-commercial, educational FM, Television and International). These are found in Part 73 of the Commission's Rules governing these various types of stations. For complete and detailed information regarding technical requirements, Part 73 should be consulted.

Authorized Power. These rules provide that the actual operating power of stations shall be maintained "as near as practicable" to that which is authorized in the license. A small degree of variation for each type of station is permitted but definite limits are prescribed. In cases of uncontrollable emergency, the power may be reduced below the stated limits for a period not to exceed ten days providing the Commission and the Engineer in Charge of the radio district are notified promptly when the emergency begins and ends and when normal licensed power is resumed.[1]

Assigned Frequency. The operation of a station must not deviate materially from its assigned frequency. Slight ranges of deviation are permitted, depending on the type of station. In standard (AM) broadcasting, the operation must be maintained within 20 cycles of the assigned frequency.[2] In FM, the allowable tolerance is 2,000 cycles above or below the assigned frequency,[3] except in the case of non-commercial, educational stations operating with 10 watts or less power, the tolerance is plus or minus 3,000 cycles.[4] In television, the carrier frequency of the visual transmitter must be maintained within 1000 cycles of the one authorized, whereas, the center frequency of the aural transmitter must be maintained 4.5 mc, plus or minus 1000 cycles, above the visual carrier frequency.[5]

Modulation Requirements. All stations are required to maintain modulation as high as possible consistent with good quality of transmission, and specific percentages of modulation are prescribed for the various kinds of stations. For detailed requirements regarding modulation, Commission Rules should be consulted.[6]

Repairing and Replacing Defective Equipment. In the event that operating equipment such as indicating instruments, monitors, etc. become defective, they must be repaired or replaced as soon as possible. If they become defective, they may be operated for a period of sixty days providing (1) log entries are made showing the time the monitor was removed and restored to service, and (2) the FCC Engineer in Charge of the radio district in which the station is located is immediately notified both after the instrument is found to be defective and after it is repaired or replaced and proper operation has been restored.[7] Informal request for additional time to complete repairs may be made of the Radio Engineer in Charge of the district in which the station is located.

While a modulation monitor is out of order, the degree of modulation of the station must be checked by suitable means as prescribed by the Rules to assure that modulation is maintained within tolerances prescribed. Where emergency conditions require operation without the use of the frequency monitor, the frequency of the station must be measured by an external source at appropriate specified intervals and the results recorded in the station log.[8]

In the event that indicating instruments fail or do not operate correctly, the Commission has prescribed the precise methods by which power shall be determined pending repair or replacement of the defective instruments.

Equipment Tests and Station Inspections. The licensees of AM and FM broadcasting stations are required to make equipment tests at least once a year, and one must be made during the four-month period preceding the date on which the renewal application is filed. The data required from these tests are set forth in the Rules and must be kept on file at the transmitter and retained for a period of two years and, upon request, be made available during that time to any duly authorized representative of the Federal Communications Commission.[9]

All licensees must make their stations available for inspection by representatives of the Commission at any reasonable hour. The Field Engineering Bureau with twenty-four field offices and twenty monitoring stations distributed throughout the country is responsible for inspections in the field.[10] The locations of these offices and monitoring stations are listed in Section 0.121; 1 RR 53: 133-159.

Requirements Regarding Operating Schedules.

a. Standard Broadcast Stations (AM)

Except on Sundays, the licensees of all standard broadcast stations (AM) must maintain a minimum operating schedule of two-thirds of the total hours they are authorized to broadcast between 6 A.M. and 6 P.M., local standard time, and two-thirds of the authorized time between 6 P.M. and midnight. An exception is made in cases of emergency due to causes over which the licensee has no control. Under such circumstances, the station may cease operation for a period not to exceed 10 days, but the Commission and the Engineer in Charge of the radio district in which the station is located must be notified in writing immediately.[11]

The station must operate or refrain from operating during the experimental period (from midnight to local sunrise) if directed by the Commission in order to facilitate frequency measurement or determine interference.[12]

If the license of a station specifies the hours of operation, this specific schedule must be adhered to except when emergencies, as mentioned above, permit cessation of operation for a limited time or when the station may be ordered by the Commission to operate or refrain therefrom during the experimental period.[13]

b. Share-Time Stations

As previously pointed out, some stations are authorized to share time on the same channel. If the licenses of such share-time stations do not specify hours of operation, the licensees must attempt to reach an agreement as to their respective time schedules. Three original copies of this written agreement must be filed by each licensee with each application for renewal of license. One copy is retained by the Commission, one sent to the Engineer in Charge of the radio district in which the station is located, and one returned to the licensee to be posted with the station license and considered as a part thereof.[14]

If the share-time license specifies a proportionate time division, the agreement must maintain this proportion. If none is specified, the licensees must agree upon a time division. Unless authorized by specific terms in the licenses, simultaneous operation of the share-time stations is not permitted.[15]

If the licenses do not specify hours of operation, the stations may agree to divide time during the experimental period. Such agreements do not have to be submitted to the Commission.[16]

The Commission will not permit a departure from the regular operating schedule set forth in the time-sharing agreement until it is superseded by another agreement signed by the licensees affected and filed in triplicate by each licensee with the Commission prior to the time of the proposed change. If time is of the essence, the schedule may be changed before the written agreement is filed, provided the Commission and the Engineer in Charge of the radio district are notified.[17]

If licensees authorized to share time cannot agree on a division, the Commission must be notified at the time renewal applications are filed. Upon receipt of such applications the Commission then designates them for hearing. Pending the outcome of the proceeding, the stations must adhere to the time schedules previously agreed upon.[18]

281

The Rules covering the broadcast stations (FM and Television) have nothing to say about share-time arrangements. It can be assumed, however, that the same basic rules relating to AM stations are applicable to them as well.

c. Daytime, Limited and Specified Hour Stations

As has already been discussed, stations with licenses which specify operation from sunrise to sunset, commence and cease operations each day in accordance with times set forth in the license. Uniform sunrise and sunset times are specified by the Commission for all the days of each month. Section 73.23 of the Rules states the operating requirements for stations classified as "limited" or "specified" hour stations.[19]

d. FM and TV Stations

All FM broadcast stations are licensed for unlimited time operation. A minimum of 36 hours per week during the hours from 6 A.M. to midnight, consisting of not less than 5 hours in any one day, except Sunday, must be devoted to broadcasting.[20]

Non-commerical educational FM stations are not required to operate on a regular schedule and no minimum number of hours of operation is specified. The Commission has said, however, that the actual operation during a license period will be taken into account in connection with the consideration of renewal applications where it appears that the channels available are insufficient to meet the demand. These same rules apply to non-commercial educational television stations operating on reserved channels.[21]

Commercial television stations are licensed for unlimited time operation. The schedule for each station is prescribed by the Commission as follows: at least two hours daily in any five broadcast days per week and a total of at least twelve hours per week during the first eighteen months of operation; at least two hours daily in any five broadcast days per week and at least sixteen, twenty, and twenty-four hours per week for each successive six-month period of operation. Thereafter, at least two hours in each of the seven days and not less than a total of twenty-eight hours per week of broadcasting is required.[22]

Time devoted to test patterns, or to aural presentations accompanied by the incidental use of fixed visual images which have no substantial relationship to the subject matter of such aural presentations, may not be considered in computing periods of programs service.[23]

Requirements Regarding Operators.   Section 318 of the Communications Act provides that no person shall operate the transmitting apparatus of any broadcast station without holding an operator's license issued by the FCC.[24] This statutory requirement has been implemented in the rules and regulations of the Commission.

Standard AM and FM Broadcast Stations.   One or more radio operators holding valid radiotelephone first-class operator licenses must be in actual charge of the transmitting equipment of a standard or FM broadcasting station and must be on duty either at the transmitter location or remote control point.[25] There is an exception to this rule. Where a broadcast station (AM) is authorized for non-directional operation, with power of 10 kilowatts or less (25 kilowatts or less for FM), it may be operated by a person with a license other than first-class if the equipment is so designed that the stability of the frequency is maintained by the transmitter itself within the limits of tolerance specified; and when none of the activities necessary to be performed to maintain normal transmission may cause off-frequency or result in any unauthorized radiation.[26]

Except when under first-class supervision, lower grade operators are permitted to make only the following adjustments of transmitting equipment:[27]

1. Those necessary to commence or terminate transmitter emissions as a routine matter.

2. External ones required as a result of variations of primary power supply.

3. External ones necessary to insure modulation within the limits required.

4. Adjustments necessary to affect any change in operating power which may be required by the station's instrument of authorization.

5. Make adjustments necessary to effect operation in accordance with a National Defense Emergency Authorization during an Emergency Action Condition.

If the transmitter apparatus is not operating in accordance with the station's authorization and none of the above adjustments is corrective, operators not holding first-class licenses and not under immediate first-class supervision are required to turn off the transmitter.[28]

As pointed out above, the licensee of a standard broadcast station must have one or more first-class operators in full time employment whose primary duties shall be to insure the proper functioning of the transmitting equipment. An operator may be employed, however, for other duties or for operation of other stations in accordance with the class of license he holds. Such duties, however, must not interfere with the proper operation of any broadcast transmitter for which he is responsible.[29]

In the event a licensee operates both a standard and FM station in the same community, a regular full-time first-class operator or operators at one station may be employed concurrently at the other, providing the performance of duties at the one does not interfere with his duties at the other.[30]

Non-Commercial Educational FM Stations. The operator requirements for non-commercial educational FM stations are largely the same as those for standard and FM stations. There are a few exceptions, as follows:

If the transmitter output is in excess of 10 watts but not greater than 1 kw, a second-class operator may perform the duties of a first-class one. If the power output is 10 watts or less, a second-class operator is adequate and he need not be in regular full-time employment at the station.[31]

Television and International Stations. One or more licensed first-class operators must be on duty at the place where the transmitting apparatus of each television and international broadcast station is located and in actual charge of its operations. This applies whether the operation is commercial or non-commercial. The operator may, at the discretion of the licensee, be employed for other duties or for the operation of another station or stations, providing these interfere in no way with his work at any television or international broadcast station for which he is responsible.[32]

Posting Licenses. All broadcast stations are required to post their licenses and any other instruments of authorization in a conspicuous place and in such manner that all terms are visible, at the place the licensee considers to be the principal control point of the transmitter. A photocopy of the license and other instruments of authorization must be posted at all other control points.[33]

The licenses of operators, regardless of classification, must also be posted at the regular place of duty. Originals (not copies) are required.

Keeping Logs. Section 303 (j) of the Communications Act gives the Commission authority to "make general rules and regulations requiring stations to keep such records of programs, transmissions of energy, communications, or signals as it may deem desirable." Pursuant to this authority, the Commission requires all broadcast stations to maintain program and operating logs. As provided in Sections 73.111, 73.281, 73.581, 73.669, and 73.781 of the Rules, the various types of broadcast stations are required to make specified entries in the program logs.[34]

Where an antenna structure is required to be lighted, the licensee must observe the tower lights at least once every 24 hours or maintain automatic equipment with indicators designed to register any failure of the lighting. The failure of any code or rotating beacon or top tower light not corrected within 30 minutes, regardless of cause, must be recorded and reported immediately by telephone or telegraph to the nearest air ways communication station or office of the Federal Aviation Administration. Similar recording must be made and notification must be given upon resumption of the required illumination.

At intervals not exceeding three months, all automatic or mechanical control devices, indicators and alarm systems associated with the tower lighting must be inspected to insure proper functioning.

The station with an antenna structure requiring illumination must make the following entries in the logs:

(a) The time the tower lights are turned on and off each day if manually controlled.

(b) The time the daily check is made, if an automatic alarm system is not provided.

(c) Entries showing the failure of a tower light and the nature of the failure; date and time the failure was observed; date, time and nature of adjustments, repairs or replacements; and identification of air ways communication station (Federal Aviation Administration) which was notified of any light failure and the date and time of such notification.[35]

Retention of Logs.   Logs for the various types of stations must be retained for a period of at least two years. Under certain conditions, the licensee may be required to keep them for a longer period. The Commission has stated that logs involving communications incident to disaster or which may be pertinent to an investigation by the Commission and about which the station has been notified, must be retained until the Commission specifically authorizes in writing their destruction. The same rule applies to retention of logs which may relate to any claim or complaint against the station until such matters have been disposed of or have been barred by the statute limiting the filing of suits.[36]

Keeping Logs in Orderly Manner.   The rules require that logs be kept in an orderly manner and be sufficiently detailed that the "data required of the particular class of station are readily available". Key letters or abbreviations, if properly explained, may be used to facilitate the keeping of the station records.

Licensees are cautioned that each station log must be kept by a competent person or persons familiar with the facts, and who is required to sign the log both when starting and going off duty. No obliterations, erasures or destruction is permitted within the period of retention. Necessary corrections can be made only by the person originating the entry who may strike out the erroneous portion of the log, initial the correction and indicate the date it is made.[37]

Uniform Definitions and Program Logs.   The Commission has adopted uniform definitions of basic program categories. Such classifications must be shown upon the face of the program log so that the licensee may submit descriptive data concerning its program service, as required by the FCC, in connection with applications for new facilities or license renewals.

As previously pointed out, the Commission recently modified its application form 303, involving changes in program categories. (See Commission's reports and orders with its explanation and rationale for adoption of new application forms and new logging requirements. 28 Fed. Reg. 1872, 25 RR 1521; 31 Fed. Reg. 448, 6 RR 2d 1631; 30 Fed. Reg. 19195, 5 RR 2d 1775).

1. FCC Rules, Section 73.52, 73.267, 73.567, 73.689, 73.765; 1 RR 53:682-683, 1048-1049, 1174-1175, 1577-1580, 1673.
2. Section 73.59, 1 RR 53:687.
3. Section 73.269, 1 RR 53:1050.
4. Section 73.569, 1 RR 53:1176.
5. Section 73.687, 1 RR 53:1572.
6. See Sections 73.55, 73.268, 73.317(f) (1), 73.687(b); 1 RR 53:684, 1050, 1131, 1571.
7. Sections 73.56(b), 73.58(b), 73.252(b) and (c), 73.253(b) and (c), 73.552(b) and (c), 73.553(b) and (c), 73.558(b) and (c) 73.688(f), 691(b); 1 RR 53:685, 1032-1033, 1162-1163, 1168, 1576-1577, 1601.
8. Sections 73.56, 73.252, 73.253, 73.553, 73.691; 1 RR 53:685, 1032-1034, 1163, 1601-1602.
9. Sections 73.47, 73.254; 1 RR 53:663, 1035-1036.
10. Section 0.121, 1 RR 53:133-139.
11. Section 73.71, 1 RR 53:701.
12. Section 73.72, 1 RR 53:701.
13. Section 73.73, 1 RR 53:701.
14. Section 73.74, 1 RR 53:701.
15. *Ibid.*
16. Section 73.76, 1 RR 53:702.
17. Section 73.77, 1 RR 53:702.
18. Section 73.78, 1 RR 53:702.
19. Section 73.23, 1 RR 53:612.
20. Section 73.261, 1 RR 53:1045.
21. Sections 73.261, 73.651(b); 1 RR 53:1045.
22. Section 73.651(a), 1 RR 53:1501.
23. *Ibid.*
24. 50 Stat. 56, c. 58.
25. Sections 73.93, 73.265; 1 RR 53:706, 1046.
26. Section 73.93(b); 1 RR 53:707.
27. *Ibid.*
28. *Ibid.*
29. Sections 73.93(d), 73.265(d); 1 RR 53:708, 1047.
30. *Ibid.*
31. Section 73.565, 1 RR 53:1171-1172.
32. Sections 73.661, 73.764; 1 RR 53:1512a.
33. Sections 73.92, 73.264, 73.564, 73.660; 1 RR 53:706, 1046, 1171, 1512a.
34. 1RR 53:721-732, 1061-1071, 1179-1185, 1513-1524, 1674-1676.
35. Sections 17.47, 17.48, 17.49; 1 RR 67:99-100.
36. Sections 73.115, 73.285, 73.585, 73.673, 73.782; 1 RR 53:732, 1071, 1184, 1523, 1675.
37. Sections 73.111, 73.281, 73.581, 73.669, 73.783, 73.784, 73.785; 1 RR 53: 721, 1061, 1179, 1513, 1676.

CHAPTER 18

FCC Rules Implementing Statutory Requirements Regarding Broadcast Programming

The Commission would be remiss in its duties if it failed, in the exercise of its licensing authority, to aid in implementing the statute, either by general rule or by individual decisions. —Former Chief Justice EARL WARREN, *354 U.S. 284.*

While Section 326 of the Communications Act prohibits the FCC from exercising censorhip over the programs presented by radio and television stations, there are a number of provisions in the law which impose requirements on broadcast licensees with respect to certain aspects of programming. Pursuant to these provisions, the Commission has adopted specific regulations which should be considered.

Station Identification. Section 303 of the Communications Act gives the FCC authority to designate call letters for all stations and to require their publication by the stations in such manner as will contribute to the efficiency of their operation and to the enforcement of the Act. Formerly, the FCC provided separate rules for identification announcements for the different broadcast stations. However, on January 19, 1970, the Commission consolidated these rules into Section 73.1201(17 RR 2d 1691), which contains the ID requirements for all AM, FM, noncommercial, educational FM, international stations and television stations. The rule reads as follows:

Station identification. - (a) When regularly required. Broadcast stations shall announce station identification: (1) at the beginning and ending of each time of operation, and (2) regularly, during operation, within 2 minutes of each hour. Standard, FM, and noncommercial educational FM broadcast stations shall, additionally, announce station identification regularly within 2 minutes of each half-hour. Television broadcast stations may make the hourly announcements either visually or aurally, but shall make the announcements at the beginning and ending of each time of operation both visually and aurally.

(b) Content. (1) Official station identification shall consist of the station's call letters immediately followed by the name of the community or communities specified in its license as the station's location.

(2) When given specific written authorization to do so, a station may include in its official station identification the name of an additional community or communities, but the community to which the station is licensed must be named first.

(3) A licensee shall not in any identification announcements, promotional announcements or any other broadcast matter either lead or attempt to lead the station's audience to believe that the station has been authorized to identify officially with cities other than those permitted to be included in official station identifications under subparagraphs (1) and (2) of this paragraph.*

(c) Channel. (1) Generally. Except as provided in subparagraph (2) of this paragraph, in making the identification announcement the call letters shall be given only on the channel of the station identified thereby.

(2) Simultaneous AM-FM broadcasts. If the same licensee operates an FM broadcast station and a standard broadcast station and simultaneously broadcasts the same programs over the facilities of both such stations, station identification announcements may be made jointly for both stations for periods of such simultaneous operation. If the call letters of the FM station do not clearly reveal that it is an FM station, the joint announcement shall so identify it.

(d) Program interruption. Licensees shall, in general, arrange their programming so as to permit the broadcast of station identification announcements at the regular times prescribed in paragraph (a) of this section without undue disruption of program continuity. Subject to this requirement, a station identification announcement need not be presented at the time it is regularly required, if to do so would objectionably break program continuity essential to the value of the program to the audience. However, program continuity is deemed to be broken, and therefore an announcement is required, if during the four-minute period in which an announcement is regularly due there is presented any non-program matter, such as commercial, public service or promotional announcements. While there may be exceptions, normally program continuity is also deemed to be broken, and an identification announcement is required, if during the four-minute period there occurs the end of a regular period in a sports event being broadcast (e. g., round, quarter, or half-inning), the end of an act in a dramatic or variety program, the intermission of a live concert, opera, recital or other musical performance presented live in its entirety, (presented simultaneously or by rebroadcast), or the end of any other musical selection.

(e) Deferred station identification. (1) If a station omits a regular station identification announcement as permitted under paragraph (d) of this sec-

*Commission interpretations may be found in a separate Public Notice issued October 30, 1967, entitled "Examples of Application of Rule Regarding Broadcast of Statements Regarding a Station's Licensed Location". (FCC 67-1132; 10 FCC 2d 407,IRR 53:2051)

tion, it shall broadcast a deferred station identification announcement at the next opportunity when it can be presented without objectionably breaking program continuity essential to the value of the program to the audience. Such opportunity is deemed to occur, at the latest, when any of the material or events mentioned in paragraph (d) of this section is presented or occurs.

(2) If no opportunity for announcement (as defined in subparagraph (1) of this paragraph) occurs after a regular station identification is omitted, a deferred station identification shall be broadcast promptly at the end of the program unless the next regular station identification is broadcast within 5 minutes after the program ends.

(f) Equipment performance measurements. Station identifications falling due during equipment performance measurements may be deferred up to a quarter of an hour.

There are special rules for international broadcast stations. Section 73. 787 requires them to make announcements at the beginning and ending of each time of broadcasting and on the hour during operation.[1] The station identification, program announcements, and oral continuity must be made "with international significance", and designed for the foreign country or countries for which the service is primarily intended.[2] These stations must comply with the provisions of Section 73. 1201(d) and (e) relating to the avoidance of program interruption for regular station identification announcements.[3]

Mechanical Reproductions. Until the latter part of 1956, FCC requirements were quite stringent with respect to identification of mechanical recordings. To make sure that the public was not deceived into believing that it was hearing live talent, all recorded programs had to be identified as such at the beginning and end of such programs and at certain specified intervals.

Following a public hearing, however, the Commission announced in October, 1956, that the rules then in effect imposed "a needless burden on broadcasters and detracted from the public's enjoyment of the programs."[4] Accordingly, the Commission amended the rules at that time requiring identification announcements only when the element of time is important and cutting down on the number and frequency required.[5]

As now in effect, the rules are uniform for standard, FM, non-commercial educational FM and television stations. They provide that no recorded program, "whether visual or aural, consisting of a speech, news, event, news commentator, forum, panel discussion, or special event in which the element of time is of special significance," may be broadcast without an appropriate announcement being made that it is recorded either at the beginning or end of the program.[6] The same rule applies to any other type of program in which the time element is important and presentation of which would create the impression that the event or program is in fact occurring simultaneously with the broadcast.[7]

Recorded programs of one minute or less need not be identified as such. Likewise, mechanical reproductions used for background music, sound effects, station program and sponsor identifications need not be announced as such.[8]

The waiver provision also applies to network programs transmitted in one time zone, recorded and rebroadcast later in another zone. However, the waiver applies only if the period of elapse between the beginning of the first and second transmissions does not exceed the time differential between the two locations.[9]

The Rules provide that when a station broadcasts network programs at a later hour in accordance with the waiver, an appropriate announcement shall be made at least once each day between the hours of 10:00 A.M. and 10:00 P.M. stating that some or all of the network programs broadcast are delayed and presented by transcription.[10]

The exception is also applicable to network programs transcribed and rebroadcast one hour later because of the time differential resulting from the adoption of daylight saving time in some areas.[11]

Sponsored Programs. Section 19 of the Radio Act of 1927 provided that "all matter broadcast by any radio station for which service, money, or any other valuable consideration is directly or indirectly paid, or promised to or charged or accepted by, the station so broadcasting, from any person, shall, at the time the same is so broadcast, be announced as paid for or furnished, as the case may be, by such person."[12]

This language was lifted verbatim from the 1927 Act and became Section 317 of the Communications Act of 1934.[13] The Commission has implemented the provisions of this section with rules which are identical for Standard, FM, television and international broadcast stations.[14] Non-commercial educational FM and television stations are not permitted to sell time to sponsors, but Section 73.621(e) of the Rules specifically makes the statutory requirements of Section 317 of the Act applicable to non-commercial educational TV stations if they carry programs "produced by or at the expense of or furnished by others".[15] While the rules governing non-commerical educational FM stations do not so state, it is assumed that the statutory requirements of Section 317 of the Act are applicable to them as well.

In the case of any political program or any discussion of public controversial issues for which any films, records, transcriptions, talent, scripts, or other materials or services are furnished directly or indirectly as an inducement to the station to carry the program, an announcement to that effect must be made at the beginning and conclusion of the program, except if the program is no longer than five minutes, only one announcement need be made either at the beginning or end.[16]

The true identity of sponsors, donors or others covered by the provisions of Section 317 must be fully and fairly disclosed. Where the station knows that an agent is arranging for the program in behalf of a third party, the announcement must reveal the identity of this third party rather than the agent.[17]

Where programs advertise commercial products or services, a mere mention of the sponsor's corporate or trade name or his product is deemed sufficient, and only one such announcement need be made during the course of the program.[18]

Even if the program is one which does not advertise a product or service, if it is paid for in whole or in part by a corporation, committee, association or other unincorporated group, or uses materials or services provided by any such organization or group in the manner described above, the announcement must disclose the name of the group. Also, in each case, the station must require that a list of the chief executive officers or members of the executive committee or the board of directors of any such organization or group be made available for public inspection at the station carrying the program.[19]

FCC Action Against "Payola" Practices.　On March 16, 1960, the Commission adopted a public notice entitled "Sponsorship Identification of Broadcast Material." The Commission indicated in this notice that on the basis of responses it had received to an inquiry of December 2, 1959, it appeared that stations had failed to comply with the requirements of Section 317 of the Communications Act and the Commission's Rules implementing it.

This action of the FCC was largely an outgrowth of "payola" practices in previous years which had evoked widespread public concern. In this notice, the Commission set forth several specific interpretations of Section 317 applicable to recordings broadcast by radio and television stations. These interpretations may be summarized as follows:

1. The receipt of any records by a station, intended by the supplier to be, or have the practical effect of being an inducement to play those particular records or any other records on the air, and the broadcast of such records, requires an appropriate announcement pursuant to Section 317.

2. Appropriate announcements must accompany all broadcast material (playing of records, etc.) where a profit is to be derived from "record hops" or other non-broadcast activities, or where recorded or other broadcast exposure is being provided in exchange for donation of records, prizes, hall rental, etc. The parties deriving financial benefit from the "record hop" must be identified as well as any other parties furnishing consideration in exchange for any of the above types of broadcast exposure.

3. An appropriate announcement must be made where transportation and accommodation expenses or equipment operation and origination expenses incurred in "remote" pickups have been paid in whole or in part by persons or organizations as an inducement to broadcast program material containing, e.g., pictures or descriptions of a place, product, service, or event. The announcement must disclose the fact that consideration was provided, and by whom, as an inducement for the broadcast presentation.

291

4. "Trade out" announcements and "plugs" violate Section 317 unless it is disclosed that the particular matter broadcast is commercial and is supported by some form of consideration.

5. "Teaser" announcements and broadcast of similar subject matter without explicit identification of the sponsor are contrary to Section 317.

6. The playing of musical selections from current motion pictures under any kind of arrangement with a local theatre or distributor, or as a "bonus" for purchase of spot announcements, without sponsorship announcement is likewise unlawful.

7. Stations must use their utmost diligence to inform themselves of situations in which their employees or independent contractors have outside financial interests which are being promoted over these stations, and to require appropriate announcements to be made as required by Section 317.[20]

FCC's Interpretation of Statute Questioned. The National Association of Broadcasters, the Federal Communications Bar Association, the networks and other segments of the broadcast industry raised questions regarding these interpretations by the Commission and formally requested further proceedings.

In April 1960, the Commission issued a *Notice of Inquiry* stating that it would consider comments as to whether clarification of its interpretations was desirable, and gave interested parties opportunity to file such comments on or before May 2, 1960.[21]

In response to the April 1, 1960 Notice, voluminous comments were filed with the Commission. Many parties particularly objected to the Commission's interpretation of Section 317 which requires that all free records, when played over a station, be accompanied with announcements identifying the donors and stating that these records are furnished without cost.

In many of the comments, it was contended that the legislative history of Section 317 did not call for such a strict interpretation. It was argued that early discussions in Congress regarding the purpose of the section as originally conceived, indicate that the section was mainly intended to prevent "disguised" advertising.[22]

Section 317 was carried over from the Radio Act of 1927. In explaining the origin and purpose of its provisions as they were stated in Section 19 of that original act, Congressman Celler, in 1926, said:

The author of the section sought to follow the law of the District of Columbia against newspapers printing disguised advertising. That law which was a rider to the Post Office Appropriation Bill, August 1912, Sixty-second Congress, second session, (Vol. 37, Stat. L. 553-554), is as follows:

All editorial or other reading matter published in any such newspaper, magazine, or periodical for the publication of which money or other valuable consideration is paid, accepted, or promised shall be plainly marked "advertisement." Any editor or publisher printing editorials or other reading matter for which compensation is paid, accepted, or promised without so marking the same, shall upon conviction in any court having jurisdiction be fined not less than $50 nor more than $500.[23]

The National Broadcasting Company argued that newspapers regularly receive gratuitous press releases and other "publicity hand-outs" from many different sources, the suppliers hoping that the information will be used to their benefit; that a portion or all of one of these press releases would not be a violation of the law. On the other hand, said NBC, if the newspaper is paid cash or other substantial consideration to run the reading material there would be a violation. It was asserted that this same principle ought to be applicable to broadcast stations.[24]

The Michigan Association of Broadcasters agreed with this point of view. In its comments to the FCC, the Association said:

We believe that this same rule of reason ought to apply to broadcast stations who receive, free of charge, records to be included in their libraries. Obviously, record companies and their distributors who make a practice of supplying these free materials to stations, have hopes that some of them will be used and that benefits therefrom will ensue. But where there is no understanding or agreement that any or all of the records will be used—no contractual obligation of any kind to play them on the station—it seems unreasonable to say that broadcast exposure without identification of the donors constitutes a violation of Section 317. As in the case of newspapers, however, if the record company or distributor *pays* the station to play the recordings a certain number of times, a broadcast announcement of this fact would be required to avoid violation of Section 317.[25]

Applicability of Section 317 to Discussion Programs. The legislative history of Section 317 does clearly show that Congress intended that the source of programs involving discussion of political or controversial issues should be identified when broadcast. There can be no doubt that the *mere* supplying of such discussion programs is sufficient to constitute "valuable consideration" in the context of Section 317, and to require sponsor identification.

In a 1958 case, the Commission made its position on this matter clear. That year, the Commission sent three Public Letters to three station licensees who had failed to reveal identity of an organization when those stations had televised kinescope summaries of Congressional hearings on a strike issue.[26] The organization had supplied the films free of charge and the stations received no material consideration except the films themselves. The Commission held that Section 317 of the Act and Section 73.654(d) of the Rules had been contravened. It was stressed that the person or group paying for or furnishing material in connection with the discussion of political matters or controversial issues of public importance should always be accurately and completely identified.

"We do not question the wisdom of this decision," said the Michigan Association of Broadcasters, "where points of view on controversial questions, especially those of a political nature, are being broadcast, the public is entitled to know who the sponsors are. Congress and the Commission have been concerned about this and, we think, rightly so. But the same reasons for this concern do not apply to pure entertainment including little or no discussion and where the consideration involved is the program itself. This is particularly true with respect to free musical recordings where there is no obligation on the part of stations to use any of the recordings."[27]

The Association further pointed out that many stations have built up large libraries of recorded music from which they draw regularly; that the current requirement that every record in these library collections (some of which contain hundreds of free records accumulated over the years) be accompanied with a commercial plug, was a serious burden on the broadcaster, degraded his program service, was offensive to the listeners, and worked seriously against the public interest.

FCC Urged To Reconsider Its Interpretation. Along with other parties in the proceeding, the MBA urged the Commission to reconsider its interpretation of Section 317 as announced on March 16, 1960, and concluded its comments as follows:

... in view of the understanding of Section 317 which has prevailed among large segments of the broadcast industry for more than thirty years, and which appears to conflict with the recent views expressed by the Commission, we earnestly hope that the Commission will not take precipitous action in the matter. We suggest that the Commission suspend the effectiveness of its recent public notice, and institute rulemaking proceedings, looking toward a more careful and studied consideration of the whole problem. This approach will ensure that all interested parties will have an opportunity to provide information and express their views.

. . . .

Presently, there are many misgivings and much confusion in the broadcast industry as to the full import of Section 317 as interpreted at various times by the FCC. Rulemaking, as proposed, would alleviate most of these misgivings and provide clarification as to requirements and procedures. This would be of immeasurable benefit to the industry. More important, the public interest unquestionably would be served.[28]

There were professed differences of opinion among the FCC Commissioners as to the applicability of Section 317. Commissioners Hyde and Lee agreed with the Commission's Public Notice of March 16, 1960 in so far as it solicited comments, but, in a separate statement, expressed the view that the Commission's interpretive ruling may have gone beyond the intent and purpose of the Statute.[29] Accordingly, they favored suspending the effective date of the ruling until the Commission could have time to study the comments filed.

Subsequently, the Eighty-Sixth Congress, at its Second Session, amended Section 317 of the Communications Act, clarifying questions as to license responsibilities regarding announcements and disclosures of payments, received in connection with the broadcast of recordings and other program materials. Also, added to the Act was Section 508 requiring the disclosure by persons other than broadcast licensees who provide or receive valuable consideration for the inclusion of any matter in a program intended for broadcast. Previously, these persons had not been directly subject to any provisions of the law. Sub-section (e) of the revised Section 317 directed the Commission to prescribe appropriate rules to implement the Congressional intent expressed in the amendment. The full text of Section 317, as revised, and Section 508 appear in Appendix I.

One effect of the new legislation was to countermand the interpretation of the Commission which would have required sponsor identification announcements in some situations, including the broadcast of free records where there is no obligation, express or implied, on the part of the station to use them.

In the light of the new legislation, on September 20, 1960, the FCC withdrew its *Notice of Inquiry* (FCC Public Notice 60.1141, No. 93746, 25 Fed. Reg. 9177). On April 27, 1961, the Commission issued a public notice (FCC 61-546, 26 Fed. Reg. 3781) in which amendments to its then existing sponsorship identification rules were proposed. After consideration of comments which were filed in the proceeding, the Commission on May 1, 1963, adopted specific regulations (25 RR 1575, 28 Fed. Reg. 4707). These regulations, which appear in Sections 73.119, 73.289, 73.654 and 73.789 carry out the provisions of Section 317 of the Communications Act, as revised, and Section 508 which was added.

Of special note is the Commission's waiver of the rule with respect to the broadcast of "feature" films. The Commission concluded that the application of the rule to such films could have a disruptive effect upon the movie industry, that in some cases it would be difficult if not impossible, for stations and networks to secure the necessary information to comply with the disclosure requirement, and that, therefore, its adoption would be contrary to the public interest. For a full statement of the Commission's rationale for granting the waiver, see the Commission's public notice mentioned above (25 RR 1579-1591,) 28 Fed. Reg. 4711-4712.

For thirty-six examples cited by the Commission, illustrating the intended effect of Section 317 of the Communications Act, see 1 RR 2d 53:951, 28 Fed. Reg. 4732.

Political Broadcasting. Section 315 of the Communications Act relating to the use of broadcasting facilities by candidates for public office, as originally adopted by Congress, was identical with Section 18 of the Radio Act of 1927.[30] While no station was obligated to carry political broadcasts, it was provided that if a station permitted any "legally qualified candidate" for public office to use its facilities, it must afford equal opportunities to all other such candidates. The section also specifically prohibited the station from censoring any material in broadcasts by political candidates.

In 1952, Congress amended Section 315 of the Communications Act by adding the provision that the charges made for broadcasts by political candidates could not exceed those made for "comparable use" of a station for other purposes.[31]

The FCC has adopted rules to carry out the provisions of Section 315 of the Act.[32] These rules are uniformly applicable to all types of broadcast stations. They incorporate the language of the statute making it optional with any station as to whether it will make its facilities available for political broadcasting, but where it does, requiring that all candidates be treated equally. Rates must be uniform and rebates are prohibited. A candidate may not be charged more than the rate a commercial advertiser would pay for comparable time to promote his business in the same area as that encompassed by the particular office for which the candidate is seeking election.

Discriminations or preferences as between candidates in "charges, practices, regulations, facilities, or services are strictly prohibited and no candidate may be subjected to any prejudice or disadvantage." No licensee can make any contract or other agreement which would have the effect of permitting one candidate to broadcast to the exclusion of others for the same office.

A complete record must be kept by the station of all requests for broadcast time by candidates for public office, together with an appropriate notation showing the disposition made by the licensee of such requests, and the charges made, if any, when broadcasting facilities are made available. These records must be retained for a period of two years and be open for public inspection.

Section 315 of the Act is applicable only to "legally qualified candidates." In the absence of statutory definition, it has been necessary for the Commission to define the term as it is used in the Rules. As described in Section 73.120 of the Rules relating to standard broadcasts stations, a "legally qualified candidate" is "any person who has publicly announced that he is a candidate for nomination by a convention of a political party or for nomination or election in a primary, special, or general election, municipal, county, state or national, and who meets the qualifications prescribed by the applicable laws to hold the office for which he is a candidate so that he may be voted for by its electorate directly or by means of delegates or electors, and who:

(1) has qualified for a place on the ballot or
(2) is eligible under the applicable law to be voted for by sticker, by writing in his name on the ballot, or other method, and
(3) has been duly nominated by a political party which is commonly known and regarded as such or
(4) makes a substantial showing that he is a bonafide candidate for nomination or office, as the case may be.

The rules with respect to treatment of political candidates on other types of stations (FM, non-commercial FM and TV) are identical to those discussed above. International broadcast stations are subject to Section 317 of the statute, but the Commission has not adopted specific rules applying it to them. It is assumed, however, should test cases arise, that the Commission would apply the same rules to international broadcasting that it does to domestic operations.

FCC's Interpretation of Section 315 Questioned. In the late fifties, the Commission's interpretation of Section 315 was seriously questioned and criticized by numerous groups, including Congress, the networks, some stations and large segments of the press. Much of this criticism was an outgrowth of a case decided by the Commission on June 15, 1959, popularly known as the "Lar Daly Case".

The case grew out of the following facts. Primary elections for the office of Mayor of Chicago were scheduled for February 24, 1959. Richard J. Daley, Mayor of Chicago, was a candidate in the Democratic Primary; Timothy P. Sheehan was a candidate in the Republican Primary; and Lar Daly was a candidate in both. Prior to election time Lar Daly filed a complaint with the Commission alleging that certain Chicago television stations had, in the course of their newscasts, shown film clips of his opponents in connection with certain events and occasions; that he had requested equal broadcasting time over these stations but that his requests had been refused.

The film clips in question, each averaging less than a minute, involved interviews with one of the candidates as to why he chose to run for the office; moving pictures of the Democratic and Republican candidates filing petitions for the race; of Mayor Richard J. Daley in connection with the selection of the speaker for the Illinois House of Representatives and another involving the selection of the site for the Democratic National Convention; and the telecasts of the two candidates making speeches of acceptance. Also, there were two short telecasts of the Mayor, one issuing an official proclamation in connection with a drive for the March of Dimes, and the other greeting President Frondizi of Argentina, on his arrival at the Chicago Midway Airport.

After careful consideration, the Commission on February 19, 1959 advised the stations involved that under Section 315 of the Communications Act, Lar Daly was entitled to equal broadcasting opportunities.

The Columbia Broadcasting System contended that the film clips were shown as part of regularly scheduled news broadcasts and were handled by the station in routine fashion; that they were not designed to advance the cause of any candidate nor were they initiated directly or indirectly by a candidate; that they were under the exclusive control of the station and each film clip was included in the particular news program in the bona fide exercise by the station of its news judgment.[33]

CBS further alleged that where a station simply broadcasts the face or voice of a candidate as part of a regular news program, selects the event to be covered and controls every aspect of the broadcast, that it is not permitting the candidate "to use" its facilities in the sense Congress intended in

Section 315. On the contrary, CBS said, in such situations the candidate is being used by the station. It was further argued that to impose a limitation on the exercise by a station of its bona fide news judgment would be a violation of free speech.[34] Numerous other arguments were advanced in support of its position.

The National Broadcasting Company and Westinghouse filed documents making many of the same points advanced by CBS.[35]

The Attorney General also opposed the Commission's interpretation and, as summarized by the Commission, his main contentions ran as follows: "that he does not support the holding that every time a candidate is shown on a regular news program, at the station's sole initiative, such showing constitutes a "use" by him since such holding might bar all direct news coverage of important campaign developments; that fair yet comprehensive news coverage can be assured not by applying Section 315 but by applying the "public interest" standard which requires fair presentation of public issues; that Section 315 does not state that any showing of a candidate on a radio or TV program entitles his opponents to "equal opportunities" to use the station's facilities; that instead it provides that "if any licensee shall permit any person . . . to use a broadcasting station it shall afford 'equal opportunities' to other candidates 'in the use of such broadcasting station'; and that this language is directed to 'use' by candidates of particular station facilities as part of their political campaign activities—not the station's reporting, as part of its news coverage, significant news events or campaign developments."[36]

In a 41 page decision adopted June 15, 1959, the Commission traced in detail the legislative history of Section 315 and dealt at great length with the arguments advanced by the petitioners.[37] Referring to the importance of the role of television in political campaigning, the Commission said:

> . . . It is generally recognized that television can be a very valuable asset to a candidate and that the potential audience which a candidate may now reach is, because of television, far in excess of what it has been in the past. We believe that television has become an integral part of political campaigns and that with newspapers it is the most universal source of information for voters about the candidates. The candidate has several roles in which he may appear on television. The most obvious appearance is as a candidate campaigning for office. Of no less importance is the candidate's appearance as a public servant, as an incumbent office holder, or as a private citizen in a non-political role. It is, of course, in these latter roles that questions are raised about the applicability of Section 315 of the Act. While not always indispensable to political success, for some purposes television may enjoy a unique superiority in selling a candidate to the public in that it may create an impression of immediacy and intimate presence, it shows the candidate in action, and it affords a potential for reaching wide audiences.[38]

In the light of these facts, the Commission reaffirmed its position that *any* appearance by a political candidate on a newscast not initiated by him constitutes a "use" of the station's facilities by the candidate within the meaning of Section 315 of the Communications Act. This interpretation, the Commission said, is compelled by the legislative history of the section and by the possible benefits and advantages which accrue in favor of a candidate who is given exposure on television.

The Commission further held that the word "use" in Section 315 is synonymous with "appearance" and the word "appearance" is essentially the same as "exposure". And the Commission refused to view the problem of equalizing advantages through exposure of candidates on television and radio newscasts as one to be resolved through application of the over-all "public interest" standard of fairness in presenting balanced programming.

The Commission did not agree with the petitioners that its interpretation involved any violation of freedom of speech or of the press. While news presentation is of great importance and vital to the public interest, a station does not have the same freedom of choice in presenting the news that a newspaper enjoys. This is because the station uses part of the radio spectrum which is public domain and its use is properly subject to Congressional control and limitations.

The following language appearing in paragraph 55 of the Commission's opinion is particularly noteworthy:

. . . we are of the opinion that there is no legal basis for exempting appearances by candidates on newscasts from Section 315, irrespective of whether the appearance was initiated by the candidate or not. We are further of the opinion that when a station uses film clips showing a candidate during the course of a newscast, that appearance of a candidate can reasonably be said to be a use, within the meaning and intent of Section 315. In short, the station has permitted a benefit or advantage to accrue to the candidate in the use of its facilities, thus placing itself under the statutory obligation to extend equal opportunities to opposing candidates in the use of its broadcasting station. In our opinion, only through this interpretation of Section 315 can Congress' unequivocal mandate that all candidates for the same office shall be treated equally be effectively carried out, taking into account the possible benefits or advantages which accrue in favor of a candidate thus given exposure on television. It may, of course, seem that such a holding is harsh or unduly rigid and that within the area of political broadcasts, it has a tendency to restrict radio and television licensees in their treatment of campaign affairs. If this be so, the short answer is that such a result follows not from any lack of sympathy on our part for the problems faced by licensees in complying with Section 315, which we are not at liberty to ignore. As the Court of Appeals observed in *Felix v. Westinghouse*, 186 F. 2d 1 (6 RR 2086), 'We must accordingly take the statute as the Congress intended it to be and leave it to that body to resolve the questions of public policy involved in the one construction or the other.'[39]

Congress, under great pressure from the broadcast industry and with the support of a substantial portion of the press, took action to resolve the questions. On September 14, 1959, Section 315 of the Communications Act was amended, specifically precluding its applicability to political candidates involved in "bona fide" newscasts.

As amended, the section now reads:

Sec. 315—(a) If any licensee shall permit any person who is a legally qualified candidate for any public office to use a broadcasting station, he shall afford equal opportunities to all other such candidates for that office in the use of such broadcasting station: provided, that such licensee shall have no power of censorship over the material broadcast under the provisions of this section. No obligation is hereby imposed upon any licensee to allow the use of its station by any such candidate. Appearance by a legally qualified candidate on any

(1) bona fide newscast

(2) bona fide news interview

(3) bona fide news documentary (if the appearance of the candidate is incidental to the presentation of the subject or subjects covered by the news documentary), or

(4) on-the-spot coverage of bona fide news events (including but not limited to political conventions and activities incidental thereto),

shall not be deemed to be use of a broadcasting station within the meaning of this subsection. Nothing in the foregoing sentence shall be construed as relieving broadcasters, in connection with the presentation of newscasts, news interviews, news documentaries, and on-the-spot coverage of news events, from the obligation imposed upon them under this Act to operate in the public interest and to afford reasonable opportunity for the discussion of conflicting views on issues of public importance.

(b) The charges made for the use of any broadcasting station for any of the purposes set forth in this section shall not exceed the charges made for comparable use of such station for other purposes.

(c) The Commission shall prescribe appropriate rules and regulations to carry out the provisions of this section.[40]

Section 2 of this amendatory act provides further that Congress will reexamine from time to time these new provisions to "ascertain whether they are effective and practicable and directs the FCC to make an annual report to the Congress setting forth (1) the information and data used by it in determining questions arising from or connected with such amendment, and (2) such recommendations as it deems necessary in the public interest."[41]

By legislation approved August 24, 1960, Congress suspended for the period of the 1960 presidential and vice-presidential campaigns the "equal opportunities" requirements of Section 315 with respect to nominees for the offices of President and Vice-President of the United States. The full text of this law appears in Appendix I.

Section 315 Primer. On April 27, 1966 the Commission adopted a so-called Section 315 Primer, "The Use of Facilities by Candidates for Public Office," which answers more than one hundred questions, as based upon the Commission's interpretations relating to applicability of Section 315 of the Act. It is a comprehensive and informative document and a valuable source of material for broadcasters and students of broadcasting. This can be found in 31 Fed. Reg. 6660, 7 RR 2d 1901-1930.

Lotteries.   Originally, Section 316 of the Communications Act prohibited the broadcasting of lottery programs or information regarding them.[42] As of September 1, 1948, this section was repealed by Congress and the substance of it incorporated in the U.S. Criminal Code. It now reads:

Broadcasting Lottery Information. Whoever broadcasts by means of any radio station for which a license is required by any law of the United States, or whoever, operating any such station, knowingly permits the broadcasting of any advertisement of or information concerning any lottery, gift enterprise, or similar scheme, offering prizes dependent in whole or in part upon lot or chance, or any list of the prizes drawn or awarded by means of any such lottery, gift enterprise, or scheme, whether said list contains any part or all of such prizes, shall be fined not more than $1,000 or imprisoned not more than one year or both.

Each day's broadcasting shall constitute a separate offense.[43]

In 1949, the Commission established rules defining and prohibiting the broadcast of lottery programs which it considered to come within the provisions of this section.[44] The rules, as originally contemplated, were uniformally applicable to all broadcasting stations, provided that an application for construction permit, license, or any other authorization for the operation of a station would not be granted where the applicant proposed to follow or continue to follow a policy or practice of broadcasting programs forbidden by the United States Criminal Code.

Programs outlawed by the Commission included those in connection with which a prize consisting of money or thing of value was awarded to any person whose selection depended in whole or in part upon lot or chance, if as a condition of winning or competing for such prize:

(1) Such winner or winners were required to furnish any money or thing of value or have in their possession any product sold, manufactured, furnished or distributed by a sponsor of a program broadcast on the station in question; or

(2) Had to answer correctly a question, the answer to which was given on a program broadcast over the station; or

(3) Had to answer the phone or write a letter in a prescribed manner or respond with a certain phrase if it had been broadcast over the station.

"Give-away" programs, so called, such as "Stop the Music", "What's My Name", and other similar features on the networks, which had attracted large national audiences, definitely fell within the ban of these rules. Two of the national networks challenged the validity of the rules in the Federal courts. They contended that the programs in question did not constitute lotteries as defined by Section 1304 of the Criminal Code, that mere participation of the home audience by simply listening to the programs did not constitute legal consideration, one of the essential elements of a lottery.

The case went to the U.S. Supreme Court on appeal. The high court, affirming the judgment of the U.S. District Court in the Southern District in New York, held that the Commission had the power to make rules to enforce Section 1304 which prohibits lotteries.[45] "Indeed," said Chief Justice Warren, speaking for the Court, "the Commission would be remiss in its duties if it failed, in the exercise of its licensing authority, to aid in implementing the statute, either by general rule or by individual decisions." But said he, "it would be stretching the statute to the breaking point to give it an interpretation that would make the give-away programs in question a crime."[46]

The Chief Justice concluded the decision as follows:

It is apparent that these so-called 'give-away' programs have long been a matter of concern to the Federal Communications Commission; that it believes these programs to be the old lottery evil under a new guise, and that they should be struck down as illegal devices appealing to cupidity and the gambling spirit. It unsuccessfully sought to have the Department of Justice take criminal action against them. Likewise, without success, it urged Congress to amend the law to specifically prohibit them. The Commission now seeks to accomplish the same result through agency regulations. In doing so, the Commission has over-stepped the boundaries of interpretation and hence has exceeded its rule making power. Regardless of the doubts held by the Commission and others as to the social value of the programs here under consideration, such administrative expansion of Section 1304 does not provide the remedy.[47]

This decision struck down those particular rules designed to ban "give-away" shows but left the Commission free to formulate rules prohibiting the broadcast of programs or information about them clearly involving all three essential elements of a lottery—prize, chance and substantial consideration. Accordingly, Section 73.122 of the Commission's Rules now in effect repeats the language of the Criminal Code and states in paragraph (b) that the determination whether a program falls within the statutory ban depends on the facts in each case but that in any event the Commission will consider a program in violation of the statute if there is connected with it a prize consisting of money or thing of value, given to a person chosen in whole or part upon lot or chance, and if the winner is required to furnish any money or thing of value or is required to possess any product sold, manufactured, furnished or distributed by a sponsor of a program broadcast on the station.[48]

Recent Lottery Cases. In 414 F2d 990, 16 RR2d 2179 (*cert.den.*, 38 *USL Week* 3285) in 1969, the Second Circuit U.S. Court of Appeals confirmed the FCC's opinion that Section 315 of the Act forbids state laws which sponsor lotteries, but remanded the Court to the Commission to provide more specific guidelines to determine more clearly the applicability of the lottery provisions to various broadcast situations. Accordingly, in a supplementary declaratory ruling, the Commission described various types of programs which are and are not permissible under the federal lottery law as interpreted by the Court's opinion. (See FCC 7-210, 43524; 18 RR2d 1915, for the Commission's report on these rulings; also see FCC *Public*

Notice, June 3, 1969, which warns against licensees broadcasting merchandising schemes which involve and promote lotteries. FCC 69-611, 31229; 16 RR2d 1559).

Obscene and Indecent Language. Section 29 of the Radio Act of 1927 provided that "no person within the jurisdiction of the United States shall utter any obscene, indecent, or profane language by means of radio communication."[49] This same prohibition was included in Section 326 of the Communications Act of 1934.[50] In 1948, the language was deleted from Section 326, and with criminal sanctions added was transferred to the United States Criminal Code and reads as follows:

Section 1464. Broadcasting obscene language. Whoever utters any obscene, indecent, or profane language by means of radio communication shall be fined no more than $10,000 or imprisoned no more than two years or both.[51]

The FCC has never formulated rules to implement this section of the Code. There was one early case in which a Federal court attempted to give specific meaning to the statute as it was originally adopted and made a part of the Radio Act of 1927. In *Duncan v. United States,* 48 F.(2d) 128 (1931), the Court said that the test of whether language used in broadcasting is obscene or indecent is whether it would arouse lewd or lascivious thoughts in the minds of listeners. Such language as "grafting thief", "doggoned thieving", "lying . . . crook", "doggone his lousy picture", etc., was not held to constitute obscenity or indecency within the meaning of Section 29 of the 1927 Act since, the court said, these expressions had no tendency to excite libidinous thought on the part of the hearers. The Court held, however, that reference to an individual as "damned" and irreverent use of the expression "By God" constituted profanity and was a violation of the law.[52]

Many programs presented over radio and television stations since 1934 have been the subject of complaints filed with the FCC by listeners, alleging that these programs were indecent, immoral, or profane. Traditionally, the FCC has associated these complaints with the official files of the stations and has reviewed them when the stations have come up for renewal of their licenses. Since there is little court opinion relating specifically to Section 1464 of the Criminal Code which prohibits obscene, indecent and profane utterance, and since the mores of communities and standards of decency differ so widely, there has been an understandable reluctance on the part of the Commission to take positive action in this area of regulation. However, there have been a few instances where it has done so.

For example, in WREC Broadcasting Service (10 RR 1323, May 26, 1955), a comparative proceeding in which there were competing applications for a construction permit to build a TV station in Memphis, Tennessee, the Commission scored a point against one of the applicants because he had carried "vulgar and suggestive" songs on his radio station (WMPS). The Commission not only spoke out against what it considered to be vulgarity but was highly critical of the applicant's "defense" of the song content:

We have found that the texts of the songs in question are vulgar and subject to double meaning. WMPS' exceptions do not persuade us to the contrary, since we have examined the texts of the songs. However, a perhaps more important point is raised by the exceptions. WMPS springs to the defense of the song content. It urges upon us that the license we confer is an open-end one which bars our examination of programming which panders to any taste, however low; and which bars any interference with management of the involved station in this regard. To state this proposition with respect to the responsibility of this Commission betrays misconception of its regulatory and licensing powers, functions and duties. Also of importance here is the failure of WMPS to recognize the dereliction involved in the broadcast of the songs and its attempt to justify their presentation on the ground of catering to "minority groups." This attitude reflects adversely upon the judgment and the sense of responsibility of the applicant WMPS, which in this proceeding seeks a permit to serve the public without, in the matter before us, evidencing a proper appreciation of the responsibility of service in the public interest which the grant of such a permit must entail (10 RR 1358).

In a 1962 case, the FCC designated for a consolidated hearing the renewal application of Station WDKD in Kingstree, South Carolina and its application for a license to cover a construction permit to change the station's antenna system. (23 RR 483, July 25, 1962). The case came to the Commission for final decision after having been heard before an Examiner who proposed that the applications be denied. One of the principal findings of the Examiner was that the station had carried "vulgar, suggestive" programs with indecent connotations.* The applicant filed exceptions to this and other findings of the Examiner. The Commission heard oral argument on the exceptions and, while not holding that the programs reached the level of obscenity under the Criminal Code (18 U. S. C. 1464), it did agree with the Examiner that the license should not be renewed because, among other things, some of the broadcast programs were "coarse, vulgar, suggestive and of indecent meaning," and "by any standards, flagrantly and patently offensive in the context of the broadcast field, and thus contrary to the public interest."

On appeal, the D. C. Court of Appeals affirmed the Commission's decision on the grounds that the licensee had misrepresented facts to the Commission, and held that this, standing alone, was sufficient justification for the Commission's decision and refused to consider the obscenity issue and passed no judgment on it.[53] Judge Wilbur Miller of the Court concurred in the result, and indicated that perhaps the reason the majority refrained from discussing the issue of obscenity was "the desire to avoid approving any Commission action which might be called censorship." However, said he, "I do not think that denying renewal of a license because of the station's broadcast of obscene, indecent or profane language—a serious criminal offense—can properly be called program censorship. But if it can be so

*Author's note: see Examiner's opinion, 23 RR 486e, for full discussion of this "smut" to which the Examiner, and subsequently the Commission, made reference.

denominated, then I think censorship to that extent is not only permissable but required in the public interest. Freedom of speech does not legalize using the public airways to peddle filth."[54] A petition for writ of certiorari to the Supreme Court was denied on October 12, 1964.[55] (Also see *In Re Pacifica Foundation*, 36 FCC 147, 1 RR2d 747 (1964), which involved program matter considered by some listeners to be indecent. The Commission, however, under the circumstances of the case, refused to disapprove a renewal of license.)

What the legal limits on obscenity in broadcasting are is not too clear. However, there can be no doubt that a program or programs containing elements of vulgarity knowingly presented by a network or station and which would be shocking to the moral standards of a substantial number of listeners would give the Commission clear legal grounds on which to question the renewal of a broadcast license or licenses. Recently, certain members of the Commission have expressed concern over a station broadcasting "four letter words" and other crude references to the "genitals." While a majority vote approved a grant of additional facilities for this station, two commissioners wrote a strong dissenting opinion, and some talk on Capitol Hill even proposed a Congressional inquiry.[56]

On April 1, 1970, the FCC imposed a one hundred dollar fine on an educational, noncommercial station, WUHY-FM, in Philadelphia for language broadcast over the station in an interview with a "rock and roll" celebrity, Jerry Garcia. During the interview, his comments were frequently interspersed with "four letter" words (see precise use of the language, 18 RR 2d 861-862). The commission stated that "we have a duty to act to prevent the widespread use on broadcast outlets of such expressions in the above circumstances. For, the speech involved has no redeeming social value, and is patently offensive by contemporary community standards, with very serious consequences to the 'public interest in the larger and more effective use of radio' (Section 303 (g). . ."

The commission further stated that "it is crucial to bear in mind the difference between radio and other media. Unlike a book . . . broadcasting is disseminated generally to the public (Section 3(o) of the Communications Act, 47 USC, Section 153(o)) under circumstances where reception requires no activity of this nature. Thus, it comes directly into the home and frequently without any advance warning of its content . . ."

Commissioner Kenneth Cox, concurred in part but dissented in part saying that the problem did not pose a problem so serious "as to justify the imposition of a sanction for the mere utterance of words." Commissioner Nicholas Johnson vehemently dissented, stating in a long opinion that it is the FCC "to adopt precise and clear guidelines for the broadcasting industry to follow in this murky area, if we are to wade into it at all—the wisdom of which I seriously question. I believe no governmental agency can punish for the content of speech by invoking statutory prohibitions which are so broad, sweeping, vague, and potentially all-encompassing that no man can foretell when, who, or with what force the commission will strike." (See majority, concurring and dissenting opinions in 18 RR 2d 860-872h. The rationale for each opinion in this case is fully set forth, and represents the latest pronouncements of the FCC commissioners.)

As mentioned in Chapter 3, the Commission has authority to suspend the license of any operator who has transmitted "signals or communications containing profane or obscene words, language or meaning." Also, the language of Section 1464 is applicable to operators or other persons having access to broadcasting facilities as well as the licensees of stations, and any violation of the section would make them subject to criminal prosecution.

False Distress Signals and Rebroadcasting. Section 325 of the Communications Act prohibits the wilful utterance or transmission of any false or fraudulent signal of distress.[57] The same section provides that no broadcasting station may rebroadcast the program or any part thereof of another broadcasting station without the express authority of the originating station.[58]

This latter provision has been implemented by Commission rules. The Commission has defined the term "rebroadcast" as the "reception by radio of the program of a radio station, and the simultaneous or subsequent retransmission of such program by a broadcast station."[59]

The licensee of a station may rebroadcast a program of another station, providing it notifies the Commission, and certifies that authority for the rebroadcast has been received from the originating station.[60]

Network Regulations. As pointed out in Chapter 3, Section 303(i) of the Act gives the Commission power to make special regulations applicable to stations engaged in network broadcasting. The FCC has implemented this and other sections of the Act by the adoption of the network regulations. Prior to their adoption, the network contracts of NBC and CBS bound the affiliated stations for a period of five years. The networks themselves, however, were bound for only a period of one year.[61] The affiliated stations were prohibited from making their facilities available to any other national network during the five year period.[62]

The standard affiliation contracts originally gave the networks an option on all the time of the station for network commercial programs, subject to certain limitations. CBS contracts provided that a station might require not less than 28 days notice before the network could preempt time for programs and a station was not required to broadcast network commercial programs for more than 50 "converted hours" in any one week. A "converted hour" was understood to be the equilvalent of one hour in the evening, two during the day, and two-thirds of an hour during Sunday afternoon. On the average, this meant that the network could preempt as many as 79 clock hours of the station's time during the week.[63]

Stations were given the right to reject a network program if it or the product advertised was objectionable, or if the station wanted to substitute a local sustaining program of public interest. NBC, however, required that the station prove that the substitution would be more in the public interest than the network program.[64]

While an affiliated station might substitute a local sustaining program for a network commercial under such conditions, it did not have the same freedom to substitute a local commercial program. If it did, it was compelled to pay to the network any increased revenue received from the substitution.[65]

Prior to the adoption of the chain broadcasting rules, there was no limitation on the number of networks which one company might own. NBC owned and operated the Blue and the Red networks with outlets in most of the major markets in the country. Nor were there restrictions on the number of stations which one network might own in the same community. NBC owned two stations in each of the following communities: New York, Chicago, Washington, and San Francisco as well as single stations in other large cities.[66]

The affiliation contracts of NBC and CBS gave the chains full control over network station rates, and there were provisions in the NBC contracts designed to prevent outlets from securing revenues from the sale of time to advertisers for national spot business at rates lower than those set forth in the network rate card.[67]

On March 18, 1938, the FCC authorized an investigation "to determine what special regulations applicable to radio stations engaged in chain or other broadcasting are required in the public interest, convenience, or necessity."[68] A committee of three FCC commissioners was appointed to make the investigation.[69]

After long and careful study, including public hearings, the Committee issued a report on June 12, 1940.[70] This report contained a draft of proposed regulations which served as a basis for oral argument before the full Commission.

After full discussion was heard from interested parties, the Commission adopted specific network regulations on May 2, 1941.[71] These were restrictive in nature and their legality and propriety were vigorously challenged by the networks in the Federal courts. One of the principal contentions made against the regulations was that the Commission was "without jurisdiction to promulgate regulations which undertake to control indirectly the business arrangements of broadcasting licensees."[72] On May 10, 1943 the U.S. Supreme Court handed down its historic decision affirming the validity of the network rules.

Some amendments were made to these rules following their adoption in 1941.[73] Since April 12, 1944, with two exceptions, no further substantive changes have been made. The regulations in effect today are as follows:

Exclusive Affiliation of Station. The Commission will not grant any application for a renewal of license or for increased or new broadcast facilities, if that station has any kind of "contract, arrangement, or understanding, express or implied, with a network organization under which the station is prevented or hindered from, or penalized for, broadcasting the programs of any other network organization."[74]

Territorial Exclusivity. The same rule applies if a station enters into any such arrangement which "prevents or hinders another station serving substantially the same area or a different area from broadcasting the network's programs not taken by the affiliate station." The Commission specifically says, however, that this does not preclude an arrangement by which the affiliate is granted the first call in its primary service area upon the programs of the network.[75]

Term of Affiliation. Network contracts are limited to two years but renewals may be made within six months prior to the commencement of a new contract period. Any kind of arrangement, express or implied, which provides for an affiliation with the network for longer than two years is strictly prohibited. These network affiliation contracts are required to be in writing and filed with the Commission, and are available for public inspection. (See Commission *Report and Order,* adopted March 21, 1969, Docket 14710, FCC 69-289; Section 1.613(a)).[76]

Option Time. This rule originally provided that no license would be granted to a station which "options for network programs any broadcast time subject to call on less than 56 days' notice, or more time than a total of three hours within each of four segments of the broadcast day." These segments of the broadcast day were described by the Commission as follows: 8: 00 a.m. to 1:00 p.m.; 1:00 p.m. to 6:00 p.m.; 6:00 p.m. to 11:00 p.m.; and 11:00 p.m. to 8:00 a.m. This meant that the affiliate might agree to give the network an option on as much as three hours of each segment of the broadcast day providing the network gave the station at least 56 days notice. Such an arrangement might not be exclusive as against other network organizations and might not prevent or hinder the station from optioning or selling *any* of its broadcast time to other network organizations. Any type of agreement preventing or hindering a station from the free scheduling of its programs or requiring that it get clearance from the network was prohibited.[77]

Subsequently, the Commission amended the option regulation for TV stations (but not AM and FM stations), so that, as of Jan. 1, 1961, option hours within each segment of the broadcast day be reduced from 3 to 2½ hours [see 25 Fed. Reg. 9051 (1960)]. More flexibility was provided for the period of advance notice required before exercise of the option. Pertinent sections of this 1961 rule, applicable to TV stations only, were:

Sec. 3.658(d). Option time. (1) (i) In no event may a station subject its time to call, under an option, for a network program to commence earlier than four weeks after notice of exercise of the option.

(ii) If a station has a written contract with one or more advertisers pursuant to which a non-network program series is being broadcast, the time so contracted shall not be callable under an option held by a network until the earlier of (*a*) the end of a 13-week waiting period or (*b*) the end of the program series so contracted.

(iii) If a station has entered into a written contract with an advertiser or advertisers for the broadcast of a non-network program scheduled to commence no later than four weeks after the network exercises its option for the same time segment, the network may not under its option require the station to substitute a network program until the earlier of (*a*) 13 weeks from the commencement of such non-network program or (*b*) the end of the program series so contracted.

(iv) If the station has contracted with more than one advertiser for the program series, the end of the program series for the purposes of this section shall be the latest of the several contract termination dates.

(2) No license shall be granted to a television broadcast station which options for network programs more than a total of 2½ hours within each of four segments of the broadcast day, as herein described. In determining the number of hours of option time, any network program which begins during the hours agreed upon by the network and station as option time and extends into non-option time, or which begins during non-option time, and extends into the hours agreed upon as option time, shall be considered as falling entirely outside option time. The broadcast day is divided into four segments, as follows: 8 a.m. to 1 p.m.; 1 p.m. to 6 p.m.; 6 p.m. to 11 p.m.; 11 p.m. to 8 a.m. (These segments are to be determined for each station in terms of local time at the location of the station but may remain constant throughout the year regardless of shifts from standard to daylight saving time or vice versa.) Time options may not be exclusive as against other network organizations and may not prevent or hinder the station from optioning or selling any or all of the time covered by the option, or other time, to other network organizations.

(3) As used in this section, an option is any contract, arrangement or understanding, express or implied, between a station and a network organization which prevents or hinders the station from scheduling programs before the network agrees to utilize the time during which such programs are scheduled, or which requires the station to clear time already scheduled when the network organization seeks to utilize the time. All time options permitted under this section must be specified clock hours, expressed in terms of any time system set forth in the contract agreed upon by the station and network organization. Shifts from daylight saving to standard time or vice versa may or may not shift the specified hours correspondingly as agreed by the station and network organization.

Following the adoption of the 1961 regulation pertaining to option time, the licensee of KTTV in Los Angeles appealed from the decision on the Commission to the United States Court of Appeals for the District of Columbia. KTTV claimed among other things, that permitting networks to option any amount of broadcasting time was a violation of the antitrust laws. The Department of Justice (which had previously expressed the view that the entire option time practice violated the Sherman antitrust law) in effect joined KTTV in the appeal.

Before the Court handed down a decision, the Commission requested that it be permitted to reconsider its action. Accordingly, on June 23, 1961, the Court remanded the case to the Commission for further proceedings. Public hearings were held and, on September 4, 1963, the Commission issued a report and order prohibiting television stations from entering into agreements that would permit the networks to option any of their broadcast time. In support of its decision, the Commission held that the practice had "anticompetitive effects," was an artificial restraint on access to particular broadcast time, involving an abdication of the licensee's duty to program his station as he deems most in the public interest. The Commission further stated the opinion that the removal of option sources, and that generally television programming would be improved since programs would have to stand or fall on their own merits. (For a full statement regarding proceedings leading up to the final decision in this case and for the full text of the Commission's report and order see FCC Docket No. 12859, 25 RR 1651-1686g).

The regulation prohibiting the TV option time practice, as adopted in 1963, is still in effect and reads as follows:

Sec. 73.658(d). Station commitment of broadcast time. No license shall be granted to a television broadcast station having any contract, arrangement, or understanding, express or implied, with any network organization, or which has the same restraining effect as time optioning. As used in this section, time optioning is any contract, arrangement, or understanding, express or implied, between a station and a network organization which prevents or hinders the station from scheduling programs before the network agrees to utilize the time during which such programs are scheduled, or which requires the station to clear time already scheduled when the network organization seeks to utilize the time.[78]

It should be pointed out that this prohibition of option time practice relates only to television and not to AM or FM stations. The rules, as originally adopted, which permit networks to option as many as three hours within each segment of the broadcast day of any AM or FM affiliate are still in effect. (See Sections 73.134 and 73.234 of the Rules, 1 RR 53:751, 1011).

Network Program Procurement Rules. On May 4, 1970, the Commission added paragraph (d) of Section 73.658 to prohibit engaging networks in domestic syndication of all television programs and restricting networks' foreign distribution of programs wholly produced by them. Also, it prohibits the recapture of network exhibition rights "if not timely exercised" (19 RR 2d 1825).

The Commission further provided that divestiture of existing network-owned syndication rights and interests is "not commanded" but the Commission stated that it would observe their effect on competition and take future action.

The Commission further added paragraph (k) to section 73.658, prohibiting television stations in the top fifty markets (where there are three operating commercial stations) from broadcasting more than three hours of network programs between 7:00 and 11:00 p.m. each day, excluding special news programs dealing with "fast-breaking news events, on-the-spot news, or paid political broadcasts by candidates." The rules are not applicable to educational, non-commercial or public broadcasting stations. (See Commissions' *Report and Order,* adopted May 4, 1970, FCC 70-466, 46636; 18 RR 2d 1825.)

Following the filing of various petitions of interested parties relating to the changes of the network rules, the Commission, on August 7, 1970, amended the rules to define the term "network" to apply only to the major networks (ABC, CBS, NBC), and to provide that the portion of the time from which network programming is excluded may not, after October 1, 1972, be filled with off-network programs, or feature films which, within two years prior to the date of the broadcast, have been previously broadcast by a station in the market. (See FCC *Memorandum Opinion and Order,* adopted August 7, 1970, FCC 70-872, 51928; 35 Fed. Reg. 13208; 19 RR 2d 1869).

Ashbook P. Bryant, in charge of the FCC Office of Network Study which has conducted research for more than ten years regarding television program procurement, in a recent article, explained the additions to Section 73.658 and has stated his reasons as to the action taken by the Commission and the intended results of the action. In part he has written:

. . . on May 4, 1970, the Commission adopted rules along these lines to provide a 'healthy impetus' to the development of the feasible maximum of diverse sources for network programming. These rules were designed to alleviate the concentration of control described in this paper and to encourage production of the widest practicable variety of programs available for television broadcasting and provide network affiliates with something more than nominal choice in the exercise of their responsibility as 'trustees' to serve the diverse needs and interests of their communities in providing television program service.

The rules will restrict the broadcast by commercial stations in the top fifty markets in which there are three or more operating commercial television stations to no more than three hours of network programs between the hours of 7:00 and 11:00 p.m. (6:00 and 10:00 Central time), thereby opening up evening time to competition among present and potential alternate program sources. Special programs concerning fast-breaking news events, on-the-spot coverage of news events, and political broadcasts were excepted from the definition of 'network program.' Also, the rules prohibit networks from engaging in the business of distributing nonnetwork programs in domestic syndication or otherwise. Networks may not acquire rights to the subsequent commercial use of programs and series which compose network programs. No longer will networks be permitted to 'compete' in the domestic syndication and nonnetwork program market; no longer will the networks be permitted to acquire, as part of the bargaining process for network exhibition, distribution and profit-sharing rights in domestic syndication and foreign distribution. They may engage in foreign distribution of programs of which they are the sole producers, but must not distribute such programs nor share in the profits from such distribution. Networks will be permitted to sell the distribution rights to their own program products to other domestic distributors.

The Commission said that an 'unhealthy situation' presently exists in television service. It emphasized that 'only three organizations (the three national television networks) control access to the crucial prime time evening schedule.' The Commission recognized that access to the top fifty markets, or a substantial share of them, is essential to the economic viability of a nonnetwork producer who proposes to compete for station time with network prime-time quality programming. It decided that the public interest would be served by curbing network occupancy of high-rated evening time and thereby giving other program sources competitive opportunity to contest for market entry by seeking the custom and favor of affiliate licensees. Independent nonnetwork producers are presently at such a competitive disadvantage that prime-time, first-run syndicated programming has virtually disappeared. 'Such programming is the key to a healthy syndication industry because it is designed for a time of day when the available audience is by far the greatest.'

The Commission also found that close network supervision of so much of the nation's programming centralizes creative control. It tends to work against the diversity of approach which would result from more independent producers developing programs in both network and syndication markets.

The Commission found that network participation in syndication, either through distribution or profit sharing, involves at least a potential conflict of interest. 'Certainly,' said the Commission, there is a 'close correlation' between the acquisition by networks of syndication and other subsidiary rights and interests and the choice of a program or series for inclusion in the networks' schedule.

The Commission said that under present conditions independent producers who desire to exhibit their product initially on a network and then offer it in domestic syndication and foreign markets must first bargain with the networks, who are their principal competitors in syndication and foreign sales, for the network exposure necessary to establish the subsequent value of their programs as valuable commercial assets in domestic syndication and foreign sales. They are usually required to grant to the networks either the distribution rights or large shares in the profits from domestic syndication and foreign distribution, or both, for the program. Similarly, a producer who seeks to distribute his programs in foreign countries must compete with the networks, who, through bargaining with the same and other independent producers, control the source of supply of the programs which constitute the staples of his market and/or share in the profits from such distribution by others. Networks do not normally accept new, untried packager-licensed programs for network exhibition unless the producer/packager is willing to cede a large part of the valuable rights and interests in subsidiary rights to the program to the network.

The Commission said:

If networks are prevented from operating as syndicators or from sharing in the profits from distribution by others in the domestic syndication market, there will no longer be any inducement to choose for network exhibition only those packager-licensed programs in which they have acquired other rights. Furthermore, producers and packagers will be enabled to fully benefit from their own initiative and presumably become more competitive and independent sources of programming since in many instances a packager cannot recoup his outlay from the first network run of a series or program and must look to the commercial uses of the program subsequent to the network run for commercial success. Relieved of the need to grant a network a large portion of his potential profit the producer's ability profitably to operate in network television will be greatly enhanced. With the expanded syndication market as a feasible alternate to network exhibition his bargaining position will be improved and he can be expected to develop into a stable and continuing alternate source of programs and ultimately to compete for network time.

The Commission pointed out that its objective was not to create 'reverse option time' for any program source, but to permit independent producers to vie with each other and with the networks for the custom and favor of stations on something approaching an even basis.

The Commission was not persuaded that the so-called 50/50 rule would have the adverse consequences which its opponents predicted. On the contrary, the Commission concluded that that proposal would accomplish 'its intended purpose without undesireable side effects.' It decided for several reasons–among them the possibility of unfavorable effects on internetwork competition–to adopt the Prime Time Access rule. The Commission will continue to observe and study the results of its present action to determine whether the rules adopted are sufficient for the purpose of adequately diversifying and multiplying sources of television programming. It published its findings regarding the 50/50 rule as an appendix to its opinion. In this regard the Commission said:

Diversity of programs and development of diverse and antagonistic sources of program service are essential to the broadcast license's discharge of his duty as 'trustee' for the public in the operation of his channel. We note that the degree of network control of their evening schedules has been steadily increasing; indeed there has been a substantial increase since we issued our Notice in 1965. This tendency should be reversed and the networks should take the lead in encouraging the inclusion of the feasible maximum of independently controlled and independently provided programs in their schedules. In this way we may more nearly achieve the goal described by Judge Learned Hand in 1942, and echoed by Justice White in 1969, of a television broadcast structure which is served 'by the widest practicable variety' of choice of programs available for broadcasting; that system which will most stimulate and liberate those who create and produce television programs and those who purvey them to the public.

The Commission's action is a landmark in regulation of television networks and their effect on the public interest in program service. A principal part of the rules —that affecting syndication and other program rights—operates directly on network organizations rather than on affiliate licensees as do the Chain Broadcasting Rules. . . .*

Right to Reject Programs.   A station cannot enter into an arrangement or contract of any kind which prevents or hinders a rejection of network programs which the station reasonably believes to be unsatisfactory or unsuitable, or which, in its opinion, is contrary to the public interest, or which prevents it from substituting one of outstanding local or national importance.[79]

Network Ownership of Stations.   Networks may not own or operate

---

Law and Contemporary Problems, Summer 1969. pp. 631-634; also see Report of the Committee on Interstate and Foreign Commerce, *Television Network Program Procurement.* H.R. No. 281, 88th Congress. 1st Session, May 8, 1963; and Second Interim Report by the Office of Network Study, *Television Network Program Procurement,* Federal Communications Commission, 1965.

more than one station of each type (AM, FM, TV) where one of the stations would cover substantially the coverage area of the other, or where the existing facilities are so "few or of such unequal desirability (in terms of coverage, power, frequency, or other related matters) that competition would be substantially restrained."[80]

Dual Network Operation. It is further provided in the Rules that the Commission will not grant a license to a station affiliated with a chain organization which maintains more than one network. This rule does not apply, however, if the networks are not operated simultaneously, or if there is no substantial overlap in the territory served by the group of stations comprising each such network.[81]

Control of Networks of Station Rates. Stations are prohibited from making any arrangements of agreements under which they are prevented or hindered by the networks from fixing or altering their rates for the sale of broadcast time other than that used by the networks.

Recommended Revisions of Network Regulations. In 1957, the Commission completed a long and comprehensive study of the network regulations. A network study group of the Commission recommended revisions of the rules designed to give station licensees greater control over their programs. The new rules relating to TV option time was an outgrowth of these recommendations. Other proposals were made which may be the subject of future action by the Commission.

Deceptive Contests. The Eighty-Sixth Congress, in 1959-60 conducted extensive public hearings with regard to the many quiz programs which had been carried by the networks and their affiliated stations. Many of these programs were found to be deceptive in character. The result was the passage of new legislation by Congress prohibiting them, as provided in Section 9 of the Communications Act Amendments, 1960, approved September 13, 1960. (See Appendix I).

1. 1 RR 53:1676.
2. *Ibid.*
3. Section 73.1201(d). See 17 RR 2d 1691.
4. FCC Docket No. 11546, effective November 7, 1956, 21 Fed. Reg. 7768; 14 RR 1541, p. 1549.
5. *Ibid.*
6. Sections 73.118(a), 73.288 and 73.653; 1 RR 53:732, 1071, 1503.
7. *Ibid.*
8. *Ibid.*
9. *Ibid.*
10. *Ibid.*
11. *Ibid.*
12. 44 Stat. 1170.
13. 48 Stat. 1089.
14. See Sections 73.119, 73.289, 73.654, 73.789; 1 RR 53:733-735, 1091-1092, 1504-1508, 1677-1681.
15. 1 RR 53:1402.
16. Sections 73.119(d), 73.289(d), 73.654(d), 73.789(d); 1 RR 53:734, 1091, 1505, 1678.
17. Sections 73.119(e), 73.289(e), 73.654(e), 73.789(e); 1 RR 53:734, 1091, 1505, 1678.
18. Sections 73.119(g), 73.289(g), 73.654(h), 73.789(g); 1 RR 53:735, 1092, 1506, 1671.
19. Sections 73.119(f), 73.289(f), 73.654(g), 73.789(f); 1 RR 53:734-735, 1092, 1505-1506, 1678.
20. Sponsorship Identification of Broadcast Material, FCC Public Notice 85460, 25 Fed. Reg. 2406 (1960); 19 RR 1569-1577.
21. In the Matter of Public Notice (FCC 60-239) dated March 16, 1960, entitled "Sponsorship Identification of Broadcast Material," FCC Docket No. 13454, 25 Fed. Reg. 2926 (1960).
22. See Hearings on H. R. 5589 before the House Committee on the Merchant Marine and Fisheries, 69th Cong., 1st Sess. (1926); also, 67 *Cong. Rec.* 5488 (House, March 12, 1926).
23. 67 *Cong. Rec.* 5488 (House, March 12, 1926).
24. See NBC Comments on file with FCC, re Public Notice 85460.
25. See MBA Comments on file with FCC, re Notice of Inquiry, FCC Docket No. 13454.
26. 17 RR 553, 556a, 556d (1958).
27. Comments of Michigan Broadcasters Assoc., *op. cit.,* pp. 4-5.
28. *Ibid.,* pp. 8-9.
29. *Op. cit.,* FCC Docket No. 13454.
30. 44 Stat. 1089 and 48 Stat. 1088.
31. 66 Stat. 717.
32. Sections 73.120, 73.290, 73.657; 1 RR 53:736-737, 1093-1094, 1508-1509.
33. See CBS pleadings filed in the *Matter of Petitions of Columbia Broadcasting Company for Reconsideration and Motions for Declaratory Rulings or Orders Relating to Applicability of Section 315 of the Communications Act of 1934, as amended, to Newscasts by Broadcast Licensees;* 18 RR 701. This opinion should be consulted for a comprehensive and detailed analysis of the legislative history of Section 315 and for a critical review of the various interpretations placed upon it.
34. *Ibid.*

35. *Ibid.*

36. *Ibid.,* p. 711.

37. *Ibid.,* pp. 701-744.

38. *Ibid.,* p. 713.

39. *Ibid.,* p. 736.

40. 73 Stat. 557. For discussions in Congress leading up to adoption of this amendment see Senate Report, Paragraph 10:1102; House Report, Paragraph 10:1103; Conference Report, Paragraph 10:1104. Also see 105 *Cong. Rec.* 13171-13195, July 28, 1959; 14863-14886, August 18, 1959; 16308-16313, September 2, 1959; and 16342-16347, September 3, 1959.

41. *Ibid.*

42. 48 Stat. 1088-1089.

43. 18 U.S.C., Section 1304.

44. Adopted August 18, 1949, FCC Docket No. 9113; effective date postponed by FCC order of September 21, 1949; 14 Fed. Reg. 5998 (1949).

45. *FCC v. A.B.C., Inc.,* 347 U.S. 284, 10 RR 2030.

46. *Ibid.,* pp. 289, 294.

47. *Ibid.,* pp. 296-297.

48. Section 73.122. 1 RR 53:739; adopted May 19, 1954, 19 Fed. Reg. 3054 (1954) effective June 26, 1954.

49. 44 Stat. 1172-1173.

50. 48 Stat. 1091.

51. 18 U.S.C., Section 1464.

52. *Duncan v. United States,* 48 F.(2d) 134.

53. E. G. Robinson, Jr. t/a Palmetto Broadcasting Company (WDKD) v. Federal Communications Commission, 334 F. 2d 534.

54. *Ibid.,* p. 537.

55. 85 S. Ct. 84.

56. *Broadcasting,* November 24, 1969, pp. 64-65.

57. 48 Stat. 1091.

58. *Ibid.*

59. Sections 73.121, 73.291, 73.655; 1 RR 53:737.

60. *Ibid.*

61. *FCC Report on Chain Broadcasting,* Commission Order No. 37, FCC Docket No. 5060, May, 1941, p. 35.

62. *Ibid.*

.63. *Ibid.,* pp. 36-37.

64. *Ibid.,* pp. 38-39.

65. *Ibid.,* pp. 39-40.

66. *Ibid.,* pp. 44-45.

67. *Ibid.,* pp. 43-44.

68. *Ibid.,* p. 1.

69. *Ibid.*

70. *Ibid.,* pp. 1-2.

71. *FCC Report on Chain Broadcasting, op. cit.* Also see 6 Fed. Reg. 2282, 2292, 5257 (1941).

72. 319 U.S. 209.

73. See 1 RR 53:201-202; 6 Fed. Reg. 5257, 8 Fed. Reg. 7355.

74. Sections 73.131 for AM broadcasting, 73.231 for FM, 73.658 for television; 1 RR 53:751, 1011, 1509-1510.

75. *Ibid.,* Sections 73.132, 73.232, 73.658(b).

76. *Ibid.,* Sections 73.133, 73.233, 73.658(c).

77. *Ibid.,* Sections 73.134, 73.234.

78. 1 RR 53:1510.
79. Sections 73.135, 73.235, 73.658(e); 1 RR 53:752, 1012, 1510.
80. Sections 73.136, 73.236, 74.658(f); 1 RR 53:752, 1012, 1510.
81. Sections 73.137, 73.237, 73.658(g); 1 RR 53:753, 1012, 1511.

CHAPTER 19

Broadcasting Programs in the Public Interest

Democracy thrives more on participation at its base than upon instruction from the top. —CLIFFORD JUDKINS DURR*

As pointed out in Chapter 3, the law directs the FCC to grant licenses and renewals thereof *only* if public interest will be served. Any violations of the specific laws and regulations pertaining to programming discussed in the preceding chapter are of course contrary to the public interest, and could constitute grounds for revocation of a station license. But compliance with these statutory and regulatory requirements is not enough. The Commission has held (and the courts have agreed) that licensees have positive resonsibilities to provide a program service that serves the needs of the community.

Early FCC Concern with Program Standards. In the late thirties, the Commission gave serious consideration to the establishment of rules governing program service for broadcasting stations.[1] A Committee of the Commission made a study of the problem and recommended that minimum standards be set as guides for licensees. In connection with this recommendation, the Committee stated:

It is very difficult to prescribe 'standards of public service' uniformly for all broadcasting stations because initiative and reasonable freedom of action are essential to the American system of broadcasting. The problem is also complicated by the fact that the requirements of broadcast service differ in the various sections of the nation, and within these sections each community presents its individual dissimilarities. Also, the economic factor is different for each class operating in different communities. While it is the primary duty of each station licensee to offer programs which will fully satisfy the public needs in the particular area served, it is obvious that some general principles might apply to the industry as a whole . . . However, it is needless to state that such standards should be minimum standards and they should be utilized solely as guides and subject to variation in accordance with changed conditions and even then should not be requirements of the Commission.[2]

* Former member of the FCC.

The Commission took no action on this proposal and no specific criteria for evaluation of program service were adopted at that time.

Some Congressmen had criticized the Commission for being lax in establishing and enforcing standards for broadcast programming; had charged that it had made little effort to require stations to operate in the public interest.[3]

In addition, during the early forties, the Commission increasingly received complaints from the public regarding program service. Many people were unhappy with the large number of broadcasts involving fortune telling, false and misleading advertising, suggestive programs bordering on obscenity, etc. The Commission received many letters complaining that stations were over-commercialized; that too little broadcast time was provided for local live talent and community organizations; that discussion of local issues was neglected and, in some cases, stations were unfair and biased in the presentation of news; and that there were two few programs of an educational, cultural and religious nature.

At long last, the FCC decided to do something positive about the situation. Accordingly, it retained Dr. Charles Siepmann, formerly with the British Broadcasting Corporation, to direct a study and come up with some proposed criteria which the Commission might establish for the evaluation of radio program service.

Adoption of the "Blue Book". The result of this study was the adoption and publication by the FCC in March, 1946 of the report, *Public Service Responsibility of Broadcast Licensees,* popularly known as the Blue Book. Essentially, what this report said was that the licensee of a broadcasting station has a primary responsibility for determining program service, but that the Commission has a statutory duty of which it may not divest itself. Accordingly, the Commission proposed in the Blue Book to give consideration to four program service factors in determining whether a station had operated in the public interest: (1) the carrying of sustaining programs to provide a "balanced" program structure; (2) the carrying of local live talent programs; (3) the carrying of programs dealing with important public issues, and (4) elimination of advertising excesses.

The Commission said that the sustaining program has five distinctive and useful functions. It helps:

1. To secure for the station or network a means by which in the overall structure of its program service it can achieve a *balanced* interpretation of public needs.

2. To provide programs which by their very nature may not be sponsored with propriety, such as some programs sponsored by religious, educational, governmental, or welfare groups.

3. To serve significant minority tastes and interests, such as providing programs of classical music or those of a literary nature.

4. To serve the needs and purposes of non-profit organizations such as educational institutions.

5. To provide a field for experiment in new types of programs, free of restrictions that obtain with reference to programs in which the advertiser's interest in selling goods predominates.

The Commission prescribed no particular percentages of time for the different program categories, but did stress that the licensee had the responsibility of attempting to achieve a "balanced program schedule" in terms of the particular needs of the community served by the station.[4]

Actually, this was no radical or drastic departure from previous FCC policy. It simply pulled together and codified some basic program factors which the Commission and its predecessor, the FRC, had evolved and applied in deciding individual cases for two decades. It did give notice to the broadcast industry, however, that in the future it would scrutinize applications more closely in terms of these specific criteria. Licensees were warned that they would be required to give an account of program performance in connection with applications for renewal of license.

New Renewal Application Form. In line with the principles stated in the Blue Book, the Commission designed a new renewal application form (303) in 1946 requiring applicants to state how much broadcast time they had devoted to the following program categories: entertainment, religious, agricultural, educational, news, discussion, talks, and miscellaneous programs.

This new form elicited information regarding the number of spot announcements carried by the station, the amount of time used for network shows and recordings, and that devoted to local live programs. The division of time as between commercial and noncommercial programs also was required to be reported.

These calculations were to be based upon an analysis of the program logs of the station for a seven-day period comprising a composite week announced by the FCC and of which days the licensees were to be given no advance notice.[5]

This application form not only required the licensee to report data reflecting past program performance but also to indicate what percentages of time for the various program classes were proposed for future operation.

Program Performance Questioned by FCC. Shortly after the Blue Book was released, the FCC withheld action on a number of applications for renewal of license where station operations did not measure up to the standards set forth. The Commission questioned whether these stations had operated in the public interest and designated their applications for public hearing.

In a 1947 case, the Commission questioned one station's performance on these grounds: (1) During the license period, it had carried a large number of commercial spot announcements, averaging more than 2,000 per week; (2) had failed to broadcast any programs dealing with controversial issues in the community; (3) had provided very little time for local live talent; and (4) had broadcast comparatively few educational programs.

In the hearing, the licensee promised to provide more time for school broadcasts, including lectures, recitals, musicals, sports, and drama. Moreover, the applicant pledged that it would devote at least 30% of its total broadcast time to local live programs, and would cut down on the quantity and frequency of commercial announcements.

In view of these promises, despite a poor record of past performance, the Commission granted the renewal application.[6]

A similar result was reached by the Commission in another 1947 case. Here again a renewal application was set down for a public hearing on essentially the same issues. The evidence adduced at the hearing showed over-commercialization, heavy use of recordings with comparatively little time devoted to broadcasts containing local live talent. But the station introduced evidence to show that it had adopted changes in program policy and had made definite commitments to provide a more varied and better "balanced" service to the community. The station received an official slap on the wrist by the FCC for inferior performance, but in view of promises to do better in the future, the Commission decided to give the station a second chance and renewed the license for another three-year period.[7]

A third Blue Book case decided in 1951 should be noted. It involved an application for renewal of a station license and a competing application for the same facility. The new applicant contended that the existing licensee had failed to keep its promises to the Commission; that station operation had fallen far below FCC program standards, and that the new applicant could provide a more worthwhile service in the public interest.

After a long and highly publicized hearing, the Commission denied the competing application and granted the renewal of license. In substance, the Commission decided that while the licensee's programming had been unbalanced in the past, improvements had now been made and a "well-rounded" service was proposed for the future. The Commission, therefore, was not disposed to prefer a new applicant and dispossess an existing licensee, when the latter recognized its substandard performance and had taken steps and made proposals under oath to improve its service.[8]

New Statement of Program Policies Adopted by the FCC. The Blue Book standards were never officially repudiated by the Commission, though subsequent rule-making proceedings led to the adoption on July 27, 1960 of a new statement of program policies and requirements. (See the full text in *Report and Statement of Policy Re: Commission en banc Programming Inquiry* in Appendix IV.)

In this report, the Commission discussed what it considered to be its regulatory powers over programming and set forth anew its views as to the responsibilities of broadcast licensees. The Commission pointed out that rules would be made "at the earliest practicable date" looking in the direction of establishing general standards and requirements to guide stations in their operations. The Commission stressed the obligation of the licensee "to make a positive, diligent and continuing effort to determine the tastes, needs and desires of the public in his community and to provide programming to meet those needs and interests."

Anticipating the adoption and publication of these guidelines, about two months earlier the Commission had announced the establishment of a new Complaints and Compliance Division in its Broadcast Bureau which would be responsible for their enforcement. Former Chairman Ford explained the reasons in an FCC Public Notice (Mimeograph No. B-88758, May 20, 1960) as follows:

We took this step because of our conviction that vigorous, timely, and systematic action in this area is essential to ensure that broadcasters fully discharge their obligation to operate in the public interest. I wish to emphasize that our decision in no way undercuts or limits the basic responsibility of licensees to take self-corrective measures, where these are required. But we believe that these self-corrective measures will be more effective—and enduring—if the Commission has adequate resources and machinery to discharge its own obligations under the Communications Act.

Our program contemplates stepping up very sharply our thoroughness and effectiveness in handling complaints. Currently, we receive 120-150 complaints weekly on broadcast matters, in addition to the matters recently brought to light, among others, by the Federal Trade Commission, by Congressional committees, and by the replies from stations and networks to our recent questionaire on Section 317 practices. To arrive at a sound judgment as to the merits of some of the practices complained of we must be able to send trained staff directly into the field to dig up the essential facts—objectively and thoroughly. While there is a place for and some utility in obtaining formal, written statements of explanation from licensees involved in individual cases, it is not an adequate substitute in many instances for direct, field investigation.

I don't want to convey the impression that the Commission has never sent investigators in the field before. However, where the complaints on their face are substantial, whether they involve an individual station or go to a general industry practice, we must have the wherewithal to look into all such substantial complaints by going to the source and drawing together all of the relevant facts—pro and con—needed to dispose of complaints on their merits. This is a prime obligation we owe to the public.

The second prong of our program involves checking into selected stations on a regular, continuing basis. We have some 1,700 stations coming up annually for renewal, and while we have some information on each of these stations when we make our renewal decisions, we do not have available an analysis in depth of the operations of each such station. We rely primarily on information, statistical and otherwise, submitted by the stations and on the presence or absence of any complaints filed against the stations or other information coming to the Commission's attention which bears on the operations of licensees.

Now, we propose to undertake an audit in detail of a limited number of selected stations so that we can have a much more penetrating and more rounded view of how effectively stations discharge their stewardship in the public interest. We intend, among other items, to check on program logs, Section 317 compliance, political broadcast records, and other pertinent station controls, records, and procedures related to the Commission's non-technical rules and regulations and other statutory and treaty requirements; to examine the extent, nature, and disposition of complaints coming directly to the stations; to ascertain whether representations made in connection with license applications are reasonably complied with, as, for example, participation by broadcast licensees in actual station management and operation.

For these station audits, we will use, as one of our tools, sample monitoring of station programs which will be compared with the logs of the stations, and the representations of the stations to the Commission, as well as a general check on station compliance with Commission rules and regulations.

If abuses are uncovered, remedial action will be required. In those cases where licensees are found to have abused their trusteeship flagrantly, provision has been made for formal hearing proceedings. Moreover, hearings in the field will be required in some cases, to provide a proper forum to determine whether the service provided by stations has been in the public interest.

The decision reached by the Commission that systematic investigation of complaints and regular station audits, including program monitoring, are required in the public interest has come only after a full consideration of all the facts. We are persuaded that without impairing the basic responsibility of licensees, the program as outlined is essential to strengthening the Commission's processes. The program undoubtedly will have a very significant impact on the industry. It should stimulate licensees to establish and maintain policies and practices more closely related to the public interest; and may well serve to raise the general level of broadcasting service.

The Commission urged that Congress provide the necessary funds ($300,000) to effectuate the proposed program in its first year.

According to former Chairman Ford:

We would have a staff of 25 persons (exclusive of secretarial and clerical assistants) who may be in the field at least half of the time. Obviously, the first year will be experimental. We cannot tell at the moment with precision the specific number of complaints we will designate for full-field investigation, or the number of stations we will audit. There are some 5,000 broadcast stations operating in 2,000 communities throughout the nation. We would do well with the proposed staff if we could reach as many as 100 communities for full audit. The stress, however, will not be placed on mechanically covering a prescribed number. Rather we intend to develop means of effectively screening various types of situations and to focus our resources where they will do the most good.

After eleven years this complaints and compliance unit is still in operation. It is clear, however, despite a limited amount of programming monitoring and study, that its investigatory and enforcement functions have never achieved the dimensions envisioned by Mr. Ford in 1960. There has been a persisting reluctance on the part of a majority of Commission members to carry on extensive surveillance activities regarding broadcast programming, and in no case in recent years has license renewal been refused solely on the grounds that the station's programs failed to measure up to the Commission's public interest criteria.

This does not mean to say, however, that the Commission and its staff have not had considerable impact on programming. The new application form, discussed in Chapter 15, calls for a great amount of program information. The mere knowledge that the Commission might exercise power to take away a license generally has had a compelling effect on stations. And what particularly can cause licensees to shudder is the Commission's practice of frequently withholding action on renewal applications if broadcast performance has not measured up to program standards as set forth in the Blue Book and in subsequent FCC policy statements. If preliminary study fails to resolve questions, the practice often has been to write stations, pointing out failure to live up to promises and to adhere to these standards and requesting explanatory comment regarding these deviations.

Educational and Religious Programs Favored. From the very beginning, the FCC has looked with favor upon the broadcasting of educational and religious programs, and has many times made pronouncements that such programming serves the public interest. There have been many times during the past twenty-five years, that the Commission has withheld action on renewal applications and placed stations on temporary licenses because they had devoted little or no time to these types of programs. And it was only after securing assurance from these stations that some such programs would be carried, that the Commission renewed their licenses on a regular basis.

The Commission and individual Commissioners have stressed in various statements and decisions that a well balanced program structure designed to meet community needs should include some broadcasts by educational institutions and religious organizations. For example, in *WKRG-TV, Inc.,* 10 RR 268 (1954), the Commission said that instructional broadcasts for in-school viewing are a type of programming to be encouraged and is illustrative of the kind of policy which "gears proposed programs to major local needs."

In *Mid-Continent Broadcasting Co. (WTIX),* FCC Public Notice No. 23360 (September 7, 1955), 12 RR 1286, the Commission had raised a question as to whether the station's license should be renewed. After deliberation, the Commission resolved the doubt in the station's favor and did renew the license without a public hearing. Former Commissioner Doerfer dissented, however, saying that the station had failed to carry any religious, educational or discussion programs and had not met the minimum program standards required by the Commission.

In 1958-59, eight radio stations in Georgia operated on temporary licenses for more than a year. Renewals were held up by the FCC because the stations had carried little or no agricultural, educational and religious programming. The Commission had under advisement the question of whether to hold public hearings. On July 15, 1959, as a leading trade journal reported it, these stations, "which had been sitting on an FCC hot seat for more than a year were removed from their uncomfortable positions."[9] By a 4 to 2 vote (one Commissioner was absent and didn't vote) all these licenses were renewed. It is assumed that the licensees made satisfactory explanations of their past performance and gave adequate assurances to the Commission that their future programming would serve the public interest.

FCC Concern with Over-All Programming. The Commission has made it clear that its chief concern is with the over-all operation of stations measured in terms of the local needs, and less in terms of individual programs or particular formats or ways in which they are presented. Broadcasters are afforded a wide range of discretion and freedom in the choice of individual programs. While possessing no power of censorship, the Commission "does review over-all operations of broadcast licensees in connection with renewal of licenses, but it does not judge the licensee's fulfillment of its public interest obligations in the light of a particular program or series of programs broadcast during a limited period of time, and it seeks to avoid any possible invasion of the discretion vested in the licensee to determine the program material to be presented and to make other decisions involved in day-to-day operations. . . ."[10]

Advertising Excesses. Over the years, a matter of concern on the part of the Commission has been what it has called "over-commercialization" of some stations. In many cases it has withheld action on renewal applications because of excessive advertising. In fact, in 1963, the Commission was moving in the direction of establishing a definite rule that would limit the amount of advertising that stations could broadcast. (See FCC Notice of Proposed Rule Making adopted May 15, 1963 (FCC 63-467; 28 Fed. Reg. 5158). However, after prolonged hearings and consideration of comments filed in the proceedings, the Commission decided not to establish a specific regulation. On January 15, 1964, the Commission issued a final report and order pointing out its continuing concern over advertising excesses in the broadcast industry, but that rather than adopt any precise standards the Commission said it would deal with the problem on a case-to-case basis. The Commission, in part, said:

Upon consideration of the record and other available information, we are convinced that the total time consumed by broadcast advertising and the extent to which such advertising is permitted to interrupt programming are two major facets of the problem of overcommercialization. We are of the view, however, that adoption of definite standards in the form of rules limiting commercial content, would not be appropriate at this time. We do not have sufficient information from which a sound set of standards of wide applicability could be evolved. . . .

We emphasize that we will give closer attention to the subject of commercial activity by broadcast stations and applicants to state their policies with regard to the number and frequency of commercial spot announcements as well as their past performance in these areas. These will be considered in our overall evaluation of station performance. Attention will be given to situations where performance varies substantially from the standards previously set forth. We also wish to emphasize that our decision not to adopt the NAB Codes at this time does not indicate that we regard them as of no value or as unsound limitations (either too much or too little).

On the contrary, one of the important considerations underlying our conclusion is that there is in existence an industry-formulated code of good practice in this field, which, while far from completely successful as a device regulating industry generally, does serve as one appropriate limitation, and which may be made more effective in the future. (1 RR 2d 1609-1610; 29 Fed Reg. 505-506).

Only a few weeks after the adoption of this report and order, the House of Representatives, by a vote of 317 to 43, approved a bill which it had had under consideration for some period of time to prohibit the FCC from setting commercial time standards. While the bill never won Senate approval, there can be no doubt that strong House opposition was a factor in persuading the Commission not to adopt any fixed regulations. (See *Broadcasting*, March 2, 1964, pp. 44-45, for a full report on Congressional proceedings and debate regarding the matter). But perhaps more important was the difficulty of devising a rule that could be applied equitably to every station and situation.

The Commission did not interpret the House action as a mandate to ignore advertising excesses. On the contrary, as reported in *Broadcasting* (March 9, 1964, p. 36) Commissioner Robert E. Lee stated that the House debate on the matter indicated a "clear directive" to examine such "excesses" in detail when broadcasters come up for renewal of their licenses.

At about this same time, in line with this belief, the Commission addressed letters to eight Florida stations requesting comment and information regarding their commercial practices. In their renewal applications, six of these stations reportedly had devoted 25 percent more of their time to commercial programs than they had previously promised. In one case, the disparity was more than 40 percent. After consideration of station responses to the letters and considerable debate among the Commissioners, in late July, 1964, the Commission, by a vote of 4 to 3, granted regular three year licenses to seven of the stations. (See *Broadcasting*, July 27, 1964, p. 34). Action on the eighth one's renewal application was deferred pending receipt of further information. It, too, however, was subsequently granted.

The Commission has continued, on a case-to-case basis, to give consideration to the advertising practices of stations when they come up for renewal of their licenses, though a number of the Commissioners have not been sympathetic with this procedure. In late 1965 and early 1966, the Commission addressed letters to several radio and TV stations because of "over-commercialization" and substantial departures from their proposed commercial policies and practices." As reported by *Broadcasting* (February 28, 1966, pp. 30-31), after considering the responses of the stations, the

Commission renewed their licenses for one year only rather than for the normal three year term.

By public notice dated March 6, 1967 (9 RR 2d, 639-640), the Commission announced the renewal of licenses of six Florida stations whose commercial practices had been under study and subject to question for a considerable period of time. However, in connection with the renewals, the Commission sent a letter to each station which read as follows:

The Commission has before it your renewal application proposing a commercial policy which would normally permit twenty minutes of commercial matter in any 60 minute segment. You state that the proposal is consonant with the needs and interests of the community.

We recognize the right of each broadcaster to make a reasoned judgment on commercial practices in terms of service to your community. We are now making a definitive judgment on the reasonableness of your commercial policy. However, we do believe that early review of your policy in actual operation would be in the public interest.

The license of your station is renewed for a three-year period ending February 1, 1970 with the requirement that, as provided in Section 308(b) of the Communications Act of 1934, as amended, you file with the Commission by August 31, 1968 a report for the 18 month period ending July 31, 1968 containing the following:

(1) Any complaints received during this period which concern your commercial practices.

(2) The total number of hours in which you have exceeded 18 minutes of commercial time, the total commercial time in each such hour, and a general statement of the reasons therefore.

(3) A statement of your commercial policies, including the steps you have taken to determine that they are consistent with the needs and interests of your community and the public interest.

Except for special circumstances, the Radio Code of the National Association of Broadcasters provides that the amount of time to be used for advertising shall not exceed eighteen minutes within any clock hour. The Commission, therefore, in the writing of these letters, appeared to be adopting the Code standard as a benchmark for license renewals. However, only six weeks later, the Commission granted an application for an FM station in Tasley, Virginia, with the applicant proposing to devote thirty-three percent of its time per hour to commercials. Commissioners Cox and Johnson dissented. Said Commissioner Johnson:

When the broadcasting industry and Congress were first considering federal regulation of broadcasting it was Secretary of Commerce Herbert C. Hoover who said, "It is inconceivable that we should allow so great a possibility for service to be drowned in advertising chatter." Who in the 1934 Congress would have predicted that its emphasis on "the public interest" in the then new Communications Act would be used to sanction 33 minutes of commercials per broadcast hour a mere 33 years later? Can the public be offered nothing save realization that, at this rate, it will be 1994 before the radio hour is totally consumed with commercials (FCC Public Notice, May 31, 1967, 10 RR 2d 144).

The situation is confusing. One thing, however, seems clear. The majority of the Commission appears not to be committed to any precise, inflexible formula with respect to the amount of broadcast time that may be devoted to advertisements, but if the amount of time substantially exceeds the limits set by the NAB Code, broadcasters should not be surprised if action on their renewal applications is delayed.

Local Live Talent Programs. In past years, the Commission attached importance to the broadcasting of local live talent programs. However, in 1966, reports indicated that a majority of the Commission had decided that they should put less emphasis on this aspect of programming and to discontinue sending letters of inquiry about it to stations. E. William Henry, then FCC chairman, and Commissioner Kenneth Cox disagreed. Mr. Henry, at the time, was quoted as saying that he thought there was "still a consensus at the Commission that broadcasters have a responsibility for presenting local live programming and that this is an area where it is appropriate for government regulation in terms of promise and performance." (See *Broadcasting,* July 5, 1965, p. 40).

Differences of Opinion as to Program Authority. Regarding advertising, local talent shows, and other types of programming there still persists decided differences of opinions among FCC commissioners as to the responsibilities of broadcasters. While some Commissioners have objected on constitutional grounds to program regulations, a majority still appears to feel that station programming should reflect licensee concern for the interests and needs of the local communities and that, legally the Commission is not precluded from considering, in this context, program performance when stations come up for renewal of their licenses.

Former Commissioner Kenneth A. Cox and Commissioner Nicholas Johnson have been particularly outspoken in their views on this subject. For example, in the March 6, 1967 action of the Commission, renewing the licenses of several stations in Florida, to which previous reference has been made, Commissioners Cox and Johnson wrote vigorous dissents, objecting particularly to the small amounts of time devoted by the stations to news, public affairs, educational, and religious programs. Former Chairman Rosel H. Hyde and former Commissioner Loevinger voted with the majority to grant the applications without further inquiry (9 RR 2d 687). They gave no reasons for their action in this case, but these reasons can readily be found in other cases where they expressed doubts as to the Commissioner's authority and to the social desirability of attempting to evaluate the merits of requests for broadcast facilities (whether original or renewal) on the basis of the amounts of time applicants have devoted to or proposed to devote to these prescribed program categories.

For example, in *Lee Roy McCourry, tra New Horizon Studios* (2 RR 2d

895, June 2, 1964), the Commission majority voted to designate for hearing an application for a new UHF station in Eugene, Oregon because the applicant did not propose to devote any time to "religious, agricultural, news, discussion or talks programming," and, upon request of the Commission, declined to offer any explanation for the omissions. Former Commissioner Loevinger disputed the legality of this action by the Commission and wrote a detailed and documented dissent with which Chairman Hyde concurred.

While these dissenting opinions appear in different cases and contexts, two relating to renewal of licenses and the other to an original application for a station, they bring out very well the strong differences of opinion among Commissioners as to the FCC's regulatory authority over broadcast programming, a controversy that has persisted more or less continuously since the FCC was created in 1934. For a study of these opinions, see 2 RR 2d 895 (1964).

Particular Types of Programs in Official Disfavor. As heretofore pointed out in Chapter 3, the old Federal Radio Commission denied a renewal application where it was shown that the owner prescribed medical treatments for listeners, basing his diagnosis simply upon symptoms recited in letters addressed to the station.[11] In another case, the FRC denied an application for renewal of license where the owner used the facilities to attack religious organizations, public officials, courts, etc., without due regard to the facts.[12]

The FCC, successor to the FRC, has never denied an application for renewal of license of a broadcast station solely on program grounds, but in many decisions it has expressed disapproval of certain types of programs as contrary to the public interest. The more objectionable ones to which the Commission has taken exception are:

Broadcasts prescribing medical treatments[13]
Broadcasts of horse racing information[14]
Advertising birth control preparations[15]
Astrology and fortune telling programs[16]
Fraudulent advertising[17]
Lottery broadcasts[19]
Obscene and vulgar programs[20]
Unwarranted attacks on persons and organizations and defamatory statements[21]
Racial and religious attacks[22]

The Federal Radio Commission enunciated the principle that broadcast stations could not be used exclusively to serve the special interests of certain individuals or groups.[23] Stations were not to be mere adjuncts of particular business enterprises;[24] nor should they become mouthpieces for certain social, economic, political, or religious philosophies to the exclusion of others.[25]

The FCC adopted and has maintained a similar policy and has insisted that broadcasting stations not be used simply as tools of special interests or for the dissemination of propaganda.

Station Advocacy Prohibited by Mayflower Decision. Prior to 1949, the FCC held to the policy that a station licensee could not be an advocate on controversial questions and did not have the privilege of editorializing as do the newspapers. In the famous *Mayflower* decision of 1940, the Commission said:

> . . . under the American system of broadcasting it is clear that responsibility for the conduct of a broadcast station must rest initially with the broadcaster. It is equally clear that with the limitations in frequencies inherent in the nature of radio, the public interest can never be served by a dedication of any broadcast facility to the support of partisan ends. Radio can serve as an instrument of democracy only when devoted to the communication of information and the exchange of ideas fairly and objectively presented. A truly free radio cannot be used to advocate the causes of the licensee. It cannot be used to support the candidacies of his friends. It cannot be devoted to the support of principles he happens to regard most favorably. In brief, the broadcaster cannot be an advocate.
>
> Freedom of speech on the radio must be broad enough to provide full and equal opportunity for the presentation to the public of all sides of public issues. Indeed, as one licensed to operate in a public domain the licensee has assumed the obligation of presenting all sides of important public questions, fairly, objectively and without bias. The public interest—not the private—is paramount. These requirements are inherent in the conception of public interest set up by the Communications Act as the criterion of regulation. And while the day to day decisions applying these requirements are the licensee's responsibility, the ultimate duty to review generally the course of conduct of the station over a period of time and to take appropriate action thereon is vested in the Commission.[26]

The Scott Case. In 1946, this philosophy of the Commission was tested by Robert Harold Scott who requested that the licenses of three California stations be revoked because they had refused to give or sell him time to broadcast his atheistic views. He contended that the existence of a Deity was a controversial matter and that he was entitled to time to dispute with religious groups who aired their views. The stations replied that this was not a controversial question, that there were comparatively few atheists and that the matter was not of sufficient public interest to justify discussion. The Commission dismissed the complaint but stated:

> We recognize that in passing upon requests for time, a station licensee is constantly confronted with most difficult problems. Since the demands for time may far exceed the amount available for broadcasting a licensee must inevitably make a selection among those seeking it for the expression of their views. He may not even be able to grant time to all religious groups who might desire the use of his facilities, much less to all who might want to oppose religion. Admittedly, a very real opportunity exists for him to be arbitrary and unreasonable, to indulge his own preference, prejudices, or whims; to pursue his own private interest or to favor those who

330

espouse his views, and discriminate against those of opposing views. The indulgence of that opportunity could not conceivably be characterized as an exercise of the broadcaster's right of freedom of speech. Nor could it fairly be said to afford the listening audience that opportunity to hear a diversity and balance of views, which is an inseparable corollary of freedom of expression. In making a selection with fairness, the licensee must, of course, consider the extent of the interest of the people in his service area in a particular subject to be discussed, as well as the qualifications of the person selected to discuss it. Every idea does not rise to the dignity of a 'public controversy,' and every organization regardless of membership or the seriousness of its purposes, is not *per se* entitled to time on the air. But an organization or idea may be projected into the realm of controversy by virtue of being attacked. The holders of a belief should not be denied the right to answer attacks upon them or their belief solely because they are few in number.

The fact that a licensee's duty to make time available for the presentation of opposing views on current controversial issues of public importance may not extend to all possible differences of opinion within the ambit of human contemplation cannot serve as the basis for any rigid policy that time shall be denied for the presentation of views which may have a high degree of unpopularity. The criterion of the public interest in the field of broadcasting clearly precludes a policy of making radio wholly unavailable as a medium for the expression of any view which falls within the scope of the constitutional guarantee of freedom of speech.[27]

The Commission Reconsiders the Mayflower Decision.   The decision of the Commission in the *Mayflower* case holding that a licensee could not be an advocate met with disfavor from some segments of the broadcast industry. The National Association of Broadcasters, for example, asked that the Commission reconsider its decision. The result was that the Commission held public hearings in March and April of 1948 to determine whether its policy should be changed.

Testimony was presented by 49 witnesses representing the broadcasting industry and various interested organizations and members of the public. On June 1, 1949, the Commission issued a report announcing that stations might editorialize providing they offered opportunities for opposing points of view. The Commission said:

... the Commission believes that under the American system of broadcasting the individual licensees of radio stations have the responsibility for determining the specific program material to be broadcast over their stations. This choice, however, must be exercised in a manner consistent with the basic policy of the Congress that radio be maintained as a medium for free speech for the general public as a whole rather than as an outlet for the purely personal or private interests of the licensee. This requires that licensees devote a reasonable percentage of their broadcasting time to the discussion of public issues of interest in the community served by their stations and that such programs be designed so that the public has a reasonable opportunity to hear different opposing positions on the public issues of interest and importance in the community. The particular format best suited for the presentation of such programs in a manner consistent with the public interest must be determined by the licensee in the light of the facts of each individual situation. Such presentation may include the identified expression of the licensee's personal viewpoint as part of the more general presentation of views or comments on various issues, but the opportunity to present such views as they may have on matters of controversy may not be utilized to achieve a partisan or one-sided presentation of issues. Licensee editorialization is but one aspect of freedom of expression by means of radio. Only insofar as it is exercised in conformity with the paramount right of the public to hear a reasonably balanced presentation of all responsible viewpoints on particular issues can such editorialization be considered to be consistent with the licensee's duty to operate in the public interest. For the licensee is a trustee impressed with the duty of preserving for the public generally radio as a medium of free expression and fair presentation.[28]

Reactions Against FCC's Current Policy on Editorialization. The policy of the Commission expressed in the editorialization opinion is still in effect. One aspect of the Commission's policy, however, has been most unpopular with some segments of the broadcast industry. It is that which requires broadcast licensees to make an affirmative effort to secure the expression of points of view opposed to those in the editorials carried by the stations. The Commission has said that it does not believe "that the licensee's obligations to serve the public interest can be met merely through the adoption of a general policy of not refusing to broadcast opposing views where a demand is made of the station for broadcast time."

The Commission has further stated "that broadcast licensees have an affirmative duty generally to encourage and implement the broadcast of all sides of controversial public issues over their facilities, over and beyond their obligation to make available on demand opportunities for the expression of opposing views. It is clear that any approximation of fairness in the presentation of any controversy will be difficult if not impossible of achievement unless the licensee plays a conscious and positive role in bringing about balanced presentation of the opposing views."[29]

Recent developments in the Fairness Doctrine. About fifteen years after the issuance of this opinion and order, on July 1, 1964, the Commission adopted a public notice setting forth a digest of its interpretive rulings on the so-called "fairness doctrine" which it had enunciated in this 1949 editorialization opinion (2 RR 2d 1901; 29 Fed. Reg. 10416).

The constitutionality of this doctrine was challenged in the U.S. Circuit Court of Appeals in the District of Columbia (Red Lion Broadcasting Co. Inc. et al., v. Federal Communications Commission and United States of America, 381 F (2d) 908, 10 RR 2d 2001), but that court upheld the validity of the doctrine on June 13, 1967.

Less than three weeks later, the Commission adopted a specific regulation requiring that stations give notice to persons, whose "honesty, character, integrity or like personal qualities" have been attacked in connection with the broadcasting of views on controversial issues of public importance. Great objection to this rule was expressed by large segments of the broadcast industry, particularly newscasters associated with networks. About one month later, the Commission amended the regulation to preclude its applicability to bona fide newscasts or on-the-spot coverage of bona fide news events. This exemption, however, was not made applicable to editorials, news commentaries, documentaries, and interviews. (See 10 RR 2d 1911; 32 Fed. Reg. 11531).

The regulation, as amended (Section 73.123, 1 RR 53:185), read as follows:

73.123. Personal attacks; political editorials. —(a) When, during the presentation of views on a controversial issue of public importance, an attack is made upon the honesty, character, integrity or like personal qualities of an identified person or group, the licensee shall, within a reasonable time and in no event later than one week after the attack, transmit to the person or group attacked (1) notification of the date, time and identification of the broadcast; (2) a script or tape (or an accurate summary if a script or tape is not available) of the attack; and (3) an offer of a reasonable opportunity to respond over the licensee's facilities.

(b) The provisions of paragraph (a) of this section shall not be applicable (i) to attack on foreign groups or foreign public figures; (ii) to personal attacks which are made by legally qualified candidates, their authorized spokesmen, or those associated with them in the campaign; and (iii) to bona fide newscasts, bona fide news interviews, and on on-the-spot coverage of a bona fide news event (including commentary or analysis contained in the foregoing programs, but the provisions of paragraph (a) shall be applicable to editorials of the licensee).

(c) Where a licensee, in an editorial, (i) endorses or (ii) opposes a legally qualified candidate or candidate or candidates, the licensee shall, within 24 hours after the editorials, transmit to respectively (i) the other qualified candidate or candidates for the same office or (ii) the candidate opposed in the editorial (1) notification of the date and the time of the editorial; (2) a script or tape of the editorial; and (3) an offer of a reasonable opportunity for a candidate or a spokesman of the candidate to respond over the licensee's facilities; provided, however, that where such editorials are broadcast within 72 hours prior to the day of the election, the licensee shall comply with the provisions of this subsection sufficiently far in advance of the broadcast to enable the candidate or candidates to have a reasonable opportunity to prepare a response and to present it in a timely fashion.

The Columbia Broadcasting System, the National Broadcasting Company, and the Radio Television News Directors Association (RTNDA) filed petitions for circuit court review of the Commission's order establishing these regulations. On September 10, 1968, the U.S. Court of Appeals, Seventh Circuit, held that they were too vague, imposed an undue burden on licensees, involved possible censorship and violated the First Amendment to the Constitution.[30] The Court, however, did not settle the question as to whether the Commission could establish any rules, or whether the fairness doctrine, as a principle, was constitutional.

Fairness Doctrine Made Applicable to Cigarette Advertising. Prior to the adoption of this regulation, as pointed out in Chapter 5, there had been increasing public concern regarding the possible health hazards resulting from cigarette smoking. A complaint was filed with the FCC alleging that a station in New York broadcast numerous advertisements for cigarette manufacturers, but afforded no opportunity for the presentation of contrasting views as to the benefits and advisability of smoking. The Commission was asked to apply the Fairness Doctrine to cigarette commercials. By letter dated June 2, 1967 (9 RR 2d 1423), the Commission informed the station that the Fairness Doctrine applied to the advertising of cigarettes and that it was required to make some time available for the discussion of the health hazards involved in smoking.

Numerous broadcasters, networks, advertisers, tobacco companies, and others, protested, and petitions were filed asking the Commission to reconsider its decision. The petitioners made the following contentions:

(A) The Fairness Doctrine violates the First and Fifth Amendments to the Constitution;

(B) Even if constitutional, it should be applied only to news programs and commentary on public issues or editorial opinion and not to advertising;

(C) The Commission's ruling is contrary to Congressional policy;

(D) No controversial issue of public importance is involved where a lawful business is advertising a lawful product, and, in the absence of any health claim in a commercial, there is no viewpoint to oppose;

(E) The requirement that stations run public service announcements pointing out the health hazards resulting from smoking debases the Fairness Doctrine and substitutes Commission fiat for licensee judgment;

(F) The ruling cannot logically be limited to cigarette smoking alone;

(G) It will have an adverse financial effect upon broadcasting, causing the cigarette industry to turn to other advertising media and will have an adverse effect on the sale of cigarettes;

(H) The ruling is procedurally bad because interested parties did not have opportunity to be heard prior to the adoption of a novel and unprecedented policy (11 RR 2d 1907).

On September 8, 1967, the Commission issued a memorandum opinion and order, rejecting all the arguments of the petitioners. After an exhaustive analysis of the matter, the Commission concluded:

There is, we believe, some tendency to miss the main point at issue by concentration on labels such as the specifics of the Fairness Doctrine or by conjuring up a parade of "horrible" extensions of the ruling. The ruling is really a simple and practical one, required by the public interest. The licensee, who has a duty "to operate in the public interest" (Section 315(a)), is presenting commercials urging the consumption of a product whose normal use has been found by the Congress and the Government to represent a serious potential hazard to public health . . . there is, we think, no question of the continuing obligation of a licensee who presents such commercials to devote a significant amount of time to informing his listeners of the other side of the matter—that however enjoyable smoking may be, it represents a habit which may cause or contribute to the earlier death of the user. This obligation stems not from any esoteric requirements of a particular doctrine but from the simple fact that the public interest means nothing if it does not include such a responsibility.

In light of all the foregoing, we conclude and find:

(a) The ruling as to the applicability of the Fairness Doctrine to cigarette advertising is within the Commission's legal authority and discretion, and is in the public interest.

(b) Petitioners have made no showing which warrants reconsideration and withdrawl of the ruling or the institution of rule making in this area.

(c) Petitioners have made no showing that relief, except as indicated in paragraph 6 above, is warranted or in the public interest; on the contrary, the grant of stay relief would be likely to cause irreparable harm to the public (11 RR 2d 1937; see full text of *Memo,* 32 Fed. Reg. 13162).

Former Commissioner Lee Loevinger voted to sustain the ruling, but wrote a concurring opinion in which he expressed some "doubts and reluctance." Commissioner Nicholas Johnson also wrote a concurring opinion responding to questions raised by Commissioner Loevinger and presenting personal views in support of the ruling.

There was an appeal to the Circuit Court of Appeals in the District of Columbia. That Court, on November 21, 1968, affirmed the Commission's authority to apply the fairness doctrine to cigarette advertising.[31] pending a Supreme Court decision (RR Report No. 21-41, October 16, 1968).

On June 9, 1969, the United States Supreme Court, by unanimous decision, upheld the validity of the Commission's policies and regulations regarding the "fairness doctrine", and their legality and constitutionality can no longer be questioned (395 U.S. 367). The decision not only validates the "fairness doctrine" and regulations which implement it, but it lays to rest many of the questions which have been raised regarding the FCC's authority over programming. Because it is a land mark decision, a major portion of it is reproduced in Appendix V.

Radio and Television Codes. The broadcasting industry has made efforts to provide effective self-regulation with respect to programming. The National Association of Radio and Television Broadcasters has adopted codes for radio and television stations. While these specific codes have not been officially approved or disapproved by the FCC, various Commissioners from time to time have informally made favorable reference to these Codes and have urged broadcasters to take action, individually and cooperatively, to improve the quality of their programs to avoid governmental controls. These NARTB codes, as recently revised, are available at nominal costs at the National Association of Broadcasters, 1771 N Street, N.W., Washington. D.C.

In Conclusion. In conclusion, it may be said that programs specifically prohibited by statute such as lotteries and broadcasts of an indecent and obscene character are contrary to the public interest and must be avoided.

But more than this, the FCC holds that the licensee has a positive responsibility to provide a program service designed to meet the varied needs of the particular community in which the station is located.

The primary responsibility for determining what this program service will be vests in the licensee. The FCC has no powers of censorship and would violate the law if it attempted to restrain a station from carrying any program or series of programs, or to impose its judgment on the day-to-day operation of the station. At the same time, it is clear that the law requires the FCC to make a decision as to whether a station has operated in the public interest when the station comes up for renewal of its license. This decision is based upon the showing made in the renewal application and any substantial complaints or commendations with respect to the station's service received from the public during the license period.

The Commission has not established any hard and fast formula applicable to every station and community. It has stressed the importance of providing a balanced program service—balanced in the sense that a reasonable effort is made to serve the religious, educational, cultural and economic needs of the community and to afford reasonable access to the microphone or camera for the expression of different points of view on important public issues.*

If the renewal application and the complaints filed against the station during the license period indicate that the station's over-all performance has fallen below these standards, and that the licensee has made little effort to ascertain community needs and interests and attempt to serve them, then questions may be raised requiring further study before action is taken on the application. The practice of the Commission in such cases has been to place the stations on temporary licenses, and through informal correspondence and investigation, elicit additional information and ascertain more fully the plans of licensees for future operations.

In most instances, these informal inquiries have resulted in a resolution of any questions raised regarding station operation and the FCC has granted the license renewals without further procedure. There have been a few cases, however, as previously pointed out, where the Commission has not been satisfied with station responses to these initial inquiries and has required licensees to go through formal public hearings in the communities where the stations are located. In these hearings a detailed and critical study of station performance is made in terms of specifically stated issues, the qualifications of the licensee are re-examined, and a written record of all

*The Commission has increasingly emphasized the importance of licensees dealing with programs which serve specific needs of the community. (See Part I, Section IV-A and IV-B of FCC Application terms. Also, FCC *Primer on Part I of Section IV-A and IV-B Concerning Ascertainment of Community Problems and Broadcast Matter to Deal with Those Problems, Notice of Inquiry,* FCC, Docket No. 18774, FCC 69-1402, 40594; also see "A Study of Broadcast Station License Renewal Application Exhibits on Ascertainment at Community Needs" by Thomas F. Baldwin, Associate Professor, Departments of Television, Radio and Communication, Michigan State University, assisted by Stuart H. Surlin, Graduate Assistant in the Department of Communication at MSU. This study was filed in this docket, and represents one of the most thorough and scientific studies that has been conducted in this field.

evidence in the proceeding is assembled and used as a basis for making a final decision in the case. If the new policies of the Commission are carried out, more careful scrutiny of program service, involving more public hearings, can be expected.

As already discussed in Chapter 15, interested parties have the opportunity of filing petitions with the FCC requesting that applications for broadcast authorizations (including renewals) be denied. At the time of filing, the applicant must give public notice in the community where the station operates. Petitions for denial may be filed within 30 days of the date the application is accepted for filing by the FCC. If the petition raises substantial questions as to whether the station has been operating in the public interest, the FCC must designate the renewal application for a public hearing. The Commission may, if it so chooses, hold the hearing in the community where the station is located and the petitioner, as well as other interested parties, may have opportunity to participate and present evidence as to whether the station has operated in the public interest and whether the station's license should be renewed. (See Appendix I for details regarding this legislation and its provisions.)*

---

*Also see recent decision of U. S. Court of Appeals, D. C., which makes it possible for listening and viewing groups to intervene as parties with legal standing and present evidence in public hearings on renewal applications. (*Office of Communications of Church of Christ et al v. Federal Communications Commission,* March 25, 1966, 359 F(2d994; 7 RR (2d) 2001). Also note activities of church and other groups conducting informal negotiations between stations and community organizations seeking program improvements and elimination of racial discrimination in broadcasting. (*Broadcasting,* July 6, 1970, p. 3).

1. Committee Report on Proposed Rules Governing Standard Broadcast stations and Standards of Good Engineering Practice, FCC Docket No. 5072-A, April 1, 1939, p. 30.

2. *Ibid.*

3. See 84th *Cong. Rec.* 1164-66, February 6, 1939.

4. *Public Service Responsibility of Broadcast Licensees,* Report of FCC, March 7, 1946.

5. See FCC's *Report, Public Service Responsibility of Broadcast Licensees,* as amended July 2, 1946, which states the definitions of program categories. In 1965, changes were made. See Form 303, IRR 98-51.

6. *Walmac Co.,* 12 FCC 91, 3 RR 1371 (1947); also see *Community Broadcasting Co.,* 12 FCC 85, 3 RR 1360 (1947).

7. *Eugene J. Roth,* 12 FCC 102, 3 RR 1377 (1947).

8. *Hearst Radio Inc.,* 6 RR 994 (1951).

9. *Broadcasting Magazine,* May 25, 1959, p. 64; also, July 20, 1959, p. 78.

10. *Captain James E. Hamilton,* 16 RR 170 (1957). Other cases in point: *Brush-Moore Newspapers, Inc.,* 11 RR 641 (1956); *Appalachian Broadcasting Co.,* 11 RR 1327 (1956); *Travelers Broadcasting Service Corporation,* 12 RR 689 (1956); *WKAT, Inc.,* 22 FCC 117, 12 RR 1 (1957).

11. See Chapter 3, Footnote 51, p. 43.

12. See Chapter 3, Footnote 55, p. 43.

13. See *Bremer Broadcasting Co.,* 2 FCC 200; other cases listed in 2 RR-M-2366e.

14. *Standard Cahill Co., Inc.,* 1 FCC 227 (1935); *Joilet Broadcasting Company,* 4 RR 1225 (1948); *American Broadcasting Company, Inc.,* 7 RR 1129 (1952). The Commission has taken the position that the *amount* of time devoted to horse racing programs and the *amount* of information presented for the benefit of betters are important in determining whether such programs are against the public interest.

15. *Knickerbocker Broadcasting Co., Inc.,* 2 FCC 76 (1935).

16. *Nellie H. and W. C. Morris,* 2 FCC 269; *Farmers and Bankers Life Insurance Corporation,* 2 FCC 455; and *Radio Broadcasting Corporation,* 4 FCC 125.

17. See *Scroggin and Company Bank,* 1 FCC 194; *Bremer Broadcasting Co.,* 2 FCC 79; *WREG Broadcasting Service,* 10 RR 1323 (1955). A cooperative arrangement has been arrived at whereby the Federal Trade Commission advises the FCC of questionable advertising broadcast over radio and television stations and the FCC communicates such information to the stations involved. See 14 RR 1262.

18. The Commission has stated that no federal law prohibits the broadcasting of advertisements for alcoholic beverages and the Commission's authority with respect to the matter is limited to the consideration of applications for renewal of license. . . . In states and localities where sale or advertising of alcoholic beverages is prohibited by law, such sale or advertising by radio would of course be contrary to the public interest. Where there are no laws prohibiting such sale or advertising, the problems raised are the same as those raised by any other program which may have limited appeal to the radio audience. In some circumstances the broadcasting of liquor advertisements may raise serious social, economic and political issues in the community, thereby imposing an obligation upon the station to make available time, if desired, to individuals or groups desiring to promote temperance and abstinence. *Broadcast Programs Advertising Alcoholic Beverages,* 5 RR 593 (1949).

19. See *KXL Broadcasters,* 4 FCC 186 (1937); also see *Metropolitan Broadcasting Corporation,* 5 FCC 501 (1938).

20. *Bellingham Publishing Co.*, 6 FCC 31, 32 (1938); also see Warner, Harry, *Radio and Television Law*, pp. 334-339.

21. *Ibid.*, pp. 384-385.

22. *KFKB Broadcasting Association, Inc. v. F.R.C.*, 60 App. D.C. 79, 47 F(2d) 670, 672 (1931).

23. *Ibid.*

24. *Third Annual Report of F.R.C.* (1929), p. 34.

25. *Ibid.*

26. *The Mayflower Broadcasting Corporation*, 8 FCC 333 (1940).

27. *Re Scott*, FCC Mimeo, 96050, July 16, 1946.

28. *In the Matter of Editorializing by Broadcast Licensees*, Docket No. 8516, 13 FCC 1246, 14 Fed. Reg. 3055, 1 RR Section 91:21 (1949).

29. *Ibid.*, p. 6.

CHAPTER 20

Changes in Ownership and Control of Stations

In passing on application for transfer of control of a broadcast licensee corporation, the Commission's primary consideration from the standpoint of public interest is not the relationship between the contract price and the items to be transferred, but rather the qualifications of the proposed transferee and its ability to provide the public with an improved broadcast service.
—7 FCC 315 (1939)

As Section 310(b) of the Communications Act provides, no license for a broadcast station may be assigned or the control of a station transferred without the prior written consent of the Commission. This section originally read:

The station license required hereby, the frequencies authorized to be used by the licensee, and the rights therein granted shall not be transferred, assigned, or in any manner either voluntarily or involuntarily disposed of, or indirectly by transfer of control of any corporation holding such license, to any person, unless the commission shall, after securing full information, decide that said transfer is in the public interest, and shall give its consent in writing.[1]

Also, as originally adopted, Section 319(b) of the Act provided that no construction permit or any rights pertaining thereto could be transferred without the consent of the Commission.

In 1952, both sections were amended. The provision relating to transfer of construction permits was deleted from 319(b) and merged with Section 310(b). The latter section now reads:

No construction permit or station license, or any rights thereunder, shall be transferred, assigned, or disposed of in any manner, voluntarily or involuntarily, directly or indirectly, or by transfer of control of any corporation holding such permit or license, to any person except upon application to the Commission and upon finding by the Commission that the public interest, convenience, and necessity will be served thereby. Any such application shall be disposed of as if the proposed transferee or assignee were making application under Section 308 for the permit or license in question; but in acting thereon the Commission may not consider whether the public interest, convenience and necessity might be served by the transfer, assignment, or disposal of the permit or license to a person other than the proposed transferee or assignee.[2]

When FCC Approval Must Be Secured. In 1948, in accordance with statutory provisions in effect at the time, the Commission released a public statement pointing out that the assignment of a license or transfer of control of a station may not be effected until after the Commission has given written consent.[3] Any kind of agreement, written or oral, or any sales of stock in a corporate licensee or changes in a partnership arrangement which shifts the major control of the station must first be approved by the Commission.

With respect to sales of stock in a licensee corporation, the Commission has stated that a transfer of control takes place requiring prior approval when:

(1) An individual stockholder gains or losses affirmative or negative control. (Affirmative control consists of control of more than 50% of voting stock; negative control consists of control of exactly 50% of voting stock.)

(2) Any family group or any individual in a family group gains or loses affirmative or negative control.

(3) Any group in privity gains or loses affirmative or negative control.

In its instructions to licensees the Commission gives the following examples of transfers of control or assignment requiring *prior* written consent:

(1) A, who owns 51% of the licensee's or permittee's stock, sells 1% or more thereof to B.

(2) X corporation, wholly owned by Y family reduces outstanding stock by purchase of treasury stock which results in family member A's individual holdings being increased to 50% or more.

(3) A and B, man and wife, each own 50% of the licensee's or permittee's stock. A sells any of his stock to B.

(4) A is a partner of the licensee company. A sells any part of his interest to newcomer B or existing partner C.

(5) X partnership incorporates.

(6) Minority stockholders form a voting trust to vote their 50% or more combined stockholdings.

(7) A, B, C, D, and E each own 20% of the stock of X corporation. A, B, and C sell their stock to F, G, and H at different times. A transfer is effected at such time as C sells 10% or more of his stock. In other words, a transfer of control occurs at such time as 50% or more of the stock passes out of the hands of the stockholders who held stock at the time the original authorization for the licensee or permittee corporation was issued.[4]

Agreements such as management contracts may involve transfers of control requiring *prior* consent of the Commission. For example, in one case the facts showed that the National Broadcasting Company had been employed as an exclusive agent of Westinghouse Electric and Manufacturing Company to supply all broadcast programs for Westinghouse stations. The Commission held that, by entering into this agreement in 1932, rights and privileges granted under the license to all intents and purposes had been transferred without the written consent of the Commission in violation of Section 310(b).[5]

The Commission had designated the renewal applications of the stations for hearing. Westinghouse petitioned for reconsideration and grant without a hearing on the grounds that the old agreement with NBC had been terminated and a new one had been made by which Westinghouse would supply its own programs for local broadcasting. With the abrogation of the 1932 contract and the pledge that henceforth the licensee would exercise control over the stations, the Commission granted the petition and renewed the licenses.[6]

Application Forms. The application forms used for requesting approval of assignments and transfers are prescribed in Section 1.329 of the Commission's Rules of Practice and Procedure. They are *FCC Form 314 (Assignment of License)* and *FCC Form 315 (Transfer of Control).*

Since the Commission is under a statutory duty to pass on the qualifications of any assignee or transferee, the considerations are substantially the same as those involved in original applications. Section 1 of these forms elicits information regarding the frequency, power, and hours of operation of the station involved. A full statement of reasons for requesting the assignment or transfer must be given by both the seller and purchaser.

Other items of information which must be submitted include original and replacement costs and present values of the station properties, a current balance sheet, and the price or consideration involved in the transaction. Copies of the contract of sale and all instruments affecting the assignment or transfer must be attached to the application.

The assignee or transferee must give information as to his legal and financial qualifications. He must submit specific and detailed data regarding funds or property furnished by parties other than the applicant and the conditions under which such financial help is provided.

A statement regarding proposed program service must be given in Section IV similar to that required in an application for a construction permit (FCC Form 301) referred to in Chapter 15.

A short form (FCC Form 316) may be used in those cases where the control shifts from one legal entity to another but where the ownership remains substantially the same. As stated in Section 1.329(b) of the Rules, this short form may be used in the following situations:

(1) Assignment from an individual or individuals (including partnerships) to a corporation owned and controlled by such individuals or partnerships without any substantial change in their relative interests;

(2) Assignment from a corporation to its individual stockholders without effect-

ing any substantial change in the disposition of their interests;

(3) Assignment or transfer by which certain stockholders retire and the interest transferred is not a controlling one;

(4) Corporate reorganization which involves no substantial change in the beneficial ownership of the corporation;

(5) Assignment or transfer from a corporation to a wholly owned subsidiary thereof or vice versa, or where there is an assignment from a corporation to a corporation owned or controlled by the assignor stockholders without substantial change in their interest; or

(6) Assignment of less than a controlling interest in a partnership.

Section 1.329 of Commission Rules states that transfer and assignment applications "should be filed with the Commission at least 45 days prior to the contemplated effective date of the assignment or transfer of control."

Section 1.330 provides that in case of death or legal disability of an individual permittee or licensee, a member of a partnership or a person controlling a corporate licensee, the Commission must be notified promptly in writing. Within 30 days, an application on short Form 316 must be filed with the Commission requesting consent to an involuntary assignment to a person or entity legally qualified to succeed to the station properties under the laws of the place having jurisdiction over the estate involved.

Financial, Contractual and Ownership Reports. So that the Commission may keep itself fully informed at all times regarding the financial status, ownership and control of stations, certain reports are required. Section 1.341 of the Rules specifies that the Licensee of each commercially operated standard, FM, television, or international broadcast station shall file with the Commission on or before April 1 of each year, on FCC Form 324, broadcast revenue and expense statements for the preceding calendar year together with a statement as to investment in tangible broadcast property as of December 31 of such year.[7]

As provided in Section 1.342, these stations must also file copies of the following contracts, instruments, and documents together with amendments, supplements, and cancellations, within 30 days of their execution.[8]

(a) Contracts relating to any kind of network service, including transcription agreements or contracts for the supplying of film for television stations which specify option time, but not contracts granting the right to broadcast music such as ASCAP, BMI, or SESAC agreements;

(b) Contracts relating to present or future ownership or control, including but not limited to the following:

(1) Articles of partnership, association, and incorporation, and changes in such instruments;

(2) Bylaws, and any instruments effecting changes in such bylaws;

(3) Any agreement, or document providing for the assignment of a license or permit or affecting, directly or indirectly, the ownership or voting rights of the common, preferred, voting or non-voting stock such as agreements for stock transfer, for issuance of new stock, or the acquisition of stock owned by the licensee or permittee. Pledges, trust agree-

ments, options to purchase stock and other executory agreements are required to be filed.

(4) Proxies with respect to stock running for a period more than a year; and those regardless of time, given without full and detailed instructions binding the nominee to act in a specified manner. For those given without such instructions, a statement must be filed showing the number of such proxies, by whom given and received, and the percentage of outstanding stock represented by each proxy. There is an exception when there are more than 50 stockholders. In such cases complete information need be filed only regarding proxies given by those who are officers or directors, or who have 1% or more of the corporation's voting stock. In cases where the licensee or permittee has more than 50 stockholders and those giving proxies are neither officers or directors nor hold 1% or more of the stock, the only information required is the name of any person voting 1% or more of the stock by proxy, the number of shares he voted in this way, and the total number of shares voted at the particular stockholders' meeting in which the proxies were involved.

(5) Mortgage or loan agreements containing provisions restricting the licensee's or permittee's freedom of operation, such as those affecting voting rights, specifying or limiting the amount of dividends payable, the purchase of new equipment, the maintenance of current assets, etc; or

(6) Any agreement reflecting a change in the officers, directors or stockholders of a corporation, other than the licensee or permittee, having an interest, direct or indirect, in the licensee or permittee.

(c) Contracts relating to the sale of broadcast time to "time brokers" for resale.

(d) Contracts relating to Subsidiary Communications Authorization Operation, except contracts granting licensees or permittees engaged in SCA the right to broadcast copyright music.

(e) Time sales contracts with the same sponsor for 4 or more hours per day, except where the length of events (such as athletic contests, musical programs, and special events) broadcast pursuant to the contract is not under control of the station.

(f) Management, consultant agreements with independent contractors; contracts relating to the utilization in a management capacity of any person other than an officer, director, or regular employee of the station; management contracts with any persons, whether or not officers, directors, or regular employees which provide for both a percentage of profits and a sharing in losses.

Agreements which need not be filed with the FCC are those with persons regularly employed as station managers or salesmen; contracts with program personnel, with chief engineers or other technical employees, with attorneys, accountants, or consulting radio engineers, performers, station representatives, labor unions, or similar agreements.

As specified in Section 1.343 of the Rules, each licensee of a standard, FM or television station, whether operating or intending to operate on a commercial or non-commercial basis, must file an Ownership Report (FCC Form 323) at the time the application for renewal of station license is required to be filed. Licensees owning more than one standard, FM, or television broadcast station need file only one ownership report at three year intervals. These reports must provide the following information as of a date not more than 30 days prior to the time they are filed with the Commission:[9]

(a) In the case of an individual, the name of such individual;
(b) Regarding a partnership, the names of the partners and the interest of each;
(c) As to a corporation, association, trust, estate, or receivership:

    (1) The name, residence, citizenship, and stockholdings of officers, directors, stockholders, trustees, executors, administrators, receivers, and members of any association.

    (2) Full information as to family relationship or business association between two or more officials and/or stockholders, trustees, executors, administrators, receivers, and members of any association;

    (3) Capitalization with a description of the classes and voting power of stock authorized by the corporate charter or other appropriate legal instrument and the number of shares of each class issued and outstanding; and

    (4) Full information on FCC Form 323 with respect to the interest and identity of any person having any direct, indirect, fiduciary, or beneficiary interest in the licensee or any of its stock. For example, where A is the beneficial owner or votes stock held by B, the same information should be furnished for A as is required for B. Or where X corporation controls the licensee, or holds 25% or more of the number of outstanding shares of either voting or non-voting stock of the licensee, the same information should be furnished with respect to X corporation as is required in the case of the licensee, together with full data as to the identity and citizenship of the person authorized to vote licensee's stock.

The same information should be supplied as to Y corporation if it controls X or holds 25% or more of the number of outstanding shares of voting or non-voting stock of X and as to Z corporation if it controls Y corporation or holds 25% or more of the number of outstanding shares of either voting or non-voting stock of Y and so on back to natural persons.

All licensees must include in the Ownership Report a list of all contracts still in effect required to be filed under Section 1.342 of the Rules as mentioned above, and must report any interest they may have in any other broadcast station.

A permittee of a station must file an Ownership Report within 30 days of the date of grant by the Commission of an application for an original construction permit containing the items of information mentioned. A supplemental Ownership Report must be filed within 30 days after any change occurs in the information required by the Ownership Report (Form 323) including:[10]

(1) Any change in capitalization or organization;
(2) Any change in officers and directors;
(3) Any transaction affecting the ownership; direct or indirect, or voting rights of licensee's or permittee's stock;

(4) Any change in the officers, directors, or stockholders of a corporation other than the licensee or permittee such as X, Y, or Z corporation described above.

Some exceptions should be noted. With respect to the ownership reports required to be reported as explained above, corporations or associations having more than 50 stockholders or members need only file the information regarding those stockholders or members who are officers or directors, and regarding others who have one percent or more of either the voting or non-voting stock of the corporation or voting rights in the association.[11]

Competing Applications in Assignment and Transfer Cases Not Permitted. As Section 310(b) of the Act now reads, if a request is made for approval of a station transfer or assignment, the Commission is not permitted to entertain and consider competing applications as is true where authority to build a station is being applied for. This, however, has not always been the case.

Several years prior to 1952, the Commission adopted a procedure requiring that all transfer and assignment applications be advertised in a local newspaper, twice weekly for at least three weeks after the filing of the application stating "the terms and conditions of the proposed assignment or transfer and the name of the proposed assignee or transferee." It was further provided that "any other person desiring to purchase the facilities upon the same terms and conditions" might file an application to this effect with the Federal Communications Commission within sixty days.

The Commission withheld action during the sixty days. If no competing applications were filed during that time, the pending one was granted if the Commission decided it was in the public interest. If a competing application was filed, the Commission might still grant the original one without a hearing if the buyer chosen by the licensee appeared to be the best qualified to operate the station and the public interest would be served. If, however, this determination could not be made, then the Commission designated the original and any competing applications for a consolidated hearing "to determine among other things which of the applicants is best qualified to operate the station in the public interest."[12]

If the Commission preferred the competing applicant, he and the licensee were given thirty days to submit a contract for the transfer of assignment on the same terms as stated in the original application or upon such other terms as stated in the original application or upon such other terms agreed upon and approved by the Commission.[13]

In 1952, Congress annulled this procedure. Section 310 (b) was amended, prohibiting competing applications in transfer and assignment cases, but still requiring that the Commission pass on the qualifications of those seeking to buy stations and to determine whether such sales would serve the public interest.

In support of the amendment, the Senate Interstate and Foreign Commerce Committee in its report to Congress, in part said:

One of the purposes of the proposed new language in this subsection is to annul the so-called Avco procedure adopted several years ago by the Commission to prevent a licensee from selling his property to a proper person of the choice but requiring an opportunity for others to make bids for any radio station proposed to be sold. The committee believes that there is no provision of present law which authorized the Commission to employ such a procedure and it deems such procedure an unwise invasion by a government agency into private business practice.

The committee regards it significant that the Commission dropped the so-called Avco procedure several months ago as unsatisfactory and a cause of undue delay in passing upon transfers of licenses. It should be emphasized that the Commission's authority to see to it that stations are operated in the public interest and to determine whether the proposed transferee possesses the qualifications of an original licensee or permittee is not impaired or affected in any degree by this subsection. In fact, the latter requirement is expressly stated. . . . [14]

"Trafficking" in Licenses. The Congress and the FCC have expressed concern from time to time over what has been called "trafficking" in licenses —the business of buying and selling stations, realizing large profits which have little relationship to the actual value of the tangible broadcast properties but are derived from what some critics are pleased to call the "exploitation" of radio and television channels in choice markets.

As early as August, 1937, Congressman Wigglesworth of Massachusetts introduced a resolution in the House looking toward an investigation of the FCC. In this resolution, reference was made to the alleged evils of monopoly in broadcasting, "trafficking in licenses, capitalization of Federal licenses at the expense of the public."[15]

Again he made reference to this problem in a speech to the House five years later in which he declared "that time after time I have stood in the well of this House and inveighed against the practice of the Commission giving its approval to the transfer of stations or the control of those stations for considerations far in excess of the value of the physical assets so transferred—a practice, in other words, involving the sale of government licenses, with all the possible dangers to the public that we have seen involved in the capitalization of licenses in other fields."[16]

On April 20, 1949, Senator Johnson of Colorado, then Chairman of the Senate Interstate and Foreign Commerce Committee, stated that it was not the intent of the Communications Act that permits and licenses should be "peddled" to second parties. "In Washington," said he, "liquor licenses are transferred for substantial sums, but broadcast licenses ought not to be sold over the bargain counter like beans in the corner grocery."[17]

The Avco Case. In 1945, The Aviation Corporation engaged primarily in the manufacturing of aircraft and airplane parts applied to the Commission for approval of the purchase of 73% of the stock of The Crosley Corporation, licensee of Station WLW in Cincinnati, Ohio. The FCC granted the application despite the fact that part of the purchase price attributable to the station facilities was not segregated from the total amount paid for the other properties of the Crosley Corporation. The price for the "entire package" was $16,060,000.00, but there was no testimony in the hearing on the application assessing any value to the broadcast properties.

With respect to the price paid for these, the majority of the Commission stated they had no jurisdiction to pass on the matter. While they suspected that the price was in excess of the fair value of the station properties and that a portion of the total consideration was being paid for the radio frequency, they said they were unable to deal with this problem since Congress had furnished no administrative standards. Until Congress, therefore, provided remedial legislation, the majority of the Commission held to the view that consideration of the price to be paid for a station should be limited to three questions:

(1) Does the price suggest trafficking in licenses? Is there evidence that the station is being acquired merely for the purpose of resale at a large profit rather than to provide a public service:

(2) Is the applicant financially qualified to pay the price?

(3) Is the price so high that the purchases would over-commercialize the operation at the expense of public service programming?

There was a dissenting opinion in the case in which two Commissioners stated that the Commission had the legal authority to pass on the purchase price of a station. They admitted that there was no set formula by which the Commission could determine whether a part of the sale price represented an exploitation of a publicly owned frequency, but they contended that the judgment should be made in terms of the circumstances of each case.[18]

One year later, in a case proposing transfer of control of broadcast facilities to a network, involving consideration of more than $3,000,000, the Commission again held that it did not have the legal power to disapprove a sale and transfer of a station simply on the grounds of price and cited its decision in the Avco case.[19] The FCC approved the deal, but again there was a dissenting opinion by the same two Commissioners who had dissented in the Avco case the year before.

In 1955, the Commission approved the assignment of a TV construction permit and the assignment of a license of a station already in operation to a single applicant at specified prices. Commissioners Webster and Bartley dissented and voted for a public hearing on the applications. In his dissent, Commissioner Webster said:

While the Communications Act provides for the assignment of a construction permit or the transfer of a corporation holding such a permit, it is silent as to whether any monetary consideration can properly be involved. Accordingly, without legal restriction in this connection, it must be assumed that certain payments are proper. However, the Commission, since its inception, has steadfastly taken the position that trafficking in frequencies is not in the public interest. But unfortunately, it has never seemed to be able to arrive at a policy under which it could determine what constitutes trafficking in frequencies, and, as a result, it has vacillated from one extreme to another.

In 1952, the Commission denied an application (BMP-5803) to extend the construction permit for Station WERL, East Rainelle, West Virginia and dismissed as moot an application (BAP-170) to assign the permit for that station on the ground that, although only a couple of thousand dollars was involved, an extension of the permit and the assignment thereof would be tantamount to a sale of the frequency. Since that time the Commission has approved assignments and transfers of bare permits where the payment of many thousands of dollars has been involved.

I do not take the position that the Commission should or could promulgate a hard and fixed rule under which it would determine what payments can legitimately be made where the assignment or transfer of a bare permit is concerned. But I think the Commission should now pause long enough in its consideration of construction permit assignments and transfers to enable it to determine whether it proposes to abandon the Commission's long-standing policy against trafficking in frequencies, and, if not, to set up some general guide for determining what constitutes trafficking of that nature. For I contend that the Commission can set up a general policy in this connection which would at least permit us to achieve a certain degree of consistency.[20]

Since this decision, Commissioner Bartley has dissented in a number of other cases where the Commission has approved sales of stations at prices much in excess of the actual value of the broadcast properties and where the sellers have had the licenses only a short period of time.[21]

Is the Transfer in the Public Interest? There are differences of opinion among authorities as to the extent to which the Commission may consider the sale price of a station in connection with transfer and assignment applications. The majority of the Commission has held the position that they have no legal authority to make a determination as to the propriety or validity of any particular price. A minority has held a contrary view.

Whichever view is correct, the basic question in all transfer cases is whether the proposed change of ownership will serve the public interest. The Commission obviously has the authority to consider this question. Price standing alone is not particularly significant. If, however, it appears that a prospective purchaser, because of the high price to be paid for the station, will "over-commercialize" his operation and neglect public service programming, or because of limited resources may have difficulty meeting installment payments and financing the operation of the station, then the Commission may properly raise the question whether the public interest will be served by approval of the transfer.

Originally, there was a great deal of concern in Congress that the ownership of stations might gravitate into the hands of a few wealthy entrepreneurs. There was a fear that those with the "bulging pocketbooks" would buy up the choice broadcasting facilities and monopoly would result.

This fear to some extent still persists, but with the multiple ownership rules now limiting the number of stations that may be owned by any one individual or group, there is less justification for the fear.

In any case, the real test is whether a transfer will serve the public interest. The question is not so much how much the purchaser pays for the station but how much service will he be able to give the community.

A bill introduced in the 86th Congress (HR 11340) proposed to amend Section 310(b) of the Communications Act prohibiting the transfer of any broadcast license held for less than three years unless, after public hearing, it is affirmatively established that, because of an unforeseen change in circumstances affecting the licensee, approval of the proposed transfer would serve the public interest.

While the Commission had reservations about the necessity of holding hearings in every transfer case, it did support the principle of the bill. On May 4, 1960, the Commission, in formal comments, said in part:

We believe that the subsection will have a salutary effect, not only in checking the practice of quick transfers by licensees tempted to traffic in licenses, but also in discouraging the entry of persons with such propensities into the broadcast field. Consequently, we believe that in the long run the policy so established will greatly simplify the problems we have encountered in transfer applications. Although we anticipate that transfer applications falling within the purview of subsection (d) may not be as numerous as in the past because of the rigid policy, and although we do expect that the required field hearings will result in some increase in the Commission's workload, we endorse the principle of the amendment.

The 86th Congress adjourned, however, without passing the bill. On December 7, 1960, the FCC issued a notice proposing to require hearings (in most cases) involving applications for assignment of licenses and transfers of control of broadcast stations within three years of their acquisition. This rule was adopted by the Commission on March 15, 1962 (23 RR 1503; 27 Fed. Reg. 2689). The rule reads as follows:

Section 1.597. Procedures on transfer and assignment applications. (a) if, upon examination, pursuant to Sections 309(a) and 210(b) of the Communications Act of 1934, as amended, of an application for Commission consent to an assignment of a broadcast construction permit or license or for a transfer of control of a corporate permittee or licensee, it appears that the station involved has been operated by the proposed assignor or transferor for less than three successive years, the application will be designated for hearing on appropriate issues pursuant to Section 309(b) of the Communications Act of 1934, as amended, unless the Commission is able to find that:

(1) The application involved a translator station only, a FM station operated for at least three years together with a Subsidiary Communications Authorization held for a lesser period; or

(2) The application involved a pro forma assignment of transfer of control; or

(3) The assignor or transferor has made an affirmative factual showing, supported by affidavits of a person or persons with personal knowledge thereof, which establishes that due to unavailability of capital, to death or disability of station principals or to other changed circumstances affecting the licensee or permittee occurring subsequent to the acquisition of the license or permit, Commission consent to the proposed assignment or transfer of control will serve the public interest, convenience and necessity.

(b) The commencement date of the three-year period set forth in paragraph (a) of this section shall be determined as follows:

(1) Where the authorizations involved in the application consist of a license and a construction permit authorizing a major change in the facilities of the licensed station (as defined in Sections 1.571, 1.572, and 1.573), the three-year period shall commence with the date of the Commission's grant of the construction permit for the modification. However, when operating authority has been issued to cover the construction permit for a major change in facility, the commencement date for calculating the length of time the station has been operated for purposes of this section shall then revert to the date the licensee received its original operating authority. A grant of authority for minor modifications in authorized facilities shall have no effect upon the calculation of this time period.

(2) Where the authorization involved in the application consists of a permit authorizing the construction of a new facility, or a license covering such a permit, the three-year period shall commence with the date or issuance of initial operating authority.

(3) Where the operating station involved in the application was obtained by means of an assignment or transfer of control (other than pro forma), the three-year period shall commence with the date of grant by the Commission of the application for said assignment or transfer of control. If the station was put in operation after such assignment or transfer, paragraph (b) (1) and (2) of this section shall apply.

(4) Where an application is filed for Commission consent to a transfer of control of a corporation holding multiple licenses and/or construction permits, the commencement date applicable to the last-acquired station shall apply to all the stations involved in the transfer, except where the application involved an FM station operated for less than three years and an AM station operated for more than three years, both serving substantially the same area. Said exception shall apply to the same circumstances where assignment applications are involved.

(c) In determining whether a broadcast interest has been held for three years, the Commission will calculate the period between the date of acquisition as specified above and the date the application for transfer or assignment is tendered for filing with the Commission.

(d) With respect to applications filed after the three-year period, the Chief of the Broadcast Bureau is directed (1) to examine carefully such applications, on a case-to-case basis, to determine whether any characteristics of trafficking remain; and (2) if so, to seek additional information by letter inquiries to the applicants, such as that which will be required to be developed and tested in the hearing process with respect to stations held less than three years.

In the proceeding which led to the adoption of this regulation, objections were filed by numerous parties in interest. One of the chief arguments advanced against adoption of the proposal was that it was a "deviation from our free enterprise system of broadcasting," and would discourage the investment of private capital in the broadcasting industry. In response the Commission stated:

... These contentions ignore the fact that the broadcast industry is one affected with a public interest, and that this Commission, within the limits of the Communications Act, is charged with the basic responsibility of considering relevant aspects of the public interest in effectuating its licensing procedures and policies. In the face of the accelerated trend in the sale of broadcast properties and of the appreciable number of transfer applications involving short-term ownership of stations, we would be remiss in our responsibilities in administering the Communications Act, if we did not effectuate the new procedure here adopted.

The Commission agrees that trafficking, standing alone, is to a considerable extent a subjective problem, and that the Commission, of course, has adequate authority to deal with it on a case-to-case basis. But these considerations do not undermine the desirability of the general procedural policy we have adopted with respect to the particular problem of possible trafficking within the initial three-year period. Moreover, the Commission is concerned not solely with trafficking, but also with the effects upon licensee responsibilities of the accelerated trend in the sales of broadcast properties and of short-term ownership of stations. ... Our remedial rule is directed to both these policy considerations. As urged by the respondents the "time factor" of three years, standing alone, cannot eradicate the trafficking problem. Accordingly, subsection (d) has been added to the rule to make it clear that the Commission will continue to examine carefully the trafficking problem in connection with transfer and assignment applications involving stations held more than three years.[22]

1. 48 Stat. 1086.

2. 66 Stat. 716.

3. Procedure on Transfer and Assignment of Licenses, 4 RR 342.

4. FCC Form 323 with instructions; Section 98, Table of Forms, 1 RR 308.

5. *Re Westinghouse Electric and Manufacturing Company*, 8 FCC 195, 196 (1940). For other cases on management contracts see network proceedings before FCC, Docket No. 5060 (1938).

6. *Ibid.*

7. 1 RR 51:206-207.

8. *Ibid.*, 51:207-208.

9. *Ibid.*, 51:206-207.

10. *Ibid.*, 51:210.

11. *Ibid.*, 51:211.

12. See Warner, *op. cit.*, Footnotes 1, 2, 3, and 4, pp. 574-576.

13. *Ibid.*

14. *Senate Report No.* 44, 82nd Cong., 1st Sess., submitted January 25, 1951, 1 RR 10:280.

15. 81 Cong. Rec., p. 9406.

16. 88 Cong. Rec., p. 551.

17. 95 Cong. Rec., p. 4783.

18. Powel Crosley, Jr. (Avco Case), 11 FCC 1 (1946). See *Re Jackman*, 5 FCC 496 (1938), and *Bulova and Henshel (Mester)* 11 FCC 137, 3 RR 125 (1946), aff'd 70 F. Supp. 118, 332 U.S. 749 (1947). Also see other cases dealing with "trafficking" in licenses digested in 2 RR M-2855-2858b.

19. *Edward J. Noble.* 11 FCC 569, 3 RR 449 (1946).

20. *E. D. Rivers, Sr.*, 12 RR 281 (1955).

21. *Telrad, Inc.*, 13 RR 1124 (1956); *Universal Broadcasting Company, Inc.*, 14 RR 569 (1956).

22. 23 RR 1507; 23 Fed. Reg. 2692. In *Harriman Broadcasting Co.*, the FCC denied an application of a former licensee because the applicant had previously engaged in trafficking in licenses and had misrepresented facts to the Commission to conceal his trafficking practices. On appeal, the Circuit Court of Appeals in the District of Columbia sustained the Commission. Said the Court: "Section 310(b) of the 1934 Act provides for Commission disapproval of any transfer contrary to the public interest. Indeed, according to the Commission regulation promulgated in 1962, trafficking is presumed until the contrary is shown, with respect to any transfer of a license where the applicant has previously dealt with licenses in a manner which adversely reflects on his character and purpose to operate in the public interest." (13 RR 2d 2073; U.S. Court of Appeals, June 20, 1968).

CHAPTER 21

Broadcaster Beware!

Licensees and their principals are expected to display a high degree of public responsibility and obedience to the law as they are in a very real sense, guardians of a public trust. —FCC, 12 RR 1225

Broadcast licenses are not granted in perpetuity. As heretofore pointed out, licensees acquire no property rights in radio or television channels. The use of these channels may be withdrawn from those who fail to comply with the law and the regulations or otherwise do not operate their stations in the public interest.

Grounds for Revoking Licenses and Issuing Cease and Desist Orders. As provided in Section 312(a) of the Communications Act, the Commission has the authority to revoke broadcast licenses or construction permits to construct stations for any of the following reasons:[1]

(1) for false statements knowingly made either in the application or in any statement of fact which may be required pursuant to Section 308;

(2) because of conditions coming to the attention of the Commission which would warrant it in refusing to grant a license or permit on an original application;

(3) for willful or repeated failure to operate substantially as set forth in the license;

(4) for willful or repeated violation of, or willful or repeated failure to observe any provision of this Act or any rule or regulation of the Commission authorized by the Act or by a treaty ratified by the United States;

(5) for violation of or failure to observe any final cease and desist order issued by the Commission under this section; or

(6) for violation of Section 1304, 1343, or 1464 of Title 18 of the United States Code.

Section 312(b) provides that "where any person (1) has failed to operate substantially as set forth in a license, (2) has violated or failed to observe any rule or regulation of the Commission authorized by this Act or by a treaty ratified by the United States, the Commission may order such person to cease and desist from such action."

However, as pointed out in Chapter 3, before a cease and desist order may be issued or a broadcast authorization (permit or license) may be revoked, the Commission must first give the permittee or licensee an opportunity to show cause why the contemplated action should not be taken. He must be supplied with a statement of the matters with which the Commission is concerned and a time and place for a public hearing must be specified. The respondent station must be given at least thirty days from the time he receives the notice to prepare for the hearing.[2]

If, after a hearing, or a waiver thereof, the Commission concludes that the station should discontinue the practice in question, or if it is decided that the offense is sufficiently serious that the permit or license should be withdrawn, an appropriate restraining or revocation order is issued. This order must recite when it is to become effective and must contain a statement of findings and the reasons therefore.[3]

In every case, where a hearing is conducted pursuant to Section 312 of the Act, the Commission must proceed with the introduction of evidence and assume the burden of proof.[4]

The provisions of Section 9(b) of the Administrative Procedure Act are made applicable to the institution of proceedings relating to revocation of licenses and the issuance of cease and desist orders. The pertinent part of Section 9(b) reads as follows:

... Except in cases of willfulness or those in which public health, interest, or safety requires otherwise, no withdrawal, suspension, revocation, or annulment of any license shall be lawful unless, prior to the institution or agency proceedings therefore, facts or conduct which may warrant such action shall have been called to the attention of the licensee by the agency in writing and the licensee shall have been accorded opportunity to demonstrate or achieve compliance with all lawful requirements. In any case in which the licensee, has, in accordance with agency rules, made timely and sufficient application for a renewal or a new license, no license with reference to any activity or a continuing nature shall expire until such application shall have been finally determined by the agency.[5]

For good cause, the Commission may institute revocation proceedings at any time against permittees and licensees and there have been numerous cases where the Commission has done so. More often, however, where misconduct is involved, the Commission has administered legal sanctions against the offending stations by refusing to grant renewal of licenses.

Misrepresentations of Facts to the Commission. One of the surest ways to jeopardize or lose a broadcast permit or license is to misrepresent or conceal essential facts from the Commission. This is illustrated by the following cases.

In 1937, the Commission refused to grant a construction permit when it was discovered that the applicant did not make frank, candid and honest disclosures as to its organizational setup, stock ownership and its connection with another station. On appeal, this action of the Commission was sustained by the U.S. Court of Appeals for the District of Columbia.[6]

In a 1940 case, the Commission revoked a station license where the applicant had made untrue statements in his original applications and had given false testimony at the hearing on these applications. The action was taken, despite the contention of the licensee that the community would be left without any local radio service.[7]

Two years later, however, the Commission refused to revoke a license where it was shown that the licensee over a period of time had misrepresented the facts regarding ownership, control and financing of the station. The countervailing facts, as recited by the Commission, were that the station had had erroneous advice from its legal counsel; had not appeared to act in bad faith; and deletion of the station license would leave the community without any local radio service and would be detrimental to the war effort.[8]

In 1947, the Commission refused to grant renewal of a station license because the licensee had concealed from the Commission various transfers of stock; had denied the existence of an oral agreement it had made to re-issue certain stock to a party who would vote it and who would serve as a director of the corporation. Also, in its original application for a construction permit, the licensee had filed a balance sheet showing over $25,000 in the bank whereas the actual amount was less than $400.

The Commission held that whatever might have been the motive, the willful concealment and misrepresentation of facts by the licensee could not be excused. The Commission further held that under the facts of the case, a showing that the station was rendering a satisfactory service was not enough to warrant a renewal of the license.[9]

In 1953, the Commission granted a renewal of license and set aside an order of revocation of a construction permit for another station where a partnership agreement and new methods of financing had not been reported promptly. The Commission concluded that the dereliction was due to ignorance and negligence and not to a deliberate desire to commit wrong. Also, the Commission noted that new owners were in charge of the two stations, were respected in the local communities, and that there was need for broadcast service in the areas involved.[10]

The Commission has emphasized that the Communications Act of 1934, as amended, "contemplates that applicants for a permit or license shall establish those qualifications which would support a finding that a grant to them would serve the public interest. This of necessity presupposes a candid, honest and complete disclosure as to all facts underlying the application and deemed by the Commission to be essential. It is also expected and required that applicants satisfactorily establish that they comprehend the responsibilities imposed upon licensees of radio broadcast stations. . . ."[11]

In *Federal Communications Commission v. WOKO, Inc.*, 329 U.S. 223, the U.S. Supreme Court expressed its point of view on the matter of concealment and misrepresentation of facts to the FCC. In that case the Commission found that station WOKO in Albany, New York had rendered an acceptable service to the community; that for a twelve year period one man and his family received all dividends paid by the licensee company though he and his family owned only 24% of the stock. The facts further showed that he was a network vice-president and had obtained the stock on assurance that he would help secure a network affiliation for the station and provide other benefits.

In reports to the FRC and later to the FCC, this family ownership was concealed and it was represented that the stock was held by others. The station's general manager appeared on behalf of the licensee at various hearings and testified falsely regarding the identity of the corporation stockholders and the shares held by each.

Upon discovery of these misrepresentations, the FCC refused to renew the station license. On appeal, the U.S. Court of Appeals for the District of Columbia reversed the Commission. The Supreme Court, however, reviewed the lower court's opinion and sustained the Commission.[12]

The licensee contended that no finding had been made that the facts concealed were material to the Commission's decision-making responsibilities. The Supreme Court answered that this was beside the point, and declared that "the fact of concealment may be more significant than the facts concealed. The willingness to deceive a regulatory body may be disclosed by immaterial and useless deceptions as well as by material and persuasive ones. We do not think it is an answer to say that the deception was unnecessary and served no purpose."[13]

Another contention made by the licensee was that a majority of its stockholders had no part or knowledge of the concealment or deception. The Court replied that "this may be a very proper consideration for the Commission in determining just and appropriate action. But as a matter of law, the fact that there are innocent stockholders can not immunize the corporation from the consequences of such deception. If officers of the corporation by such mismanagement waste its assets, presumably the state law affords adequate remedies against the wrongdoers. But in this as in other matters, stockholders entrust their interests to their chosen officers and often suffer for their dereliction. Consequences of such acts cannot be escaped by a corporation merely because not all of its stockholders participated."[14]

The final language of the opinion, reflecting the Supreme Court's attitude toward misrepresentation or concealment of facts and the scope of the Commission's authority in this regard, should be noted:

Lastly, and more importantly, the Court of Appeals suggested that in order to justify refusal to renew, the Commission should have made findings with respect to the quality of the station's service in the past and its equipment for good service in the future. Evidence of the station's adequate service was introduced at the hearing. The Commission on the other hand insists that in administering the Act it must rely upon the reports of licensees. It points out that this concealment was not caused by slight inadvertence nor was it an isolated instance, but that the station carried on the course of deception for approximately twelve years. It says that in deciding whether the proposed operations would serve public interest, convenience or necessity, consideration must be given to the character, background and training of all parties having an interest in the proposed licensee, and that it cannot be required to exercise the discretion vested in it to entrust the responsibilities of a licensee to an applicant guilty of a systematic course of deception.

We cannot say that the Commission is required as a matter of law to grant a license on a deliberately false application even if the falsity were not of this duration and character, nor can we say that refusal to renew the license is arbitrary and capricious under such circumstances. It may very well be that this station has established such a standard of public service that the Commission would be justified in considering that its deception was not a matter that affected its qualifications to serve the public. But it is the Commission, not the courts, which must be satisfied that the public interest will be served by renewing the license. And the fact that we might not have made the same determination on the same facts does not warrant a substitution of judicial for administrative discretion since Congress has confided the problem to the latter. We agree that this is a hard case, but we cannot agree that it should be allowed to make bad law.[15]

Unlawful Assignment of Control. As explained in Chapter 20, Section 310(b) makes it unlawful to transfer the control of a station without the consent of the Commission. In some instances licenses have been lost because of this violation.

In *United States Broadcasting Corporation,* 2 FCC 208 (1935), applications for license renewal and for full time operation were denied where it appeared the station had carried on a mediocre program service, was in financial difficulties and where there had been a transfer of control without the consent of the Commission.[16]

In another case, the Commission revoked a license where there had been two unauthorized transfers of control, at least one of which was willful; where incomplete and erroneous ownership reports had been filed, some stock transfers had not been reported, and the officers, directors and stockholders had been negligent and indifferent to their responsibilities to the public and the Commission.[17]

There have been many instances involving violations of Section 310(b) where the Commission has granted renewal of licenses. In such cases, the Commission has resolved doubts in favor of the licensees because of countervailing factors. For example, in *Farmers Broadcasting Service, Inc.,* 8 RR 415 (1953), 50 percent of the stock in the licensee company was issued to new stockholders without the Commission's consent and there was failure to report intention to sell additional stock. The Commission decided however that there was no active concealment of facts and that the errors committed were not deliberate but due to ignorance of corporate procedure.[18] Considering all the circumstances, the Commission approved a renewal of the station's license.

In a 1953 case, applications for transfer of control and renewal of license were granted despite the fact there had been misrepresentations to the Commission and an unauthorized transfer of control. Any doubts were resolved in favor of the licensee for the reason that the offenses had been committed some years in the past and the perpetrators of the illegal acts no longer were connected with the management of the station and a useful and needed broadcast service was being provided the public[19]

The Commission decided in 1956 that a prior unauthorized shift of control was not a bar to license renewal where the change was more technical than actual; that the same persons, a family group, continued to own the corporation in which one now had a majority interest, and where the same management and operating policies were still in effect.[20]

Illegal Delegation of Control over Radio Programs. Any kind of arrangement by which the licensee delegates or abdicates its responsibility for programming violates section 310(b) of the Act and may result in a loss of license. For example, in a 1948 case, the Commission held that a contract by which a city, licensee of a station, transferred to a private commercial organization substantial control over about 85% of the broadcast time, with the right of the latter to seek injunctive relief in case of breach or threatened breach by the city, was an abdication of the licensee's duties in violation of the law. The city was required to rid itself of the contract and regain control of the station.[21]

In 1949, the Commission announced the reservations of broadcast time by sellers of stations to be illegal. The Commission declared that "under the Act a station licensee is fully responsible for the operation and control of his station and he cannot properly divest himself by contract or otherwise of such responsibility. The obligation to operate in the public interest is the licensee's alone. It is not in the public interest and is inconsistent with the nature of the rights conferred by a license for owners of radio stations as part of the consideration for the transfer of such stations to reserve a right to the use of radio time on the station being sold, to attempt to obtain a right of reverter of license, or to obtain other rights which under the Act can be exercised only by licensees."[22]

The Commission has implemented this policy with the following specific regulation (Section 73.241):

Special rules relating to contracts providing for reservation of time upon sale of a station.—(a) No license, renewal of license, assignment of license, or transfer of control of a corporate licensee shall be granted or authorized to a standard broadcast station which has a contract, arrangement or understanding, express or implied, pursuant to which, as consideration or partial consideration for the assignment of license or transfer of control, the assignor of a station license or the transferor of stock, where transfer of a corporate licensee is involved, or the nominee of such assignor or transferor retains any right of reversion of the license or any right to the reassignment of the license in the future, or reserves the right to use the facilities of the station for any period whatsoever.[23]

In a 1950 case, the Commission stated that the licensee is responsible for the selection of programs and must maintain a continuous and positive control over programming. Retention of a negative or veto control with the delegation of responsibility to a time broker is not sufficient.[24]

Violations of the Communications Act. Violations of law in general as they relate to character qualifications of broadcast licensees have already been discussed in Chapter 13. Licensees of course are expected to observe strictly all provisions of the Communications Act itself. Failure to do so can lead to serious consequences.

There are penal provisions which should be mentioned. Section 501 of the Act provides that "any person who willfully and knowingly does or causes or suffers to be done" anything prohibited or declared to be unlawful, or likewise fails to do anything required, shall, upon conviction, be fined not more than $10,000 or be imprisoned for a term not more than one year, or both. In case of second offenses, the term of imprisonment may be extended to two years.[25]

As pointed out in Chapter 3, it is the responsibility of U.S. District Attorneys to carry out under the direction of the Attorney General all necessary proceedings for the enforcement of this and other provisions of the Communications Act.[26]

While the Commission itself has no authority to enforce criminal sanctions, as previously pointed out, it does have the power to revoke licenses or may refuse to renew them where violations of the Act are involved.

Violations of FCC Rules and Regulations. In the business and programming affairs and technical operation of the station, management must be alert at all times to make sure that FCC rules and regulations are strictly observed. Section 502 of the Communications Act specifies penalties for willful violation of these rules. It reads:

> Any person who willfully and knowingly violates any rule, regulation, restriction, or condition made or imposed by the Commission under authority of this Act, or any rule, regulation, restriction, or condition made or imposed by any international radio or wire communications treaty or convention, or regulations annexed thereto, to which the United States is or may hereafter become a party, shall, in addition to any other penalties provided by law, be punished, upon conviction thereof, by a fine of not more than $500 for each and every day during which such offense occurs.[27]

Here again we are dealing with criminal provisions of the statute, responsibility for the enforcement of which vests in the Attorney General. The Commission, however, has the authority to revoke or refuse to renew licenses for violations of its rules the same as it may for violation of any of the provisions of the Communications Act.

In an early 1932 case, the U.S. Court of Appeals of the District of Columbia sustained a decision of the Federal Radio Commission, denying license renewal because the station involved had violated regulations by using excessive power, by permitting the station to be operated by a person not having a license and had not met the requirements as to announcement of station call letters and identification of phonograph records.[28]

In 1935, the FCC denied a renewal application where it appeared, among other things, that the station's transmitter was not being properly modulated and spare parts were such that they could not be used for replacement.[29]

In other situations, stations have lost their licenses for failing to maintain operating schedules as required by the Commission, for defective equipment and repeated violations of technical rules, for failure to log the names of political speakers, and for not requiring station personnel to sign station logs, etc.[30]

The Commission has taken into account extenuating circumstances and has set aside revocation orders or granted renewal of licenses despite infractions of rules. For example, in a 1949 case, the Commission revoked the license of a station because of almost 150 technical irregularities. The order of revocation, however, subsequently was set aside, because the licensee was operating from a new site and a special inspection had shown that the violations had been corrected.[31]

Likewise, in a Puerto Rican case, a revocation order was set aside where there had been numerous engineering violations. Extenuating circumstances included attempts at improvements in technical operation. Also, the station had been in operation only a short time and the Commission thought there was a good prospect that it would continue to improve its service. Moreover, there was no evidence that the misconduct in question was willful or deliberate.[32]

Forfeitures. By a 1960 amendment of Section 503 of the Act, the Commission is empowered to impose forfeitures (1) for willful and repeated failure of a station to operate substantially as authorized; (2) for failure to observe any rule or regulation of the Commission or to comply with any final cease or desist order; (3) for violation of Section 317(c) or Section 509(a) (4) of the Act or Section 1304, 1343, or 1464 of Title 18 of the United States Code. No forfeiture liability, however, may attach until the licensee has received written notice and has had an opportunity to show in writing why he should not be held liable. (See Appendix I, Section 503 and 504 of the Act, for details regarding maximum penalties and administrative procedure.)

Since the amendment to the law was enacted in 1960, the FCC has frequently imposed penalties and forfeitures on stations for a variety of reasons. Some examples are: failure to identify sponsors as required by Section 317 of the Communications Act (*United Television Inc.*, 1 RR 2d 509; *WHAS, Inc.*, 2 RR 2d 869; *Glen Harmon Corp.*, 6 RR 2d 653; *Lotus Broadcasting Corp.*, 11 RR 2d 680); unauthorized transfers of control in violation of Section 310(b) of the Act (*Arthur C. Schofield*, 5 RR 2d 164; *Victor Valley Broadcasters, Inc.*, 6 RR 2d 968); deceptive programming contrary to Section 509 of the Act (*Eastern Broadcasting Corp.*, 10 RR 2d 393); fraudulent billing practices, prohibited by Sections 73.112 and 73.124 of the Commission's rules (*WBZB Broadcasting Service, Inc.*, 11 RR 2d 254); violations of various technical regulations (*North County Broadcasting Co., Inc.*, 11 RR 2d 42; *Robert J. Martin*, 11 RR 2d 425; *WHIH, Inc.*, 11 RR 2d 677); delay in filing renewal applications (*Lakeland FM Broadcasting, Inc.*, 11 RR 2d 599; *Warner Robins Broadcasting Co., Inc.*, 11 RR 2d 601); alleged obscenity, *Broadcasting*, July 13, 1970, p. 33.

These fines or forfeitures have ranged from $100 for failure to file renewal applications on time to $10,000 for broadcasting deceptive programming. A maximum limit of $10,000 for forfeitures is set by the statute. Fines less than this amount may vary, depending upon the severity of the offense as determined by the Commission. There has been recent discussion at the FCC regarding the possibility of increasing the amount of fines, and it appears that a recommendation may be made to Congress to amend the law to make this possible (See *Broadcasting*, January 26, 1970, p. 5).

Network Regulations. The network regulations have already been discussed in Chapter 18. A historic case involving violation of these regulations was *Don Lee Broadcasting System*, 14 FCC 993, 5 RR 1179 (1950). In that case, the Commission found that the network in question had forced its affiliates to "accept arrangements under which they could not freely accept programs from another network organization;" had pressured them "to agree to accept regularly network programs on less than 56 days' notice," and "to treat as network option time far more than the 3 hours in each of the segments of the broadcast day permitted by the rules." The record in the case further showed that the affiliates were compelled to surrender, contrary to the regulations, their rights to reject network programs which they reasonably believed to be contrary to the public interest and their right to substitute programs of outstanding local importance for network programs. As the Commission said, "in order to force the affiliates to comply with the network demands, the affiliates were subjected to unremitting and insistent pressure from the network in the form of written and oral communications, 'follow up' activities on the part of network officials, and, on occasion, implied threats to cancel station network affiliation. In at least one instance, moreover, the network refused to grant an affiliation with a new station if it were managed by a manager of another of its affiliates who had, in the past, proved 'uncooperative' with respect to the network's demands to relinquish local option time, and to shift programs, and had shown reluctance to accept the network's judgment as to what constituted good programming for the local station." [33]

Despite these violations of the network rules as shown by the record, the Commission concluded:

We find ourselves in a difficult situation in deciding this case. This is not due to any deficiency in the record for we are convinced that the attitude which responsible Don Lee officers displayed in this record with respect to the Commission's chain broadcasting regulations—an attitude which can at best be characterized as one of indifference—warrants critical examination of the qualifications of the applicant to be a broadcast licensee. We are, however, faced with the important practical difficulties in this case which arise from the fact that the only sanction we have to apply is denial of license—an action which will put the licensee out of business. Except (in an aggravated case), the Commission is reluctant to impose a sentence on a licensee which not only terminates his existing operations but would preclude him from holding any other radio licenses. Had we the authority to order a suspension, assess a penalty or impose some other sanction less than a 'death sentence' we should have no hesitancy whatsoever in doing so in this case. In view of the foregoing, we are disposed to afford Don Lee a final chance to demonstrate its ability to comply with the Commission's rules and regulations in the light of the enunciation of their scope and import in this decision. In reaching this conclusion, the Commission has given careful consideration to the affidavit filed by Lewis Allen Weiss on January 6, 1949, in which he undertook to personally guarantee that, in the future, Don Lee would not, in any manner, violate the Commissioner's chain broadcasting regulations.[34]

Had the Commission been empowered to assess penalties (as it is now) at the time this case was decided, it no doubt would have assessed one against the network involved. Now having sanctions less than the "death sentence", the Commission may be able to deal more effectively with willful and repeated violations of network regulations should they occur.

In deciding this Don Lee case, the Commission stated what it considered to be the basic purpose and policy underlying the chain broadcasting regulations of which all broadcasters should be aware and careful to observe:

. . . These regulations were promulgated to insure that the licensees of radio stations who become affiliated with the various networks did not, formally or informally, surrender control of the day-to-day operation of their stations to the networks. Licensee responsibility is an integral part of the statutory scheme for regulating the radio industry under which persons or groups are granted limited renewable franchises to utilize the radio spectrum for broadcasting in the public interest. In granting licenses the Commission considers the operational plans and policies proposed by the licensee; the licensee's ability to carry out his proposals; his ties with the community in which the station is located; and all other facets of the licensee's character and qualifications to own and operate the station and serve the community in which it is located; and all other facets of the licensee's character and qualifications to own and operate the station and serve the community in which the station is located; and all other facets of the licensee's character and qualifications to own and operate the station and serve the community in which it is located. Pursuant to this careful evaluation the Commission seeks to choose those applicants who propose an operation best calculated to serve the public interest and best qualified to carry out the proposed plans. The Communications Act makes the individual licensee responsible for the operation of his station and requires that he maintain control of that operation in order to carry out the proposals made to the Commission. Unless the licensee retains complete control of his station, the Commission has no one whom it can hold responsible for the operation of the station and the Commission's statutory duty to insure that broadcast licensees operate their stations in the public interest would be effectively frustrated.

The network regulations are designed to insure that control of the individual stations is not forfeited to a network organization and with which such stations are affiliated. The networks, as such, are not licensed by the Commission and are under no statutory obligation to serve the public interest. The chain broadcasting regulations, therefore, are designed to govern the conduct of the individual stations rather than the networks. Thus they provide that no license shall be issued to a station which violates any of the regulations. Where, however, a station has been induced to violate one or more of the regulations because of pressure or coercion from a network, it is the network which is primarily responsible for the violations of the regulations. For an individual station does not deal with a network as an equal, particularly when it is a small station. Consequently, when a network, which has induced its affiliated stations to violate the regulations, is also the licensee of various radio stations, serious questions are raised as to the qualifications of that network to continue as a licensee of such broadcasting stations even though since its operation of its own stations does not come within the scope of the chain broadcasting rules, the network's activities do not involve any violations of the rules with respect to its own stations.

The chain broadcasting regulations have clear application not only to prohibited relationships between network and stations which are expressed in formal written agreements, but to prohibited relationships which may be established through tacit understandings or courses of conduct which have the same effect as formal written agreements. The regulations enjoin stations from 'having any contract, arrangement, or understanding, express or implied' which establish the specified prohibited relationships. A tacit understanding imposed by a network upon it affiliates under which the stations affiliated with the network are expected to operate and do in fact generally operate contrary to the provisions of the chain broadcasting regulations is as much a violation of those rules as if the forbidden course of conduct were the result of a formally written contract spelling out the forbidden practices.[35]

Defamation. The common law and state statutes recognize the right of every man to be protected from false and defamatory references. In legal parlance, a defamatory imputation is one which tends to lower a man's reputation among responsible and respectable people, or causes him to be shunned or avoided, or to become the object of contempt, hatred or ridicule. Such a derogatory reference broadcast from a radio or television station may subject the station to an action for damages in a state court.

Traditionally, two types of defamation have been recognized by the courts—slander and libel. Slander involves spoken words, whereas libel consists of written or printed words or pictures. More liability attaches to the latter because of its permanence of form and greater damaging effects.

When are defamatory remarks on radio and television slanderous and when are they libelous? This has been a troublesome and controversial matter. It has been held that a defamatory radio or television broadcast read from a script was libelous in character.[36] In 1956, a New York court sustained a complaint which alleged a libelous statement on television not based upon a prepared script.[37]

In this New York case, the specific question was raised whether a telecast not read from a prepared script constituted libel or slander. The Court said in part:

This precise question has not been passed upon by our appellate courts, not apparently in any other jurisdiction. *Hartmann v. Winchell* (supra) held that the 'utterance of defamatory remarks, *read from a script* into a radio microphone and broadcast constitutes libel' (296 N.Y. at P. 298; italics supplied). It expressly did not reach the question 'whether broadcasting defamatory matter which has not been reduced to writing should be held to be libelous because of the potentially harmful and widespread effects of such defamation' (p. 300).[38]

The New York Court concluded that the defamatory remarks, though not read from a script and though extemporaneous in character, nevertheless constituted libel because of the likelihood of "aggravated injury" inherent in the medium of broadcasting.[39] The *North Carolina Law Review* for April, 1958 reviewed the development of the law on whether televised defamation is libel or slander and concluded that the New York Court was correct.[40]

The weight of opinion in recent years seems to be that all broadcast defamation should be classified as libel on the grounds that the potential for harm should be the important factor and not permanence of form.[41] Some writers, however, have taken the opposing view.[42]

In any case, whether the defamation be classified as slander or libel, all broadcasters must use due care to see that false and derogatory statements do not go out over the air. In a number of early radio cases, the doctrine of absolute liability for defamation as applied to newspapers was followed by the courts.[43] In a 1939 case, however, a Pennsylvania court refused to follow this doctrine. The facts of this case were that NBC had leased its facilities to an advertising agency which in turn had engaged Al Jolson as the featured entertainer on a sponsored program presented over the network. The script of the particular program in question was prepared in advance and was submitted to the network and approved. While the program was in progress, Jolson deviated from the script and made an extemporaneous remark to the effect that the Plaintiff operated a "rotten hotel." The Plaintiff brought an action for defamation and was awarded $15,000 by a jury in the lower court.

On appeal, the judgment was reversed, the higher court holding that "a broadcasting station that leases its time and facilities to another whose agents carry on the program is not liable for an interjected defamatory remark where it appears that it exercised due care in the selection of the lessee, and having inspected and edited the script, had no reason to believe an extemporaneous defamatory remark would be made.[44]

With respect to defamation by radio and television, the laws in the various states vary and courts are not uniform in their construction of the statutes. All licensees, however, should be familiar with the laws as applied in the states where their stations operate. Management should be particularly careful to see that no statements go out over the air which, for example, falsely accuse persons of crimes, impute immoral conduct, suggest the existence of an infectious or loathsome disease, or do harm to a person in his profession or business, etc. Generally, whether broadcast licensees are liable for such statements depends upon whether the statements are true or false, the degree of care exercised by the licensee in connection with any questionable broadcast, and whether the utterances are made by station employees or by outside persons having no official connection with the station.

Political Broadcasting. In Chapter 18, mention was made of Section 315 of the Communications Act relating to the use of broadcast facilities by political candidates. The language in the section which prohibits the station from censoring any material used in such broadcasts has been troublesome. In 1951, the FCC held that the broadcaster has no authority to censor a broadcast by a political candidate, whether on the ground that it contains defamatory matter or for any other reason. The Commission warned that all licensees would thereafter be expected to comply fully with this provision of the law.[45]

Since that time a number of suits have been filed in state courts against broadcast stations charging defamation in political broadcasts and asking damages for alleged injuries. These cases have held that the stations are immune from such damage suits since they are prohibited from censoring the broadcasts of the political candidates.[46] There has been language in some of these cases, however, which indicates that the courts might have allowed damage claims had the facts been different. For example, in a 1955 case decided by the Connecticut Supreme Court of Errors, it was held that the defendant radio station was not liable for damages. The Court said the station was immune under the circumstances but implied the decision might have been otherwise had it been shown that the defendant company "maliciously permitted its facilities to be used, or that it knew that the facts stated were false and yet allowed the broadcast, or otherwise acted in bad faith."[47]

In a 1958 North Dakota case, the Supreme Court in that state pointed out that Section 315 of the Communications Act states "in clear and specific language that where candidates for political office are permitted to use the facilities of a station such 'shall have no power of censorship.' "[48] The Court further said that "since power of censorship of political broadcasts is prohibited it must follow as a corollary that the mandate prohibiting censorship includes the privilege of immunity from liability for defamatory statements made by the speakers.[49] The Court further reasoned that it "could not believe that it was the intent of Congress to compel a station to broadcast libelous statements and at the same time subject it to the risk of defending actions for damages.[50]

There was language in the case, however, which suggested possible exceptions. The Court quoted from an Illinois case in which the U.S. Supreme Court had referred to "narrowly limited classes of speech, the prevention of which have never thought to raise any constitutional problem. These include the lewd and obscene, the profane, and libelous and the insulting or 'fighting' words—those which by their very utterance inflict injury or tend to incite to an immediate breach of the peace. It has been well observed that such utterances are no essential part of any exposition of ideas, and are of such slight social value as a step to truth that any benefit that may be derived from them is clearly outweighed by the social interest in order and morality."[51]

This case was appealed to the U.S. Supreme Court and the decision of the North Dakota Court was affirmed. The Supreme Court held that a broadcasting station may not censor defamatory statements contained in speeches broadcast by legally qualified candidates for public office, and the licensee of the station is immune from any liability for such statements.[52] This decision of the high court laid to rest any question regarding the matter and now provides an unequivocal mandate which all stations may follow.

1. 66 Stat. 716-717. See Section 6 of Communications Act Amendments, 1960, for recent changes in 312(a)

2. *Ibid.*

3. *Ibid.*

4. *Ibid.*

5. 60 Stat. 237 at 242.

6. *Great Western Broadcasting Association v. FCC,* 68 App. D.C. 119, 94 F.(2d) 244 (1937).

7. *Revocation of Station License of Station WSAL,* 8 FCC 34 (1940).

8. *Panama City Broadcasting Company,* 9 FCC 208 (1942). See also *Ocala Broadcasting Company, Inc.,* 9 FCC 223 (1942).

9. *Broadcasting Service Organization, Inc.,* 11 FCC 1057, 3 RR 979 (1947).

10. *Big State Broadcasting Corporation,* 8 RR 161 (1953).

11. *Balboa Radio Corporation,* 6 RR 649 (1953).

12. 329 U.S. 223.

13. *Ibid.,* p. 227.

14. *Ibid.*

15. *Ibid.,* pp. 228-229.

16. 2 FCC 208 (1935).

17. *Station KWIK,* 6 RR 567 (1950); also see *Station WXLT,* 6 RR 378 (1950); *Station KXXL,* 5 RR 1206 (1950).

18. Also see *Joseph C. Calloway,* 5 FCC 345 (1938); *J. L. Robinson,* 5 FCC 623 (1938); *John R. Frazier,* 5 FCC 649 (1938); *East Texas Broadcasting Co.,* 8 FCC 479 (1941); *ABC-Paramount Merger Case,* 8 RR 541 (1953).

19. *St. Joseph Valley Broadcasting Corp.,* 8 RR 766 (1953).

20. *News Publishing Co.,* 13 RR 1061 (1956).

21. *WOAX, Inc.,* 12 FCC 960; 4 RR 344 (1948).

22. *In the Matter of Promulgation of Special Rules Relating to Contracts Providing for Reservation of Time upon Sale of Station,* Docket No 8774, 14 Fed. Reg. 179 (1949).

23. Section 73.241, 1 RR 53:1017.

24. *Master Broadcasting Corp.,* 6 RR 621 (1950).

25. 48 Stat. 1100.

26. *Ibid.,* 1043.

27. 48 Stat. 1100-1101.

28. *Brohy v. FRC,* 61 App. D.C. 204, 59 F. (2d) 879 (1932).

29. *United States Broadcasting Corporation,* 2 FCC 208 (1935).

30. See *Greater Kampeska Radio Corp.,* 5 FCC 514 (1938); affirmed 71 App. D.C. 117, 108 F. (2d) 5 (1939); *Charles C. Carlson,* 12 FCC 902; 3 RR 1887 (1948); *Radio Station WPBP,* 4 RR 1087 (1948).

31. *Radio Station WINZ,* 5 RR 715 (1949).

32. *Inter-American Radio Corporation* 7 RR 676 (1951).

33. *Don Lee Broadcasting System,* 14 FCC 993, 5 RR 1179 (1950).

34. *Ibid.,* pp. 1010-1011.

35. *Ibid.*

36. *Hartman v. Winchell,* 296 NY 298, 73 N.E. (2d) 30; Also *Gearhart v. WSAZ, Inc.,* U.S. District Court, E.D. Ky., March 9, 1957, 150 F. Supp. 98.

37. *Shor v. Billingsley, et al,* New York Supreme Court, New York County, November 28, 1956, 158 NY 5 (2d) 476, 14 RR 2053.

38. *Ibid.,* 14 RR 2054.

39. *Ibid.,* 2054-2056.

40. 36 *N.C.L. Rev.* 355 (April, 1958); also see the *University of Kansas City Law Review,* 26 *U.K.C.L. Rev.* 69 (December, 1957).

41. 37 *B.L.L. Rev.* 378 (1957); 32 *Tulane L. Rev.* 136 (December 1957); 71 *Harv. L. Rev.* 384 (December 1957); 43 *Corn. L. Q.* 320.

42. See 31 *St. John's Law Review* 314 (May, 1957).

43. *Sorenson v. Wood,* 123 Neb. 348, 243 N.W. 82 (1932), appeal dismissed *sub. nom; KFAB Broadcasting Co. v. Sorenson,* 290 U.S. 599 (1933); *Coffee v. Midland Broadcasting Co.,* 8 F. Supp. 889 (W.D. Mo., 1934); *Knickerbocker Broadcasting Co.,* 179 Misc. 787, 38 N.Y.S. (2d) 985 (1942).

44. *Summit Hotel Co. v. National Broadcasting Co.,* 336 Pa. 182 (1939).

45. *WDSU Broadcasting Corporation,* 7 RR 766 (1951).

46. *Farmers Educational and Cooperative Union of America,* North Dakota Supreme Court, April 3, 1958, 17 RR 2001; also, *Lamb v. Sutton, et. al.,* U.S. District Court, M.D. Tenn., July 29, 1958, Civil Actions No. 1925, 1936, 17 RR 2099.

47. *Charles Parker Company v. Silver City Crystal Co.,* Conn. Supreme Court of Errors, August 1, 1955, 12 RR 2057 at 2062. In *Dansell v. Voice of New Hampshire, Inc.,* New Hampshire Supreme Court, Merrimack County, April 29, 1954, Equity No. 123, 10 RR 2045, the Court actually held that Section 315 of the Communications Act did not prohibit the censorship of libelous material in a political broadcast or protect the station against liability for libel or slander. The Court said only the censorship of words as to their political and partisan trend is prohibited by Section 315.

48. *Farmers Educational and Cooperative Union of America,* North Dakota Division v. WDAY, Inc., N.D. Sup. Ct., 17 RR 2007.

49. *Ibid.,* p. 2008.

50. *Ibid.,* p. 2007.

51. *Beaubarnais v. Illinois,* 343 U.S. 250, 96 L. Ed. 919, 72 S. Ct. 725.

52. 18 RR 2135 (June 29, 1959).

CHAPTER 22

Copyright and Other Legal Restrictions on Broadcast Use of Program Materials

The notion of property starts, I suppose, from confirmed possession of a tangible object and consists in the right to exclude others from interference with the more or less free doing with it as one wills. But in copyright, property has reached a more abstract expression. . . . The grant of this extraordinary right is that the person to whom it is given has invented some new collocation of visible or audible points—of lines, colors, sounds or words. The restraint is directed against reproducing this collocation, although but for the invention and the statute any one would be free to combine the contents of the dictionary, the elements of the spectrum, or the notes of the gamut in any way that he had the wit to devise. . . . —JUSTICE HOLMES

The creative works of others may not be used by radio and television stations except with the permission of the owners and under the conditions which they prescribe. Even though these works have not been copyrighted, they are protected prior to duplication for sale by common law as interpreted and applied in the several states.

Once these original materials are placed on the market for general sale, statutory copyright must be relied on for protection against their unauthorized use.

Dramatic and Dramatico-Musical Materials. Section 1 (d) of the U.S. Copyright Code confers the following exclusive rights regarding the performance of dramatic works:

To perform or represent the copyrighted work publicly if it be a drama or, if it be a dramatic work and not reproduced in copies for sale, to vend any manuscript or any record whatsoever thereof; to make or to procure the making of any transcription or record thereof by or from which, in whole or in part, it may in any manner or by any method be exhibited, performed, represented, produced, or reproduced; and to exhibit, perform, represent, produce, or reproduce it in any manner or by any method whatsoever.[1]

The courts have definitely established that these performance rights apply to operas, operettas, musical comedies, or other dramatic-musical works as well as ordinary dramas and stage plays. Any radio or television adaptions of these various dramatic forms are subject to the same exclusive rights.

It has also been clearly established that motion picture and kinescopic photoplays fall within this category and the exhibition of them on television without license would infringe Section 1 (d) quoted above.

There is some question as to whether the provisions of this section are applicable to the exhibition of what may be termed non-dramatic motion pictures and kinescopes. However, some authorities believe that the courts will lean in that direction and hold the unauthorized exhibition of such materials as illegal.[2]

It is the "public performance" of the above types of material which is prohibited without the permission of the owners. The courts have held that radio and television broadcasts are "public performances" within the meaning of the statute.[3] All broadcast stations, therefore, whether they be commercial or noncommercial, must secure clearances from the copyright owners before putting such materials on the air.

Music Materials. In the case of dramatic works as described above, unauthorized "public performace" is enough to infringe the Copyright Code. In the case of musical compositions and mechanical recordings, not dramatic in character, there is the added requirement that they be publicly performed "for profit." All commercial stations operating for profit must secure clearances for such musical compositions and recordings. It has been held that the unlicensed broadcast of a copyrighted musical composition by means of a phonograph recording on a sustaining program of a non-profit radio station, which devoted a third of its time to advertising programs and used the revenue to defray operating costs, was a "performance for profit" within the meaning of the Copyright Act, entitling the copyright owner to an injunction and damages.

The facts of this case were that Debs Memorial Fund, Inc. owned and operated Station WEVD in Brooklyn, New York, and was organized as a business corporation under Article 2 of the Stock Corporation Law of New York. The Fund had by-laws providing for non profit sharing operation, with all profits and surplus being used for the enlargement of the station's facilities and for improving the educational and cultural activities thereof. The Court stated that the basic purpose of the Fund was philanthropic and educational.

The Court held that "it can make no difference that the ultimate purposes of the corporate defendant were charitable or educational. Both in the advertising and sustaining programs, Debs was engaged in an enterprise which resulted in profit to the advertisers and to an increment to its own treasury whereby it might repay its indebtedness and avoid an annual deficit." The reasoning of the Court seemed to be that by providing a musical

371

program such as the one in question, the station increased its number of listeners and made it more desirable as a station for paid advertising.[4]

The question arises whether the same rule applies to educational radio and television stations which operate on a strictly non-profit and non-commercial basis. The answer appears to be no. There is an important difference between these stations and the Debs one in that they are prohibited from carrying any advertising at all. Also, the FCC rules definitely preclude any type of commercial or profit-making operation on the part of educational stations using reserved channels. Therefore, it appears that they are not required to get permission to use copyrighted music or recordings thereof from the owners.

The American Society of Composers, Authors, and Publishers. Radio and television stations generally draw upon the resources of the American Society of Composers, Authors, and Publishers for recorded music. This society has a large repertoire of copyrighted music which is available for use by stations under contractual arrangements and on payment of an annual license fee.

The following definition of "users of music" appears in the current Articles of Association of the Society:

'User' means any person, firm or corporation who or which
1. owns or operates an establishment or enterprise where copyrighted musical compositions are performed publicly for profit, or
2. is otherwise directly engaged in giving public performance of copyrighted musical compositions for profit.

In 1946, ASCAP attempted to enlarge its licensing activities to include educational institutions. Several schools in the East reluctantly entered into contracts with the Society paying annual fees for the use of music in the Society's repertoire. But some educational organizations strenuously objected and refused to accede to a demand for payment of a license fee.[5] Negotiations resulted in ASCAP arrangements favorable to the educators.

The term "user" as presently defined by the society includes all commercial broadcast stations, but would not appear to include non-commercial stations operated by non-profit institutions. The standard practice for educational stations is to secure ASCAP licenses for nominal fees with freedom to use all the music in the ASCAP repertoire so long as no public performance for profit is involved.

What has just been said must be qualified. The ASCAP contracts state that members are assigned the public performance rights "of the separate numbers, songs, fragments or arrangements, melodies or selections forming part or parts of musical plays and dramatico-musical compositions, but that the owner reserves and excepts from the assignment the right of performance of musical plays and dramatico-musical compositions in their entirety, or any part of such plays or dramatico-musical compositions on the legitimate stage."[6]

What this means is that the ASCAP license gives the broadcast station the right to use the separate songs and parts of musical plays, operas, operettas, oratorios, and the like, but not the right to use these dramatico-musical compositions in their entirety or any parts of them if they are picked up and tramsmitted from the "legitimate stage."

The rights for the performance of these dramatico-musical works in their entirety or parts thereof on the legitimate stage are spoken of as "grand rights." They are not assigned to ASCAP but are retained by the copyright proprietor, and no public presentation of the works in their totality or parts on the legitimate stage, either on a profit or non-profit basis, can be made without his consent. Securing such consent in each individual case is a matter of negotiation between station management and the copyright owner.

It should be mentioned that music may not be integrated on the sound track of motion picture film or kinescope and used by broadcast stations without the consent of the copyright holder.

Broadcast Music, Inc. BMI, the competing organization of ASCAP, charges license fees in terms of station rate cards. An important difference between the BMI and ASCAP contracts is that with the former the broadcaster obtains both "grand" and "small" rights in all musical compositions in the BMI repertoire for both radio and television.

Since educational broadcast stations do not sell time and have no rate cards, they are able to negotiate contracts with BMI for performance rights without charge except for the payment of a nominal annual fee the same as assessed by ASCAP.

Performing and Recording Rights to Literary Works. On July 17, 1952, Congress amended Title 17 of the U.S. Copyright Code to extend to authors the performing and recording rights in non-dramatic literary works, the law becoming effective January 1, 1953. The amendment gives to such authors exclusive rights as follows:

(c) To deliver, authorize the delivery of, read, or present the copyrighted work in public for profit if it be a lecture, sermon, address or similar production, or other nondramatic literary work; to make, procure the making of any transcription or record thereof by or from which, in whole or in part, it may in any manner or by any method be exhibited, delivered, presented, produced, or reproduced; and to play or perform it in public for profit, and to exhibit, represent, produce, or reproduce it in any manner or by any method whatsoever. . . . [7]

Under the law prior to this amendment, the writers of poems, short stories, magazine articles or novels were imperfectly protected against the unauthorized performance of their works. It was pointed out to Congress that if poems, short stories, magazine articles or novels were published in book form first, the copyright statute gave no performance protection. Congress responded with proposed legislation designed to remedy this situation.

The legislation as originally introduced would have granted copyright protection even if a performance were "non-profit" in character.[8] The effects of such legislation would have barred a teacher from reading excerpts from a copyrighted book in the classroom, a minister from reading such materials in the pulpit, or a speaker from doing the same at a civic meeting. When these effects were pointed out, the bill was changed to limit the copyright protection to *performances for profit* only.[9] As the law reads, therefore, it is not a violation of the copyright law for a broadcasting station operating noncommercially to use copyrighted material, whether in the form of poems, short stories, magazine articles or similar publications. This rule applies to live shows produced by a non-commercial educational station or to the use of transcriptions of this material.

While there is some difference of opinion among authorities, this amendment appears to provide that no person may make a transcription or recording of a copyrighted work without payment of royalties. This applies whether or not the purpose of making the recording is "non-profit" or not. Recordings can be made *only* when the permission of the copyright owner has been obtained. Accordingly, neither a commercial or noncommercial station may make a transcription of a literary work without prior clearance from the author, nor may it copy a record or a transcription which it has received without securing appropriate clearances.

Kinds of Materials Which May be Copyrighted.   The following types of materials may be copyrighted and all commercial radio and TV stations should make sure they have been cleared before using them in broadcasts. [10]

(a)   Books, including composite and cyclopedic works, directories, gazetteers, and other compilations.

(b)   Periodicals, including newspapers.

(c)   Lectures, sermons, addresses prepared for oral delivery.

(d)   Dramatic or dramatico-musical compositions.

(e)   Musical compositions, including words and music.

(f)   Maps and charts.

(g)   Works of art; models or designs for works of art.

(h)   Reproductions of works of art.

(i)   Drawings or plastic works of a scientific or technical character.

(j)   Photographs.

(k)   Prints and pictorial illustrations including prints or labels used for articles of merchandise.

(l)   Motion picture photoplays.

(m)   Motion pictures other than photoplays.

(n)   Scripts.

With the exceptions previously pointed out, educational stations operating strictly on a non-profit basis may use copyrighted materials without securing clearance.*

The Doctrine of Fair Use. The limited use of published copyrighted materials for purposes of review and criticism is permissable. Where brief references or quotations from such works are used on educational broadcasts, no problem is involved. Whether there is fair use depends on the nature and purpose of the quotations, the quantity quoted and the extent to which the material might prejudice the use or sale of the original work. Obviously the presentation of a full-length copyrighted play or dramatico-musical in a telecourse on dramatic literature or music appreciation would not be fair use. However, a few short quotations or characterizations used for illustrative purposes would constitute fair use.

No clearly defined rules with respect to fair use can be stated. In *Shapiro, Bernstein and Company, Inc. v. Collier and Son,* the Court stated some general principles that are helpful: "The extent and relative value of the extracts; the purpose and whether the quoted portions might be used as a substitute for the original work; the effect upon the distribution and objects of the original work."[11]

Protection of Program Ideas. The Courts have held that radio and television ideas which have been reduced to tangible and concrete form and possessing the attributes of novelty and originality are considered protectable interests. Both common law and statutory copyright law afford protection. Should an unauthorized use of a concrete original idea be attempted, the offender may be liable for legal damages and may be enjoined in a court of equity from further use of the program idea or format.[12]

In order for the creator of the program to avail himself of judicial protection he should, at once, reduce to writing the concrete facts regarding the basic ideas and format of the program. This statement should contain the name of the creator of the program, the date of its origination, descriptive facts regarding its format indicating its originality and novelty. The statement should include assertions by the creator that the program idea is the result of independent and creative effort on his part, that he claims a prop-

*For several years, Congress has had under consideration revision of the copyright laws. These proposals, if adopted, may impose greater restrictions on the use of copyrighted materials for educational broadcasting and instructional closed circuit systems. Also, despite the Supreme Court decision in June, 1968 (392 U.S. 398-401) holding that CATV systems are not required to pay royalty payments, a Senate bill is pending which may result in legislation requiring cable operators to pay royalty fees. At this point, there are differences of opinion among leaders in Congress, and what the outcome will be is not sure. Students interested in proposals to overhaul the copyright laws should read the following: S.543. 91st Congress. 1st Sess., January 10, 1969, a bill for the general revision of the copyright law, title 17 of the United States Code, and for other purposes: S. 543 (Committee Print), December 10, 1969; "The Wired Nation," Ralph Lee Smith, *The Nation,* May 18, 1970, 582-606; "Cable TV Legislation," Frederick W. Ford, former President, National Cable TV Association, *Television Digest,* June 15, 1970, Vol. 10:24; "Board Memo on Legislation," Frederick W. Ford, National Cable TV Association, April 19, 1969.

erty interest therein and that it is not to be used without his permission. The statement should be dated and retained in his files for future reference and use.

If the program idea or any scripts, films, or kinescopes pertaining thereto are permitted to be used by others, it should be made perfectly clear in writing that no property rights therein are being given up; and that, under no circumstances, can any use be made without the written consent of the proprietor. Nothing should be done which may be construed as making the program idea available for general use.

Unfair Competition. In an early case, *International News Service v. Associated Press,* 248 U.S. 215 (1918), the Supreme Court extended the doctrine of unfair competition to cover misappropriation of another's goods —"to misappropriation of what equitably belongs to a competitor."

The facts of this case were that the Plaintiff and Defendant were rival news gathering agencies. The International News Service copied news items from the bulletin boards and early editions of the Associated Press and telegraphed these items to its subscribers on the West Coast.

The Court held that while Associated Press could assert no property right in news as against the general public, as against a competitor, there was a kind of quasi-property right. The Court said that AP had acquired these rights in its news:

> . . . as the result of organization and the expenditure of labor, skill, and money and which is salable by complainant for money, and that defendant in appropriating it and selling it as his own is endeavoring to reap where it has not sown . . . Stripped of all disguises, the process amounts to an unauthorized interference with the normal operation of complainant's legitimate business precisely at the point where the profit is to be reaped, in order to divert a material portion of the profit from those who have earned it to those who have not; with special advantage to defendant in the competition because of the fact that it is not burdened with any part of the expense of gathering the news. The transaction speaks for itself, and a court of equity ought not to hesitate long in characterizing it as unfair competition in business.[13]

The doctrine of this case has been extended to enjoin a broadcasting station from pirating news from a newspaper. The Associated Press brought an injunction against KVOS, a radio station in Bellingham, Washington, claiming that the station was engaged in unfair competition when it broadcast the news contained in member papers before the papers could be distributed to their subscribers. The U.S. Circuit Court of Appeals for the Ninth Circuit sustained the injunction.[14] Also, stations have invoked this doctrine against competing stations who have appropriated to their use without permission the content of sports programs.[15]

While the law of unfair competition has and may be invoked by broadcast stations, Harry Warner has observed that "the public policy which abhors monopolies aided by the pragmatic experience of the courts precludes the wholesale substitution of common law and statutory copyright by the law of unfair competition. It is submitted that the law of unfair competition should be invoked to protect intellectual property when the latter is outside the protective scope of common law and statutory copyright. Thus unfair competition complements statutory copyright; it cannot and should not be employed where the copyright law provides a remedy."[16]

Right of Privacy. The right of privacy may be defined as the right of every person to "be left alone", to demand that his private affairs shall not be exhibited to the public without his consent. It assures him private existence and protection from public gaze.[17]

This right of privacy has been given wide legal recognition by courts. In New York it has been sanctioned by statute in relation to advertising. The New York law reads:

Section 50, Article 3 of the Civil Rights Law.—Right of Privacy.—a person, firm, or corporation that uses for advertising purposes, or for the purpose of trade, the name, portrait, or picture of any living person without having first obtained the written consent of such person, or if a minor, of his or her parent or guardian, is guilty of a misdemeanor.

Broadcasting stations are under obligation to respect an individual's right of privacy. Under certain conditions, however, an individual may lose this right for example, by becoming a public figure, or becoming a part of a news event, or by being involved in court proceedings or other official matters of public interest.

Dr. Frederick S. Siebert has provided a succinct statement on this subject with respect to television which is helpful and informative:[18]

Television stations, both commercial and noncommercial, are facing an entirely new set of problems in the area of privacy because of the visual presentation.

All types of stations undoubtedly have the right to broadcast pictorial material about news events and persons in the news. This right, however, does not guarantee to the station the privilege of access with cameras and recording equipment to all types of news events. News events occurring in public places may be reported both by camera and recorder. Public places include streets, parks, and other sites to which every member of the public has access without payment or restriction.

Most news occurrences, however, take place in what might be called semiprivate places, such as government buildings, sports arenas, or controlled-admission halls. Television stations may report events occurring in such sites only with the permission of the authority controlling admission to the site.

The right of the individual to protest televising his person depends on whether or not he is currently newsworthy and on whether or not the cameraman has legal access to the site. For example, an educational station may not televise the picture of a person without his consent unless he is in the news. The station, however, if

377

given permission to televise a football game, does not have to get permission from each individual player or from each member of the audience who might appear on the screen.

The Right of Privacy and the Courts. The doctrine of right of privacy is a relatively new legal concept. As already mentioned, courts generally recognize the principle, but there are often differences of opinion among judges as to when the individual's privacy ends and the public's right to know begins. For example, there is considerable controversy as to what extent radio and television shall have access to trials. Some courts take the position that the mass media have no constitutional right to require trial participants to submit to photography or sound recordings. They hold it is an invasion of the right of privacy. Also, they object on the grounds that it is an interference with court procedure that may prevent the defendant from getting a fair trial.[19] While the American Bar Association has had the matter under study, its Special Committee on Canons of Ethics has recently recommended only minor changes in the language of Canon 35 "without in any way qualifying its adamantine prohibition against photographing, broadcasting, or televising of courtroom proceedings other than ceremonial proceedings such as the formal portions of naturalization proceedings."[20]

On the other hand, some courts are moving in the direction of loosening the restrictions against electronic journalism. Their position is that the defendant gives up his right of privacy when he becomes involved in a public trial and, in recognition of the public's right to be informed, broadcast media should have access to the courtroom.[21]

As Dr. Siebert has pointed out, the two basic questions a radio or television station must consider in connection with individual privacy, are (1) whether the person subjected to broadcast exposure is a part of a situation or event which is clearly newsworthy, and (2) whether the photographer or recorder has legal access to the site. Also, since broadcast media have a special obligation to serve community needs, the question must always be considered, whether the public's right to know does not take precedence over the individual's desire to be free of public gaze.

1. 61 Stat. 652 (1947).

2. See Warner, Harry P., *Radio and Television Law* (New York, 1953), p. 315, for discussion of this point; also see 66 Stat. 753 (1952), which may be invoked to protect motion pictures other than photoplays.

3. *Select Theaters Corporation v. Ronzoni Marcaroni Co.*, 59 U.S.P.Q. 288 (DC NY 1943); *Associated Music Publishers v. Debs Memorial Radio Fund*, 46F Supp. 829 (DC NY 1942), affirmed, 141 F(2d) 852 (2d cir. 1944) *cert.* denied 323 U.S. 766.

4. *Ibid.*

5. See Warner, *op. cit.*, pp. 403-404.

6. ASCAP agreement with members executed in 1941 and expiring in 1965. See Warner, *op. cit.*, for full discussion of these ASCAP contracts.

7. 66 Stat. 752.

8. HR 3589, 82nd Congress, 1st Session, introduced April 6, 1951.

9. HR 1160, 82nd Congress, 1st Session (1951), accompanied HR 3589.

10. See Warner, *op. cit.*, Chapter III, "The Subject Matter of Copyright Protection", pp. 40-91, for detailed and authoritative discussion re materials which must be cleared before used on radio or television stations.

11. *New York Tribune, Inc. v. Otis and Company*, 39 F. Supp. 67 (DC NY 1941).

12. *Stanley v. Columbia Broadcasting System*, 35 Cal. (2d) 653, 221 P. (2d) 73 (1950); *Cole v. Phillips H. Lord, Inc.*, 262 App. Div. 116, 28 NYS (2d) 404, (1941); 16 *University of Chicago Law Review* 323 (1949).

13. 39 Sup. Ct. Reporter, 72-73.

14. *Associated Press v. KVOS*, Fed. Supp. 279 (1934); also see 80 F (2) 575 (1935).

15. *Pittsburgh Athletic Co. v KQV Broadcasting Co.*, 24 F. Supp. 490 (WD Pa. 1938); Also, *Mutual Broadcasting System, Inc. v. Muzak Corp.*, 177 Misc. 489, 30 NYS (2d) 419 (Sup. Ct. 1941); and *Southwestern Broadcasting Co. et al, v. Oil Center Broadcasting Co.*, 210 SW (2d) 230 (Texas Civ. App. 1947).

16. Warner, *op. cit.*, p. 931.

17. 4 *Harvard Law Review* 193, 195; *Melvin V. Reid* 112 Cal. App. 285, 297 Pac. 91 (1931).

18. Siebert, Frederick S., "Clearance, Rights and Legal Problems of Educational Radio and Television Stations". National Association of Educational Broadcasters (1955).

19. See *Atlanta Newspapers, Inc., et. al. v. Grimes et al.*, Georgia Superior Court, April 14, 1959; also see 43 A. B. A. J. 419 (May, 1957); *Tribune Review Publishing Co. v. Thomas*, 153 F. Supp. 486 (W.D. Pa., 1957); and 330 P. (2d) 734 (Okla. Crim. App. 1958).

20. 16 FCC B. J. No. 1, 66.

21. See "The Right to Report by Television," by Fred S. Siebert, 34 *Journalism Quarterly* 333 (Summer, 1957); also in same issue, "Equality of Access for Radio in Covering Washington News," by Theodore F. Koop of CBS, p. 338; and "Electronic Journalism in the Colorado Courts," by Hugh B. Terry of KLZ. Denver, p. 341.

PART VI

A Look to the Future

CHAPTER 23

Overcoming Barriers to Effective Broadcast Regulation

... The mountain of work of the Commission never shows any signs of letting up. We are on a tyrannical treadmill of en banc *meetings, executive sessions, oral arguments and —interspersed with trips up to Capitol Hill. And apparently there are more trips to the Hill to be added to our treadmill.* —WAYNE COY*

In the first edition of this book, the writer made reference to a long and comprehensive study of FCC made by a Legislative Oversight Subcommittee of the House Committee on Interstate and Foreign Commerce.[1] Though the report of that study received comparatively little publicity at the time it was issued, certain recommendations it made later were adopted by Congress and the FCC which made possible more effective regulation.

One proposal of the Subcommittee urged Congress to amend Section 5 (c) of the Communications Act to provide wider latitude for consultation by the Commission with members of its staff in the preparation of decisions. In support of this proposal, it was said:

This so-called 'separation of functions' required by the Communications Act precludes both commissioners and hearing examiners from the use of Commission personnel for advice and consultation when problems arise. Yet, the Commission is expected to perform the function of providing the final decision in each case, based on a massive body of evidence, summaries of evidence provided by the 'review staff,' with whom they are equally unable to consult, and upon whatever further information in the way of proposed findings and conclusions, exception, and supporting reasons they receive from the pleadings of the interested parties.

As a result of this situation, the Commission is provided with a staff of experts, with whom it cannot consult without reopening the record, allowing the interested parties to be present, giving opportunity for reply, and needlessly adding to the size and volume of testimony which, in all probability, in the more difficult cases, already extends to thousands of pages. The judicial imputation of expertise to Commission decisions under these circumstances is in effect a legal fiction.[2]

*Former chairman of the FCC; now deceased.

As the law then stood, the Commission was precluded from consulting with the General Counsel, Chief Engineer, Chief Accountants and their staffs to secure information and advice in preparation of decisions. This restriction seriously handicapped the Commission in disposing of the large volume of cases that had to be decided. Both quantity and quality of output were affected.

As this writer stated in 1961, there seemed to be no valid reason why members of the Commission should not be free to call upon appropriate members of the staff for help and advice, so long as those staff members had not been engaged, directly or indirectly, in the prosecution or investigation of a case.[3]

In 1961, Congress amended the Communications Act to remedy the situation. The provisions of Section 409c(2) of the law, the effect of which had been to cut off the Commission from consultation with its principal legal, engineering and accounting officers, were eliminated.[4] Likewise, the prohibition against one examiner discussing a case for which he was responsible with another examiner or other staff member who was in no way involved in the case was abolished.[5] The bar against any person involved in the preparation or presentation of a case for hearing or review thereof, from making any additional presentation to an examiner or the Commission was quite properly retained.[6]

Furthermore, in the interest of giving the Commission greater access to the staff for consultation, in 1961, Congress repealed Section 5(c) of the Communications Act.[7] This section had prevented the Commission from seeking the advice and counsel of personnel in the so-called Review Section of the Commission. The law previously provided that the function of these experts was to prepare for the Commission summaries of evidence presented in adjudicatory hearings, and, prior to oral argument, compile facts relevant to exceptions and replies thereto filed by the parties in the proceedings. The review staff, however, was not permitted to make any recommendations for action and could prepare memoranda, decisions and orders only in accordance with specific directions of the Commission. Except for personnel in the Commissioners' offices, the law further prohibited any employee not a member of the review staff from performing any of the functions of the review staff.

As pointed out by the House Report on the 1961 Communications Amendments, the restrictive provisions in the law resulted in waste and inefficiency, because they had the effect "of depriving the Commission of the full assistance which the personnel of the review staff was capable of furnishing.[8]

It seems clear that the repeal of Section 5(c) and the amendment of Section 409(c) have had a beneficial effect. It has speeded up the handling of some adjudicatory cases and has made available to the Commission and the examiners important sources of information, advice and expertise which have been helpful in decision making. At the same time, legal safeguards against *ex parte* communications have been retained to protect the judicial process and comply with the Administrative Procedure Act.

Responsibility of Commissioners for Preparing Opinions. Another suggestion of the Legislative Oversight Committee which has now been effectuated was that one Commissioner should take responsibility for preparing the opinion in each adjudicatory case, with the rotation principle followed to distribute equally the work load among the Commissioners. In all Federal court cases, one judge prepares and delivers the opinion of the Court. The Committee suggested that this practice might very well be followed in those cases where Commissioners are acting in a judicial capacity.

As this writer pointed out in the first edition of this volume, for a number of reasons this proposal seemed to have merit:

The involvement of an individual Commissioner in the actual writing and signing of an opinion, permitting him to draw freely upon staff resources for information and advice, would definitely place responsibility at the Commission level. This might do much to restore public confidence in the agency, which, to some extent, has suffered because of a widespread belief that the staff and not the Commission itself plays the major role in deciding cases. Such personal involvement would stimulate the critical faculties of the Commissioner, give him a better knowledge of the facts and a deeper understanding of the issues in the case. This no doubt would contribute to the quality and soundness of opinions and make for greater consistency in Commission decisions.[9]

In line with the Subcommittee's proposal, the Commission in recent years has followed the practice of having an individual Commissioner supervise the preparation of majority opinions and in many cases his name appears on the title page.

Previously, with the Commissioners being insulated to a large extent from staff personnel and with so many matters coming to the Commission for decision, it was virtually impossible for them to participate actively in the writing of opinions. But with the establishment of the Review Board and its assuming responsibility for handling interlocutory and other matters, and with the repeal of Section 5(c) of the Act giving Commissioners wider latitude for staff consultation, the problem of the Commissioners having time to participate in the preparing of decisions has been greatly alleviated.

Service Fees for Broadcasters. The Legislative Oversight Committee made another important proposal which the Commission has now put into effect. The Committee proposed that thought be given to the establishment of a fee system, charging broadcasters for special services and privileges they receive from the government. In 1963, the Commission adopted such a system. The history leading up to this action was a long and tortuous one.

As early as 1929, the old Federal Radio Commission received a Congressional slap on the wrist for not working out a system of service fees to be charged applicants for broadcasting facilities. In response, the Chairman of the FRC transmitted to the Senate such a proposal.[10] Congressional interest, however, flagged and the proposal was kept in cold storage for three years.

In 1932, Senator Dill recommended an amendment to the Radio Act which would impose nominal charges upon applicants for broadcast facilities and defray most of the operational costs of the FRC.[11] In support of this amendment he had said in a special report to the Senate that he thought the proposed fees were entirely just, "because without governmental regulation the interference between radio stations would amount to chaos so far as radio reception is concerned." He further explained that the radio stations charged for the use of their facilities and could "well afford to help pay the cost of regulation." [12]

Nothing happened legislatively, but after the FCC was established, there was a resurgence of this type of advocacy in Congress. With the expansion of radio and with mounting profits in the industry, the halls of Congress reverberated more frequently with oratory alleging excessive profiteering and exploitation of publicly owned radio channels and urging that commercial interests be required to pay something for these valuable franchises and to help defray the costs of governmental regulation.[13]

FCC Rebuked by Congress. Rebuked for not bringing to Congress a proposal, the FCC began a comprehensive study of the matter.[19] While this was going on, the House in 1941 approved a bill which would have imposed taxes ranging from 5 to 15 percent on net annual sales of radio time above $100,000.[14]

But the Senate Finance Committee under powerful pressure from the broadcasting industry, refused to go along with the House bill or the FCC proposal and again no legislation was passed.[15]

The following year, Congressman Wigglesworth rebuked the FCC for not recommending a tax plan in lieu of that which had been repudiated by the Committee the year before. He referred to the $30,000,000 net profits then accruing to the broadcast industry on an investment of only $40,000,000. "It seems to me entirely illogical and unreasonable," he complained, "to allow the industry to continue to obtain any such return from licenses for which they pay nothing under present conditions in this country."[16]

As the broadcasting industry expanded after the War, Congressional grumbling against free use and commercial exploitation of publicly owned radio channels continued. In March, 1950, again responding to the persistent needling of Congress and at the specific request of the Senate Committee on Expenditures in the Executive Departments, the FCC submitted a report classifying its activities for which service fees might be assessed. These included processing all broadcast applications; all authorizations for telephone and telegraph services under FCC jurisdiction; equipment tests, station inspections, and miscellaneous filings such as petitions, motions, etc.[17]

Two years later, in a House debate on whether to cut the FCC's annual budget by $2,000,000, Congressman O'Konski from Wisconsin stated that he knew something about the FCC because he happened to be in the radio industry. "There is no reason under the sun," said he, "why the Federal Communications Commission should cost the taxpayers of this country one cent. . . .For as profitable a business as the radio and television business, it is incredible that they get their licenses for free."

"I know of one television station," he continued, "that was built at a total construction cost of $150,000, and a few weeks after they passed the requirements they sold that station for a million and a quarter dollars. They paid not one red penny for that license. . . .Let us give the Federal Communications Commission the money they need to let this industry expand and grow. But at the same time let us make the radio and television industry foot the bill.[18]

Less than seven months before, Congress had passed the Independent Offices Appropriation Act of 1952 authorizing the head of each governmental agency to prescribe by regulation such fees and charges as he determined to be fair and equitable "taking into consideration direct and indirect costs to the government, value to the recipient, public policy or interest served, and other pertinent facts.[19]

Persistent Congressional Pressure Brings FCC Action. With this enabling legislation applicable to administrative agencies in general, plus the persistent urging by Congressmen for twenty years that broadcasters and other communication companies operating across state lines should bear the cost of their regulation, the FCC at last felt there was a clear directive from Capitol Hill to take positive action. Accordingly, the Commission issued a notice of proposed rule-making, published in the *Federal Register* on February 3, 1954.[20]

This notice proposed to divide all applications for broadcast authorizations into two main categories. In one, a fee of $325 was to be charged for each broadcast application involving major analysis and action. In the other, a fee of $50.00 was proposed for applications requiring less time and effort to process, such as those involving minor changes in broadcasting equipment.

A schedule of smaller charges was proposed for handling applications for various types of radio stations used by ships, airplanes, land transportation, amateurs, etc. Fees also were included for applications from manufacturers asking for type approval of various kinds of broadcasting equipment and for inspections of radio stations on ships at sea.

In addition, a schedule of charges was set forth for applications from telephone and telegraph companies regulated by the FCC, involving acquisition, construction or extension of facilities, ranging from 30 to 350 dollars.

Congressional Reaction. And now what was the reaction of Congress? Were there speeches commending the Commission for finally doing what it so often had been scolded for not doing? No such eloquence emanated from Capitol Hill. On the contrary, a week before the deadline for filing comments in the proceeding, the Senate Interstate and Foreign Commerce Committee, which exercises legislative jurisdiction over the FCC, unanimously passed a resolution and transmitted it to the Chairman of the Commission, saying that it had concluded, after inquiry, that any departure from the existing structure of licensing should be resolved specifically by the Congress itself and that the FCC should suspend the proceeding. [21]

This struck the fatal blow. Dispite the enabling legislation passed only three years before and the intermittent agitations of Congress for service fees for almost three decades, the Commission simply could not buck the unanimous opposition of this powerful Senate committee. The case was dismissed and the piles of official papers accumulated by the FCC in the proceeding were consigned to the docket graveyard.[22]

Eight years went by before the Commission made another attempt to charge service fees. On August 3, 1961, the Chairman of the House Interstate and Foreign Commerce Committee agreed that under Title V of the Independent Offices Appropriation Act of 1952 the Commission did have the authority to establish a fee system.[23] During 1962, the Department of Defense and the Federal Aviation Agency adopted service charges and cited this Appropriation Act as their authority for their actions.[24] With new Congressional support and action by other federal agencies, the Commission, on February 16, 1962, despite strong opposition from some segments of the broadcast industry, did revive the matter. Hearings were held, and on May 6, 1963 an order was issued announcing a fee schedule for applications filed with the Commission.[25] The order was revised and adopted September 25, 1963.[26] Application of the fee schedule was postponed until March 17, 1964 pursuant to a stay imposed by the Court of Appeals for the Seventh Circuit on December 31, 1963 which was later vacated. On July 10, 1964, the Court held that the fees were valid and that the Commission had not exceeded its authority as alleged by the National Association of Broadcasters and other parties having radio and TV interests. [27] Subsequently, on July 1, 1970, the Commission adopted a new fee schedule designed to return to the government approximately the amount of appropriated funds expended by the Commission each year. Renewal license fees were abolished and a system of annual operating fees was established instead. CATV operations were also made subject to the payment of operating fees (19 RR 2d 1801).

Position of Hearing Examiner Should be Appraised. Giving the Commission wider latitude to consult with its staff, active participation in decision preparation by Commissioners and the establishment of a fee system have improved the regulatory situation at the FCC. Some other recommendations made by the Legislative Oversight Committee, to which reference was made in the first edition of this book, have not yet been put into effect, but, in the opinion of this writer, they still merit consideration. One of the Subcommittee's proposals called for a reexamination of the position of the

Hearing Examiner in the Commission. The Subcommittee raised questions regarding the operation of the present examiner system as established under the Administrative Procedure Act in 1952, particularly the method of recruiting hearing officers which required approval of their qualifications by the Civil Service Commission. The Subcommittee suggested considering the establishment of an independent "Office of Federal Administrative Practice" to perform this function. In this connection, the Report of the Subcommittee stated:

It would seem that the recruitment and selection of the desired caliber of hearing examiner requires that such tasks be performed by an agency having a major and continuing interest in the field of administrative proceedings. In this way a full understanding of the problem involved in such proceedings and of the capacities required for hearing examiners would be brought to bear in the consideration of what men should be retained as examiners.[28]

The Report further recited that "it has been frequently observed that proceedings before such hearing examiners are of too great length, as is often the opinion of the hearing examiner himself," and suggested that the Congress might be helpful "in the direction of eliminating irrelevant and immaterial matters, which currently take up undue time in administrative proceedings."[29] This proposal still seems to merit consideration.

Ex Parte Representations in Adjudicatory Cases Should be Clearly Prohibited by Law. Another proposal urged by the Subcommittee was that additional legislation be enacted prohibiting the making of any *ex parte* or extra record representation to any commissioner or any employee of the Commission regarding any proceeding of an adjudicatory character. The Subcommittee recommended that this be made applicable to all persons including members of Congress and the executive branch of the government. Any oral or written communications regarding such cases would be required to be made a part of the official record. A failure to comply with these requirements would result in severe civil and criminal penalties. These rules against *ex parte* representations are applicable to Federal courts and certainly they ought to be applicable to administrative agencies and Congress in so far as adjudicatory proceedings are concerned.

Differences Between Commissions and Courts Should Be Recognized.
A word of caution is appropriate here. The important differences between regulatory commissions such as the FCC and courts should be clearly understood. The FCC, as presently constituted, is far more than a court. It is a public service agency, not only obliged to decide cases, but to conduct experimentation and research and under the continuing obligation to promote "the larger and more effective use of radio in the public interest."[30] The doors of the Commission, therefore, should always be open to members of the public seeking information about the problems of broadcasting, and Commissioners and members of their staff should be free to discuss these

problems with outside persons so long as they do not relate to matters in hearing status.

FCC Must Keep Itself Informed. Also, there is another important point to remember. If wise policies and regulations are to be adopted, the Commission and its staff must keep fully informed regarding developments in the communications field. It would not be desirable, therefore, to isolate and insulate them from the public to the same extent as judges who deal only with adjudicatory matters. They should be free to move with intelligent discretion outside Commission walls and talk freely with those who are in a position to provide information that will be helpful in meeting the complex regulatory problems relating to broadcasting and other communication services.

The competent FCC official will make a clear distinction between his legislative and judical functions. In this sense he has a more difficult job than the judge who serves solely as an adjudicator, and whose official purview is always limited to the written record. The competent Commissioner knows when to talk and when not to talk. He has the obligation of silence and limited vision in adjudicatory cases, but he also has the obligation of communication and wide observation in other areas of his responsibility.

Any legislation, therefore, prohibiting extra-record representations should make this distinction in functions perfectly clear. Should there be the least statutory ambiguity in this respect, the effect would be to restrain and restrict the FCC official in important areas of responsibility outside the judicial realm where he ought to be mobile, inquisitive and communicative.

Standards of Conduct for Commission Officials and Employees Established. Despite what has been said above, members of the Commission and their employees have an obligation to maintain independent judgment in their work, and to adhere strictly to all requirements of the law and orders of the government having to do with official conduct. As the Commission itself has said:

The effectiveness of the Commission in serving the public interest depends upon the extent to which the Commission holds the confidence and esteem of the Nation's citizens. To hold the public confidence, unusually high standards of honest, integrity, impartiality, and conduct must be maintained within the Commission and all officers and employees must not only obey the literal requirements of the Federal laws and orders governing official conduct, but also show by their conduct that they support the ethical principles which underlie these laws and regulations. The avoidance of misconduct and conflicts of interest on the part of the Commission employees through informed judgment is indispensable to the maintenance of these standards . . .[31]

On December 15, 1965, as authorized by the Communications Act and pursuant to Executive Order No. 11222, dated May 8, 1965, and in accordance with Civil Service regulations, the Commission issued an order establishing standards of conduct for itself and employees. All persons doing business or anticipating doing business with the Commission would do well to consult these standards. They are recited in Part 19 of the Commission's Rules, Sections 19.735-101 to 19.735-413, inclusive; 1 RR 15:19-15:38. Congress might well enact legislation applicable to its members restricting them in their contacts with FCC regarding adjudicatory matters, as was recommended by the Legislative Oversight Committee.

FCC's Authority Over Broadcast Programming Should Be Clarified.
Additional legislation of a fundamental nature is needed which was not mentioned in the Report of the House Subcommittee on Legislative Oversight. Of paramount importance is the need for statutory clarification as to the Commission's authority relating to programs carried by broadcast stations.

While the Courts have held that under the present law the Commission does have legislative authority to consider program service in the exercise of its licensing functions, there is some vagueness and ambiguity in the wording of the statute that has been troublesome. Section 326 of the Communications Act says the Commission cannot censor programs. Well, what is censorship? The courts have clearly held that the term, when interpreted in connection with the provisions of the Act, prohibits critical review by the FCC of particular programs carried by stations except where violation of specific laws such as the indecency or lottery statutes may be involved. They have not, however, precluded FCC review of the over-all performance of a station when it comes up for renewal of its license.

Despite this, there has been a tremendous amount of speaking and writing in and out of Congress for the past twenty-five years to the effect that Congress never really intended to give the Commissioner the power. As previously pointed out, one of the former Commissioners stated that the FCC exceeds its authority when it requires applicants for broadcast facilities to file any program information except where infractions against lottery laws and the like are involved[32] On the other hand, other Commissioners have stated that the Commission has a positive duty to review the over-all programming of a station when it comes up for renewal of its license.[33] Congress ought to eliminate the confusion by legislation to the extent constitutionally possible. There ought not to be a continuing debate over what the Commission's authority is.

Increasing Work Load Requires Additional FCC Personnel. In the first edition of this volume, published in 1961, the large volume of business at the FCC and the limited facilities to take care of the business were pointed out. Since then the work load has become much larger but the amount of personnel and facilities have not kept pace with the increase.

For the year ending June 30, 1959, the FCC received and processed more than 12,000 broadcast applications for new AM, FM and TV stations, and for authority to modify existing operations.[34] In 1968, the number had jumped to 18,321.[35] In 1959, it received more than 250,000 additional applications for authority to operate aviation, marine, public safety, industrial, land transportation, citizen's, amateur and disaster radio services.[36] In 1968, the number of applications for such stations received by the FCC was more than a half million, and the number of authorized stations had reached the grand total of 1,723,098 with more than six million transmitters in operation.[37]

In 1959, the Commission handled about 25,000 complaints of station interference and conducted more than 15,000 investigations involving a sizeable number of field inspections.[38] In 1968, it received and disposed of almost 40,000 such complaints and conducted almost twice as many field investigations.[39]

Besides the variety and multiplicity of services provided in the broadcasting and safety and special services fields, its regulatory responsibilities with respect to telephone, telegraph and other common carrier communications continue to increase at a rapid rate. In a little less than a decade, the number of applications from telephone and telegraph companies for new facilities and for extension and enlargement of existing ones increased from about 5,000 filed with the FCC in 1957[40] to more than 11,000 in 1967,[41] and as of June 30, 1938, there were 4,242 additional applications pending which had not been finally processed by the Commission.[42]

Added to all this is the increasing volume of regulatory work relating to the activities of the Communications Satellite Corporation and the community antenna systems (there were nearly 2,000 CATV systems operating in the United States as of March 29,1968),[43] plus increasing monitoring services and technical research, and participation in domestic and international conferences galore.

This service, plus much more not mentioned, is provided to broadcasting and common carrier industries whose worth runs into many billions of dollars. The broadcasting industry alone, had a gross income of more than three billion dollars during the calendar year 1966, [44]three times more than it was in 1959.[45] The telephone industry, which had a plant investment of more than 41 billion dollars and operating revenues of more than 14 billion dollars in 1966, had more than doubled its income in the ten year period.[46] The telegraph industry, with a plant investment of almost 800 million dollars and annual income in 1966, showed considerable expansion during the same period.[47]

To all this must be added the cable and radio companies under the jurisdiction of the FCC which provide international telephone and telegraph service with yearly income running more than one hundred million dollars, and which handle annually more than 30 million telegraph and TELEX messages, and almost ten million telephone calls.[48]

1967 and 1968 reports indicate continued growth in plant investment and substantial increases in income in the broadcast and telecommunication industries.[49]

To regulate these vast industries which, over-all, have more than doubled in size and income during the last decade, the FCC, for the fiscal year 1968 received only $19,170,000* in appropriations,[50] and despite the tremendous growth of the communications industries the FCC had only 1,470 employees to regulate these industries, which was only about 300 more than it had in 1959.[51]

As this writer pointed out in the 1961 edition of this book, and here again re-emphasizes, it becomes readily apparent that one of the main reasons the Commission does not do a better job of regulating these huge industries is that its resources are still pathetically inadequate.

It simply is impossible for the Commission to handle this enormous volume of business in the most efficient manner with the limited facilities available. Not only the general public, but the broadcasting industry itself suffers from this situation. For example, in the past, there often have been protracted delays in the processing of applications for new stations or modifications of existing facilities. The decisions in important cases have been held up for months (and even years) because of lack of personnel. Petitions from industry for changes in rules often must be kept in a pending status for inordinate periods of time because there isn't the manpower available to evaluate them and act on them. Often broadcasters who have spent large amounts of money in competitive proceedings must remain in suspense for months waiting for an overworked staff to digest the records and get the cases ready for Commission action.

Special Competency of FCC Commissioners Required. Additional money and a larger staff are, of course, only part of the answer to the problem of securing efficient broadcast regulation. The more important consideration is the securing of personnel, both at the Commission and staff levels, *competent* to deal with the increasingly complex regulatory problems at the FCC.

Generally speaking, since the creation of the FCC in 1934, the members of the Commission have been high-caliber men. (See biographical material relating to present and past commissioners in Appendix II.) Their qualifications have compared favorably with those of members of the numerous other independent commissions and boards of the Federal government. But there have been times when appointments to the FCC, as well as other agencies of government, have been motivated more by political and partisan considerations than by genuine concern for high and special qualifications needed to perform the duties of public office.

While political considerations have played some part in the appointment of Federal judges, traditionally there has been a concern that persons appointed to these judicial offices should have special qualifications for their jobs. They must have unquestioned integrity, a high sense of public responsibility, and the special training, experience and skills needed to perform in a judicial role. Where attempts have been made to appoint persons not

*This figure was increased some in 1969 and 1970. Fees have helped, but still not enough.

measuring up to these standards, bar associations and other professional groups interested in the proper administration of justice have vigorously protested. Generally, public opinion in this country demands a high degree of competency of those who must pass judgment on the behavior and rights of citizens and who must settle multifarious and complicated questions of law in our democratic society.

No less should be demanded of persons who serve on commissions such as the FCC. In fact, in some respects, they ought to have even higher qualifications. An FCC commissioner must act in a three-fold capacity. He must serve in a legislative role in the formulation of rules and regulations to implement laws passed by Congress. He must see that these rules are administered properly. And he must serve as judge in many cases coming within the jurisdiction of the FCC. He is required to wear three hats and he must be able to change these hats when the duties of his office require.

Communications media have become increasingly important in American life. This fact becomes so very real when we contemplate what the situation would be if we suddenly were deprived of all telephone, telegraph, and radio communication. The FCC has tremendous legislative, administrative and judicial powers with respect to a large part of these facilities. And since the jurisdiction of courts is very much limited, this means that the decisions of the Commission are to a large extent final. Their decisions crucially affect the position and operational pattern of these media as they function to meet the needs of the nation.

The men, therefore, who serve on the FCC should have the highest qualifications. They should have superior intellects with demonstrated ability to do creative, constructive and objective thinking. Their educational and professional backgrounds should be such that they have developed a deep and profound understanding and appreciation of the critically important role that mass media play in a free, democratic society. And above all, they should have unquestioned personal integrity, a high sense of social responsibility, and a capacity for independent thought and action. The regular term of an FCC Commissioner is now only seven years. Quite often it is less than this when the commissioner is appointed to fill an unexpired term. It would be well to give consideration to lengthening this period to ten or possibly twelve years. This longer tenure, in addition to providing more financial security, would give a commissioner more time to become familiar with the complex regulatory problems of the agency and to make his maximum contribution to its operations. It would also be more conducive to his exercise of independent judgment since he would not be subject as often to the political hazards and ordeal that usually accompany reappointment.

Still more important, commissioners, like judges, should be free of pressures from Congress, the White House, and the industries they regulate. Many competent men are hesitant to accept positions on regulatory commissions for fear they may not be able "to call the shots as they see them."

As is the case with Federal judges, they should be fully insulated and protected from outside pressures and intimidations and free to perform their tasks with the knowledge that they will not have to suffer reprisals of any sort because of any official decisions made or actions taken.

To guard against commission "packing" tendencies, Congress and professional groups particularly concerned with FCC operations should scrutinize most carefully each appointment and reappointment to the agency at the time it is made. No person should be approved for membership on the Commission, who has committed himself to take direction from any party leadership or who might be inclined to become a "rubber stamp" for the party in power or become the spokesman for any special interest group.

Congress and the FCC. A larger staff and higher standards for the selection of Commissioners will go far in improving the quality of broadcast regulation. There is another problem, however, that must be solved if the FCC is ever to achieve maximum efficiency. It has to do with the attitude and relationship of Congress toward the agency. It is a situation so serious that it deserves special consideration.

It has now been more than ten years since a Congressional Subcommittee on Legislative Oversight terminated its investigative activities in Washington. There can be no doubt that the work of the Subcommittee and subsequent studies of the FCC by other Congressional committees have been helpful in drawing attention to some of the serious regulatory problems of the Commission and have revealed some misfunction and malpractice that needed correction. As pointed out in the first part of this chapter, some improvements have been made in line with suggestions made by the Subcommittee. There can be no doubt that more recent Congressional activities and recommendations have had a constructive influence on FCC behavior. Ironically, however, the very Congress that has brought to light the unhappy conditions at the FCC and has made remedial suggestions has had a great deal to do with creating these conditions. The long-standing antipathy which Congress has manifested with respect to the agency has made it difficult for the FCC to achieve the high level of performance of which it is capable.

The Investigation-Ridden FCC. Probably no other agency of the Federal government has been the object of as much vilification and prolonged investigation by Congress as has the FCC. In fact, its bath of fire brought on by the spectacular exploits of the House Subcommittee on Legislative Oversight in the fifties and the highly publicized Congressional threats and surveillance in the sixties have been but a continuation of an ordeal to which the bedraggled agency has been subject more or less constantly since Sam Rayburn breathed the breath of life into it in 1934.

It may surprise many to know that the FCC has been under Congressional investigation or the threat of one virtually every year since it was established. The same may be said of its predecessor, the Federal Radio Commission, created in 1927 but which succumbed after six years of pelting from angry and hostile law-makers in Washington.

The Radio Act of 1927 established the Federal Radio Commission with authority to assign radio frequencies, grant, renew and revoke licenses and, within limitations, to set standards and make rules for the operation of radio stations. But Congress was never happy with this original "traffic cop of the air." Almost from the very beginning, it seemed to be viewed by its progenitors on Capitol Hill as a delinquent creature, not to be trusted, and requiring frequent discipline.

Shortly after it was created, a resolution was introduced in the House to investigate the agency.[52] Subsequently, a similar resolution was introduced in the Senate, to authorize an investigation of its personnel, records, documents, and decisions, "with particular reference to the conduct and deportment of the several members of the Commission while engaged in exercising judicial or quasi-judicial functions under the Radio Act of 1927. . . ."[53]

A few days later, Senator Huey P. Long requested the Senate to make a formal inquiry of the FRC with respect to its handling of a radio case involving conflicting interests in Shreveport and New Orleans, based upon allegations that the decision had been "changed and rechanged, reversed and re-reversed by reason of pressure exerted from the White House."[54]

Early Attacks of the FCC. But the move of the "kingfish" from Louisiana to bring the FRC to public trial didn't materialize. Before there was time to get the inquisition under way, the agency had drawn its last breath, and its functions had been swallowed up by the newly created FCC, empowered by Congress to regulate all interstate and foreign communication by means of wire or radio, including the vast telephone and telegraph industries.

This new agency had the initial blessing of New Dealers in Washington. However, Roosevelt's signature on the Communications Act of 1934 was hardly dry before the FCC was under severe attack from irate Congressmen. They took it to the proverbial woodshed frequently, and during the first seven years of its life introduced eleven different resolutions in the House and Senate to subject it to formal investigation.[55]

There was an incredible ambivalence exhibited by Congress in its attacks against the FCC during that early period. A good example of this was the behavior of Congress before and after the Commission adopted the network regulations in May, 1941. For fifteen years prior to their adoption, in virtually every session of Congress, the evils of monopoly in the broadcasting industry were oratorically deplored and the FCC was frequently chided for not riding herd on network practices. Accordingly, as previously discussed, in 1938, the FCC instituted a general investigation of the broadcasting industry, its particular target being the operations of the radio networks.

Interestingly enough, while the Commission was carrying on this rigorous proceeding and was promulgating these regulations, no fewer than six resolutions were introduced in the Congress to investigate the distraught agency.[56] These various investigatory moves were aided and abetted by a growing number of unsuccessful and disgruntled (and in some cases embittered) applicants for radio stations. But much of this probing spirit in Congress resulted from complaints of powerful (and at times vindictive) leadership in the broadcasting industry, unhappy with governmental controls, and infuriated by the possibility of stricter regulations.

The rules, as finally adopted by the FCC, were relatively mild in light of the strong position taken by Congress against radio monopoly and its insistence for more than a decade that network operations be regulated. Despite this, the regulations evoked a flood of critical comment from Capitol Hill castigating the Commission for assuming arbitrary powers over the program and business affairs of networks and stations. Almost immediately, a resolution was introduced in the Senate to investigate the FCC to determine whether the regulations were arbitrary and capricious, abridged the rights of free speech, and violated the First Amendment.[57]

Shortly thereafter, the Supreme Court issued the famous Felix Frankfurter opinion (to which reference has already been made) upholding the legality of the regulations. But it afforded the FCC with no relief from the Congressional flail. On the contrary, it intensified the hostility of the dissident Congressmen who were now determined to drive the "bureaucratic rascals" from Washington.

The Cox Investigation. The inquisitional scene shifted from the Senate to the House where the stage had been set for a full dress and spectacular probe of the FCC. The stage manager for this sensational drama was the tempestuous Congressman Eugene Cox from Georgia. In early January, 1943, he introduced House Resolution No. 21 to set up a select committee to scrutinize the organization, personnel and activities of the FCC.[58] Within three weeks, the House had approved the resolution and Congressman Cox was appointed to direct the show.[59]

The fierce and sensational manner in which he and Eugene Garey, the Committee's first general counsel, carried on the investigation attracted national attention. As for the FCC, it was a demoralizing and bitter experience. Members of the Commission and its staff, not yet recovered from a decade of almost uninterrupted ordeal in their relations with Congress, were now pulled away from their normal regulatory duties and were required to prepare loads of informational data for the Select Committee and were interrogated under oath regarding FCC policies and procedures.

The author remembers most vividly the intensity with which the House Committee pressed their charges against the Commission. The morale of the employees dropped to an abysmally low point. He recalls the weary and frustrated feelings of a staff which had long cringed under the Congressional whip-lash for failure to control network practices, and now was flayed by the same Congress for attempting to regulate those practices, and was accused of exceeding its powers and meddling in the business affairs of stations and networks.

While the Commission writhed under this torturous treatment, FCC sympathizers at the White House and other political powers in Washington interceded backstage. Counter forces were set in action in the House and the Senate. The charge was made that Congressman Cox had accepted a $2500 interest in a new radio station in his home state after having used his Congressional position to influence the Commission to grant the application.[60]

Embarrassed by this accusation (no formal charges were ever made against him), he resigned as Chairman of the Committee in a diatribe which he emitted to his colleagues and to packed galleries in the House Chamber, September 30, 1943.[61]

He was succeeded as Chairman by Congressman Lea of California.[62] General Counsel Garey carried on for another five months and concluded that he had had enough. Senator Warren Magnuson (then a member of the lower House and on the Committee) had complained publicly that the FCC had been investigated for 13 months, that 1800 pages of testimony had been taken, with half of it consisting of words from counsel and Committee members, and all before the Commission was permitted to present its case.[63] In a huff, Mr. Garey withdrew from the Committee.[64] His parting shot was that the investigation was being converted into a "sheer whitewashing affair," wholly responsive to political pressures and dominated by political expediency."[65]

He was succeeded by John J. Sirica, who tried to pump new life into the investigation. By this time, however, the counter forces in Congress had taken full command. Unable to develop the kind of report which he thought the facts required, he resigned on November 28, 1944, stating that he did not want anyone to be able to say that he was a party to a "whitewash."[66]

The final report of the Select Committee was submitted to the House on January 2, 1945.[67] It contained no startling disclosures of FCC misconduct. In fact, it was the opinion of some experts who had followed the proceedings closely that the report pretty much absolved the Commission from the charges made against it.

The "Blue Book" Controversy.   The year that followed was one of the few in the history of the FCC that the *Congressional Record* shows no formal moves to investigate the agency. The respite, however, was short lived, and the Commission had hardly had time to draw a deep breath before it was under severe attack from Congressional Hill. And here again Congress demonstrated its remarkable facility for chameleon-type behavior.

One of the complaints of some Congressmen for many years had been that the Commission had been lax in establishing and enforcing standards for broadcast programming; that despite many complaints, the Commission had made little effort to require stations to operate in the public interest.

At long last, the FCC decided to do something about it. Paul A. Porter, brilliant and imaginative, and with an impressive record as a public official, received the Presidential nod for chairmanship of the Commission. During his tenure which lasted a little over a year, he brought in Dr. Charles Siepmann, formerly with the British Broadcasting Corporation, to direct a study and come up with some proposed criteria which the Commission might establish for the evaluation of radio program service.

The result of this study was the adoption and publication by the FCC in March, 1946 of the report, *Public Service Responsibility of Broadcast Licensees,* popularly known as the Blue Book and which was discussed in Chapter 19.

Congressional reaction to this FCC publication was immediate. Despite his previous castigation of the Commission for failure to set general standards, and even before he had time to read the Blue Book carefully, Congressman Wigglesworth of Massachusetts made derogatory reference to it in a House speech, saying that some people construed it as "indicating an interest on the part of the FCC to assume unlawful control over what the people shall or shall not hear over the air."[68] He further declared that "there is imperative need for improvement in standards of administration by the Commission and for remedial legislation. Both are essential to impartial and efficient regulation and to equality of opportunity and freedom of speech over the radio . . ."[69]

Not to be outdone, fiery Senator Tobey of New Hampshire dropped a companion resolution in the Senatorial hopper to determine how much the FCC had censored and controlled programs of broadcasting stations, and the extent it had restricted or might restrict freedom of speech as guaranteed by the Constitution of the United States.[70] A short time later, Congressman Wolverton of New Jersey gave the House notice that he was introducing a resolution to authorize an inquiry and complete study of the FCC.[71]

It was shortly after this that the writer was appointed Chief of the Renewals and Revocation Section of the Commission. It was his job, with the help of a small staff, to process all renewal applications of broadcast stations and recommend appropriate action to the Commission in terms of the program criteria set forth in the Blue Book.

He served in the position for about four years but felt handicapped because of conflicting attitudes in the Commission and on Capitol Hill. While the courts had said the FCC had the responsibility to exercise authority in the program field, some Congressmen persisted in saying publicly that the Commission was guilty of censorship when it did so and that it had misconstrued the original intent of Congress.

Needless to say, this cleavage militated against any real, effective application of the program criteria which the Commission had enunciated, and engendered a kind of frustration and impuissance which, except for a few cases, made the approval of renewal applications pretty much of an automatic process.

Since the Cox investigations there have been frequent threats and intimidations which have tended to keep the Commission and its staff in a state of anxiety and frustration.[72] Congressional intrusions and ambivalence have continued to make it difficult for the FCC to formulate positive policies and take effective action on matters relating to the public interest. All too often have the energies and resources of the Commission been diverted from important regulatory tasks by investigating rigmarole which makes the headlines but which, in too many instances, has failed to serve useful and constructive purposes.

What makes the situation worse is the awareness of the Commission that in the establishment of basic policies, whatever road it may take, the rigmarole is likely to result and Commission character is likely to be impugned. This accounts in part for the Commission's tendency to delay action of important matters such as the clear channel case and toll TV which were the subject of so much heated controversy in Congress for many years.

It is not meant by the writer to suggest that Congress should not be concerned about the conduct of administrative agencies. Unquestionably, one of the important functions of Congress is to investigate and expose inefficiency and irresponsibility in public administration. The investigative process, however, carried on more or less continuously over a long period of time can have a most damaging effect on a federal agency. This has been the case with the FCC. At no time in its thirty-seven years of life has it in fact been independent in its operations. While some Congressional inquiries have been constructive in character and have been enormously helpful to the FCC, there have been too many of a destructive nature, designed to serve special interests in and outside Congress. Their punitive and often inquisitional character over a long period of time has created in the public mind an image of depravity with respect to the FCC that severely handicaps the agency in the exercise of its functions. It is the opinion of the writer that until Congress changes its own ways and corrects this situation, the FCC will never begin to approach its full capacity for achievement and public service.

The White House and the FCC. This is also true with respect to the White House and its staff. As previously pointed out, members of the FCC are appointed by the President who designates the Chairman. It is only natural, therefore, that Commissioners should feel some sense of loyalty to the executive leadership at 1600 Pennsylvania Avenue. Members of the Commission also know full well that if their conduct is not pleasing to the President, he is not likely to reappoint them. This has a subtle but none the less real influence on the thinking and actions of Commissioners—an influence which does not exist with respect to Federal judges who have life tenure and owe no allegiance to any individual or group.

Extending the terms of office of FCC members as suggested above would be helpful. The real solution, however, must come from a deep and profound concern at the White House for responsible and efficient administration. While there have been many meritorious appointments to the FCC and other independent commissions in Washington, there have been some in both Republican and Democratic administrations which were motivated largely by political expediency. In these cases, not enough consideration was given to the special competencies required to perform the difficult tasks of a government agency whose functions vitally affect the lives of all the American people.

No person should be appointed to the FCC simply because he has been helpful to the party, or simply because he has associated with and has the support of some special interest group, or because he is a friend of the President or a Congressman or other leaders in the party. While it is not meant to suggest that such things constitute disqualifying factors, quite obviously they should not be major considerations in appointing men to administer the highly important and complicated affairs at the FCC.

Once competent men are appointed who meet the high qualification tests suggested, they should be completely independent in the performance of their duties and free to make decisions without pressures or reprisals of any sort from the White House or any other political source. In this respect, they should have the same protection as that enjoyed by the courts.

The Total Citizenship Has a Responsibility. The FCC itself, Congress and the White House must bear their appropriate share of the responsibility for the failure of broadcast regulation to reach the highest level of efficiency in this country. To point the finger of criticism at these agencies alone, however, would be most unfair and would oversimplify the problem. The total citizenship has a responsibility.

Studies of the Special Subcommittee on Legislative Oversight of the House Committee on Interstate and Foreign Commerce clearly revealed a shocking disregard by many citizens for moral and ethical values which traditionally have been basic to American culture. In the feverish, competitive struggle of special interest groups to gain control and capitalize on scarce natural resources such as radio and television channels, all too often contestants have succumbed to the temptation to ignore the ground rules and resort to *ex parte* pressures to win the victory.

Another manifestation of the growing indifference to ethical standards among our citizenship were the exposures in the fifties of the deceptive tactics employed in certain quiz shows carried by the networks. While the networks and sponsors of those shows deserved criticism for the colossal hoax perpetrated on the American people, it must not be overlooked that it never could have happened without the participation of individual citizens, willing to bemean themselves to secure quickly the big dazzling cash rewards.

Irresponsibility and misconduct in government mirror to some extent the general lack of concern for and a breakdown in the moral code. As citizens, we can hardly expect our governmental officials who serve us in Washington to exhibit a higher standard of moral and ethical conduct than we ourselves exhibit. If the citizen representing himself or some group rushes to Washington and contrives a situation where he can make *ex parte* representations to a Commissioner, or enlists the aid of a Congressman or a member of the White House staff to secure a favorable decision from the FCC, he is just as guilty of misconduct as a Special Assistant to the President or a Congressman would be if he made a call to the FCC for the purpose of influencing the outcome of a case.

The problem, therefore, of overcoming barriers to effective broadcast regulation is the responsibility of all the people and not just those who represent us in the nation's Capital. In fact, the very preservation of all democratic government depends to a large extent upon the moral choices made by individual citizens.

A Report to the former President of Michigan State University from its Committee on the Future of the University highlighted this point and stressed the importance of university training along this line:

> If educated persons are to be effective citizens in the world, they must be prepared to make difficult moral choices as individuals and as members of social groups. A democracy cannot survive unless its members recognize their responsibilities for the ethical as well as the technical implications of the public and private decisions being made. The university is not an institution for indoctrination, but the university experience should equip the student to examine his ethical position and to analyze and define the value systems necessary to the maintenance of a free society.[73]

Not only universities, but education at all levels should recognize here one of its most challenging opportunities to meet one of the most critical needs of our time.

Final Suggestion for Improving Broadcast Regulation. The last proposal for improving broadcast regulation comes out of the Final Report of the President's Task Force on Communications Policy issued December 7, 1968.[74] This study covered a sixteen months period and involved the work of fifteen departments and agencies of the Federal Government and a large number of consultants in and outside the government. Important recommendations of this task force included the enactment of legislation creating a new agency in the Executive Branch of the Federal government, which would have over-all responsibility for allocating the radio spectrum for both government and non-government uses.

The FCC would be relieved of the complex managerial tasks related to civilian uses of the spectrum which it now performs and could devote more time and energy to its regulatory responsibilities. The Task Force envisioned "substantial benefits on all sides from consolidated spectrum management functions" lodged in a new entity in the Executive Branch of the Government:

> . . . the management structure and operations would benefit by eliminating duplicate offices, personnel, research facilities, data collection and analysis facilities, and other resources; this increased efficiency would result in more comprehensive and sorely needed management capabilities. Private users would benefit from this improved management capability, because more spectrum resources could be made available within virtually every area of use. Government users would likewise benefit

in those areas where their needs are greatest, and should incur little or no loss in communications capability in any area. Finally, the public would benefit from the increased spectrum resources made available for both public and private use, in terms of added services and/or reduced rates.[75]

In answer to the argument that unification of spectrum management would encroach upon the FCC's exercise of regulatory responsibilities in broadcasting and common carrier services, the Task Force said:

> . . . This argument is predicated on the notion that spectrum allocation and assignment is a fundamental determinant of the structure and performance of these sectors, and therefore cannot be separated from FCC's broadcast licensing and common regulatory role. However, after careful analysis, we have concluded that this concern is not well founded.
>
> The FCC's responsibilities in the field of broadcasting, such as determining the proper number, location, and qualifications of broadcast entities and regulating their operations, are quite distinct from responsibilities for managing use of the spectrum. While policies underlying these functions may occasionally conflict or overlap, the crucial fact is they represent distinctly separate activities which can properly be performed by different agencies.
>
> An Executive Branch spectrum manager and the FCC should encounter no major obstacles in working out together (under the watchful eye of Congress) any needed changes in the existing broadcast station allotment plan which would appropriately reflect the objectives of both agencies. We have no reason to expect that disagreement would frequently arise on the need for such changes given (a) the present stage of broadcast development, (b) the present station allotment plan (essentially unchanged for over 15 years), (c) the recognition by the FCC in recent proceedings of the potential benefits of releasing certain unused portions of the UHF broadcast band to other services, and (D) the unlikely prospect of any major modifications to the existing allotment plan in the near term. The Commission would continue to license broadcast stations, according to the existing station allotment plan.[76]

The Report of the President's Task Force runs more than four hundred pages. It contains many recommendations which have important implications for the development of both domestic and international communications, for conservation of the radio spectrum and more effective utilization thereof, and for improvement of regulation. It is highly recommended for reading by all students and practitioners of broadcasting.

1. Emery, Walter B., *Broadcasting and Government: Responsibilities and Regulations*, Michigan State University Press, East Lansing, Michigan, 1961, pp. 303-312.

2. *Regulation of Broadcasting, Half Century of Government Regulation of Broadcasting and the Need for Further Legislative Action;* a study for the Committee on Interstate and Foreign Commerce, House of Representatives, 85th Congress, Second Session on H. Res. 99, United States Government Printing Office, Washington, 1958, pp. 157-158.

3. Emery, p. 304.

4. Public Law 87-192, approved August 31, 1961, 75 Stat. 420-422, Section 1, 1 RR 10:150; also see House Report No. 723, 87th Congress, 1st Session, submitted July 17, 1961, 1 RR 10:449; and Senate Report No. 576, 87th Congress, 1st Session, submitted July 19, 1961; 1 RR 10:461-10:462.

5. Administrative Procedure Act; see Senate Report, *Ibid;* Public Law 89-554, 89th Congress, 2d Session, approved September 6, 1966, 5 USC, Section 554 (d); 1 RR 25:16.

6. *Ibid.*

7. 75 Stat. 420, Section 1; 1 RR 10:22-24.

8. House Report, *Ibid.*

9. Emery, pp. 304-305.

10. See 70 *Cong. Rec.* 5058, March 2, 1929 and 72 *Cong. Rec.* 342, December 10, 1929. Also see Senate Document No. 47, 71st Congress, 2nd Session, 1929, for the full text of the FRC Chairman's letter.

11. See 70 *Cong. Rec.* 542, December 16, 1932.

12. Senate Report No. 564, pp. 11-12, 72nd Congress, 1st Session.

13. See speech on floor of House by Congressman Lawrence J. Connery, April 11, 1938, 83 *Cong. Rec.* 5284; also see discussion of Congressman Richard B. Wigglesworth, February 6, 1939, 84 *Cong. Rec.* 1164-1166.

14. See remarks of Congressman Wigglesworth, 88 *Cong. Rec.* 551, January 22, 1942.

15. *Ibid.*, pp. 551-552.

16. *Ibid.*

17. 96 *Cong. Rec.* A1914-A1915, March 8, 1950.

18. 98 *Cong. Rec.* 2538-2539, March 19, 1952.

19. 59 Stat. 597.

20. 19 Fed. Reg. 622-624.

21. 100 *Cong. Rec.* 3782, March 24, 1954.

22. FCC *Annual Report,* 1954, p. 16.

23. 107 *Cong. Rec.* 14587-88; also see 25 RR 1561.

24. See Federal Register of January 13, 1962, p. 401 (FR 62-405) and May 26, 1962, pp. 4955 (FR 62-5109).

25. 25 RR 1559;28 Fed. Reg. 4758.

26. 25 RR 1574a; 28 Fed. Reg. 10921.

27. Aeronautical Radio, Inc. v. United States, 2 RR 2d 2073, U. S. Court of Appeals, Seventh Circuit, July 10, 1964.

28. *Regulation of Broadcasting, op. cit.* p. 169.

29. *Ibid.*, p. 170.

30. Section 303(g), Communications Act of 1934, 48 Stat. 1082.

31. Section 19.753-101, Commission Rules; 1 RR 15:20.

32. However, Commissioner Craven did vote to approve the Report and Statement of the Commission adopted July 27, 1960, which reads in part:
In the fulfillment of his obligation the broadcaster should consider the tastes,

needs and desires of the public he is licensed to serve in developing his programming and should exercise conscientious efforts not only to ascertain them but also to carry them out as well as he reasonably can. He should reasonably attempt to meet all such needs and interests on an equitable basis. Particular areas of interest and types of appropriate service may, of course, differ from community to community, and from time to time. However, the Commission does expect its broadcast licensees to take the necessary steps to inform themselves of the real needs and interests of the areas they serve and to provide programming which in fact constitutes a diligent effort, in good faith, to provide for those needs and interests.

33. "The Role of the FCC in Programming," address of Commissioner Frederick W. Ford before the West Virginia Broadcasters Association, White Sulphur Springs, West Virginia, August 28, 1959, FCC Mimeograph No. 77193. Commissioners Cox and Johnson, as shown in Chapter 19, hold similar views.

34. FCC *Annual Report,* 1959, pp. 75, 105.

35. *Ibid.,* 1968, p. 18.

36. *Ibid.,* 1959, pp. 75, 105.

37. *Ibid.,* 1968, pp. 146-147.

38. *Ibid.,* 1959, p. 142.

39. *Ibid.,* 1968, pp. 150-151.

40. *Ibid.,* 1959, p. 128.

41. *Ibid.,* 1968, p. 139.

42. *Ibid.*

43. "The Potential of Cable Television," remarks by Frederick W. Ford, former President, National Cable Television Association, before the Telecommications Symposium of the Broadcast Advertising Club of Chicago, March 29, 1968.

44. FCC *Annual Report,* 1967, p. 170.

45. *Ibid.,* 1959, pp. 125-127.

46. *Ibid.,* 1967, p. 203.

47. *Ibid.,* p. 73.

48. *Ibid.,* pp. 79-81.

49. *Ibid.,* 1968, pp. 53-55.

50. *Ibid.,* 1968, p. 11.

51. *Ibid.*

52. H. Res. 80, 75 *Cong. Rec.* 1057, December 21, 1931.

53. 78 *Cong. Rec.* 965, May 28, 1934.

54. *Ibid.,* p. 10558.

55. See House Res. 394, 80 *Cong. Rec.* 456, January 15, 1936; Senate Res. 245, 80 *Cong. Rec.* 3427, March 9, 1936; House Res. 442, 80 *Cong. Rec.* 3468, March 9, 1936; House Res. 313, 81 *Cong. Rec.* 8880, August 14, 1937; House Res. 321, 81 *Cong. Rec.* 9295, August 16, 1937; House Res. 342, 81 *Cong. Rec.* 9683, August 21, 1937; Senate Res. 149,81 *Cong. Rec.* 6786-6787, July 6, 1937; House Res. 365, 82 *Cong. Rec.* 720, December 2, 1937; House Res. 70 and 72, 84 *Cong. Rec.* 805, January 25, 1939; Senate Res. 251, 86 *Cong. Rec.* 3731, April 1, 1940; House Res. 51, 87 *Cong. Rec.* 79, January 8, 1941.

56. In addition to resolutions listed in previous footnote, see Senate Res. 251, 86 *Cong. Rec.* 3731, April 1, 1940; House Res. 51, 87 *Cong. Rec.* 79, January 8, 1941.

57. See Senate Res. 133, 87 *Cong. Rec.* 3950-51, May 13, 1941.

58. See House Res. 21 introduced by Congressman Cox, 89 *Cong. Rec.* 26, January 6, 1943; unanimously approved by the House Rules Committee.

59. See 89 *Cong. Rec.* 235.

60. See resignation speech of Congressman Cox made on the House floor making reference to this charge, September 30, 1943, 89 *Cong. Rec.* 7937.

61. *Ibid.*

62. 89 *Cong. Rec.* 8035, October 4, 1943.

63. 90 *Cong. Rec.* 2123, February 29, 1944.

64. *Broadcasting*, February 28, 1944, p. 9.

65. *Ibid.*

66. *Ibid.*, December 4, 1944, p. 16.

67. *Ibid.*, January 28, 1945, p. 13.

68. 82 *Cong. Rec.* 2219, March 13, 1946.

69. *Ibid.*

70. Senate Res. 307, 92 *Cong. Rec.* 9803-9804, July 24, 1946.

71. 93 *Cong. Rec.* 2899, March 31, 1947.

72. See *Broadcasting*, January 27, 1969, pp. 66-72; March 10, 1969, pp. 23-28; November 24, 1969, pp. 64-65; November 17, 1969, pp. 38-39.

73. A Report to the former President of Michigan State University, East Lansing, Michigan, 1959.

74. *Final Report of President's Task Force on Communications Policy*, December 7, 1968, U. S. Government Printing Office, Washington, D. C.

75. *Ibid.*, Chapter VI, pp. 55-56.

76. *Ibid.*, pp. 56-58.

APPENDIX I

Communications Act of 1934, as Amended*

AN ACT

To provide for the regulation of interstate and foreign communication by wire or radio, and for other purposes.

Be it enacted by the Senate and House of Representatives of the United States of America in Congress assembled,

Title I—General Provisions

PURPOSES OF ACT; CREATION OF FEDERAL COMMUNICATIONS COMMISSION

SECTION 1. For the purpose of regulating interstate and foreign commerce in communication by wire and radio so as to make available, so far as possible, to all the people of the United States a rapid, efficient, Nation-wide, and world-wide wire and radio communication service with adequate facilities at reasonable charges, for the purpose of the national defense, for the purpose of promoting safety of life and property through the use of wire and radio communication, and for the purpose of securing a more effective execution of this policy by centralizing authority heretofore granted by law to several agencies and by granting additional authority with respect to interstate and foreign commerce in wire and radio communication, there is hereby created a commission to be known as the "Federal Communications Commission", which shall be constituted as hereinafter provided, and which shall execute and enforce the provisions of this Act.

APPLICATION OF ACT

SEC. 2. (a) The provisions of this Act shall apply to all interstate and foreign communication by wire or radio and all interstate and foreign transmission of energy by radio, which originates and/or is received within the United States, and to all persons engaged within the United States in such communication or such transmission of energy by radio, and to the licensing and regulating of all radio stations as hereinafter provided; but it shall not apply to persons engaged in wire or radio communication or transmission in the Philippine Islands or the Canal Zone, or to wire or radio communication or transmission wholly within the Philippine Islands or the Canal Zone.

(b) Subject to the provisions of section 301, nothing in this Act shall be construed

*Only parts of the Act relating to broadcasting have been included. The full text of the Act can be secured at nominal cost from the U. S. Government Printing Office, Washington, D. C. Also it is reproduced in Statutes at Large and Pike and Fisher I RR 10:11-177.

to apply or to give the Commission jurisdiction with respect to (1) charges, classifications, practices, services, facilities, or regulations for or in connection with intrastate communication service by wire or radio of any carrier, or (2) any carrier engaged in interstate or foreign communication solely through physical connection with the facilities of another carrier not directly or indirectly controlling or controlled by, or under direct or indirect common control with such carrier, or (3) any carrier engaged in interstate or foreign communication solely through connection by radio, or by wire and radio, with facilities, located in an adjoining State or in Canada or Mexico (where they adjoin the State in which the carrier is doing business), or another carrier not directly or indirectly controlling or controlled by, or under direct or indirect common control with such carrier, or (4) any carrier to which clause (2) or clause (3) would be applicable except for furnishing interstate mobile radio land vehicles in Canada or Mexico; except that sections 201 through 205 of this Act, both inclusive, shall, except as otherwise provided therein, apply to carriers described in clause (2), (3) and (4).

DEFINITIONS

SEC. 3. For the purposes of this Act, unless the context otherwise requires—

(a) "Wire communication" or "communication by wire" means the transmission of writing, signs, signals, pictures, and sounds of all kinds by aid of wire, cable, or other like connection between the points of origin and reception of such transmission, including all instrumentalities, facilities, apparatus, and services (among other things, the receipt, forwarding, and delivery of communications) incidental to such transmission.

(b) "Radio communication" or "communication by radio" means the transmission by radio of writing, signs, signals, pictures, and sounds of all kinds including all instrumentalities, facilities, apparatus, and services (among other things, the receipt, forwarding, and delivery of communications) incidental to such transmission.

(c) "Licensee" means the holder of a radio station license granted or continued in force under authority of this Act.

(d) "Transmission of energy by radio" or "radio transmission of energy" includes both such transmission and all instrumentalities, facilities, and services incidental to such transmission.

(e) "Interstate communication" or "interstate transmission" means communication or transmission (1) from any State, Territory, or possession of the United States (other than the Philippine Islands and the Canal Zone), or the District of Columbia, to any other State, Territory, or possession of the United States (other than the Philippine Islands and the Canal Zone), or the District of Columbia, (2) from or to the United States to or from the Philippine Islands or the Canal Zone, insofar as such communication or transmission takes place within the United States, or (3) between points within the United States but through a foreign country; but shall not, with respect to the provisions of Title II of this Act (other than Section 223 thereof,) include wire or radio communication between points in the same State, Territory, or possession of the United States, or the District of Columbia, through any place outside thereof, if such communication is regulated by a State commission.

(f) "Foreign communication" or "foreign transmission" means communication or transmission from or to any place in the United States to or from a foreign country, or between a station in the United States and a mobile station located outside the United States.

(g) "United States" means the several States and Territories, the District of

408

Columbia, and the possessions of the United States, but does not include the Philippine Islands or the Canal Zone.

(h) "Common carrier" or "carrier" means any person engaged as a common carrier for hire, in interstate or foreign radio transmission of energy, except where reference is made to common carriers not subject to this Act; but a person engaged in radio broadcasting shall not, insofar as such person is so engaged, be deemed a common carrier.

(i) "Person" includes an individual, partnership, association, joint-stock company, trust, or corporation.

(j) "Corporation" includes any corporation, joint-stock company, or association.

(k) "Radio station" or "station" means a station equipped to engage in radio communication or radio transmission of energy.

(l) "Mobile station" means a radio-communication station capable of being moved and which ordinarily does move.

(m) "Land station" means a station, other than a mobile station, used for radio communication with mobile stations.

(n) "Mobile service" means the radio-communication service carried on between mobile stations and land stations, and by mobile stations communicating among themselves.

(o) "Broadcasting" means the dissemination of radio communications intended to be received by the public, directly or by the intermediary of relay stations.

(p) "Chain broadcasting" means simultaneous broadcasting of an identical pro gram by two or more connected stations.

(q) "Amateur station" means a radio station operated by a duly authorized person interested in radio technique solely with a personal aim and without pecuniary interest.

(r) "Telephone exchange service" means service within a telephone exchange, or within a connected system of telephone exchanges within the same exchange area operated to furnish to subscribers intercommunicating service of the character ordinarily furnished by a single exchange, and which is covered by the exchange service charge.

(s) "Telephone toll service" means telephone service between stations in different exchange areas for which there is made a separate charge not included in contracts with subscribers for exchange service.

(t) "State commission" means the commission, board, or official (by whatever name designated) which under the laws of any State has regulatory jurisdiction with respect to intrastate operations of carriers.

(u) "Connecting carrier" means a carrier described in clause (2) of section 2 (b).

(v) "State" includes the District of Columbia and the Territories and possessions.

(w) (1) "Ship" or "vessel" includes every description of watercraft or other artificial contrivance, except aircraft, used or capable of being used as a means of transportation on water, whether or not it is actually afloat.

(2) A ship shall be considered a passenger ship if it carries or is licensed or certified to carry more than twelve passengers.

(3) A cargo ship means any ship not a passenger ship.

(4) A passenger is any person carried on board a ship or vessel except (1) the officers and crew actually employed to man and operate the ship, (2) persons employed to carry on the business of the ship, and (3) persons on board a ship when they are carried, either because of the obligation laid upon the master to carry shipwrecked, distressed, or other persons in like or similar situations or by reason of any circumstance over which neither the master, the owner, nor the charterer (if any) has control.

(5) "Nuclear ship" means a ship provided with a nuclear powerplant.

(x) "Radiotelegraph auto alarm" on a ship of the United States subject to the provisions of Part II of Title III of this Act means an automatic alarm receiving apparatus which responds to the radiotelegraph alarm signal and has been approved by the Commission. "Radiotelegraph auto alarm" on a foreign ship means an automatic alarm receiving apparatus which responds to the radiotelegraph alarm signal and has been approved by the government of the country in which the ship is registered: Provided, that the United States and the country in which the ship is registered are parties to the same treaty, convention, or agreement prescribing the requirements for such apparatus. Nothing in this Act or in any other provision of law shall be construed to require the recognition of a radiotelegraph auto alarm as complying with Part II of Title III of this Act, on a foreign ship subject to such part, where the country in which the ship is registered and the United States are not parties to the same treaty, convention, or agreement prescribing the requirements for such apparatus.

(y) (1) "Operator" on a ship of the United States means, for the purpose of Parts II and III of Title III of this Act, a person holding a radio operator's license of the proper class as prescribed and issued by the Commission.

(2) "Operator" on a foreign ship means, for the purpose of Part II of Title III of this Act, a person holding a certificate as such of the proper class complying with the provisions of the radio regulations annexed to the International Telecommunication Convention in force, or complying with an agreement or treaty between the United States and the country in which the ship is registered.

(z) (1) "Radio officer" on a ship of the United States means, for the purpose of Part II of Title III of this Act, a person holding at least a first or second class radiotelegraph operator's license as prescribed and issued by the Commission. When such person is employed to operate a radiotelegraph station aboard a ship of the United States, he is also required to be licensed as a "radio officer" in accordance with the Act of May 12, 1948 (46 USC, Section 229 a-h).

(2) "Radio officer" on a foreign ship means, for the purpose of Part II of Title III of this Act, a person holding at least a first or second class radiotelegraph operator's certificate complying with the provisions of the radio regulations annexed to the International Telecommunication Convention in force.

(aa) "Harbor" or "port" means any place to which ships may resort for shelter or to load or unload passengers or goods, or to obtain fuel, water, or supplies. This term shall apply to such places whether proclaimed public or not and whether natural or artificial.

(bb) "Safety convention" means the International Convention for the Safety of Life at Sea in force and the regulations referred to therein.

(cc) "Station license", "radio station license", or "license" means that instrument of authorization required by this Act or the rules and regulations of the Commission made pursuant to this Act, for the use or operation of apparatus for transmission of energy, or communications, or signals by radio, by whatever name the instrument may be designated by the Commission.

(dd) "Broadcast station", "broadcasting station", or "radio broadcast station" means a radio station equipped to engage in broadcasting as herein defined.

(ee) "Construction permit" or "permit for construction" means an instrument or authorization required by this Act or the rules and regulations of the Commission made pursuant to this Act for the construction of a station or the installation of apparatus, for the transmission of energy, or communications, or signals by radio, by whatever names the instrument may be designated by the Commission.

(ff) "Great Lakes Agreement" means the agreement for the promotion of safety on the Great Lakes by means of radio in force and the regulations referred to therein.

SEC. 4. (a) The Federal Communications Commission (in this Act referred to as the "Commission") shall be composed of seven commissioners appointed by the President, by and with the advice and consent of the Senate, one of whom the President shall designate as chairman.

(b) Each member of the Commission shall be a citizen of the United States. No member of the Commission or person in its employ shall be financially interested in the manufacture or sale of radio apparatus or of apparatus for wire or radio communication; in communication by wire or radio or in radio transmission of energy; in any company furnishing services or such apparatus to any company engaged in communication by wire or radio or to any company manufacturing or selling apparatus used for communication by wire or radio; or in any company owning stocks, bonds, or other securities of any such company; nor be in the employ of or hold any official relation to any person subject to any of the provisions of this Act, nor own stocks, bonds, or other securities of any corporation subject to any of the provisions of this Act. Such commissioners shall not engage in any other business, vocation, profession or employment. Any such commissioner serving as such after one year from the date of enactment of the Communications Act Amendments, 1952, shall not for a period of one year following the termination of his services as a Commissioner represent any person before the Commission in a professional capacity, except that this restriction shall not apply to any commissioner who has served the full term for which he was appointed. Not more than four commissioners shall be members of the same political party.

(c) The commissioners first appointed under this Act shall continue in office for the terms of one, two, three, four, five, six, and seven years, respectively, from the date of the taking effect of this Act, the term of each to be designated by the President, but their successors shall be appointed for terms of seven years and until their successors are appointed and have qualified, except that they shall not continue to serve beyond the expiration of the next session of Congress subsequent to the expiration of said fixed term of office; except that any person chosen to fill a vacancy shall be appointed only for the unexpired term of the commissioner whom he succeeds. No vacancy in the Commission shall impair the right of the remaining commissioners to exercise all the powers of the Commission.

(d) Each commissioner shall receive an annual salary of $10,000, payable in monthly installments.*

(e) The principal office of the Commission shall be in the District of Columbia, where its general sessions shall be held; but whenever the convenience of the public or of the parties may be promoted or delay or expense prevented thereby, the Commission may hold special sessions in any part of the United States.

(f) (1) The Commission shall have authority, subject to the provisions of the civil-service laws and the Classification Act of 1949, as amended, to appoint such officers, engineers, accountants, attorneys, inspectors, examiners, and other employees as are necessary in the exercise of its functions.

(2) Without regard to the civil-service laws, but subject to the Classification Act of 1949, each commissioner may appoint a legal assistant, an engineering assistant, and a secretary, each of whom shall perform such duties as such commissioner shall direct. In addition, the chairman of the Commission may appoint, without regard

*This subsection (d) has been superseded by 5 U. S. C. Sections 5314(19), 5315(57). Pursuant to recommendations of the President submitted to Congress in accordance with Section 225(h) of Pub. L. 90-206, approved December 16, 1967, 81 Stat. 644, the annual rate for the Chairman is now $40,000 and for other members $38,000.

to the civil-service laws, but subject to the Classification Act of 1949, an administrative assistant who shall perform such duties as the chairman shall direct.

(3) The Commission shall fix a reasonable rate of extra compensation for overtime services of engineers in charge and radio engineers of the Field Engineering and Monitoring Bureau of the Federal Communications Commission, who may be required to remain on duty between the hours of 5 o'clock postmeridian and 8 o'clock antemeridian or on Sundays or holidays to perform services in connection with the inspection of ship radio equipment and apparatus for the purposes of Part II of Title III of this Act or the Great Lakes Agreement, on the basis of one-half day's additional pay for each two hours or fraction thereof of at least one hour that the overtime extends beyond 5 o'clock postmeridian (but not to exceed two and one-half days' pay for the full period from 5 o'clock postmeridian to 8 o'clock antemeridian) and two additional days' pay for Sunday or holiday duty. The said extra compensation for overtime services shall be paid by the master, owner, or agent of such vessel to the local United States collector of customs or his representative, who shall deposit such collection into the Treasury of the United States to an appropriately designated receipt account: Provided, That the amounts of such collections received by the said collector of customs or his representatives shall be covered into the Treasury as miscellaneous receipts; and the payments of such extra compensation to the several employees entitled thereto shall be made from the annual appropriations for salaries and expenses of the Commission: Provided further, That to the extent that the annual appropriations which are hereby authorized to be made from the general fund of the Treasury are insufficient, there are hereby authorized to be appropriated from the general fund of the Treasury such additional amounts as may be necessary to the extent that the amounts of such receipts are in excess of the amounts appropriated: Provided further, That such extra compensation shall be paid if such field employees have been ordered to report for duty and have so reported whether the actual inspection of the radio equipment or apparatus takes place or not: And provided further, That in those ports where customary working hours are other than those hereinabove mentioned, the engineers in charge are vested with authority to regulate the hours of such employees so as to agree with prevailing working hours in said ports where inspections are to be made, but nothing contained in this proviso shall be construed in any manner to alter the length of a working day for the engineers in charge and radio engineers or the overtime pay herein fixed.

(g) The Commission may make such expenditures (including expenditures for rent and personal services at the seat of government and elsewhere, for office supplies, law books, periodicals, and books of reference, for printing and binding) for land for use as sites for radio monitoring stations and related facilities, including living quarters where necessary in remote areas, for the construction of such stations and facilities, and for the improvement, furnishing, equipping and repairing of such stations and facilities, and of laboratories and other related facilities (including construction of minor subsidiary buildings and structures not exceeding $25,000 in any one instance) used in connection with technical research activities, as may be necessary for the execution of the functions vested in the Commission and as from time to time may be appropriated for by Congress. All expenditures of the Commission, including all necessary expenses for transportation incurred by the commissioners or by their employees, under their orders, in making any investigation or upon any official business in any other places than in the city of Washington, shall be allowed and paid on the presentation of itemized vouchers therefor approved by the chairman of the Commission or by such other member or officer thereof as may be designated by the Commission for that purpose.

(h) Four members of the Commission shall constitute a quorum thereof. The Commission shall have an official seal which shall be judicially noticed.

(i) The Commission may perform any and all acts, make such rules and regulations, and issue such orders, not inconsistent with this Act, as may be necessary in the execution of its functions.

(j) The Commission may conduct its proceedings in such manner as will best conduce to the proper dispatch of business and to the ends of justice. No commissioner shall participate in any hearing or proceeding in which he has a pecuniary interest. Any party may appear before the Commission and be heard in person or by attorney. Every vote and official act of the Commission shall be entered of record, and its proceedings shall be public upon the request of any party interested. The Commission is authorized to withhold publication of records or proceedings containing secret information affecting the national defense.

(k) The Commission shall make an annual report to Congress, copies of which shall be distributed as are other reports transmitted to Congress. Such report shall contain: (1) Such information and data collected by the Commission as may be considered of value in the determination of questions connected with the regulation of interstate and foreign wire and radio communication and radio transmission of energy; (2) Such information and data concerning the functioning of the Commission as will be of value to Congress in appraising the amount and character of the work and accomplishments of the Commission and the adequacy of its staff and equipment; provided, that the first and second annual reports following the date of enactment of the Communications Act Amendments, 1952, shall set forth in detail the number and caption of pending applications requesting approval of transfer of control or assignment of a broadcasting station license, or construction permits for new broadcasting stations, or for increases in power, or for changes of frequency of existing broadcasting stations at the beginning and end of the period covered by such reports; (3) (Repealed);* (4) An itemized statement of all funds expended during the preceding year by the Commission, of the sources of such funds, and of the authority in this Act or elsewhere under which such expenditures were made; and (5) Specific recommendations to Congress as to additional legislation which the Commission deems necessary or desirable, including all legislative proposals submitted for approval to the Director of the Bureau of the Budget.

(1) All reports of investigations made by the Commission shall be entered of record, and a copy thereof shall be furnished to the party who may have complained, and to any common carrier or licensee that may have been complained of.

(m) The Commission shall provide for the publication of its reports and decisions in such form and manner as may be best adapted for public information and use, and such authorized publications shall be competent evidence of the reports and decisions of the Commission therein contained in all courts of the United States and of the several States without any further proof or authentication thereof.

(n) Rates of compensation of persons appointed under this section shall be subject to the reduction applicable to officers and employees of the Federal Government generally.

(o) For the purpose of obtaining maximum effectiveness from the use of radio and wire communications in connection with safety of life and property, the Commission shall investigate and study all phases of the problem and the best methods of obtaining the cooperation and coordination of these systems.

---

*Section K (3) was deleted by Pub. L. No. 554 (82d Cong.), July 16, 1952, 74 Stat. 245, 249, which formerly required the Commission to report as to new employees and persons leaving the Commission's employ during the preceding year.

SEC. 5. (a) The member of the Commission designated by the President as chairman shall be the chief executive officer of the Commission. It shall be his duty to preside at all meetings and sessions of the Commission, to represent the Commission in all matters relating to legislation and legislative reports, except that any Commissioner may present his own or minority views or supplemental reports, to represent the Commission in all matters requiring conferences or communications with other governmental officers, departments or agencies, and generally to coordinate and organize the work of the Commission in such manner as to promote prompt and efficient disposition of all matters within the jurisdiction of the Commission. In the case of a vacancy in the office of the Chairman of the Commission, or the absence or inability of the chairman to serve, the Commission may temporarily designate one of its members to act as Chairman until the cause or circumstance requiring such designation shall have been eliminated or corrected.

(b) Within six months after the enactment of the Communications Act Amendments, 1952, and from time to time thereafter as the Commission may find necessary, the Commission shall organize its staff into (1) integrated bureaus, to function on the basis of the Commission's principal workload operations, and (2) such other divisional organizations as the Commission may deem necessary. Each such integrated bureau shall include such legal, engineering, accounting, administrative, clerical, and other personnel as the Commission may determine to be necessary to perform its functions.

(c) [Repealed].

(d) (1) When necessary to the proper functioning of the Commission and the prompt and orderly conduct of its business, the Commission may, by published rule or by order, delegate any of its functions (except functions granted to the Commission by this paragraph and by paragraphs (4), (5), and (6) of this subsection) to a panel of Commissioners, an individual commissioner, an employee board, or an individual employee, including functions with respect to hearing, determining, ordering, certifying, reporting, or otherwise acting as to any work, business, or matter, except that in delegating review functions to employees in cases of adjudication (as defined in the Administrative Procedure Act), the delegation in any such case may be made only to an employee board consisting of three or more employees referred to in paragraph (8). Any such rule or order may be adopted, amended, or rescinded only by a vote of a majority of the members of the Commission then holding office. Nothing in this paragraph shall authorize the Commission to provide for the conduct, by any person or persons other than persons referred to in clauses (2) and (3) of Section 7(a) of the Administrative Procedure Act, of any hearing to which such Section 7(a) applies.

(2) As used in this subsection (d) the term "order, decision, report, or action" does not include an initial, tentative, or recommended decision to which exceptions may be filed as provided in Section 409(b).

(3) Any order, decision, report, or action made or taken pursuant to any such delegation, unless reviewed as provided in paragraph (4), shall have the same force and effect, and shall be made, evidenced, and enforced in the same manner, as orders, decisions, reports, or other actions of the Commission.

(4) Any person aggrieved by any such order, decision, report or action may file an application for review by the Commission within such time and in such manner as the Commission shall prescribe, and every such application shall be passed upon by the Commission. The Commission, on its own initiative, may review in whole or in part, at such time and in such manner as it shall determine any order, decision, report, or action made or taken pursuant to any delegation under paragraph (1).

(5) In passing upon applications for review, the Commission may grant in whole or in part, or deny such applications without specifying any reasons therefor. No such application for review shall rely on questions of fact or law upon which the panel of Commissioners, individual Commissioner, employee board, or individual employee has been afforded no opportunity to pass.

(6) If the Commission grants the application for review, it may affirm, modify, or set aside the order, decision, report, or action, or it may order a rehearing upon such order, decision, report, or action in accordance with Section 405.

(7) The filing of an application for review under this subsection shall be a condition precedent to judicial review of any order, decision, report, or action made or taken pursuant to a delegation under paragraph (1). The time within which a petition for review must be filed in a proceeding to which Section 402(a) applies, or within which an appeal must be taken under Section 402(b), shall be computed from the date upon which public notice is given of orders disposing of all applications for review filed in any case.

(8) The employees to whom the Commission may delegate review functions in any case of adjudication (as defined in the Administrative Procedure Act) shall be qualified, by reason of their training, experience, and competence, to perform such review functions, and shall perform no duties inconsistent with such review functions. Such employees shall be in a grade classification or salary level commensurate with their important duties, and in no event less than the grade classification or salary level of the employee or employees whose actions are to be reviewed. In the performance of such review functions such employees shall be assigned to cases in rotation so far as practicable and shall not be responsible to or subject to the supervision or direction of any officer, employee, or agent engaged in the performance of investigative or prosecuting functions for any agency.

(9) The secretary and seal of the Commission shall be the secretary and seal of each panel of the Commission, each individual Commissioner, and each employee board or individual employee exercising functions delegated pursuant to paragraph (1) of this subsection.

(e) Meetings of the Commission shall be held at regular intervals, not less frequently than once each calendar month, at which times the functioning of the Commission and the handling of its work load shall be reviewed and such orders shall be entered and other action taken as may be necessary or appropriate to expedite the prompt and orderly conduct of the business of the Commission with the objective of rendering a final decision (1) within three months from the date of filing in all original application, renewal, and transfer cases in which it will not be necessary to hold a hearing, and (2) within six months from the final date of the hearing in all hearing cases; and the Commission shall promptly report to the Congress each such case which has been pending before it more than such three- or six-month period, respectively, stating the reasons therefor.

TITLE III—PROVISIONS RELATING TO RADIO

PART I—GENERAL PROVISIONS

LICENSE FOR RADIO COMMUNICATION OR TRANSMISSION OF ENERGY

SECTION 301. It is the purpose of this act, among other things, to maintain the control of the United States over all the channels of interstate and foreign radio transmission; and to provide for the use of such channels, but not the ownership thereof, by persons for limited periods of time, under licenses granted by Federal authority, and no such license shall be construed to create any right, beyond the terms, conditions, and periods of the license. No person shall use or operate any apparatus for the transmission of energy or communications or signals by radio (a) from one place in any Territory or possession of the United States or in the District of Columbia to another place in the same Territory, possession, or District; or (b) from any State, Territory, or possession of the United States, or from the District of Columbia to any other State, Territory, or possession of the United States; or (c) from any place in any State, Territory, or possession of the United States, or in the District of Columbia, to any place in any foreign country or to any vessel; or (d) within any State when the effects of such use extend beyond the borders of said State, or when interference is caused by such use or operation with the transmission of such energy, communications, or signals from within said State to any place beyond its borders, or from any place beyond its borders to any place within said State, or with the transmission or reception of such energy, communications, or signals from and/or to places beyond the borders of said State; or (e) upon any vessel or aircraft of the United States; or (f) upon any other mobile stations within the jurisdiction of the United States, except under and in accordance with this Act and with a license in that behalf granted under the provisions of this Act.

DEVICES WHICH INTERFERE WITH RADIO RECEPTION

Section 302. (a) The Commission may, consistent with the public interest, convenience, and necessity, make reasonable regulations governing the interference potential of devices which in their operation are capable of emitting radio frequency energy by radiation, conduction, or other means in sufficient degree to cause harmful interference to radio communications. Such regulations shall be applicable to the manufacture, import, sale, offer for sale, shipment, or use of such devices.

(b) No person shall manufacture, import, sell, offer for sale, ship, or use devices which fail to comply with regulations promulgated pursuant to this section.

(c) The provisions of this section shall not be applicable to carriers transporting such devices without trading in them, to devices manufactured solely for export, to the manufacture, assembly, or installation of devices for its own use by a public utility engaged in providing electric service, or to devices for use by the Government of the United States or any agency thereof. Devices for use by the Government of the United States or any agency thereof shall be developed, procured, or otherwise acquired, including offshore procurement, under United States Government criteria, standards, or specifications designed to achieve the common objective of reducing interference to radio reception, taking into account the unique needs of national defense and security.

GENERAL POWERS OF COMMISSION

SEC. 303. Except as otherwise provided in this Act, the Commission from time to time, as public convenience, interest, or necessity requires, shall—

(a) Classify radio stations;

(b) Prescribe the nature of the service to be rendered by each class of licensed stations and each station within any class;

(c) Assign bands of frequencies to the various classes of stations, and assign frequencies for each individual station and determine the power which each station shall use and the time during which it may operate;

(d) Determine the location of classes of stations or individual stations;

(e) Regulate the kind of apparatus to be used with respect to its external effects and the purity and sharpness of the emissions from each station and from the apparatus therein;

(f) Make such regulations not inconsistent with law as it may deem necessary to prevent interference between stations and to carry out the provisions of this Act: *Provided, however,* That changes in the frequencies, authorized power, or in the times of operation of any station, shall not be made without the consent of the station licensee unless, after a public hearing, the Commission shall determine that such changes will promote public convenience or interest or will serve public necessity, or the provisions of this Act will be more fully complied with;

(g) Study new uses for radio, provide for experimental uses of frequencies, and generally encourage the larger and more effective use of radio in the public interest;

(h) Have authority to establish areas or zones to be served by any station;

(i) Have authority to make special regulations applicable to radio stations engaged in chain broadcasting;

(j) Have authority to make general rules and regulations requiring stations to keep such records of programs, transmissions of energy, communications, or signals as it may deem desirable;

(k) Have authority to exclude from the requirements of any regulations in whole or in part any radio station upon railroad rolling stock, or to modify such regulations in its discretion;

(l) (1) Have authority to prescribe the qualifications of station operators, to classify them according to the duties to be performed, to fix the forms of such licenses, and to issue them to such citizens or nationals of the United States as the Commission finds qualified, except that in issuing licenses for the operation of radio stations on aircraft the Commission may, if it finds that the public interest will be served thereby, waive the requirement of citizenship in the case of persons holding United States pilot certificates or in the case of persons holding foreign aircraft pilot certificates which are valid in the United States on the basis of reciprocal agreements entered into with foreign governments;

(2) Notwithstanding Section 301 of this Act and paragraph (1) of this subsection, the Commission may issue authorizations, under such conditions and terms as it may prescribe, to permit an alien licensed by his government as an amateur radio operator to operate his amateur radio station licensed by his government in the United States, its possessions, and the Commonwealth of Puerto Rico provided there is in effect a bilateral agreement between the United States and the alien's government for such operation on a reciprocal basis by United States amateur radio operators: provided, that when an application for an authorization is received by the Commission, it shall notify the appropriate agencies of the Government of such fact, and such agencies shall forthwith furnish to the Commission such information in their possession as bears upon the compatibility of the request with the national security: and provided further, that the requested authorization may then be granted unless the Commission shall determine that information received from such agencies necessitates denial of the request. Other provisions of this Act and of the Administrative Procedure Act shall not be applicable to any request or application for or modification, suspension, or cancellation of any such authorization.

(m) (1) Have authority to suspend the license of any operator upon proof sufficient to satisfy the Commission that the licensee—

(A) Has violated any provision of any Act, treaty, or convention binding on the United States, which the Commission is authorized to administer, or any regulation made by the Commission under any such Act, treaty, or convention; or

(B) Has failed to carry out a lawful order of the master or person lawfully in charge of the ship or aircraft on which he is employed; or

417

(C) Has willfully damaged or permitted radio apparatus or installations to be damaged; or

(D) Has transmitted superfluous radio communications or signals or communications containing profane or obscene words, language, or meaning, or has knowingly transmitted—

(1) False or deceptive signals or communications, or

(2) A call signal or letter which has not been assigned by proper authority to the station he is operating; or

(E) Has willfully or maliciously interfered with any other radio communications or signals; or

(F) Has obtained or attempted to obtain, or has assisted another to obtain or attempt to obtain, an operator's license by fraudulent means.

(2) No order of suspension of any operator's license shall take effect until fifteen days' notice in writing thereof, stating the cause for the proposed suspension, has been given to the operator licensee who may make written application to the Commission at any time within said fifteen days for a hearing upon such order. The notice to the operator licensee shall not be effective until actually received by him, and from that time he shall have fifteen days in which to mail the said application. In the event that physical conditions prevent mailing of the application at the expiration of the fifteen-day period, the application shall then be mailed as soon as possible thereafter, accompanied by a satisfactory explanation of the delay. Upon receipt by the Commission of such application for hearing, said order of suspension shall be held in abeyance until the conclusion of the hearing which shall be conducted under such rules as the Commission may prescribe. Upon the conclusion of said hearing the Commission may affirm, modify, or revoke said order of suspension.

(n) Have authority to inspect all radio installations associated with stations required to be licensed by any Act or which are subject to the provisions of any Act, treaty, or convention binding on the United States, to ascertain whether in construction, installation, and operation they conform to the requirements of the rules and regulations of the Commission, the provisions of any Act, the terms of any treaty or convention binding on the United States, and the conditions of the license or other instrument of authorization under which they are constructed, installed, or operated.

(o) Have authority to designate call letters of all stations;

(p) Have authority to cause to be published such call letters and such other announcements and data as in the judgment of the Commission may be required for the efficient operation of radio stations subject to the jurisdiction of the United States and for the proper enforcement of this Act;

(q) Have authority to require the painting and/or illumination of radio towers if and when in its judgment such towers constitute, or there is a reasonable possibility that they may constitute, a menace to air navigation. The permittee or licensee shall maintain the painting and/or illumination of the tower as prescribed by the Commission pursuant to this section. In the event that the tower ceases to be licensed by the Commission for the transmission of radio energy, the owner of the tower shall maintain the prescribed painting and/or illumination of such tower until it is dismantled, and the Commission may require the owner to dismantle and remove the tower when the Administrator of the Federal Aviation Agency determines that there is a reasonable possibility that it may constitute a menace to air navigation.

(r) Make such rules and regulations and prescribe such restrictions and conditions, not inconsistent with law, as may be necessary to carry out the provisions of this Act, or any international radio or wire communications, treaty or convention, or regulations annexed thereto, including any treaty or convention insofar as it relates to the use of radio, to which the United States is or may hereafter become a party.

(s) Have authority to require that apparatus designed to receive television pictures broadcast simultaneously with sound be capable of adequately receiving all frequencies allocated by the Commission to television broadcasting when such apparatus is shipped in interstate commerce, or is imported from any foreign country into the United States, for sale or resale to the public.

WAIVER BY LICENSEE

SEC. 304. No station license shall be granted by the Commission until the applicant therefor shall have signed a waiver of any claim to the use of any particular frequency or of the ether as against the regulatory power of the United States because of the previous use of the same, whether by license or otherwise.

GOVERNMENT-OWNED STATIONS

SEC. 305. (a) Radio stations belonging to and operated by the United States shall not be subject to the provisions of sections 301 and 303 of this Act. All such Government stations shall use such frequencies as shall be assigned to each or to each class by the President. All such stations, except stations on board naval and other Government vessels while at sea or beyond the limits of the continental United States, when transmitting any radio communication or signal other than a communication or signal relating to Government business, shall conform to such rules and regulations designed to prevent interference with other radio stations and the rights of others as the Commission may prescribe.

(b) Radio stations on board vessels of the United States Maritime Commission or the Inland and Coastwise Waterways Service shall be subject to the provisions of this title.

(c) All stations owned and operated by the United States, except mobile stations of the Army of the United States, and all other stations on land and sea, shall have special call letters designated by the Commission.

(d) The provision of Sections 301 and 303 of this Act notwithstanding, the President may, provided he determines it to be consistent with and in the interest of national security, authorize a foreign government, under such terms and conditions as he may prescribe, to construct and operate at the seat of government of the United States a low-power radio station in the fixed service at or near the site of the embassy or legation of such foreign government for transmission of its messages to points outside the United States, but only (1) where he determines that the authorization would be consistent with the national interest of the United States and (2) where such foreign government has provided reciprocal privileges to the United States to construct and operate radio stations within territories subject to its jurisdiction. Foreign government stations authorized pursuant to the provisions of this subsection shall conform to such rules and regulations as the President may prescribe. The authorization of such stations, and the renewal, modification, suspension, revocation, or other termination of such authority shall be in accordance with such procedures as may be established by the President and shall not be subject to the other provisions of this Act or of the Administrative Procedure Act.

FOREIGN SHIPS

SEC. 306. Section 301 of this Act shall not apply to any person sending radio communications or signals on a foreign ship while the same is within the jurisdiction of the United States, but such communications or signals shall be transmitted only in accordance with such regulations designed to prevent interference as may be promulgated under the authority of this Act.

SEC. 307. (a) The Commission, if public convenience, interest, or necessity will be served thereby, subject to the limitations of this Act, shall grant to any applicant therefor a station license provided for by this Act.

(b) In considering applications for licenses, and modifications and renewals thereof, when and insofar as there is demand for the same, the Commission shall make such distribution of licenses, frequencies, hours of operation, and of power among the several states and communities as to provide a fair, efficient and equitable distribution of radio service to each of the same.

(c) The Commission shall study the proposal that Congress by statute allocate fixed percentages of radio broadcasting facilities to particular types or kinds of non-profit radio programs or to persons identified with particular types or kinds of non-profit activities, and shall report to Congress, not later than February 1, 1935, its recommendations together with the reasons for the same.

(d) No license granted for the operation of a broadcasting station shall be for a longer term than three years and no license so granted for any other class of station shall be for a longer term than five years, and any license granted may be revoked as hereinafter provided. Upon the expiration of any license, upon application therefor, a renewal of such license may be granted from time to time for a term of not to exceed three years in the case of broadcasting licenses and not to exceed five years in the case of other licenses, if the Commission finds that public interest, convenience and necessity would be served thereby. In order to expedite action on applications for renewal of broadcasting station licenses and in order to avoid needless expense to applicants for such renewals, the Commission shall not require any such applicant to file any information which previously has been furnished to the Commission or which is not directly material to the considerations that affect the granting or denial of such application, but the Commission may require any new or additional facts it deems necessary to make its findings. Pending any hearing and final decision on such application and the disposition of any petition for rehearing pursuant to Section 405, the Commission shall continue such license in effect. Consistently with the foregoing provisions of this subsection, the Commission may by rule prescribe the period or periods for which licenses shall be granted and renewed for particular classes of stations, but the Commission may not adopt or follow any rule which would preclude it, in any case involving a station of a particular class, from granting or renewing a license for a shorter period than that prescribed for stations of such class if, in its judgment, public interest, convenience, or necessity would be served by such action.

(e) No renewal of an existing station license in the broadcast or the common carrier services shall be granted more than thirty days prior to the expiration of the original license.

SEC. 308. (a) The Commission may grant construction permits and station licenses, or modifications or renewals thereof, only upon written application therefore received by it: provided, that (1) in cases of emergency found by the Commission involving danger to life or property or due to damage to equipment, or (2) during a national emergency proclaimed by the President or declared by the Congress and during the continuance of any war in which the United States is engaged and when such action is necessary for the national defense or security or otherwise in furtherance of the war effort, or (3) in cases of emergency where the Commission finds, in the non-broadcast services, that it would not be feasible to secure renewal applications from existing licensees or otherwise to follow normal licensing procedure, the Commission may grant construction permits and station licenses, or modifications or renewals thereof, during the emergency so found by the Commission or during the continuance of any such national emergency or war, in such manner and upon such terms and conditions as the Commission shall by regulation prescribe, and without the filing of a formal application, but no authorization so granted shall continue in effect beyond the period of the emergency or war requiring it: providing further that the Commission may issue by cable, telegraph, or radio a permit for the operation of a station on a vessel of the United States at sea, effective in lieu of a license until said vessel shall return to a port of the continental United States.

(b) All applications for station licenses, or modifications or renewals thereof, shall set forth such facts as the Commission by regulation may prescribe as to the citizenship, character, and financial, technical, and other qualifications of the applicant to operate the station; the ownership and location of the proposed station and of the stations, if any, with which it is proposed to communicate; the frequencies and the power desired to be used; the hours of the day or other periods of time during which it is proposed to operate the station; the purposes for which the station is to be used; and such other information as it may require. The Commission, at any time after the filing of such original application and during the term of any such license, may require from an applicant or licensee further written statements of fact to enable it to determine whether such original application should be granted or denied or such license revoked. Such application and/or such statement of fact shall be signed by the applicant and/or licensee.

(c) The Commission in granting any license for a station intended or used for commercial communication between the United States or any Territory or possession, continental or insular, subject to the jurisdiction of the United States, and any foreign country, may impose any terms, conditions, or restrictions authorized to be imposed with respect to submarine-cable licenses by section 2 of an Act entitled "An Act relating to the landing and the operation of submarine cables in the United States", approved May 24, 1921.

ACTION UPON APPLICATIONS; FORM OF AND CONDITIONS ATTACHED TO LICENSES

SEC. 309. (a) Subject to the provisions of this section, the Commission shall determine, in the case of each application filed with it which Section 308 applies, whether the public interest, convenience, and necessity will be served by the granting of such application, and, if the Commission, upon examination of such application and upon consideration of such other matters as the Commission may officially notice, shall find that public interest, convenience and necessity would be served by the granting thereof, it shall grant such application.

(b) Except as provided in subsection (c) of this section, no such application—

(1) for an instrument of authorization in the case of a station in the broadcasting or common carrier services, or

(2) for an instrument of authorization in the case of a station in any of the following categories:

(A) fixed point-to-point microwave stations (exclusive of control and relay stations used as integral parts of mobile radio systems),

(B) industrial radio positioning stations for which frequencies are assigned on an exclusive basis,

(C) aeronautical en route stations,

(D) aeronautical advisory stations,

(E) airdrome control stations,

(F) aeronautical fixed stations, and

(G) such other stations or classes of stations, not in the broadcasting or common carrier services, as the Commission shall by rule prescribe, shall be granted by the Commission earlier than thirty days following issuance of public notice by the Commission of the acceptance for filing of such application or of any substantial amendment thereof.

(c) Subsection (b) of this section shall not apply—

(1) to any minor amendment of an application to which such subsection is applicable, or

(2) to any application for—

(A) a minor change in the facilities of an authorized station,

(B) consent to an involuntary assignment or transfer under Section 310(b) or to an assignment or transfer thereunder which does not involve a substantial change in ownership or control,

(C) a license under Section 319(c) or, pending application for or grant of such license, any special or temporary authorization to permit interim operation to facilitate completion of authorized construction or to provide substantially the same service as would be authorized by such license,

(D) extension of time to complete construction of authorized facilities,

(E) an authorization of facilities for remote pickups, studio links and similar facilities for use in the operation of a broadcast station,

(F) authorizations pursuant to Section 325(b) where the programs to be transmitted are special events not of a continuing nature,

(G) a special temporary authorization for non-broadcast operation not to exceed thirty days where no application for regular operation is contemplated to be filed or not to exceed sixty days pending the filing of an application for such regular operation, or

(H) an authorization under any of the proviso clauses of Section 308(a).

(d) (1) Any party in interest may file with the Commission a petition to deny any application (whether as originally filed or as amended) to which subsection (b) of this section applies at any time prior to the day of Commission grant thereof without hearing or the day of formal designation thereof for hearing; except that with respect to any classification of applications, the Commission from time to time by rule may specify a shorter period (no less than thirty days following the issuance of public notice by the Commission of the acceptance of for filing of such application or of any substantial amendment thereof), which shorter period shall be reasonably related to the time when the applications would normally be reached for processing. The petition shall contain specific allegations of fact sufficient to show that the petitioner is a party in interest and that a grant of the application would be prima facie inconsistent with subsection (a). Such allegations of fact shall, except for those of which official notice may be taken, be supported by affidavit of a person or persons with personal knowledge thereof. The applicant shall be given the opportunity to file reply in which allegations of fact or denials thereof shall similarly be supported by affidavit.

(2) If the Commission finds on the basis of the application, the pleadings filed, or other matters which it may officially notice that there are no substantial and material questions of fact and that a grant of application would be consistent with subsection (a), it shall make the grant, deny the petition, and issue a concise statement of the reasons for denying the petition which statement shall dispose of all substantial issues raised by the petition. If a substantial and material question of fact is presented or if the Commission for any reason is unable to find that grant of the

application would be consistent with subsection (a), it shall proceed as provided in subsection (e).

(e) If, in the case of any application to which subsection (a) of this section applies, a substantial and material question of fact is presented or the Commission for any reason is unable to make the finding specified in such subsection, it shall formally designate the application for hearing on the ground or reasons then obtaining and shall forthwith notify the applicant and all other known parties in interest of such action and the grounds and reasons therefor, specifying with particularity the matters and things in issue but not including issues or requirements phrased generally. When the Commission has so designated an application for hearing the parties in interest, if any, who are not notified by the Commission of such action may acquire the status of a party to the proceeding thereon by filing a petition for intervention showing the basis for their interest not more than thirty days after publication of the hearing issues or any substantial amendment thereto in the *Federal Register*. Any hearing subsequently held upon such application shall be a full hearing in which the applicant and all other parties in interest shall be permitted to participate. The burden of proceeding with the introduction of evidence and the burden of proof shall be upon the applicant, except that with respect to any issue presented by a petition to deny or a petition to enlarge the issues, such burdens shall be as determined by the Commission.

(f) When an application subject to subsection (b) has been filed, the Commission, notwithstanding the requirements of such subsection, may, if the grant of such application is otherwise authorized by law and if it finds that there are extraordinary circumstances requiring emergency operations in the public interest and that delay in the institution of such emergency operations would seriously prejudice the public interest, grant a temporary authorization, accompanied by a statement of its reasons therefor, to permit such emergency operations for a period not exceeding ninety days, and upon making like findings may extend such temporary authorization for one additional period not to exceed ninety days. When any such grant of a temporary authorization is made, the Commission shall give expeditious treatment to any timely filed petition to deny such application and to any petition for rehearing of such grant filed under Section 405.

(g) The Commission is authorized to adopt reasonable classifications of applications and amendments in order to effectuate the purposes of this section.

(h) Such station licenses as the Commission may grant shall be in such general form as it may prescribe, but each license shall contain, in addition to other provisions, a statement of the following conditions to which such license shall be subject:

(1) The station license shall not vest in the licensee any right to operate the station nor any right in the use of the frequencies designated in the license beyond the term thereof nor in any other manner than authorized therein.

(2) Neither the license nor the right granted thereunder shall be assigned or otherwise transferred in violation of this Act.

(3) Every license issued under this Act shall be subject in terms to the right of use or control conferred by section 606 of this Act.

LIMITATION ON HOLDING AND TRANSFER OF LICENSES

SEC. 310. (a) The station license required hereby shall not be granted to or held by—

(1) Any alien or the representative of any alien;

(2) Any foreign government or the representative thereof;

(3) Any corporation organized under the laws of any foreign government;

(4) Any corporation of which any officer or director is an alien or of which more than one-fifth of the capital stock is owned of record or voted by aliens or

their representatives or by a foreign government or representative thereof, or by any corporation organized under the laws of a foreign country;

(5) Any corporation directly or indirectly controlled by any other corporation of which any officer or more than one-fourth of the directors are aliens, or of which more than one-fourth of the capital stock is owned of record or voted, after June 1, 1935, by aliens, their representatives, or by a foreign government or representative thereof, or by any corporation organized under the laws of a foreign country, if the Commission finds that the public interest will be served by the refusal or the revocation of such license.

Nothing in this subsection shall prevent the licensing of radio apparatus on board any vessel, aircraft, or other mobile station of the United States when the installation and use of such apparatus is required by Act of Congress or any treaty to which the United States is a party.

Notwithstanding paragraph (1) of this subsection, a license for a radio station on an aircraft may be granted to and held by a person who is an alien or a representative of an alien if such person holds a United States pilot certificate or a foreign aircraft pilot certificate which is valid in the United States on the basis of reciprocal agreements entered into with foreign governments.

Notwithstanding Section 301 of this Act and paragraphs (1) and (2) of this subsection, the Commission may issue authorizations, under such conditions and terms as it may prescribe, to permit an alien licensed by his government as an amateur radio operator to operate his amateur radio station licensed by his government in the United States, its possessions, and the Commonwealth of Puerto Rico provided there is in effect a bilateral agreement between the United States and the alien's government for such operation on a reciprocal basis by United States amateur radio operators: provided, that when an application for an authorization is received by the Commission, it shall notify the appropriate agencies of the Government of such fact, and such agencies shall forthwith furnish to the Commission such information in their possession as bears upon the compatibility of the request with the national security: and provided further, that the requested authorization may then be granted unless the Commission shall determine that information received from such agencies necessitates denial of the request. Other provisions of this Act and of the Administrative Procedure Act shall not be applicable to any request or application for or modification, suspension, or cancellation of any such authorization.

(b) No construction permit or station license, or any rights thereunder, shall be transferred, assigned, or disposed of in any manner, voluntarily or involuntarily, directly or indirectly, or by transfer of control of any corporation holding such permit or license, to any person except upon application to the Commission and upon finding by the Commission that the public interest, convenience and necessity will be served thereby. Any such application shall be disposed of as if the proposed transferee or assignee were making application under Section 308 for the permit or license in question; but in acting theron the Commission may not consider whether the public interest, convenience and necessity might be served by the transfer, assignment, or disposal of the permit or license to a person other than the proposed transferee or assignee.

SPECIAL REQUIREMENTS WITH RESPECT TO CERTAIN APPLICATIONS
IN THE BROADCASTING SERVICE

SEC. 311. (a) When there is filed with the Commission any application to which Section 309(b) (1) applies, for an instrument of authorization for a station in the broadcasting service, the applicant—

(1) shall give notice of such filing in the principal area which is served or is to be served by the station; and

(2) if the application is formally designated for hearing in accordance with Section 309, shall give notice of such hearings in such area at least ten days before commencement of such hearing.

The Commission shall by rule prescribe the form and content of the notices to be given in compliance with this subsection, and the manner and frequency with which such notices shall be given.

(b) Hearings referred to in subsection (a) may be held at such places as the Commission shall determine to be appropriate, and in making such determination in any case the Commission shall consider whether the public interest, convenience or necessity will be served by conducting the hearing at a place in, or in the vicinity of, the principal area to be served by the station involved.

(c) (1) if there are pending before the Commission two or more applications for a permit for construction of a broadcasting station, only one of which can be granted, it shall be unlawful, without approval of the Commission, for the applicants or any of them to effectuate an agreement whereby one or more of such applicants withdraws his or their application or applications.

(2) The request for Commission approval in any such case shall be made in writing jointly by all the parties to the agreement. Such request shall contain or be accompanied by full information with respect to the agreement, set forth in such detail, form and manner as the Commission shall by rule require.

(3) The Commission shall approve the agreement only if it determines that the agreement is consistent with the public interest, convenience or necessity. If the agreement does not contemplate a merger, but contemplates the making of any direct or indirect payment to any party thereto in consideration of his withdrawal of his application, the Commission may determine the agreement to be consistent with the public interest, convenience or necessity only if the amount or value of such payment, as determined by the Commission, is not in excess of the aggregate amount determined by the Commission to have been legitimately and prudently expended and to be expended by such applicant in connection with preparing, filing, and advocating the granting of his application.

(4) For the purposes of this subsection an application shall be deemed to be "pending" before the Commission from the time such application is filed with the Commission until an order of the Commission granting or denying it is no longer subject to rehearing by the Commission or to review by any court.

ADMINISTRATIVE SANCTIONS

SEC. 312. (a) The Commission may revoke any station license or construction permit—

(1) for false statements knowingly made either in the application of or in any statement of fact which may be required pursuant to Section 308;

(2) because of conditions coming to the attention of the Commission which would warrant it in refusing to grant a license or permit on an original application;

(3) for willful or repeated failure to operate substantially as set forth in the license;

(4) for willful or repeated violation of, or willful or repeated failure to observe, any provision of this Act or any rule or regulation of the Commission authorized by this Act or by a treaty ratified by the United States; and

(5) for violation of or failure to observe any final cease and desist order issued by the Commission under this section; or

(6) for violation of Section 1304, 1343, or 1464 of Title 18 of the United States Code.

(b) Where any person

(1) has failed to operate substantially as set forth in a license.

(2) has violated or failed to observe any of the provisions of this Act, or Section 1304, 1343 or 1464 of Title 18 of the United States Code, or

(3) has violated or failed to observe any rule or regulation of the Commission authorized by this Act or by a treaty ratified by the United States, the Commission may order such person to cease and desist from such action.

(c) Before revoking a license or permit pursuant to subsection (a), or issuing a cease and desist order pursuant to subsection (b), the Commission shall serve upon the licensee, permittee or person involved an order to show cause why an order of revocation or a cease and desist order should not be issued. Any such order to show cause shall contain a statement of the matters with respect to which the Commission is inquiring and shall call upon said licensee, permittee or person to appear before the Commission at a time and place stated in the order, but in no event less than thirty days after the receipt of such order, and give evidence upon the matter specified therein; except that where safety or life or property is involved, the Commission may provide in the order for a shorter period. If after hearing, or a waiver thereof, the Commission determines that an order of revocation or a cease and desist order should issue, it shall issue such order which shall include a statement of the findings of the Commission and the grounds and reasons therefor, and specify the effective date of the order, and shall cause the same to be served on said licensee, permittee, or person.

(d) In any case where a hearing is conducted pursuant to the provisions of this section, both the burden of proceeding with the introduction of evidence and the burden of proof shall be upon the Commission.

(e) The provisions of Section 9(b) of the Administrative Procedure Act which apply with respect to the institution of any proceeding for the revocation of a license or permit shall apply also with respect to the institution, under this section, of any proceeding for the issuance of a cease and desist order.

APPLICATION OF ANTITRUST LAWS; REFUSAL OF LICENSES AND PERMITS IN CERTAIN CASES

SEC. 313. (a) All laws of the United States relating to unlawful restraints and monopolies and to combinations, contracts, or agreements in restraint of trade are hereby declared to be applicable to the manufacture and sale of and to trade in radio apparatus and devices entering into or affecting interstate or foreign commerce and to interstate or foreign radio communications. Whenever in any suit, action, or proceeding, civil or criminal, brought under the provisions of any of said laws or in any proceedings brought to enforce or to review findings and orders of the Federal Trade Commission or other governmental agency in respect of any matters as to which said Commission or other governmental agency is by law authorized to act, any licensee shall be found guilty of the violation of the provisions of such laws or any of them, the court, in addition to the penalties imposed by said laws, may adjudge, order, and/or decree that the license of such licensee shall, as of the date the decree or judgment becomes finally effective or as of such other date as the said decree shall fix, be revoked and that all rights under such license shall thereupon cease: *Provided, however,* That such licensee shall have the same right of appeal or review as is provided by law in respect of other decrees and judgments of said court.

(b) The Commission is hereby directed to refuse a station license and/or the permit hereinafter required for the construction of a station to any person (or to any person directly or indirectly controlled by such person) whose license has been revoked by a court under this section.

PRESERVATION OF COMPETITION IN COMMERCE

SEC. 314. After the effective date of this Act no person engaged directly, or indirectly through any person directly or indirectly controlling or controlled by, or under direct or indirect common control with, such perons, or through an agent, or otherwise, in the business of transmitting and/or receiving for hire energy, communications, or signals by radio in accordance with the terms of the license issued under this Act, shall by purchase, lease, construction, or otherwise, directly or indirectly, acquire, own, control, or operate any cable or wire telegraph or telephone line or system between any place in any State, Territory, or possession of the United States or in the District of Columbia, and any place in any foreign country, or shall acquire, own, or control any part of the stock or other capital share or any interest in the physical property and/or other assets of any such cable, wire, telegraph, or telephone line or system, if in either case the purpose is and/or the effect thereof may be to substantially lessen competition or to restrain commerce between any place in any State, Territory, or possession of the United States, or in the District of Columbia, and any place in any foreign country, or unlawfully to create monopoly in any line of commerce; nor shall any person engaged directly, or indirectly through any person directly or indirectly controlling or controlled by, or under direct or indirect common control with, such person, or through an agent, or otherwise, in the business of transmitting and/or receiving for hire messages by any cable, wire, telegraph, or telephone line or system (a) between any place in any State, Territory, or possession of the United States, or in the District of Columbia, and any place in any foreign country, or shall acquire, own, or control any part of the stock or other capital share or any interest in the physical property and/or other assets of any such radio station, apparatus, or system, if in either case the purpose is and /or the effect thereof may be to substantially lessen competition or to restrain commerce between any place in any State, Territory, or possession of the United States, or in the District of Columbia, and any place in any foreign country, or unlawfully to create monopoly in any line of commerce.

FACILITIES FOR CANDIDATES FOR PUBLIC OFFICE

Sec. 315. (a) If any licensee shall permit any person who is a legally qualified candidate for any public office to use a broadcasting station, he shall afford equal opportunities to all other such candidates for that office in the use of such broadcasting station: *provided,* that such licensee shall have no power of censorship over the material broadcast under the provisions of this section. No obligation is hereby imposed upon any licensee to allow the use of its station by any such candidate. Appearance by a legally qualified candidate on any—

(1) bona fide newscast
(2) bona fide news interview,
(3) bona fide news documentary (if the appearance of the condidate is incidental to the presentation of the subject or subjects covered by the news documentary), or
(4) on-the-spot coverage of bona fide news events (including but not limited to political conventions and activities incidental thereto)

Shall not be deemed to be use of a broadcasting station within the meaning of this subsection. Nothing in the foregoing sentence shall be construed as relieving broadcasters, in connection with the presentation of newscasts, news interviews, news documentaries, and on-the-spot coverage of news events, from the obligation imposed upon them under this Act to operate in the public interest and to afford reasonable opportunity for the discussion of conflicting views on issues of public importance.*

(b) The charges made for the use of any broadcasting station for any of the purposes set forth in this section shall not exceed the charges made for comparable use of such station for other purposes.

(c) The Commission shall prescribe appropriate rules and regulations to carry out the provisions of this section.**

MODIFICATION BY COMMISSION OF CONSTRUCTION PERMITS OR LICENSES

SEC. 316. (a) Any station license or construction permit may be modified by the Commission either for a limited time or for the duration of the term thereof, if in the judgment of the Commission such action will promote the public interest, convenience and necessity, or the provisions of this Act or of any treaty ratified by the United States will be more fully complied with. No such order of modification shall become final until the holder of the license or permit shall have been notified in writing of the proposed action and the grounds and reasons therefor, and shall have been given reasonable opportunity, in no event less than thirty days, to show cause by public hearing, if requested, why such order of modification should not issue; provided, that where safety of life or property is involved, the Commission may by order provide for a shorter period of notice.

(b) In any case where a hearing is conducted pursuant to the provisions of this section, both the burden of proceeding with the introduction of evidence and the burden of proof shall be upon the Commission.***

* By Pub. L. No. 86-274, approved September 14, 1959, 73 Stat. 557, Congress amended subsection (a). Section 2 of this amendatory act reads as follows:
Sec. 2. (a) The Congress declares its intention to reexamine from time to time the amendments to Section 315(a) of the Communications Act of 1934 made by the first Section of this Act, to ascertain whether such amendment has proved to be effective and practicable.
(b) To assist the Congress in making its reexaminations of such amendment, the Federal Communications Commission shall include in each annual report it makes to Congress a statement setting forth (1) the information and data used by it in determining questions arising from or connected with such amendment, and (2) such recommendations as it deems necessary in the public interest.
**Pub. L. 86-677 (S. J. Res. 207, approved August 24, 1960) provides:
Resolved by the Senate and House of Representatives of the United States of America in Congress assembled, that that part of Section 315(a) of the Communications Act of 1934, as amended, which requires any licensee of a broadcast station who permits any person who is a legally qualified candidate for any public office to use a broadcasting station to afford equal opportunities to all other such candidates for that office in the use of such broadcasting station, is suspended for the period of the 1960 presidential and vice-presidential campaigns with respect to nominees for the offices of President and Vice-President of the United States. Nothing in the foregoing shall be construed as relieving broadcasters from the obligation imposed upon them under this Act to operate in the public interest.
(2) The Federal Communications Commission shall make a report to the Congress, not later than March 1, 1961, with respect to the effect of the provisions of this joint resolution and any recommendations the Commission may have for amendments to the Communications Act of 1934 as a result of experience under the provisions of this joint resolution.
***Former Section 316 was repealed September 1, 1948, Pub. L. No. 772 (80th Cong.), 62 Stat. 862. The substance of it was incorporated in 18 U. S. C. 1304, which reads:
Sec. 1304. Broadcasting Lottery Information. Whoever broadcasts by means of any radio station for which a license is required by any law of the United States, or whoever, operating

SEC. 317. All matter broadcast by any radio station for which service, money, or any other valuable consideration is directly or indirectly paid, or promised to or charged or accepted by, the station so broadcasting, from any person, shall, at the time the same is so broadcast, be announced as paid for or furnished, as the case may be, by such person: provided, that "service or other valuable consideration" shall not include any service or property furnished without charge or at a nominal charge for use on, or in connection with, a broadcast unless it is so furnished in consideration for an identification in a broadcast of any person, product, service, trademark or brand name beyond an identification which is reasonably related to the use of such service or property on the broadcast.

(2) Nothing in this section shall preclude the Commission from requiring that an appropriate announcement shall be made at the time of the broadcast in the case of any political program or any program involving the discussion of any controversial issue for which any films, records, transcriptions, talent, scripts, or other material or service of any kind have been furnished, without charge or at a nominal charge, directly or indirectly, as an inducement to the broadcast of such program.

(b) In any case where a report has been made to a radio station, as required by Section 508 of this Act, of circumstances which would have required an announcement under this section had the consideration been received by such radio station, an appropriate announcement shall be made by such radio station.

(c) The licensee of each radio station shall exercise reasonable diligence to obtain from its employees, and from other persons with whom it deals directly in connection with any program or program matter for broadcast, information to enable such licensee to make the announcement required by this Section.

(d) The Commission may waive the requirement of an announcement as provided in this Section in any case or class of cases with respect to which it determines that the public interest, convenience, or necessity does not require the broadcasting of such announcement.

(e) The Commission shall prescribe rules and regulations to carry out the provisions of this section.

OPERATION OF TRANSMITTING APPARATUS

SEC. 318. The actual operation of all transmitting apparatus in any radio station for which a station license is required by this Act shall be carried on only by a person holding an operator's license issued hereunder. No person shall operate any such apparatus in such station except under and in accordance with an operator's license issued to him by the Commission: provided, however, that the Commission if it shall find that the public interest, convenience or necessity will be served thereby may waive or modify the foregoing provisions of this section for the operation of any station except (1) stations for which licensed operators are required by international agreement, (2) stations for which licensed operators are required for safety purposes,

---

such a station, knowingly permits the broadcasting of, any advertisement of or information concerning any lottery, gift enterprise, or similar scheme, offering prizes dependent in whole or in part upon lot or chance, or any list of the prizes drawn or awarded by means of any such lottery, gift enterprise, or scheme, whether said list contains any part or all of such prizes, shall be fined not more than $1,000 or imprisoned not more than one year, or both. Each day's broadcasting shall constitute a separate offense.

(3) stations engaged in broadcasting (other than those engaged solely in the functions of rebroadcasting the signals of television broadcast stations), and (4) stations operated as common carriers on frequencies below thirty thousand kilocycles: provided further, that the Commission shall have power to make special regulations governing the granting of licenses for the use of automatic radio devices and for the operation of such devices.

CONSTRUCTION PERMITS

SEC. 319 (a) No license shall be issued under the authority of this Act for the operation of any station the construction of which is begun or is continued after this Act takes effect, unless a permit for its construction has been granted by the Commission. The application for a construction permit shall set forth such facts as the Commission by regulation may prescribe as to the citizenship, character, and the financial, technical, and other ability of the applicant to construct and operate the station, the ownership and location of the proposed station and of the station or stations with which it is proposed to communicate, the frequencies desired to be used, the hours of the day or other periods of time during which it is proposed to operate the station, the purpose for which the station is to be used, the type of transmitting apparatus to be used, the power to be used, the date upon which the station is expected to be completed and in operation, and such other information as the Commission may require. Such application shall be signed by the applicant.

(b) Such permit for construction shall show specifically the earliest and latest dates between which the actual operation of such station is expected to begin, and shall provide that said permit will be automatically forfeited if the station is not ready for operation within the time specified or within such further time as the Commission may allow, unless prevented by causes not under the control of the grantee.

(c) Upon the completion of any station for the construction or continued construction of which a permit has been granted, and upon it being made to appear to the Commission that all the terms, conditions, and obligations set forth in the application and permit have been fully met, and that no cause or circumstance arising or first coming to the knowledge of the Commission since the granting of the permit would, in the judgment of the Commission, make the operation of such station against the public interest, the Commission shall issue a license to the lawful holder of said permit for the operation of said station. Said license shall conform generally to the terms of said permit. The provisions of Section 309(a), (b), (c), (d), (e), (f), and (g), shall not apply with respect to any station license the issuance of which is provided for and governed by the provisions of this subsection.

(d) A permit for construction shall not be required for Government stations, amateur stations, or mobile stations. With respect to stations or classes of stations other than Government stations, amateur stations, mobile stations, and broadcasting stations, the Commission may waive the requirement of a permit for construction if it finds that the public interest, convenience or necessity would be served thereby; provided, however, that such waiver shall apply only to stations whose construction is begun subsequent to the effective date of the waiver. If the Commission finds that the public interest, convenience and necessity would be served thereby, it may waive the requirement of a permit for construction of a station that is engaged soley in rebroadcasting television signals if such station was constructed on or before the date of enactment of this Act.

DESIGNATION OF STATIONS LIABLE TO INTERFERE WITH DISTRESS SIGNALS

SEC. 320. The Commission is authorized to designate from time to time radio stations the communications or signals of which, in its opinion, are liable to interfere with the transmission or reception of distress signals of ships. Such stations are required to keep a licensed radio operator listening in on the frequencies designated for signals of distress and radio communications relating thereto during the entire period the transmitter of such station is in operation.

DISTRESS SIGNALS AND COMMUNICATIONS

SEC. 321 (a) The transmitting set in a radio station on shipboard may be adjusted in such a manner as to produce a maximum radiation, irrespective of the amount of interference which may thus be caused, when such station is sending radio communication or signals of distress and radio communications relating thereto.

(b) All radio stations, including Government stations and stations on board foreign vessels when within the territorial waters of the United States, shall give absolute priority to radio communications or signals relating to ships in distress; shall cease all sending on frequencies which will interfere with hearing a radio communication or signal of distress, and, except when engaged in answering or aiding the ship in distress, shall refrain from sending any radio communications or signals until there is assurance that no interference will be caused with the radio communications or signals relating thereto, and shall assist the vessel in distress, so far as possible, by complying with its instructions.

INTERCOMMUNICATION IN MOBILE SERVICE

SEC. 322. Every land station open to general public service between the coast and vessels or aircraft at sea shall, within the scope of its normal operations, be bound to exchange radio communications or signals with any ship or aircraft station at sea; and each station on shipboard or aircraft at sea shall, within the scope of its normal operations, be bound to exchange radio communications or signals with any other station on shipboard or aircraft at sea or with any land station open to general public service between the coast and vessels or aircraft at sea; provided, that such exchange of radio communication shall be without distinction as to radio systems or instruments adopted by each station.

INTERFERENCE BETWEEN GOVERNMENT AND COMMERCIAL STATIONS

SEC. 323. (a) At all places where Government and private or commercial radio stations on land operate in such close proximity that interference with the work of Government stations cannot be avoided when they are operating simultaneously, such private or commercial stations as do interfere with the transmission or reception of radio communications or signals by the Government stations concerned shall not use their transmitters during the first fifteen minutes of each hour, local standard time.

(b) The Government stations for which the above-mentioned division of time is established shall transmit radio communications or signals only during the first fifteen minutes of each hour, local standard time, except in case of signals or radio communications relating to vessels in distress and vessel requests for information as to course, location, or compass direction.

431

Sec. 324. In all circumstances, except in case of radio communications or signals relating to vessels in distress, all radio stations, including those owned and operated by the United States, shall use the minimum amount of power necessary to carry out the communication desired.

FALSE DISTRESS SIGNALS; REBROADCASTING; STUDIOS OF FOREIGN STATIONS

Sec. 325. (a) No person within the jurisdiction of the United States shall knowingly utter or transmit, or cause to be uttered or transmitted, any false or fraudulent signal of distress, or communication relating thereto, nor shall any broadcasting station rebroadcast the program or any part thereof of another broadcasting station without the express authority of the originating station.

(b) No person shall be permitted to locate, use, or maintain a radio broadcast studio or other place or apparatus from which or whereby sound waves are converted into electrical energy, or mechanical or physical reproduction of sound waves produced, and caused to be transmitted or delivered to a radio station in a foreign country for the purpose of being broadcast from any radio station there having a power output of sufficient intensity and/or being so located geographically that its emissions may be received consistently in the United States, without first obtaining a permit from the Commission upon proper application therefor.

(c) Such application shall contain such information as the Commission may by regulation prescribe, and the granting or refusal thereof shall be subject to the requirements of section 309 hereof with respect to applications for station licenses or renewal or modification thereof, and the license or permission so granted shall be revocable for false statements in the application so required or when the Commission, after hearings, shall find its continuation no longer in the public interest.

CENSORSHIP; INDECENT LANGUAGE

Sec. 326. Nothing in this Act shall be understood or construed to give the Commission the power of censorship over the radio communications or signals transmitted by any radio station, and no regulation or condition shall be promulgated or fixed by the Commission which shall interfere with the right of free speech by means of radio communication.*

ADMINISTRATION OF RADIO LAWS IN TERRITORIES AND POSSESSIONS

Sec. 329. The Commission is authorized to designate any officer or employee of any other department of the Government on duty in any Territory or possession of the United States other than the Philippine Islands and the Canal Zone, to render therein such services in connection with the administration of the radio laws of the United States as the Commission may prescribe: *Provided,* That such designation shall be approved by the head of the department in which such person is employed.

*The prohibition against indecent programming was deleted by Pub. L. No. 772 (80th Cong.), 62 Stat. 862, September 1, 1948 and the substance was incorporated in 18 U. S. C. 1464, which reads:
Sec. 1464—Broadcasting Obscene Language. Whoever utters any obscene, indecent, or profane language by means of radio communication shall be fined not more than $10,000 or imprisoned not more than two years, or both.

Section 330. (a)   No person shall ship in interstate commerce, or import from any foreign country into the United States, for sale or resale to the public, apparatus described in paragraph (s) of Section 303 unless it complies with rules prescribed by the Commission pursuant to the authority granted by that paragraph. Provided, that this section shall not apply to carriers transporting such apparatus without trading in it.

(b) For the purposes of this section and Section (s)—

(1) The term "interstate commerce" means (A) commerce between any State, the District of Columbia, the Commonwealth of Puerto Rico, or any possession of the United States, (B) commerce between points in the same State, the District of Columbia, the Commonwealth of Puerto Rico, or possession of the United States but through any place outside thereof, or (C) commerce wholly within the District of Columbia or any possession of the United States.

(2) The term "United States" means the several States, the District of Columbia, the Commonwealth of Puerto Rico, and the possessions of the United States, but does not include the Canal Zone.

PART IV—GRANTS FOR NONCOMMERCIAL EDUCATIONAL BROADCASTING FACILITIES; CORPORATION FOR PUBLIC BROADCASTING

SUBPART A - GRANTS FOR FACILITIES

DECLARATION OF PURPOSE

Section 390. The purpose of this subpart is to assist (through matching grants) in the construction of noncommercial educational television or radio broadcasting facilities.

AUTHORIZATION OF APPROPRIATIONS

Section 391. There are authorized to be appropriated for the fiscal year ending June 30, 1963, and each of the four succeeding fiscal years such sums, not exceeding $32,000,000 in the aggregate, as may be necessary to carry out the purposes of Section 390. There are also authorized to be appropriated for carrying out the purposes of such section, $10,500,000 for the fiscal year ending June 30, 1968, $12,500,000 for the fiscal year ending June 30, 1969, and $15,000,000 for the fiscal year ending June 30, 1970. Sums appropriated pursuant to this section shall remain available for payment of grants for projects for which applications, approved under Section 392, have been submitted under such section prior to July 1, 1971.

GRANTS FOR CONSTRUCTION

Section 392.—(a) For each project for the construction of noncommercial educational television or radio broadcasting facilities there shall be submitted to the Secretary an application for a grant containing such information with respect to such project as the Secretary may by regulation require, including the total cost of such project and the amount of the Federal grant requested for such project, and providing assurance satisfactory to the Secretary—

(1) that the applicant is (A) an agency or officer responsible for the supervision

of public elementary or secondary education or public higher education within that State, or within a political subdivision thereof, (B) in the case of a project for television facilities, the State noncommercial educational television agency or, in the case of a project for radio facilities, the State educational radio agency, (C) a college or university deriving its support in whole or in part from tax revenues, (D)(i) in the case of a project for television facilities, a nonprofit foundation, corporation, or association which is organized primarily to engage in or encourage noncommercial educational television broadcasting and is eligible to receive a license from the Federal Communications Commission for a noncommercial educational broadcasting station pursuant to the rules and regulations of the Commission in effect on April 12, 1962, or (ii) in the case of a project for radio facilities, a nonprofit foundation, corporation, or association which is organized primarily to engage in or encourage noncommercial educational radio broadcasting and is eligible to receive a license from the Federal Communications Commission; or meets the requirements of clause (i) and is also organized to engage in or encourage such radio broadcasting and is eligible for such a license for such a radio station; or (E) a municipality which owns and operates a broadcasting facility transmitting only noncommercial programs;

(2) that the operation of such educational broadcasting facilities will be under the control of the applicant or a person qualified under paragraph (1) to be such an applicant;

(3) that necessary funds to construct, operate, and maintain such educational broadcasting facilities will be available when needed;

(4) that such broadcasting facilities will be used only for educational purposes; and

(5) that, in the case of an application with respect to radio broadcasting facilities, there has been comprehensive planning for educational broadcasting facilities and services in the area the applicant proposes to serve and the applicant has participated in such planning, and the applicant will make the most efficient use of the frequency assignment.

(b) The total of the grants made under this part from the appropriation for any fiscal year for the construction of noncommercial educational television broadcasting facilities and noncommercial educational radio broadcasting facilities in any State may not exceed 8-½ per centum of such appropriation.

(c)(1) In order to assure proper coordination of construction of noncommercial educational television broadcasting facilities within each State which has established a State educational television agency, each applicant for a grant under this section for a project for construction of such facilities in such State, other than such agency, shall notify such agency of each application for such a grant which is submitted by it to the Secretary, and the Secretary shall advise such agency with respect to the disposition of each such application.

(2) In order to assure proper coordination of construction of noncommercial educational radio broadcasting facilities within each State which has established a State educational radio agency, each applicant for a grant under this section for a project for construction of such facilities in such State, other than such agency, shall notify such agency of each application for such a grant which is submitted by it to the Secretary, and the Secretary shall advise such agency with respect to the disposition of each such application.

(d) The Secretary shall base his determinations of whether to approve applications for grants under this section and the amount of such grants on criteria set forth in regulations and designed to achieve (1) prompt and effective use of all noncommercial educational television channels remaining available, (2) equitable geographical distribution of noncommercial educational television broadcasting facilities or noncommercial educational radio broadcasting facilities, as the case may be, throughout the

States, and (3) provision of noncommercial educational television broadcasting facilities or noncommercial educational radio broadcasting facilities, as the case may be, which will serve the greatest number of persons and serve them in as many areas as possible, and which are adaptable to the broadcast educational uses.

(e) Upon approving any application under this section with respect to any project, the Secretary shall make a grant to the applicant in the amount determined by him, but not exceeding 75 per centum of the amount determined by the Secretary to be the reasonable and necessary cost of such project. The Secretary shall pay such amount from the sum available therefore, in advance or by way of reimbursement, and in such installments consistent with construction progress, as he may determine.

(f) If, within ten years after completion of any project for construction of educational television or radio broadcasting facilities with respect to which a grant has been made under this section—

(1) the applicant or other owner of such facilities ceases to be an agency, officer, institution, foundation, corporation, or association described in subsection (a)(1), or

(2) such facilities cease to be used for noncommercial educational television purposes or noncommercial educational radio purposes, as the case may be (unless the Secretary determines, in accordance with regulations, that there is good cause for releasing the applicant or other owner from the obligation so to do), the United States shall be entitled to recover from the applicant or other owner of such facilities the amount bearing the same ratio to the then value (as determined by agreement of the parties or by action brought in the United States district court for the district in which such facilities are situated) of such facilities, as the amount of the Federal participation bore to the cost of construction of such facilities.

RECORDS

Section 393.—(a) Each recipient of assistance under this subpart shall keep such records as may be reasonably necessary to enable the Secretary to carry out his functions under this subpart, including records which fully disclose the amount and the disposition by such recipient of the proceeds of such assistance, the total cost of the project or undertaking in connection with which such assistance is given or used, and the amount and nature of that portion of the cost of the project or undertaking supplied by other sources, and such other records as will facilitate an effective audit.

(b) The Secretary and the Comptroller General of the United States, or any of their duly authorized representatives, shall have access for the purpose of audit and examination to any books, documents, papers, and records of the recipient that are pertinent to assistance received under this subpart.

RULES AND REGULATIONS

Section 394. The Secretary is authorized to make such rules and regulations as may be necessary to carry out this subpart, including regulations relating to the order of priority in approving applications for projects under Section 392 or to determining the amounts of grants for such projects.

PROVISION OF ASSISTANCE BY FEDERAL COMMUNICATIONS COMMISSION

Section 395. The Federal Communications Commission is authorized to provide such assistance in carrying out the provisions of this subpart as may be requested by the Secretary. The Secretary shall provide for consultation and close cooperation with the Federal Communications Commission in the administration of his functions under this subpart which are of interest to or affect the functions of the Commission.

SUBPART B - CORPORATION FOR PUBLIC BROADCASTING

CONGRESSIONAL DECLARATION OF POLICY

Section 396.—(a) The Congress hereby finds and declares—
(1) that it is in the public interest to encourage the growth and development of noncommercial educational radio and television broadcasting, including the use of such media for instructional purposes;
(2) that expansion and development of noncommercial educational radio and television broadcasting and of diversity of its programming depend on freedom, imagination, and initiative on both the local and national levels;
(3) that the encouragement and support of noncommercial educational radio and television broadcasting, while matters of importance for private and local development, are also of appropriate and important concern to the Federal Government;
(4) that it furthers the general welfare to encourage noncommercial educational radio and television broadcast programming which will be responsive to the interests of people both in particular localities and throughout the United States, and which will constitute an expression of diversity and excellence;
(5) that it is necessary and appropriate for the Federal Government to complement, assist, and support a national policy that will most effectively make noncommercial educational radio and television service available to all the citizens of the United States;
(6) that a private corporation should be created to facilitate the development of educational radio and television broadcasting and to afford maximum protection to such broadcasting from extraneous interference and control.

CORPORATION ESTABLISHED

(b) There is authorized to be established a nonprofit corporation, to be known as the "Corporation for Public Broadcasting," which will not be an agency or establishment of the United States Government. The Corporation shall be subject to the provisions of this section, and, to the extent consistent with this section, to the District of Columbia Nonprofit Corporation Act.

BOARD OF DIRECTORS

(c)(1) The Corporation shall have a Board of Directors (hereinafter in this section referred to as the "Board"), consisting of fifteen members appointed by the President, by and with the advice and consent of the Senate. Not more than eight members of the Board may be members of the same political party.
(2)The members of the Board (A) shall be selected from among citizens of the United States (not regular fulltime employees of the United States) who are eminent in such fields as education, cultural and civic affairs, or the arts, including radio and television; (B) shall be selected so as to provide as nearly as practicable a broad representation of various regions of the country, various professions and occupa-

tions, and various kinds of talent and experience appropriate to the functions and responsibilities of the Corporation.

(3) The members of the initial Board of Directors shall serve as incorporators and shall take whatever actions are necessary to establish the Corporation under the District of Columbia Nonprofit Corporation Act.

(4) The term of office of each member of the Board shall be six years except that (A) any member appointed to fill a vacancy occurring prior to the expiration of the term for which his predecessor was appointed shall be appointed for the remainder of such term; and (B) the terms of office of members first taking office shall begin on the date of incorporation and shall expire, as designated at the time of their appointment, five at the end of two years, five at the end of four years, and five at the end of six years. No members shall be eligible to serve in excess of two consecutive terms of six years each. Notwithstanding the preceding provisions of this paragraph, a member whose term has expired may serve until his successor has qualified.

(5) Any vacancy in the Board shall not affect its power, but shall be filled in the manner in which the original appointments were made.

ELECTION OF CHAIRMAN; COMPENSATION

(d)(1) The President shall designate one of the members first appointed to the Board as Chairman; thereafter the members of the Board shall annually elect one of their number as Chairman. The members of the Board shall also elect one or more of them as a Vice Chairman or Vice Chairmen.

(2) The members of the Board shall not, by reason of such membership, be deemed to be employees of the United States. They shall, while attending meetings of the Board or while engaged in duties related to such meetings or in other activities of the Board pursuant to this subpart be entitled to receive compensation at the rate of $100 per day including travel time, and while away from their homes or regular places of business they may be allowed travel expenses, including per diem in lieu of subsistence, equal to that authorized by law (5 USC §5703) for persons in the Government service employed intermittently.

OFFICERS AND EMPLOYEES

(e)(1) The Corporation shall have a President, and such other officers as may be named and appointed by the Board for terms and at rates of compensation fixed by the Board. No individual other than a citizen of the United States may be an officer of the Corporation. No officer of the Corporation, other than the Chairman and any Vice Chairman, may receive any salary or other compensation from any source other than the Corporation during the period of his employment by the Corporation. All officers shall serve at the pleasure of the Board.

(2) Except as provided in the second sentence of subsection (c)(1) of this section, no political test or qualification shall be used in selecting, appointing, promoting, or taking other personnel actions with respect to officers, agents, and employees of the Corporation.

NONPROFIT AND NONPOLITICAL NATURE OF THE CORPORATION

(f)(1) The Corporation shall have no power to issue any shares of stock, or to declare or pay any dividends.

437

(2) No part of the income or assets of the Corporation shall inure to the benefit of any director, officer, employee, or any other individual except as salary or reasonable compensation for services.

(3) The Corporation may not contribute to or otherwise support any political party or candidate for elective public office.

PURPOSES AND ACTIVITIES OF THE CORPORATION

(g)(1) In order to achieve the objectives and to carry out the purposes of this subpart, as set out in subsection (a), the Corporation is authorized to—

(A) facilitate the full development of educational broadcasting in which programs of high quality, obtained from diverse sources, will be made available to noncommercial educational television or radio broadcast stations, with strict adherence to objectivity and balance in all programs or series of programs of a controversial nature;

(B) assist in the establishment and development of one or more systems of interconnection to be used for the distribution of educational television or radio programs so that all noncommercial educational television or radio broadcast stations that wish to may broadcast the programs at times chosen by the stations;

(C) assist in the establishment and development of one or more systems of noncommercial educational television or radio broadcast stations throughout the United States;

(D) carry out its purposes and functions and engage in its activities in ways that will most effectively assure the maximum freedom of the noncommercial educational television or radio broadcast systems and local stations from interference with or control of program content or other activities.

(2) Included in the activities of the Corporation authorized for accomplishment of the purposes set forth in subsection (a) of this section are, among others not specifically named—

(A) to obtain grants from and to make contracts with individuals and with private, State, and Federal agencies, organizations, and institutions;

(B) to contract with or make grants to program production entities, individuals, and selected noncommercial educational broadcast stations for the production of, and otherwise to procure, educational television or radio programs for national or regional distribution to noncommercial educational broadcast stations;

(C) to make payments to existing and new noncommercial educational broadcast stations to aid in financing local educational television or radio programming costs of such stations, particularly innovative approaches thereto, and other costs of operation of such stations;

(D) to establish and maintain a library and archives of noncommercial educational television or radio programs and related materials and develop public awareness of and disseminate information about noncommercial educational television or radio broadcasting by various means, including the publication of a journal;

(E) to arrange, by grant or contract with appropriate public or private agencies, organizations, or institutions, for interconnection facilities suitable for distribution and transmission of educational television or radio programs to noncommercial educational broadcast stations;

(F) to hire or accept the voluntary services of consultants, experts, advisory boards, and panels to aid the Corporation in carrying out the purposes of this section;

(G) to encourage the creation of new noncommercial educational broadcast

438

stations in order to enhance such service on a local, State, regional, and national basis;

(H) conduct (directly or through grants or contracts) research, demonstrations, or training in matters related to noncommercial educational television or radio broadcasting.

(3) To carry out the foregoing purposes and engage in the foregoing activities, the Corporation shall have the usual powers conferred upon a nonprofit corporation by the District of Columbia Nonprofit Corporation Act, except that the Corporation may not own or operate any television or radio broadcast station, system, or network, community antenna television system, or interconnection or program production facility.

AUTHORIZATION FOR FREE OR REDUCED RATE INTERCONNECTION SERVICE

(h) Nothing in the Communications Act of 1934, as amended, or in any other provision of law shall be construed to prevent United States communications common carriers from rendering free or reduced rate communications interconnection services for noncommercial educational television or radio services, subject to such rules and regulations as the Federal Communications Commission may prescribe.

REPORT TO CONGRESS

(i) The Corporation shall submit an annual report for the preceding fiscal year ending June 30 to the President for transmittal to the Congress on or before the 31st day of December of each year. The report shall include a comprehensive and detailed report of the Corporation's operations, activities, financial condition, and accomplishments under this section and may include such recommendations as the Corporation deems appropriate.

RIGHT TO REPEAL, ALTER, OR AMEND

(j) The right to repeal, alter, or amend this section at any time is expressly reserved.

FINANCING

(k)(1) There are authorized to be appropriated for expenses of the Corporation for the fiscal year ending June 30, 1969, the sum of $9,000,000, to remain available until expended.

(2) Notwithstanding the preceding provisions of this section, no grant or contract pursuant to this section may provide for payment from the appropriation for the fiscal year ending June 30, 1969, for any one project or to any one station of more than $250,000.

RECORDS AND AUDIT

(1)(1)(A) The accounts of the Corporation shall be audited annually in accordance with generally accepted auditing standards by independent certified public accountants or independent licensed public accountants certified or licensed by a regulatory authority of a State or other political subdivision of the United States.

The audits shall be conducted at the place or places where the accounts of the Corporation are normally kept. All books, accounts, financial records, reports, files, and all other papers, things, or property belonging to or in use by the Corporation and necessary to facilitate the audits shall be made available to the person or persons conducting the audits; and full facilities for verifying transactions with the balances or securities held by depositories, fiscal agents and custodians shall be afforded to such person or persons.

(B) The report of each such independent audit shall be included in the annual report required by subsection (i) of this section. The audit report shall set forth the scope of the audit and include such statements as are necessary to present fairly the Corporation's assets and liabilities, surplus or deficit, with an analysis of the changes therein during the year, supplemented in reasonable detail by a statement of the Corporation's income and expenses during the year, and a statement of the sources and application of funds, together with the independent auditor's opinion of those statements.

(2)(A) The financial transactions of the Corporation for any fiscal year during which Federal funds are avilable to finance any portion of its operations may be audited by the General Accounting Office in accordance with the principles and procedures applicable to commercial corporate transactions and under such rules and regulations as may be prescribed by the Comptroller General of the United States. Any such audit shall be conducted at the place or places where accounts of the Corporation are normally kept. The representatives of the General Accounting Office shall have access to all books, accounts, records, reports, files, and all other papers, things, or property belonging to or in use by the Corporation pertaining to its financial transactions and necessary to facilitate the audit, and they shall be afforded full facilities for verifying transactions with the balances or securities held by depositories, fiscal agents, and custodians. All such books, accounts, records, reports, files, papers and property of the Corporation shall remain in possession and custody of the Corporation.

(B) A report of each such audit shall be made by the Comptroller General to the Congress. The report to the Congress shall contain such comments and information as the Comptroller General may deem necessary to inform Congress of the financial operations and condition of the Corporation, together with such recommendations with respect thereto as he may deem advisable. The report shall also show specifically any program, expenditure, or other financial transaction or undertaking observed in the course of the audit, which, in the opinion of the Comptroller General, has been carried on or made without authority of law. A copy of each report shall be furnished to the President, to the Secretary, and to the Corporation at the time submitted to the Congress.

(3)(A) Each recipient of assistance by grant or contract, other than a fixed price contract awarded pursuant to competitive bidding procedures, under this section shall keep such records as may be reasonably necessary to fully disclose the amount and the disposition by such recipient of the proceeds of such assistance, the total cost of the project or undertaking in connection with which such assistance is given or used, and the amount and nature of that portion of the cost of the project or undertaking supplied by other sources, and such other records as will facilitate an effective audit.

(B) The Corporation or any of its duly authorized representatives, shall have access for the purpose of audit and examination to any books, documents, papers, and records of the recipient that are pertinent to assistance received under this section. The Comptroller General of the United States or any of his duly authorized representatives shall also have access thereto for such purpose during any fiscal year for which Federal funds are available to the Corporation.

DEFINITIONS

Section 397. For the purposes of this part—

(1) The term "State" includes the District of Columbia, the Commonwealth of Puerto Rico, the Virgin Islands, Guam, American Samoa, and the Trust Territory of the Pacific Islands.

(2) The term "construction", as applied to educational television broadcasting facilities, or educational radio broadcasting facilities means the acquisition and installation of transmission apparatus (including towers, microwave equipment, boosters, translators, repeaters, mobile equipment, and video-recording equipment) necessary for television broadcasting, or radio broadcasting, as the case may be, including apparatus which may incidentally be used for transmitting closed circuit television programs, but does not include the construction or repair of structures to house such apparatus. In the case of apparatus the acquisition and installation of which is so included, such term also includes planning therefor.

(3) The term "Secretary" means the Secretary of Health, Education and Welfare.

(4) The terms "State educational television agency" and "State educational radio agency" mean, with respect to television broadcasting and radio broadcasting, respectively, (A) a board or commission established by State law for the purpose of promoting such broadcasting within a State, (B) a board or commission appointed by the Governor of a State for such purpose if such appointment is not inconsistent with State law, or (C) a State officer or agency responsible for the supervision of public elementary or secondary education or public higher education within the State which has been designated by the Governor to assume responsibility for the promotion of such broadcasting; and, in the case of the District of Columbia, the term "Governor" means the Board of Commissioners of the District of Columbia and, in the case of the Trust Territory of the Pacific Islands, means the High Commissioner thereof.

(5) The term "nonprofit" as applied to any foundation, corporation, or association, means a foundation, corporation, or association, no part of the net earnings of which inures, or may lawfully inure, to the benefit of any private sharcholder or individual.

(6) The term "Corporation" means the Corporation authorized to be established by subpart B of this part.

(7) The term "noncommercial educational broadcast station" means a television or radio broadcast station, which (A) under the rules and regulations of the Federal Communications Commission in effect on the date of enactment of the Public Broadcasting Act of 1967, is eligible to be licensed or is licensed by the Commission as a noncommercial educational radio or television broadcast station and which is owned and operated by a public agency or nonprofit private foundation, corporation, or association or (B) is owned and operated by a municipality and which transmits only noncommercial programs for educational purposes.

(8) The term "interconnection" means the use of microwave equipment, boosters, translators, repeaters, communication space satellites, or other apparatus or equipment for the transmission and distribution of television or radio programs to noncommercial educational television or radio broadcast stations.

(9) The term "educational television or radio programs" means programs which are primarily designed for educational or cultural purposes.

Section 398. Nothing contained in this part shall be deemed (1) to amend any other provision of, or requirement under this Act; or (2) to authorize any department, agency, officer, or employee of the United States to exercise any direction, supervision, or control over educational television or radio broadcasting, or over the Corporation or any of its grantees or contractors, or over the charter or bylaws of the Corporation, or over the curriculum, program of instruction, or personnel of any educational institution, school system, or educational broadcasting station or system.

EDITORIALIZING AND SUPPORT OF POLITICAL CANDIDATES PROHIBITED

Section 399. No noncommercial educational broadcasting station may engage in editorializing or may support or oppose any candidate for political office.

TITLE IV—PROCEDURAL AND ADMINISTRATIVE PROVISIONS

JURISDICTION TO ENFORCE ACT AND ORDERS OF COMMISSION

SECTION 401. (a) The district courts of the United States shall have jurisdiction, upon application of the Attorney General of the United States at the request of the Commission, alleging a failure to comply with or a violation of any of the provisions of this Act by any person, to issue a writ or writs of mandamus commanding such person to comply with the provisions of this Act.

(b) If any person fails or neglects to obey any order of the Commission other than for the payment of money, while the same is in effect, the Commission or any party injured thereby, or the United States, by its Attorney General, may apply to the appropriate district court of the United States for the enforcement of such order. If, after hearing, that court determines that the order was regularly made and duly served, and that the person is in disobedience of the same, the court shall enforce obedience to such order by a writ of injunction or other proper process, mandatory or otherwise, to restrain such person or the officers, agents, or representatives of such person, from further disobedience of such order, or to enjoin upon it or them obedience to the same.

(c) Upon the request of the Commission it shall be the duty of any district attorney of the United States to whom the Commission may apply to institute in the proper court and to prosecute under the direction of the Attorney General of the United States all necessary proceedings for the enforcement of the provisions of this Act and for the punishment of all violations thereof, and the costs and expenses of such prosecutions shall be paid out of the appropriations for the expenses of the courts of the United States.

(d) The provisions of the Expediting Act, approved February 11, 1903, as amended, and of section 238 (1) of the Judicial Code, as amended, shall be held to apply to any suit in equity arising under Title II of this Act, wherein the United States is complainant.

PROCEEDINGS TO ENJOIN, SET ASIDE, ANNUL OR SUSPEND ORDERS
OF THE COMMISSION

SEC. 402. (a) Any proceeding to enjoin, set aside, annul, or suspend any order of the Commission under this Act (except those appealable under subsection (b) of this section) shall be brought as provided by and in the manner prescribed in Public Law 901, Eighty-first Congress, approved December 29, 1950.

(b) Appeals may be taken from decisions and orders of the Commission to the United States Court of Appeals for the District of Columbia in any of the following cases:

(1) By any applicant for a construction permit or station license whose application is denied by the Commission.

(2) By any applicant for the renewal or modification of any such instrument of authorization whose application is denied by the Commission.

(3) By any party to an application for authority to transfer, assign, or dispose of any such instrument of authorization, or any rights thereunder, whose application is denied by the Commission.

(4) By any applicant for the permit required by Section 325 of this Act whose application has been denied by the Commission, or by any permittee under said section whose permit has been revoked by the Commission.

(5) By the holder of any construction permit or station license which has been modified or revoked by the Commission.

(6) By any other person who is aggrieved or whose interests are adversely affected by any order of the Commission granting or denying any application described in paragraphs (1), (2), (3) and (4) hereof.

(7) By any person upon whom an order to cease and desist has been served under Section 312 of this Act.

(8) By any radio operator whose license has been suspended by the Commission.

(c) Such appeal shall be taken by filing a notice of appeal with the court within thirty days from the date upon which public notice is given of the decision or order complained of. Such notice of appeal shall contain a concise statement of the nature of the proceedings as to which the appeal is taken; a concise statement of the reasons on which the appellant intends to rely, separately stated and numbered; and proof of service of a true copy of said notice and statement upon the Commission. Upon filing of such notice, the court shall have jurisdiction of the proceedings and of the questions determined therein and shall have power, by order, directed to the Commission or any other party to the appeal, to grant temporary relief as it may deem just and proper. Orders granting temporary relief may be either affirmative or negative in their scope and applications so as to permit either the maintenance of the status quo in the matter in which the appeal is taken or the restoration of a position or status terminated or adversely affected by the order appealed from and shall, unless otherwise ordered by the court, be effective pending hearing and determination of said appeal and compliance by the Commission with the final judgment of the court rendered in said appeal.

(d) Within thirty days after the filing of an appeal, the Commission shall file with the court the record upon which the order complained of was entered, as provided in Section 2112 of Title 28, United States Code.

(e) Within thirty days after the filing of any such appeal, any interested person may intervene and participate in the proceedings had upon said appeal by filing with the court a notice of intention to intervene and a verified statement showing the nature of the interest of such party, together with proof of service of true copies of said notice and statement, both upon appellant and upon the Commission. Any person who would be aggrieved or whose interest would be adversely affected by a reversal or modification of the order of the Commission complained of shall be considered an interested party.

(f) The record and briefs upon which any such appeal shall be heard and determined by the court shall contain such information and material, and shall be prepared within such time and in such manner as the court may by rule prescribe.

(g) At the earliest convenient time the court shall hear and determine the appeal upon the record before it in the manner prescribed by Section 10 (e) of the Administrative Procedure Act.

(h) In the event that the court shall render a decision and enter an order reversing the order of the Commission, it shall remand the case to the Commission to carry out the judgment of the court and it shall be the duty of the Commission, in the absence of the proceedings to review such judgment, to forthwith give effect thereto, and unless otherwise ordered by the court, to do so upon the basis of the proceedings already had and the record upon which said appeal was heard and determined.

(i) The court may, in its discretion, enter judgment for costs in favor of or against an appellant, or other interested parties intervening in said appeal, but not against the Commission, depending upon the nature of the issues involved upon said appeal and the outcome thereof.

(j) The court's judgment shall be final, subject, however, to review by the Supreme Court of the United States upon writ of certiorari on petition therefor under Section 1254 of Title 28 of the United States Code, by the appellant, by the Commission, or by any interested party intervening in the appeal, or by certification by the court pursuant to the provisions of that section.

INQUIRY BY COMMISSION ON ITS OWN MOTION

SEC. 403. The Commission shall have full authority and power at any time to institute an inquiry, on its own motion, in any case and as to any matter or thing concerning which complaint is authorized to be made, to or before the Commission by any provision of this Act, or concerning which any question may arise under any of the provisions of this Act, or relating to the enforcement of any of the provisions of this Act. The Commission shall have the same powers and authority to proceed with any inquiry instituted on its own motion as though it had been appealed to by complaint or petition under any of the provisions of this Act, including the power to make and enforce any order or orders in the case, or relating to the matter or thing concerning which the inquiry is had, excepting orders for the payment of money.

REPORTS OF INVESTIGATIONS

SEC. 404. Whenever an investigation shall be made by the Commission it shall be its duty to make a report in writing in respect thereto, which shall state the conclusions of the Commission, together with its decision, order, or requirement in the premises; and in case damages are awarded such report shall include the findings of fact on which the award is made.

REHEARINGS

Section 405. After an order, decision, report, or action has been made or taken in any proceeding by the Commission, or by any designated authority within the Commission pursuant to a delegation under Section 5(d)(1), any party thereto, or any other person aggrieved or whose interests are adversely affected thereby, may petition for rehearing only to the authority making or taking the order, decision, report, or action; and it shall be lawful for such authority, whether it be the Commission or other authority designated under Section 5(d)(1), in its discretion, to grant such a rehearing if sufficient reason therefor be made to appear. A petition for rehearing must be filed within thirty days from the date upon which public notice is given of the order, decision, report, or action complained of. No such application shall excuse any person from complying with or obeying any order, decision, report, or action of the Commission, or operate in any manner to stay or postpone the enforcement thereof, without the special order of the Commission. The filing of a petition for rehearing shall not be a condition precedent to judicial review of any such order, decision, report, or action, except where the party seeking such review (1) was not a party to the proceedings resulting in such order, decision, report, or action, or (2) relies on questions of fact or law upon which the Commission, or designated authority within the Commission, has been afforded no opportunity to pass. The Commission, or designated authority within the Commission, shall enter an order, with a concise statement of the reasons therefor, denying a petition for rehearing or granting such petition, in whole or in part, and ordering such further proceedings as may be appropriate: Provided, that in any case where such petition relates to an instrument of authorization granted without a hearing, the Commission, or designated authority within the Commission, shall take such action within ninety days of the filing of such petition. Rehearings shall be governed by such general rules as the Commission may establish, except that no evidence other than newly discovered evidence, evidence which has become available only since the original taking of evidence, or evidence which the Commission or designated authority within the Commission believes should have been taken in the original proceeding shall be taken on any rehearing. The time within which a petition for review must be filed in a proceeding to which Section 402(a) applies, or within which an appeal must be taken under Section 402(b) in any case, shall be computed from the date upon which public notice is given of orders disposing of all petitions for rehearing filed with the Commission in such proceeding or case, but any order, decision, report, or action made or taken after such rehearing reversing, changing, or modifying the original order shall be subject to the same provisions with respect to rehearing as an original order.

GENERAL PROVISIONS RELATING TO PROCEEDINGS— WITNESSES AND DEPOSITIONS

Section 409.—(a) In every case of adjudication (as defined in the Administrative Procedure Act) which has been designated by the Commission for hearing, the person or persons conducting the hearing shall prepare and file an initial, tentative, or recommended decision, except where such person or persons become unavailable to the Commission or where the Commission finds upon the record that due and timely execution of its functions imperatively and unavoidably require that the record be certified to the Commission for initial or final decision.

(b) In every case of adjudication (as defined in the Administrative Procedure Act) which has been designated by the Commission for hearing, any party to the proceeding shall be permitted to file exceptions and memoranda in support thereof to the initial, tentative, or recommended decision, which shall be passed upon by the Commission or by the authority within the Commission, if any, to whom the function of passing upon the exceptions is delegated under Section 5(d)(1): Provided, however, that such authority shall not be the same authority which made the decision to which the exception is taken.

(c) (1) In any case of adjudication (as defined in the Administrative Procedure Act) which has been designated by the Commission for a hearing, no person who has participated in the presentation or preparation for presentation of such case at the hearing or upon review shall (except to the extent required for the disposition of ex parte matters as authorized by law) directly or indirectly make any additional presentation respecting such case to the hearing officer or officers or to the Commis-

445

sion or to any authority within the Commission to whom, in such case, review functions have been delegated by the Commission under Section 5(d)(1), unless upon notice and opportunity for all parties to participate.

(2) The provision in subsection (c) of Section 5 of the Administrative Procedure Act which states that such subsection shall not apply in determining applications for initial licenses, shall not be applicable hereafter in the case of applications for initial licenses before the Federal Communications Commission.

(d) To the extent that the foregoing provisions of this section and Section 5(d) are in conflict with the provisions of the Administrative Procedure Act, such provisions of this section and Section 5(d) shall be held to supersede and modify the provisions of that Act.

(e) For the purposes of this Act the Commission shall have the power to require by subpena the attendance and testimony of witnesses and the production of all books, papers, schedules of charges, contracts, agreements, and documents relating to any matter under investigation. Witnesses summoned before the Commission shall be paid the same fees and mileage that are paid witnesses in the courts of the United States.

(f) Such attendance of witnesses, and the production of such documentary, evidence, may be required from any place in the United States, at any designated place of hearing. And in case of disobedience to a subpena the Commission, or any party to a proceeding before the Commission, may invoke the aid of any court of the United States in requiring the attendance and testimony of witnesses and the production of books, papers, and documents under the provisions of this section.

(g) Any of the district courts of the United States within the jurisdiction of which such inquiry is carried on may, in case of contumacy or refusal to obey a subpena issued to any common carrier or licensee or other person, issue an order requiring such common carrier, licensee, or other person to appear before the Commission (and produce books and papers if so ordered) and give evidence touching the matter in question; and any failure to obey such order of the court may be punished by such court as a contempt thereof.

(h) The testimony of any witness may be taken, at the instance of a party, in any proceeding or investigation pending before the Commission, by deposition, at any time after a cause or proceeding is at issue on petition and answer. The Commission may also order testimony to be taken by deposition in any proceeding or investigation pending before it, at any stage of such proceeding or investigation. Such depositions may be taken before any judge of any court of the United States, or any United States commissioner, or any clerk of a district court, or any chancellor, justice, or judge of a supreme or superior court, mayor, or chief magistrate of a city, judge of a county court, or court of common pleas of any of the United States, or any notary public, not being of counsel or attorney to either of the parties, nor interested in the event of the proceeding or investigation. Reasonable notice must first be given in writing by the party or his attorney proposing to take such deposition to the opposite party or his attorney of record, as either may be nearest, which notice shall state the name of the witness and the time and place of the taking of his deposition. Any person may be compelled to appear and depose, and to produce documentary evidence, in the same manner as witnesses may be compelled to appear and testify and produce documentary evidence before the Commission, as hereinbefore provided.

(i) Every person deposing as herein provided shall be cautioned and sworn (or affirm, if he so request) to testify the whole truth, and shall be carefully examined. His testimony shall be reduced to writing by the magistrate taking the deposition, or under his direction, and shall, after it has been reduced to writing, be subscribed by the deponent.

(j) If a witness whose testimony may be desired to be taken by deposition be in a foreign country, the deposition may be taken before an officer or person designated by the Commission, or agreed upon by the parties by stipulation in writing to be filed with the Commission. All depositions must be promptly filed with the Commission.

(k) Witnesses whose depositions are taken as authorized in this Act, and the magistrate or other officer taking the same, shall severally be entitled to the same fees as are paid for like services in the courts of the United States.

(l) No person shall be excused from attending and testifying or from producing books, papers, schedules of charges, contracts, agreements, and documents before the Commission, or in obedience to the subpena of the Commission, whether such subpena be signed or issued by one or more commissioners, or in any cause or proceeding, criminal or otherwise, based upon or growing out of any alleged violation of this Act, or of any amendments thereto, on the ground or for the reason that the testimony or evidence, documentary or otherwise, required of him may tend to incriminate him or subject him to a penalty or forfeiture; but no individual shall be prosecuted or subjected to any penalty or forfeiture for or on account of any transaction, matter, or thing concerning which he is compelled, after having claimed this privilege against self-incrimination, to testify or produce evidence, documentary or otherwise, except that any individual so testifying shall not be exempt from prosecution and punishment for perjury committed in so testifying.

(m) Any person who shall neglect or refuse to attend and testify, or to answer any lawful inquiry, or to produce books, papers, schedules of charges, contracts, agreements, and documents, if in his power to do so, in obedience to the subpena or lawful requirement of the Commission, shall be guilty of a misdemeanor and upon conviction thereof by a court of competent jurisdiction shall be punished by a fine of not less than $100 nor more than $5,000, or by imprisonment for not more than one year, or by both such fine and imprisonment.

Title V—Penal Provisions—Forfeitures

GENERAL PENALTY

SECTION 501. Any person who willfully and knowingly does or causes or suffers to be done any act, matter, or thing, in this Act prohibited or declared to be unlawful, or who willfully and knowingly omits or fails to do any act, matter, or thing in this Act required to be done, or willfully and knowingly causes or suffers such omission or failure, shall, upon conviction thereof, be punished for such offense, for which no penalty (other than a forfeiture) is provided in this Act, by a fine of not more than $10,000 or by imprisonment for a term not exceeding one year, or both; except that any person having been once convicted of an offense punishable under this Section, who is subsequently convicted of violating any provision of this Act punishable under this Section, shall be punished by a fine of not more than $10,000 or by imprisonment for a term not exceeding two years or both.

VIOLATIONS OF RULES, REGULATIONS, AND SO FORTH

SEC. 502. Any person who willfully and knowingly violates any rule, regulation, restriction, or condition made or imposed by the Commission under authority of this Act, or any rule, regulation, restriction, or condition made or imposed by an international radio or wire communications treaty or convention, or regulations annexed thereto, to which the United States is or may hereafter become a party, shall, in addition to any other penalties provided by law, be punished, upon conviction thereof, by a fine of not more than $500 for each and every day during which such offense occurrs.

FORFEITURES

Sec. 503. (a) Any person who shall deliver messages for interstate or foreign transmission to any carrier, or for whom as sender or receiver, any such carrier shall transmit any interstate or foreign wire or radio communication, who shall knowingly by employee, agent, officer, or otherwise directly or indirectly, by or through any means or device whatsoever, receive or accept from such carrier any sum of money or any other valuable consideration as a rebate or offset against the regular charges for transmission of such messages as fixed by the schedules of charges provided for in the Act, shall in addition to any other penalty provided by this Act forfeit to the United States a sum of money three times the amount of money so received or accepted and three times the value of any other consideration so received and accepted, to be ascertained by the trial court; and in the trial of said action all such rebates or other considerations so received or accepted for a period of six years prior to the commencement of the action may be included therein, and the amount recovered shall be three times the total amount of money, or three times the total value of such consideration, so received or accepted, or both, as the case may be.

(b) (1) Any licensee or permittee of a broadcast station who—

(A) Willfully or repeatedly fails to operate such station substantially as set forth in his license or permit,

(B) willfully or repeatedly fails to observe any of the provisions of this Act or of any rule or regulation of the Commission prescribed under authority of this Act or under authority of any treaty ratified by the United States,

(C) fails to observe any final cease and desist order issued by the Commission,

(D) violates Section 317 (c) or Section 509 (a) (4) of this act, or

(E) violates Section 1304, 1343, or 1464 of Title 18 of the United States Code, shall forfeit to the United States a sum not to exceed $1,000. Each day during which such violation occurs shall constitute a separate offense. Such forfeiture shall be in addition to any other penalty provided by this Act.

(2) No forfeiture liability under paragraph (1) of this subsection (b) shall attach unless a written notice of apparent liability shall have been issued by the Commission and such notice has been received by the licensee or permittee or the Commission shall have sent such notice by registered or certified mail to the last known address of the licensee or permittee. A licensee or permittee so notified shall be granted an opportunity to show in writing, within such reasonable period as the Commission shall by regulations prescribe why he should not be held liable. A notice issued under this paragraph shall not be valid unless it sets forth the date, facts, and nature of the act or omission with which the licensee or permittee is charged and specifically identifies the particular provision or provisions of the law, rule, or regulation or the license, permit, or cease and desist order involved.

(3) No forfeiture liability under paragraph (1) of this subsection (b) shall attach for any violation occurring more than one year prior to the date of issuance of the notice of apparent liability and in no event shall the forfeiture imposed for the acts or omissions set forth in any notice of apparent liability exceed $10,000.

PROVISIONS RELATING TO FORFEITURES

Sec. 504. (a) The forfeitures provided for in this Act shall be payable into the Treasury of the United States, and shall be recoverable in a civil suit in the name of the United States brought in the district where the person or carrier has its principal operating office or in any district through which the line or system of the carrier runs; provided, that any suit for the recovery of a forfeiture imposed pursuant to the provisions of this Act shall be a trial de novo; provided further, that in the case of forfeiture by a ship, said forfeiture may also be recoverable by way of libel in any district in which such ship shall arrive or depart. Such forfeitures shall be in addition to any other general or specific penalties herein provided. It shall be the duty of the various district attorneys, under the direction of the Attorney General of the United States, to prosecute for the recovery of forfeitures under the Act. The costs and expenses of such prosecutions shall be paid from the appropriation for the expenses of the courts of the United States.

(b) The forfeitures imposed by Parts II and III of Title III and Sections 503(b) and 507 of this Act shall be subject to remission or mitigation by the Commission, upon application therefor, under such regulations and methods of ascertaining the facts as may seem to it advisable, and, if suit has been instituted, the Attorney General, upon request of the Commission, shall direct the discontinuance of any prosecution to recover such forfeitures; provided, however, that no forfeiture shall be remitted or mitigated after determination by a court of competent jurisdiction.

(c) In any case where the Commission issues a notice of apparent liability looking toward the imposition of a forfeiture under this Act, that fact shall not be used, in other proceedings before the Commission, to the prejudice of the persons to whom such notice was issued, unless (i) the forfeiture has been paid, or (ii) a court of competent jurisdiction has ordered payment of such forfeiture, and such order has become final.

VENUE OF OFFENSES

Sec. 505. The trial of any offense under this Act shall be in the district in which it is committed; or if the offense is committed upon the high seas, or out of the jurisdiction of any particular state or district, the trial shall be in the district where the offender may be found or into which he shall be first brought. Whenever the offense is begun in one jurisdiction and completed in another it may be dealt with, inquired of, tried, determined, and punished in either jurisdiction in the same manner as if the offense had been actually and wholly committed therein.

COERCIVE PRACTICES AFFECTING
BROADCASTING

Sec. 506. (a) It shall be unlawful, by the use or express or implied threat of the use of force, violence, intimidation, or duress, or by the use or express or implied threat of use of other means to coerce, compel, or constrain or attempt to coerce, compel, or constrain a licensee—

(1) to employ or agree to employ, in connection with the conduct of the broadcasting business of such licensee, any person or persons in excess of the number of employees needed by such licensee to perform actual services; or

(2) to pay or give or agree to pay or give any money or other thing of value in lieu of giving, or on account of failure to give, employment to any person or persons, in connection with the conduct of the broadcasting of such licensee, in excess of the number of employees needed by such licensee to perform actual services; or

(3) to pay or agree to pay more than once for services performed in connection with the conduct of the broadcasting business of such licensee; or

(4) to pay or give or agree to pay or give any money or other thing of value for

449

services, in connection with the conduct of the broadcasting business of such licensee, which are not to be performed; or

(5) to refrain, or agree to refrain, from broadcasting or from permitting the broadcasting of a non-commercial educational or cultural program in connection with which the participants receive no money or other thing of value for their services, other than their actual expenses, and such licensee neither pays nor gives any money or other thing of value for the privilege of broadcasting such program nor receives any money or other thing of value on account of the broadcasting of such program; or

(6) to refrain, or agree to refrain, from broadcasting or permitting the broadcasting of any radio communication originating outside of the United States.

(b) It shall be unlawful, by the use or express or implied threat of the use of force, violence, intimidation or duress, or by the use of express or implied threat of the use of other means to coerce, compel, or constrain or attempt to coerce, compel, or constrain a licensee or any other person—

(1) to pay or agree to pay any exaction for the privilege of, or on account of, producing, preparing, manufacturing, selling, buying, renting, operating, using, or maintaining recordings, transcriptions, or mechanical, chemical, or electrical reproductions, or other articles, equipment, machines, or materials, used or intended to be used in broadcasting or in the production, preparation, performance, or presentation of a program or programs for broadcasting; or

(2) to accede to or impose any restriction upon such production, preparation, manufacture, sale, purchase, rental, operation, use, or maintenance, if such restriction is for the purpose of preventing or limiting the use of such articles, equipment, machines, or materials in broadcasting or in the production, preparation, performance, or presentation of a program or programs for broadcasting; or

(3) to pay, or agree to pay any exaction on account of the broadcasting, by means of recordings or transcriptions, of a program previously broadcast, payment having been made, or agreed to be made, for the services actually rendered in the performance of such program.

(c) The provisions of subsection (a) or (b) of this section shall not be held to make unlawful the enforcement or attempted enforcement, by means lawfully employed, of any contract right heretofore or hereafter existing or of any legal obligation heretofore or hereafter incurred or assumed.

(d) Whoever willfully violates any provision of subsection (a) or (b) of this section shall, upon conviction thereof, be punished by imprisonment for not more than one year or by a fine of not more than $1,000, or both.

(e) As used in this section the term "licensee" includes the owner or owners, and the person or persons having control or management, of the radio station in respect of which a station license was granted.

DISCLOSURE OF CERTAIN PAYMENTS

Sec. 508. (a) Subject to subsection (d), any employee of a radio station who accepts or agrees to accept from any person (other than such station), or any person (other than such station), who pays or agrees to pay such employee, any money, service, or other valuable consideration for the broadcast of any matter over such station shall, in advance of such broadcast, disclose the fact of such acceptance or agreement to such station.

(b) Subject to subsection (d), any person who, in connection with the production or preparation of any program or program matter which is intended for broadcasting over any radio station, accepts or agrees to accept, or pays or agrees to pay, any money, service or other valuable consideration for the inclusion of any matter as a part of such program or program matter, shall, in advance of such broadcast, disclose the fact of such acceptance or payment or agreement to the payee's employer, or to the person for whom such program or program matter is being produced, or to the licensee of such station over which such program is broadcast.

(c) Subject to subsection (c), any person who supplies to any other person any program or program matter which is intended for broadcasting over any radio station shall, in advance of such broadcast, disclose to such other person any information of which he has knowledge, or which has been disclosed to him, as to any money, service or other valuable consideration which any person has paid or accepted, or has agreed to pay or accept, for the inclusion of any matter as a part of such program or program matter.

(d) The provisions of this section requiring the disclosure of information shall not apply in any case where, because of a waiver made by the Commission under Section 317(d), an announcement is not required to be made under Section 317.

(e) The inclusion in the program of the announcement required by Section 317 shall constitute the disclosure required by this section.

(f) The term "service or other valuable consideration" as used in this section shall not include any service or property furnished without charge or at a nominal charge for use on, or in connection with, a broadcast, or for use on a program which is intended for broadcasting over any radio station, unless it is so furnished in consideration for an indentification in such broadcast or in such program of any person, product, service, trademark, or brand name beyond an identification which is reasonably related to the use of such service or property in such broadcast or such program.

(g) Any person who violates any provision of this section shall, for each such violation, be fined not more than $10,000 or imprisoned not more than one year, or both.

PROHIBITED PRACTICES IN CASE OF CONTESTS OF INTELLECTUAL KNOWLEDGE, INTELLECTUAL SKILL, OR CHANCE

Sec. 509 (a) It shall be unlawful for any person, with intent to deceive the listening or viewing public—

(1) to supply to any contestant in a purportedly bona fide contest of intellectual knowledge or intellectual skill any special and secret assistance whereby the outcome of such contest will be in whole or in part prearranged or predetermined;

(2) by means of persuasion, bribery, intimidation, or otherwise, to induce or cause any contestant in a purportedly bona fide contest of intellectual knowledge or intellectual skill to refrain in any manner from using or displaying knowledge or skill in such contest, whereby the outcome therof will be in whole or in part prearranged or predetermined;

(3) to engage in any artifice or scheme for the purpose of prearranging or predetermining in whole or in part the outcome of a purportedly bona fide contest of intellectual knowledge, intellectual skill, or chance;

(4) to produce or participate in the broadcasting of, to offer to a licensee for broadcasting, or to sponsor, any radio program, knowing or having reasonable ground for believing that, in connection with a purportedly bona fide contest of intellectual knowledge, intellectual skill, or chance constituting any part of such program, any person has done or is going to do any act or thing referred to in paragraph (1), (2) or (3) of this subsection;

(5) to conspire with any other person or persons to do any act or thing prohibited by paragraph (1), (2), (3), or (4) of this subsection, if one or more of such persons do any act to effect the object of such conspiracy.

(b) For the purpose of this section—

(1) the term "contest" means any contest broadcast by a radio station in connection with which any money or any other thing of value is offered as a prize or prizes to be paid or presented by the program sponsor or by any other person or persons, as announced in the course of the broadcast;

(2) the term "the listening or viewing public" means those members of the public who, with the aid of radio receiving sets, listen to or view programs broadcast by radio stations.

(c) Whoever violates subsection (a) shall be fined not more than $10,000 or imprisoned not more than one year, or both.

UNAUTHORIZED PUBLICATION OF COMMUNICATIONS

Sec. 605. No person receiving or assisting in receiving, or transmitting, or assisting in transmitting, any interstate or foreign communication by wire or radio shall divulge or publish the existence, contents, substance, purport, effect, or meaning thereof, except through authorized channels of transmission or reception, to any person other than the addressee, his agent, or attorney, or to a person employed or authorized to forward such communication to its destination, or to proper accounting or distributing officers of the various communicating centers over which the communication may be passed, or to the master of a ship under whom he is serving, or in response to a subpoena issued by a court of competent jurisdiction, or on demand of other lawful authority; and no person not being authorized by the sender shall intercept any communication and divulge or publish the existence, contents, substance, purport, effect, or meaning of such intercepted communication to any person; and no person not being entitled therto shall receive or assist in receiving any interstate or foreign communication by wire or radio and use the same or any information therein contained for his own benefit or for the benefit of another not entitled thereto; and no person having received such intercepted communication or having become acquainted with the contents, substance, purport, effect, or meaning of the same or any part thereof, knowing that such information was so obtained, shall divulge or publish the existence, contents, substance, purport, effect, or meaning of the same or any part thereof, or use the same or any information therein contained for his own benefit or for the benefit of another not entitled thereto—provided, that this section shall not apply to the receiving, divulging, publishing, or utilizing the contents of any radio communication broadcast, or transmitted by amateurs or others for the use of the general public, or relating to ships in distress.

WAR EMERGENCY—POWERS OF PRESIDENT

Sec. 606. (a) During the continuance of a war in which the United States is engaged, the President is authorized, if he finds it necessary for the national defense and security, to direct that such communications as in his judgment may be essential to the national defense and security shall have preference or priority with any carrier subject to this Act. He may give these directions at and for such times as he may determine, and may modify, change, suspend, or annul them and for any such purpose he is hereby authorized to issue orders directly, or through such person or persons as he designates for the purpose, or through the Commission. Any carrier complying with any such order or direction for preference or priority herein authorized shall be exempt from any and all provisions in existing law imposing civil or criminal penalties, obligations, or liabilities upon carriers by reason of giving preference or priority in compliance with such order or direction.

(b) It shall be unlawful for any person during any war in which the United States is engaged to knowingly or willfully, by physical force or intimidation by threats of physical force, obstruct or retard or aid in obstructing or retarding interstate or foreign communication by radio or wire. The President is hereby authorized, whenever in his judgment the public interest requires, to employ the armed forces of the United States to prevent any such obstruction or retardation of communication: provided, that nothing in this section shall be construed to repeal, modify, or affect either Section 6 or Section 20 of an Act entitled "An Act to Supplement Existing Laws Against Unlawful Restraints and Monopolies, and for Other Purposes."

(c) Upon proclamation by the President that there exists war or a threat of war, or a state of public peril or disaster or other national emergency or in order to preserve the neutrality of the United States, the President, if he deems it necessary in the interest of national security or defense, may suspend or amend, for such time as he may see fit, the rules and regulations applicable to any or all stations or devices capable of emitting electromagnetic radiations within the jurisdiction of the United States as prescribed by the Commission, and may cause the closing of any station for radio communication, or any device capable of emitting electromagnetic radiations between 10 kilocycles and 100,000 megacycles, which is suitable for use as a navigational aid beyond 5 miles, and the removal therefrom of its apparatus and equipment, or he may authorize the use or control of any such station or device and/or its apparatus and equipment, by any department of the Government under such regulations as he may prescribe upon just compensation to the owners. The authority granted to the President, under this subsection, to cause the closing of any station or device and the removal therefrom of its apparatus and equipment, or to authorize the use or control of any station or device and/or its apparatus and equipment, may be exercised in the Canal Zone.

(d) Upon proclamation by the President that there exists a state or threat of war involving the United States, the President, if he deems it necessary in the interest of the national security and defense, may, during a period ending not later than six months after the termination of such state or threat of war and not later than such earlier date as the Congress by concurrent resolution may designate, (1) suspend or amend the rules and regulations applicable to any or all facilities or station and its apparatus and equipment by any department of the Government under such regulations as he may prescribe, upon just compensation to the owners.

(e) The President shall ascertain the just compensation for such use or control and certify the amount ascertained to Congress for appropriation and payment to the person entitled thereto. If the amount so certified is unsatisfactory to the person entitled thereto, such person shall be paid only 75 per centum of the amount and shall be entitled to sue the United States to recover such further sum as added to such payment of 75 per centum will make such amount as will be just compensation for the use and control. Such suit shall be brought in the manner provided by paragraph 20 of Section 24, or by Section 145, of the Judicial Code, as amended.

(f) Nothing in subsections (c) or (d) shall be construed to amend, repeal, impair, or affect existing laws or powers of the states in relation to taxation or the lawful police regulations of the several states, except wherein such laws, powers, or regulations may affect the transmission of government communications, or the issue of stocks and bonds by any communication system or systems.

(g) Nothing in subsection (c) or (d) shall be construed to authorize the President to make any amendment to the rules and regulations of the Commission which the Commission would not be authorized by law to make; and nothing in subsection (d) shall be construed to authorize the President to take any action the force and effect of which shall continue beyond the date after which taking of such action would not have been authorized.

(h) Any person who willfully does or causes or suffers to be done any act prohibited pursuant to the exercise of the President's authority under this section, or who willfully fails to do any act which he is required to do pursuant to the exercise of the President's authority under this section, or who willfully causes or suffers such failure, shall, upon conviction thereof, be punished for such offense by a fine of not more than $5,000, except that any person who commits such an offense with intent to injure the United States or with intent to secure an advantage to any foreign nation, shall, upon conviction thereof, be punished by a fine of not more than $20,000 or by imprisonment for not more than 20 years, or both.

FCC Chronology and Leadership from 1934 to 1970

EARLY FCC LEADERSHIP

On March, 1958, Dr. Bernard Schwartz, who had formerly served as Legal Counsel for the House Subcommittee on Legislative Oversight investigating the FCC and other federal agencies, was quoted as having said to a Harvard Law School audience that these agencies had become "political dumping grounds for lame duck Congressmen" and that the caliber of appointments had been extremely low during the last 20 years.[1] Since he was primarily concerned with the activities of the FCC during his short-lived tenure with the Committee, we may assume that he had this agency mainly in mind when he made the derogatory remark.

With respect to the FCC, it cannot be properly said that the agency has been a "dumping ground" for lame duck Congressmen. In fact, of the 43 persons who have served on the Commission, only two served in Congress prior to their appointments. Nor is it correct to say that the caliber of appointments generally has been extremely low. On the contrary, with some exceptions, those appointed to the FCC have been well qualified for their jobs.

THE FIRST DEMOCRATIC MEMBERS

The first FCC Chairman was Democrat *Eugene Octave Sykes.* He was from Mississippi, and prior to coming to Washington had served for eight years as a member of the Supreme Court of that state. He was appointed as an original member of the Federal Radio Commission in 1927 and continued in that office until the creation of the FCC in 1934 when Roosevelt made him Chairman of the new agency.[2]

Other original Democratic members who served under Mr. Sykes were Commissioner *Irvin Stewart* from Texas, attorney and educator, with a distinguished record as a professor at the University of Texas and American University, plus four years experience as Chief of the Electrical Communication Treaty Division in the Department of State and participation in several important international radio conferences, and who, because of his vast knowledge in the communications field and his writing skill, had been called upon by Congress to play a major role in drafting the Communications Act; *Paul A. Walker,* distinguished attorney who had achieved a national reputation as an able public utility regulator in his home state of Oklahoma, and aging attorney *Hampson Gary* who had had a long career in government and

[1] *New York Times,* March 29, 1959, p. 36.
[2] *Who's Who in America,* 1940-41, p. 2518.

who resigned as Commissioner after less than six months of service.[3]

The first Republican members were *Thaddeus Harold Brown* from Ohio, an attorney who had served as a member of the Ohio Civil Service Commission, had been Secretary of State in Ohio for four years and who, just prior to his FCC appointment, had been Vice-Chairman of the Federal Radio Commission; *Norman Stanley Case*, an attorney and former governor of Rhode Island and personal friend of Roosevelt when the latter was Governor of New York; and *George Henry Payne* from New York, author and journalist, and at one time Republican candidate for Governor in New York.

Mr. Sykes served as Chairman of the FCC only eight months. He continued as a Commissioner but stepped down as Chairman on March 9, 1935, and was succeeded by *Anning S. Prall*, a Democrat from New York State, who had served terms in Congress and previously was Commissioner of Taxes and Assessments in New York City and, at one time, had been President of the Board of Education there.

On July 23, 1937 Chairman Prall died and was succeeded by *Frank Ramsey McNinch* of North Carolina. Mr. McNinch had had a distinguished record as a governmental administrator and long experience in the field of utility regulation. With a professional background which included service as a member of the North Carolina House of Representatives and as Mayor of Charlotte, he accepted appointment to the Federal Power Commission in 1930. President Roosevelt designated him as Chairman of the FPC at the suggestion of the President and took over the leadership of the FCC on October 1, 1937.

He remained at the FCC helm for a little less than two years when he resigned on August 31, 1939 to become Special Assistant to the Attorney General.

With the exception of Mr. Garey who resigned after a few months of service and Mr. Stewart whose short term expired June 30, 1937, all original members were still on the Commission when McNinch switched to the Justice Department.[4]

EARLY PROBLEMS AND ACCOMPLISHMENTS

The first five years were difficult and turbulent ones for these commissioners. The Commission had to be organized, the vast broadcasting and tele-communications industries had to be brought under regulatory controls, and the basic operational pattern of the Commission had to be established.

During the first year of its life, the Commission conducted hearings pursuant to Section 307(c) of the Communications Act and, as mentioned in Chapter 3, made a report to Congress with recommendations against requiring fixed percentages of broadcast facilities for educational purposes.

The Commission issued orders requiring licensees to file information regarding the ownership of broadcasting stations. Telephone and telegraph companies under the jurisdiction of the Commission were ordered to report current services, rates, contracts, and stock ownership. Under the leadership of Paul A. Walker, then Chairman of the Telephone Division, the Commission carried on an investigation of the American Telephone and Telegraph Company for three years which brought about substantial reductions in long distance telephone rates.[5]

[3]Biographical material regarding these early Commissioners is taken from *Who's Who in America,* and press releases of the FCC.
[4]Biographical material regarding these early Commissioners is taken from *Who's Who in America* and press releases of the FCC.
[5]FCC Report, *Investigation of the Telephone Industry in the United States,* June 14, 1939, p. 602.

New rules and engineering standards for AM broadcast stations were approved.[6] Important hearings on radio frequency allocations were completed during this early period. Negotiations with other North American countries regarding the cooperative use of the radio spectrum and the avoidance of objectionable interference across national boundaries were completed. The result was the signing of the North American Regional Broadcasting Agreement in Havana on December 13, 1939.[7]

This was the period in which Mae West programs evoked wide-spread protests, and when Orson Wells caused "terror and fright" among millions of listeners with his "War of the Worlds" program. The Commission was pressed by the public to scrutinize more closely the programming of stations when they came up for renewal of their licenses.[8]

AN ANGRY CONGRESS

The problems of the Commission during these early days were aggravated by a hostile Congress. This antipathy was a carry over from the days of the Federal Radio Commission. That original "traffic cop of the air," as it was called, was never popular with Congress. As pointed out in Chapter 23, the FCC seemed to be even less popular. During the first four years of its life, it was the object of frequent charges and attacks from angry Congressmen. Growing dissatisfaction with the FCC's operations prompted the introduction of numerous resolutions in Congress to investigate the FCC.

THE CONTROVERSIAL MR. FLY

This was the unhappy situation which *James Lawrence Fly* faced when he took over the administrative reins of the FCC from Mr. McNinch on September 1, 1939. He was particularly well trained for the rough five years ahead. His educational and professional background included graduation from the U. S. Naval Academy, an LL.B. degree from Harvard and the practice of law in New York and Massachusetts. From 1929 to 1934, he was Special Assistant to the Attorney General and served as government counsel in actions involving restraint of trade under the Federal anti-trust laws. From 1934 to 1937, he headed up the legal department of the Tennessee Valley Authority and was its General Counsel for two years prior to his appointment as Chairman of the FCC on September 1, 1939.[9]

Less than three months after Mr. Fly took office, the Commission began public hearings on an order to investigate the radio networks. Despite vigorous and venomous protests from the broadcast industry. Mr. Fly was determined to see the investigation through to the bitter end. While the proceeding was under way, he was the subject of scathing attacks from industry spokesmen who were infuriated by his testy manner and the possibilities of stricter regulations.

He also received much tongue-lashing from Capitol Hill, and from 1939 to 1943, while he was in command at the FCC, no fewer than five resolutions were introduced in Congress to investigate the distraught agency. These various investigatory moves were aided and abetted by a growing number of unsuccessful and disgruntled (and

[6]Rules and Regulations of the FCC, published in mimeograph form, FCC mimeograph No. 30764, Nov. 28, 1938. Also see *Fifth Annual Report of FCC* (1939).
[7]The full text of the agreement as approved by the signatories on December 13, 1939 appears in 1 RR 41:11-43.
[8]See Warner, Harry. *Radio and Television Law* (Washington, 1948), pp. 337-39.
[9]*Who's Who in America,* 1938-1939, p. 916.

in some cases embittered) applicants for radio stations.

After prolonged hearings, in May, 1941, the Commission adopted its historic *Report on Chain Broadcasting*, establishing the network regulations.[10]

By this time, Commissioner Brown no longer was with the Commission, having encountered political difficulties on Capitol Hill and failing to secure confirmation of his reappointment by the Senate. *Frederick I. Thompson*, a Democrat and Newspaper publisher from Alabama, had been appointed and began service with the FCC on April 13, 1939. *Ray C. Wakefield*, an attorney and Republican from California and formerly Chairman of the public service commission of that state, took the oath of office on March 22, 1941. These new members joined Chairman Fly and Commissioners Walker and Payne in adoption of the majority report approving the network regulations.

As previously pointed out, *T. A. M. Craven*, who began his first term as Commissioner on August 25, 1937, vigorously dissented from the majority report and was joined in the dissent by Commissioner Case.

Chairman Fly was on the receiving end of much of the criticism which these network regulations evoked from Congress and the broadcast industry. Already bruised and battered by three years of the ordeal, he appeared before the Senate Interstate and Foreign Commerce Committee and adamantly denied the charges made against the Commission.[11]

Shortly thereafter, the Supreme Court issued the famous Felix Frankfurter opinion (*National Broadcasting Co. vs. U. S.*, 319 U.S. 190, May 10, 1943), upholding the legality of the regulations. But powerful political and economic forces had now combined to force the resignation of Mr. Fly. But he by no means was about to resign. He was determined to weather the storm, "come hell or high water."

He had the sympathetic support of *Clifford J. Durr* who had come on the Commission in November, 1941, about the time the network investigation began. Mr. Durr was a Democrat from Alabama. He was a brilliant lawyer, having graduated from the law school at the University of Alabama and later completed a degree in jurisprudence at Oxford University under a Rhodes scholarship. From 1933 to 1941, he had held a number of important legal positions in the Federal government. He was General Counsel and Director of the Defense Plant Corporation at the time of his appointment to the FCC.[12] He was a liberal in the true sense of the word and intensely devoted to the public interest.

Despite the prolonged pounding inflicted on him by the Cox Committee (discussed in Chapter 23), Mr. Fly did not give up his FCC job until December 1944. He resigned just a few weeks before the Committee released its report absolving the Commission of most of the major charges made against it.

WAR-TIME ACTIVITIES

While much of Mr. Fly's time and energy as Chairman was taken up with matters pertaining to the investigation, he and the other commissioners carried heavy administrative duties during the War. The Board of War Communications, cooperating with the Office of Civilian Defense and other governmental agencies and the military establishment, made important contributions to the war effort.

Also, it was during this period that the Commission held hearings on the proposed merger of the Postal Telegraph and Western Union companies. After consideration

[10]FCC, *Report on Chain Broadcasting*, Commission Order No. 37, Docket No. 5060, May, 1941.

[11]Hearings before the Senate Committee on Interstate Commerce on S. Res. 113, 77th Congress, First Session, June 2 to 20, 1941, pp. 10106.

[12]*Broadcasting*, March 17, 1958, p. 54.

of a long and involved record in the proceeding, the Commission approved the consolidation and thereby made possible a stabilization of the telegraph industry.[13]

Because of the continued growth of newspaper ownership of radio stations during the late thirties, the Commission under the leadership of Mr. Fly instituted a full scale investigation to determine whether a monopoly in mass media was developing. There was pressure from some sources for the establishment of rules which would impose limitations on newspaper ownership of stations.

After long public hearings in which the press strongly opposed any rules which would discriminate against newspapers, the Commission issued a report which it submitted to Congress.[14] No rules were established. The Commission simply said that in the future, each case involving newspaper ownership and raising questions of monopoly, would be decided on its merits. This policy enunciated under Mr. Fly's leadership has continued, more or less, to be the policy of the Commission ever since.[15]

POST-WAR LEADERSHIP

Following Mr. Fly's resignation on November 11, 1944, *Ewell Kirk Jett* was appointed interim Chairman. Prior to his appointment as a Commissioner, he had served as Chief Engineer. He had had a distinguished career as a radio engineer in the Navy, the Federal Radio Commission and the FCC, covering a span of 35 years. He had been a bulwark of strength down through the years in helping meet the many difficult engineering problems with which the Commission had been faced.[16]

But he was eager to retire from government service and had no desire to take over the full duties of Chairman. Accordingly, his interim appointment was terminated in about six weeks and he was succeeded by *Paul A. Porter* who had received the Presidential nod for the position.

Who's Who in America for 1944 gives the highlights of Mr. Porter's previous career as follows: He was educated at Kentucky Wesleyan College and University of Kentucky Law College. Later, he worked for several years as a newspaper reporter and editor. From 1934 to 1937, he was Special Counsel in the Department of Agriculture; and from 1937 to 1942 was Washington Counsel for the Columbia Broadcasting System. Subsequently, he was Deputy Administrator in charge of the rent division of the Office of Price Administration and at the time of his appointment to the FCC was Assistant Director of the Office of Economic Stabilization.[17]

Although Mr. Porter was with the Commission only a little over a year, some very significant developments occurred while he was there regarding frequency allocations for FM and TV broadcasting. With the War coming to a close, the Commission, under the previous leadership of Mr. Fly, had initiated public hearings relating to the allocation of frequencies above 25 megacycles. Mr. Porter and the Commission followed through with a number of important reports based upon these hearings.

On June 27, 1945, the Commission allocated the 88 to 108 megacycle band as the "permanent home" for FM broadcasting, reserving the first twenty channels in

[13]10 FCC 148-198, September 27, 1943.
[14]The hearings were conducted for a total of 25 days between July 23, 1941 and February 12, 1942. The record consisted of 3400 pages and 400 exhibits. 54 witnesses were called. See "The Newspaper Radio Decision" 7 *FCC Bar Journal* (1944), 11, 13.
[15]See Warner, *op. cit.*, pp. 205 to 212, for good discussion of the newspaper ownership hearings, the decision of the FCC and the problems involved.
[16]*Who's Who in America*, 1940-41, p. 1390.
[17]*Ibid.*, 1946-47, p. 1889.

the band for noncommercial, educational broadcasting.[18]

After further hearings, on September 12 and 20, 1945, the Commission published rules and regulations and standards of good engineering practice governing the commercial FM broadcast service.[19]

It was also in connection with this proceeding, that the Commission allocated the 44 to 88 and 174 to 216 megacycle bands to television. Following hearings which began on October 4, 1945, the Commission, on November 21, 1945, made available thirteen VHF channels for commercial television with UHF channels provided for experimentation and future development.[20]

THE "BLUE BOOK" CONTROVERSY

Mr. Porter also gave leadership in the preparation and publication of the industry-shaking "Blue Book." Before he came on the scene, for years, certain Congressmen had been complaining that the Commission had been lax in establishing and enforcing standards for radio programs; that despite many complaints, little effort had been made to require stations to serve the "public interest."[21]

Commissioner Durr, who had already been on the Commission more than three years, felt strongly that something positive should be done about it. He was quite articulate and vocal in the expression of his views and had much to do with establishing a climate of receptivity in the Commission for definite action. Typical of his thinking was a speech he made during the War in which he said:

In thinking of radio, we are too much inclined to think in terms of what radio can bring to the people—a one-way pipeline of news, ideas, and entertainment—and too little in terms of its value as an outlet through which the people may express themselves. Democracy thrives more on participation at its base than upon instruction from the top . . . Round-table discussion of local problems by local people, and town meetings in which local people participate, may be as exciting and as important as similar types of programs on national and international affairs participated in by authorities of national or international reputation. Moreover, while programs by the local music society, the college department of music, the policemen's band, or the local little theater may not reach the technical perfection of similar performances by a national symphony orchestra or Hollywood professionals, they bring to the community a sense of participation and an awareness of cultural values that can never be piped in from studios in New York or Hollywood.

The world is now in the midst of a major crisis, greater than any that has heretofore occurred in its history. Following the war, when tremendous economic, political, and cultural adjustments will have to be made, the pattern of the future will depend upon our ability to make these adjustments in the right way. In this country, we are dedicated to the principles of democracy. If the pattern of the future is to be a democratic pattern, it cannot be imposed from the top; it must be based upon the desires, beliefs, and feelings of the people themselves. Democracy can function only in an atmosphere of full information and frank discussion. In determining the course of the future, radio can plan its part for good or evil, depending upon whether it is the voice of the few or an outlet for full information and free expression, as uncurbed by commercial as by political restraints.[22]

Mr. Durr believed that some minimum program standards should be set up by the Commission to be applied when stations come up for renewal of their licenses. Mr.

[18]Report of FCC on Allocations from 44 to 108 megacycles. Docket No. 6651, June 27, 1945.
[19]See Report of FCC, No. 84371, August 24, 1945.
[20]Report of the Commission Re. Promulgation of Rules and Regulations and Standards of Good Engineering Practice for Commercial Television Broadcast Stations (Docket No. 6780., Nov. 21, 1945).
[21]See speech of Congressman Wigglesworth on house Floor; 84 *Cong. Rec.* 1164-1166, Feb. 6, 1939.
[22]Durr, Clifford Judkins, "Freedom of Speech for Whom," FCC Mimeograph No. 79855.

Porter agreed, and during his one year tenure as FCC Chairman, Dr. Charles Seipmann, formerly with the British Broadcasting Corporation, was brought in to direct a study and come up with some criteria which the Commission might establish for the evaluation of radio program service.

The result of this study was the adoption and publication by the FCC in March, 1946 of the report, *Public Service Responsibility of Broadcast Licensees,* fully discussed in previous Chapters.

Only a few weeks before this report was released, Paul Porter resigned to accept the position of OPA Administrator. He was replaced by a brilliant young man then only thirty-two years of age, *Charles Ruthven Denny, Jr.,* who had been appointed Commissioner shortly after Mr. Porter received the Chairmanship.

Mr. Denny had a brilliant record as a student at Amherst and at Harvard Law School. He was admitted to the District of Columbia Bar in 1936, practiced law in the District for two years, and then joined the Department of Justice as an attorney. He was appointed Special Assistant to the Attorney General in 1941 and came to the FCC as Assistant General Counsel the following year.[23]

Not yet thirty years of age, he quickly acquired a masterful knowledge of regulatory problems at the FCC and demonstrated unusual administrative and organizational ability. He was made General Counsel in October, 1942 and during the next two years spent much of his time representing the Commission in the hearings conducted by the Congressional Select Committee to which reference has already been made.[24]

His stellar performance in these hearings was credited as having been an important factor in the issuance of the report by that committee which acquitted the Commission of most of the charges made against it. There can be no doubt that the favorable impression he made on Congress as well as his efficient handling of legal matters within the Commission accounted for his appointment to the Commission on March 30, 1945.[25] With the departure of Mr. Porter, it was only logical that Mr. Denny should succeed him.

He was appointed Acting Chairman on February 26, 1946.[26] He continued in an acting capacity until December 4 of the same year when the President gave him full status as Chairman.[27]

Only a few weeks after he was appointed Acting Chairman, the Blue Book was issued. Industry and Congressional reaction was immediate. It was charged that the document had been adopted without rule-making proceedings and was therefore illegal; that it constituted censorship and violated Section 326 of the Communications Act and the First Amendment to the Constitution.[28]

Judge Thurman Arnold, former member of the United States Circuit Court of Appeals for the District of Columbia, took an opposite point of view. Speaking for the American Civil Liberties Union over the CBS network on June 1, 1946, he commended the FCC for its action. Said he, in part:

The Commission announced that hereafter in issuing and in renewing the licenses of broadcasting stations it would give particular attention to the program service that the station had been giving the public . . . The Commission followed the simple principle that this valuable public grant should be given to those who gave more public service in preference to those who

[23] *Who's Who in America,* 1946-47, p. 599.
[24] See *FCC Log. A Chronology of Events in the History of the Federal Communications Commission from its Creation on June 19, 1934, to July 2, 1956;* compiled by the FCC Office of Reports and Information.
[25] *Ibid.,* p. 45
[26] *Ibid.,* p. 49.
[27] *Ibid.,* p. 52.
[28] Senate Resolution 307 introduced by the late Senator Tobey to investigate FCC control over radio programming was an outgrowth of these charges. See *Cong. Rec.,* 9803, 9804, July 24, 1946.

gave less. The absence of such a standard in the past has been responsible for the abuses of our forums of the air. It is difficult to see how any rational man can quarrel with this sort of protection of the public interest, as a condition of a public grant.[29]

The Commission, under Mr. Denny's leadership, set up machinery to apply the criteria set forth in the Blue Book. Licensees were put on notice that their program service would be measured in terms of these criteria when their stations came up for renewal of their licenses.

Shortly thereafter, a number of hearings on renewal applications were held. Some stations received slaps on the wrist for over-commercialization or for not providing what the Commission called a "balanced program service." In no case, however, was a single renewal application denied for failure to adhere to Blue Book standards.[30]

Nevertheless, the very fact that the Commission had announced its intention to apply these program standards and, in a few instances, had required stations to go through expensive public hearings before their licenses were renewed, gave force and sanction to the standards which most licensees felt it would be risky to ignore.

A number of other significant actions were taken by the Commission while Mr. Denny was Chairman. Measures were adopted to streamline and speed up the processing of applications.[31] New rules for educational FM stations were adopted.[32] The international tele-communications conference began in Atlantic City on May 16, 1947 and continued until October 3 of the same year with Chairman Denny presiding.[33]

A COMMERCIAL BROADCASTER BECOMES CHAIRMAN

A treaty having been signed by all the participants, Mr. Denny resigned in October, 1947 as Chairman of the FCC to accept a position as General Counsel of the National Broadcasting Company.[34]

Commissioner Paul A. Walker, was appointed Acting Chairman less than one month later and held the position until December 26, 1947, when President Truman gave the Chairmanship to *Wayne Coy*.[35]

Like some of his predecessors, Mr. Coy had an impressive background. He graduated from Franklin (Indiana) College in 1926. He began his newspaper career at the age of 16 as a reporter, and later served as city editor of the *Franklin Star* and became editor and publisher of the *Delphi Citizen*.

In 1933, he was made a secretary to Governor McNutt of Indiana, directed the Governor's Commission on Unemployment Relief, and organized and administered Indiana's first Welfare Department. In 1935, he was appointed Indiana State Administrator and Regional Administrator for the Works Progress Administration. Two years later he went to the Philippines as administrative assistant to Mr. McNutt, then United States High Commissioner to those islands. Subsequently, Mr. Coy was made Assistant Administrator of the Federal Security Agency, followed by an assignment in 1941 as Special Assistant to the President and White House Liaison officer with the Office of Emergency Management.

[29]Speech of Thurman Arnold over CBS Network, June 1, 1946, incorporated in *Congressional Record* by Congressman Hugh B. Mitchell. 92 *Cong. Rec.* A 3120-21, June 3, 1946.
[30]See *Walmac Co.*, 12 FCC 91, 3 RR 1371 (1947); *Eugene J. Roth*, 12 FCC 102, 3 RR 1377 (1947); *Hearst Radio, Inc.*, 6 RR 994 (1951).
[31]*FCC Log, op. cit.*, pp. 50-51.
[32]*Ibid.*, p. 56.
[33]*Ibid.*, p. 58.
[34]*Ibid.*
[35]*Ibid.*, p. 59.

In 1942, he was appointed Assistant Director of the Budget, a position which he held until February, 1944 when he left government service to become assistant to the publishers of the *Washington Post* and director of the paper's radio stations WINX-AM and WINX-FM.

Mr. Coy had been active on a number of committees of the National Association of Broadcasters. In 1946 and 1947, he headed an industry committee which cooperated with the Federal Communications Commission on the simplification of broadcast application forms. He had long been interested in frequency modulation broadcasting and had served as an officer and director of FM Broadcasters, Inc.[36]

Mr. Coy served as Chairman for four years. During this time, the Commission grappled with many difficult regulatory problems. On September 20, 1948, the Commission initiated public hearings on possible expansion of television broadcasting to include the UHF bands, the addition of color, and other improvements.[37] Shortly thereafter, all TV applications were "frozen" pending study of the general TV situation.[38] Long and exhaustive hearings were held intermittently, and after the issuance of five reports covering different phases of the TV proceeding, the Commission began the preparation of its final report and order looking toward lifting the television "freeze," adding 70 UHF channels, adopting a nation-wide allocation table with assignment of both VHF and UHF channels to communities throughout the country, and reserving 242 channels for education.[39]

Mr. Durr did not seek reappointment when his term expired on June 30, 1948 and had no opportunity to participate in these television hearings. His intelligent and constructive efforts, however, in behalf of educational broadcasting continued to have effect. The understanding and enthusiasm which he generated in the Commission with respect to educational FM carried over into the television proceedings and no doubt was an important factor in the Commission's decision to reserve television channels for education.

In this connection, the late Commissioner *Frieda B. Hennock,* who replaced Mr. Durr,[40] should be mentioned. She was a democrat from New York where she had practiced law and had been active in politics before coming to the Commission. She soon exhibited an active interest in reserving TV channels for education. Her animated and zealous advocacy during the hearings attracted nation-wide attention, and many have credited her with playing a major role in the Commission's decision to make the reservations.

In connection, with the channel allocations and the establishment of a nationwide plan for television, there were many thorny technical problems. The knowledge and advice of Commissioners *Edwin M. Webster* and *George A. Sterling,* both career men who had served the Commission in an engineering capacity for many years, were most helpful in working out these problems.

One of the controversial questions that the Commission had to consider in the television proceeding was whether to establish a fixed table of assignments for the country at large with definite mileage separations for stations on the same or adjacent channels, or to provide that assignments would be made in terms of local demand and needs. The majority report resolved the question in favor of the fixed table. *Robert Jones,* a Republican from Ohio and a former Congressman, who became a Commissioner on September 5, 1947, dissented vigorously. The majority contended that the adoption of the fixed table of assignments would make for

[36]FCC Biographical Sketch of Chairman Wayne Coy, Mimeograph No. 14931, December 29, 1947.
[37]*FCC Log, op. cit.,* p. 62.
[38]*Ibid.*
[39]*Ibid.,* p. 75-76.
[40]*Ibid.,* p. 62

administrative simplicity and would provide for a more equitable and effective distribution of television facilities. Commissioner Jones disagreed. In concluding his dissenting opinion he said:

... Efficient distribution of channels and the provision of the maximum number of television stations have been sacrificed to achieve a misleading appearance of simplicity of administration. The public interest, convenience and necessity have been abandoned to the theoretical convenience of the Commission. The small communities are to be subjected to rules drawn upon considerations applicable primarily or wholly to large cities. The apparent simplicity of administration is an illusion that will disappear as soon as the number and complexity of conflicting applications under the standards emerge. The Commission thinks it has eliminated Section 307(b)* contests between cities (it has not eliminated them all); but by creating a scarcity of frequencies it has created a bigger problem in each city where there will surely be more applicants than there are channels. The administrative burden created by competitive applicants for the limited number of frequencies by this artificial scarcity or channel assignments will far outweigh the administrative burden they are trying to eliminate.[41]

Other important accomplishments of the Commission under the Coy administration should be noted. Of special importance was the adoption of the famous report authorizing broadcasters to editorialize subject to their affording broadcast time for the expression of opposing views.[42] The Commission underwent a reorganization; administrative and prosecutory functions were separated; hearing examiners were appointed in line with the Administrative Procedure Act, requiring that they act in a judicial capacity and decide cases independently. New bureaus were established to take care of expanding broadcast services and many new rules and regulations were adopted to cover these services.[43]

The Wayne Coy administration came to a close when he resigned on February 21, 1952 to go into the television business. He was succeeded by *Paul A. Walker* whose tenure as Chairman lasted for eighteen months, and whose professional career is hereinafter presented in detail as a special case study in public administration.

ROBERT TAYLOR BARTLEY IS APPOINTED TO THE FCC

Shortly after Mr. Walker's appointment, on March 6, 1952, *Robert Taylor Bartley*, a Democrat from Texas, was appointed to the Commission. He came directly from Capitol Hill where he had been serving as Administrative Assistant to the Speaker of the House Sam Rayburn.

Following his college work at Southern Methodist University, he served on the research and investigative staff of the House Committee on Interstate and Foreign Commerce, and later held staff appointments at the FCC and the Securities and Exchange Commission. Subsequently, he became Vice-President of the Yankee Network, Inc. and before going to Capitol Hill was with the National Association of Broadcasters for five years.[44] He is now serving his third term which will expire June 30, 1972.

*Section 307(b) of the Communications Act provides that "in considering applications for licenses, and modifications and renewals thereof, when and insofar as there is demand for the same, the Commission shall make such distribution of licenses, frequencies, hours of operation, and of power among the several states and communities as to provide a fair, efficient, and equitable distribution of radio service to each of the same.
[41]*FCC Sixth Report and Order;* 17 Fed. Reg. 3905, 4100, May 2, 1952.
[42]*In the Matter of Editorializing by Broadcasting Licensees,* FCC Docket No. 8516; 13 FCC 1246; 14 Fed. Reg. 30 55; 1 RR 91:21 (1949).
[43]*FCC Log, op. cit.,* 65-82.
[44]Biographical Sketch of Robert T. Bartley, FCC Public Notice 73828, March 6, 1952.

He has decried censorship and is repelled by the idea that the Commission should tell the broadcasters what particular programs they should or should not carry. But he has made clear his belief that the Communications Act not only gives the Commission the authority to review program performance but imposes a definite responsibility on it to exercise this authority when stations file their renewal applications. In such program review, he thinks the Commission should be concerned with such matters as whether the station has been fair in presenting both sides of public issues and in presenting news programs. There can be no question that he believes in the "fairness doctrine" which was recently upheld by the U. S. Supreme Court. Also, where there is over-commercialization (especially if the use of "artificial audience-stealing gimmicks" is involved) or if the broadcaster seems more concerned with making a "fast buck" than providing public service, the Commissioner has not hesitated to question whether the station is serving the public interest.[45] In a Report and Order adopted on January 15, 1964, the Commission expressed its concern regarding overcommercialization, stated that it had legal authority to prevent it, and that, while it would not establish rules at that time imposing limitations, it would continue to deal with the subject on a case-by-case basis. Mr. Bartley, along with the six other commissioners, voted to approve the Report and Order.[46]

Mr. Bartley has exhibited a consistent concern regarding monopoly and multiple ownership and undue concentrations of control in the broadcast industry. For example, he refused to vote for the approval of the proposed giant merger of the International Telephone and Telegraph Company and the American Broadcasting Company (discussed more fully later) on the grounds that the Commission had failed to give adequate consideration to the possible effects of such a merger on the structure of competitive broadcasting in the country. "This merger," said he, "would place a major share of our national broadcast service—particularly our television service—under the direct ultimate control of an expanding conglomerate corporation, international in scope, heterogeneous in character and largely extraterritorial in orientation and operation, with the inherent danger of the broadcast operations becoming a tool of and image builder for the corporate conglomerate and little attention given to the local needs of the public which the broadcast operations are charged with serving."[47]

Again, in a more recent case, in which the Morman Church was granted a renewal of its KSL license in Salt Lake City, he voted for a hearing to find out, in the light of the licensee's interrelated commercial interests, whether "there is an undesirable concentration of control of mass media or a situation which would tend" to concentrate economic domination in the Salt Lake City market.[48]

Since he was appointed to the Commission in March, 1952, several men have served as chairman of the FCC. Mr. Bartley frequently has been mentioned in the press as a prospect for the job when vacancies have occurred. It does not appear, however, that he has been an aggressive candidate for the chairmanship and seems to be well satisfied to remain in a commissioner's role.

Shortly after Mr. Bartley's original appointment, Robert Jones resigned to enter the practice of law and was replaced on October 14, 1952 by *Eugene H. Merrill,* a Democrat from Utah. The latter remained on the Commission for only six months when he was replaced on April 15, 1953 by *John C. Doerfer,* a Republican from Wisconsin.

[45]*Broadcasting,* August 6, 1956. p. 77.
[46]1 RR 2d 1607.
[47]9 RR 2d 30-45.
[48]15 RR 2d 465; also see *Broadcasting,* January 27, 1969, pp. 28-29.

With the election of a Republican administration, *Rosel Hyde*, who had been a member of the Commission since April, 1946 (he was appointed to fill the unexpired term of *William H. Wills* who on April 18, 1953, died after being on the Commission only nine months), was elevated to the Chairmanship by President Eisenhower to succeed Commissioner Walker who had retired. Mr. Hyde was appointed Chairman for the specified term of one year only, a limitation on tenure that no president before or since has imposed on the office.

The new FCC chief was a seasoned veteran in the field of broadcast regulation. He was a member of the staff of the old Federal Radio Commission and had been associated with the FCC since its creation in 1934. He had held legal positions in the agency, beginning with that of Assistant Attorney and continuing progressively in positions of Associate Attorney, Attorney, Attorney Examiner, Senior Attorney, Principal Attorney, Assistant General Counsel, and General Counsel, and following the demise of Mr. Mills, as pointed out above, was appointed a member of the Commission.[49]

He had participated in many hearings of a regulatory and adjudicatory nature, took part in the first general frequency allocation proceedings conducted by the Federal Radio Commission in 1928 and in similar hearings carried on by the FCC in 1935. He played an active role in the network investigation of 1938 and the proceedings which resulted in the establishment of regular FM and TV broadcasting in 1941. And, as a member of the Commission, he was an important participant in the 1949-52 television hearings which resulted in the establishment of a nationwide table of TV assignments.[50]

He also had taken leadership in various international telecommunication conferences. He was a member of the United States delegation to the Third Inter-American Telecommunications Conference at Rio de Janeiro in 1945, and was Chairman of the United States delegation to the Third North American Regional Broadcasting Conference in 1949-1950 which effected a new broadcasting agreement for that region.[51]

His educational background included attendance at the Utah Agricultural College in 1920-21 and graduation from the George Washington University law school in 1929. He was admitted to the District of Columbia bar in 1928 and licensed to practice before the U. S. Supreme Court in 1945.[52]

While Mr. Hyde was serving his first stint as Chairman there were a number of important developments which should be noted. TV processing lines were established to speed up action on pending applications. A code of ethics for FCC employees was adopted. A $65,000,000 increase in interstate telephone rates became effective. The license term for TV stations was extended from one to three years. The multiple ownership rules were amended, limiting control by one group or interest to seven AM, seven FM, and seven TV stations, with ownership of VHF stations limited to five. Domestic telegraph rates were increased, yielding additional annual income to Western Union of $10,000,000.[53]

REPUBLICAN ROBERT E. LEE IS APPOINTED

About six months following Mr. Hyde's one year designation as Chairman, on October 6, 1953, *Robert E. Lee*, a Republican from the District of Columbia was

[49]FCC Public Notice 34398, July 1956.
[50]*Ibid.*
[51]*Ibid.*
[52]*Ibid.*
[53]FCC Log, *op. cit.* Also, see *FCC Annual Report,* 1954.

appointed to the Commission. Prior to his appointment he had done important administrative work with the FBI, and for a time was Director of Surveys and Investigations for the House Committee on Appropriations.

He was born in Chicago and studied Commerce and Law at De Paul University. He had considerable experience with business concerns in an auditing capacity prior to his government experience.[54]

His appointment to the FCC was contested by a substantial number of Senators. It was alleged by some that he lacked broadcast experience. Others were fearful that he might attempt to impose strict controls on the broadcast media. There can be no doubt that some on Capitol Hill opposed him because of his friendship for and past associations with Senator McCarthy, whose behavior at the time had outraged many Congressmen and a substantial number of people throughout the country.

After much debate, the Senate confirmed his appointment by a vote of 58 to 25. Following confirmation, the February 1, 1954 issue of *Broadcasting* carried a report on an interview with him in which he was quoted as expressing confidence in the "free-enterprise radio-TV system." He expressed the view that the FCC must be "in the driver's seat but light on the reins." He further said that "as long as broadcasters stay within the law they will have no trouble with me. I hope no station in any part of the U. S. feels even remotely that I would encourage it to carry a certain program as against another."[55]

Eight months later, he warned the broadcasters that they would need to find a way to clean their own house or the sins of the few would bring "the walls of the temple crumbling down on the heads of the vast majority of this great industry."[56]

He expressed concern about over-commercialization in broadcasting, the abuses of the "pitch" advertisers and the "growing cancer" in the form of advertising in bad taste.[57]

Mr. Lee has been re-appointed twice to the Commission and his present term does not expire until June 30, 1974. Down through the years he has stressed the importance of self-regulation as opposed to censorship and governmental control of broadcast programming, and in the judgments he is required to make he has said that he relies heavily on the broadcasting code of the National Association of Broadcasters.[58] But he has further pointed out that not all broadcasters live up to the code, that a few disregard the interests of the people, and by doing so they invite censorship.[59]

While he feels it is the duty of the broadcaster to determine and meet the programming needs of the community, he has observed that the courts have upheld the Commission's authority to review and evaluate past programming when stations come up for renewal of their licenses. And, if the record of performance is clearly below standard, as evidenced by a volume of complaints from listeners, he believes it is the duty of the Commission to take remedial action in the public interest.[60]

He has been particularly concerned about some TV programming which he considers indecent and obscene. In a recent case, where the majority of the Commission approved an application for a license for additoinal broadcast facilities, he joined with another commissioner in a strong dissent. He took exception to the reading of a poem over one of the licensee's stations which he said contained "four letter words" and "crude terms for genitals."[61]

[54]Biographical Sketch of Commissioner Robert E. Lee, FCC Public Notice 33738, July 2, 1956.
[55]*Broadcasting,* February 1, 1954, p. 50.
[56]*Ibid.,* September 27, 1954, p. 40.
[57]*Ibid.*
[58]*Ibid.,* May 19, 1969, p. 52.
[59]*Ibid.*
[60]*Ibid.,* pp. 49-50.
[61]*Ibid.,* November 3, 1969, p. 30; also see November 24, p. 64.

Upon expiration of Mr. Hyde's one year term as Chairman, the President having failed to act, the Commission continued Mr. Hyde's position by electing him Acting Chairman.[62] He continued in an acting capacity until the President appointed *George C. McConnaughey* on October 4, 1954.[63]

Mr. McConnaughey, a resident of Ohio, had been Chairman of the Renegotiation Board prior to his appointment as head of the FCC. His formal education included an LL.B. from Western Reserve University. He was admitted to the Ohio Bar in 1924. After practicing law for two years, he was employed by the city of Cleveland in a legal capacity from 1926 to 1928. From 1939 to 1945, he was chairman of the Ohio Public Utilities Commissin and for three years during this period, served as chairman of the Ohio War Transportation Committee. He was president of the National Association of Railroad and Utilities Commissioners in 1944-45.[64]

Mr. McConnaughey's administration as Chairman lasted about two years and nine months. Some developments during that period should be mentioned. FM broadcasters were authorized to engage in supplemental "functional music" operations. A study of network operations was initiated. Rule making proceedings to consider the problems of UHF were instituted. The Commission called a public conference to consider the technical problems of UHF, out of which developed an industry committee known as TASO. This organization made allocations studies for more than two years and reported important data to the Commission in 1959.[65]

At no previous period in the history of the Commission was there more intense rivalry for the acquisition of broadcasting facilities. Applicants for television stations spent hundreds of thousands of dollars in competitive proceedings. With some channels being sought valued at as high as ten million dollars each, enormous pressures of an extrajudicial character were brought to bear on Congress, the White House and the FCC to influence decisions in highly controversial cases.

COMMISSION APPOINTMENTS UNDER THE MCCONNAUGHEY REGIME

During the McConnaughey administration, *Richard Alfred Mack,* a Democrat from Florida and Chairman of the Public Service Commission of that state became an FCC commissioner replacing Freida B. Hennock, whose term had expired on June 30, 1955.

About a year later, *T. A. M. Craven* was re-appointed for a second term. As previously pointed out he had served one term from 1937 to 1944 and then left the commission to engage in private radio engineering consulting in Washington, D. C.

As mentioned in Chapter 3, he had opposed the adoption of the network regulations more than seventeen years before on the grounds that they involved control of programs and business practices of broadcast licensees. Also, as heretofore indicated, he took the position that the Commission exceeds its authority when it requires licensees to supply program information in terms of certain categories which are set forth in the renewal application form. He stated:

From my point of view the Commission's position in this entire matter is patently both illegal and impractical. For, here the Commission prescribes what programs it considers to be in the best interest of the public and, by this prescription, creates either an artificial demand or an artificial need, or both—which does violence to principles of freedom of expression; to the clear

---

[62]*FCC Log, op. cit.,* p. 94.
[63]*Ibid.,* p. 97.
[64]*Who's Who in America,* 1958-59, p. 1830.
[65]*FCC Log, op. cit.,* pp. 97-112.

statutory principle that choice of programs is the licensee's exclusive duty and responsibility; to every social aspect of programming as it applies to the varying tastes, customs, needs, and demands of the many communities of this nation; and to the economic well-being of the stations themselves.

The answer to this Commission-created problem is simple, legal, and practical. The Commission should discontinue using program proposals as one of the criteria on which it bases its approval or disapproval of an application for a broadcast permit or renewal of license. Only for the purpose of determining whether the law would be or is being violated by programming should an applicant or a respondent in a revocation proceeding be required to file program proposals or practices. Otherwise the Commission should leave the task of programming in the public interest exclusively to the licensee where it belongs as a matter of right and duty.[66]

CHAIRMAN MCCONNAUGHEY RETIRES

Mr. McConnaughey's term expired on June 30, 1957 and he left the Commission to practice law. Prior to his departure, Congress, through its special House Committee on Legislative Oversight, was preparing to make serious charges against the Commission with particular respect to its handling and disposition of several important TV cases. It was this foreboding situation which *John Charles Doerfer* faced when he moved into the Chairman's office in July, 1957 and which plagued him and the Commission almost constantly during the three year period that he headed the agency.

JOHN CHARLES DOERFER'S DEMISE AS FCC CHAIRMAN*

On June 19, 1960, the Federal Communications Commission was twenty-six years old. To put it mildly, its life had been hectic.

This agency that regulates all broadcasting and a vast portion of the telephone and telegraph industries in the country, since its birth in 1934, had been viewed more or less continuously by its progenitors on Capitol Hill as a delinquent child— congenitally weak and depraved, and requiring frequent discipline.

It has been under formal investigation by Congress or the threat of one every year since it was created. In fact, its bath of fire brought on by the spectacular exploits of the House Subcommittee on Legislative Oversight was but a continuation of the ordeal to which the bedraggled Commission had been subject most of its life.

Its general popularity rating had never been high. The broadcast industry had often complained bitterly because of FCC regulations, particularly when they related to programming. Other groups had denounced the Commission for not imposing stricter program controls. It had been called almost everything in the book —incompetent, irresponsible, morally corrupt, bureaucratic, left wingish and even subversive.

The eleven men who had previously served as Chairman of the FCC had been clobbered unmercifully. One died in office. Three succumbed shortly after leaving the job. Of those still alive in 1960 two related that they suffered serious health impairment as a result of the experience.

With the possible exception of James Lawrence Fly who ruled the FCC roost

[66]Notice of Proposed Rule Making, In the Matter of Section IV (Statement of Broadcasting Application Forms, 301, 303, 314, and 315), FCC Docket No. 12673, adopted November 19, 1958; 1 RR 98:26.

*This portrait of Mr. Doerfer first appeared in the March 1960 issue of the *Telefilm Magazine.* It was reprinted with a few editorial changes by permission of *Telefilm.* Minor changes again have been made in the statement as it appears in the revised edition of this book.

during the early forties, no chairman had a rougher time than John Charles Doerfer who resigned on March 10, 1960. He held the position for almost three years (the average term for FCC chairmen had been less than two years), and the hot seat kept him jumping most of the time.

He was appointed a member of the Commission in 1953 and was designated Chairman in July, 1957, replacing George McConnaughey who left the job to practice law. Even before President Eisenhower gave him the nod for the top post, the House Subcommittee on Legislative Oversight already had Doerfer and several other FCC Commissioners targeted for investigational fire. Dr. Bernard Schwartz, the "rule or ruin" professor (as he was later called by Congressman Harris), then Chief Counsel for the Subcommittee, had his staff searching the FCC files for evidence of villainy. And with the use of concealed tape recorders in their interviews at the FCC, they were conducting try-outs for the leading characters to be featured in the sensational drama to follow.

A few months later, the big show opened in the House Office Building on Capitol Hill. In a confidential memo prepared for the Subcommittee, Dr. Schwartz had accused the FCC Chairman and several other members of the Commission of official misconduct, undue fraternization with the broadcast industry, and fraud against the government. The memo had been leaked to the press without Doerfer having received any prior official notice of the charges. He was incensed, and appeared before the Subcommittee in public hearings to answer the charges.

Normally a mild man, he was in an angry mood as he faced a battery of news-hungry reporters and clicking cameras and began his testimony that afternoon on February 3, 1959. While he didn't question the right of a Congressional committee to investigate the Commission, he was deeply aggrieved and provoked by what he considered to be the irresponsible and sleuth-like tactics of Professor Schwartz and his staff. "It is my right," he declared, "as a public official and as a citizen to object strongly to the process of smearing reputations by distortions and innuendo."

With vocal acidity he referred to the "confidential" memo of Dr. Schwartz which had charged that he and other members of the Commission had failed to act with judicial propriety and were guilty of undue association with the broadcast industry.

"This memorandum," he said, "makes it appear that the members of the FCC are judges and only judges. It implies that most of their time is spent in deciding cases between litigants. . . . Probably ten per cent of our work involves litigated matters. In such cases, we sit as judges. When I *sit* as judge, I *act* as judge. When I have matters for decision between litigants, I do not discuss these matters with either side, or, for that matter, with anyone. But when I am a legislator looking for information to solve some of the great problems confronting communications in the country, I will talk to anyone . . . in my office . . . on the steps of the Capitol or at lunch with him at any public restaurant . . ."

With impassioned utterance (which brought applause from the crowded hearing room), he said that he "came to Washington a man of modest means. I am still a man of modest means. I followed my conscience in deciding every matter that came before me. I have done the best I know how and I am willing to subject my record to the sharpest scrutiny . . ."

With the conclusion of Mr. Doerfer's opening statement, the spotlight shifted to Dr. Schwartz. With dramatic ferocity, the probing professor grilled Chairman Doerfer for nearly three days. Among other things, he wanted to know if Doerfer had made trips at the expense of organizations regulated by the FCC. Doerfer readily admitted that he had made some, but was quick to point out that he was permitted to do so by Section 4(b) of the Communications Act which specifically provided that an FCC commissioner might accept a "reasonable honorarium or compensation" for the "presentation or delivery of publications or papers."*

*Section 4(b) has since been repealed by Congress.

But what about the trips he had made when he had received expense money from the group he addressed and at the same time had been reimbursed by the government for these expenses? With a kind of "mousetrap" finality in his voice, the professor wanted to know if Chairman Doerfer thought Section 4(b) of the Act permitted him to make a profit at government expense.

Mr. Doerfer's face flashed fire at this innuendo. "That's a nasty way to put it," he indignantly replied. He explained that if a group offered him a reasonable honorarium or compensation for making a speech, which included a sum equal to what he could legitimately claim from the government, it was perfectly proper for him to accept it, and in no sense was there any violation of the law.

He further testified that in each case where he had received honorariums plus government reimbursement for expenses, his trips had had a double purpose. He explained that on all such trips he not only made speeches, but spent considerable time making studies and inspections of an official nature.

Never once during the three day ordeal did Doerfer wince under the whiplash of cross-examination. With clear conscience and indomitable courage, he stoutly defended his actions and denied every charge made against him.

Shortly thereafter, Dr. Schwartz resigned as Chief Counsel under pressure from the Subcommittee which had become increasingly unhappy with his methods of operation. No punitive action of any kind was taken against Mr. Doerfer although there was a strong feeling on the part of some Congressman that he was unfit to continue in office. Despite all the furor on Capitol Hill, two other commissioners against whom the professor had made similar charges of misconduct, were subsequently re-appointed to the FCC for seven year terms and were confirmed by Congress with little difficulty.

While many people feel that Mr. Doerfer should have been more aloof in his relations with the broadcast industry, it is clear from the record that he violated no laws. There was no evidence that any of his decisions in official matters were affected by *ex parte* influences. While some may disagree with him as to how much a commissioner should associate informally with persons connected with industries regulated by the FCC (this writer certainly does), no thinking person, fully understanding the functions and responsibilities of the agency, would argue that a commissioner should be restricted to the same extent as a judge.

As Doerfer pointed out, an FCC official has important duties of a legislative and rule-making character. These require that he be free to move with intelligent discretion outside Commission walls and talk with those who are in a position to give him information about the problems of the communications industry. Except in adjudicatory cases, in important matters about which there is public interest and concern, he should be free to express his personal views and discharge his statutory duty to "encourage the larger and more effective use of radio in the public interest."

Until he resigned March 10, he and his colleagues at the FCC were so busy with pressing regulatory matters that there was little time for him to brood over episodes of the past. The stack of agenda items which the FCC then and must still consider at its regular meetings each week often measures a foot high. Some items, of course, are disposed of quickly. On the other hand, many involve highly technical questions and perplexing matters of public policy, requiring careful and prolonged study.

For example, during the last year of his administration the problem of frequency allocation demanded increasing time and attention. How could the limited radio spectrum be better divided and made to serve more effectively our growing civilian and military needs? How could this be done in the face of growing demands of other countries for larger slices of the spectrum to meet their needs?

Finding satisfactory answers to these questions was time-consuming and brain-racking. Mr. Doerfer and two other commissioners found it necessary to travel abroad to negotiate with other countries and attempt to work out allocation agreements.

Related to the general allocation problem was the long standing, hotly contested issue whether to break up the clear channels and provide more frequencies for new stations in areas not then receiving adequate primary radio service. It had been hanging fire for fifteen years and a decision was long over-due.

Mr. Doerfer and his fellow commissioners proposed to authorize new Class II stations on these clear channel stations and other broadcast interests vigorously opposed it. But the proposal, some time after Mr. Doerfer's departure from the Commission, as pointed out in Chapter Eight, finally did prevail, and was sustained by the Supreme Court.

During the last part of Mr. Doerfer's term, the Commission held extensive hearings, precipitated largely by public concern at that time over the quiz scandals. During the month of December, 1958, the FCC commissioners listened to witnesses complain about these deceptive programs, about payola practices, over-commercialization, crime thrillers and various other types of broadcasting.

As Chairman, Mr. Doerfer expressed the view that some of the grave charges of wide-spread corruption and deception in the broadcast industry were canards. He agreed, however, that there had been some reprehensible practices, and he believed that measures should be taken by the government to prevent their recurrence. In line with this belief, he went along with other commissioners in proposing, in February, 1959, that rules be adopted to prohibit television stations from carrying rigged programs, unless announcement was made by the station at the beginning and end of such programs that they were rigged, in fact were not spontaneous, and did not involve genuine contest of intellectual skill or knowledge.

Furthermore, the Commission under his leadership proposed a rule which would deny a license to any TV station having a contract with a network unless the station received assurance that any network program of this type would be accompanied by announcements describing its true nature.

Mr. Doerfer hoped that these rules would be adopted.* He was troubled, however, by the incessant demands of some segments of the public that the FCC prescribe specific program standards and attempt or define "program balance" for all radio and television stations.

Shortly before President Eisenhower made him FCC Chairman in 1957, in a speech to the Catholic Institute of the Press in New York City, he compared the American system of broadcasting to systems in several other countries where government plays a more dominant role. In making comparision, he said, "the American way of broadcasting is, and promises to continue to be, a greater power for good because it is a free system. The people themselves are given the opportunity of developing their own programs, freedom to express their thoughts and ideas, and the power to discourage poor programming quickly and effectively by turning off the dials."

He further avowed that "the Federal Communications Commission has very limited power over programming." But he "sees no obstacle in such a limitation because it reasserts the tremendous faith of the American people in preserving the freedom of expressing themselves with a minimum of governmental interference."

Despite his belief that the FCC had limited authority with respect to programming, he was willing to take corrective action where the violation of specific statutes were involved. For example, in December 1958, he and his colleagues ordered a station in Denver to show cause why its license should not be revoked, on the basis

*As pointed out in Chapter Eighteen, Congress, on September 13, 1960, passed Public L. 87-448, which was approved May 11, 1962, 76 Stat. 68, prohibiting deceptive programming such as Chairman Doerfer had in mind and thereby making rules unnecessary.

of a complaint that the station had carried off-color and indecent language, in violation of the Criminal Code which specifically forbids such language.

He summed up his views regarding the FCC's powers over broadcasting in these words:

Congress did provide for Federal regulation of the radio spectrum in the public interest. This is mainly a problem of allocating the radio spectrum between broadcasting and other communication services. Assignment of radio frequencies is made to private persons or corporations so as to effect an efficient and equitable distribution among the several states and communities.

The licensees were to have a license for three-year periods subject to renewal if they can show that they have programmed in the public interest. Specifically, licensees are prohibited from broadcasting obscene, indecent or profane matter, or any information in the conduct of a lottery, or denying equal opportunities to political candidates.

Apart from this, the Federal Communications Commission has little power over programming—especially over a single program." (May 5, 1957, FCC Mimeo. No. 44910).

In a speech before the presidents of state broadcasting associations on February 25, 1959, he pointed out that the American system of broadcasting is not subsidized by the taxpayers' money. "It is financed by businessmen who are seeking a profit," he declared. "This needs no apology. It is the philosophy of the Communications Act and of our form of government. There are those who contend that the profit motive in broadcasting should be substituted by a government whip—not a big rawhide one—but just a *little one* for the time being."

He didn't agree. As he told these state presidents, he believed the "solutions for higher levels of all programming are essentially grass roots problem. They must grow out of felt needs and not be imposed by the infusion of an insipid system from some government hierarchy."

Despite his feeling that government should play a limited role in broadcasting, as Chairman of the FCC he often expressed his views publicly as to what constitutes good programming. He said that it should not only serve "the cultural, spiritual, educational and entertainment needs of the public," but also "should preserve for the people uncensored news and discussion of public problems."

As a public official, he felt that it was his duty to encourage and lend endorsement to high quality programs. He was eager, as he said, to use his position in every legitimate way to help the industry and the general public to the end that their interests would be better served.

It had long been a practice of the FCC to hold informal conferences with representatives of the telephone industry. These discussions, he believed often resulted in improved telephone service and reductions in rates. In fact, shortly before, the Bell company, through informal negotiations with the FCC, agreed to substantial cuts in charges for some calls. Mr. Doerfer could see no good reason why the broadcast industry and the FCC might not carry on informal negotiations and, avoiding arbitrary standards set by governmental fiat, thereby achieve improved program service.

With the thought of being helpful along this line, he proposed in January 1959, that the three networks work out a cooperative arrangement by which each would make available a minimum of one hour per week, during good listening time, for informational, educational and cultural programming.

As a result, the networks did enter into such an agreement which was to be effective the second week of November following the political conventions and general election. But the agreement was abandoned shortly without achieving any practical results.

While there are many who would disagree as to the quality of his performance at the FCC, certainly John Doerfer came to his job with an outstanding professional background. He came to the Commission with a fine collegiate record and long years of successful professional experience as an accountant, lawyer and public servant.

He was born in West Allis, Wisconsin, a suburb of Milwaukee. His parents were of German extraction, his father having come to this country when he was four years of age. As a child, Doerfer attended parochial schools in West Allis. At an early age, he was selling newspapers and working as a caddy on the golf courses to make part of his expenses. His father was a skilled machinist and had a reasonably good income, but with seven children to support he was unable to provide his family with much more than the basic necessities. John Doerfer, therefore, was compelled to make his own way through high school and college.

He peddled ice in the summer time in Madison, Wisconsin to help defray his expenses as a student at the University of Wisconsin. After graduation there, he entered the Marquette Law School in 1931 and completed his J.D. degree in 1934 with *cum laude* honors.

He was quiet and studious and highly respected by the faculty and students for his fine personal qualities and scholastic ability. He was known for his friendly disposition and ability to get along well with his fellow students and instructors. His classmates elected him president of the Senior Class in the Law School.

Prior to his law school years, he married Ida M. Page, a charming and intelligent girl who was born in Vermont but had been reared in Wisconsin. In addition to carrying a full course of study in law, he worked long hours as an accountant to take care of his school and family expenses. (Mr. and Mrs. Doerfer have two grown sons.)

Those who knew him in those early years, report that he was mild and modest, but that he never backed away from a fight where important principles were involved.

After graduation from law school, he practiced law in West Allis. He was elected Chairman of the Junior Bar Association in Milwaukee and later served as Chairman of the Public Utilities Section of the Wisconsin Municipal League.

He was elected City Attorney of West Allis. In his practice before the Wisconsin Public Service Commission, he specialized in public utility cases and, in 1949, was appointed Chairman of that commission.

It was his four year record of performance in this job that attracted the attention of the White House in 1953, and led to his appointment to the FCC the same year, replacing Paul A. Walker from Oklahoma who retired after nineteen years of service.

As previously pointed out, Mr. Doerfer was under almost constant surveillance by the House Committee on Legislative Oversight while he was Chairman of the Commission. In 1957 he was severely questioned by this committee regarding a visit in the home of George B. Storer, owner of a number of broadcast stations. Some time later, he made another trip to Florida and was a guest on Mr. Storer's yacht for several nights. This second trip was the subject of critical interrogation by several members of the House Committee when Mr. Doerfer appeared before the committee on March 4, 1960, to testify regarding what steps the FCC had taken to curb payola practices in the broadcast industry. For almost three hours, without one minute of recess, he was peppered with questions. Congressman Moss of California devoted a third of the time to cross-examination designed to show the impropriety of his accepting gratuities from Mr. Storer. It was a grueling experience for the Chairman, but he maintained a remarkable calm and restraint which were the object of comment by numerous observers at the hearing.

Mr. Doerfer responded to questions by saying that he had a right to choose his friends, that he had the right to make social contacts with any persons providing they were not involved in adjudicatory proceedings before the FCC, and that, while there might be differences of opinion, he did not feel that he had done anything wrong and that his conscience was perfectly clear.

When asked if he intended to resign as Chairman of the FCC following the three hour ordeal, he angrily replied that he had no such intention. But the rigors of Congressional scrutiny inevitably take their toll. No man can last for long as Chairman of the FCC. Mr. Doerfer, with all his courage, was no exception.

On the morning of March 4, this writer, on assignment, spent an hour and a half with the former Chairman in his office. During this interview he gave no indication that he intended to resign. It was the wood-shed treatment that he received from the Harris committee on Capitol Hill that afternoon, because of his visit with Mr. Storer on the yacht, that aroused White House concern and precipitated his demise as Chairman of the most controversial and investigation-ridden agency in the federal government.

THE MACK SCANDAL

More than a year before Mr. Doerfer's ignominious exit from the FCC, Commissioner Mack was under serious surveillance and attack from Capitol Hill. He was accused of having sold his vote to a winning applicant in a competitive television proceeding. Bernard Schwartz, the chief counsel of the House Legislative Oversight Subcommittee, who, as previously pointed out, had locked horns with Mr. Doerfer in sessions of the Subcommittee pressed the charges with a ferocity which attracted national attention.

A memorandum which Dr. Schwartz had prepared as a "confidential" document but which was leaked to the *New York Times* in January, 1958, alleged among other things that Mr. Mack and some other Commissioners had been captives of the broadcast industry, that they undoubtedly had accepted gifts and travel expenses from parties involved in adjudicatory proceedings and from broadcasters whom they were required to regulate (See *New York Times*, January 23, 1958, pp. 1, 14 and January 28, p. 16).

In the midst of this furore, under pressure from Congressional leadership as well as the White House, and with a criminal indictment pending against him, he resigned March 3, 1958.

Shortly thereafter, President Eisenhower appointed *John S. Cross*, an Arkansas Democrat, to serve the remainder of Mr. Mack's term. Mr. Cross was sworn in as Commissioner on May 23, 1958. At the time of his appointment he was Assistant Chief of the Telecommunications Division of the State Department. He had received a degree in electrical engineering from Alabama Polytechnic Institute in 1923. He had had a long career as a construction engineer, having held important positions with the South Carolina and Michigan state highway departments and the National Park Service.

FCC CHAIRMAN, FREDERICK WAYNE FORD*

Succeeding Mr. Doerfer as Chairman on March 15, 1960 was a lawyer's lawyer, as one of his former colleagues described him . . . *Frederick Wayne Ford* . The fifty-year old soft-spoken Ford (that was his age at the time) had served the FCC as Commissioner since his appointment to that post by President Dwight D. Eisenhower thirty months before. Held in high esteem by the FCC legal staff and by many communications lawyers in Washington who practice before the Commission, he was considered "no patsy for the industry."

His philosophy for broadcast regulation was quite different from his predecessor,

*The author collaborated with the Editor of *Telefilm* in the writing of this portrait of Mr. Ford as it appeared in the original edition of this book, and was reprinted with the Editor's permission. Some minor changes in the piece have been made as it appears in this revised edition.

John C. Doerfer, whose resignation was asked for and received by President Eisenhower. In a speech which he made to the West Virginia Broadcasters Association entitled "The Role of the FCC in Programming," in August following his appointment as Chairman, he reviewed the legislative history of the Radio Act of 1927 and the Communications Act of 1934, as well as important judicial decisions and the consistent practice of the old Radio Commission and the FCC. He expressed the view that the Commission's authority in this field was crystal clear and has definite responsibility to evaluate the over-all program service of a station in terms of the public interest when that station comes up for renewal of its license. The former chairman seriously questioned the legal authority of the FCC to regulate programs, except where they violate specific statutes such as those forbidding lotteries and indecent presentations. Doerfer often got worked up emotionally about obscenity on-the-air, but made it clear that he doubted the FCC's power to establish general standards or "guidelines" for broadcast programming. The legal basis for his doubt was Section 326 of the Communications Act which forbids the Commission from censoring programs. Doerfer not only doubted the FCC's legal power, but he questioned the propriety of general surveillance in view of our traditional concern in this country for free speech as guaranteed by the First Amendment. From a social point of view, Doerfer objected to it. Furthermore, he did not think it was possible to set forth program criteria, applicable to all communities, because of the multiplicity and variety of cultural tastes in this country.

Contrary to Doerfer, Ford, West Virginia Republican, believed the Commission not only *could* set up some guidelines for the industry but *should* do so. "It has been my view for a long time," said he, in the speech at White Sulphur Springs, West Virginia, "that it is highly unfair for the Commission to lie in ambush, so to speak, while practices are developing which violate its concept of the public interest, convenience and necessity, and then make an example of an uninformed broadcaster. I believe, rather it is generally our duty to inform the public through appropriate orders or reports of the criteria we expect to apply in advance of action against an individual broadcaster," he continued.

On February 11, 1960, Ford, in a speech before the Television and Radio Advertising Club of Philadelphia on "Programming . . . The Commission and Its Broadcast Licensees" in regard to the development within the Commission of a reasonably well-defined policy of reviewing programs, stated:

. . . the greatest freedom will be assured the broadcaster in programming his station and at the same time the Commission will perform its function of protecting the public interest, convenience and necessity with the minimum of interference to that freedom.

Following his graduation from the University of West Virginia Law School in 1934, with scholastic honors, he entered private law practice for several years before coming to Washington to serve in the general counsel's office of the Federal Security Administration in 1939. From there he went to the Office of Price Administration in 1942, later joining the U.S. Army Air Force. After several years of military service, he was discharged as a major and came back to Washington in 1946. After a short period of service with the OPA, he joined the FCC legal staff in 1947 in the Hearing and Review Sections.

Mr. Ford became Chief of the Hearing Division of the FCC in 1951 and, while serving in that capacity, he served as FCC co-counsel in two of the most important hearing cases ever conducted by the FCC. He had a major responsibility in the now-famous Paramount case, in which Paramount Television Productions and its subsidiary companies were seeking renewal of station licenses and were asking for authority to build new television stations. He also assumed important legal responsibilities in the celebrated Richards case, in which George (Dick) Richards was charged with news-slanting on three clear channel stations, KMPC, Hollywood, WJR, Detroit, and WGAR, Cleveland.

Regarding the Paramount case, the Paramount companies had been involved in anti-trust litigation for more than 20 years. These companies were charged with monopolistic practices and restraints of trade, both at federal and state levels. On May 3rd, 1948, the U.S. Supreme Court handed down a decision finding Paramount substantially guilty of the charges, including price-fixing conspiracies and block-booking.

Paramount was required to split into two companies, one to be concerned with pictures and the other with theatres. The FCC was concerned that Paramount's monopolistic practices might carry over into the television field. The FCC received reports to the effect that Paramount and other motion picture companies had refused to make any of their films available for use by television stations.

Fred Ford was one of the principal attorneys for the FCC in the hearings on the broadcast applications of Paramount. The case went on for many days before an FCC examiner. Ford and his aides had prepared for the hearings with meticulous care.

The Commission ultimately granted the Paramount applications and subsequently approved a merger of Paramount with the American Broadcasting Company, and the Commission held that the policies of the motion picture company (Paramount) with respect to their past use of film talent or stories on television did not constitute a bar to a grant of license and transfer applications.

No case in the history of the FCC has received more nation-wide publicity than the Richards' case. Benedict Cottone, then General Counsel of the FCC, was the principal attorney, with his capable right hand man, Fred Ford.

The hearing extended over a three-year period. Two hundred and ninety witnesses were heard in over a hundred days of testimony. More than 18,000 pages of testimony were taken. Mr. Richards spent a reported two million dollars in behalf of his own defense.

Mr. Richards died and the case came to an inconclusive end. The FCC Examiner in the case issued a brief opinion, holding that the death of Richards "had rendered the proceedings moot." The Commission, accordingly, renewed the licenses of the stations.

One can only speculate what the Examiner might have done, had Mr. Richards lived. But it should be pointed out that Mr. Ford and other FCC counsel in the case had in their proposed findings of fact and law (document ran more than 300 pages), recommended that the licenses of these stations be revoked. Some of the language in that document which bears the Ford name was a key to what might be expected of the new FCC chairman in the field of program regulation:

For a broadcaster to treat the facilities licensed to him as a tool for the exploitations of his personal, private, political, social and economic beliefs in a manner which denies or suppresses expression or opportunity for expression of contrary points of view, or in a manner which creates difficult obstacles to the equal presentation of such contrary points of view over that broadcaster's facilities, would in fact constitute the exercise by the broadcaster of a power of 'thought control' through the utilization of a facility entrusted to his use by the public . . .

The language of this document also makes it clear that Mr. Ford did not hold the view then, at least in the context of the Richards case, that the statutory bar against censorship precluded the Commission from judging the program service of a station to determine whether it had served the public interest. In fact, some of his statements during his term as Chairman were quite similar to those which appeared in that 1951 document:

"It is provided in the Communications Act (Section 326)," reads that weighty treatise, "that there shall be no censorship by the government of the communications transmitted over a radio station. The language of this provision is plain. Simply put, it means that the Commission may not restrain any station in its intention to broadcast or not to broadcast any particular material subject to such exceptions as pertain to lotteries, obscene and profane language and broadcast by candidates for public offices. But the act provides just as plainly that the Commission may not grant a license to any person unless that license will be used in the public interest. (Section 309). The same requirement is applied to a broadcaster who seeks renewal of his license (Section 307 (d)). In the latter case, the test of whether the broadcaster who seeks a renewal of his license may be expected in the future to serve the public interest, in his past conduct and the record of his past operations. This has been aptly put by the courts in the language of the scriptures: 'By their fruits ye shall know them.' " (Matt. VII:20).

Ford endorsed the plan to require licensees up for renewal not only to submit logs for the required week but also state in narrative form what the community's needs are and how the licensee has met them. He did not openly take sides on the proposal by Representative Oren Harris of the House Oversight Subcommittee, that the FCC actually monitor licensees on a nationwide basis (this issue divided Harris and Doerfer), but after he became Chairman, a new unit in the Commission was created to do selective monitoring of programs.

Ford had spent most of his adult years working for the government (20 years, including four in the Air Force, which elevated him from second lieutenant to major). As an attorney at the FCC and the Justice Department (four years) he was involved in investigatory and adversary proceedings that required considerable aloofness from the parties involved. His performances over the years had exhibited a judicial temper and a clear understanding between judicial and administrative processes.

ACTIVITIES OF FCC DURING THE FORD ADMINISTRATION

During the one year Mr. Ford served as Chairman, he was able to avoid the political woodshed treatment and burning at the stake which had befallen some of his predecessors. While he held the top post, a number of important developments affecting broadcast regulation occurred.

Congress was especially active. The Communications Act was amended enabling the FCC to waive requirements for prior construction permits for translator and booster stations which were discussed in Chapter Eleven (Public L. No. 97, 86th Congress, approved July 7, 1960, 74 Stat. 363); passed a joint resolution suspending for the time of the campaign the equal facilities requirement of Section 315 of the Act as it applied to the nominees for President and Vice-President and which resulted in the great Nixon-Kennedy debates (Public L. 86-677, approved August 24, 1960, 74 Stat. 554); amended the Act requiring disclosure of payments for broadcast of certain matter and prohibiting deception in broadcast contests (Public L. 86-752, approved September 13, 1960, 74 Stat. 889).

Among the significant actions taken by the FCC during Mr. Ford's administration was the adoption on September 14, 1960 of rules applicable to TV stations, reducing the number of hours of network option time and giving stations the right to reject network programs and substitute others believed to have greater local or national importance (20 RR 1568; 25 Fed. Reg. 9051),* an amendment to the Rules on November 16, 1960 requiring that applicants for broadcast facilities give public notice of the filing of their applications *(FCC 27th Annual Report, Fiscal Year 1961);* a proposal to Congress on February 11, 1961 that legislation be enacted to enable

---

*It should be pointed out that Mr. Ford objected to this action and joined with Commissioners Hyde and Bartley in a dissent to that part of the Commission's order relating to option time.

the Commission to regulate community antenna TV systems, and one week later granted authority for trial operations of toll TV in Hartford, Connecticut *(FCC 27th Annual Report, Fiscal Year 1961,* p. 152).

MEMORABLE MR. MINOW—BROADCASTING: "A VAST WASTELAND"

In June, 1960, President Eisenhower appointed *Charles Henry King,* a Republican from Michigan and Dean of the Detroit College of Law, to fill the unexpired term of John Doerfer. However, because the November elections were imminent, the Senate adjourned without confirming his appointment. He was serving a recess appointment when the newly elected President Kennedy, in early 1961, replaced him with *Newton Norman Minow,* a young lawyer from Chicago. At the same time Mr. Ford stepped down as Chairman and the President designated Mr. Minow to succeed him in that office. Since Mr. Ford's term as commissioner still had almost four years to run, he chose to continue as a Republican member under the new Democratic administration.

Mr. Minow, when he assumed the Chairmanship on March 2, 1961, was only 34 years of age and was the second youngest commissioner and chairman in history (Charles Denny was a few months younger when he was designated Chairman in 1946). Sixteen men have served as Chairman of the FCC since it was created in 1934 but for the short time Mr. Minow was at the helm, none evoked more public response than he. Shortly after he became Chairman, addressing the delegates to the 39th Annual Convention of the National Association of Broadcasters, he warned that while he was "unalterably opposed to government censorship," broadcasters would be held to strict account when their licenses came up for renewal, that they would be required to live up to their promises regarding programming, and would be expected to do a much better job in the public interest.

Shock waves swept over this assembly of 2,000 broadcast executives and operators when this "brash" and assertive young man declared:

. . . When television is good, nothing—not the theatre, not the magazines or newspapers—nothing is better.

But when television is bad, nothing is worse. I invite you to sit down in front of your television set when your station goes on the air and stay there without a book, magazine, newspaper, profit and loss sheet or rating book to distract you—and keep your eyes glued to that set until the station signs off. I can assure you that you will observe a vast wasteland.

You will see a procession of game shows, violence, audience participation shows, formula comedies about totally unbelievable families, blood and thunder, mayhem, violence, sadism, murder, western badmen, western good men, private eyes, gangsters, more violence, and cartoons. And, endlessly, commercials—many screaming, cajoling, and offending. And most of all, boredom. True, you will see a few things you will enjoy. But they will be very, very few. And if you think I exaggerate, try it.

. . . .

. . . I did not come to Washington to idly observe the squandering of the public's airwaves. I intend to take the job of chairman of the FCC very seriously. There will be times perhaps when you will consider that I take myself or my job too seriously.

Now, how will these principles be applied? Clearly, at the heart of the FCC's authority lies its power to license, to renew or fail to renew, or to revoke a license. As you know, when your license comes up for renewal, your performance is compared with your promises. I understand that many people feel that in the past licenses were often renewed *pro forma.* I say to you now; renewal will not be *pro forma* in the future. There is nothing permanent or sacred about a broadcast license.[66]

[66]*Broadcasting,* May 15, 1960, pp. 58-59.

Who was this young "upstart" who dared to threaten disciplinary action against a powerful and defiant industry? He was born in Milwaukee and attended public schools there. This was followed by a period of military service which included his helping to install a telephone line linking India with China.

Upon release from active duty, he attended Northwestern University where he received a B. S. degree in 1949 and an LL. B. in 1950. In the law school he served as Editor of the *Law Review* and was named the outstanding student in his graduating class, receiving the Wigmore Award.

After a short period of law practice in Chicago in early 1951, he was appointed law clerk to the then Chief Justice of the U. S. Supreme Court, Fred M. Vinson, which position he held until he became assistant to the then Governor of Illinois, Adlai E. Stevenson. In 1955, he joined with Stevenson in establishing a new law firm in Chicago, which later merged with Paul, Weiss, Wharton, and Garrison, with offices in New York and Washington.[67]

Mr. Minow had become closely associated with the Kennedy family, both socially and politically. Being a friend of Robert Sargent Shriver, brother-in-law of Jack Kennedy, having worked closely in political campaigns with Robert Kennedy, and having a high regard for the new President and his political ideals, together with Minow's professional and civic background, made his choice for the FCC job a natural and logical one.

Among his many civic affiliations he was on the junior board of the National Conference of Christians and Jews, was a member of the Northwestern University Alumni Association, was active in the Chicago Bar Association, had lectured widely to schools and colleges on a variety of subjects and public issues. In October, 1960, he was selected as one of the ten outstanding men of Chicago by the Junior Chamber of Commerce and Industry in that city.[68]

As might be expected, the two years of Mr. Minow's administration (March 2, 1961 to June 1, 1963) was marked by intensified Commission action to require broadcasters to live up to their promises and provide a service in keeping with the program criteria which the FCC had enunciated in 1960 (see Appendix IV). For example, on June 28, 1961, he and the other Commissioners denied an application for a new FM station at Elizabeth, N. J., on the grounds that it failed to determine the programming needs of the community intended to be served.[69] This decision was affirmed by the Court of Appeals in the District of Columbia.[70]

During the two years of Mr. Minow's administration, the Commission stepped up its disciplinary actions against a sizeable number of stations. In 1962-63, five licenses were revoked, applications of eight stations for renewal of their licenses were denied, and seventeen others were involved in formal proceedings to determine whether their licenses should be renewed. Ten stations received short term renewals and twenty others had to pay fines for failure to comply with regulations.[71]

But this was only part of the story. During the fiscal year 1963, because of questions raised by the Commission and its staff regarding station performance, action on 476 renewal applications was deferred pending further study and resolution of these questions.[72] And, in the annual report for that year, the Commission reported that the public was showing a "growing awareness of the obligations of broadcast licensees," as evidenced by the fact that more than 20,000 expressions of

[67]Biographical Sketch of Chairman Newton N. Minow of the Federal Communications Commission, Press Release 16741.
[68]*Ibid.*
[69]30 FCC 1021; 20 RR 951.
[70]*Henry, et. al. Suburban Broadcasters v. Federal Communications Commission,* U. S. Court of Appeals, District of Columbia Circuit, March 29, 1962.
[71]Federal Communications Commission, *29th Annual Report for Fiscal Year 1963,* pp. 49-50.
[72]*Ibid.,* p. 51.

opinion on broadcasting or broadcast regulation had been received, compared to 12,000 the previous year.[73]

The Commission further stated that 42 per cent of these communications involved complaints about programming, that an additional 29 per cent pertained to advertising, overcommercialization, and loud, false, and misleading advertisements. The Commission also mentioned receiving a large number of letters of a complimentary character which, the Commission said, were largely prompted by pre-renewal announcements on stations inviting listeners to write their opinions of the service. Others, said the Commission, came as a result of "direct pleas broadcast by certain performers and licensees for members of their audiences to send letters on their behalf."[74]

The FCC report further pointed out that as a result of complaints received, investigations were conducted in 21 states involving 51 stations and two networks. "Inquiry subjects", said the Commission, "included character qualifications of licensees, unauthorized transfer of control of stations, lotteries, double billing, rigged contests, 'payola,' and 'plugola,' horserace broadcasting believed to be used for illegal gambling, antitrust practices, violations of the fairness doctrine, and various technical violations."[75]

The Commission was busy in other ways while Mr. Minow was there. The Clear Channel proceeding was concluded and thirteen channels were opened up for secondary stations; standards for the conduct of FCC employees were revised and improved; extensive inquiry of network practices was carried on; a new Research and Education Division in the Broadcast Bureau was established to encourage the development of educational broadcasting; public hearings and inquiries on program service in Chicago, Illinois and Omaha, Nebraska were conducted; a Review Board was established and an Executive Director was appointed, and other moves were made to streamline and improve operations.[76]

He and other members of the Commission presented testimony before Congressional committees concerning proposed legislation to require all TV receivers to have both VHF and UHF bands, to amend Section 315 of the Act relating to broadcasts by political candidates, and to provide new laws for communications satellite control. They were likewise called before these committees to testify regarding the use of the media to disseminate horse racing information and the relationship of the media to juvenile delinquency.[77]

TWO NEW COMMISSIONERS LEND HELPING HANDS

While Mr. Minow waged his campaign to improve the broadcast landscape, two new commissioners with similar interest and zeal came on the scene—*E. William Henry* and *Kenneth A. Cox*. Mr. Henry, a Democrat from Tennessee, took office on October 2, 1962, replacing John Cross whose term had expired. Mr. Cox, a Democrat from the state of Washington, who had been serving as Chief of the FCC Bureau since March 9, 1961, moved up as a commissioner on March 26, 1963. He took the position of T. A. M. Craven, who, at the age of 70, had retired from government service.

Mr. Henry received his elementary education in Memphis, Tennessee. He received a B. A. degree from Yale University in 1951 and after a tour of military duty in the Korean War, he received an LL. B. from Vanderbilt University where

[73]*Ibid.*, p. 47.
[74]*Ibid.*
[75]*Ibid.*
[76]See FCC Annual Reports, 1961, 1962, 1963.
[77]*Ibid.*

he served as associate editor of the *Law Review* and was elected to the Order of Coif, the national honor society of the legal profession.

He was admitted to the Tennessee State Bar in 1957, practiced law in both state and federal courts and was active in bar associations at local, state and national levels. He found time to participate in numerous civic activities including those concerned with civil rights in Memphis where he was practicing law at the time of his appointment to the FCC. Of special note was his activities as representative to the Nationalities Division of the Democratic National Committee in Washington during the Kennedy campaign of 1960.[78]

Mr. Cox was born in Topeka in 1916, received his B. A. and LL. B. degrees from the University of Washington and an M. A. degree in law from the University of Michigan where he was an Assistant Professor for a short period of time.

His later professional experience prior to his employment as Chief of the Broadcast Bureau at the FCC included law practice in Seattle, service as Special Counsel to the Senate Interstate and Foreign Commerce Committee in charge of the Committee's Television Inquiry in 1956-57, and periodically, thereafter, special consultant jobs for the Committee.[79]

MR. HENRY BECOMES CHAIRMAN

As Chairman, Mr. Minow received ideological support from Mr. Cox as Chief of the Broadcast Bureau and from Mr. Henry as Commissioner. But the triumvirate didn't last very long. About two months after Mr. Cox was sworn in as Commissioner, Mr. Minow resigned, and the President designated Mr. Henry to succeed him as FCC chief.

With Mr. Minow's departure on June 2, 1963, it seemed reasonable to expect that regulatory policies at the Commission would continue to be pretty much the same. This turned out to be the case. The day after Mr. Henry moved into the Chairman's office, this writer interviewed him and he stated that since the "vast wasteland" speech he thought that broadcast programming had improved. But despite this, he felt that "broadcasters still had along way to go." Responding to a question as to whether the Commission should prescribe program standards for stations, he replied:

This is, of course, at the heart of many of the problems that we have at the Commission. I think the Commission has a very distinct concern with programming, and thus with the types of programs that go out over the air. The reason we are concerned is because this, after all, is the end product of broadcasting. Programming is the thing in which the public is interested —about the only thing in which the public is or should be interested. The methods by which we exercise our concern is the problem.

As far as I am concerned, our efforts here at the Commission should be directed toward evaluating and influencing the manner by which the broadcasters are serving the interests and needs of the people. If broadcasters, as they have often done in the past, seek only to use broadcasting as a medium of advertising, as a medium of money-making, to the exclusion of public service programming, then I think we have a right to be concerned. We are here as representatives of the people to see that their needs and interests are met. If only a certain portion of the public is having its needs and interests met, then under our rules of procedure we can step in and inquire of broadcasters as to why, and ask them to take steps to do better. And I think any time a broadcaster or anyone else says that the Federal Government is getting too much concerned with programming, we should examine this criticism very closely to see why it is and what direction our concern is taking. I think certainly all the action that I may have direct control over will be aimed at program diversity, at greater choice, greater freedom of expression, and not the restriction of that expression. This, after all, should really be our concern.[80]

[78]Biographical Sketch of E. William Henry, FCC Press Release 36270, June 2, 1963.
[79]FCC Public Notice—G, 1525, March 9, 1961.
[80]"E. William Henry, New FCC Chairman—An Interview and Portrait," Walter B. Emery,

With respect to Section 315 of the Act which forbids the Commission from censoring programs, he said:

> . . . I think it's very important to see what direction our regulatory action is taking before it is criticised as censorship. All my concern with programming is aimed at creating a climate for greater freedom of expression, not restricting it, and therefore, my efforts as a regulator are exactly the opposite of censorship.[81]

He, like his predecessor, expressed a great interest in educational broadcasting and intended to give it his full support. "I think," said he, "that educational stations have an important role to play. The reason is that, in many instances, they fulfill the need for variety that you don't always get on commercial broadcasting. This is true in most every community where there is an educational outlet, where controversial matters are involved, or where matters relating to minority tastes such as modern art and ballet can be treated in some detail. I think anything we can do to promote educational broadcasting is very worthwhile. And certainly under my tenure at the Commission I intend to do all I can to promote it."

He expressed an interest not only in the content of educational programs but the way in which they are presented:

> We not only should encourage educational broadcasters to deal with controversial subjects and participate in community affairs, but we should encourage them to be showmen in the sense that they don't do any good unless someone listens to them. And they can learn a lot from commercial broadcasters in this regard, perhaps improve their efforts at fund raising, and so on. I think, in general, they are doing an excellent job.[82]

With respect to the Commission's authority over programming, Mr. Cox's views were much the same as those expressed by Mr. Henry when he was Chairman. Usually the two men could be found in the same voting camp when questions came up regarding program performance, and in some instances, Mr. Cox was even more severe with regard to station accountability.[83]

Mr. Cox, whose term expired June 30, 1970, consistently took the position that the Commission has the authority and responsibility to give consideration to programming when stations come up for renewal of their licenses. He did not believe this constitutes censorship. He made his position clear in a speech to the Twenty-Third Annual Convention of the National Religious Broadcasters in January, 1966:

> The public has invested billions of dollars in broadcast receivers to gain access to the program services provided by radio and television stations. While our basic allocations policies are vital, and our engineering and other technical regulations are important, this is true only to the extent that they, and our other policies, produce a communications system which really serves and satisfies as many public interests and needs as can be accommodated within the limited spectrum available and supported by the advertising—and other more limited—funds available for this purpose. I submit that judgment in this area must involve programming in the kind of broad terms set forth in the Commission's 1960 Programming Policy Statement.
>
> . . . I therefore believe that Congress intended the Commission to administer its general public interest authority in the programming field, as in all other areas of communications, but then added a specific command that it not censor or interfere with the right of free speech. In any event, I don't think our general efforts to insure that broadcasters ascertain and serve the needs of their communities constitute censorship or interfere with free speech.
>
> . . . While it is true that the programming issues are often of secondary importance, it seems clear to me that if we have no business at all considering programming, the Courts would have long since acted to save the time of all concerned by pointing out that we should not be

[81] *Ibid.*, p. 20.
[82] *Ibid.*
[83] See 2 RR 2d 1003, July 13, 1964.

cluttering up the records with such matters. They have never done this—and to my knowledge no broadcaster has sought to raise the issue more directly. . . .[84]

LEE LOEVINGER IS APPOINTED TO THE COMMISSION

Holding quite opposite views on broadcast regulation of programs to Henry and Cox was *Lee Loevinger*, a Democrat from Minnesota with a penchant for scholarship and rhetorical finesse, who took the oath of office as Commissioner on June 11, 1963. No other member of the FCC has ever exhibited more of a studious flare than he. While one might disagree with him ideologically, his pronouncments usually were based on extensive study and research.

Prior to his appointment, he had served for two years as Assistant Attorney General in charge of the Antitrust Division in the Department of Justice. Before that, he was an Associate Justice of the Minnesota Supreme Court.

He came to the Commission with an impressive educational and professional background. He was born in St. Paul on April 24, 1913, attended elementary and secondary schools in the twin-city area, graduated from the University of Minnesota in 1933 *(summa cum laude)* and three years later completed his LL.B. degree.[85]

He took sharp issue with Chairman Henry and Commissioner Cox regarding the Commission's role in broadcast programming. This was pointedly brought out in his concurring statement accompanying the Commission's action adopting new broadcast application forms in 1965 which had been in process of preparation for several years. Commissioners Bartley and Hyde refused to go along with the action and it was only by the Loevinger vote that the forms were adopted. But as his concurring opinion made clear he very reluctantly voted to approve them:

I agree with Commissioner Hyde that the Commission should not undertake regulation of the program content of broadcasting. Regulation of program content is objectionable on both constitutional and philosophical grounds . . .

It seems obvious that, as Commissioner Hyde points out, the programming reporting form constitutes a kind of regulatory device or procedure. The form now in use requires a specification of precise percentages of program time devoted and to be devoted to seven specific categories of program classification. The new form calls for a specification of only minimum amounts of time to be devoted to two specific categories and one general or miscellaneous category. In this respect the new form seems to me to be a very considerable improvement over the one now in use. I do object to the requirement that all programs be classified in the log on the basis of some ten categories. Despite the disclaimer in the form that this requirement "is not intended to establish a formula for station operation" this undoubtedly will serve at least to exert influence toward establishing a formula for station operation and may serve as the basis for Commission coercion to conformity with Commission ideas on this subject . . .

It is apparent from the division of Commission opinion regarding this matter that the new programming form cannot be promulgated without my vote . . . It is frequently the case in the practical administration of government that to insist on perfection or unanimity is to frustrate all improvement. We must, therefore, be satisfied to achieve progress without perfection and consensus without unanimity. Since the new program form seems to me to represent a considerable improvement over the one now in use, I concur in its promulgation despite what I consider to be significant defects.[86]

He also expressed the opinion that the FCC exceeded its authority when it required broadcasters to supply information regarding the amounts of time they

[84]"The FCC, the Constitution, and Religious Broadcast Stations," Kenneth A. Cox, before the Twenty-Third Annual Convention, National Religious Broadcasters, January 26, 1966; also see his article in October, 1965, issue of *George Washington Law Review*, pp. 196-217.
[85]Biographical Sketch of Lee Loevinger, FCC Release 36813, June 11, 1963,—G.
[86]5 RR 2d 1782-1783, September 15, 1965.

484

devote to religious programs. This belief is based upon the constitutional principle of separation of church and state.[87]

Unlike Mr. Minow who had spoken of the "vast wasteland" in broadcasting, he expressed the view that generally broadcasters give the public what it wants and are doing a reasonably good job.[88] In a lengthy speech at an NAB Regional Conference on October 17, 1967, he discussed what he called the "reflective-projective" theory of broadcasting. "Most of those," said he "who articulate the demand for democracy and service to the public interest, and who are accustomed to influence policy and social action in this manner, are of an intellectual elite. Such leaders think of democracy as a system in which they define the public interest and the public is persuaded to accept or acquiesce in leadership views. But in fact the public wants to see its own image in the mass media mirrors, not the image of intellectual leaders ... Perhaps the smudged, commonplace, homely, slightly unattractive picture that we get of ourselves from mass media is providing us with a common image and a common cultural bond that we could not get from a more elegant and more attractive portrait."[89]

At a news conference in Los Angeles on September 16, 1967, he stated that the American system of broadcasting is "the most free system" in the world and that the broadcasters by and large were doing a good job reporting the facts regarding the Vietnam situation and the civil disorders in the United States.[90]

FCC ACTIONS DURING THE HENRY ADMINISTRATION

The Commission had three of its most active and productive years while Mr. Henry was head. There was no let up in enforcement activities (revocations, forfeitures, short term renewals, etc.).[91] The number of questions concerning the handling of controversial issues and editorializing increased substantially, and on July 6, 1964, the Commission issued an extensive public notice on "Applicability of the Fairness Doctrine in the Handling of Controversial Issues of Public Importance," including a legislative history of the subject and a digest of FCC rulings.[92] There was continued inquiry of network practices with particular reference to program production and restraints on competition.[93] Rule-making proceedings were instituted looking toward requiring full disclosure of ownership and control of stock held by banks and brokerage houses for the benefit of mutual funds, trusts, etc.,[94] and restrictions on multiple ownership of TV stations in the large markets were proposed.[95]

In the interest of avoiding delay in competitive proceedings and promoting consistency in decision, the Commission, on July 28, 1965, adopted a "Policy Statement on Comparative Broadcast Hearings."[96] As previously mentioned, the Commission adopted new and revised application forms for AM and FM stations,[97] and adopted rules requiring stations to maintain files containing copies of applications and owner-

[87] *Ibid.* Commissioners Henry and Cox disagreed. Commissioner Cox's views appear in the October, 1965 issue of the *George Washington Law Review*, pp. 196-217.
[88] *Ibid.* September 18, 1967, p. 54.
[89] "The Ambiguous Mirror: The Reflective-Projective Theory of Broadcasting and Mass Communications", Lee Loevinger, NAB Conference, Atlanta, Georgia, October 17, 1967, pp. 24-25.
[90] *Broadcasting*, September 18, 1967, p. 54.
[91] See FCC Annual Reports, 1963, 1964, 1965.
[92] 2 RR 2d 1901-1926; 29 Fed. Reg. 10416.
[93] 4 RR 2d 1589, March 19, 1965; 30 Fed. Reg. 4065.
[94] *FCC Thirtieth Anniversary Report*, pp. 61-62; 29 Fed. Reg. 13211.
[95] 5 RR 2d 1609, June 21, 1965; 30 Fed. Reg. 8166.
[96] 5 RR 2d 1901.
[97] 5 RR 2d 1773.

ship reports which have been submitted to the Commission, and to make them available for public inspection in the community where the main studios are located.[98]

With more than 1700 CATV systems in operation in 1965, the FCC was being pressed by broadcasters to restrict their operations. In April, 1965, the Commission adopted carriage and nonduplication rules applicable to all these systems, both microwave and nonmicrowave. At the same time, it instituted a general inquiry and rule making proceedings concerning CATV systems and their effects on the broadcasting industry.[99]

Mention should be made of the Commission's concern with and activities relating to satellite communication with which Mr. Henry was greatly interested and gave his full support. In 1965, the Commission authorized the Communications Satellite Corporation (COMSAT) to begin commercial operation and approved applications for international common carriers for authority to lease channels in the system.[100] Commercial service was inaugurated June 28, 1965 when President Johnson talked with European officials over the facilities of Early Bird, positioned in synchronous orbit 22,300 miles above the equator in the middle of the Atlantic Ocean. One year later a total of 52 countries had signed agreements and had become members of the International Telecommunication Satellite Consortium (INTELSAT).[101]

WADSWORTH REPLACES FORD ON THE COMMISSION

Fred Ford left the Commission on December 31, 1964, to accept a position as President of the National Community Television Association at an annual salary of $50,000.[102] It was not until May 5, 1965 thereafter that *James J. Wadsworth*, a Republican from New York, replaced him on the Commission, having been appointed by President Johnson a short time before.

During his early professional career he had served ten years in the New York State Legislature. He served as a defense plant executive during the Second World War. Subsequently, he held various jobs with the Federal government, successively was Deputy and Permanent U. S. Representative to the United Nations, and distinguished himself as a consultant and writer in areas having to do with the problems of international relations and world peace.[103]

After being appointed and prior to confirmation by the Senate, Mr. Wadsworth characterized himself as a "moderate to liberal Republican."[104] His conduct for the short time he was at the FCC would seem to fit that label. He was not one to make many public speeches, but hints of his regulatory philosophy are to be found in some important decisions made by the Commission during his brief tenure as a Commissioner. For example, much to the surprise of many broadcasters he joined with Commissioners Johnson and Bartley in denying the renewal application of television station WHDH in Boston and granting the license to competing applicant Boston Broadcasters, Inc.[105] However, he voted with the majority to grant the renewal application of WLBT(TV) in Jackson, Mississippi which had been contested by the Office of Communications of the United Church of Christ and community groups in Jackson.[106]

[98]4 RR 2d 1665, March 31, 1965.
[99]4 RR 2d 1679, April 22, 1965.
[100]*FCC 31st Annual Report,* p. 41.
[101]*FCC 32nd Annual Report,* p. 38.
[102]*Broadcasting,* November 23, 1964, p. 72.
[103]Biographical Sketch of Commissioner James J. Wadsworth, FCC Public Notice, December 8, 1967.
[104]*Broadcasting* , March 29, 1965, p. 36.
[105]15 RR 2d 411-442.

Unlike the majority at the Commission he, along with Robert E. Lee, was unwilling to vote for an inquiry of broadcasting operations by "conglomerates" because he felt it would yield no worthwhile results.[107]

HYDE BECOMES CHAIRMAN A SECOND TIME

Following Mr. Henry's departure from the Commission on May 1, 1966, Mr. Hyde assumed the duties of his office on an acting basis until June 27, 1966, when President Johnson gave him full status as Chairman. At the time of this appointment, he had served continuously as a Commissioner since 1945 and, as previously pointed out, had served as head of the agency for a year in 1953-54 during the Eisenhower administration.

His elevation to the Chairmanship in 1966 was unique in two respects. Mr. Hyde is the only man to occupy with full status the office more than once, and the only one to be appointed by both Republican and Democratic presidents.

From the time he became Chairman in 1966 until he retired on October 31, 1969, life at the FCC was hectic. At no previous time in the history of the Commission were the ideological conflicts among its members sharper and more pronounced. Intensifying these FCC rifts was the almost constant surveillance and intermeddling of Congress, aided and abetted by the critical clamor and outcries of the broadcast industry, the cable operators, the trade press and other special interests, not to mention an aroused and sometimes hostile public. The FCC offices in Washington were even picketed by a disgruntled group led by a Reverend Carl McIntire, protesting an FCC requirement that he follow the "fairness doctrine" with respect to broadcasting of programs dealing with controversial issues of public importance.[108]

THE "ACTIVISTS"—COMMISSIONERS COX AND JOHNSON

In the midst of and taking an active part in the FCC fracas was Commissioner *Kenneth Cox,* who, prior to Mr. Hyde's appointment as Chairman, had already achieved a reputation in the broadcast industry as a "hardline regulator." His ideological and "activist" partner was a young, outspoken intellectual, *Nicholas Johnson,* a Democrat from Iowa, appointed by President Johnson to replace Mr. Loevinger whose term expired on June 30, 1966. Mr. Johnson took the oath of office just three days after Mr. Hyde became Chairman.

At the time, he was only 31 years of age, and was the youngest person ever to be a member of the Commission. Before taking the FCC job he had been a Maritime Administrator (1964-66), had been an associate member of a law firm in Washington, D. C. (1963-64), a professor of law at the University of California, teaching administrative law and economic regulation (1960-63), was law clerk to Associate Justice Hugo L. Black of the U. S. Supreme Court (1959-60) and to Judge John R. Brown of the U. S. Court of Appeals for the Fifth Circuit (1958-59).

His formal education included an LL. B. degree from the University of Texas. As an undergraduate student he achieved membership in Phi Beta Kappa, was an honors graduate in the Law School, and was editor of the Texas Law Review. He was elected to the Order of the Coif and to Phi Delta Phi, and became a member of the Phi Eta Sigma and Pi Sigma Alpha honorary fraternities.[109]

[106]13 RR 2d 769.
[107]1 RR 53: CXII.
[108]*Broadcasting,* January 1, 1968, p. 29.
[109]Biographical Sketch of Commissioner Nicholas Johnson, FCC News Release, January, 1968.

Except perhaps for Clifford Durr, the Rhodes Scholar member from Alabama during the Fly regime, no member of the FCC, including former Commissioner Cox, has been more committed to a strict and hard line of broadcast regulation than has Commissioner Johnson. Needless to say, this has not made him popular with large segments of the broadcast industry or with the trade press.

There was an amusing cartoon in the editorial section of the December 15, 1969 issue of *Broadcasting* magazine, one of the leading trade journals in the broadcasting field. Two characters are portrayed by the artist in this cartoon. One, a large, well-fed, harried-looking fellow, depicted as the president of a broadcasting company, is sitting at his desk and looking across at another man, a small, stubby creature of the garrulous type, who apparently is the president's assistant. They evidently have been engaged in acrimonious conversation regarding money matters and FCC regulations. With hostility in his eyes and a threatening forward movement, the executive shouts at his "no-good," loquacious assistant: "If you quote Nicholas Johnson to me once more, I'll have you killed."[110]

What makes this cartoon in *Broadcasting* particularly significant and interesting, is the fact that in the editorial columns of 31 issues of this weekly magazine in 1968 and 1969, Mr. Johnson was criticized or excoriated for something he had written, said or done in an official capacity. The magazine, which often has accused him of indulging in invective and name-calling, variously described him in its editorials for those years as "brash," "naive," "stupid," "self-appointed savior," "crackdowner," "top banana," "hortatory," "a bureaucrat," "avid publicity seeker," "neophyte," "comsummate nuisance," "spreader of anti-commercial venom," "trouble-maker," "activist maneuverer," "arrogant," "a devisive force," and "noisiest dissenter."[111]

Commissioner Kenneth Cox, his former "partner in dissent," as described by *Broadcasting*, also received top billing of a derogatory character in the editorials of the magazine. Though the scoldings were somewhat less severe than those of Johnson, Cox was upbraided for his views and actions in 21 issues published in 1968-69.[112]

In contrast to the attacks against Commissioners Cox and Johnson, the magazine, during this period, in ten issues, made lauditory references to Chairman Hyde. Little reference in editorials, complimentary or otherwise, was made to other FCC members. Commissioner Bartley did come in for some ribbing because of his negative views in certain cases regarding monopoly and concentrations of control of broadcast facilities.[113]

In general, the reasons for the Cox and Johnson castigations by *Broadcasting* and some other trade journals are much the same as they were for the attacks by these publications against former FCC "activist" members Walker, Durr, Fly, Minow, and Henry—their insistence that the airways are public property, that broadcast monopolies must be strictly controlled and competition preserved, that licensees are

---

[110] *Broadcasting*, December 15, 1969, p. 90.
[111] See *Broadcasting*, last page of each issue, February 19, April 22, April 29, May 6, June 10, July 22, August 5, September 16, September 23, October 7, October 14, October 28, November 11, November 25, 1968; January 13, March 17, May 12, May 19, May 26, July 14, July 21, August 25, September 1, September 15, September 22, November 17, December 15, 1969.
[112] See *Broadcasting*, last page of each issue, March 11, April 29, May 20, July 8, July 22, August 5, October 14, November 11, November 25, 1968; January 13, January 20, May 19, May 26, July 14, August 4, August 18, September 15, November 10, December 29, 1969.
[113] See *Broadcasting*, references to Chairman Hyde, last page of each issue, April 8, May 6, June 17, 1968; February 17, May 19, June 9, June 16, August 4, September 18, November 3, December 22, 1969; references to Commissioner Bartley, June 3, 1968, May 19, 1969; references to Commissioner Robert E. Lee, July 28, September 16, 1968, December 29, 1969; references to Commissioner Rex Lee, July 29, 1968.

obligated to provide programs in terms of community needs and interests, be fair in the presentation of points of view on controversial issues of public importance, and their belief that the Commission has the authority and the duty to set minimum program standards and require stations to live up to them, all of which, in referring to Mr. Johnson, *Broadcasting* has described as "espousal of rigid control of pro grams and business affairs—a sort of socialism."[114]

Contributing further to these journalistic diatribes was the caustic criticism by these so-called "activists" leveled at their more conservative fellow commissioners, vehemently expressed at times in dissenting opinions and public speeches.[115] And especially provoking the ire of the trade press and broadcasting industry has been Mr. Johnson's use of invective, such as when he referred to some segments of the broadcast industry as "media barons," and when, at frequent times, he has questioned their motives and practices.[116]

Despite the name calling by some trade journals and broadcasters, many perceptive and knowledgable opinion leaders and journalists have expressed high praise for commissioner Johnson and former commissioner Cox for their independence of mind and spirit and their dedication to the public interest. (See *Wall Street Journal*, April, 10, 1969, p. 18; *Saturday Review*, April 12, 1969, p. 91; *Educational Broadcasting Review*, June, 1969, p. 43.)

H. REX LEE IS APPOINTED TO THE COMMISSION

On October 28, 1968, *H. Rex Lee*, a Democrat from the District of Columbia, made his appearance on the FCC stage, having been appointed by President Johnson to replace Lee Loevinger, whose term had expired on June 30 of that year. At the time of this appointment, he was Assistant Administrator of the Agency for International Development. Prior to his AID experience, he had served as Governor of American Samoa for six years during which time he helped transform what had been previously called a "Pacific slum" into a "showplace of the South Seas."

Also, among his accomplishments in Samoa was the establishment of an elaborate TV system, especially designed for instructional and educational purposes.

He has been one of the quiet commissioners; so far has made comparatively few speeches, and has made few headlines. With his experience in Samoa developing a TV system for educational and instructional uses, it was to be expected that he would give his support to the further development of educational broadcasting in the United States. One of the first speeches he made after becoming a Commissioner was one he gave before the National Association of Educational Broadcasters in which he reviewed developments in the Samoan project and gave his blessing to the expanded educational uses of broadcast media in the United States.

He has indicated some interest in a standard of evaluation that would attach importance to local live programming.[117] Also, it is noteworthy that in December, 1969, that he joined with Commissioners Bartley, Cox and Johnson in approving a pilot questionnaire to be sent to six large companies engaged in broadcasting, the purpose of which was to elicit information on the effects of conglomerate ownership particularly on program service and on competition in the broadcast industry.[118]

---

[114]*Broadcasting*, June 10, 1968, p. 80.
[115]See dissenting opinion of Commissioner Johnson in ABC-Merger case, 9 RR 2d 46-86; also see *Broadcasting*, February 6, 1967, p. 94, June 10, 1968, p. 80, September 1, 1969, September 22, 1969, p. 86.
[116]*Broadcasting*, February 24, 1969, p. 94; also see *Atlantic Monthly*, June, 1968, pp. 43-51.
[117]17 RR 2d 305; also see *Broadcasting*, September 15, 1969, p. 108.
[118]*Broadcasting*, December 22, 1969, p. 17.

Despite the furore that characterized Mr. Hyde's administration, under his leadership the Commission achieved some noteworthy results. There was much heated debate on important regulatory issues in and outside the Commission (this in itself had much educational value), but some long standing questions which had been pending and unresolved for years were finally settled by the FCC and approved by the courts. For example, the validity of the "fairness doctrine" and the regulations implementing it was decided once and for all. Despite tremendous pressure from powerful groups in Congress and the broadcast industry Mr. Hyde would not retreat from his original position favoring the doctrine and regulations. In an address before the International Radio and Television Society in New York, September 22, 1967, he said he was "puzzled" by the reaction in some quarters to the Commission's action adopting the regulations:

All that the commission did was to codify policies that had been outstanding for many years and which have not interfered with the effective operation of the broadcasting industry during these years.[119]

He defended the procedures embodied in Commission rules relating to application of the "fairness doctrine." And, said he, "surely, no broadcaster would claim the right to editorialize against a person's candidacy and not afford the opportunity for rebuttal." Furthermore, if a person's character, honesty or integrity is attacked in a program involving the discussion of a controversial issue, it seemed elementary to him—under the concept of fairness—that the person attacked should have an opportunity to respond if he wishes. And, said the former Chairman, "It seems equally elementary that he cannot respond if he does not know what was said about him."

He thought there should be specific regulations so that broadcasters will be informed regarding the mechanics of compliance, and so the Commission can deal more effectively with those few who "flagrantly violate fairness policies."

Regarding the application of the "fairness doctrine" to the advertising of cigarettes, Chairman Hyde noted that there were "highly respected reports" on smoking asserting that the use of cigarettes is hazardous to health and that as a matter of "conscience" broadcasters have an obligation to inform the public, particularly teen-agers.[120]

In a conversation the author had with him following the Supreme Court's decision sustaining the Commission's fairness doctrine rules,[121] Mr. Hyde expressed some pride in the part he had played and the support given by his fellow commissioners.

During his administration, another long-standing matter which had rested on the FCC regulatory door step for thirteen years (what to do about toll television) was finally resolved. Despite tremendous pressures and interventions from Capitol Hill and the powerful lobby of theatre owners and UHF entrepreneurs, Mr. Hyde finally joined with five other commissioners and approved the service on a regular basis. Commissioner Rex Lee did not participate and Commissioner Bartley, who simply wrote a one sentence dissent, objected to the action because he believed "that valuable spectrum space should not be used for subscription TV.[122]

On September 30, 1969, the U. S. Court of Appeals for the District of Columbia unanimously upheld the Commission's authority to authorize the toll TV service and

[119]Speech before the International Radio and Television Society, New York, September 22, 1967; also see report in *Broadcasting*, September 25, 1967, p. 76.
[120]*Ibid.*
[121]Red Lion Broadcasting Co., Inc., etc., et al., Petitioners, v. FCC et al and United States et al, Petitioners v. Radio Television News Directors Ass. et al, decided June 9, 1969.
[122]14 RR 2nd 1731, December 12, 1968.

490

held that the regulations governing its operation were legal and proper.[123]

No more complex and perplexing question has ever faced the Commission than what to do about Community Antenna systems (CATV). For sometime before Mr. Hyde became Chairman the FCC had agonized over the problems, and initially was reluctant to assume regulatory control. Congress was entreated to enact legislation clarifying the Commission's authority in the matter. Prior to and during the two years that Mr. Hyde was at the helm, the Commission was involved in a series of rule-making proceedings regarding the matter. There was strong opposition from the CATV industry and from Congress questioning the Commission's authority to regulate in the field.

Despite these objections and pressures, Mr. Hyde remained steadfast in his position that the public interest required some CATV regulation to give protection to the established system of broadcasting, and he was supported in the main by his fellow commissioners.[124]

As in the case involving the "fairness doctrine", the courts upheld the Commission's regulatory policies in the CATV area. (See Chapter 11 for discussion of court cases.)

LANDMARK CASES DECIDED DURING HYDE ADMINISTRATION

Three historic cases which the Commission decided while Mr. Hyde was Chairman involved the proposed merger of the American Broadcasting System (ABC) and the International Telephone and Telegraph Company (ITT), (7 FCC 2d 245 (1966), 9 FCC 2d 546 (1947), 9 RR 2d 12, 10 RR 2d 289; the application for renewal of license of WHDH-TV in Boston (15 RR 2d 411-442), and application for renewal of license of Station WLBT-TV in Jackson, Mississippi (5 RR 2d 2050.)

In the ABC-ITT case, one of the important issues was whether the merger of these two giant companies would violate anti-trust laws and work against competition in the broadcast industry. Chairman Hyde together with Commissioners Loevigner, Robert E. Lee and Wadsworth, concluded, on the basis of showings made by the parties that the competitive position of ABC would actually be strengthened, that with increased facilities it would be able to provide more and better program service in the public interest. Commissioners Bartley and Johnson each issued strong dissenting opininons with which Commissioner Cox substantially agreed. Bartley and Cox were particularly vehement in their opposition, arguing, among other things, that the Commission acted hastily without the benefit of "a full evidentiary hearing" (only an oral argument was held by the Commission), and that competition and the public interest would be "significantly harmed" by the merger. In his dissent Mr. Johnson, in part, said:

It will place one of the three largest purveyors of news and opinion in America under the control of one of the largest conglomerate corporations in the world; a company that derives 60 percent of its earnings from foreign sources, and 40 percent of its domestic income from defense and space contracts. The possibility that the integrity of one news judgment of ABC would be affected by the economic interests of ITT is a real threat, without regard to the character of the present management of ITT and ABC and their protestations that no possibility of harm exists . . .[125]

[123]*National Association of Theatre Owners and Joint Committee Against Toll TV, Petitioners v. Federal Communications Commission and the United States of America, Respondents, Zenith Radio Corporation and Teco, Inc. Intervenors,* decided September 30, 1969, United States Court of Appeals.
[124]See 11 RR 2d 1570, adopted October 24, 1969, 34 Fed. Reg. 17651.
[125]See 9 RR 49-50; also see *Broadcasting*, January 8, 1968, pp. 34-35 for discussion and report on cancellation of the merger plans.

The opinion of Mr. Hyde and other approving members did not prevail. The U.S. Justice Department took exception to the Commission's action and filed a petition for court review. This prompted ABC and ITT to abandon their plans and the merger never materialized. It seems clear that the dissenting opinions of Commissioners Johnson and Bartley had some influence on the Justice Department in its decision to ask the courts to disapprove the proposed union, and, in turn, caused the companies to give up the project and discontinue the fight which would have been long and which, judicially, seemed to offer little promise for ultimate success.

In the Jackson, Mississippi case, involving the application for renewal of license of Station WLBT (TV), Mr. Hyde voted with the majority to grant the renewal. The United Church of Christ appealed the decision on the grounds that it and other groups had been refused an opportunity to participate as parties and present evidence in the proceeding. The Court remanded the case for further hearings and ordered the Commission to give the appellants legal standing and allow them to present evidence in the proceeding. The examiner who heard the case the second time issued an opinion recommending that the license be renewed and, again, the Commission sustained his opinion and granted a renewal of the license.

Mr. Hyde voted with the FCC majority. A second appeal was made by the Church group and the Court of Appeals in the last decision written by Justice Burger before he became Chief Justice of the U. S. Supreme Court, reversed the Commission and in effect, vacated the license, and directed that new applicants be invited to compete for the facility. The Court was severely critical of the Examiner who conducted the second hearing:

The impatience with the public intervenors, hostility toward their efforts to satisfy a surprisingly strict standard of proof, plain errors in rulings and findings lead us, albeit reluctantly, to the conclusion that it will serve no useful purpose to ask the commission to reconsider the examiner's actions and its own decision and order under a correct allocation of proof. The administrative conduct reflected in this record is beyond repair.[126]

In the Boston case, involving the renewal application of WHDH, Mr. Hyde participated but in the final show down (the case had a long and tortuous history), Mr. Hyde abstained. The decision caused great concern in the broadcast industry since it seemed to encourage community groups to contest and compete for licenses at renewal time.[127]

HYDE SUPPORTS EDUCATIONAL BROADCASTING

As a commissioner and as Chairman during two different periods, Mr. Hyde consistently and enthusiastically supported noncommercial, educational broadcasting. He along with men like Commissioner Bartley questioned the propriety of strict surveillance and review of station operations to achieve "balance" and variety in programming. This, he thought, could be more appropriately attained by unhampered competition and by encouraging the broadcast development of the communications industry, with a significant component consisting of stations devoted to the educational and instructional uses of the media. To the very end of his career at the FCC, he gave his enthusiastic support to the educational and instructional uses of the media, as reflected in many of his official actions and in speeches to a variety of business, educational and cultural groups.

[126]16 RR (2d) 2095, June 20, 1969; also see *Broadcasting*, June 30, 1969, pp. 21-22 for report on case.
[127]15 RR 2d 411.

As much of the foregoing discussion shows the final two years of the Hyde administration was a turbulent time for the Commission. There was intense and often sharp controversy among the commissioners and a large amount of complaints from industry, and, as usual, much belligerent intervention from Congress. But despite the heat generated, it is significant and heartening that there were no charges of "sellouts" and no challenges of substance against the integrity of commissioners as was the case in some previous FCC administrations. Mr. Hyde's points of view, as expressed in some decisions were vigorously and even heatedly opposed by certain commissioners, but there is no evidence of name-calling or attempts on his part to belittle the character of these dissenters or to interfere with their rights and responsibilities to call the regulatory shots as they saw them.

HYDE RETIRES—A NEW ERA OF REGULATION BEGINS

Mr. Hyde completed his regular term on June 20, 1969. However, President Nixon requested that he remain on the job until his successor could be chosen. Mr. Wadsworth, whose regular term did not expire until June 30, 1971, chose to resign to accept an appointment as a member of the delegation to the International Telecommunications Satellite Conference. Mr. Hyde's official duties ended Friday, October 31, 1969 when *Dean Burch,* a 41 year old Republican from Tucson, Arizona was sworn in as his successor. Six days later, *Robert Wells,* a 50 year old Republican from Garden City, Kansas, assumed his duties as commissioner replacing Mr. Wadsworth.

Mr. Burch is a lawyer and formerly served as Administrative Assistant to Senator Goldwater and later was Chairman of the Republican National Committee during the Goldwater presidential campaign.

He served in the army from 1946 to 1948 and is a lieutenant colonel in the Army Reserve in the judge advocate's branch. His educational background includes a law degree from the University of Arizona and his record in civic activities is an impressive one.[128]

Mr. Wells was in the broadcasting business prior to his FCC appointment. He owns real estate and hardware and variety stores in Garden City. In 1955, he won an award from the State Junior Chamber of Commerce in Kansas for his outstanding citizenship.[129]

As reported by a trade journal, Chairman Burch has characterized himself as no political philosopher, but as a mechanic—a doer who puts philosophy to work.[130] At this writing it is too early to predict with accuracy what his attitude will be on important regulatory matters. However, some of his recent statements are suggestive. For example, five weeks after he became Chairman, as reported by the press, he publicly declared that he was opposed to the notion that broadcast program quality can be upgraded by proscription from Washington, and while he said he had not made up his mind, he suggested that the diversification issue was overgrown with theory and he seemed less than fascinated with the idea of breaking up multimedia combinations without facts to back up any such splits.[131]

In line with these ideas, it is noteworthy that a few weeks after his appointment, he signed an FCC letter (approved by the full Commission), in response to an inquiry

---

[128] *Broadcasting,* September 1, 1969, pp. 21-22.
[129] *Ibid.*
[130] *Ibid.*
[131] *Broadcasting,* December 8, 1969, pp. 36-37.

by a private citizen, making it clear that the Commission would not make any move to censor news reporters and analysts. The inquiry was made following the attack by Vice President Spiro T. Agnew of network news operations.[132]

A month later, along with Commissioners Wells and Robert E. Lee, he voted against sending "pilot questionnaires" to conglomerates owning broadcasting properties as a follow-up of studies previously instituted by the Commission. His opinion did not prevail, since, as previously mentioned, commissioners Bartley, Cox, Johnson and H. Rex Lee, the Democratic members, constituting at that time a majority, voted to approve sending out the questionnaires.[133]

It is interesting to note that Mr. Wells sided with the new Chairman and together with Robert E. Lee supported the minority view. Mr. Wells, as reported by the press, based his objection to the pilot project on the grounds that the information to be gathered would not warrant the expense of time and money, and that the information desired could be elicited when the "conglomerate" stations came up for renewal of their licenses.[134]

REGULATORY EXPECTATIONS UNDER NEW LEADERSHIP

As the Commission is presently constituted, and with the expiration of Mr. Cox's term on June 30, 1970 and his replacement with a Republican, one might reasonably predict that broadcasters for the next two or three years may be subject to much less regulation than they have had in the past. However, as a student of FCC history, this writer hesitates to prophesy. There are many factors and forces which influence the FCC and the behavior of its members. Capitol Hill, with its loud, conflicting and often demanding pressures and edicts; with rivalries in the broadcast industry itself and pressures brought to bear on the Commission and on the White House and Congress, not to mention the increasingly active concern with Commission regulatory policies by a multiplicity of private groups and organizations—all these and many other variables make forecasts of the regulatory weather at the FCC difficult.

There is one prospect, however, that seems fairly certain. If Mr. Johnson continues on the Commission until the expiration of his term, June 30, 1973, (according to press reports he has indicated he intends to serve out his term), and with Mr. Bartley not coming up for renewal until 1971, and if Rex Lee stays on until the end of his term in 1975, the Republican majority (after June 30, 1970 when Mr. Cox is replaced) will face some interesting and stimulating challenges. It is reasonable to expect that the clash and climate of controversy at the FCC will be heated and even stormy at times, and trade journals will continue to have exciting copy to stimulate readership and increase circulation.

SPECIAL CASE STUDY IN FCC LEADERSHIP
PAUL ATLEE WALKER
CHAMPION OF THE PUBLIC INTEREST*

It was hot and humid in Washington, D. C. the afternoon of June 30, 1953. Despite the heat and humidity, a large number of government employees and

---

[132]*Ibid.*, November 4, 1969, p. 56.
[133]*Broadcasting*, December 2, 1969, p. 17
[134]*Ibid.*, p. 18.
*The author knew Mr. Walker for many years; worked with him as his legal assistant when he was a member and Chairman of the FCC. This study is partially based upon a book the author wrote about him, *Paul A. Walker of the FCC: An Appreciation* (Lancaster Press, 1946). Mr. Walker retired from the FCC in 1953. He died November 2, 1965.

representatives of the communications industry gathered in the New Post Office Building on historic Pennsylvania Avenue to pay tribute to a retiring public official.

The guest of honor was Paul Atlee Walker, whose nineteen years of service as an FCC commissioner officially came to an end at five o'clock that day.

As Walker sipped soft punch and mingled with his friends, there was a remarkable alertness and joviality in his manner that belied his seventy-one years. A rigorous half century of public life had left some physical marks, but there was no bitterness on his countenance, no rancor in his speech. His conversation was amiable and gracious. And when the FCC staff presented him with a scroll and gold watch as tokens of esteem, he was deeply touched and visibly overcome with gratitude.

One short hour of congratulations and good wishes and the party was over. As the big clock in the tower of the Old Post Office Building across Twelfth Street struck five, most of the guests were leaving, to be caught up in the mad rush of traffic which, at that hour, fans out in all directions from downtown Washington as government workers hurry to their suburban homes. But a few of the old-timers lingered to visit longer with the Commissioner. For they knew that when he left his office that day, not only would a great public career come to an end, but it would mark the close of an important and dramatic era in which government for two decades had played a positive and dynamic role in the field of communications.

The circumstances of Paul Walker's early life had prepared him for a role of leadership during this historic era. Born in a Pennsylvania log house in 1881, the son of a Quaker farmer who had been impoverished by the depression at that time, he had known much discomfort and hardship in his childhood. Farms were foreclosed, unemployment stalked the land, and there was hunger everywhere. These conditions made an indelible mark on Walker's mind.

By the time he was eighteen he was decrying the abuses of uncontrolled capitalism." In 1899, in a speech to his graduating class at Southwestern State Normal School in California, Pennsylvania, he declared that "a man backed by ambition and greed, holding in his grasp the happiness of millions, should not be permitted to increase his power by continued extortion, if the power of the state can prevent it."

The next twelve years were busy ones as he prepared himself for the big job ahead. During this time, he completed a Ph. B at the University of Chicago, taught and directed athletics in an Illinois High School, served as principal of an Oklahoma high school, and completed a law degree at the University of Oklahoma.

His formal education completed, he opened a law office in Shawnee, Oklahoma. It was here he made his first political race. He ran for Justice of the Peace and was elected by an overwhelming majority.

After a few months at this job, he ran for County Judge. "I had no cash," he has related, "so I went to the bank and borrowed enough to buy a horse. I rode that animal all over the country; covered every district. I talked to farmers in their homes and in the fields. I helped them milk their cows. I spoke from cotton wagons, at picnics and pie suppers. My campaign slogan was honesty and justice for all with special favors to none.

"In the Democratic primary, I was nominated by a huge majority. Sometime later, two election officials came to me and said they could carry a certain district for me in the general election, but that in order to do it, they would have to have some money. My reply was: 'Gentlemen, in the first place, I have no money. In the second place, if I did, it wouldn't be right to give it to you. You are election officials in that district and responsible for counting the votes. I might be accused of bribery.' "

If he had dealt differently with these money-seeking election officials, he might have won the race. He was defeated by 102 votes. A change of only 52 votes would have made him winner. But he would not compromise his principles to achieve the victory.

When he refused to take part in or sanction what he thought might be interpreted as a misdeed, he set a pattern for his life from which he never deviated. In the years that followed, he had opportunities to join questionable financial enterprises, but he scrupulously avoided them. He turned down many social invitations, not necessarily because he suspected that those doing the entertaining had ulterior motives, but more because he feared the public, to whom he was responsible, might misunderstand.

Walker lost no time grieving over his political defeat. Oklahoma was a young and growing state. If he could not be county judge, he knew there would be other challenging opportunities for public service.

There was an industrial boom. In 1910, the state was producing over 250,000 barrels of oil daily. A year later, 110 fields had been established and Oklahoma was producing one-third of the world's supply. With an abundance of coal, lead, clays, timber, building stone and other raw materials, manufacturing had gotten a good start. New railroads were being constructed. The telephone industry, electric light and power plants, and other public utilities were growing rapidly.

With the growth of business in the state there was a corresponding expansion in the powers of government. The Oklahoma Corporation Commission needed a competent lawyer to head up its campaign to cut the costs of public utilities and conserve the state's natural resources.

This was precisely the kind of challenge Walker was looking for. He was offered the job. He quickly accepted and began work at the State Capitol on January 1, 1915.

In the fifteen years that followed, he waged an almost continuous fight with the gas and light companies to secure lower rates and improve service for the people of Oklahoma. He assisted in getting the legislature to pass a law giving authority to the Commission to enforce oil and natural gas conservation measures. He also served as special counsel for the Commission in its war against freight rate discriminations.

As a result of these activities, he was urged to run for membership on the Commission. He made the race in 1930 and was an easy winner. "My campaign was pretty well made before I announced that I would run," he has related. "As special counsel for the Commission, I had handled the freight rate cases for farmers, oil producers, and for almost every major industry in the state. As a result, three-fourths of the newspapers supported me without my requesting it."

After his election, he was chosen by other members of the Commission to serve as Chairman. He immediately launched an investigation of gas rates in the state. He thought they were much too high. Oklahoma was in the worst throes of depression. Many people could not pay their utility bills and their service was being cut off.

Shortly after the probe began, a man came to see him about the gas rate matter. "He asked me to have lunch with him," Paul Walker remembers. "I said, 'yes, I'll have lunch with you, but each man will pay for his own meal, and we'll eat in the Capitol cafeteria.'

"As we ate lunch, he said he couldn't understand my position on the rate matter and wanted to know what I expected to get out of it by carrying on the fight. 'Not a thing,' was my emphatic answer, 'except to see that the people of Oklahoma are treated right.' He did not seem to understand that a public official could be motivated by an unselfish desire to serve the people."

It is no overstatement to say that Paul Walker almost stood alone at times in these battles for rate reductions. Often opposed by other members of the Oklahoma Commission, and frequently denounced by the utilities, he, nevertheless, stood firm for what he considered to be the rights and interests of the people. He did not want to hurt the utilities, but he felt it was his duty to see that the consuming public got a square deal and he worked uncompromisingly toward this end.

In response to a joint resolution of the state legislature in 1933, he started an official inquiry of rates and practices of telephone companies operating in Oklahoma. He has recounted some of the difficulties involved. "In determining whether certain charges for telephone service were reasonable, we were handicapped because we could not get all the facts. It was discovered that the American Telephone and Telegraph Company with headquarters in New York, was charging its subsidiaries in Oklahoma large management fees, yet we had no jurisdiction over the New York company which would permit us to examine the books of that company to determine the basis for such a charge."

He, like many other state utility commissioners, became convinced that the only way to achieve effective regulation of the communications industries operating across state lines was to establish a new Federal agency with which state commissions could cooperate. When Congress was considering legislation to create the FCC, he appeared before the House Committee on Interstate and Foreign Commerce and declared that "the ramifications of the holding companies made it an impossibility for the state commissions to get anywhere in a telephone rate investigation," and that "if there is to be effective regulation at all of the telephone business, it must be brought about through the Federal Commission."

President Roosevelt had been fully briefed on Walker's philosophy, background and special talents when, in 1934, he telephoned from the White House and asked if he could accept appointment as a member of the newly created FCC. He knew that Walker had the exact qualifications for this rugged assignment. He expected an affirmative answer and he got it! In a few weeks Walker took the oath of office in the new, air-conditioned Post Office Building in Washington, expensively equipped by James Farley with handsome furniture and fancy, brass cuspidors.*

Walker promptly called on President Roosevelt and presented a proposal for a comprehensive investigation of the telephone industry. The President was agreeable. A resolution was submitted to Congress and $750,000 was appropriated for the investigation (later increased to $1,500,000).

Walker immediately was under pressure to make political appointments. How he resisted this pressure is typified by an incident that happened in his office shortly after the investigation got under way. A high government official called on him to *demand* that his cousin be employed for one of the key jobs. After a few minutes of fiery verbal exchange, the Commissioner, fearless and determined, got up from his seat. The high politico knew it was time to go. Mumbling threats, he moved toward the door. His eyes piercing, and biting his words, the Commissioner retorted with finality: "There will be no politics in this investigation. I will not recommend the appointment."

Walker was eager to choose competent persons and perfect an efficient organization. By October, 1935, nearly 200 accountants and engineers had been employed and were studying the books and operations of the Bell System. Public hearings were held intermittently from March, 1936 to June, 1937. Company officials were interrogated on profits, dividends, labor policies, lobby and propaganda methods and other matters coming within the scope of the inquiry.

On December 2, 1936, the Commission announced that as a result of informal discussions with the Company, rates had been reduced to the extent that telephone subscribers would save 12 million dollars a year.

The final report on the investigation was submitted to Congress on June 14, 1939. It disclosed that telephone rate reductions "in excess of thirty million dollars were effected in the interest and for the benefit of the American telephone-using public."

A week after the report was made, President Roosevelt reappointed Walker for

*The cuspidors were found to be unnecessary and later were removed from the building. The writer often has wondered what happened to these expensive items.

a second term on the Commission. Without objection, the Senate confirmed the appointment on June 29, 1939. A few days before, Congressman Jed Johnson brought applause from the House when he referred to the "unusual mental attainments" of Paul Walker and said that the "nation needs more men of his caliber in public life."

Paul Walker's interest in communications was not limited to telephone service. While much of his time and energy were taken up with the telephone investigation during the early years of his FCC career, he kept a close eye on the expanding broadcasting industry.

Two years before the telephone investigation was completed, speeches were being made in the halls of Congress condemning "radio monopoly." The increasing fury of Congressional criticism prompted the Commission to order a probe of the billion-dollar radio industry.

Paul Walker had an important hand in determining the scope of the inquiry, which covered contractual relations between networks and their affiliates, monopolistic practices in the broadcasting industry, and network control of station programming. He was appointed a member of the Commission committee to carry on the investigation. More than seventy sessions of public hearings were held. Walker was present at all but three of them and took an active part in the questioning of witnesses.

The outcome was the adoption of network regulations (still in effect) designed to break the grip of network control over station affiliates and require these stations to exercise greater responsibility over programming.

The network regulations evoked a storm of protest from the broadcast industry. Their validity was contested in the courts. It was alleged that the Commission exceeded its statutory authority, and that the rights of free speech had been abridged in violation of the First Amendment. But the Supreme Court didn't agree and the regulations were confirmed in May of 1943.

Following the Supreme Court decision, the president of one of the networks stated that under the Court's interpretation of the law the Commission could now do whatever it wanted to do in regulating the business practices and programs of broadcasters. But Walker didn't see it this way. He never felt that the Frankfurter opinion went this far. He construed the opinion to mean that the Commission had to pass on the qualifications of applicants for broadcast facilities and, in connection with license renewals, review the overall operation of stations and determine whether they had operated in the public interest. In fact, in 1946, he voted to approve the famous Blue Book about which there has been so much discussion in Washington. This document, which has never been officially repudiated by the FCC, set forth some general criteria to be used in determining whether stations have kept their promises and discharged their public responsibilities. And, in the opinion of this writer, if Walker were on the Commission today he would take a firm position against the deception and over-commercialization which have characterized many radio and TV programs in recent years. There would be no question in his mind that the Commission has the authority and the responsibility to prohibit, through its licensing functions, such deplorable practices.

Despite the strong positions he had taken regarding some of the policies of the telephone and broadcasting industries, he came through the Congressional investigations of the forties unscathed. While charges and counter-charges were being made, with the Commission under scorching attack from Congress and special interests, Paul Walker fearlessly continued to "call the shots" as he saw them. Notwithstanding the inquisitorial atmosphere which pervaded Washington, not once was his integrity officially questioned.

He went through the long and exhaustive public hearings which led to the adoption of the nation-wide television table with assignment of more than 2,000 TV channels throughout the country. He was greatly impressed with the showing made by educators in their appeal for reserved channels. While the proceeding was pending, however, he refrained from any extra-judicial, loud-mouthed advocacy. He waited until all the evidence was in before making up his mind on this and other phases of the hearing.

Paul Walker was passed up a half dozen times before he was finally made Chairman of the FCC. Because of his adamantine qualities and his unswerving devotion to the public interest, he was not always popular with some powerful political and economic interests. When matters of principle were involved, he was not one to pull his punches. For example, in 1943, he strongly rebuked a large utility concern for what he thought was gross mistreatment of a small, independent telephone company. "The wrongs committed," said he, ". . . will unless corrected, remain forever a reminder to the public of the arbitrary and hurtful actions which can be perpetrated by a powerful monopoly. The ultimate effect of such actions will be to destroy completely public trust and confidence in utility management . . ."

Such strong words tended to give segments of the communications industry an image of Walker as a "big corporation foe." This was a false image, of course, because those who were close to him knew that he was a real friend to the American free enterprise system. Nevertheless, the hostile attitude held by a few vested interests had its effect on the White House and militated against his appointment to the Chairmanship of the FCC.

Whatever may be said against Mr. Truman, it was to his credit that he recognized the true worth of Walker as a public administrator and, on February 28, 1952, elevated him to the top FCC position.

Walker had just passed his 71st birthday. He was cautioned by his associates to take it easy. Much younger men had succumbed to the strain of the office, he was reminded. Despite the warnings, he seemed to work harder the next fourteen months than ever before and he seemed to thrive on the responsibility.

Under his administration, the television freeze was lifted and the wild scramble for television channels began. For several months he and the FCC staff were working day and night setting up machinery to process more than 700 applications for new stations already on file with the Commission.

Just seven months after his appointment, the Commission announced that 200 TV stations had been authorized, and that the number of pending applications had increased to nearly 900. The legal battle for valuable channels in the big market was feverish and intense. In one case involving competing applications, Walker was commanded to appear in the late Senator McCarthy's office and, in star chamber fashion, the Senator attempted coercive tactics. But Walker was fearless and unyielding. He respected Senators regardless of their character or party affiliation, but no power on earth could make him do what he thought was wrong.

With the election of the Republican administration, he stepped down as Chairman and was replaced by Rosel Hyde, a Republican from Idaho, who, as a member of the staff and the Commission, had worked with Walker since the agency was created in 1934.

Walker retired from the Commission in 1953. After a brief period of law practice in Washington, D.C., he and his family returned to Oklahoma, taking up residence in Norman, where, for the remainder of his life, he enjoyed the associations of many old friends on the faculty and staff at the University of Oklahoma. He died on November 2, 1965 at the age of eighty-four.

Federal Trade Commission Guides, Program Monitoring and Liaison Procedures Between the FCC and FTC

GUIDES AGAINST DECEPTIVE PRICING

The following guides have been adopted by the Federal Trade Commission *for the use of its staff* in the evaluation of pricing representations in advertising.[1] While the guides do not purport to be all inclusive, they are directed toward the elimination of existing major abuses and are being released to the public in the interest of obtaining voluntary, simultaneous and prompt cooperation by those whose practices are subject to the jurisdiction of the Federal Trade Commission.

In determining whether or not pricing practices are violative of the laws administered by the Commission, the facts in each matter are considered in view of the requirements of the Federal Trade Commission Act, as amended, and principles enunciated by the Courts in the adjudication of cases. The foremost of these principles are:

1. Advertisements must be considered in their entirety and as they would be read by those to whom they appeal.
2. Advertisements as a whole may be completely misleading although every sentence separately considered is literally true. This may be because things are omitted that should be said, or because advertisements are composed or purposely printed in such a way as to mislead.
3. Advertisements are not intended to be carefully dissected with a dictionary at hand, but rather to produce an impression upon prospective purchasers.
4. Whether or not the advertiser knows the representations to be false, the deception of purchasers and the diversion of trade from competitors is the same.
5. A deliberate effort to deceive is not necessary to make out a case of using unfair methods of competition or unfair or decptive acts or practices within the prohibition of the statute.
6. Laws are made to protect the trusting as well as the suspicious.
7. Pricing representations, however made, which are ambiguous will be read favorably to the accomplishment of the purpose of the Federal Trade Commission Act, as amended, which is to prevent the making of claims which have the tendency and capacity to mislead.

---

[1]For the purposes of these Guides "Advertising" includes any form of public notice which uses a claim for a product, however such representation is disseminated or utilized.

FEDERAL TRADE COMMISSION
WASHINGTON 25

BUREAU OF INVESTIGATION
OFFICE OF
CHIEF PROJECT ATTORNEY

Gentlemen: In re: *Commercial Broadcasts*

Pursuant to statutory authority the Federal Trade Commission is engaged in the review of current radio and television advertising, and requests that you forward to the Radio and Television, Advertising Unit, Federal Trade Commission, Washington 25, D. C., typed script representing the commercial text of all advertising originating in your studios and disseminated through your facilities on the following date(s):

Commercial continuities submitted should include those announcements, statements, and testimonials tending to or intended to create a demand for, or to induce the purchase of, any article of commerce, whether such commercial script opens, is interspersed with, or concludes a program. If commercial continuities are in a foreign language you are requested to submit an English translation of the continuities.

Date of dissemination and station call letters should be printed, stamped, or written, preferably at the bottom of each sheet of commercial continuity. Legible carbon copies of commercial continuities are acceptable. The advertiser's name and address should be indicated where not part of the script. Electrical transcriptions or films need not be transcribed. It will be sufficient to list the sponsor, the product advertised and the agency from which it is received.

Non-commercial script (i.e., without any commercial objective) covering lectures and similar programs, which are purely educational, religious, civic or political need not be submitted. Further, you may omit forwarding commercial advertising continuities of local banking institutions, building and loan associations, transportation companies, including local taxi services, local hotels, restaurants, theatres, night clubs, and mortuary establishments.

Please mail return promptly, in packages weighing not more than 4 lbs. each, and use the enclosed government franks for mailing. Please prepare the enclosed transmittal form FTC-R-6 covering individual station material, to distinguish your network material sent by originating key stations.

Enclosures
FTC-R-7
L-3813 rev.; the 1970 form letter has been modified in some words. But the content is essentially the same.

LICENSEE RESPONSIBILITY WITH RESPECT TO THE BROADCAST
OR FALSE, MISLEADING OR DECEPTIVE ADVERTISING*

1. The first issue of a new Federal Trade Commission publication, "Advertising Alert," is enclosed with copies of this Notice which are being mailed to all broadcast

* FCC 61-1316
11836
Public Notice, November 7, 1961.

licensees. The Federal Communications Commission and the Federal Trade Commission have undertaken this program believing that it will be of great benefit to all broadcasters in assisting them to fulfill their obligation to sift out fraudulent and deceptive advertising matter, to the Commissions themselves in their respective enforcement activities, and eventually to the general public. Subsequent issues of the "Alert," to be mailed directly by the Federal Trade Commission on a regular basis, will bring to all broadcast licensees notice as to advertising matter which is the subject of corrective action by FTC. In addition, the "Alert" will frequently discuss in considerable detail a particular problem area with which the FTC is concerned. These discussions and notices will familiarize licensees with various deceptive practices so that they will be able to recognize them and take appropriate steps to protect the public against them.

2. As you know, the Commission has always held that a licensee's duty to protect the public from false, misleading or deceptive advertising is an important ingredient of his operation in the public interest. In its Report and Statement of Policy, re: Commission En Banc Programming Inquiry dated July 29, 1960, the Commission set forth the responsibility with regard to false and misleading advertising in the following terms:

"Broadcasting licensees must assume responsibility for all material which is broadcast through their facilities. This includes all programs and advertising material which they present to the public. With respect to advertising material the licensee has the additional responsibility to take all reasonable measures to eliminate any false, misleading or deceptive matter. . . . This duty is personal to the licensee and may not be delegated."

It is the hope of this Commission and of the FTC that the program here instituted will be of assistance to licensees in carrying out this responsibility.

3. The "Alert" will contain information pertaining to Complaints and Orders which have been issued by the Federal Trade Commission. If there is submitted to a licensee advertising matter which has been the subject of an FTC *Complaint*, he should realize that, although no final determination has been made that the advertising in question is false or deceptive, a question has been raised as to its propriety, and he should therefore exercise particular care in deciding whether to accept it for broadcast. An *Order* issued by the Federal Trade Commission against an advertiser, which has become final, is a formal determination by that agency that the particular advertising in question is false or deceptive. Should it come to this Commission's attention that a licensee has broadcast advertising which is known to have been the subject of a final Order by the FTC, serious question would be raised as to the adequacy of the measures instituted and carried out by the licensee in the fulfillment of his responsibility, and as to his operation in the public interest.

4. In this regard, particular attention is directed to the fact that licensee responsibility is not limited merely to a review of the advertising copy submitted for broadcast, but that the licensee has the additional obligation to take reasonable steps to satisfy himself as to the reliability and reputation of every prospective advertiser and as to his ability to fulfill promises made to the public over the licensed facilities. The fact that a particular product or advertisement has not been subject of Federal Trade Commission action in no way lessens the licensee's responsibility with regard to it. On the contrary, it is hoped that the information received from these "Alerts" will make it possible for licensees to recognize questionable enterprises, claims, guarantees, and the like, and where deemed inappropriate for broadcast, to bring them to the attention of the Federal Trade Commission for possible further investigation.

5. The Commission hopes that this program will help licensees in carrying out their responsibilities and we will welcome any comments and suggestions as to how it is felt this program might be enhanced so as to enable licensees to give greater protection to the public and thus render an even more valuable service to their communities.

Adopted: November 1, 1961

HOW FTC MONITORING SYSTEM OPERATES*

Because of numerous inquiries, it appears appropriate to explain the [Federal Trade] Commission's advertising monitoring program. All commercial radio and television broadcasting stations receive requests to submit scripts, which accounts for the many inquiries.

The major networks furnish typed scripts covering one week of broadcasts each month. These account for all commercials centrally originating, and explain why the individual broadcaster is asked only for commercials originating in his studio. These network commercials are requested frequently because they generally represent the advertising of greatest public interest due to the number of persons exposed.

Individual television stations submit copy four times each year. Radio broadcasters furnish copy one, two or four times a year according to a formula based primarily on the size of the listening audience. Advertising broadcast over facilities reaching a large metropolitan area, for example, obviously reflects substantially greater public interest than that transmitted by a station even with equal power but reaching only a rural, limited audience.

Requests to individual stations are for a 24-hour period in each instance. They are scheduled so that copy is received daily from stations located throughout the country. One station may receive two requests fairly close together but that station will normally find a longer lapse until the next, and requests for the year will total no more than four. Successive requests normally will cover different days of the week.

When it is particularly inconvenient for a station to furnish copy for a specified date, a letter of explanation ordinarily will permit substitution of an alternate date. Some broadcasters prefer simply to tape the day's commercials. This practice is acceptable.

Upon receipt of these continuities, every one is read and considered carefully. A staff of four monitors reads about 50,000 scripts a month, many of them several pages in length. A substantial number of these is segregated and routed for further attention.

By examining advertisements segregated by these monitors, attorneys determine whether Commission Orders to Cease and Desist, and Stipulations, are being violated. Other commercials are analyzed to determine the effectiveness of Trade Practice Rules and the Guides program. Many are selected and routed to attorneys for further attention because the experienced eye of the monitor detects claims which the Commission has found to be unlawful in previous cases, or which appear to be questionable for other reasons.

By means of this monitoring program, a continuing review of advertising by industries is maintained. All advertising for a type of product, or type of claim, is assembled. This permits a comprehensive study of an entire segment of advertising, isolation of problems, and selection of the best manner of coping with them.

The monitoring program is an invaluable aid in determining which current indus-

* FTC, Advertising Alert No. 2.
February 12, 1962.

try practices most require attention. The program also is useful in the investigation and trial of cases by providing a steady flow of current advertising. The information also helps in the policing of compliance with outstanding orders.

Advertising for alcoholic beverages is segregated and forwarded to the Bureau of Internal Revenue, which has primary jurisdiction over such advertising.

The review of written continuities is supplemented by some direct monitoring of broadcasts. This is done on a regular and continuing spot check basis in Washington. Also, all professional employees report questionable advertising coming to their attention as they are stationed or travel throughout the country.

The foregoing discussion relates to radio and television commercials, but printed advertising receives comparable attention. A cross section sampling of newspapers is supplied daily. Copies are requested from papers scattered geographically, representing large metropolitan areas and rural communities, those directed primarily to specialized trades, etc. A similar approach is employed in surveying magazine advertising.

BROADCAST LICENSEES CAUTIONED ABOUT IMPROPER USE OF BROADCAST RATINGS*

As a part of its continuing liaison with the Federal Trade Commission, this Commission [FCC] has determined that notice should be given to its broadcast licensees concerning possible improper use of broadcast ratings in advertising campaigns.

Information has come to the attention of the Commission, as a result of hearings recently held by the Special Subcommittee on Investigations of the House Committee on Interstate and Foreign Commerce and through complaints, that some licensees have made improper use of broadcast ratings. The Commission recognizes, of course, that audience research is an important selling tool in efforts to obtain advertiser support. It is not the intention of the Commission to discourage valid audience research or its proper use by broadcast licensees in their selling campaigns.

In using audience research, however, the licensee must act responsibly. He therefore has an obligation to take reasonable precautions to insure that a survey which he uses in an advertising campaign is valid (e.g., that it is properly conceived, reasonably free from bias, has an adequate sample). He also has an obligation to act responsibly in the use he makes of the survey. He may not, for example, quote a portion of the survey out of context so as to leave a false and misleading impression of the relative ranking of his station in the market.

As is made clear in the Public Notice issued this day by the Federal Trade Commission [page 11:210], failure to act responsibly may constitute an unfair method of competition, or an unfair or deceptive act or practice in violation of the Federal Trade Commission Act. The Commission intends ordinarily to refer complaints dealing with questionable use of broadcast ratings to the Federal Trade Commission for that agency's consideration.

In determining whether a licensee is operating in the public interest, the Commission will take into account any findings or order to cease and desist of the Federal Trade Commission concerning the use of broadcast ratings by a licensee.

Adopted: June 12, 1963

* FCC 63-544
35611
Public Notice, June 13, 1963.

APPENDIX IV

Report and Statement of Policy Re: Commission *en banc* Programming Inquiry*

The Commission en banc, by Commissioners Ford (Chairman), Bartley, Lee, Craven and Cross, with Commissioner Hyde dissenting and Commissioner King not participating, adopted the following statement on July 27, 1960:

On October 3, 1957 the Commission's Network Study Staff submitted its report on network broadcasting. While the scope and breadth of the network study as set forth in Order Number 1 issued November 21, 1955 encompassed a comprehensive study of programming, it soon became apparent that due to factors not within the control of the staff or the committee consideration of programming would be subject to substantial delay making it impracticable that the target dates for the over-all report could be met in the program area. The principal reasons were: (a) the refusal of certain program distributors and producers to provide the committee's staff with certain information which necessitated protracted negotiations and ultimately legal action (FCC v. Ralph Cohn, et al., 154 F. Supp, 899 [15 RR 2085]); and (b) the fact that a coincidental and collateral investigation into certain practices was instituted by the Department of Justice. Accordingly the network study staff report recommended that the study of programming be continued and completed. The Director of the Network Study in his memorandum of transmittal of the Network Study Report stated:

The staff regrets that it was unable to include in the report its findings and conclusions in its study of programming. It is estimated that more than one-fourth of the time of the staff was expended in this area. However, the extended negotiations and litigation with some non-network program producers relative to supplying financial data necessary to this aspect of the study made it impossible to obtain this information from a sufficient number of these program producers to draw definitive conclusions on all the programming issues. Now that the Commission's right to obtain this information has been sustained, it is the hope of the staff that this aspect of the study will be completed and the results included in a supplement to the report. Unless the study of programming is completed, the benefit of much labor on this subject will have been substantially lost.

As a result, on February 26, 1959, the Commission issued its "Order for Investigatory Proceeding," Docket No. 12782. That Order stated that during the course of the Network Study and otherwise, the Commission had obtained information and data regarding the acquisition, production, ownership, distribution, sale, licensing and exhibition of programs for television broadcasting. Also, that that information and data had been augmented from other sources including hearings before Committee of Congress and from the Department of Justice, and that the Commission had determined that an overall inquiry should be made to determine the facts with respect to the television network program selection process. On November 9, 1959, the proceeding instituted by the Commission's Order of February 26, 1959 was amended and enlarged to include a general inquiry with respect to programming to

*25 F.R. 7291, August 3, 1960.

determine, among other things, whether the general standards heretofore laid down by the Commission for the guidance of broadcast licensees in the selection of programs and other material intended for broadcast are currently adequate; whether the Commission should, by the exercise of its rule-making power, set out more detailed and precise standards for such broadcasters; whether the Commission's present review and consideration in the field of programming and advertising are adequate, under present conditions in the broadcast industry; and whether the Commission's authority under the Communications Act of 1934, as amended, is adequate, or whether legislation should be recommended to Congress.

This inquiry was heard by the Commission en banc between December 7, 1959, and February 1, 1960, and consumed 19 days in actual hearings. Over 90 witnesses testified relative to the problems involved, made suggestions and otherwise contributed from their background and experience to the solution of these problems. Several additional statements were submitted. The record in the en banc portion of the inquiry consisted of 3,775 pages of transcript plus 1,000 pages of exhibits. The Interim Report of the staff of the Office of Network Study was submitted to the Commission for consideration on June 15, 1960.

The Commission will make every effort to expedite its consideration of the entire docket proceeding and will take such definitive action as the Commission determines to be warranted. However, the Commission feels that a general statement of policy responsive to the issues in the en banc inquiry is warranted at this time.

Prior to the en banc hearing, the Commission had made its position clear that, in fulfilling its obligation to operate in the public interest, a broadcast station is expected to exercise reasonable care and prudence with respect to its broadcast material in order to assure that no matter is broadcast which will deceive or mislead the public. In view of the extent of the problem existing with respect to a number of licensees involving such practices as deceptive quiz shows and payola which had become apparent, the Commission concluded that certain proposed amendments to our Rules as well as proposed legislation would provide a basis for substantial improvements. Accordingly, on February 5, 1960, we adopted a Notice of Proposed Rule Making to deal with fixed quiz and other non-bona fide contest programs involving intellectual skill. These rules would prohibit the broadcasting of such programming unless accompanied by an announcement which would in all cases describe the nature of the program in a manner to sufficiently apprise the audience that the events in question are not in fact spontaneous or actual measures of knowledge or intellectual skill. Announcements would be made at the beginning and end of each program. Moreover, the proposed rules would require a station, if it obtained such a program from networks, to be assured similarly that the network program has an accompanying announcement of this nature. This, we believe, would go a long way toward preventing any recurrence of problems such as those encountered in the recent quiz show programs.

We have also felt that this sort of conduct should be prohibited by statute. Accordingly, we suggested legislation designed to make it a crime for anyone to wilfully and knowingly participate or cause another to participate in or cause to be broadcast a program of intellectual skill or knowledge where the outcome thereof is prearranged or predetermined. Without the above-described amendment, the Commission's regulatory authority is limited to its licensing function. The Commission cannot reach networks directly or advertisers, producers, sponsors and others who, in one capacity or another, are associated with the presentation of radio and television programs which may deceive the listening or viewing public. It is our view that this proposed legislation will help to assure that every contest of intellectual skill or knowledge that is broadcast will be in fact a bona fide contest. Under this proposal, all those persons responsible in any way for the broadcast of a deceptive program of this type would be penalized. Because of the far reaching effects of radio and television, we believe such sanctions to be desirable.

The Commission proposed on February 5, 1960 that a new section be added to the Commission's rules which would require the licensee of radio broadcast stations to adopt appropriate procedures to prevent the practice of payola amongst his employees. Here again the standard of due diligence would have to be met by the licensee. We have also approved on February 11 the language of proposed legislation which would impose criminal penalties for failure to announce sponsored programs, such as payola and others, involving hidden payments or other considerations. This proposal looks toward amending the United States Code to provide fines up to $5,000 or imprisonment up to one year, or both, for violators. It would prohibit the payment to any person or the receipt of payment by any person for the purpose of having as a part of the broadcast program any material on either a radio or television show unless an announcement is made as a part of the program that such material has been paid for or furnished. The Commission now has no direct jurisdiction over the employees of a broadcast station with respect to this type of activity. The imposition of a criminal penalty appears to us to be effective manner for dealing with this practice. In addition, the Commission has made related legislative proposals with respect to fines, temporary suspension of licenses and temporary restraining orders.

In view of our mutual interest with the Federal Trade Commission and in order to avoid duplication of effort, we have arrived at an arrangement whereby any information obtained by the FCC which might be of interest to FTC will be called to that Commission's attention by our staff. Similarly, FTC will advise our Commission of any information or data which it acquires in the course of its investigations which might be pertinent to matters under jurisdiction of the FCC. This is an understanding supplemental to earlier liaison arrangements between FCC and FTC.

Certain legislative proposals recently made by the Commission as related to the instant inquiry have been mentioned. It is appropriate now to consider whether the statutory authority of the Commission with respect to programming and program practices is, in other respects, adequate.

In considering the extent of the Commission's authority in the area of programming it is essential first to examine the limitations imposed upon it by the First Amendment to the Constitution and Section 326 of the Communications Act.

The first Amendment to the United States Constitution reads as follows:

Congress shall make no law respecting an establishment of religion or prohibiting the free exercise thereof; or abridging the freedom of speech, or of the press; or the right of the people peaceably to assemble, and to petition the Government for a redress of grievances.

Section 326 of the Communications Act of 1934, as amended, provides that:

Nothing in this chapter [Act] shall be understood or construed to give the Commission the power of censorship over the radio communications or signals transmitted by any radio station, and no regulation or condition shall be promulgated or fixed by the Commission which shall interfere with the right of free speech by means of radio communication.

The communication of ideas by means of radio and television is a form of expression entitled to protection against abridgement by the First Amendment to the Constitution. In United States v. Paramount Pictures, 334 U. S. 131, 166 (1948) the Supreme Court stated:

We have no doubt that moving pictures, like newspapers and radio are included in the press whose freedom is guaranteed by the First Amendment.

As recently as 1954 in Superior Films v. Department of Education, 346 U.S. 587, Justice Douglas in a concurring opinion stated:

507

Motion pictures are, of course, a different medium of expression than the radio, the stage, the novel or the magazine. But the first Amendment draws no distinction between the various methods of communicating ideas.

Moreover, the free speech protection of the First Amendment is not confined solely to the exposition of ideas nor is it required that the subject matter of the communication be possessed of some value to society. In Winters v. New York, 333 U.S. 507, 510 (1948) the Supreme Court reversed a conviction based upon a violation of an ordinance of the City of New York which made it punishable to distribute printed matter devoted to the publication of accounts of criminal deeds and pictures of bloodshed, lust or crime. In this connection the Court said:

> We do not accede to appellee's suggestion that the constitutional protection for a free press applies only to the exposition of ideas. The line between the informing and the entertaining is too elusive for the protection of that basic right . . . Though we can see nothing of any possible value to society in these magazines, they are as much entitled to the protection of free speech as the best of literature.

Notwithstanding the foregoing authorities, the right to the use of the airwaves is conditioned upon the issuance of a license under a statutory scheme established by Congress in the Communications Act in the proper exercise of its power over commerce.[1] The question therefore arises as to whether because of the characteristics peculiar to broadcasting which justifies the government in regulating its operation through a licensing system, there exists the basis for a distinction as regards other media of mass communication with respect to application of the free speech provisions of the First Amendment? In other words, does it follow that because one may not engage in broadcasting without first obtaining a license, the terms thereof may be so framed as to unreasonably abridge the free speech protection of the First Amendment?

We recognize that the broadcasting medium presents problems peculiar to itself which are not necessarily subject to the same rules governing other media of communication. As we stated in our Petition in Grove Press, Inc. and Readers Subscription, Inc. v. Robert K. Christenberry (Case No. 25, 861) filed in the U.S. Court of Appeals for the Second Circuit, "radio and TV programs enter the home and are readily available not only to the average normal adult but also to children and to the emotionally immature . . . Thus, for example, while a nudist magazine may be within the protection of the First Amendment . . . the televising of nudes might well raise a serious question of programming contrary to 18 U.S.C. §1464 . . . Similarly, regardless of whether the 'four-letter words' and sexual description, set forth in 'Lady Chatterley's Lover,' (when considered in the context of the whole book) make the book obscene for mailability purposes, the utterance of such words or the depiction of such sexual activity on radio or TV would raise similar public interest and Section 1464 questions." Nevertheless it is essential to keep in mind that "the basic principles of freedom of speech and the press like the First Amendment's command do not vary."[2]

Although the Commission must determine whether the total program service of broadcasters is reasonably responsive to the interests and needs of the public they serve, it may not condition the grant, denial or revocation of a broadcast license upon its own subjective determination of what is or is not a good program. To do so would "lay a forbidden burden upon the exercise of liberty protected by the Constitution."[3] The Chairman of the Commission during the course of his testimony

[1]NBC v. United States, 319 U.S. 190 (1943)
[2]Burstyn v. Wilson, 343 U.S. 495, 503, (1952).
[3]Cantwell v. Connecticut, 310 U.S. 926, 307.

recently given before the Senate Independent Offices Subcommittee of the Committee on Appropriations expressed the point as follows:

> Mr. Ford. When it comes to questions of taste, unless it is downright profanity or obscenity, I do not think that the Commission has any part in it.
>
> I don't see how we could possibly go out and say this program is good and that program is bad. That would be a direct violation of the law.[4]

In a similar vein Mr. Whitney North Seymour, President-elect of the American Bar Association, stated during the course of this proceeding that while the Commission may inquire of licensees what they have done to determine the needs of the community they propose to serve, the Commission may not impose upon them its private notions of what the public ought to hear.[5]

Nevertheless, several witnesses in this proceeding have advanced persuasive arguments urging us to require licensees to present specific types of programs on the theory that such action would enhance freedom of expression rather than tend to abridge it. With respect to this proposition we are constrained to point out that the First Amendment forbids governmental interference asserted in aid of free speech, as well as governmental action repressive of it. The protection against abridgement of freedom of speech and press flatly forbids governmental interference, benign or otherwise. The First Amendment "while regarding freedom in religion, in speech and printing and in assembling and petitioning the government for redress of grievances as fundamental and precious to all, seeks only to forbid that Congress should meddle therein." (Powe v. United States, 109 F. (2d) 147).

As recently as 1959 in Farmers Educational and Cooperative Union of America v. WDAY, Inc. 360 U. S. 525, the Supreme Court succinctly stated:

> . . . expressly applying this country's tradition of free expression to the field of radio broadcasting, Congress has from the first emphatically forbidden the Commission to exercise any power of censorship over radio communication.

An examination of the foregoing authorities serves to explain why the day-to-day operation of a broadcast station is primarily the responsibility of the individual station licensee. Indeed, Congress provided in Section 3(h) of the Communications Act that a person engaged in radio broadcasting shall not be deemed a common carrier. Hence, the Commission in administering the Act and the courts in interpreting it have consistently maintained that responsibility for the selection and presentation of broadcast material ultimately devolves upon the individual station licensee, and that the fulfillment of the public interest requires the free exercise of his independent judgment. Accordingly, the Communications Act "does not essay to regulate the business of the licensee. The Commission is given no supervisory control of the programs, of business management or of policy . . . Congress intended to leave competition in the business of broadcasting where it found it . . ."[6] The regulatory responsibility of the Commission in the broadcast field essentially involves the maintenance of a balance between the preservation of a free competitive broadcast system, on the one hand, and the reasonable restriction of that freedom inherent in the public interest standard provided in the Communications Act, on the other.

In addition, there appears a second problem quite unrelated to the question of censorship that would enter into the Commission's assumption of supervision over

---

[4]Hearings before the Subcommittee of the Committee on Appropriations, United States Senate, 86th Congress, 2nd Session on H.R.11776 at page 775.
[5]Memorandum of Mr. Whitney North Seymour, Special Counsel to the National Association of Broadcasters at page 7.
[6]FCC v. Sanders Brothers, 309 U.S. 470, 475 (1940)

program content. The Commission's role as a practical matter, let alone a legal matter, cannot be one of program dictation or program supervision. In this connection we think the words of Justice Douglas are particularly appropriate.

The music selected by one bureaucrat may be as offensive to some as it is soothing to others. The news commentator chosen to report on the events of the day may give overtones to the news that pleases the bureaucrat but which rile the ... audience. The political philosophy which one radio sponsor exudes may be thought by the official who makes up the programs as the best for the welfare of the people. But the man who listens to it ... may think it marks the destruction of the Republic ... Today it is a business enterprise working out a radio program under the auspices of government. Tomorrow it may be a dominant, political or religious group. ... Once a man is forced to submit to one type of program, he can be forced to submit to another. It may be but a short step from a cultural program to a political program ... The strength of our system is in the dignity, resourcefulness and the intelligence of our people. Our confidence is in their ability to make the wisest choice. That system cannot flourish if regimentation takes hold.[7]

Having discussed the limitations upon the Commission in the consideration of programming, there remains for discussion the exceptions to those limitations and the area of affirmative responsibility which the Commission may appropriately exercise under its statutory obligation to find that the public interest, convenience and necessity will be served by the granting of a license to broadcast.

In view of the fact that a broadcaster is required to program his station in the public interest, convenience and necessity, it follows despite the limitations of the First Amendment and Section 326 of the Act, that his freedom to program is not absolute. The Commission does not conceive that it is barred by the Constitution or by statute from exercising any responsibility with respect to programming. It does conceive that the manner or extent of the exercise of such responsibility can introduce constitutional or statutory questions. It readily concedes that it is precluded from examining a program for taste or content, unless the recognized exceptions to censorship apply: for example, obscenity, profanity, indecency, programs inciting to riots, programs designed or inducing toward the commission of crime, lotteries, etc. These exceptions, in part, are written into the United States Code and, in part, are recognized in judicial decision. See Sections 1304, 1343 and 1464 of Title 18 of the United States Code (lotteries, fraud by radio, utterance of obscene, indecent or profane language by radio). It must be added that such traditional or legislative exceptions to a strict application of the freedom of speech requirements of the United States Constitution may very well also convey wider scope in judicial interpretation as applied to licensed radio than they have had or would have as applied to other communications media. The Commission's petition in the Grove case, supra, urged the court not unnecessarily to refer to broadcasting, in its opinion, as had the District Court. Such reference subsequently was not made though it must be pointed out there is no evidence that the motion made by the FCC was a contributing factor. It must nonetheless be observed that this Commission conscientiously believes that it should make no policy or take any action which would violate the letter or the spirit of the censorship prohibitions of Section 326 of the Communications Act.

As stated by the Supreme Court of the United States in Joseph Burstyne, Inc. v. Wilson, supra:

... Nor does it follow that motion pictures are necessarily subject to the precise rule governing any other particular method of expression. Each method tends to present its own peculiar problem. But the basic principles of freedom of speech and the press, like the First Amendment's command, do not vary. Those principles, as they have frequently been enunciated by this Court, make freedom of expression the rule.

[7]Public Utilities Commission v. Pollak, 343 U.S. 451, 468, Dissenting Opinion.

A review of the Communications Act as a whole clearly reveals that the foundation of the Commission's authority rests upon the public interest, convenience and necessity.[8] The Commission may not grant, modify or renew a broadcast station license without finding that the operation of such station is in the public interest. Thus, faithful discharge of its statutory responsibilities is absolutely necessary in connection with the implacable requirement that the Commission approve no such application for license unless it finds that "public interest, convenience and necessity would be served." While the public interest standard does not provide a blueprint of all the situations to which it may apply, it does contain a sufficiently precise definition of authority so as to enable the Commission to properly deal with the many and varied occasions which may give rise to its application. A significant element of the public interest is the broadcaster's service to the community. In the case of NBC v. United States, 319 U. S. 190, the Supreme Court described this aspect of the public interest as follows:

An important element of public interest and convenience affecting the issue of a license is the ability of the licensee to render the best practicable service to the community reached by broadcasts . . . The Commission's licensing function cannot be discharged, therefore, merely by finding that there are no technological objections to the granting of a license. If the criterion of 'public interest' were limited to such matters, how could the Commission choose between two applicants for the same facilities, each of whom is financially and technically qualified to operate a station? Since the very inception of federal regulation by radio, comparative considerations as to the services to be rendered have governed the application of the standard of 'public interest, convenience or necessity.'

Moreover, apart from this broad standard which we will further discuss in a moment, there are certain other statutory indications.

It is generally recognized that programming is of the essence of radio service. Section 307(b) of the Communications Act requires the Commission to "make such distribution of licenses . . . among the several States and communities as to provide a fair, efficient and equitable distribution of radio service to each of the same." Under this section the Commission has consistently licensed stations with the end objective of either providing new or additional programming service *to* a community, area or state, or of providing a new or additional "outlet" for broadcasting *from* a community, area or state. Implicit in the former alternative is increased radio reception; implicit in the latter alternative is increased radio transmission and, in this connection, appropriate attention to local live programming is required.

Formerly by reason of administrative policy, and since September 14, 1959, by necessary implications from the amended language of Section 315 of the Communications Act, the Commission has had the responsibility for determining whether licensees "afford reasonable opportunity for the discussion of conflicting views on issues of public importance." This responsibility usually is of the generic kind and thus, in the absence of unusual circumstances, is not exercised with regard to particular situations but rather in terms of operating policies of stations as viewed over a reasonable period of time. This, in the past, has meant a review, usually in terms of filed complaints, in connection with the applications made each three year period for renewal of station licenses. However, that has been a practice largely traceable to workload necessities, and therefore not so limited by law. Indeed the Commission recently has expressed its views to the Congress that it would be desirable to exercise a greater discretion with respect to the length of licensing periods within the maximum three year license period provided by Section 307(d). It has also initiated rulemaking to this end.

The foundation of the American system of broadcasting was laid in the Radio Act

[8]Sections 307(d), 308, 309, inter alia.

of 1927 when Congress placed the basic responsibility for all matter broadcast to the public at the grass roots level in the hands of the station licensee. That obligation was carried forward into the Communications Act of 1934, and remains unaltered and undivided. The licensee, is, in effect, a "trustee" in the sense that his license to operate his station imposes upon him a nondelegable duty to serve the public interest in the community he had chosen to represent as a broadcaster.

Great confidence and trust are placed in the citizens who have qualified as broadcasters. The primary duty and privilege to select the material to be broadcast to his audience and the operation of his component of this powerful medium of communication is left in his hands. As was stated by the Chairman in behalf of this Commission in recent testimony before a Congressional Committee.[9]

Thus far Congress has not imposed by law an affirmative programming requirement on broadcast licensees. Rather, it has heretofore given licensees a broad discretion in the selection of programs. In recognition of this principle, Congress provided in Section 3(h) of the Communications Act that a person engaged in radio broadcasting shall not be deemed a common carrier. To this end the Commission in administering the Act and the courts in interpreting it have consistently maintained that responsibility for the selection and presentation of broadcast material ultimately devolves upon the individual station licensee and that the fulfillment of such responsibility requires the free exercise of his independent judgment.

As indicated by former President Hoover, then Secretary of Commerce, in the Radio Conference of 1922-25:

The dominant element for consideration in the radio field is, and always will be, the great body of the listening public, millions in number, country wide in distribution. There is no proper line of conflict between the broadcaster and listener, nor would I attempt to array one against the other. Their interests are mutual, for without the one the other could not exist.

There have been few developments in industrial history to equal the speed and efficiency with which genius and capital have joined to meet radio needs. The great majority of station owners today recognize the burden of service and gladly assume it. Whatever other motive may exist for broadcasting, the pleasing of the listener is always the primary purpose. . . .

The greatest public interest must be the deciding factor. I presume that few still dissent as to the correctness of this principle, for all will agree that public good must ever balance private desire; but its acceptance leads to important and far-reaching practical effects, as to which there may not be the same unanimity, but from which, nevertheless, there is no logical escape.

The confines of the licensee's duty are set by the general standard "the public interest, convenience or necessity."[10] The initial and principal execution of that standard, in terms of the area he is licensed to serve, is the obligation of the licensee. The principal ingredient of such obligation consists of a diligent, positive and continuing effort by the licensee to discover and fulfill the tastes, needs and desires of his service area. If he has accomplished this, he has met his public responsibility. It is the duty of the Commission, in the first instance, to select persons as licensees who meet the qualifications laid down in the Act, and on a continuing basis to review the operations of such licensees from time to time to provide reasonable assurance to the public that the broadcast service it receives is such as its direct and justifiable interest requires.

Historically it is interesting to note that in its review of station performance the Federal Radio Commission sought to extract the general principles of broadcast service which should (1) guide the licensee in his determination of the public interest and (2) be employed by the Commission as an "index" or general frame of reference in evaluating the licensee's discharge of his public duty. The Commission attempted no precise definition of the components of the public interest but left the discern-

[9]Testimony of Frederick W. Ford, May 16, 1960 before the Subcommittee on Communications of the Committee on Interstate & Foreign Commerce, United States Senate.
[10]Cf. Communications Act of 1934, as amended, inter alia, Secs. 307, 309.

ment of its limit to the practical operation of broadcast regulation. It required existing stations to report the types of service which had been provided and called on the public to express its views and preferences as to programs and other broadcast services. It sought information from as many sources as were available in its quest of a fair and equitable basis for the selection of those who might wish to become licensees and the supervision of those who already engaged in broadcasting.

The spirit in which the Radio Commission approached its unprecedented task was to seek to chart a course between the need of arriving at a workable concept of the public interest in station operation, on the one hand, and the prohibition laid on it by the First Amendment to the Constitution of the United States and by Congress in Section 29 of the Federal Radio Act against censorship and interference with free speech, on the other. The Standards or guidelines which evolved from that process, in their essentials, were adopted by the Federal Communications Commission and have remained as the basis for evaluation of broadcast service. They have in the main, been incorporated into various codes and manuals of network and station operation.

It is emphasized, that these standards or guidelines should in no sense constitute a rigid mold for station performance, nor should they be considered as a Commission formula for broadcast service in the public interest. Rather, they should be considered as a Commission formula for broadcast service in the public interest. Rather, they should be considered as indicia of the types and areas of service which, on the basis of experience, have usually been accepted by the broadcasters as more or less included in the practical definition of community needs and interests.

Broadcasting licensees must assume responsibility for all material which is broadcast through their facilities. This includes all programs and advertising material which they present to the public. With respect to advertising material the licensee has the additional responsibility to take all reasonable measures to eliminate any false, misleading, or deceptive matter and to avoid abuses with respect to the total amount of time devoted to advertising continuity as well as the frequency with which regular programs are interrupted for advertising messages. This duty is personal to the licensee and may not be delegated. He is obligated to bring his positive responsibility affirmatively to bear upon all who have a hand in providing broadcast matter for transmission through his facilities so as to assure the discharge of his duty to provide an acceptable program schedule consonant with operating in the public interest in his community. The broadcaster is obligated to make a positive, diligent and continuing effort, in good faith, to determine the tastes, needs and desire of the public in his community and to provide programming to meet those needs and interests. This again, is a duty personal to the licensee and may not be avoided by delegation of the responsibility to others.

Although the individual station licensee continues to bear legal responsibility for all matter broadcast over his facilities, the structure of broadcasting, as developed in practical operation, is such—especially in television—that, in reality, the station licensee has little part in the creation, production, selection and control of network program offerings. Licensees place "practical reliance" on networks for the selection and supervision of network programs which, of course, are the principal broadcast fare of the vast majority of television stations throughout the country.[11]

In the fulfillment of his obligation the broadcaster should consider the tastes, needs and desires of the public he is licensed to serve in developing his programming and should exercise conscientious efforts not only to ascertain them but also to carry them out as well as he reasonably can. He should reasonably attempt to meet all such

[11]The Commission, in recognition of this problem as it affects the licensees, has recently recommended to the Congress enactment of legislation providing for direct regulation of networks in certain respects.

needs and interests on an equitable basis. Particular areas of interest and types of appropriate service may, of course, differ from community to community, and from time to time. However, the Commission does expect its broadcast licensees to take the necessary steps to inform themselves of the real needs and interests of the areas they serve, and to provide programming which in fact constitutes a diligent effort, in good faith, to provide for those needs and interests.

The major elements usually necessary to meet the public interest, needs and desires of the community in which the station is located as developed by the industry, and recognized by the Commission, have included: (1) Opportunity for Local Self-Expression, (2) The Development and Use of Local Talent, (3) Programs for Children, (4) Religious Programs, (5) Educational Programs, (6) Public Affairs Programs, (7) Editorialization by Licensees, (8) Political Broadcasts, (9) Agricultural Programs, (10) News Programs, (11) Weather and Market Reports, (12) Sports Programs, (13) Service to Minority Groups, (14) Entertainment Programming.

The elements set out above are neither all-embracing nor constant. We reemphasize that they do not serve and have never been intended as a rigid mold or fixed formula for station operation. The ascertainment of the needed elements of the broadcast matter to be provided by a particular licensee for the audience he is obligated to serve remains primarily the function of the licensee. His honest and prudent judgments will be accorded great weight by the Commission. Indeed, any other course would tend to substitute the judgment of the Commission for that of the licensee.

The programs provided first by "chains" of stations and then by networks have always been recognized by this Commission as of great value to the station licensee in providing a well-rounded community service. The importance of network programs need not be re-emphasized as they have constituted an integral part of the well-rounded program service provided by the broadcast business in most communities.

Our own observations and the testimony in this inquiry have persuaded us that there is no public interest basis for distinguishing between sustaining and commercially sponsored programs in evaluating station performance. However, this does not relieve the station from responsibility for retaining the flexibility to accommodate public needs.

Sponsorship of public affairs, and other similar programs may very well encourage broadcasters to greater efforts in these vital areas. This is borne out by statements made in this proceeding in which it was pointed out that under modern conditions sponsorship fosters rather than diminishes the availability of important public affairs and "cultural" broadcast programming. There is some convincing evidence, for instance, that at the network level there is a direct relation between commercial sponsorship and "clearance" of public affairs and other "cultural" programs. Agency executives have testified that there is unused advertising support for public affairs type programming. The networks and some stations have scheduled these types of programs during "prime time."

The Communications Act[12] provides that the Commission may grant construction permits and station licenses, or modifications or renewals thereof, "only upon written application" setting forth the information required by the Act and the Commission's Rules and Regulations. If, upon examination of any such application, the Commission shall find the public interest, convenience and necessity would be served by the granting thereof, it shall grant said application. If it does not so find, it shall so advise the applicant and other known parties in interest of all objections to the application and the applicant shall then be given an opportunity to supply

[12]Section 308(a).

514

additional information. If the Commission cannot then make the necessary finding, the application is designated for hearing and the applicant bears the burden of providing proof of the public interest.

During our hearings there seemed to be some misunderstanding as to the nature and use of the "statistical" data regarding programming and advertising required by our application forms. We wish to stress that no one may be summarily judged as to the service he has performed on the basis of the information contained in his application. As we said long ago:

It should be emphasized that the statistical data before the Commission constitute an index only of the manner of operation of the stations and are not considered by the Commission as conclusive of the over-all operation of the stations in question.

Licensees will have an opportunity to show the nature of their program service and to introduce other relevant evidence which would demonstrate that in actual operation the program service of the station is, in fact, a well rounded program service and is in conformity with the promises and representations previously made in prior applications to the Commission.[13]

As we have said above, the principal ingredient of the licensee's obligation to operate his station in the public interest is the diligent, positive and continuing effort by the licensee to discover and fulfill the tastes, needs and desires of his community or service area, for broadcast service.

To enable the Commission in its licensing functions to make the necessary public interest finding, we intend to revise Part IV of our application forms to require a statement by the applicant, whether for new facilities, renewal or modification, as to: (1) the measures he has taken and the effort he has made to determine the tastes, needs and desires of his community or service area, and (2) the manner in which he proposes to meet those needs and desires.

Thus we do not intend to guide the licensee along the path of programming; on the contrary the licensee must find his own path with the guidance of those whom his signal is to serve. We will thus steer clear of the bans of censorship without disregarding the public's vital interest. What we propose will not be served by pre-planned program format submissions accompanied by complimentary references from local citizens. What we propose is documented program submissions prepared as the result of assiduous planning and consultation covering two main areas: first, a canvass of the listening public who will receive the signal and who constitute a definite public interest figure; second, consultation with leaders in community life—public officials, educators, religious, the entertainment media, agriculture, business, labor—professional and eleemosynary organizations, and others who bespeak the interests which make up the community.

By the care spent in obtaining and reflecting the views thus obtained, which clearly cannot be accepted without attention to the business judgment of the licensee if his station is to be an operating success, will the standard of programming in the public interest be best fulfilled. This would not ordinarily be the case if program formats have been decided upon by the licensee before he undertakes his planning and consultation, for the result would show little stimulation on the part of the two local groups above referenced. And it is the composite of their contributive planning, led and sifted by the expert judgment of the licensee, which will assure to the station the appropriate attention to the public interest which will permit the Commission to find that a license may issue. By his narrative development, in his application, of the planning, consulting, shaping, revising, creating, discarding and evaluation of programming thus conceived or discussed, the licensee discharges the public interest

[13]Public Notice (98501), September 20, 1946, "Status of Standard Broadcast Applications."

facet of his business calling without Government dictation or supervision and permits the Commission to discharge its responsibility to the public without invasion of spheres of freedom properly denied to it. By the practicality and specificity of his narrative the licensee facilitates the application of expert judgment by the Commission. Thus, if a particular kind of educational program could not be feasibly assisted (by funds or service) by educators for more than a few time periods, it would be idle for program composition to place it in weekly focus. Private ingenuity and educational interest should look further, toward implemental suggestions of practical yet constructive value. The broadcaster's license is not intended to convert his business into "an instrumentality of the federal government",[14] neither, on the other hand, may he ignore the public interest which his application for a license should thus define and his operations thereafter reasonably observe.

Numbers of suggestions were made during the en banc hearings concerning possible uses by the Commission of codes of broadcast practices adopted by segments of the industry as part of a process of self-regulation. While the Commission has not endorsed any specific code of broadcast practices, we consider the efforts of the industry to maintain high standards of conduct to be highly commendable and urge that the industry persevere in these efforts.

The Commission recognizes that submissions, by applicants, concerning their past and future programming policies and performance provide one important basis for deciding whether—in so far as broadcast services are concerned—we may properly make the public interest finding requisite to the grant of an application for a standard, FM or television broadcast station. The particular manner in which applicants are required to depict their proposed or past broadcast policies and services (including the broadcasting of commercial announcements) may therefore, have significant bearing upon the Commission's ability to discharge its statutory duties in the matter. Conscious of the importance of reporting requirements, the Commission on November 24, 1958 initiated proceedings (Docket No. 12673) to consider revisions to the rules prescribing the form and content of reports on broadcast programming.

Aided by numerous helpful suggestions offered by witnesses in the recent en banc hearings on broadcast programming, the Commission is at present engaged in a thorough study of this subject. Upon completion of that study we will announce, for comment by all interested parties, such further revisions to the present reporting requirements as we think will best conduce to an awareness, by broadcasters, of their responsibilities to the public and to effective, efficient processing, by the Commission, of applications for broadcast licenses and renewals.

To this end, we will initiate further rule making on the subject at the earliest practicable date.

Adopted: July 27, 1960.

SEPARATE STATEMENT OF COMMISSIONER HYDE

I believe that the Commission's "Interim Report and Statement of Policy" in Docket No. 12782 misses the central point of the hearing conducted by the Commission en banc, December 7, 1959, to February 1, 1960.

It reiterates the legal position which was taken by the Federal Radio Commission in 1927, and which has been adhered to by the Federal Communications Commission since it was organized in 1934. This viewpoint was accepted by the executives of the leading networks and by most other units of the broadcasting industry as well as the National Association of Broadcasters. The main concern requiring a fresh

---

[14]The defendant is not an instrumentality of the federal government but a privately owned corporation. McIntire v. Wm. Penn Broadcasting Co., 151 F. (2d) 597, 600.

approach is what to do in the light of the law and the matters presented by many witnesses in the hearings. This, I understand, is to be the subject of a rule-making proceeding still to be initiated. I urged the preparation of an appropriate rule-making notice prior to the preparation of the instant statement.

I also disagree with the decision of the Commission to release the document captioned "Interim Report by the Office of Network Study, Responsibility for Broadcast Matter, Docket No. 12782." Since it deals in part with a hearing in which the Commission itself sat en banc, I feel that it does not have the character of a separate staff-study type of document, and that its release with the Commission policy statement will create confusion. Moreover, a substantial portion of the document is concerned with matter still under investigation process in Docket 12782. I think issuance of comment on these matters under the circumstances is premature and inappropriate.

The Fairness Doctrine and Personal Attack Regulations Sustained by the U. S. Supreme Court

For many years the FCC has been committed to a policy of requiring broadcast stations to present both sides of important public issues. In 1967, the Commission promulgated regulations requiring stations to afford opportunity for reply to persons or groups whose character or integrity has been attacked in a broadcast involving controversial discussion. The Red Lion Company, licensee of radio station WGCB, challenged the constitutional and statutory validity of this policy. Similarly, the Radio and Television News Directors Association objected to the regulations relating to personal attacks. The Red Lion company appealed to the U. S. Court of Appeals for the District of Columbia. RTNDA appealed to the U. S. Court of Appeals for the Seventh Circuit.

The D. C. court upheld the Commission's decision in the Red Lion case. On the other hand, the Seventh Circuit court sustained the objections of RTND. Red Lion and the FCC, both losers in the lower courts, asked for Supreme Court review.

The petitions were granted, and on June 9, 1969, the high court handed down a decision affirming both the Commission's policy and its personal attack regulations and laying to rest, once and for all, any question as to their constitutionality or legality. Some important parts of the landmark decision follows. In the interest of brevity, most of the footnotes and citations therein have been omitted. Students are urged to read the full text of the opinion which appears in 395 U. S. 367.

SUPREME COURT OF THE UNITED STATES

Nos. 2 AND 717.—OCTOBER TERM, 1968.

Red Lion Broadcasting Co., Inc., etc., et al., Petitioners,		On Writ of Certiorari to the United
2	*v.*	States Court of Appeals for the
Federal Communications Commission et al.		District of Columbia Circuit.

United States et al., Petitioners,		On Writ of Certiorari to the United
717	*v.*	States Court of Appeals for the
Radio Television News Directors Association, et al.		Seventh Circuit.

[June 9, 1969.]

MR. JUSTICE WHITE delivered the opinion of the Court.

The Federal Communications Commission has for many years imposed on radio and television broadcasters the requirement that discussion of public issues be presented on broadcast stations, and that each side of those issues must be given fair coverage. This is known as the fairness doctrine, which originated very early in the history of broadcasting and has maintained its present outlines for some time. It is an obligation whose content has been defined in a long series of FCC rulings in particular cases, and which is distinct from the statutory requirement of § 315 of the Communications Act[1] that equal time be allotted all qualified candidates for public office. Two aspects of the fairness doctrine, relating to personal attacks in the context of controversial public issues and to political editorializing, were codified more precisely in the form of FCC regulations in 1967. The two cases before us now, which were decided separately below, challenge the constitutional and statutory bases of the doctrine and component rules. *Red Lion* involves the application of the fairness doctrine to a particular broadcast, and *RTNDA* arises as an action to review the FCC's 1967 promulgation of the personal attack and political editorializing regulations, which were laid down after the *Red Lion* litigation had begun.

I.
A.

The Red Lion Broadcasting Company is licensed to operate a Pennsylvania radio station, WGCB. On November 27, 1964, WGCB carried a 15-minute broadcast by Reverend Billy James Hargis as part of a "Christian Crusade" series. A book by Fred J. Cook entitled "Goldwater—Extremist on the Right" was discussed by Hargis, who said that Cook had been fired by a newspaper for fabricating false charges against city officials; that Cook had then worked for a Communist-affiliated publication; that he had defended Alger Hiss and attacked J. Edgar Hoover and the Central Intelligence Agency; and that he had now written a "book to smear and destroy Barry Goldwater."[2] When Cook heard of the broadcast he concluded that he had been personally attacked and demanded free reply time, which the station refused. After an exchange of letters among Cook, Red Lion, and the FCC, the FCC declared that the Hargis broadcast constituted a personal attack on Cook; that Red Lion had failed to meet its obligation under the fairness doctrine as expressed in *Times-Mirror Broadcasting Co.*, 24 P & F Radio Reg. 404 (1962), to send a tape, transcript, or summary of the broadcast to Cook and offer him reply time; and that the station must provide reply time whether or not Cook would pay for it. On review in the Court of Appeals for the District of Columbia,[3] the FCC's position was upheld as constitutional and otherwise proper. 381 F. 2d 908 (1967).

B.

Not long after the *Red Lion* litigation was begun, the FCC issued a Notice of Proposed Rule Making, 31 Fed. Reg. 5710, with an eye to making the personal attack aspect of the fairness doctrine more precise and more readily enforceable, and also to specify its rules relating to political editorials. After considering written comments supporting and opposing the rules, the FCC adopted them substantially as proposed, 32 Fed. Reg. 10303. Twice amended, 32 Fed. Reg. 11531, 33 Fed. Reg. 5362, the rules were held unconstitutional in the *RTNDA* litigation by the Court of Appeals for the Seventh Circuit on review of the rule-making proceeding as abridging the freedoms of speech and press. 400 F. 2d 1002 (1968). (The Court then cited the FCC Rules which are stated on pp. 000 and need not be repeated here.)

C.

Believing that the specific application of the fairness doctrine in *Red Lion*, and the promulgation of the regulations in *RTNDA*, are both authorized by Congress and enhance rather than abridge the freedoms of speech and press protected by the First Amendment, we hold them valid and constitutional, reversing the judgment below in *RTNDA* and affirming the judgment below in *Red Lion*.

II.

The history of the emergence of the fairness doctrine and of the related legislation shows that the Commission's action in the *Red Lion* case did not exceed its authority, and that in adopting the new regulations the Commission was implementing congressional policy rather than embarking on a frolic of its own.

A.

Before 1927, the allocation of frequencies was left entirely to the private sector, and the result was chaos.[4] It quickly became apparent that broadcast frequencies constituted a scarce resource whose use could be regulated and rationalized only by the Government. Without government control, the medium would be of little use because of the cacaphony of competing voices, none of which could be clearly and predictably heard.[5] Consequently, the Federal Radio Commission was established to allocate frequencies among competing applicants in a manner responsive to the public "convenience, interest, or necessity."[6]

Very shortly thereafter the Commission expressed its view that the "public interest requires ample play for the free and fair competition of opposing views, and the Commission believes that the principle applies . . . to all discussions of issues of importance to the public." *Great Lakes Broadcasting Co.*, 3 F. R. C. Ann. Rep. 32, 33 (1929), rev'd on other grounds, 37 F. 2d 993, cert. dismissed, 281 U. S. 706 (1930). This doctrine was applied through denial of license renewals or construction permits, both by the FRC, *Trinity Methodist Church, South v. FRC*, 62 F. 2d 850

(C. A. D. C. Cir. 1932), cert. denied, 288 U. S. 599 (1933), and its successor FCC, *Young People's Association for the Propagation of the Gospel,* 6 F. C. C. 178 (1938). After an extended period during which the licensee was obliged not only to cover and to cover fairly the views of others, but also to refrain from expressing his own personal views, *Mayflower Broadcasting Corp.,* 8 F. C. C. 333 (1941), the latter limitation on the licensee was abandoned and the doctrine developed into its present form.

There is a twofold duty laid down by the FCC's decisions and described by the 1949 Report on Editorializing by Broadcast Licensees, 13 F. C. C. 1246 (1949). The broadcaster must give adequate coverage to public issues, *United Broadcasting Co.,* 10 F. C. C. 515 (1945), and coverage must be fair in that it accurately reflects the opposing views. *New Broadcasting Co.,* 6 P & F Radio Reg. 258 (1950). This must be done at the broadcaster's own expense if sponsorship is unavailable. *Cullman Broadcasting Co.,* 25 P & F Radio Reg. 895 (1963). Moreover, the duty must be met by programming obtained at the licensee's own initiative if available from no other source. *John J. Dempsey,* 6 P & F Radio Reg. 615 (1950); see *Metropolitan Broadcasting Corp.,* 19 P & F Radio Reg. 602 (1959); *The Evening News Assn.,* 6 P & F Radio Reg. 283 (1950). The Federal Radio Commission had imposed these two basic duties on broadcasters since the outset, *Great Lakes Broadcasting Co.,* 3 F. R. C. Ann. Rep. 32 (1929), rev'd on other grounds, 37 F. 2d 993, cert. denied, 281 U. S. 706 (1930); *Chicago Federation of Labor v. FRC,* 3 F. R. C. Ann. Rep. 36 (1929), aff'd 41 F. 2d 422 (C. A. D. C. Cir. 1930); *KFKB Broadcasting Assn. v. FRC,* 47 F. 2d 670 (C. A. D. C. Cir. 1931), and in particular respects the personal attack rules and regulations at issue here have spelled them out in greater detail.

When a personal attack has been made on a figure involved in a public issue, both the doctrine of cases such as *Red Lion* and *Times-Mirror Broadcasting Co.,* 24 P & F Radio Reg. 404 (1962), and also the 1967 regulations at issue in *RTNDA* require that the individual attacked himself be offered an opportunity to respond. Likewise, where one candidate is endorsed in a political editorial, the other candidates must themselves be offered reply time to use personally or through a spokesman. These obligations differ from the general fairness requirement that issues be presented, and presented with coverage of competing views, in that the broadcaster does not have the option of presenting the attacked party's side himself or choosing a third party to represent that side. But insofar as there is an obligation of the broadcaster to see that both sides are presented, and insofar as that is an affirmative obligation, the personal attack doctrine and regulations do not differ from preceding fairness doctrine. The simple fact that the attacked men or unendorsed candidates may respond themselves or through agents is not a critical distinction, and indeed, it is not unreasonable for the FCC to conclude that the objective of adequate presentation of all sides may best be served by allowing those most closely affected to make the response, rather than leaving the response in the hands of the station which has attacked their candidacies, endorsed their opponents, or carried a personal attack upon them.

B.

The statutory authority of the FCC to promulgate these regulations derives from the mandate to the "Commission from time to time, as public convenience, interest, or necessity requires" to promulgate "such rules and regulations and prescribe such restrictions and conditions . . . as may be necessary to carry out the provisions of this chapter. . . ." 47 U. S. C. § 303 and § 303 (r).[7] The Commission is specifically directed to consider the demands of the public interest in the course of granting licenses, 47 U. S. C. §§ 307 (a), 309 (a); renewing them, 47 U. S. C. § 307; and modifying them. *Ibid.* Moreover, the FCC has included among the conditions of the Red Lion license itself the requirement that operation of the station be carried out in the public interest, 47 U. S. C. § 309 (h). This mandate to the FCC to assure that broadcasters operate in the public interest is a broad one, a power "not niggardly but expansive," *National Broadcasting Co. v. United States,* 319 U. S. 190, 219 (1943), whose validity we have long upheld. *FCC v. Pottsville Broadcasting Co.,* 309 U. S. 134, 138 (1940); *FCC v. RCA Communications, Inc.,* 346 U. S. 86, 90 (1953); *FRC v. Nelson Bros. Bond & Mortgage Co.,* 289 U. S. 266, 285 (1933). It is broad enough to encompass these regulations.

The fairness doctrine finds specific recognition in statutory form, is in part modeled on explicit statutory provisions relating to political candidates, and is approvingly reflected in legislative history.

In 1959 the Congress amended the statutory requirement of § 315 that equal time be accorded each political candidate to except certain appearances on news programs, but added that this constituted no exception *"from the obligation imposed upon them under this Act to operate in the public interest and to afford reasonable opportunity for the discussion of conflicting views on issues of public importance."* Act of September 14, 1959, § 1, 73 Stat. 557, amending 47 U. S. C. § 315 (a) (emphasis added). This language makes it very plain that Congress, in 1959, announced that the phrase "public interest," which had been in the Act since 1927, imposed a duty on broadcasters to discuss both sides of controversial public issues. In other words, the amendment vindicated the FCC's general view that the fairness doctrine inhered in the public interest standard. Subsequent legislation enacted into law and declaring the intent of an earlier statute is entitled to great weight in statutory construction.[8] And here this principle is given special force by the equally venerable principle that the construction of a statute by those charged with its execution should be followed unless there are compelling indications that it is wrong,[9] especially when Congress has refused to alter the administrative construction.[10] Here, the Congress has not just kept its silence by refusing to overturn the administrative construction,[11] but has ratified it with positive legislation. Thirty years of consistent administrative construction left undisturbed by Congress until 1959, when that construction was expressly accepted, reinforce the natural conclusion that the public interest language of the Act authorized the Commission to require licensees to use their stations for discussion of public issues, and that the FCC is free to implement this requirement by reasonable rules and regulations which fall short of abridgment of the freedom of speech and press, and of the censorship proscribed by § 326 of the Act.[12]

The objectives of § 315 themselves could readily be circumvented but for the complementary fairness doctrine ratified by § 315. The section applies to campaign appearances by candidates, and not by family, friends, campaign managers, or other supporters. Without the fairness doctrine, then, a licensee could ban all campaign appearances by candidates themselves from the air[13] and proceed to deliver over his station entirely to the supporters of one slate of candidates, to the exclusion of all others. In this way the broadcaster could have a far greater impact on the favored candidacy than he could by simply allowing a spot appearance by the candidate himself. It is the fairness doctrine as an aspect of the obligation to operate in the public interest, rather than § 315, which prohibits the broadcaster from taking such a step.

The legislative history reinforces this view of the effect of the 1959 amendment. Even before the language relevant here was added, the Senate report on amending § 315 noted that "broadcast frequencies are limited and, therefore, they have been necessarily considered a public trust. Every licensee who is fortunate in obtaining a license is mandated to operate in the public interest and has assumed the obligation of presenting important public questions fairly and without bias." S. Rep. No. 562, 86th Cong., 1st Sess., 8-9 (1959). See also, specifically adverting to Federal Communications Commission doctrine, *id.*, at 13.

. . . .

When the Congress ratified the FCC's implication of a fairness doctrine in 1959 it did not, of course, approve every past decision or pronouncement by the Commission on this subject, or give it a completely free hand for the future. The statutory authority does not go so far. But we cannot say that when a station publishes a personal attack or endorses a political candidate, it is a misconstruction of the public interest standard to require the station to offer time for a response rather than to leave the response entirely within the control of the station which has attacked either the candidacies or the men who wish to reply in their own defense. When a broadcaster grants time to a political candidate, Congress itself requires that equal time be offered to his opponents. It would exceed our competence to hold that the Commission is unauthorized by the statute to employ a similar device where personal attacks or political editorials are broadcast by a radio or television station.

In light of the fact that the "public interest" in broadcasting clearly encompasses the presentation of vigorous debate of controversial issues of importance and concern to the public; the fact that the FCC has rested upon that language from its very inception a doctrine that these issues must be discussed, and fairly; and the fact that Congress has acknowledged that the analogous provisions of § 315 are not preclusive in this area, and knowingly preserved the FCC's complementary efforts, we think the fairness doctrine and its component personal attack and political editorializing regulations are a legitimate exercise of congressionally delegated authority. The Communications Act is not notable for the precision of its substantive standards and in this respect the explicit provisions of § 315, and the doctrine and rules at issue here which are closely modeled upon that section, are far more explicit than the generalized "public interest" standard in which the Commission ordinarily finds its sole guidance, and which we have held a broad but adequate standard before. *FCC v. RCA Communications, Inc.,* 346 U. S. 86, 90 (1953); *National Broadcasting Co. v. Pottsville Broadcasting Co.,* 309 U. S. 134, 138 (1940); *FRC v. Nelson Bros, Bond & Mortgage Co.,* 289 U. S. 266, 285 (1933). We cannot say that the FCC's declaratory ruling in *Red Lion,* or the regulations at issue in *RTNDA,* are beyond the scope of the congressionally conferred power to assure that stations are operated by those whose possession of a license serves "the public interest."

III.

The broadcasters challenge the fairness doctrine and its specific manifestations in the personal attack and political editorial rules on conventional First Amendment grounds, alleging that the rules abridge their freedom of speech and press. Their contention is that the First Amendment protects their desire to use their allotted frequencies continuously to broadcast whatever they choose, and to exclude whomever they choose from ever using that frequency. No man may be prevented from saying or publishing what he thinks, or from refusing in his speech or other utterances to give equal weight to the views of his opponents. This right, they say, applies equally to broadcasters.

A.

Although broadcasting is clearly a medium affected by a First Amendment interest, *United States v. Paramount Pictures, Inc.,* 334 U. S. 131, 166 (1948), differences in the characteristics of new media justify differences in the First Amendment standards applied to them.[15] *Joseph Burstyn, Inc. v. Wilson,* 343 U. U. 495, 503 (1952). For example, the ability of new technology to produce sounds more raucous than those of the human voice justifies restrictions on the sound level, and on the hours and places of use, of sound trucks so long as the restrictions are reasonable and applied without discrimination. *Kovacs v. Cooper,* 336 U. S. 77 (1949).

Just as the Government may limit the use of sound amplifying equipment potentially so noisy that it drowns out civilized private speech, so may the Government limit the use of broadcast equipment. The right of free speech of a broadcaster, the user of a sound truck, or any other individual does not embrace a right to snuff out the free speech of others. *Associated Press v. United States,* 326 U. S. 1, 20 (1945).

When two people converse face to face, both should not speak at once if either is to be clearly understood. But the range of the human voice is so limited that there could be meaningful communications if half the people in the United States were talking and the other half listening. Just as clearly, half the people might publish and the other half read. But the reach of radio signals is imcomparably greater than the range of the human voice and the problem of interference is a massive reality. The lack of know-how and equipment may keep many from the air, but only a tiny fraction of those with resources and intelligence can hope to communicate by radio at the same time if intelligible communication is to be had, even if the entire radio spectrum is utilized in the present state of commercially acceptable technology.

It was this fact, and the chaos which ensued from permitting anyone to use any frequency at whatever power level he wished, which made necessary the enactment of the Radio Act of 1927 and the Communications Act of 1934,[16] as the Court has noted at length before. *National Broadcasting Co. v. United States,* 319 U. S. 190, 210-214 (1943). It was this reality which at the very least necessitated first the division of the radio spectrum into portions reserved respectively for public broadcasting and for other important radio uses such as amateur operation, aircraft, police, defense, and navigation; and then the subdivision of each portion, and assignment of specific frequencies to individual users or groups of users. Beyond this, however, because the frequencies reserved for public broadcasting were limited in number, it was essential for the Government to tell some applicants that they could not broadcast at all because there was room for only a few.

Where there are substantially more individuals who want to broadcast than there are frequencies to allocate, it is idle to posit an unabridgeable First Amendment right to broadcast comparable to the right of every individual to speak, write, or publish. If 100 persons want broadcast licenses but there are only 10 frequencies to allocate, all of them may have the same "right" to a license; but if there is to be any effective

[15]The general problems raised by a technology which supplants atomized, relatively informal communication with mass media as a prime source of national cohesion and news were discussed at considerable length by Zechariah Chafee in Government and Mass Communications (1947). Debate on the particular implications of this view for the broadcasting industry has continued unabated. A compendium of views appears in Freedom and Responsibility in Broadcasting (Coons ed.) (1961). See also Kalven, Broadcasting, Public Policy, and the First Amendment, 10 J. of Law and Econ. 15 (1967); Ernst, The First Freedom 125-180 (1946); Robinson, Radio Networks and the Federal Government, especially at 75-87 (1943). The considerations which the newest technology brings to bear on the particular problem of this litigation are concisely explored by Louis Jaffe in The Fairness Doctrine, Equal Time, Reply to Personal Attacks, and the Local Service Obligation; Implications of Technological Change (U.S. Government Printing Office 1968).

[16]The range of controls which have in fact been imposed over the last 40 years, without giving rise to successful constitutional challenge in this Court, is discussed in Emery, Broadcasting and Government: Responsibilities and Regulations (1961); Note, Regulation of Program Content by the FCC, 77 Harv. L. Rev. 701 (1964).

communication by radio, only a few can be licensed and the rest must be barred from the airways. It would be strange if the First Amendment, aimed at protecting and furthering communications, prevented the Government from making radio communication possible by requiring licenses to broadcast and by limiting the number of licenses so as not to overcrowd the spectrum.

This has been the consistent view of the Court. Congress unquestionably has the power to grant and deny licenses and to delete existing stations. *Federal Radio Commission v. Nelson Bros. Bond & Mortgage Co.*, 289 U. S. 266 (1933). No one has a First Amendment right to a license or to monopolize a radio frequency; to deny a station license because "the public interest" requires it "is not a denial of free speech." *National Broadcasting Co. v. U. S.*, 319 U. S. 190, 227 (1943).

By the same token, as far as the First Amendment is concerned those who are licensed stand no better than those to whom licenses are refused. A license permits broadcasting, but the licensee has no constitutional right to be the one who holds the license or to monopolize a radio frequency to the exclusion of his fellow citizens. There is nothing in the First Amendment which prevents the Government from requiring a licensee to share his frequency with others and to conduct himself as a proxy or fiduciary with obligations to present those views and voices which are representative of his community and which would otherwise, by necessity, be barred from the airwaves.

This not to say that the First Amendment is irrelevant to public broadcasting. On the contrary, it has a major role to play as the Congress itself recognized in § 326, which forbids FCC interference with "the right of free speech by means of radio communications." Because of the scarcity of radio frequencies, the Government is permitted to put restraints on licensees in favor of others whose views should be expressed on this unique medium. But the people as a whole retain their interest in free speech by radio and their collective right to have the medium function consistently with the ends and purposes of the First Amendment. It is the right of the viewers and listeners, not the right of the broadcasters, which is paramount. See *FCC v. Sanders Bros. Radio Station*, 309 U. S. 470, 475 (1940); *FCC v. Allentown Broadcasting Corp.*, 349 U. S. 358, 361-362 (1955); Z. Chafee, Government and Mass Communications 546 (1947). It is the purpose of the First Amendment to preserve an uninhibited marketplace of ideas in which truth will ultimately prevail, rather than to countenance monopolization of that market, whether it be by the Government itself or a private licensee. *Associated Press v. United States*, 326 U. S. 1, 20 (1945); *New York Times Co. v. Sullivan*, 376 U. S. 254, 270 (1964); *Abrams v. United States*, 250 U. S. 616, 630 (1919) (Holmes, J., dissenting). "[S]peech concerning public affairs is more than self-expression; it is the essence of self-government." *Garrison v. Louisiana*, 379 U. S. 64, 74-75 (1964). See Brennan, The Supreme Court and the Meiklejohn Interpretation of the First Amendment, 79 Harv. L. Rev. 1 (1965). It is the right of the public to receive suitable access to social, political, esthetic, moral, and other ideas and experiences which is crucial here. That right may not constitutionally be abridged either by Congress or by the FCC.

B.

Rather than confer frequency monopolies on a relatively small number of licensees, in a Nation of 200,000,000, the Government could surely have decreed that each frequency should be shared among all or some of those who wish to use it, each being assigned a portion of the broadcast day or the broadcast week. The ruling and regulations at issue here do not go quite so far. They assert that under specified circumstances, a licensee must offer to make available a reasonable amount of broadcast time to those who have a view different from that which has already been expressed on his station. The expression of a political endorsement, or of a personal attack while dealing with a controversial public issue, simply triggers this time-sharing. As we have said, the First Amendment confers no right on licensees to prevent others from broadcasting on "their" frequencies and no right to an unconditional monopoly of a scarce resource which the Government has denied others the right to use.

In terms of constitutional principle, and as enforced sharing of a scarce resource, the personal attack and political editorial rules are indistinguishable from the equal-time provision of § 315, a specific enactment of Congress requiring stations to set aside reply time under specified circumstances and to which the fairness doctrine and these constituent regulations are important complements. That provision, which has been part of the law since 1927, Radio Act of 1927, c. 169, § 18, 44 Stat. 1162, 1170, has been held valid by this Court as an obligation of the licensee relieving him of any power in any way to prevent or censor the broadcast, and thus insulating him from liability for defamation. The constitutionality of the statute under the First Amendment was unquestioned.[17] *Farmers Educ. & Coop. Union v. WDAY,* 360 U. S. 525 (1959).

Nor can we say that it is inconsistent with the First Amendment goal of producing an informed public capable of conducting its own affairs to require a broadcaster to permit answers to personal attacks occurring in the course of discussing controversial issues, or to require that the political opponents of those endorsed by the station be given a chance to communicate with the public. Otherwise, station owners and a few networks would have unfettered power to make time available only to the highest bidders, to communicate only their own views on public issues, people and candidates, and to permit on the air only those with whom they agreed. There is no sanctuary in the First Amendment for unlimited private censorship operating in a medium not open to all. "Freedom of the press from governmental interference under the First Amendment does not sanction repression of that freedom by private interests." *Associated Press v. U. S.,* 326 U. S. 1, 20 (1944).

C.

It is strenuously argued, however, that if political editorials or personal attacks will trigger an obligation in broadcasters to afford the opportunity for expression to speakers who need not pay for time and whose views are unpalatable to the licensees, then broadcasters will be irresistibly forced to self-censorship and their coverage of controversial public issues will be eliminated or at least rendered wholly ineffective. Such a result would indeed be a serious matter, for should licensees actually eliminate their coverage of controversial issues, the purposes of the doctrine would be stifled.

At this point, however, as the Federal Communications Commission has indicated, that possibility is at best speculative. The communications industry, and in particular the networks, have taken pains to present controversial issues in the past, and even now they do not assert that they intend to abandon their efforts in this regard.[18] It would be better if the FCC's encouragement were never necessary to

[17]This has not prevented vigorous argument from developing on the constitutionality of the ancillary FCC doctrines. Compare Barrow, The Equal Opportunities and Fairness Doctrine in Broadcasting: Pillars in the Forum of Democracy, 37 U. Cin. L. Rev. 447 (1968), with Robinson, The FCC and the First Amendment: Observations on 40 Years of Radio and Television Regulation, 52 Minn. L. Rev. 67 (1967), and Sullivan, Editorials and Controversy: The Broadcaster's Dilemma, 32 Geo. Wash. L. Rev. 719 (1964).

[18]The President of the Columbia Broadcasting System has recently declared that despite the Government, "we are determined to continue covering controversial issues as a public service, and exercising our own independent news judgment and enterprise. I, for one, refuse to allow that judgment and enterprise to be affected by official intimidation." Stanton, Keynote Ad-

induce the broadcasters to meet their responsibility. And if experience with the administration of these doctrines indicates that they have the net effect of reducing rather than enhancing the volume and quality of coverage, there will be time enough to reconsider the constitutional implications. The fairness doctrine in the past has had no such overall effect.

That this will occur now seems unlikely, however, since if present licensees should suddenly prove timorous, the Commission is not powerless to insist that they give adequate and fair attention to public issues. It does not violate the First Amendment to treat licenses given the privilege of using scarce radio frequencies as proxies for the entire community, obligated to give suitable time and attention to matters of great public concern. To condition the granting or renewal of licenses on a willingness to present representative community views on controversial issues is consistent with the ends and purposes of those constitutional provisions forbidding the abridgment of freedom of speech and freedom of the press. Congress need not stand idly by and permit those with licenses to ignore the problems which beset the people or to exclude from the airways anything but their own views of fundamental questions. The statute, long administrative practice and cases are to this effect.

Licenses to broadcast do not confer ownership of designated frequencies, but only the temporary privilege of using them. 47 U. S. C. § 301. Unless renewed, they expire within three years. 47 U. S. C. § 307 (d). The statute mandates the issuance of licenses if the "public convenience, interest or necessity will be served thereby." 47 U. S. C. § 307(a). In applying this standard the Commission for 40 years has been choosing licensees based in part on their program proposals. In *F. R. C. v. Nelson Bros. Bond and Mortgage Co.*, 289 U. S. 266, 279 (1933), the Court noted that in "view of the limited number of available broadcasting frequencies, the Congress has authorized allocation and licenses." In determining how best to allocate frequencies, the Federal Radio Commission considered the needs of competing communities and the programs offered by competing stations to meet those needs; moreover, if needs or programs shifted, the Commission could alter its allocations to reflect those shifts. *Id.*, at 285. In the same vein, in *F. C. C. v. Pottsville Broadcasting Co.*, 309 U. S. 134, 137-138 (1940), the Court noted that the statutory standard was a supple instrument to effect congressional desires "to maintain . . . a grip on the dynamic aspects of radio transmission" and to allay fears that "in the absence of governmental control the public interest might be subordinated to monopolistic domination in the broadcasting field." Three years later the Court considered the validity of the Commission's chain broadcasting regulations, which among other things forbade stations from devoting too much time to network programs in order that there be suitable opportunity for local programs serving local needs. The Court upheld the regulations, unequivocally recognizing that the Commission was more than a traffic policeman concerned with the technical aspects of broadcasting and that it neither exceeded its powers under the statute nor transgressed the First Amendment in interesting itself in general program format and the kinds of programs broadcast by licensees. *National Broadcasting Co. v. United States*, 319 U. S. 190 (1943).

D.

The litigants embellish their first amendment arguments with the contention that the regulations are so vague that their duties are impossible to discern. Of this point it is enough to say that, judging the validity of the regulations on their face as they are presented here, we cannot conclude that the FCC has been left a free hand to

---

dress, Sigma Delta Chi National Convention, Atlanta, Georgia, November 21, 1968. Problems of news coverage from the broadcaster's viewpoint are surveyed in Wood, Electronic Journalism (1967).

vindicate its own idiosyncratic conception of the public interest or of the requirements of free speech. Past adjudications by the FCC give added precision to the regulations; there was nothing vague about the FCC's specific ruling in *Red Lion* that Fred Cook should be provided an opportunity to reply. The regulations at issue in *RTNDA* could be employed in precisely the same way as the fairness doctrine was in *Red Lion.* Moreover, the FCC itself has recognized that the applicability of its regulations to situations beyond the scope of past cases may be questionable, 32 Fed. Reg. 10303, 10304 and n. 6, and will not impose sanctions in such cases without warning. We need not approve every aspect of the fairness doctrine to decide these cases, and we will not now pass upon the constitutionality of these regulations by envisioning the most extreme applications conceivable, *United States v. Sullivan,* 332 U. S. 689, 694 (1948), but will deal with those problems if and when they arise.

We need not and do not now ratify every past and future decision by the FCC with regard to programming. There is no question here of the Commission's refusal to permit the broadcaster to carry a particular program or to publish his own views; of a discriminatory refusal to require the licensee to broadcast certain views which have been denied access to the airways; of government censorship of a particular program contrary to § 326; or of the official government view dominating public broadcasting. Such questions would raise more serious first amendment issues. But we do hold that the Congress and the Commission do not violate the First Amendment when they require a radio or television station to give reply time to answer personal attacks and political editorials.

E.

It is argued that even if at one time the lack of available frequencies for all who wished to use them justified the Government's choice of those who would best serve the public interest by acting as proxy for those who would present differing views, or by giving the latter access directly to broadcast facilities, this condition no longer prevails so that continuing control is not justified. To this there are several answers.

Scarcity is not entirely a thing of the past. Advances in technology, such as microwave transmission, have led to more efficient utilization of the frequency spectrum, but uses for that spectrum have also grown apace. Portions of the spectrum must be reserved for vital uses unconnected with human communication, such as radionavigational aids used by aircraft and vessels. Conflicts have even emerged between such vital functions as defense preparedness and experimentation in methods of averting midair collisions through radio warning devices. "Land mobile services" such as police, ambulance, fire department, public utility, and other communications systems have been occupying an increasingly crowded portion of the frequency spectrum and there are, apart from licensed amateur radio operators' equipment, 5,000,000 transmitters operated on the "citizens' band" which is also increasingly congested. Among the various uses for radio frequency space, including marine, aviation, amateur, military, and common carrier users, there are easily enough claimants to permit use of the whole with an even smaller allocation to broadcast radio and television uses than now exists.

Comparative hearings between competing applicants for broadcast spectrum space are by no means a thing of the past. The radio spectrum has become so congested that at times it has been necessary to suspend new applications. The very high frequency television spectrum is, in the country's major markets, almost entirely occupied, although space reserved for ultra high frequency television transmission, which is a relatively recent development as a commercially viable alternative, has not yet been completely filled.

The rapidity with which technological advances succeed one another to create more efficient use of spectrum space on the one hand, and to create new uses for that space by ever growing numbers of people on the other, make it unwise to speculate on the future allocation of that space. It is enough to say that the resource is one of considerable and growing importance whose scarcity impelled its regulation by an agency authorized by Congress. Nothing in this record, or in our own researches, convinces us that the resource is no longer one for which there are more immediate and potential uses than can be accommodated, and for which wise planning is essential. This does not mean, of course, that every possible wavelength must be occupied at every hour by some vital use in order to sustain the congressional judgment. The substantial capital investment required for many uses, in addition to the potentiality for confusion and interference inherent in any scheme for continuous kaleidoscopic reallocation of all available space may make this unfeasible. The allocation need not be made at such a breakneck pace that the objectives of the allocation are themselves imperiled.

Even where there are gaps in spectrum utilization, the fact remains that existing broadcasters have often attained their present position because of their initial government selection in competition with others before new technological advances opened new opportunities for further uses. Long experience in broadcasting, confirmed habits of listeners and viewers, network affiliation, and other advantages in program procurement give existing broadcasters a substantial advantage over new entrants, even where new entry is technologically possible. These advantages are the fruit of a preferred position conferred by the Government. Some present possibility for new entry by competing stations is not enough, in itself, to render unconstitutional the Government's effort to assure that a broadcaster's programming ranges widely enough to serve the public interest.

In view of the prevalence of scarcity of broadcast frequencies, the Government's role in allocating those frequencies, and the legitimate claims of those unable without governmental assistance to gain access to those frequencies for expression of their views, we hold the regulations and ruling at issue here are both authorized by statute and constitutional. The judgment of the Court of Appeals in *Red Lion* is affirmed and that in *RTNDA* reversed and the causes remanded for proceedings consistent with this opinion.

It is so ordered.

Not having heard oral argument in these cases, MR. JUSTICE DOUGLAS took no part in the Court's decision.*

*See FCC General Counsel's *Memorandum* regarding the Red Lion decision above. It is an excellent interpretation of the decision which sets "at rest the long-continuing controversy as to the Commission's authority to interest itself in general program format and the kinds of programs broadcast by licensees" (20 RR 2d 81, September 2, 1969, released October 9, 1970, 20 RR 2d 377).

APPENDIX VI

On February 18, 1971, the Commission adopted a primer to clarify and provide guidelines as to the requirements and policies with respect to ascertainment of community problems by broadcast applicants.

FEDERAL COMMUNICATIONS COMMISSION
PRIMER

ON

PART I

SECTION IV-A AND IV-B OF APPLICATIONS FORMS

CONCERNING

ASCERTAINMENT OF COMMUNITY PROBLEMS

AND

BROADCAST MATTER TO DEAL WITH THOSE PROBLEMS

A. General

1. QUESTION: With what applications does this Primer apply in answering Part I, Section IV (A or B) of the application forms?
ANSWER: With applications for:
a. construction permit for new broadcast stations;
b. construction permit for a change in authorized facilities when the station's proposed field intensity contour (Grade B for television, 1 mV/m for FM, or 0.5 mV/m for AM) encompasses a new area that is equal to or greater than 50% of the area within the authorized field intensity contours.
c. construction permit or modification of license to change station location;
d. construction permit for satellite television station, including a 100% satellite;
e. the assignee's or transferee's portion of applications for assign-

ment of broadcast license or transfer of control, except in *pro forma* cases where Form 316 is appropriate.

Educational organizations filing applications for educational noncommercial stations are exempt from the provisions of this Primer.

2.   QUESTION: If Section IV (A or B) has been recently submitted, must an applicant conduct a new ascertainment of community problems and submit a new Section IV?

ANSWER: Needless duplication of effort will not be required. Prior filings within the year previous to the tender of the present application will generally be acceptable, where they were filed by the same applicant, for the same station or for another station in the same community and there are no significant coverage differences involved. Parties relying on previous filings must specifically refer to the application relied on and state that in their judgment there has been no change since the earlier filing. Proposed assignors and transferors of control are not required to file Part I even where they must file other parts of Section IV.

3.   QUESTION: What is the general purpose of Part I, Section IV-A or IV-B?

ANSWER: To show what the applicant has done to ascertain the problems, needs and interests of the residents of his community of license and other areas he undertakes to serve (See Question 6, below), and what broadcast matter he proposes to meet those problems, needs and interests, as evaluated. The word "Problems" will be used subsequently in this Primer as a short form of the phrase "problems, needs and interests." The phrase "to meet community problems" will be used to include the obligation to meet, aid in meeting, be responsive to, or stimulate the solution for community problems.

4.   QUESTION: How should ascertainment of community problems be made?

ANSWER: By consultations with leaders of the significant groups in the community to be served and surrounding areas the applicant has undertaken to serve, and by consultations with members of the general public. In order to know what significant groups are found in a particular community, its composition must be determined, see Question and Answer 9. The word "group" as used here is broad enough to include population segments, such as racial and ethnic groups, and informal groups, as well as groups with formal organization.

5.   QUESTION: Can an applicant rely upon long-time residency in or familiarity with, the area to be served instead of making a showing that he has ascertained community problems?

ANSWER: No. Such an ascertainment is mandatory.

6.   QUESTION: Is an applicant expected to ascertain community problems outside the community of license?

ANSWER: Yes. Of course, an applicant's principal obligation is to ascertain the problems of his community of license. But he should

531

also ascertain the problems of the other communities that he undertakes to serve, as set forth in his response to Question 1 (A) (2) of Section IV-A or IV-B. Applicants for stations licensed to more than one city, or for channels assigned to two or more cities, or proposed transferees or assignees of stations which have obtained waiver of the station identification rules to permit secondary identification with additional cities, are expected to ascertain problems in each of the cities. If an applicant chooses not to serve a major community that falls within his service contours a showing must be submitted explaining why. However, no major city more than 75 miles from the transmitter site need be included in the applicant's ascertainment, even if the station's contours exceed that distance.

7. QUESTION: Must the ascertainment of community problems for the other areas the applicant undertakes to serve be as extensive as for the city of license?

ANSWER: No. Normally, consultations with community leaders who can be expected to have a broad overview of community problems would be sufficient to ascertain community problems.

8. QUESTION: Should an applicant for a major change in facilities (see Answer 1(b), above) make a new ascertainment of community problems for the entire service area or just the additional area to be served?

ANSWER: Only the additional area to be served need be subjected to a new ascertainment of community problems. Only communities or areas covered by Question and Answer 6 need be ascertained, to the extent indicated in Answer 7.

9. QUESTION: How does an applicant determine the composition of his city of license?

ANSWER: The applicant may use any method he chooses, but guesswork or estimates based upon alleged area familiarity are inadequate. Current date from the U.S. Census Bureau, Chamber of Commerce and other reliable studies or reports are acceptable. The applicant must submit such data as is necessary to indicate the minority, racial, or ethnic breakdown of the community, its economic activities, governmental activities, public service organizations, and any other factors or activities that make the particular community distinctive.

10. QUESTION: If the applicant shows consultations with leaders of groups and organizations that represent various economic, social political, cultural and other elements of the community, such as government, education, religion, agriculture, business, labor, the professions, racial and/or ethnic groups, and eleemosynary organizations, is the applicant still required to submit a showing in support of its determination of the composition of the community?

ANSWER: Yes. The purpose of requiring a determination of the community is to inform the applicant and the Commission what groups comprise the community. The applicant must use that information to select those who are to be consulted as representatives of those groups. That determination may be challenged on a showing, including supporting data, that a significant group has been omitted. The

532

"significance" of a group may rest on several criteria, including its size, its influence, or its lack of influence in the community.

B. **Consultations with Community Leaders and Members of the General Public.**

11(a). QUESTION: Who should conduct consultations with community leaders?

ANSWER: Principals or management-level employees. In the case of newly formed applicants who have not hired a full staff and are applying for new stations, or for transfer or assignment of an authorization, principals, management-level employees, or prospective management-level employees, must be used to consult with community leaders.

11(b). QUESTION: Who should consult with members of the general public?

ANSWER: Principals or employees. In the case of newly formed applicants who have not hired a full staff and are applying for new stations, or for transfer or assignment of an authorization, principals, employees or prospective employees may conduct consultations. If consultations are conducted by employees who are below the management level, the consultation process must be supervised by principals, management-level employees, or prospective management-level employees. In addition, the applicant may choose to use a professional research or survey service to conduct consultations with members of the general public.

12. QUESTION: To what extent may a professional research or survey service be used in the ascertainment process?

ANSWER: A professional service would not establish a dialogue between decision-making personnel in the applicant and community leaders. Therefore, such a service may not be used to consult community leaders. However, a professional service, as indicated in Answer 11(b), may be used to conduct consultations with the general public. A professional service may also be used to provide the applicant with background data, including information as to the composition of the city of license. The use of a professional research or survey service is not required to meet Commission standards as to ascertaining community problems. The applicant will be responsible for the reliability of such a service.

13(a). QUESTION: With what community leaders should consultations be held?

ANSWER: The applicant has already determined the composition of the community, and should select for consultations those community leaders that reflect that composition. Groups with the greatest problems may be the least organized and have the fewest recognized spokesmen. Therefore, additional efforts may be necessary to identify their leaders so as to better establish a dialogue with such groups and better ascertain their problems.

13(b). QUESTIONS: With what members of the general public should consultations be held?

ANSWER: A random sample of members of the general public should be consulted. The consultations should be designed to further ascer-

533

tain community problems which may not have been revealed by consultations with community leaders. In addition to a random sample, if the applicant has reason to believe that further consultation with a particular group may reveal further insight into its problems, he is encouraged to consult with additional members of that group.

14.   QUESTION: How many should be consulted?

ANSWER: No set number or formula has been adopted. Community leaders from each significant group must be consulted. A sufficient number of members of the general public to assure a generally random sample must also be consulted. The number of consultations will vary, of course, with the size of the city in question and the number of distinct groups or organizations. No formula has been adopted as to the number of consultations in the city of license compared to other communities falling within the station's coverage contours. Applicants for stations in relatively small communities that are near large communities are reminded that an ascertainment of community problems primarily in the larger community raises a question as to whether the station will realistically serve the smaller city, or intends to abandon its obligation to the smaller city.

15.   QUESTION: When should consultations be held?

ANSWER: In preparing applications for major changes in the facilities of operating stations, a complete new ascertainment must be made within six (6) months prior to filing the application. Applicants for a new facility, or the party filing the assignee or transferee portion of an application for assignment or transfer, are also required to hold consultations within six (6) months prior to filing an appropriate application.

16.   QUESTION: Is a showing on the ascertainment of community problems defective if leaders of one of the groups that comprise the community, as disclosed by the applicant's study, are not consulted?

ANSWER: The omission of consultation with leaders of a significant group would make the applicant's showing defective, since those consulted would not reflect the composition of the community.

17.   QUESTION: In consultations to ascertain community problems, may a preprinted form or questionnaire be used?

ANSWER: Yes. A questionnaire may serve as a useful guide for consultations with community leaders, but cannot be used in lieu of personal consultations. Members of the general public may be asked to fill out a questionnaire to be collected by the applicant. If the applicant uses a form or questionnaire, a copy should be submitted with the application.

18.   QUESTION: In consulting with community leaders to ascertain community problems, should an applicant also elicit their opinion on what programs the applicant should broadcast?

ANSWER: It is not the purpose of the consultations to elicit program suggestions. (See Question and Answer 3.) Rather, it is to ascertain what the person consulted believes to be the problems of the community from the standpoint of a leader of the particular group or organization. Thus, a leader in the educational field would be a useful source of information on educational matters; a labor leader, on labor matters; and a business leader on business matters. However, it is also recognized that individual leaders may have significant comments outside their respective fields, and the applicant should consider their comments with respect to all community problems. The applicant has the responsibility for determining what broadcast matter should be presented to meet the ascertained community problems as he has evaluated them.

19. QUESTION: If, in consulting with community leaders and members of the general public, an applicant receives little information as to the existence of community problems, can he safely assume that only a few problems actually exist?

ANSWER: No. The assumption is not safe. The applicant should re-examine his efforts to determine whether his consultations have been designed to elicit sufficient information. Obviously, a brief or chance encounter will not provide adequate results. The person interviewed should be specifically advised of the purpose of the consultation. The applicant should note that many individuals, when consulting with a broadcast applicant, either jump to the conclusion that the applicant is seeking programming preferences, or express community problems in terms of exposure or publicity for the particular group or groups with which they are affiliated. The applicant may properly note these comments, but should ask further questions designed to elicit more extensive responses as to community problems.

20. QUESTION: In responding to Part I of Section IV-A or IV-B how should the applicant identify the community leaders consulted?

ANSWER: By name, position, and/or organization of each. If further information is required to clearly identify a specific leader, it should be submitted.

21. QUESTION: Should the information elicited from a community leader, from the standpoint of the group he represents, be set forth after his name?

ANSWER: It is not required, but the applicant may find it desirable. The information can be set forth in a general list of community problems.

C. Information Received.

22. QUESTION: Must all community problems which were revealed by the consultations be included in the applicant's showing?

ANSWER: All ascertained community problems should be listed, whether or not he proposes to treat them through his broadcast matter. An applicant need not, however, list comments as to community problems that are clearly frivolous.

D. Applicant's Evaluation

23. QUESTION: What is meant by an "applicant's evaluation" of information received as to community problems?

ANSWER: The applicant's evaluation is the process by which he determines the relative importance of the community problems, and the extent to which he can present broadcast matter to meet the problems.

24. QUESTION: Is the applicant's evaluation to be included in his application?

ANSWER: It is not required. Where the applicant's broadcast matter does not appear to be sufficiently responsive to the community problems disclosed by his consultations, the applicant may be asked for an explanation by letter or inquiry from the Commission. See Questions and Answers 25 and 26.

25. QUESTION: Must an applicant plan broadcast matter to meet all community problems disclosed by his consultations?

ANSWER: Not necessarily. However, he is expected to determine in good faith which of such problems merit treatment by the station. In determining what kind of broadcast matter should be presented to meet those problems, the applicant may consider his program format and the composition of his audience, but bearing in mind that many problems affect and are pertinent to diverse groups of people.

26. QUESTION: If an applicant lists a number of community problems but in his evaluation determines that he will present broadcast matter to meet only one or two of them, would the proposal be defective?

ANSWER: A *prima facie* question would arise as to how the proposal would serve the public interest, and the applicant would have the burden of establishing the validity of his proposal.

27. QUESTION: As a result of the evaluation process, is an applicant expected to propose broadcast matter to meet community problems in proportion to the number of people involved in the problem?

ANSWER: No. For example, the applicant, in his evaluation (see Question and Answer 23) might determine that a problem concerning a beautification program affecting all the people would not have the relative importance and immediacy of a problem relating to inadequate hospital facilities affecting only a small percentage of the community, but in a life-or-death way.

E. Broadcast Matter to Meet the Problems as Evaluated

28. QUESTION: What is meant by "broadcast matter"?

ANSWER: Programs and announcements.

29. QUESTION: In the application, must there be a showing as to *what* broadcast matter the applicant is proposing to *what* problem?

ANSWER: Yes. See Public Notice of August 22, 1968, Fcc 68–847, 13 RR 2d 1303. The applicant should give the description, and anticipated time segment, duration and frequency of broadcast of the program or program series, and the community problem or problems which are to be treated by it. An appropriate way would be to list the broadcast matter and, after it, the particular problem or problems the broadcast matter is designed to meet. Statements such as "programs will be broadcast from time to time to meet community problems," or "news, talk and discussion programs will be used to meet community problems," are clearly insufficient. Applicants should note that they are expected to make a positive, diligent and continuing effort to meet community problems. Therefore, they are expected to modify their broadcast matter if warranted in light of changed community problems. If announcements are proposed, they should be identified with the community problem or problems they are designed to meet.

30. QUESTION: Can an applicant specify only announcements and no programs to meet community problems?

ANSWER: A proposal to present announcements only would raise a question as to the adequacy of the proposal. The applicant would have the burden of establishing that announcements would be the most effective method for meeting the community problems he proposes to meet. If the burden is not met by the showing in the application, it will be subject to further inquiry.

31. QUESTION: What is meant by devoting a "significant proportion" of a station's programming to meet community problems? [*City of Camden* 18 Fcc 2d 412, 421, 16 RR 2d 555, 568 (1969]

ANSWER: There is no single answer for all stations. The time required to deal with community problems can vary from community to community and from time to time within a community. Initially, this is a matter that falls within the discretion of the applicant. However, where the amount of broadcast matter proposed to meet community problems appears patently insufficient to meet significantly the community problems disclosed by the applicant's consultations, he will be asked for an explanation by letter of inquiry from the Commission.

32. QUESTION: Can station editorials be used as a part of licensee's efforts to meet community problems?

ANSWER: Yes.

33. QUESTION: Can news programming be considered as programming to meet community problems?

ANSWER: Yes. However, they can not be relied upon exclusively. Most broadcast stations, of course, carry news programs regardless of community problems. News programs are usually considered by the people to be a factual report of events and matters—to keep the public informed—and, therefore, are not designed primarily to meet community problems.

34. QUESTION: If an applicant proposes a specialized format (all news, rock and roll, religious, etc.), must it present broadcast matter to meet community problems?

ANSWER: Yes. The broadcast matter can be fitted into the format of the station.

35. QUESTION: May an applicant rely upon activities other than programming to meet community problems?

ANSWER: No. Many broadcasters do participate personally in civic activities, but the Commission's concern must be with the licensee's stewardship of his broadcast time in serving the public interest.

36.   QUESTION: Are there any requirements as to when broadcast matter meeting community problems should be presented?

ANSWER: The applicant is expected to schedule the time of presentation on a good faith judgment as to when it could reasonably be expected to be effective.

APPENDIX VII

List of Available Current FCC Publications

In its *34th Annual Report/Fiscal Year 1968*, the Federal Communications Commission provides a list of currently available Commission printed publications. This list includes the title and price of each publication, which the Commission states is subject to change without notice. Those parts of the list relating to broadcasting are reproduced below. Requests for these publications should be addressed to the Superintendent of Documents, U. S. Government Printing Office, Washington, D. C. 20402. Remittance should be made by check or money order and made payable to that office.

Communications Act of 1934

	Price
Revised to Sept. 13, 1960 (plus the Administrative Procedure Act, the Judicial Review Act, and selected sections of the Criminal Code pertaining to broadcasting)	$1.00
Packet No. 1, revised pages to Communications Act, September 1960 to December 1961	.25
Packet No. 2, revised pages to Communications Act, December 1961 to October 1962 (includes Communications Satellite Act of 1962)	.30
Packet No. 3, revised pages to Communications Act, October 1962 to December 1964	.15
Packet No. 4, revised pages to Communications Act, December 1964 to November 1967	.30

Federal Communications Commission Reports

Pamphlets issued weekly. Contain decisions, reports, public notices and other documents of the FCC. Annual subscription price of the weekly pamphlets is $14.00. Foreign mailing is $4.00 additional. Price information for single pamphlets and back issues will be supplied by the Superintendent of Documents on request.
Bound volumes of decisions and reports exclusive of annual reports.

FIRST SERIES

Volume	Date	Price
15	July 7, 1950 to June 28, 1951	$4.00
16	July 18, 1951 to June 25, 1952	3.00
17	July 24, 1952 to June 26, 1953	3.50
18	June 30, 1953 to June 30, 1954	3.00
19	July 1, 1954 to June 30, 1955	4.25
20	July 1, 1955 to June 30, 1956	4.50

21	July 1, 1956 to Dec. 31, 1956	3.50
22	January 11, 1957 to July 5, 1957	5.00
23	July 12, 1957 to December 27, 1957	3.00
24	January 10, 1958 to July 3, 1958	2.50
25	July 11, 1958 to January 9, 1959	4.75
26	January 16, 1959 to July 2, 1959	3.25
27	July 10, 1959 to January 8, 1960	3.25
28	January 15, 1960 to July 8, 1960	3.25
29	July 15, 1960 to December 30, 1960	4.50
30	January 13, 1961 to July 7, 1961	3.75
31	July 14, 1961 to January 5, 1962	4.00
32	January 12, 1962 to July 6, 1962	4.25
33	July 13, 1962 to December 29, 1962	3.25
34	January 11, 1963 to July 5, 1963	4.00
35	July 12, 1963 to December 27, 1963	3.00
36	January 17, 1964 to July 6, 1964	5.00
37	July 17, 1964 to January 8, 1965	4.00
38	January 22, 1965 to July 9, 1965	4.50

SECOND SERIES

1	July 7, 1965, to December 27, 1965	5.25
2	January 3, 1966, to March 25, 1966	3.75
3	April 1, 1966, to June 24, 1966	4.25
4	July 1, 1966, to September 23, 1966	4.25
5	September 30, 1966, to December 23, 1966	4.25
6	December 30, 1966, to March 3, 1967	4.00
7	March 17, 1967, to May 12, 1967	4.25
8	May 19, 1967, to August 4, 1967	4.75
	Cumulative Index Digest to volumes 1 through 7	8.50

Federal Register Publications

Code of Federal Regulations, Title 47—Telecommunications, Chapter I, Federal Communications Commission, revised as of January 1, 1968.

	Price
Subchapter A—General	$1.00
Subchapter B—Common Carrier Services	1.50
Subchapter C—Broadcast Radio Services	1.00
Subchapter D—Safety and Special Radio Services	1.50

NOTE: Subchapters reprinted annually.

Federal Register, published daily except Sunday, Mondays, and days following official Federal holidays; contains documents amending rules, proposed amendments, and miscellaneous notices. Subscription is $1.50 per month or $15 per year, payable in advance. Single copies vary in price. Remit check or money order made payable to Superintendent of Documents, Government Printing Office, Washington, D.C. 20402.

Volumes of FCC Rules and Regulations by Categories

Available on subscription basis from Superintendent of Documents, U.S. Government Printing Office, Washington, D.C. 20402. Subscription price is for an indefinite period and includes basic volume plus all amendments to be mailed to subscribers by the Superintendent of Documents when issued. Parts are not sold separately, nor can they be supplied by the Commission. Domestic subscription includes U.S. territories, Canada, and Mexico. Address requests to Superintendent of Documents, U.S. Government Printing Office, Washington, D.C. 20402.

VOLUME I—(January 1968)

Part 0, Commission Organization.
Part 1, Practice and Procedure.
Part 13, Commercial Radio Operators.
Part 17, Construction, Marking, and Lighting of Antenna Structures.
Part 19, Employee Responsibilities and Conduct. $4 ($5 foreign).

VOLUME II—(May 1966)

Part 2, Frequency Allocation and Radio Treaty Matters: General Rules and Regulations.
Part 5, Experimental Radio Services (Other Than Broadcast).
Part 15, Radio Frequency Devices.
Part 18, Industrial, Scientific, and Medical Equipment. $2 ($2.75 foreign).

VOLUME III—(March 1968)

Part 73, Radio Broadcast Services.
Part 74, Experimental, Auxiliary, Special Broadcast and other Program Distribution Service. (Former pt. Nos. 3 and 4 respectively.) $7 ($8.75 foreign).

VOLUME IV—(July 1964)

Part 81, Stations on Land in Maritime Services.
Part 83, Stations on Shipboard in Maritime Services.
Part 85, Public Fixed Stations and Stations of the Maritime Services in Alaska. (Former pt. Nos. 7, 8, and 14, respectively.) $3 ($4.25 foreign).

VOLUME V—(January 1964)

Part 87, Aviation Services.
Part 89, Public Safety Radio Services.
Part 91, Industrial Radio Services.
Part 93, Land Transportation Radio Services. (Former pt. Nos. 9, 10, 11, and 16, respectively.) $3.75 ($4.75 foreign).

VOLUME VI—(October 1966)

Part 95, Citizens Radio Service.
Part 97, Amateur Radio Service.
Part 99, Disaster Communications Service. (Former pt. Nos. 12, 19, and 20, respectively.) $1.25 ($1.75 foreign).

VOLUME VII—(May 1966)

Part 21, Domestic Public Radio Services (Other Than Maritime Mobile).
Part 23, International Fixed Public Radio Communication Services.
Part 25, Satellite Communications. (Pt. 23 was formerly pt. 6) $2 ($2.75 foreign).

541

Reports, statistics and miscellaneous publications

Available on request to Commission unless otherwise indicated.

General

Title	Price
**Annual Reports of the Commission	Varies per edition
**Statistics of Communications Common Carriers	$.60
**Television Network Program Procurement Report	
2d Interim Report, Part 2	2.25
**Report of the Advisory Committee for the Land	
Mobile Radio Services:	
Vol. 1	.40
Vol. 2, Parts 1 and 2	2.25

ADM Bulletin No. 1—List of Printed Publications for Sale
INF Bulletin No. 1–B—How to Apply for a Broadcast Station
INF Bulletin No. 2–B—Broadcast primer
INF Bulletin No. 3–G—What You Should Know About the FCC
INF Bulletin No. 4–G—Radio Station, Frequency and Equipment Lists
INF Bulletin No. 6–G—Radio Publications and Services
INF Bulletin No. 7–G—A Short History of Electrical Communication
INF Bulletin No. 11–S—Safety and Special Radio Services Primer
INF Bulletin No. 12–C—Common Carrier Primer
INF Bulletin No. 13–G—Radio Station Call Signs
INF Bulletin No. 14–G—Regulation of Wire and Radio Communication
INF Bulletin No. 15–G—Frequency Allocation
INF Bulletin No. 16–B—Educational Television
INF Bulletin No. 17–G—Memo to All Young People Interested in Radio
INF Bulletin No. 18–G—Letter to a Schoolboy
INF Bulletin No. 19–G—FCC Field Engineering Services
INF Bulletin No. 20–G—Subscription TV and the FCC
INF Bulletin No. 21–B—Educational Radio

Engineering and Technical

OCE Bulletin No. 5—Type Approved Miscellaneous Equipment
OCE Bulletin No. 7—Type Approved Medical Diathermy Equipment
OCE Bulletin No. 8—Industrial Radio Frequency Heaters Require Periodic Inspection
OCE Bulletin No. 10—Attachments to Type Approved Equipment Illegal
OCE Bulletin No. 11—Does my Transmitter Need a License?
OCE Bulletin No. 12—Operation in the Broadcast Band Without a License
OCE Bulletin No. 13—Type Approved Wireless Microphones and Telemetering Transmitters
OCE Bulletin No. 15—Type Acceptance Program
OCE Bulletin No. 16—Information Relative to the Filing of Formal Applications in the Experimental Radio Service
OCE Bulletin No. 17—Applications in the Experimental Radio Services Involving Air Force Contracts
OCE Bulletin No. 19—FCC Test Procedure for Wireless Microphones and Telemetering Devices Submitted For Type Approval under Part 15.
Radio Equipment List

**Available through purchase from Government Printing Office

Broadcasting Services

Annual AM–FM Broadcast Financial Data
Annual TV Broadcast Financial Data
Survey of Political Broadcasting (biennial)
**Figure M–3, Estimate AM-Ground Conductivity of the United States
*Annual Canadian Television Station List
*Mexican Television Station List (periodically)
*Changes in Table of Allocations (periodically)
*Recapitulative List of Foreign Broadcast Assignments (Canadian/Mexican)
*Recapitulative List of U.S. Broadcast Assignments
*Change List Notification of Foreign Assignments (Canadian/Mexican)
*Change List Notification of U.S. Assignments
Amendment (Supplement) to TV Station Allocations re Canadian/United States TV 1952
    Agreement

Safety and Special Radio Services

Recommended Radio Operating Techniques and Procedures for Land Mobile Services except
    Common Carrier
SS Bulletin 1001—Citizens Radio Service
SS Bulletin 1001a—How to Use CB Radio
SS Bulletin 1001c—Citizens Radio Service License Serial Numbers
SS Bulletin 1001d—Use of Citizens Radio By Telephone Answering Services and Similar
    Organizations
SS Bulletin 1001e—Citizens radio Service and Civil Defense
SS Bulletin 1001f—Licensing of Clubs in the Citizens Radio Service
SS Bulletin 1001g—Citizens Radio Service-Selecting Class C and Class D Station Equipment
SS Bulletin 1002—Aircraft Radio Station
SS Bulletin 1002a—Aeronautical Advisory Stations
SS Bulletin 1002c—Aeronautical Public Service Stations
SS Bulletin 1003—Amateur Radio Service
SS Bulletin 1003b—Amateur Radio Operation Away From the Licensed Location
SS Bulletin 1003c—International Amateur Radiocommunication
SS Bulletin 1003d—Assignment of Amateur Radio Station Call Signs
SS Bulletin 1003e—Renewal of Amateur Radio License
SS Bulletin 1003f—Reciprocal Amateur Operation
SS Bulletin 1004—Land Transportation Radio Services
SS Bulletin 1005—Industrial Radio Services
SS Bulletin 1006a—Use of the Same Transmitting Equipment by More Than One Station
    Licensee in the Public Safety, Industrial and Land Transportation Radio Services
SS Bulletin 1007—Ship Radiotelephone and Radar
SS Bulletin 1009—Public Safety Radio Services
SS Bulletin 1035—Study Questions for Amateur Novice Class Examination
SS Bulletin 1065—Mutual Recognition of Certain Mobile and Amateur Radio Licenses Issued
    by the United States or Canada
SS Bulletin 1097—Notice to Licensees and Operators of Land Mobile Radio Stations

Field Engineering Services

Study Guide and Reference Material for Commercial Radio Operator Examinations
FE Bulletin No. 1—Information Pertaining to FCC Rules Governing Operation of Industrial
    Heating Equipment

*Available to public through FCC duplicating contractor.
**Available through purchase from Government Printing Office.

FE Bulletin No. 3—Digest of Radio Regulations and Instructions for Restricted Radiotelephone Operators

FE Bulletin No. 4—Information Concerning Commercial Radio Operator Licenses and Permits

FE Bulletin No. 6—The Organization of Citizens Radio Groups for Self Regulation

FE Bulletin No. 6a—Citizens Radio Service Interference Problems and Suggested Solutions

FE Bulletin No. 8—Television Reception and Interference

FE Bulletin No. 15—Assistance to Radio Stations, Laboratories, and Radio Organizations in Locating Sources of Interference to Radio Reception

FE Bulletin No. 18—Radio Certification of Boats Carrying More Than Six Passengers for Hire

FE Bulletin No. 22—Notice to Applicant for Restricted Radiotelephone Operator Permit

Bibliography

BOOKS:

Agee, Warren. (ed.). *Mass Media in a Free Society.* Lawrence: University Press of Kansas, 1969.

Archer, Gleason L. *Big Business and Radio.* New York: The American Historical Company, 1939.

————. *History of Radio to 1926.* New York: The American Historical Society, 1938.

Arons, Leon, and Mark A. *Television and Human Behavior.* New York: Appleton-Century-Crofts, 1963.

Barnouw, Erik. *A Tower in Babel* . New York: Oxford University Press, 1966.

————. *Mass Communication: Television, Radio, Film, Press.* New York: Rinehart, 1956.

————. *The Golden Web: A History of Broadcasting in the United States, 1933-1953.* New York: Oxford University Press, 1968.

Barrett, Donald N. (ed.). *Values in America.* Notre Dame, Ind.: University of Notre Dame Press, 1961.

Barrett, Edward W. *Truth Is Our Weapon.* New York: Funk and Wagnalls Company, 1953.

Bernstein, Marvin H. *Regulating Business by Independent Commission.* Princeton, N. J.: Princeton University Press, 1955.

Bogart, Leo. *The Age of Television* . New York: Frederick Ungar Publishing Company, 1956.

Bryson, Lyman. *The Communication of Ideas.* New York: Harper and Brothers, 1948.

Bureau of the Census. *Telephones and Telegraphs.* Washington, D. C.: U. S. Government Printing Office, 1902.

Carnegie Commission on Educational Television. *Public Television: A Program for Action.* New York: Harper & Row, 1967.

Casson, Herbert N. *The History of the Telephone.* Chicago: A. C. McClung, 1910.

Center for the Study of Democratic Institutions. *Broadcasting and Government Regulation in a Free Society.* Santa Barbara, Calif.; 1959.

————. *Fair Trial vs. A Free Press.* Santa Barbara, Calif., 1965.

Chafee, Zechariah, Jr. *Freedom of Speech and Press.* New York: Freedom Agenda, 1955.

————. Government and Mass Communications. Chicago: University of Chicago Press, 1947.

Chase, Francis, Jr. *Sound and Fury.* New York: Harper and Brothers, 1942.

Chester, Edward W. *Radio, Television and American Politics.* New York: Sheed and Ward, 1969.

Chester, Giraud, and Garrison, Garnet. *Radio and Television* (Rev. ed.). New York: Appleton-Century. Crofts, Inc., 1963.

Clark, David G., and Hutchison, Earl R. (eds.). *Mass Media and the Law: Freedom and Restraint,* New York: Wiley-Interscience, John Wiley and Sons, 1970.

Commission on Freedom of the Press. *A Free and Responsible Press.* Chicago: University of Chicago Press, 1947.

Coons, John E., (ed.). *Freedom and Responsibility in Broadcasting.* Evanston, Ill.: Northwestern University Press, 1961.

545

Dale, Edgar. *Can You Give the Public What It Wants?* New York: The World Book Encyclopedia and Cowles Education Corporation, 1967.

Daugherty, William, and Janawitz, Morris. *A Psychological Warfare Case Book.* Baltimore, Md.: Johns Hopkins Press, 1958.

DeFluer, Melvin L. *Theories of Mass Communication* (Rev. ed.). New York: David McKay, 1970.

Dizard, Wilson P. *The Strategy of Truth: The Story of the U.S. Information Agency.* Washington, D. C.: Public Affairs Press, 1961.

Dunlap, Orrin E., Jr. *Communications in Space: From Wireless to Satellite Relay.* New York: Harper and Brothers, 1962.

——————. *Dunlap's Radio and Television Almanac.* New York: Harper and Brothers, 1951.

Emery, Walter B. *National and International Systems of Broadcasting: Their History, Operation and Control.* East Lansing: Michigan State University Press, 1969.

Elliott, William Y. (ed.). *Television's Impact on American Culture.* East Lansing: Michigan State University Press, 1956.

Ernst, Morris Leopold. *The First Freedom.* New York: The Dial Press, Inc., 1935.

——————, and Seagle, William. *To the Pure: A Study of Obscenity and the Censor.* New York: The Viking Press, Inc., 1929.

Filgate, John Thomas. *Theory of Radio Communication.* Brooklyn: Radio Design Publishing Company, 1929.

Fore, William F. *Image and Impact.* New York: Friendship Press, Inc., 1970.

Frankfurter, Felix. *The Public and Its Government.* New York: Oxford University Press, 1930.

Friendly, Fred W. *Due to Circumstances Beyond Our Control.* New York Random House, 1967.

Gillmor, Donald M., and Barron, Jerome A. *Mass Communication Law: Cases and Comment.* American Case Book Series. St. Paul, Minn.: West Publishing Company, 1969.

Gordon, George N.; Falk, Irving, and Hodapp, William. *The Idea Invaders.* New York: Hastings House, 1963.

Haiman, Franklyn S. *Freedom of Speech: Issues and Cases.* New York: Random House, 1967.

Hand, Learned. *The Spirit of Liberty: Papers and Addresses of Learned Hand.* New York: Alfred A. Knopf, 1952.

Head, Sydney. *Broadcasting in America.* Boston: Houghton Mifflin, 1956.

Herring, James M., and Gross, Gerald C. *Telecommunications: Economics and Regulation.* New York: McGraw-Hill, 1936.

Holt. Robert T. *Radio Free Europe.* Minneapolis: University of Minnesota Press, 1958.

Husing, Ted. *Ten Years Before the Mike.* New York: Holt, Rinheart, Winston, Inc., 1935.

Hyneman, Charles S. *Bureaucracy in a Democracy.* New York: Harper and Brothers, 1950.

Johsnon, Nicholas. *How to Talk Back to Your Television Set.* Boston: Little, Brown and Company, 1970.

Kahn, Frank J. *Documents of American Broadcasting.* New York: Appleton-Century-Crofts, 1968.

Kelly, Frank. *Who Owns the Air?* Santa Barbara, Calif.: Center for the Study of Democratic Institutions, 1964.

Kendrick, Alexander. *Prime Time: The Life of Edward R. Murrow.* Boston: Little, Brown, 1969.

Kerwin, Jerome Gregory. *The Control of Radio.* Chicago: University of Chicago Press, 1934.

Kingsbury, John E. *The Telephone and Telephone Exchanges.* New York: Longmans, Green, and Company, Inc., 1915.

Koenig, Allen E. (ed.). *Broadcasting and Bargaining: Labor Relations in Radio and Television.* Madison: The University of Wisconsin Press, 1970.

————, and Hill, Ruane B. (eds.). *The Farther Vision: Educational Television Today.* Madison: The University of Wisconsin Press, 1967.

Kraus, Sidney. (ed.). *The Great Debates.* Bloomington: Indiana University Press, 1962.

Lacy, Dan. *Freedom and Communications.* (2nd ed.). Urbana: University of Illinois Press, 1965.

Landis, James M. *Report on Regulatory Agencies to the President-Elect.* Washington, D. C.: December, 1960.

Landry, Robert J. *This Fascinating Radio Business.* Indianapolis: The Bobbs, Merrill Company, Inc., 1946.

Levin, Harvey J. *Broadcast Regulation and Joint Ownership of Media.* New York: New York University Press, 1960.

Lippmann, Walter. *Essays in Public Philosophy.* Boston: Little, Brown and Company, 1955.

MacNeal, Harry B. *The Story of Independent Telephony.* Washington, D. C.: The Independent Pioneer Telephone Association, n. d.

Mathison, Stuart L., and Walker, Philip M. *Computer and Telecommunications: Issues in Public Policy.* Englewood Cliffs, N.J.: Prentice-Hall, 1970.

McGinniss, Joe. *The Selling of the President 1968.* New York: Trident Press, 1969.

Mill, John Stuart. *On Liberty.* Alburey Castell. (ed.). New york: Appleton-Century-Crofts, 1947.

Minow, Newton N. *Equal Time: The Private Broadcasters and the Public Interest.* Lawrence Laurent. (ed.), New York: Atheneum, 1964.

Morecroft, John H. *Elements of Radio Communication.* New York: John Wiley and Sons, Inc., 1934.

Morse, Edward Lind. *Samuel F. B. Morse, Letters and Journals.* Boston: Houghton Mifflin Company, Inc., 1914.

Moser, Julius G., and Lannie, Richard A. *Radio and the Law.* Los Angeles: Parker, 1947.

Murray Edelman. *The Licensing of Radio Services in the United States.* Urbana: University of Illinois Press, 1950.

National Association of Broadcasters. *Broadcasting and the Bill of Rights.* Washington, D. C.: National Association of Broadcasters, 1947.

Nye, Russel B. *This Almost Chosen People: Essays in the History of American Ideas.* East Lansing: Michigan State University Press, 1966.

Oleck, Howard L. *Non-Profit Corporations and Associations.* Englewood Cliffs, New Jersey: Prentice-Hall, Inc., 1956.

Paulu, Burton. *Radio and Television Broadcasting on the European Continent.* Minneapolis: University of Minnesota Press, 1967.

Pennybacker, John H., and Braden, Waldo W. (eds.). *Broadcasting and the Public Interest.* New York: Random House, 1969.

Pike and Fischer. *Radio Regulation.* Washington, D. C.: 1945—.

Pilpel, Harriet, and Zavin, Theodora. *Rights and Writers, A Handbook of Literary and Entertainment Law.* New York: E. P. Dutton and Company, Inc., 1960.

Rhyne, Charles S. *Municipal Regulations, Taxation and Use of Radio.* Washington, D. C.: National Institute of Municipal Law Officers, 1955.

Rivers, William L., and Schramm, Wilbur. *Responsibility in Mass Communications.* New York: Harper and Row, 1969.

Robinson, Thomas Porter. *Radio Networks and the Federal Government.* New York: Columbia University Press, 1943.

Rosenbloom, Joel. "Authority of the Federal Communications Commission," in *Freedom and Responsibility in Broadcasting.* John E. Coons. (ed.), Evanston, Ill.: Northwestern University Press, 1961.

Salomon, Leon I. *The Independent Federal Regulatory Commissions.* New York: H. W. Wilson Company, 1959.

Sargent, William. *Battle for the Mind.* New York; Doubleday and Company, 1957.

Schramm, Wilbur. *Communications in Modern Society.* Urbana: University of Illinois Press, 1948.

————. Mass Communications. Urbana: University of Illinois Press, 1949.

Schwartz, Bernard. *The Professor and the Commissions.* New York: Alfred A. Knopf, Inc., 1959.

Seldes, Gilbert. *The Public Arts.* New York: Simon and Schuster, 1956.

Shaffner, Tal. P. *The First Quarter Century of American Broadcasting.* Kansas City: Midland Publishing Company, 1946.

Shayon, Robert Lewis. (ed.). *The Eighth Art.* New York: Holt, Rinehart and Winston, 1962.

Siebert, Frederick S. *Clearance, Rights and Legal Problems of Educational Radio and Television Stations.* Washington, D. C.: National Association of Educational Broadcasters, 1955.

————. Peterson, Theodore, and Schramm, Wilbur. *Four Theories of the Press.* Urbana: University of Illinois Press, 1956.

Siepmann, C. A. *Radio's Second Chance.* Boston: Little, Brown and Company, 1946.

————. *Radio, Television and Society.* New York: Oxford University Press, 1950.

Simonson, Solomon. *Crisis in Television: A Study of the Private Judgment in the Public Interest.* New York: Living Books, 1966.

Skornia, Harry J., and Kitson, Jack William. *Problems and Controversies in Television and Radio: Basic Readings.* Palo Alto, Calif.: Pacific Books, 1968.

————. *Television and Society.* New York: McGraw-Hill, 1965.

Smead, Elmer A. *Freedom of Speech by Radio and Television.* Washington, D. C.: Public Affairs Press, 1959.

Steiner, Gary A. *The People Look at Television: A Study of Audience Attitudes.* New York: Knopf, 1963.

Summers, Harrison B. (ed.). *Radio Censorship* . New York: H. W. Wilson Company, 1939.

————. and Summers, Robert E. *Broadcasting and the Public.* Belmont, Calif.: Wadsworth, 1966.

Thompson, Robert L. *Wiring a Continent.* Princeton, New Jersey: Princeton University Press, 1947.

University of Chicago. *Print, Radio and Film in a Democracy.* Chicago: University of Chicago Press, 1942.

University of Michigan Law School. *Lectures on Communication Media, Legal and Policy Problems.* Ann Arbor: University of Michigan, 1955.

Urban, George R. (ed.). *Scaling the Wall: Talking to Eastern Europe.* Detroit: Wayne State University Press, 1964.

Warner, Harry P. *Radio and Television Law.* Albany, N. Y.: Matthew Bender and Company, Inc., 1948.

————. *Radio and Television Rights.* Albany, N. Y.: Matthew Bender and Company, Inc., 1953.

White, Leonard Dupee. *Introduction to the Study of Public Administration* . New York: The Macmillan Company, 1955.

Wincor, Richard. *Literary Property.* New York: Clarkson N. Potter, Inc., 1967.
World Radio-TV Handbook. (24th ed.). Hvidovre, Denmark: H. P. J. Meakin, 1970.
Wright, Charles R. *Mass Communication, A Sociolgocial Perspective.* New York: Random House, 1959.

PERIODICALS—GENERAL

Agee, W. K. "Cross-Channel Ownership," *Journalism Quarterly,* XXVI (December 1949), 410-416.
Anello, Douglas A., and Cahill, Robert V. "Legal Authority of the FCC to Place Limits on Broadcast Advertising," *Journal of Broadcasting,* VII (Fall 1963), 285-303.
Armstrong, Edwin H. "A Method of Reducing Disturbances in Radio Signaling by a System of Frequency Modulation," *Proceedings of the Institute of Radio Engineers,* May 1936, 689.
Barron, Jerome, A. "The Meaning and Future of Red Lion," *Educational Broadcasting Review,* III (December 1969), 9-16.
Bendiner, Robert. "The FCC—Who Will Regulate the Regulators?" *The Reporter,* XVII (September 19, 1957), 26-30.
Berelson, Bernard. "The Great Debate on Cultural Democracy." *Studies in Public Communication No. 3. Chicago: University of Chicago, 1961.*
Berkman, Dave. *"A Modest Proposal: Abolishing the FCC,"* Columbia Journalism *Review,* IV (Fall 1965), 34-36.
Bryant, Ashbrook P. "Responsibility for Broadcast Matter," *Journal of Broadcasting,* V (Winter 1960-61), 3016-
Bundy, McGeorge. "Educational TV: A National Awakening," *NAEB Journal,* XXVI (May-June 1967), 47-54.
Butler, James J. "Radio Can be Denied on Monopoly Ground," *Editor and Publisher,* LXXXIII (January 28, 1950), 9.
Carson, Saul. "The Richards' Licenses," *New Republic,* CXXXI (August 8, 1949), 22-23.
Carter, Roy E., Jr. "Radio Editorializing Aboard the New Mayflower," *Journalism Quarterly,* XXVIII (Fall 1951), 49-53.
Cox, Kenneth A. "Broadcasters as Revolutionaries," *Television Quarterly,* VI (Winter, 1967), 13-19.
————. "Does the FCC Really Do Anything?" *Journal of Broadcasting,* XI (Spring 1967), 97-113.
Emery, Walter B. "Broadcasting Rights and Responsibilities in Democratic Society," *NAEB Journal;* XXIV (March-April 1965), 72-84.
————. "Government's Role in the American System of Broadcasting," *Television Quarterly,* I (February 1968), 17-21.
————. "Is There a Constitutional Flaw in the Public Broadcasting Act of 1967?" *Educational Broadcasting Review,* II (February 1968), 17-21.
————. Legal Restrictions on Use of Program Materials," *Journal of Broadcasting,* IV (Summer 1960), 241-252.
————. "Nervous Tremors in the Broadcast Industry," *Educational Broadcasting Review,* III (June 1969), 43-51.
————. "The FCC: Its Powers, Functions, and Personnel," *Journal of Broadcasting,* II (Summer 1958), 225-239.
Fisher, John. "TV and Its Critics," *Harper's,* CCIX (July 1958), 10-14.
Ford, Frederick W. "Cable TV Legislation: History, Analysis and Recommendations," *Television Digest,* X (June 15, 1970), 1-6.
————. "Television: Divided or United—Some Problems in Television Growth," address before the 13th Annual Convention of the National Community

Television Association, Philadelphia, Pennsylvania, June 18, 1964.
————. "The Fairness Doctrine," *Journal of Broadcasting,* VIII (Winter 1963-64), 3-16.
————. "The Meaning of the 'Public Interest, Convenience or Necessity,' " *Journal of Broadcasting,* V (Summer 1961), 205-218.
Gelman, Morris J. "The Future of Television: Will Wire Take Over?" *Television,* XXII (Ddecember 1965), 27-31 and 68-77.
Goldin, H. H. "Economic and Regulatory Problems in the Broadcast Field," *Land Economics,* XXX (1954), 223-233.
Gompertz, Kenneth; Cooney, Stuart, and Tuber, richard. "A Bibliography of Articles on Broadcasting in Law Periodicals, 1920-1968," *Journal of Broadcasting,* XIV, (Winter 1969-70); published in association with the *Federal Communications Bar Journal,* XXXIII (1969).
Gould, J. "Commissioner Johnson: 9 Month Record as Dissenter," *New York Times,* (March 26, 1967), II, 29:1.
————. "FCC Duties Should be Confined to Common Carrier Cases with Broadcasting Supervision Shifted to a New Agency," *New York Times,* (June 26, 1966), II, 15.
"Government by Commission: FCC and its Radio Rules: Case Study of Bureaucracy in Action," *Fortune,* XXVII (May 1943), 86-89.
Holt, Darrel. "The Origin of 'Public Interest' in Broadcasting," *Educational Broadcasting Review,* I (October 1967), 15-19.
Hoover, Herbert. "Radio Gets a Policeman," *American Heritage,* VI (August 1955), 73-76.
Houn, Franklin W. "Radio Broadcasting and Propaganda in Communist China," *Journalism Quarterly,* XXXIV (Summer 1957), 366-377.
"How to Protect Citizen Rights in Television and Radio," New York: Office of Communication, United Church of Christ, 1970.
Jansky, C. M., Jr. "The Contribution of Herbert Hoover to Broadcasting, I (Summer 1957), 241-249.
Johnson, Nicholas. "Crisis in Communications," *Television Quarterly,* VI (Winter 1967), 21-28.
————. "The Why of Public Broadcasting," *Educational Broadcasting Review,* I (December 1967), 5-10.
Kahn, Frank. "Economic Regulation of Broadcasting as a Utility," *Journal of Broadcasting,* VII (Spring 1963), 97-112.
Koop, Theodore F. "Equality of Access for Radio in Covering Washington News," *Journalism Quarterly,* XXXIV (Summer 1957), 338-340.
Kurtz, Robert S. "The Right to Privacy: A Legal Guidepost to Television Programming," *Journalism of Broadcasting,* VI (Summer 1962), 243-254.
Lawrence, Edmund. "Radio and the Richards' Case," *Harper's,* CCV (July 1959), 82-87.
Leigh, R. B. "Policing the Commentator: Case of FCC Chairman Fly and Congressman Cox," *Harper's,* CXL (January 1945), 97-
Levin, Harvey J. "Competition Among the Mass Media and the Public Interest," *Public Opinion Quarterly,* XVIII (Spring 1954), 62-79.
Lichty, Lawrence W. "The Impact of FRC and FCC Commissioners' backgrounds on the regulations of Broadcasting, VI (Spring 1962), 97-110.
Loevinger, Lee. "Broadcasting and Religious Liberty," *Journal of Broadcasting,* IX (Winter 1964-65), 3-23.
————. "The Lexonomics of Telecommunications," *Journal of Broadcasting,* XI (Fall 1967), 285-311.
————. "The Limits of Technology in Broadcasting," *Journal of Broadcasting,* X (Fall 1966), 285-298.

————. "The Role of Law in Broadcasting," *Jorunal of Broadcasting*, VIII (Spring 1964), 113-126.

Mannes, Marya. "The Networks and the FCC," *The Reporter* (March 29, 1962), 19-23.

Marks, Leonard H. "Communications Satellites: New Horizons for Broadcasters," *Journal of Broadcasting*, IX (Spring 1965), 97-101.

McMahon, Robert S. "Harris Subcommittee Report: Fifty Years of Broadcasting Regulation," *Journal of Broadcasting*, III (Winter 1958-1959), 56-87.

Meyers, H. "The FCC's Expanding, Demanding Universe," *Fortune*, LXXVIII (June 1966), 151-

Minow, Newton N. Address before the National Association of Broadcasters' Public Affairs/Editorializng Conference, Washington, D. C., (March 1, 1962).

————. "The Role of the Federal Communications Commission in Recent Developments in the Communications Industry." Address to National Association of Broadcasters, Chicago (April 2, 1963).

Oppenheimer, Walter D. "Television and the Right of Privacy," *Journal of Broadcasting*, I (Spring 1957).

Paglin, Max D. "Some Regulatory and International Problems Facing Establishment of Communication Satellite Systems," *Journal of Broadcasting*, VI (Fall 1962), 285-294.

Pierson, W. Theodore. "The Active Eyebrow—A Changing Style for Censorship," *Television Quarterly*, I (February 1962), 14-21.

————. "What Is the American System of Broadcasting?" *Journal of Broadcasting*, X (Summer 1966), 191-198.

Pressman, Gabe; Shayon, Robert Lewis, and Schulman, Robert. "The Responsible Reporter," *Television Quarterly*, III (Spring 1964), 8-26.

"Racial Justice in Broadcasting: A Report of a Program to Combat Discrimination Practices by Broadcast Licensees Against Blacks and Other Minorities by Means of Programming and Employment Practices," New York: Office of Communication, United Church of Christ, (1970).

Ripley, Joseph M. "Policies and Practices Concerning Broadcasts of Controversial Issues," *Journal of Broadcasting*, IX (Winter, 1964-65), 25-32.

Rosenburg, Herbert H. "Program Content," *Western Political Quarterly*, II (September 1949), 375-401.

Schlesinger, Arthur, Jr. "How Drastically has Television Changed Our Politics?" *TV Guide*, (October 22, 1966), 6-10.

Seymour, Whitney N. "Authority of the FCC over Broadcast Content," *Journal of Broadcasting*, IV (Winter, 1959-60), 18-26.

Sherrill, R. B. "A. B. C. & I. T. T., Marriage in Haste," *The Nation*, CCIV (March 20, 1967), 361-364.

Siebert, Frederick S. "The Right to Report by Television," *Journalism Quarterly*, XXXIV (Summer 1957), 333-337.

Siepmann, C. A. "Scramble for Air Time," *The Nation*, CLXXVIII (May 15, 1944), 422-424.

Smith, Ralph Lee. "The Wired Nation," *The Nation*, CCX (May 18, 1970), 582-606.

Smith, Robert Franklin. "Madame Commissioner," *Journal of Broadcasting*, XII (Winter 1967-68), 69-81.

Sperry, Robert. "A Selected Bibliography of Works on the Federal Communications Commission," *Journal of Broadcasting*, XII (Winter, 1967-68), 83-93.

Stanley, Earl R. "Revocation, Renewal of License, and Fines and Forfeiture Cases before the Federal Communications Commission," *Journal of Broadcasting*, VIII (Fall 1964), 371-382.

Tebbel, J. "Freedom of the Air: Myth or Reality?" *Saturday Review,* XLV (April 14, 1962), 56.

Terry, Hugh B. "Electronic Journalism in the Colorado Courts," *Journalism Quarterly,* XXXIV (Summer 1957), 459-462.

"The War We're Losing—The Communications Crisis: What Persuaders Can Do," *Printers' Ink,* CCLXXX (September 14, 1962), 27-73.

U. S. Supreme Court. "The 'Red Lion' Decision," *Journal of Broadcasting,* XIII (Fall 1969), 415-432.

Walker, Paul A., and Emery, Walter B. "Post War Communications and Speech Education," *Quarterly Journal of Speech,* XXX (December 1944), 399-402.

Weeks, Lewis E. "The Radio Election of 1924," *Journal of Broadcasting,* VIII (Summer 1964), 233-243.

Wolfe, G. Joseph. "Norman Baker and KTNT," *Journal of Broadcasting,* XII (Fall 1968), 389-399.

Yoder, R. M. "They Track Down Outlaw Broadcasters," *Saturday Evening Post,* CCXXIV (December 1, 1951), 17-19; (December 8, 1951), 34.

Zeidenberg, Leonard. "Is the FCC Obsolete?" *Television,* XXIII (October 1966), 27-31, 51-57.

LEGAL PERIODICALS:

Anello, Douglas A., and Gross, Kenneth W. "The Legislative Picture 1965: Bills Affecting the Broadcast Industry," *Federal Communications Bar Journal,* XIX (1964-1965), 111-126.

Austin, Douglas V. "Governmental Censorship in Radio and Television Broadcasting," Public Utilities Fortnightly, LXXVI (August 19, 1965), 27-42.

Baker, Warren E. "Policy by Rule or *Ad Hoc* Approach—Which should It Be?" *Law and Contemporary Problems,* XXII (Autumn 1957), 611-625.

Barrow, Roscoe L. "Antitrust and the Regulated Industry: Promoting Competition in Broadcasting," *Duke Law Journal,* MCMLXIV (Spring 1964) 282-302.

————. "Network Broadcasting—The Report of the FCC Network Study Staff," *Law and Contemporary Problems,* XXII (Autumn 1957), 611-625.

Bechtel, Gene A. "FCC Procedure in Acquiring AM, FM, and TV Licenses," *American Bar Association Law Notes,* Miscellaneous Section, II (July 1966).

Bell, David S. "Impact of Quality Programming on FCC Licensing," *Louisiana Law Review,* XXIII, (December 1962), 85-106.

Blair, Forbes W. "The Permutable Law of Strike Applications," *Federal Communications Bar Journal,* XXIII (1969), 24-38.

Blake, Jonathan D. "Red Lion Broadcasting Co. v. FCC: Fairness and the Emperor's New Clothes," *Federal Communications Bar Journal,* XXIII (1969), 75-92.

Borchardt, Kurt. "Organizational Use of Administrative Organization and Procedure for Policy-Making Purposes: Six Case Studies and Some Conclusions," *The George Washington Law Review,* XXX (March 1962), 429-466.

Brennan, Patrick (ed.). "Federalism and the Control of Criminal Law," *Journal of Criminal Law, Criminology and Police Science,* XLIX (March-April 1959), 579-580.

"Broadcaster Immune from Liability for Libelous Statements Made by a Political Candidate," *Maryland Law Review,* XIX (Fall 1959), 345-347.

Brown, Ralph S., Jr. "Character and Candor Requirements for FCC Licensees," *Law and Contemporary Problems,* XXII (Autumn 1957), 644-657.

Cahill, Robert V. " 'Fairness' and the FCC," *Federal Communications Bar Journal,* XXI (1967), 17-25.

"CATV and Copyright Liability," *Harvard Law Review*, LXXX (May 1967), 1514-1537.

Cole, John P., Jr. "Community Antenna Television, the Broadcaster Establishment, and the Federal Regulator," *American University Law Review*, XIV (June 1965), 124-145.

Collins, Daniel F. "Judicial Review of FCC Decisions, 1968-1969," *Federal Communications Bar Journal*, XXIII (1969), 57-67.

Colon, Frank T. "The Court and the Commissions: *Ex parte* Contacts and the Sangamon Valley Case, *Federal Communications Bar Journal*, XIX (1964-1965), 67-87.

"Communications Satellite Act of 1962," *Harvard Law Review*, LXXVI (December 1962), 388-400.

Courtney, Jeremiah, and Blooston, Arthur. "Development of Mobile Radio Communications—The Workhorse Radio Services," *Law and Contemporary Problems*, XXII (Autumn 1957), 626-643.

Cox, Kenneth. "The FCC, the Constitution, and Religious Broadcasting Programming," *The George Washington Law Review*, XXXIV (December 1965), 196-218.

Dean, III, John W. "Political Broadcasting: The Communications Act of 1934 Reviewed," *Federal Communications Bar Journal*, XX (1966), 16-43.

"Diversifications and the Public Interest: Administrative Responsibility of the FCC," *Yale Law Journal*, LXVI (January 1957), 365-396.

Doerfer, John C. "Legislation Affecting the Federal Regulatory Process," *Federal Communications Bar Journal*, XVII (1959), 5-20.

Doyle, Stephen E. "Do We Really Need a Federal Department of Telecommunications?" *Federal Communications Bar Journal*, XXI (January 1957), 365-396.

Epstein, David. "Copyright Protection and Community Antenna Television Systems," *Federal Communications Bar Journal*, XIX (1964-1965), 97-108.

Ernest, G. Lane. " 'Equal Time' Provisions: Has Broadcasting Come of Age?" *Colorado Law Review*, XXXVI (Winter 1964), 257-268.

"Fairness, Freedom and Cigarette Advertising: A Defense of the Federal Communications Commission," *Columbia Law Review*, LXVII (December 1967), 1470-1489.

"False Advertising: Use of Mock-Ups in Television Demonstrations: Scope of Effective Regulation by the FTC," *UCLA Law Review*, X (January 1963), 417-425.

"FCC Attacks Radio Give-Away Program," *Stanford Law Review*, I (April 1949), 475-485.

"FCC Disclaims Power to Limit Competition in Broadcasting," *Columbia Law Review*, LVII (November 1957), 1036-1038.

"FCC Fairness Doctrine—Applicability to Advertising," *Iowa Law Review*, LIII (October 1967), 480-491.

"FCC Jurisdiction over CATV: A Need for Reins?" *Georgetown Law Review*, LVI (January 1968), 597-608.

"FCC May Properly Consider Past Competitive Practices of Newspaper Applicant as Basis for Denial of Radio License," *Harvard Law Review*, LXIII (Autumn 1957), 672-696.

"Federal Communications Act—Jesuit University Is Not Considered Representative of Alien in Determining Eligibility to Hold Station License, *Harvard Law Review*, LXXII (April 1959), 1172-1173.

"Federal Communications Commission and Regulation of CATV," *New York University Law Review*, XLIII (March 1968), 117-139.

Fisher, Ben C. "Communications Act Amendments, 1952—An Attempt to Legislate Administrative Fairness," *Law and Contemporary Problems,* XXII, (Autumn 1957), 672-696.

Ford, Frederick W. "The Impact of Judicial Review on the Federal Communications Commission," *West Virginia Law Review,* LXIII (December 1960), 25-39.

Greenberg, Edward. "Wire Television and the FCC's Second Report and Order on CATV Systems," *Journal of Law and Economics,* X (October 1967), 181-192.

Griffith, Emlyn I. "Mayflower Rule—Gone But Not Forgotten," *Cornell Law Quarterly,* XXXV (Spring 1950), 574-591.

"Gross Receipt Tax on Radio Stations," *Stanford Law Review,* I (June 1949), 741-756.

Hansen, Victor R. "Broadcasting and the Antitrust Laws," *Law and Contemporary Problems,* XXII (Autumn 1957), 572-583.

Harum, Albert E. "Broadcast Defamation: A Reformation of the Common Law Concepts," *Federal Communications Bar Journal,* XXI (1967), 73-91.

"Imitation of Comedian's Voice in Television Commercial May Constitute Defamation or Unfair Competition But Not Invasion of Privacy," *Harvard Law Review,* LXXVI (June 1963), 1685-1691.

Irion, H. Gifford. "FCC Criteria for Evaluating Competing Applicants," *Minnesota Law Review,* XLIII (January 1959), 479-498.

———. " 'Need for Broadcast Service'—A Key Phrase in Communications Laws," *Federal Communications Bar Journal,* XIX (1964-65), 479-498.

Jentz, Gaylord A. "Federal Regulation of Advertising: False Representations of Composition, Character, or Source and Deceptive Television Demonstrations," *American Business Law Journal,* VI (Spring 1968), 409-428.

Johnson, John A. "Satellite Communications: The Challenge and the Opportunity for International Cooperation," *Federal Communications Bar Journal,* XIX (1964-1965), 88-96.

Johnson, Nicholas. "Public Interest and Public Broadcasting: Looking at Communications as a Whole," *Washington University Law Quarterly,* MCMLXVII (Fall 1967), 480-492.

Kahn, Frank J. "Economic Injury and the Public Interest," *Federal Communications Bar Journal,* XXIII (1969), 182-201.

Kalodner, Howard L., and Vance, Verne W., Jr. "The Relations Between Federal and State Protection of Literary and Artistic Property," *Harvard Law Review,* LXXII (April 1959), 1079-1128.

Kalvin, Jr., Harry. "Broadcasting, Public Policy and the First Amendment," *Journal of Law and Economics,* X (October 1967), 15-49.

Kennedy, Roger. "Programming Content and Quality," *Law and Contemporary Problems,* XXII (Autumn 1957), 479-498.

Knickerbocker, Daniel C., Jr. "Licensee's Right to Hearing on Modification of License," *Cornell Law Quarterly,* XXXIV (1949), 608-615.

LeDuc, Don R. "The FCC v. CATV et al: A Theory of Regulatory Reflex Action," *Federal Communications Bar Journal,* XXIII (1969), 93-109.

"Legal Problems of Educational Television," *Yale Law Journal,* LXVII (February 1958), 639-673.

Leventhal, Normal P. "Caution: Cigarette Commercials May Be Hazardous to Your Licenses—The New Aspect of Fairness," *Federal Communications Bar Journal,* XXII (1968), 55-124.

Levin, Harvey J. "Broadcast Regulation and Intramedium Competition," *Virginia Law Review,* XLV (November 1959), 1104-1138.

———. "Regulatory Efficiency, Reform and the FCC," *Georgetown Law Journal,* L (Fall 1961), 1-50.

Loevinger, Lee. "Issues in Program Regulation,' *Federal Communications Bar Journal*, XX (1966), 3-15.

Lovett, Lee G. "*Ex Parte* and the FCC: The New Regulations," *Federal Communications Bar Journal*, XXI (1967), 54-62.

Lynd, Robert D. "Banzhaf v. FCC: Public Interest and the Fairness Doctrine," *Federal Communications Bar Journal*, XXIII (1969), 39-55.

McCullough, Robert G. "Right of Privacy as Subject to Qualified Privilege of Television News Broadcaster," *Washington and Lee Law Review*, XIII (1956), 255-264.

McGowan, John J. "Competition, Regulation, and Performance in Television Broadcasting," *Washington University Law Quarterly*, MCMLXVII (Fall 1967), 499-520.

Meyer, Elizabeth. "Responsible Representatives of the Listening Public Have Standing as 'Persons Aggrieved'," *Wayne Law Review*, XIII (Winter 1967), 377-384.

Monroe, Jr., William B. "The Case for Television in the Courtroom," *Federal Communications Bar Journal*, XXI (1967), 48-53.

Palmer, John C.; Smith, James R., and Wade, Edwin L. "Community Antenna Television: Survey of a Regulatory Problem," *Georgetown Law Journal*, LVII (Fall 1963), 136-176.

Peck, Cornelius J. Regulation and Control of *Ex Parte* Communications with Administrative Agencies," *Harvard Law Review*, LXXVI (December 1962), 233-274.

Pike and Fischer. *Radio Regulation*. Washington, D. C.: 1945—.

Powell, Jon T. "The Czech Crisis and International Broadcasting in Perspective," *Federal Communications Bar Journal*, XXIII (1969), 3-23.

———. "Satellites, Sovereignty and Speculation," *Federal Communications Bar Journal*, XXII (1968), 218-235.

———. "U. S. Television and Southern Rhodesia: Issues of Basic Rights," *Federal Communications Bar Journal*, XXIII (1969), 122-139.

"Radio: Broadcasting 'Obviously Offensive and Patently Vulgar' Material Warrants FCC Denial of License Renewal," *Minnesota Law Review*, XL (January 1963), 465-473.

Ramey, Carl R. "Federal Communications Commission and Broadcast Advertising: An Analytical Review," *Federal Communications Bar Journal*, XX (1966), 71-116.

"Regulation of Program Content by the FCC," *Harvard Law Review*, LXXVII (February 1964), 701-706.

Remmers, Donald H. "Recent Legislative Trends in Defamation by Radio," *Harvard Law Review*, LXIV (March 1951), 727-758.

Robinson, Glen O. "FCC and the First Amendment: Observations on 40 Years of Radio and Television Regulation," *Minnesota Law Review*, LII (November 1967), 67-163.

Rollo, Reed T. "Enforcement Provisions of the Communications Act," *Federal Communications Bar Journal*, XVIII (1963), 45-48.

Roth, George F. "Shareholder Control and FCC Regulation of Corporate Broadcast Licensees," *Wisconsin Law Review*, (1967), 774-780.

Salant, Richard S. "The Functions and Practices of a Television Network," Law and Contemporary Problems, XXII (Autumn 1957), 584-610.

Schwartz, Bernard. "Contemporary Television and the Chancellor's Foot," *Georgetown Law Journal*, XLVII (Summer 1959), 655-699.

Schwartz, Herman. "Comsat, the Carriers, and the Earth Stations: Some Problems with Melding Variegated Interests," *Yale Law Review*, LXXVI (January 1967), 441-484.

Schwartz, Louis, and Woods, Robert A. "One Year in the Life of the Three Year Rule," *Federal Communications Bar Journal,* XIX (1964-65), 3-12.

Segal, P. M. "Recent Trends in Censorship of Radiobroadcast Programs," *Rocky Mountain Law Review,* XX (June 1948), 366-380.

Segal, P. M., and Warner, Harry P. "Ownership of Broadcasting Frequencies: A Review," *Rocky Mountain Law Review,* XIX (February 1947), 111-122.

Sheehan, Dennis W. "Broadcaster's Immunity from Liability for Political Defamation," *Georgetown Law Review,* XLVIII (Spring 1960), 544-562.

"Simulation of Entertainer's Voice in Television Commercial Gives Rise to Cause of Action for Defamation and Unfair Competition," *Fordham Law Review,* XXXI (December 1962), 385-390.

Singer, Richard G. "Church of Christ: Standing and the Evidentiary Hearing," *George Law Journal,* LV (November 1966), 264-284.

Smythe, Dallas W. "Facing Facts About the Broadcast Business," *University of Chicago Law Review,* XX (1952), 96-106.

Spievack, Edwin B. "Presidential Assault on Telecommunications," *Federal Communications Bar Journal,* XXIII (1969), 155-181.

"Standing of Television Viewers to Contest FCC Orders: the Private Action Goes Public," *Columbia Law Review,* LXVI (December 1966), 1511-1528.

"State Regulation of Radio and Television," *Harvard Law Review,* LXXIII (December 1959), 386-405.

Stukas, William B. "Federal Communications Commission and Program Regulation —Violation of the First Amendment?" *Nebraska Law Review,* XLI (June 1962), 826-846.

Suelflow, James E. "Subscription Television, Part I—What Are the Chances of Success?" *Public Utilities Fortnightly,* (June 22, 1967), 23-28.

———. "Subscription Television, Part II—Should Subscription Television Be Regulated?" *Public Utilities Fortnightly,* LXXX (July 6, 1967), 23-28.

Tannenbaum, Samuel W. "Titles in the Entertainment field," *American Bar Association Journal,* XLV (May 1959), 459-462.

Taylor, Jr., Reese H. "The Case for State Regulation of CATV Distribution Systems," *Federal Communications Bar Journal,* XXIII (1969), 110-121.

"Television Broadcasting and Copyright Law; The Community Antenna Controversy," *St. John's Law Review,* XLI (October, 1966), 225-239.

"Temporary Authorizations in the FCC," *Georgetown Law Journal,* LVI (January 1968), 575-583.

Thomas, Jr., Lowell S. "Federal Communications Commission: Control of 'Deceptive Programming,' " *University of Pennsylvania Law Review,* CVIII (April 1960), 868-892.

Toohey, Daniel W. "Newspaper Ownership of Broadcast Facilities," *Federal Communications Bar Journal,* XX (1966), 44-57.

Tower, Charles H. "The Portrayal of Crime on Television," *American Bar Association, Section, Criminal Law Proceedings,* (1960), 31-44.

"Transit Broadcasting: The Problem of the Captive Audience," *Columbia Law Review,* LI (January 1951), 108-118.

Trask, George G. "The Palace of Humbug—A Study of FCC Policies Relating to Group Ownership of Television Stations," *Federal Communications Bar Journal,* XXII (1968), 185-217.

"Use of the Stay on Appeals from the Federal Communications Commission," *Virginia Law Review,s* XXXV (February 1949), 236-242.

Warner, Harry P. "Legal Protection of the Content of Radio and TV Program Content," *Iowa Law Review,* (Fall 1950), 14-28.

Webbink, Douglas W. "How Not to Measure the Value of a Scarce Resource: The

Land-Mobile Controversy," *Federal Communications Bar Journal,* XXIII (1969), 202-209.

Willis, J. A. "Judicial Review of FCC Decisions," *Federal Communications Bar Journal,* XX (1966), 169-174.

"Wire Mire: The FCC and CATV," *Harvard Law Review* LXXIX, (December 1965), 366-390.

GOVERNMENT PUBLICATIONS:

Federal Communications Commission. *Annual Reports,* 1934-. Washington, D. C.: U. S. Government Printing Office.

———. *An Economic Study of Standard Broadcasting.* Washington, D. C.: U. S. Government Printing Office, 1947.

———. *The Communications Act of 1934 with Amendments and Index Thereto.* Washington, D. C.: U. S. Government Printing Office, 1961. (Supplementary Packets 1 through 4, published from 1961 to 1967, reporting amendments during that period, are also available).

———. *Decisions and Reports of the Federal Communications Commission of the United States,* 1934 to 1949, and 1958-. Washington, D. C.: U. S. Government Printing Office.

———. *Public Service Responsibility of Broadcast Licenses* ("Blue Book"), March 7, 1946.

———. *Report on Chain Broadcasting;* Commission Order No. 37, Docket No. 5060, May 1941.

———. *Second Interim Report by the Office of Network Study; Television Network Program Procurement, Part II.* Washington, D. C.: U. S. Government Printing Office, 1965.

Office of the Federal Register, National Archives and Records Service, General Services Administration. *Code of Federal Regulations: Title 47—Telecommunication,* Parts 0 to 19 and 70 to 79. Washington, D. C.: U. S. Government Printing Office. (This Publication contains FCC rules and regulations pertaining to FCC organization, practice and procedure, and to the operation of radio services; revised and codified as of January 1, 1969).

U. S. Congress. 78th Cong., House. *Investigation of the Federal Communications Commission.* Hearings before the Select Committee to Investigate the Federal Communications Commission, 1943-1945. Washington, D. C.: U. S. Government Printing Office, 1945.

———. 83rd Cong., 1st Sess. Senate. *Workload of the Federal Communications Commission.* Hearings before Committee on Interstate and Foreign Commerce, May 18, 1953. Washington, D. C.: U. S. Government Printing Office, 1953.

———. 83rd Cong., 2d Sess. Senate. *Status of UHF and Multiple Ownership of TV Stations.* Hearings before the Subcommittee on Communications of the Committee on Interstate and Foreign Commerce on S. 3095, May 19, 20, 21, June 15, 16, 17, 18, and 22, 1954. Washington, D. C.: U. S. Government Printing Office, 1954.

———. 84th Cong., 1st Sess. Senate. *Imposition of Administrative Fines by the FCC.* Hearings before the Interstate and Foreign Commerce Committee on S. 1549, June 21, 1955. Washington, D. C.: U. S. Government Printing Office, 1955.

———. 85th Cong., 1st Sess. House. *Regulation of Broadcasting: Half a Century of Government Regulation of Broadcasting and the Need for Further Legislative Action: A Study for the Committee on Interstate and Foreign Commerce* Washington, D. C.: U. S. Government Printing Office, 1958.

————. 85th Cong., 2nd Sess. House Report 1602. *The Federal Communications Commission.* Interim Report of the Subcommittee on Legislative Oversight of the House Committee on Interstate and Foreign Commerce, April 4, 1958. Washington, D. C.: U. S. Government Printing Office, 1958.

————. 86th Cong., 1st Sess. Senate. *Educational Television.* Hearings before the Committee on Interstate and Foreign Commerce on S. 12 (A Bill to Expedite the Utilization of Television Transmission Facilities in our Schools and Colleges, and in Adult Training Programs), January 27 and 28, 1959. Washington, D. C.: U. S. Government Printing Office, 1959.

————. 86th Cong., 1st Sess. Senate. *Educational Television.* Report from the Committee on Interstate and Foreign Commerce to Accompany S. 12 (House Report 56), February 26, 1959. Washington, D. C.: U. S. Government Printing Office, 1959.

————. 86th Cong., 2d Sess. House. *Communications Act Amendments Clarifying Regularity Authority.* Report from Committee on Interstate and Foreign Commerce to Accompany S. 1740 (Senate Report 2148), August 24, 1960. Washington, D. C.: U. S. Government Printing Office, 1960.

————. 86th Cong., 2d Sess. House. *Independent Regulatory Commissions:* (Comparative Operating Data for Years 1949 and 1959. Compilation from Commission Reports and Answers to June 3, 1960, Subcommittee Questionnaire Showing Workload; Personnel; Turnover; Backlog; Number of Cases Determined; Regulatory Problems and Appropriations of Civil Aeronautics Board, Federal Communications Commission, Federal Power Commission, Federal Trade Commission, Interstate Commerce Commission, and Securities and Exchange Commission). A Print of the Special Subcommittee on Legislative Oversight of the Committee on Interstate and Foreign Commerce, December 1960. Washington, D. C.: U. S. Government Printing Office, 1960.

————. 86th Cong., 2d Sess. House. *Independent Regulatory Commissions.* Report of the Special Subcommittee on Legislative Oversight of the Committee on Interstate and Foreign Commerce (Pursuant to Section 136 of the Legislative Reorganization Act of 1946, Public Law 601, 79th Congress, and House Resolution 56, as Amended, 86th Congress), January 3, 1961. Washington, D. C.: U. S. Government Printing Office, 1961.

————. 86th Cong., 2d Sess. House. Responsibilities of Broadcasting Licensees and Station Personnel. Hearings before a Subcommittee of the Committee on Interstate and Foreign Commerce on Payola and other Deceptive Practices in the Broadcasting Field, February 8, 9, 10, 15, 16, 17, 18, 19, and March 4, 1960. Washington, D. C.: U. S. Government Printing Office, 1960.

————. 86th Cong., 2nd Sess. Senate Report 692. *Redefining Duties of FCC Staff.* Report from Committee on Interstate and Foreign Commerce to Accompany S 1738, August 12, 1959. Washington, D. C.: U. S. Government Printing Office, 1959.

————. 86th Cong., 1st Sess. Senate. *VHF Booster and Community Antenna Legislation.* Hearings before Subcommittee of the Committee on Interstate and Foreign Commerce. Part I on S. 1739, S. 1741, S. 1801, S. 1886 and S. 2303, June 30, July 1, 7, 9, 1959. Part II on S. 2653, October 27-30, and December 15-16, 1959. Washington, D. C.: U. S. Government Printing Office, 1959, 1960.

————. 87th Cong., 1st Sess. Senate. *Freedom of Communications.* Final Report of the Committee on Commerce, prepared by its Subcommittee of the Subcommittee on Communications, pursuant to S. Res. 305, 86th Congress (Senate Report 994, Part 5), January 9, 1962. Washington, D. C.: U. S. Government Printing Office, 1962.

————. 87th Cong., 1st Sess. Senate Report 478. *Reorganization Plan No. 4 of 1961 (FCC).* Report from Committee on Government Operations to Accompany S. Res. 147, June 28, 1961. Washington, D. C.: U. S. Government Printing Office, 1961.

————. 89th Cong., 1st Sess. House. *Regulation of Community Antenna Television.* Hearings before Subcommittee of the Committee on Interstate and Foreign Commerce on H. R. 7715, May 2 and June 2-4, 1965. Washington, D. C.: U. S. Government Printing Office, 1966.

————. 89th Cong., 2d Sess. House. *Regulation of Community Antenna Television.* Hearings before Subcommittee on H. R. 14201, March 22-24 and April 5-7, 1966. Washington, D. C.: U. S. Government Printing Office, 1966.

————. 90th Cong., 1st Sess. House. *Copyright Law Revision.* Report from the Committee on the Judiciary to Accompany H. R. 2512 (House Report 83), March 8, 1967. Washington, D. C.: U. S. Government Printing Office, 1967.

————. 90th Cong., 1st Sess. Senate. *The Public Television Act of 1967.* Hearings before the Subcommittee on Communications of the Committee on Commerce on S. 1160, April 11-14, 25-28, 1967. Washington, D. C.: U. S. Government Printing Office, 1967.

————. 90th Cong., 2d Sess. Senate. *The FCC's Actions and the Broadcasters' Operations in Connection with the Commission's Fairness Doctrine.* Staff Report for the Subcommittee on Communications of the Committee on Commerce, prepared under the direction of Robert Lowe, Washington, D. C.: U. S. Government Printing Office, 1967.

United States Information Agency. *Annual Reports,* 1954-. Washington, D. C.: U. S. Government Printing Office.

PH. D. DISSERTATIONS:

Gwyn, Robert. *Broadcast Networks and Public Policy.* University of Illinois, 1963.

Hartenberger, Werner K. *Cameras in the Courtroom: The Role of the Broadcast Media in the Free Press-Fair Trial Controversy.* Wayne State University, 1966.

Kittross, John M. *Television Frequency Allocation Policy in the United States.* University of Illinois, 1960.

McDougald, William Worth. *Federal Regulation of Political Broadcasting: A History and Analysis.* Ohio State University, 1964.

McMahon, Robert S. *Federal Regulation of Radio and Television Broadcast Industry in the United States,* 1927-1950. Ohio State University, 1959.

Mullally, Donald P. *A Legislative, Administrative and Judicial History of the Fairness Doctrine in Television and Radio Broadcasting.* Michigan State University, 1968.

Newbill, Mickie L. *Competition and Program Balance.* Michigan State University, 1963.

Price, John F. *The Legislative History of Educational Television Facilities Proposed in the United States Congress: A Rhetorical-Critical Study,* Michigan State University, 1964.

Schmid, William Thomas. *A Historical Analysis of the Educators' Request for Non-Commercial Television Channel Reservations in the United States,* Ohio State University, 1970.

Smith, Thomas Herman. *A Description and Analysis of the Early Diffusion of Color Television in the United States.* Ohio State University, 1970.

Stern, Robert H. *The FCC and Television: The Regulatory Process in an Environment of Rapid Technical Innovation.* Harvard University, 1951.

Weeks, Lewis Elton. *Order out of Chaos: The Formative Years of American Broadcasting, 1920-1927.* Michigan State University, 1962.

Index

Administrative Procedure Act: as prescribed by hearings, 266; 269.

Advertising: alcoholic beverages by, 338; cases involving overcommercialization, 326–327; early use of radio for, 21; FCC statement of policies re overcommercialization, 325–328; legislative history of ban on cigarette commercials, 79–80; listeners offended by, 26.

Alcoholic beverages: advertising of, 338.

Alien ownership: *See* Licenses.

AM applications: FCC declared a freeze, 122–123.

Amateur radio: dimensions, 6; early operations, 20.

American Broadcasting Company: merger with Paramount Company, 240.

American Committee for Liberation: *See* Radio Liberty.

American Council on Education, 155.

American Forces Network (Europe): audience and programming, 180–183; creation of, 178; facilities, 179; organization and personnel, 178.

American Institute of Electrical Engineers: report of, 17.

American Society of Composers, Authors and Publishers, 372–373.

American Telephone and Telegraph Company: early uses of broadcasting, 24, 32; established, 17; inaugurates regular service across U.S., 18.

Antenna towers: marking and lighting, 275.

Anti-Trust Division: prosecutes offenders of criminal laws, 87–88.

Anti-trust laws: applicable to broadcasting, 87; effect on character qualifications, 234, 236–240.

Appeals: from Commission action to U.S. Court of Appeals of District of Columbia, 268–269; from examiners' opinions, 267; grounds for, 86–87; to Court of Appeals, 86–87; to U.S.

Supreme Court, 269; who may file, 268.

Applicants (decisional factors when involved in competitive cases): broadcast experience, 245; legal qualifications for, 233–236; local ownership, 245; programming, 246–249; record of performance, 246.

Applications for construction permits: controversial programming required, 261–263; form used and information and showing required, 258–263; processing procedure for, 263–266; when public hearings require action on, 267–268.

Applications for licenses to cover permits: requirements for grants thereof, 272–277.

Armed Forces Television (Europe): dimensions of, 168.

Armstrong, Edwin H.: inventor of FM, 126, 147.

Arnold, Thurman: speaks in behalf of "Blue Book," 462–463.

ASCAP: *See* American Society of Composers, Authors, and Publishers.

Assignment of License: also *see* Transfer of Control; application forms, 342–343; application procedures, 350–352; competing applications not permitted, 346–347; FCC prior approval required, 340–341; three year rule, 351–352.

Atlantic cable, 15.

AT&T: *See* American Telephone and Telegraph Company.

Auxiliary stations: application procedure, 191; boosters, 194–195; eligibility for licenses for translator stations, 193; remote pick-ups, 187–188; repeaters, authorized by Congressional enactment, 196–197; studio links and intercity relays, 189–191; UHF translators, restrictions on site of, 193; VHF translators, 192–193.

AVCO cases, 348–349.

Bartley, Robert Taylor: FCC Commissioner, 464–465.

Bell, Alexander Graham: demonstrates telephony, 15–16.

Bell System: early organization, 17; growth of, 17.

"Blue Book": *See Public Service Responsibility of Broadcast Licensees*

Boosters: *See* Auxiliary Stations.

Bori, Lucretia: opera star, 21.

Brinkley, John R.: license renewal denied, 48–49; medical broadcasts of, 22–23.

Broadcast Bureau: organization of functions, 61.

Broadcast channels: equitable distribution required, 43; public ownership thereof, 42–43.

Broadcast Music Inc., 373.

Broadcast regulations: Congressional action related to, 383–389, 395–400; difference of viewpoints, 6–7; proposals to improve, 389, 391–395, 402–403; when states are permissible, 90–93.

Broadcasting: early celebrities, 21, 30–31; early competition, 23; early criticism from listeners, 25–26; early educational uses, 22; early experimental attempts, 20–21; early hucksters, 22–23; early religious uses, 22; free competition recognized, 42; municipal regulations, 90; state controls, 90–93.

Brown, Harold: FCC Commissioner, 456.

Bryan, William Jennings: early broadcasts of, 22.

Bryant, Ashbrook P.: views regarding network program procurement, 311–313.

Buchanan, James: transmits cable message to England, 15.

Cable Television Bureau: organization and functions, 63.

Cantor, Eddie, 30.

Caruso, Enrico: early broadcast, 20.

Case, Norman Stanley: dissents to adoption of network regulations, 50; FCC Commissioner, 456.

CATV: *See* Community Antenna TV Systems; size of industry, 6.

Cease and Desist orders: grounds for, 354–364.

Celler Emanuel: monopoly protests, 25.

Censorship: early complaints, 25; FCC may not exercise, 46.

Channels: clear, 111; local, 112; regional, 111–112.

Chase, Francis: recounts chaos in the air waves, 23–24.

Cigarette advertising: also *see* Fairness Doctrine; Surgeon General's report, 78.

Citizen groups: early complaints of broadcasting, 25–26.

Citizens radio: dimensions, 6.

Class I Station (AM): defined, 112.

Class II Station (AM): defined 112.

Class III Station (AM): defined, 113.

Class IV Station (AM): defined, 113; power increased, 113–114.

Clay, Lucius D.: organized Radio Free Europe by, 170.

Clear Channel Broadcasting Service: petition filed, 115.

Clear Channel Case, 114–117.

Codes: Radio and Television, 337, 335.

Community problems: ascertainment of, 530.

Commissioners (FCC): competency and qualifications, 393; law against staff consultation with, repealed, 383–385; preparing opinions by, 385.

Committee for Free Europe, Inc.: *See* Radio Free Europe (RFE).

Common Carrier Bureau: organization and functions, 61–62.

Communication Act of 1934: allocation of frequencies and terms of licenses, 420; amended to provide for FCC reorganization, 59–61; announcement of sponsored programs, 429; application of anti-trust laws and revocation of licenses, 426–427; application of the Act, 407–408; application procedure for licenses, 420–423; coercive practices affecting broadcasting, 449–450; construction permits or licenses, 428, 430; Corporation for Public Broadcasting, 436–442; deceptive programs involving contests, 451–452; definitions of terms, 408–410; devices which interfere with radio reception, 416; disclosure of certain payments for programs, 450–451; false distress signals prohibited, 432; FCC administrate sanctions, 425–426; FCC may not exercise censorship, 432; general powers of the FCC stated, 419; grants for noncommercial education facilities, 433–436; interference between government and commercial stations, 431; license waiver required, 419; limitations on holding and transfer of licenses, 432–424; monopoly condemned and condoned, 41–42; operation of transmitting apparatus, 429; organization and functions of the FCC, 414–415; penal provisions and forfeitures, 447–449; powers of President under war conditions, 452–454; procedural and administrative provisions, 442–447; prohibiting monopolies which interfere with competition in commerce, 427; provisions for licenses and restrictions thereof, 415–416; provisions relate to government-owned stations, 419–420; provisions relating to broadcasts of political candidates, 427–428; provisions relating to the FCC, 411–413; unauthorized publication of communications, 452.

Communication media: early history of, 13.

Communications Satellite Corporation (COMSAT): establishment of, 175; growth of satellite communications, 175; legislative powers and objectives, 175–177; manager of International Telecommunications Satellite Consortium (INTELSAT), 178; subject to FCC authority, 176–177.

Community Antenna TV Systems: See CATV, congressional concern for, 199–200, 215; congressional proposals to require royalty fees, 375; copyright laws not applicable, 204–205; cross-ownership of CATV and TV stations, 203; FCC assumes regulatory jurisdiction, 199; growth and number of, 198–199; judicial sanction of FCC to regulate, 214; program requirements, 202–203; recent FCC actions relating thereto, 203–204; regulations and restrictions, 202–203.

Competitive hearings: See Applicants.

Complaints and Compliance Division (Broadcast Bureau): established, 322.

Congress: angry with FCC, 457; appropriation for experimental telegraph line, 13; concerned about FCC workload, 59–60; influence on broadcast advertising of cigarettes, 79–80; influence on FCC, 85–86; investigatory activities re FCC, 395–400.

Contractual arrangements: reports of, FCC required, 343–344.

Copyright laws: proposals pending in Congress, 375.

Copyright restrictions, 370–375.

Corporation for Public Broadcasting: creation of, 83, 436; financing, 83, 439; nonpolitical and nonprofit character, 83, 437–438, 432; organization and staff, 437; purposes, 83, 436, 438.

Coughlin, Charles E.: network broadcasts, 31.

Council of Chief State School Officers, 156.

Court review: See Federal Communications Commission.

Courts: enforce compliance with broadcasting laws and regulations, 86; review actions of FCC, FTC and FDA, 86–87.

Cox, Eugene: See Cox investigation.

Cox, Kenneth: comment of, re overcommercialization, 327; concerning utterance of

obscene language, 305; FCC commissioner, 487–488.

Cox Investigation, 397–400.

Coy, Wayne: 383; a commercial broadcaster becomes FCC Chairman, 462–464.

Craven, T.A.M.: FCC commissioner, 458, 468–469, 481; opposes FCC program controls, 46–47, 50.

Cross, Milton J., 30–31.

Damrosch, Walter: network broadcasts, 31.

Daytime Broadcasters Association: petition filed, 115.

Daytime stations: ask for authority to operate before sunrise, 119–120; pre-sunrise service authorized by FCC, 121–122.

Deceptive contests, 314, 451–452.

Declaration of Human Rights: See Radio Free Europe (RFE).

Defamation, 364–366.

Defense Commissioner: functions, 66–67.

Deforest, Lee W.: early radio transmissions of, 20.

Denney, Charles R.: 162; FCC Chairman, 461–462.

Department of Health, Education and Welfare: functions, 83.

Dingell, John D.: proposes FCC controls of networks, 44.

Diversification of ownership: See Multiple Ownership.

Doctrine of fair use, 375.

Doerfer, John C.: demise as Chairman, 469–475; FCC Chairman, 465–468; under congressional investigation and fire, 470–473.

Don Lee case: See Network Regulations.

Dramatico-musical materials: restrictions on use, 370–371.

Durr, Clifford Judkins: 318; FCC Commissioner, 458, 460.

Educational broadcasting: aided by funds of Department of Health, Education and Welfare, 83; congressional aid, 6; dimensions, 6.

Educational FM stations: classes and frequency assignments, 144–146; eligibility and requirements, 142–145; growth, 140–142; operator requirements, 283; proposed assignment changes, 145–146; purposes and character, 140.

Educational stations: broadcast of recordings and copyrighted music not required to pay royalty fees, 372.

Educational television: early developments, 155–157; eligibility and operating requirements, 157–159; purposes and character, 157; recent growth, 156; rules regarding noncommercial aspects of programs clarified, 157–159.

Equipment: inspections and tests of, 280; repairing and replacing defective equipment, 280; safety requirements, 274–275; tests of, 276; type acceptance, 275.

Electromagnetic waves: nature of, 99–100.

Emergency Communications Systems Branch: functions, 67.

Emergency Relocation Board: organization and functions, 67–68.

ETV Facilities Act of 1962, 83, 433–436.

Examiners: freedom to consult with staff, 384.

Ex Parte representations, 389.

Experimental broadcast stations: allocation of frequencies for, 221; application and licensing procedure, 220–221; developmental, 220; facsimile, 220; renewal applications and showing required, 222; research studies conducted, 223–224; technical requirements, 221–223; television, 220.

Experimental radio stations: application and licensing procedure, 216–217; character specified, 216; classifications, 216; conducting research studies, 219–220; operational requirements, 217–218; reporting requirements to FCC, 218; student authorizations, 218–219.

Fairness Doctrine: 332–337; Appendix V; FCC General Counsel's *Memorandum* relating thereto, 529; made applicable to cigarette advertising, 333–335; U.S. Supreme Court decision, 518–529.

False Distress signals: prohibited by law, 306.

FCC: *See* Federal Communications Commission.

FCC Commissioners: how appointed, 54; limitations of activities, 54–55; qualifications, 54; salaries, 54; terms of office, 54.

Federal Aviation Administration: subject to approval of antenna towers, 275.

Federal Cigarette Labeling and Advertising Act, 79.

Federal Communications Commission: accessibility to wide information needed, 390; also *see* Congress; annual reports to Congress, 55–56; appointment of personnel, 56; authority should be clarified; chronology of, 455–494; current publications of, 530–539; divisions abolished, 57; early leadership, 455–456; early problems and accomplishments, 456–457; established, 34; expenditures, 56; facilities and workload, 68–69; how

business transacted, 55; limits of authority, 40–41; must be guided by public interest, 50; original staff organization, 56–57; powers enumerated, 43–48; problems of workload, 392–393; program controls, 46–47; staff delegations of authority, 65–66; staff organization, 61–68; staff reorganized, 58–61; standards of conduct, 340–391; subject to court review, 51; tripart functions of, 389–390; under investigation, 395–400.

Federal Radio Commission: rules established, 30–31.

Federal Trade Commission: administrative procedures, 76–66; advertising alerts, 501–503; basic functions, 72–73; bi-partisan character, 72; commissioners, 72; condemnation of monopoly, 25; cooperative arrangements with FCC, 501–502; creation of, 72; duties of, 72; form letter to elicit advertising continuity, 501; guides against deceptive advertising, 500; how monitoring operates 81–82, 503–504; improper ratings cautioned, 504; objectional advertising defined, 73–76, 77–78; working arrangement with Food and Drug Administration, 83; workload, 80.

Field Engineering Bureau: organization and functions, 62–63.

Films: showing on television stations not required to disclose movie owners under section 317 of the Act, 295.

Financial Reports: licenses required, 343.

Fines and Forfeitures, 361–362.

Fly, James Lawrence: Controversial FCC Chairman, 457; wartime leadership, 458–459.

Folsom, Marian B.: supporter for educational television, 156.

Food and Drug Administration: cooperative arrangement with FTR, 83; corrective procedures, 83; functions, 82; organization and staff, 82–83; powers, 82.

Ford Foundation, 156.

Ford, Frederick Wayne: concern for programming in the public interest, 322–323; FCC Chairman, biography of, 475–479; speech on FCC role in programming, 405.

Frankfurter, Felix: inadequate regulation stated, 32.

Frequencies: FCC classifications of, 102–104; propagation characteristics of, 101; range of, 101.

Frequency Broadcast Station (FM): number of, 6.

Frequency Modulation Stations (FM): advantages over AM, 126; allocation and assignment of channels, 131–132; classes of stations, 131–132; duplication of FM and AM programming, 134–135; minimum mileage separations, 133–134; operation requirements, 282–283; pattern and decline of growth, 127–128; postwar problems, 127; restrictions on use of channels, 133; revision of rules, 129; *see* Educational FM stations; *see* subsidiary Communications authorizations; table of assignments, 132–133.

FTR: *See* Federal Trade Commission.

Fund for Adult Education, 156.

Gary, Hampson: FCC Commissioner, 455–456.

General Counsel: organization and functions, 64; *see* Red Lion Case.

General Electric Company: early broadcasting interests, 24.

Give-away shows: ban of by FCC overruled by Supreme Court, 302; rules against FCC, 302.

Grange, Harold "Red": sports announcer, 21.

"Ham" radio: *See* Amateur radio.

Harding, Warren G.: early broadcast, 21.

Harris, Oren: proposes Frequency Allocation Board, 106; proposes network controls, 44.

Hearing Examiner: reexamination of position proposed, 388–389.

Hennock, Frieda B.: activist in favor of educational TV, 463.

Henry, E. William: FCC actions under leadership of, 485–486; FCC Chairman, 481–485.

Holmes, Oliver Wendell, 40, 370.

Hoover, Herbert: attempts to regulate radio, 26–28; calls radio conferences, 28–29; regulatory philosophy, 29; study commission, 59.

Horse racing: broadcasts of, 338.

Husing, Ted: sports announcer, 31.

Hyde, Rosel H.: accomplishments, 490–493; opposed program regulation, 328; serves as FCC Chairman two periods, 466, 487–494.

Hyneman, Charles S.: comments on inefficiency of staff, 58–59.

Indecent Language: *See* Obscene Language.

Instructional Television Fixed Stations: elegibility for licenses, 198; frequency assignments, 197; number of, 197; purposes of; 197; regulations, 197–198.

Intelsat, 6; *See* Communications Satellite Corporation (COASAT).

Intercity Relays (Studio links): *See* auxiliary stations.

Interdepartmental Radio Advisory Committee, 84–85.

Interference: early problems, 26.

Intermittent Service Area: intensity requirements, 118.

International Broadcast Stations: application forms and qualifications of applicants, 162–163; assignment of frequencies, 163; call letters and locations, 165; conditions for commercial programs, 164; interference to foreign stations, 163; operational requirements, 164–165; operator requirements, 284; purposes defined by FCC, 162.

Irion, Gifford: comments on comparative cases, 252–254.

Jamming: from foreign broadcasts to Voice of America, 167.

Jessel, George, 30.

Jeff, Ewell Kirk: FCC Commissioner, 459.

Johnson, John: Vice-President, COMSAT, 175, 185.

Johnson, Lyndon, 178.

Johnson, Nicholas: comment of, re excessive advertising, 327–328; concerning obscene language, 305–306; FCC Commissioner, 487–488.

Joint Committee on Toll Television, 206.

Joint Council on Educational Television, 206; 155, 160–161.

Jones, Robert: FCC Commissioner, 463–464.

Justice Department, U.S.: enforces provisions of the Communications Act, 87.

Kaltenborn, H. V., 21.

Koop, Theodore F.: on access for covering news, 379.

Kreisler, Fritz: early microphone celebrity, 21.

La Follette, Robert: complaints of censorship, 25.

Landry, Robert J.: recounts early days of hucksterism, 23.

"Lar Daly Case," 297–299.

Lea, Congressman: Chairman, Committee to investigate FCC, 398.

Lea, H. Rex: FCC Commissioner, 489.

Lee, Robert E.: Comment of, re excessive advertising, 326; FCC Commissioner, 466–467.

Ownership reports: licenses required, 343–346.

Paramount Pictures, Inc.: involved in antitrust violations, 237–240.
Pay TV: *See* Subscription Television.
"Payola" practices, 291.
Personal attacks: regulations relating to, 332; also *see* Appendix V.
Petitions for reconsideration of commissions' decisions, 268.
Pirating news, 376.
Political broadcasting: announcement of sponsorship, 290, 293; FCC regulations concerning broadcasts of candidates, 296–297; legislative history of, 295–296, 297–300; stations not libel for broadcasts of political candidates, 366–367.
Political Candidates: FCC may not censor broadcasts of, 366–367; involved in news casts, 300.
Porter, Paul A.: FCC Chairman, 459–460; sponsors study of program criteria, 398–399.
Prall, Anning S.: FCC Chairman, 456.
President, U.S.: appointive powers, 54, 85, 411; assigns radio frequencies used by Federal agencies, 84, 419; delegations of authority, 84–85; emergency powers, 84, 452.
Presidential Task Force: *Final Report,* 108, 402–403.
Presidents Task Force on Communications Policy, 402–403.
Prettyman, E. Barrett, 244.
Primary Service Area: field intensity requirements, 117–118.
Profane language: cases involving, 303.
Program regulation: courts recognized, 48–50; early legislative history, 47–48.
Programming: advertising excesses, *see* Advertising: cases involving public interest, 320–321; conflicting views of FCC Commissioners re regulatory authority over, 328–329; FCC concern for balanced programming, 325; FCC concern with standards, 318–319; FCC enforcement procedures, 322–324; FCC policy statement, 321–322; FCC guidelines for, 321–322, 505–517; horse racing information, 338; involving atheistic views, *see* Scott Case; local live talent, 328; responsibilities of broadcast licenses, 335–337; station advocacy approved by FCC, 331–332; types favored by FCC, 324; types of, opposed by FCC, 329.
Protection of program ideas, 375–376.

Public Responsibility of Broadcast Licensees: adoption of report, 460–461; analyzed, 319; problems of enforcement, 320–321.

Radio Act of 1927: adopted, 29; provisions, 29–30.
Radio Corporation of America: early network broadcasting, 24.
Radio Free Europe (RFE): audience response to, 171; committed to Declaration of Human Rights, 171; creation by Committee for Free Europe, Inc., 170; efforts in behalf of East-West relations, 171; offices and facilities, 170; philosophy and criteria for programming, 171–172; program services, 170–171.
Radio in the American Sector (RIAS): ownership and control, 168; program services, 168–169; transmission facilities, 168.
Radio Liberty: monitoring and recording foreign broadcasts, 173; nature and purposes of organization, 172–175; programming services, 173–174; research facilities, 173; transmission facilities, 173.
Radio Moscow: hours of broadcasting, 184.
Radio Peking: hours of operation, 184.
Radio spectrum: conservation of, 105; for more effective utilization, 105–108.
RCA: *See* Radio Corporation of America
Rebroadcasting: not permissable without authority, 306.
Recording: *See* Mechanical reproductions.
Red Lion Case, 53: also *see* Fairness Doctrine.
Remote Pickups: *See* Auxiliary Stations.
Repeaters: *See* Auxiliary Stations.
Review Board: organization and functions, 63–64.
Review Section (FCC): restrictions of, against consulting commissions, 384.
Revocation of licenses: grounds for, *see* Licences.
Right of privacy, 377–378.
Rights: dramatic works, 370–371; grand, 370–371, 373; literary works, 373–374; music, 371–372.
Rogers, Will, 30.
Roosevelt, Franklin D.: appoints committee to plan national communications policy, 33.

Safety and Special Radio Services: dimensions, 6.
Safety and Special Radio Services Bureau: organization and functions, 62.

569